Instruments of EU Corporate Governance

European Company Law Series

VOLUME 19

Editor

Steef M. Bartman, Attorney-at-Law, Emeritus Professor of Company Law at Leiden Law School and Professor of Corporate Group Liability at Maastricht University, the Netherlands.

Introduction

The European Company Law Series is closely linked to the bimonthly journal European Company Law, also published by Kluwer Law International.

Contents/Subjects

The series covers subjects of company law in a broad sense, including insolvency, co-determination and securities law. Topical issues such as merger control, corporate governance, and piercing the corporate veil have been covered.

Objective of Series

Analysis of topical or complex subjects in European company law.

Readership

Academics; regulators; practitioners.

The titles published in this series are listed at the end of this volume.

Instruments of EU Corporate Governance

Effecting Changes in the Management of Companies in a Changing World

Edited by

Hanne S. Birkmose
Mette Neville
Karsten Engsig Sørensen

Wolters Kluwer

Published by:
Kluwer Law International B.V.
PO Box 316
2400 AH Alphen aan den Rijn
The Netherlands
E-mail: lrs-sales@wolterskluwer.com
Website: www.wolterskluwer.com/en/solutions/kluwerlawinternational

Sold and distributed by:
Wolters Kluwer Legal & Regulatory U.S.
920 Links Avenue
Landisville, PA 17538
United States of America
E-mail: customer.service@wolterskluwer.com

ISBN 978-94-035-4162-4

e-Book: ISBN 978-94-035-4173-0
web-PDF: ISBN 978-94-035-4174-7

Editors

Hanne S. Birkmose is head of department and a professor of Law at the Department of Law, University of Southern Denmark. Her research areas include Company Law – in particular, International Company Law and EU Company Law – and Corporate Governance, and she has written several national and international articles within these areas. She is also the author of books on UCITS (Undertakings for Collective Investment in Transferable Securities) and Alternative Investment Funds in Denmark. Recently, she has mainly worked with shareholder activism, the role of institutional shareholders, and sustainable finance. She is an academic member of the ECGI (European Corporate Governance Institute, Brussels), the Nordic Company Law Network, and the Nordic Corporate Governance Network.

Mette Neville is professor at the Department of Management, Aarhus University, Denmark and director of the Centre for Small- and Medium-sized Enterprises (CeSME), https://mgmt.au.dk/smv, which is an interdisciplinary research centre that focuses on growth and development in SMEs, including the value creation of the board. She leads several major research projects in collaboration with the SMEs, such as 'The SME board as a Digital Catalyst': https://mgmt.au.dk/smv/digital-katalysator, and Rethink Now (Gentænk NU) https://mgmt.au.dk/smv/gentaenk-nu. She is the head of the Board Educations offered by Aarhus University, including a Board education with a focus on SMEs, and Education for the Chairman of the Board, and she has extensive board experience herself. She is a member of several councils and committees, for example, the SME Board for Digital Transformations (appointed by the Minister for Industry, Business, and Financial Affairs), Chairman of the Disciplinary Committee at OMX Commodities, Norway (financial energy market for Norway, Denmark, Sweden and Finland, and she is a member of the expert panel of the Financial Supervisory Authority's Board of Directors.

Karsten Engsig Sørensen is a professor at the Department of Law, Aarhus University, Denmark. He holds a Danish law degree, a PhD (on European Union (EU) Company Law), and a Danish Dr. Jur. (on joint ventures). Furthermore, he holds an LLM from the University of Exeter. His research is mainly focused on EU Law and Company Law, and within these areas he has published several books and articles in both Danish and English. In addition, he has been the editor of several books on Company Law, EU Law, and WTO Law appearing on, *inter alia*, Kluwer Law International, DJØF Publishing, and Cambridge University Press. He is one of the two editors of the SSRN e-journal on Nordic and European Company Law, and a member of the Nordic Network for Company Law.

Contributors

Hanna Almlöf is an assistant professor in Business Law at the Department of Management and Engineering, Linköping University, Sweden. Her main research focus is on small and medium-sized companies that are owner-managed or family-owned. She is a research fellow at CeFEO – Centre for Family Entrepreneurship and Ownership – located at Jönköping International Business School and the Ratio Institute, Stockholm. She is a member of the Nordic Network for Company Law, the Research Panel for Company and Securities law at Stockholm Centre for Commercial Law, and the European Foundation Research Network.

Alexandra Andhov is an associate professor in Corporate Law and Law and Technology at the Faculty of Law, Copenhagen University, Denmark. Her research focuses on questions of corporate law, corporate governance, capital markets, law and technology from an interdisciplinary and comparative perspective. Her main research interest lies in the integration of legal, economic, and technological analysis, with particular emphasis on more sustainable, inclusive democratic and fair markets. She has published articles on these topics in numerous European and US law journals and reviews. She has also published chapters in anthologies published by the leading publishing houses. In 2019, she was a Fulbright Scholar at Cornell Law School, and she has held visiting posts at various institutions, including the Oxford Law School and University of Turin. She is a member of various organizations and societies, among others the American Society of Comparative Law, and IDA (the Danish Society of Engineers).

Iris H.-Y. Chiu is professor of Corporate Law and Financial Regulation at University College London (UCL). She is director of the UCL Centre of Ethics and Law and advances the public and stakeholder engagement of the Centre's agenda relating to a wide range of issues concerning law, regulation, governance, and ethics in business and finance. She has published extensively in the areas of corporate governance and financial regulation, including The Foundations and Anatomy of Shareholder Activism (2010), Investment Management and Corporate Governance (2017), The Legal Framework for Internal Control in Banks and Financial Institutions (2015), and Banking Law and Regulation (2019). She is a Research Fellow of the ECGI, and most recently, a Senior Scholar at the European Central Bank's Legal Research Programme.

Prof. Blanaid Clarke holds the McCann FitzGerald Chair in Corporate Law at Trinity College, Dublin. Her research interests include corporate law, governance, ethics, takeover regulation, and financial services law, and she has published extensively in these areas. She is deputy chairman of the Irish Banking Culture Board and the Irish representative on the Organisation for Economic Co-operation and Development's (OECD's) Corporate Governance Committee. She is also a member of the European Securities and Markets Authority's (ESMA's) Takeover Bids Network, the Sustainable Market Actors Research Network, and the European Model Company Act (EMCA) Group. She is currently a vice president of the Academic Board of the European Banking Institute. Previously, she was a member of the Irish Central Bank Commission (2010–2018), ESMA's Securities Markets Stakeholder Group (2018–2020), the European Commission's Informal Expert Group on Company Law (2014–2018), and its Reflection Group on the Future of EU Company Law (2010–2011).

Matteo Gargantini is assistant professor (tenure-track) of Business Law at the University of Genoa, Italy. Previously, he was assistant professor of European Economic Law at the University of Utrecht and senior research fellow at the Max Planck Institute Luxembourg for Procedural Law. Matteo has also served at Consob, the Italian Securities and Exchange Commission. He is a member of the Consultative Working Group (CWG) of the ESMA Corporate Finance Standing Committee (CFSC). He holds the Italian National Academic Qualification as full professor of business law and as associate professor of law and economics and financial markets law.

Carsten Gerner-Beuerle is a professor of Commercial Law at University College London. He held visiting positions at various universities in Europe and the United States, including the London School of Economics, King's College London, Humboldt University Berlin, the University of California at Berkeley, and Duke University. Carsten has published widely on issues of capital markets regulation, corporate law, and law and finance. He is admitted to the bar in Germany and the United Kingdom, regularly advises a German law firm on matters of corporate law and corporate insolvency, and has prepared studies for the European Commission and the European Parliament on the reform of corporate governance, financial regulation, and private international law.

Jesper Lau Hansen, dr. jur., is a professor of Company Law and Financial Markets Law at the University of Copenhagen, Faculty of Law. He was a member of the Commission's Reflection Group and has been appointed twice to its continuation, the Informal Company Law Expert Group (ICLEG). He served as an academic member on the first two Stakeholder Groups attached to ESMA, in the last round as its chairman. In respect of Danish law, he has served as an independent expert on the committee that prepared the new 2009 Companies Act and on various other committees concerned with financial law.

Bastiaan Kemp is professor of Corporate Governance and Corporate Regulation at the Faculty of Law of Maastricht University and an attorney-at-law at Loyens & Loeff, Amsterdam. In addition, he is a professorial fellow and vice-academic director at the Institute for Corporate Law, Governance, and Innovation Policies, a member of the editorial boards of the Dutch corporate law journal 'Maandblad voor Ondernemingsrecht' and European Company Law and a member of the corporate law advisory committee of the Dutch Bar Association and the Royal Association of Dutch Civil Law Notaries. His research is mainly focused on the regulation of the dynamic between shareholders and boards and on corporate litigation.

Jukka Mähönen is a professor of Law at the University of Oslo Faculty of Law, a deputy head of the Research Group Sustainability Law and leader of University of Oslo research project Futuring Sustainable Nordic Business Models, and a professor of Cooperative Law at the University of Helsinki Faculty of Law, and a principal investigator in Academy of Finland research project Shaping, fixing, and making markets via IPR: regulating sustainable innovation ecosystems (SHARE). He holds LLM (Berkeley), MSc (Econ.) (Turku), LLLic. (Turku), and LLD (Turku) degrees. He teaches company and cooperative law, private global governance, and law and economics. His research interests are in company and cooperative law, securities law, accounting and auditing law, tax law, and economic analysis of law. Recently he has worked with institutional investors, corporate purpose, financial and sustainability reporting, and sustainability. He is also looking for possibilities of new sustainable business models.

Florian Möslein is director of the Institute for Law and Regulation of Digitalisation (www.irdi.institute) and professor of Law at the Philipps-University Marburg, where he teaches Contract Law, Company Law, and Capital Markets Law. He previously held academic positions at the Universities of Bremen, St. Gallen, and Berlin, and visiting fellowships in Italy (Florence, European University Institute), the US (NYU, Stanford, and Berkeley) and Australia (Sydney and Melbourne). Having graduated from the Faculty of Law in Munich, he also holds academic degrees from the University of Paris-Assas (licence en droit) and London (LLM in International Business Law). He has published three monographs and more than eighty articles and book contributions, and he has edited seven books. His current research focus is on regulatory theory, corporate sustainability, and the legal challenges of the digital age.

Jessica Östberg is an associate professor and head of department for Company Law at Stockholm University. She was a post doc fellow at the University of Oxford, with an affiliation with Christ Church, during the period from September 2017 to August 2018. Her research areas include Company Law and Corporate Governance, with a special focus on the duties of directors and shareholders and the purpose of the company. She has written several articles within these areas. She is a member of the board of directors of Stockholm Centre for Commercial Law (SCCL) and a Head of the Research Panel for Company Law and Securities Law at SCCL. She is also an academic member of the ECGI, Brussels and a member of the Nordic Company Law Network.

Jessica Schmidt is a professor of Civil Law, German, European and international company and capital markets law at the University of Bayreuth, Germany. Her research areas include German and European company law as well as European private law, private international law, and comparative law. She is a member of Informal Expert Group on Company Law and Corporate Governance of the European Commission. Moreover, she is a member of ECGI, of the INSOL Europe Academic Management board and of various other academic associations.

Michele Siri is a full professor of Business Law at the University of Genoa, Italy and director of the Jean Monnet Centre of Excellence EUSFIL, European Union Sustainable Finance and Law. Since 2017 he has held a Jean Monnet Chair on European Union Financial and Insurance Markets Regulation. Since 2018 he has been a member of the Board of Appeal of the European Supervisory Authorities, of which he was appointed as chairman in 2021. He is an academic member of the advisory committee of the Italian Financial Markets Authority (CONSOB). He is also an adjunct professor at the Luigi Bocconi University of Milan and the LLM programme in EU Financial Regulation at the Frankfurt School of Finance & Management.

Beate Sjåfjell is professor of Law at the University of Oslo, Faculty of Law, and visiting professor at College of Europe, European Legal Studies Department. She is founder and head of the Oslo Faculty's research group Sustainability Law (2022–2027), building on a decade of work in the research group Companies, Markets and Sustainability (2012–2022). She is a member of the European Commission's Informal Group of Company Law Experts (2020–2024), and she coordinates international networks and projects, including Daughters of Themis: International Network of Female Business Scholars. Her main publications include Innovating Business for Sustainability: Regulatory Approaches in the Anthropocene (co-edited with Carol Liao and Aikaterini Argyrou; Edward Elgar Publishing 2022), The Cambridge Handbook of Corporate Law, Corporate Governance and Sustainability (co-edited with Christopher M. Bruner; Cambridge University Press 2019), and Creating Corporate Sustainability. Gender as an Agent of Change (co-edited with Irene Lynch Fannon; Cambridge University Press 2018). Many of her research papers are available on SSRN.

Christoph Van der Elst is professor of Business Law and Economics at Tilburg University, the Netherlands, and at Ghent University, Belgium and is a European Corporate Governance Institute research associate. He is a member of the Belgian Bar (Cottyn) and advised many different government agencies at national and international level. His current research interests are corporate governance, corporate voting, shareholder engagement, and company law and DLT, all topics on which he has published widely in academic and professional journals.

Charlotte Villiers is a professor of Company Law and Corporate Governance at the University of Bristol Law School. She publishes on various aspects of corporate governance and the relationship between company law and corporate governance, and accounting law and reporting, including analyses of the rise of sustainability reporting in national and EU legislation. She was a member of the global research team on the Sustainable Market Actors for Responsible Trade (SMART) Project led by the University of Oslo, for which she wrote papers on the issue of accounting and integrated reporting.

Summary of Contents

Table of Contents

CHAPTER 1
Introduction

Hanne S. Birkmose & Karsten Engsig Sørensen

§1.01 THE AIM OF THE BOOK

This book aims to analyse the different instruments that legislators and others have used to promote good corporate governance in European companies. These corporate governance instruments have developed over time and are still evolving.

Good corporate governance has always been an embedded part of company law, but over the years, the role has become even more explicit. Thus, issues such as the structure of management, appointment of directors, decision-making, and control of management have from the outset been part of company law. A new era started when separate recommendations or codes were developed addressing corporate governance issues. This development started in Europe with the Cadbury Code from 1992, which was soon followed in other European countries. These codes were soft-law instruments but made potent by reporting requirements. They were initially focussed on listed companies, and thus started a development where the corporate governance debate was usually more focussed on listed companies than non-listed companies.

Another era was initiated by the financial crisis, after which the European Union (EU) took a much larger role in formulating corporate governance policies and instruments. Thus, it is natural that large parts of this book focus on EU corporate governance. But given that the harmonisation is still very limited (and patchy) and often in the form of soft law, there is still a large role for national law to play, and consequently national experiences from Member States and some third countries are also included. The EU's approach to corporate governance in listed companies after the financial crisis was that the established corporate governance framework was inefficient and not able to resolve the traditional principal-agent problem. Thus, in addition to traditional instruments being re-framed, the EU also found that there was a need for new instruments, often focussing on enhancing the role of (certain) shareholders.

Moreover, new perspectives on corporate governance have challenged the established framework. The focus was not only on solving the traditional principal-agent problem but also on solving other types of tension among company stakeholders. Most recently the issue of sustainable corporate governance, i.e., how corporate governance may become more long-termed and able to balance the interest of different stakeholders, has dominated much of the debate. To achieve this agenda, national and EU regulators have used – or proposed to use – some of the more traditional instruments of corporate governance, such as the composition of the board or remuneration, by adding a new dimension to these. But we also see that there are new instruments forthcoming, such as reporting and certification, that with or without the legislators' intervention may help to achieve these aims.

These developments bode great changes, first and foremost for European listed companies. The discussion of corporate governance instruments in small and medium-sized enterprises (SMEs) has however been almost non-existent at EU level and for most parts limited at national level. However, the question is whether there is a need for a differentiated approach and how best to take account of the difficulties of applying corporate governance practices across the range of sizes and types of companies, and whether there is a need for different legislative or soft-law instruments. For example, SMEs are often owner-managed or family firms. This reduces the need for monitoring, but their ownership and management structures often lead to other challenges of which many are linked to internal governance problems, for example, lack of governance structures, processes, and competences that enable them to respond strategically to the rapid changes in the business environment, for example, digitalisation, sustainability, etc.

The main focus of this book is on the developments in the instruments used to promote good corporate governance. This includes both an analysis of instruments that have been there for a long time, and an analysis of newer and emerging instruments. Traditionally, the main target of these instruments has been the directors (or boards) and most often those in listed companies. Some instruments do not focus on the board but on other stakeholders that may affect changes in corporate governance, and consequently, these instruments rely on a more subtle indirect approach. This includes instruments that address the role of auditors, shareholders, institutional investors, public authorities, etc. Each of these presents some potential, but due to their indirect nature, they also call for a critical analysis of their effect. Finally, the effect of any of the instruments outlined will depend on how it is ensured that the addressee (board or other stakeholders) comply with these and here a range of different methods or instruments are also used.

The book is divided into three parts. The first part focusses on the instruments that stipulate or underpin the duties of directors or the board, the second part addresses instruments that use more indirect methods by not addressing the directors or board but instead addressing other stakeholders that may affect the behaviour of the two. Finally, the third part focusses on some of the instruments used to ensure compliance with the instruments dealt with in the first two parts. In the following sections, there will be a short overview of each part and finally some overall conclusions.

§1.02 ADDRESSING THE DUTIES OF DIRECTORS

The most straightforward way of affecting how directors act is to impose duties on directors. In company law, there are many such duties imposed on directors either to handle certain tasks or to abstain from such. Duties of this nature are likely to have an effect on corporate governance. But there are other duties imposed on directors in which the effect is somewhat more complex and debatable, and these are the subjects discussed in the first part of the book.

Company law will often explicitly or implicitly outline the overall duties of directors. Such duties may be formulated differently, and their effect on management, and thus corporate governance, can be hard to determine. Therefore, the first two chapters of part 1 are dedicated to this topic, as they address the topic from different angles. However, directors are also imposed a range of other duties that may affect their performance. Some of the more important duties are addressed in the subsequent chapters in this part.

In Chapter 2, *Jessica Östberg* addresses the overall duty of directors to act in the interest of the company in which they serve. This duty is often used as a synthesis of the duty of loyalty and duty of care that directors have in most jurisdictions. The author starts by outlining the theoretical framework formed by the shareholder value and stakeholder value theories that indicates different approaches to what the overall duties of the directors should be. However, these differences are often softened by modified versions or application. This point is illustrated by the comparative overview of directors' duties in the United States (US), United Kingdom (UK), and some of the EU Member States that is provided by the chapter. Given the intangible nature of the overall duty to act in the interest of the company, it is likely that this duty has little consequence for management in practice. But as the author points out, the negative component to the duty to act in the interest of the company does offer some protection against disloyal and damaging behaviour by the directors. It is more difficult to evaluate the effect of the positive component of the duty, but the author points out that it may have an effect in at least two situations, i.e., where the company is approaching insolvency and when a takeover is imminent.

Chapter 3, written by *Beate Sjåfjell,* focusses on the ongoing debate on whether the overall duties of directors should reflect a duty to act sustainably. The introduction of such a duty has recently been suggested by the report produced by Ernst & Young for the Commission entitled 'Study on directors' duties and sustainable corporate governance',[1] and it has been picked up by the Commission in its recent proposal for a directive on corporate sustainability due diligence.[2] The chapter takes its starting point by assuming that such a duty should be introduced and discusses how it should be formulated and be given effect. The author first discusses how the concepts of 'sustainable value creation' and 'planetary boundaries' can be used to establish a general duty. Next, she addresses the question of how such a general duty is integrated

1. The report was published 29 July 2020 and is available at https://op.europa.eu/en/publication-detail/-/publication/e47928a2-d20b-11ea-adf7-01aa75ed71a1/language-en
2. *See* COM(2022) 71, in particular Article 25.

into the duties of the board, since this is crucial if such a general duty should become operational. The author is not convinced that the Commission's proposal for a directive on corporate sustainability due diligence incorporates the duty in the most expedient way, and she points to alternative ways of doing this. Finally, the author examines how a duty to conduct due diligence may work as a tool in making such a general duty operational. Also, here she finds that there is room for improvement.

In Chapter 4, *Karsten Engsig Sørensen* addresses a different form of duties imposed on companies and often also directors: procedural rules regulating how directors make decisions. Such procedural rules have been part of national company law for a long time, but it is only in more recent time that an awareness has occurred of the fact that such rules may be a powerful corporate governance instrument. The author points out different types of procedural rules and their purpose. These are grouped first as rules on allocation of tasks, next as rules on how to make decisions or solve tasks, and finally transparency rules. There are examples in EU law of all types and even more in national law. The author then discusses the potential advantages of using such rules. Apart from ensuring more effective and objective decisions, they may strengthen other corporate governance measures; they may inspire confidence among stakeholders, and they may prevent some of the risks associated with decision-making in groups. But as the author points out there may also be potential negative effects, such as cost and the fact that not all procedures will fit all companies. So, the use of procedural rules should be used with care, and the author in his conclusion points out some guiding principles for their successful use.

Another way of addressing the duties of directors is to make recommendations of how the board best go about governing the company. This is what the corporate governance codes are doing, and this instrument is addressed by *Matteo Gargantini* and *Michele Siri* in Chapter 5. First, the authors analyse how soft law and self-regulation works in corporate governance codes. In doing so, they also point out that there have been several drivers that have resulted in a convergence in corporate governance codes. Next, the chapter outlines the span of the typical provisions found in codes. It becomes clear that codes often supplement several of the other corporate governance instruments analysed in this book, and in doing so make use of different instruments in their effort to promote good corporate governance. The impact of the codes, however, depends on how they are 'enforced': or being soft-law instruments how the boards are induced to comply with these. This is discussed by the authors addressing both the role of the 'comply or explain' mechanism and other formal and informal types of 'enforcement'. The authors end the chapter by discussing the future role of corporate governance codes. They conclude, *inter alia*, that the inventiveness of the codes as pioneers of best practices has faded, and instead legislators have played a more proactive role in corporate governance. As a result, the role of the codes is likely to become a supporting role in the alignment to the spirit of legal provisions.

Finally, another duty imposed on directors is the duty to report on different aspects of the companies' activities or strategies. In Chapter 6, *Charlotte Villiers* explores how and to what extent reporting requirements may shape corporate governance in EU companies. First, the author tracks how reporting requirements have rapidly developed in the EU in recent years. Whereas financial reporting primarily served the interest of shareholders, the newer reporting requirements also have the purpose of encouraging stewardship and responsible business. Next, the author considers how the evolving reporting requirements may either support or even influence corporate governance practices and structures. She points out that reporting may be instrumental first as a process for measuring corporate and managerial behaviours and impacts and reporting on them, second as a mechanism of corporate governance which requires an account from the managers to the stakeholders of decisions made and of the company's position, and third, as a mechanism for corporate governance, to bring about or achieve particular corporate governance goals.

§1.03 INDIRECT REGULATION OF CORPORATE GOVERNANCE

The second part of the book focusses on the instruments that have more indirectly influenced the working of the board. Instead of imposing duties on the directors, the setup in which they operate is changed. Many of those instruments discussed here – but not all – are relying on external actors or the market as such to keep management in check.

The company board or boards play(s) an essential role in corporate governance, and in particular, their composition is a key to ensuring that the directors can perform their duties properly and effectively. In Chapter 7, *Jessica Schmidt* discusses how EU law addresses board composition, assesses the pros and cons of the different initiatives, and explores areas for potential future legislation. The author finds that the EU initiatives have two characteristics. For one, the various harmonisation measures have often been initiated by corporate scandals or crisis situations, but sometimes also by political motivations (e.g., the directive on gender balance on boards). Moreover, the EU legislator has clearly focused on companies which are most important economically and financially: listed companies and companies in the financial sector. This has led to a kind of 'mosaic harmonisation', which leads the author to ask whether it would not be time to abandon the current 'piecemeal' approach and strive for a more streamlined and coherent framework.

Chapter 8 continues the discussion on the role of the board, but with a special focus on boards in SMEs. In many Member States, SMEs are the backbone of many economies, and therefore it is of great socio-economic importance that SMEs are properly governed so that their full potential is released. It requires that corporate governance problems in SMEs must be identified as they are very different from those in listed companies. In this contribution, *Mette Neville* discusses whether the board in particular has the potential to enhance good corporate governance in SMEs as ownership and management structures are some of the most important contextual factors in companies. Here SMEs differ greatly from many larger companies and the traditional problem of conflicting interests of owners and managers, which can arise when managers (agents) manage a company on behalf of the owners (principals) is absent. Rather, SMEs are typically closely held with one or a few owners, and the Achilles heel will often be conflicts among shareholders. As shareholders are often part of the management and/or board, conflicts will directly affect the management of the company. Other corporate governance problems in SMEs are linked to the internal operations of the company, as the owner-manager is often the main decision-maker. However, in her chapter, Neville finds that boards have the potential to create value also in SMEs in the form of better governance if certain challenges are overcome. The challenges discussed not only relate to SMEs not having a board in the first place, their composition, and the members' competences but also the boards' way of working and barriers constructed by the owners. A different aspect of the debate covered by the chapter is the choice of regulatory instruments to enhance the role of the board in SMEs. Hard law may be part of the solution where it is possible to reduce the flexibility of company legislation regarding the management structures of SMEs. Rather, the author points to the owner(s) as key to the solution, but also that differentiated codes aimed at SMEs that are flexible and encompass the heterogeneity of SMEs can contribute to the creating of value in the many SMEs in the Member States.

In Chapter 9, *Christoph Van der Elst* discusses another key aspect of corporate governance – remuneration – a discussion which dates back even before the modern corporate governance era. However, as the author shows in the chapter, remuneration as a corporate governance instrument has been applied in different ways during the different waves of interests in directors' pay. First, in the pre-corporate governance era, compensation was embedded in the managerialist governance approach of companies, while later in the 20th century the shareholder wealth maximisation perspective became dominant and compensation packages were used as an instrument for increasing shareholder wealth. Lately, due to the still increasing level of directors' pay, the say on pay mechanism must mitigate exaggerated compensation. At the same time, compensation also serves other interests, most recently sustainability goals. The struggle to frame compensation as an effective corporate governance instrument is also reflected in the prominent role compensation has in most corporate governance codes. The author shows, however, that these codes differ greatly, in terms of what is perceived as best practice in relation to remuneration of non-executive directors even though the overall corporate governance environments are largely similar. These differences are hard to explain, but the author shows that they do have a direct effect on the behaviour of companies. Consequently, he argues that in the lack of convincing arguments for one best practise, development of company remuneration specific policies for non-executive directors, which the shareholders regularly assess at the annual general meeting, could be the new 'best practice'.

The role of the shareholders in the governance of companies has increasingly been debated after the financial crisis. In Chapter 10, *Bastiaan Kemp* discusses the new role of shareholders and the general meeting. He points to two trends that define the role of the general meeting as a corporate governance instrument. On the one hand, the general meeting has come to play a less prominent role over time as an instrument for information and dialogue, while on the other hand, there is a growing concern about how companies act as part of the society. The latter trend gives more room to the interest of the stakeholders and in the view of the author creates a corporate governance environment of stakeholder pluralism, which puts pressure on the traditional principal-agent understanding. Rather, new principal-agent relationships emerge. Based on a law and economics analysis of these relationships, the author finds that although the stakeholders are given a more prominent role it is not to be recommended that the shareholder general meeting is replaced by a general meeting of stakeholders. Rather, he argues that the traditional shareholder general meeting can play a key role in ensuring good governance also in a world characterised by stakeholder pluralism. Such a role would require that shareholders are imposed a duty to focus on the interest of the company and all its stakeholders. To ensure that shareholders not only focus on their own interests, he introduces two mechanisms to ensure that the shareholders adhere to this broader duty: (i) creating or enhancing the possibility for stakeholders to enforce this duty through the courts and (ii) instating a system of mandatory cooperation among the corporate bodies when exercising control rights.

The role of minority shareholders in corporate governance is the topic of Chapter 11 written by *Hanna Almlöf*. Her focus is on owner-managed SMEs where the existence of minority shareholders may create conflicts that will also affect the management of the company. She first explores the theoretical tension between the minority and controlling shareholder(s) in SMEs and the origins for the conflicts that may emerge. The author then shows how company law – often with mixed results – try to prevent, counteract, or solve such conflicts, and here she focuses on three different stages: the entry stages where the minority shareholders enter the company, the next stage when the company is running and finally, the stage where the minority shareholder wants to exit the company. She shows how different rights including rights to information, procedural rights, and exit rights are used in different jurisdictions, and she concludes that most often these rights do not provide the optimal solution. She therefore exploits new ways of empowering minority shareholders that may prove more effective. First, she suggests the use of formal and informal decision arenas outside the fora stipulated by company law such as, for instance, family constitutions. Such arenas may play a crucial role in aligning the interest of shareholders, and the board may take a guiding and supporting role in this process. Next, she suggests that the minority shareholders could be given a right to be a member of the board of the company. The author proposes that this should not be dictated in company law, but company law should provide this solution as an opt-in rule. Lastly, she suggests an increased use of redemption of shares as a solution to ensuring minority shareholders an exit right. These suggestions would help to prevent or solve shareholder conflicts that may affect the management of the company, but several of the proposals also suggest that the board may have a crucial role to play in preventing and solving such conflicts and therefore add another dimension to good corporate governance in SMEs.

In Chapter 12, *Iris H-Y Chiu* picks up on another aspect of the changing corporate governance landscape and discusses the corporate governance role of institutional investors. Institutional investors have been given an increasingly prominent role in corporate governance by EU regulators, and this chapter discusses the nature of these EU policy developments and argues that the tenets are shifting from perceiving institutional shareholders within their 'agency' relationship with corporate management, to one of institutions having a key 'representative capacity' to discipline corporate behaviour. In her analysis of this development, the author finds that policymakers seem to be seeking a 'trickle-down' effect, so that institutions' exercise of their governance role continues to be based on the 'agency-based' paradigm, but at the same time also achieves social benefit. Placing policy reforms between two conceptions of the corporate governance role of institutional investors creates ambiguity. However, the author also finds that policy reforms for institutional shareholders seem to be shifting from a framing based in corporate law to one based in capital markets regulation. Such a shift also has implications for institutions' corporate governance roles, as regulating institutions' 'representative capacity' in capital market regulations imply that their incentives are steered towards a form of investment management conduct that secures social good. Adoption of financial regulation as the paradigm for regulating institutional investment conduct can allow for clearer regulative steers to affect institutional investors' corporate governance roles. Although the author finds that there are hints of such an approach, the actual effect on institutional behaviour is yet to be seen.

The theory of the market for corporate control (MCC) suggests that a company which is poorly managed renders the company vulnerable to a takeover at a price below its real value by a bidder who will replace existing management, turn the company around, and reap the rewards. This is the starting point for Chapter 13, in which *Blanaid Clarke* discusses the relevance of the MCC as an EU corporate governance mechanism in a market that faces increased protectionism and a weakening of globalisation. Her analysis opens with a discussion of the assumptions on which the MCC rests and the embedded weakness in these assumptions followed by an exploration of a number of unresolved issues in the theory. Next, importance of a competitive MCC is examined. This includes an examination of the role of defensive measures introduced by management. In the EU, the takeover bids directive marked a new era in the attempt to create an open and efficient MCC, and the author considers first the extent to which the MCC is enshrined in the directive and second the manner in which it has been implemented in Member States. Based on these analyses, the author concludes that there are serious doubts as to the effectiveness of a board neutrality rule such as the one introduced by the directive. Finally, the author explores whether the MCC has stood the test of time and in particular how the 2008 Global Financial Crisis, the emergence of private equity, and the Pandemic has added to our understanding of the MCC and its implications. She argues that these crises have highlighted the choice between open markets and protectionism and that a degree of balance is required as part of a holistic approach to takeover regulation so that the benefits to be derived from hostile takeovers are retained whilst some of the unintended consequences are avoided. Finding such a balance will be a significant challenge. In her final conclusion the author finds, that while it is evident that the MCC has been accepted as an important external governance mechanism, it should not be seen as a complete substitute for internal governance. Rather it may compliment it.

In the final chapter of part 2 of the book, *Florian Möslein* discusses certification of companies as a corporate governance instrument. Such schemes serve as regulatory instruments that aim to leverage sustainable and responsible entrepreneurship. Similar to the discussion of the MCC in the previous chapter, certification functions as an external corporate governance mechanism, as it relies on the market – consumers and investors – to pressure companies to demand more sustainable entrepreneurial activities. Certification may bring out sustainability information that otherwise may be difficult to obtain and assess by allowing the market to steer the behaviour of companies. In Chapter 14, Möslein opens with a presentation of the US scheme of Certified B Corporations, which have been particularly successful. This is followed by a presentation of other prominent schemes and a dissemination of how they differ from one another in four dimensions that are critical to their functioning. Taking an outside-in perspective on the certification schemes, the author argues that they also need to be understood in the interaction with other measures that aim to promote sustainability and social entrepreneurship. These include new sustainability-oriented company forms, disclosure of non-financial reporting, and certification of (financial) products. Finally, it is explored how certification schemes interact with the broader corporate governance framework, in particular corporate governance codes. In his conclusion, the author finds that while certification schemes and corporate governance codes share similarities, it is precisely due to these similarities that their regulatory relationship is delicate. Today, they sometimes overlap or even contradict each other, and if they are to achieve their regulatory (sustainability) goals, they need to be reconciled with each other. Given the variety of private and public rule-setters and regulatory approaches, the author concludes that such regulatory consistency is difficult, if not impossible to reach.

§1.04 ENFORCEMENT AND ITS EFFECT ON GOVERNANCE

Enforcement of the different corporate governance instruments has already been addressed briefly in several of the chapters mentioned earlier, but in the third and last part of the book, this topic is the focus point of the chapters. Each instrument often presents its own problem when it comes to enforcement, but in the last four chapters the authors address some of the overarching enforcement mechanisms. However, the focus is on enforcement directed at directors, and the instruments focusing on affecting corporate governance although external actors will often need to be contemplated differently.

In Chapter 15, *Carsten Gerner-Beuerle* addresses the question of how shareholder litigation may work as a tool to enforce good corporate governance. Conventional wisdom has it that this is a powerful tool and consequently, there have been reforms of national law to facilitate such litigation. But recent empirical studies primarily from the US has questioned whether shareholder litigation has the desired effect, and the purpose of the chapter is to develop a framework that makes it easier to compare shareholder enforcement rights across countries. After having identified three factors that make it difficult to capture and quantify legal rules, the author gives an overview of the building blocks that form the system regulating directors' duties and their enforcement. The building blocks are then applied to the enforcement of the duty of care, showing the different factors that may affect the strength of the duty of care and the level of enforcement of these duties. Using Delaware and France as examples, he concludes that France may be lower than Delaware when it comes to the level of enforcement, but that France has a higher score on the level of the duty of care. The theoretical framework developed in the chapter may thus be used to capture and quantify the effect of fiduciary duties and the mechanisms governing their enforcement.

Auditors are not part of management, but they have an important role in overseeing management and the audit reports they make are likely to enhance the rules that ensure good corporate governance. Thus, in Chapter 16 *Jukka Mähönen* discusses the different roles of the auditors and how they have changed over time, often driven by corporate scandals. As a starting point, it is argued that audit will only work as a successful enforcement of corporate governance standards if the auditor will report to the shareholders of at least some discovered breaches. The probability that the auditors will report a discovered breach depends partly on the auditors' independence, but also that they have the right skills to perform their duties and the quality of the tools they use in their work, would they be law based, social norm based, or a hybrid. A related discussion that the chapter covers is what the auditors should audit. It is argued by the author that the auditors' traditional role to audit *financial accounts* represents a paradox: financial accounts represent the past by definition, and therefore investors and other parties interested in the company's prospects rely on information, which is not audited, such as interim earnings reports, financial analysts' forecasts, and privately obtained information, all out of scope of auditor influence. Thus, the author stresses the importance of the additional reporting requirements, such as the management report, non-financial statement, and a corporate governance statement, which certain companies must disclose. The auditors' role in relation to these additional disclosures differs, though, which may weaken the credibility of reports on internal control. Thus, in the final section of the chapter, the auditor discusses the European Commission's proposal for a Corporate Sustainability Reporting Directive, which includes important changes in the regulatory framework and especially for the duties of auditors. In his conclusion, the author welcomes this development as an important means of strengthening the role of the external auditor as an agent in the corporate governance context.

The possible public enforcement of directors' duties is addressed by *Jesper Lau Hansen* in Chapter 17. First the author asks whether there is a need for public enforcement, as the existing possibilities which mostly consist of private enforcement may be sufficient to enforce the duties. Taking the aftermath of the recent financial crisis into consideration, the author observes that in Denmark there was litigation against directors in a bank, resulting in personal liability for some of them. Another effective private enforcement mechanism that has been applied is the removal of directors and the reputational damages that this brings. He does accept, however, that there are indications that it may be costly and difficult to pursue pecuniary claims through the courts, and that this may warrant to consider public enforcement of and additional or supplementary tools for enforcing directors' duties. In considering this question, the author starts by pointing out the fact that states are vastly more powerful than individuals, and therefore any public enforcement mechanism should be subject to limitation that ensures that there is no abuse of power. The author then discusses different forms of public enforcement, including criminal prosecutions, the public enforcement of directors' duties used in Australia, and investigations conducted based on request from minority shareholders or initiated by a public authority. He also points out that much enforcement takes place when the public, for instance, the tax authorities, uses private enforcement mechanisms to pursue damages against directors. The author concludes that criminal enforcement or proceedings that require the same safeguards as criminal proceedings may not be optimal for enforcement of directors' duties, and instead he argues that the best way to supplement private enforcement is for the public to use the system of private enforcement and to use investigations as an instrument to establish whether there are any violations of duties that warrant criminal or civil proceedings.

In the last chapter of the book, Chapter 18, *Alexandra Andhov* discusses how our changing world pushes companies to re-think and re-design their businesses by embracing digital solutions relating to corporate governance. Her chapter takes a starting point in many of the existing corporate governance instruments, which have been discussed throughout the book, and from here the author explores their possible digitalisation and how digitalisation may affect their implementation. However, she also warns that before companies fully embrace various digital solutions to digitalise corporate governance, it is important to be aware of inherent technological risks and limitations. These are examined from both positive and normative perspectives by critically reviewing novel technological corporate governance solutions through the lens of a corporate governance purpose. In doing so, she in particular asks whether technology can provide a solution for particular corporate governance 'pain points'. First, four critical pain points are identified: Division of control and ownership; role of the boards, their composition and accountability; disclosure, transparency and market manipulation; and compliance, sustainability, and protection of (diverse) stakeholders. Next, these pain points are explored through a digital lens that includes a number of technical advancements from simple software solutions to complex systems based on blockchain or AI. In her conclusion, she points at the important role of the board if companies and corporate governance is to improve from the use of technology. Boards need to understand the technology, and they need to take an active role when adopting and implementing technology that carries out any part of the corporate governance. It makes one wonder, if the digital deficit in SME boards discussed in Chapter 8 is not a challenge in most company boards today.

§1.05 CONCLUSIONS

The account of different instruments shows the wide range of approaches that are used to achieve the overall goal of promoting good corporate governance. These instruments often provide different results, and therefore they may be used to achieve different goals under the overall heading of 'good corporate governance'. There seems to have been two main drivers in their developments: first, they are adjusted according to the development of best practices, including knowledge gained on what works and what does not work. Next, they have developed as the emphasis and goals of corporate governance have changed over time, for instance, by the emphasis on more shareholder engagement, the focus on long-time value creation, sustainability, etc. Some instruments seem to have been adjusted and enhanced throughout this development (for instance, reporting, composition of the board, and remuneration), some are new instruments added more recently and still in their infant stage (certification and digitalisation), and some instruments have been in decline (the market for corporate control and maybe corporate governance codes).

It is also clear that most instruments will not achieve much on their own, which is why a mix of instruments is desirable or in some cases necessary. Even though a book focussing on different corporate governance instruments may draw an incomplete picture of how corporate governance works in practice, the insight into the working of each instrument could provide knowledge of what each instrument may achieve and thus when to use them and how to mix them.

Enforcement of corporate governance instruments is addressed in several chapters of the book. It seems that for many instruments there are often problems of ensuring enforcement and/or problems with establishing whether the exiting enforcement mechanism is sufficient or not. The reason for this is likely to be the nature of corporate governance rules which are formulated either as vague duties or as recommendations that were never intended to be enforced in the traditional way. Other instruments work indirectly, for instance, by establishing procedures that management should follow, and which will hopefully result in a particular behaviour, or by inducing other actors to act in a way that will eventually reflect on the way directors are performing their duties. For such indirect instruments, strict enforcement of the rules does not guarantee the desired effect on corporate governance. The last part of the book addresses the enforcement mechanisms undertaken by key corporate governance stakeholders such as shareholders, auditors, or public entities. They show that all of these mechanisms have shortcomings, and although digitalisation and technological developments are often pictured as game changers, it is still too early to say how the development will enhance the implementation of the different corporate governance instruments. The fact that enforcement seems to develop very cautiously raises the question whether this is an intentional reluctance. There may be a fear that too much enforcement will either make directors too cautious to be optimal for running a successful business, may not have any substantial effect on corporate governance because of the indirect nature of the instrument or may make directors adopt rules that do not work, even if they would work in other companies.

PART I Addressing the Duties of Directors

CHAPTER 2

The Duty to Act in the Interest of the Company

Jessica Östberg

§2.01 INTRODUCTION

In many jurisdictions, directors of a limited liability company have a duty of loyalty and a duty of care. The duties are often understood as implying a duty to act *in the interest of the company*.[1] Since the company is an artificial legal person, it is not fully clear how this duty should be understood. The meaning of the duty has accordingly been discussed extensively in recent decades, and the debate has intensified as a result of the increased focus on corporate sustainability.[2]

1. *See* for a comparative overview of directors' duties, Carsten Gerner-Beuerle and Edmund-Philipp Schuster, *Mapping Directors' Duties: Strategies and Trends in the EU*, Boards of Directors in European Companies – Reshaping and Harmonising Their Organisation and Duties (Hanne Birkmose, et al. eds, Kluwer Law International B.V. 2013).
2. *See*, e.g., Lucian A. Bebchuk and Roberto Tallarita, *The Illusory Promise of Stakeholder Governance*, Harvard Law School Program on Corporate Governance Working Paper 2020-1, 11 (December 2020); Colin Mayer, *Prosperity: Better Business Makes the Greater Good* (Oxford University Press 2018); Colin Mayer, *Ownership, Agency and Trusteeship*, ECGI Law Working Paper No 488/2020 (11 December 2019); Alex Edmans, *Grow the Pie: How Great Companies Deliver Both Purpose and Profit* (Cambridge University Press 2020); Beate Sjåfjell, *Sustainable Value Creation Within Planetary Boundaries – Reforming Corporate Purpose and Duties of the Corporate Board*, University of Oslo, Faculty of Law Legal Studies Research Paper Series No. 2020-20 (4 August 2020); Edward Rock, *For Whom Is the Corporation Managed in 2020?: The Debate Over Corporate Purpose*, 76, European Corporate Governance Institute – Law Working Paper No. 515/2020 (1 May 2020); David Kershaw and Edmund Schuster, *The Purposive Transformation of Company Law*, LSE Law, Society and Economy Working Papers 4/2019, 4–6; Michael C. Jensen, *Value Maximization, Stakeholder Theory, and the Corporate Objective Function*, Tuck Business School Working Paper No. 01-09; Harvard NOM Research Paper No. 01-01; Harvard Business School Working Paper No. 00-058, 8–21, 9 (October 2001) and Rolf Skog, *The Importance of Profit in Company Law – A Comment from a Swedish Perspective*, 12 (4) ECFR, 563–571 (2015).

This chapter provides an analysis and discussion of certain topics and trends relating to the duty to act in the interest of the company, with the ultimate aim of concluding to which extent it may contribute to good corporate governance.

The chapter starts with a brief description of directors' duties. Thereafter the theoretical framework, above all the shareholder value theory and the stakeholder theory, is outlined. This section is followed by a comparative overview covering the United States (US), the United Kingdom (UK), and a few European Union (EU) countries. When discussing the meaning of the duty to act in the interest of the company, a distinction is in some jurisdictions made between solvent and insolvent companies, since the creditors (and not the shareholders) have the greatest outcome in the company's business in insolvent companies. Insolvent companies are therefore dealt with under a separate section following the comparative overview. The chapter concludes with a discussion and some final remarks.

There is some focus on listed companies. Accordingly, some rules discussed govern only listed companies, such as the corporate governance codes. In some jurisdictions, a special corporate form has been introduced in order to promote corporate sustainability, so-called *benefit corporations*. The regulation covering benefit corporations is not discussed in this chapter, mainly due to space restrictions.[3]

§2.02 DIRECTORS' DUTIES: THE BASICS

The corporate governance system consists of rules that create as well as provide solutions to the so-called principal-agency problem, which is inherent in the structure of a listed company.[4] A well-functioning corporate governance system aims at least at reducing the agency-costs by providing rules that make monitoring, deterrence, and compliance more effective.[5] In recent years, sustainability has in some jurisdictions been added to the concept of corporate governance and the term *good corporate governance* has been introduced.[6] The duty of loyalty and the duty of care form part of

---

3. The benefit corporation has been analysed by Jill Fisch and Steven Davidoff Solomon, *The ''Value of a Public Benefit Corporation*, Research Handbook on Corporate Purpose and Personhood (Elizabeth Pollman and Robert B. Thompson, eds., 2021). *See* also Ofer Eldar, *Designing Business Forms to Pursue Social Goals*, 106 Va. L. Rev. 937, 964–968 (2020) and Leo Strine, *Leo Strine, Jr. Wants Corporations to be Good Citizens* (22 September 2020) https://www.clientsmart.net/blog /leo-strine-jr-wants-corporations-to-be-good-citizens, visited on 14 April 2022.
4. *See* regarding the principal-agency problem Adolf Augustus Berle and Gardiner Colt Means, *The Modern Corporation and Private Property*, 71 (The Macmillan 1932), and Michael Cole Jensen and William H. Meckling, *The Theory of the Firm: Managerial Behavior, Agency costs and Ownership*, J. Financ. Econ. (1976). In companies with a controlling shareholder, the principal is the minority shareholders and the controlling shareholder the agent.
5. *See* Stephen M. Bainbridge, *Corporate Governance after the Financial Crisis*, 3 (Oxford University Press 2012).
6. *See, e.g.*, OECD/G20 Principles of Corporate Governance (2015) para. 9: 'Corporate governance involves a set of relationships between a company's management, its board, its shareholders and other stakeholders. Corporate governance also provides the structure through which the objectives of the company are set, and the means of attaining those objectives and monitoring performance are determined.' *See also* the Swedish corporate governance code (2020) Section I, 1. Aims.

the corporate governance system; they restrict the discretion of the directors and aim at protecting the company and its shareholders from negligent, opportunistic, and disloyal behaviour by the directors.[7] One function of the duties is accordingly to reduce agency costs.

In many jurisdictions, the duties are based on the contractual, agency-like relationship between the company and each of the directors, a relationship that is based on trust and confidence.[8] The duties are consequently often owed to *the company* and not to individual shareholders, not even the majority, which means that the duties may be enforced primarily by the company, or by minority shareholders by way of derivative action.[9]

The exact inter-relationship between the duty of loyalty and the duty of care is not fully clear and varies to some extent between jurisdictions. Some basic features and differences may however be established.

The *duty of loyalty* implies that the directors must act in the interest of *the company*.[10] This means, first of all, that a director may not act in his or her own interest or in the interest of another party, for example, by the usurpation of corporate opportunities or unfair self-dealing.[11] This negative component of the duty has attracted much attention in case law, not least in the US, and in some countries it is regulated at least partly in the statutory company act.[12] It is of fundamental importance for the company considering the trustful relationship between the director and the company. A breach of this duty is a serious breach, and there is often a presumption that a director has acted negligently; it may even be a criminal offense.[13]

In many jurisdictions, the aforementioned applies also in corporate groups. This means that directors should observe the interest of the company to which the director has been appointed to, and consequently not the interest of the group or a group company.[14] There are, however, jurisdictions in which the interests of the group or a

7. *See, e.g.*, Jessica Östberg, *Styrelseledamöters lojalitetsplikt: särskilt om förbudet att utnyttja affärsmöjligheter* 143 (Jure Förlag 2016).
8. *See, e.g.*, Mark Arnold, *General Duties of Directors*, Company Directors: Duties, Liabilities and Remedies (Simon Mortimore QC, ed., 2 ed Oxford University Press 2013) 223–228 and *Bristol and West Building Society v Mothew* [1998] Ch1, 18 A.
9. *See, e.g.*, Section 170 (1) UK Companies Act 2006 (CA 2006); Paul L. Davies et al., *Gower Principles of Modern Company Law*, 251 (Sweet & Maxwell 2021); Arnold, *supra* n. 8, at 228–229; Gerner-Beuerle and Schuster, *supra* n. 1, at 21 and Östberg, *supra* n. 7, at 139 with further references.
10. *See, e.g.*, Section 172 CA 2006; *Patient Care Services, S.C. v. Segal* (1975), 32 Ill.App.3d 1021, 337 N.E.2d 471; *Guth v. Loft*, 5 A.2d 503 (Del. 1939) and Östberg, *supra* n. 7, at 66.
11. *See, e.g.*, Gerner-Beuerle and Schuster, *supra* n. 1, at 11 and *Guth v. Loft*, 5 A.2d 503 (Del. 1939).
12. *See, e.g.*, Fletcher Cyclopedia of the Law of Corporations §§ 861 and 913; *Guth v. Loft*, 5 A.2d 503 (Del. 1939); Section 175 CA 2006, § 88 German Stock Corporation Act (Aktiengesetz vom 6. September 1965 (BGBl. I S. 1089) (AktG) and Chapter 8 Section 23 Swedish Companies Act (2005:551) (SCA).
13. For example, under Swedish law an intentional breach of the duty of loyalty may be punished as 'disloyalty to principal,' (Sw. *trolöshet mot huvudman)*, Chapter 10 Section 5 Swedish Criminal Code (1962:700).
14. This is, for example, the case under UK, Finnish, and Swedish law, *see* regarding groups, e.g., Klaus J. Hopt, *Groups of Companies: A Comparative Study of the Economics, Law, and Regulation of Corporate Groups*, The Oxford Handbook of Corporate Law and Governance (Jeffrey N.

group company may or must be considered. This is the case in, for example, Germany, France, and Italy. In France, the concept of the 'interest of the group' is recognized, and in Germany there is a *Konzernrecht* of a special nature.[15]

In many jurisdictions, the duty of loyalty also has a positive component, implying that the directors must act (in good faith) to *promote* the best interests of the company.[16] This part of the duty is more complex, since it is not fully clear exactly how the concept 'the interests of the company' should be understood and since it involves business judgment. It is sometimes considered part of the duty of care.[17] Some scholars have argued that the company has an interest of its own[18] and others that the interest of the company must correspond with physical persons actually having an interest in the company.[19] Some argue that primarily the interest of the shareholders is relevant. Others argue, however, that it covers all (or some) of the company's stakeholders' interests.[20] The debate regarding the interest of the company is consequently strongly related to the law and economics theory of shareholder value versus stakeholder theory, theories which is outlined in the subsequent section. The duty is furthermore closely related to the corporate purpose, as discussed further in §2.03 [C].

The *duty of care* is above all related to *how* the duty is performed, and it relates to both the decision-making process and the monitoring and oversight of the management.[21] In many jurisdictions it implies, *inter alia*, that decisions must be duly prepared and evaluated,[22] and that the management must be monitored with a certain standard of care.[23]

The (positive) duty to promote the interest of the company is related to the business judgment rule, which is applicable in one way or another in many

---

Gordon and Wolf-Georg Ringe eds, Oxford University Press 2018) 603–633, 611. For Finnish law, *see* the Supreme court cases HD 2004:69 and 2004:115 and for Swedish law Östberg, *supra* n. 7, at 84 with further references.

15. *See* for corporate groups, e.g., Hopt, *supra* n. 14, at 612 et seq. and John Armour et al., *Report on the Recognition of the Interest of the Group* (2016), available at https://papers.ssrn.com/abstract=2888863.
16. *See, e.g.*, Section 172 CA 2006; Davies et al., *supra* n. 9, at 286 and Chris Brummer and Leo E. Strine Jr., *Duty and Diversity*, 75(1) Vand. L. Rev. (2022). For Swedish law, *see* the Supreme court case NJA 2013 p. 117.
17. *See, e.g.*, Art. 25 of the Proposal for a Directive of the European Parliament and of the Council on Corporate Sustainability Due Diligence and amending Directive (EU) 2019/1937 (COM(2022) 71 (final) (CSDD).
18. *See* regarding this question, e.g., Günther Teubner, *Unternehmensinteresse – das gesellschaftliche Interesse des Unternehmens "an sich"?*, ZHR 148, 470–488 (1984). *See* also the Finnish scholar Lars-Erik Taxell, *Aktiebolagets organisation*, 13 (Åbo Akademi 1983), who claimed that the company has its own interest which includes financial stability and development opportunities. This view has been expressly rejected by the Swedish supreme court in NJA 2013 p. 117, para. 21.
19. *See* further §2.03 [A] *infra*.
20. *See* further §2.03 [B] *infra*.
21. *See, e.g.*, David Kershaw, *The Foundations of Anglo-American Corporate Fiduciary Law*, 200 (Cambridge University Press 2018); *Fletcher Cyclopedia of the Law of Corporations* §1011 and Gerner-Beuerle and Schuster, *supra* n. 1, at 3. In English law, the duty of care is regulated in Section 174 CA 2006 and in German law, in § 93 AktG.
22. *See* Kershaw, *supra* n. 21, at 200–217. *See also* Östberg, *supra* n. 7, at 322–323.
23. *See* Kershaw, *supra* n. 21, at 217–228 and 229 et seq.

jurisdictions. This rule protects the directors from liability, if the decision was duly prepared and evaluated and was taken in the honest belief that it was in line with the best interests of the company.[24]

§2.03 THE THEORETICAL FRAMEWORK[25]

[A] The Theory of Shareholder Value

The theory of shareholder value, or sometimes shareholder primacy, was established in case law in the US already in the beginning of the 20th century.[26] It was later confirmed, *inter alia*, in the widely cited case *Dodge v. Ford Motor Co.*[27] One of its strongest supporters was Milton Friedman, who published a famous article in New York Times in 1970 with the title 'The Social Responsibility of Business Is to Increase Its Profits'.[28] Friedman claimed that the only responsibility of businessmen is to conduct the business in accordance with the desires of the shareholders, in other words to make as much money as possible, while conforming to law as well as ethical custom.[29] In his view, different stakeholders' interests should mainly be protected by legislation.[30]

According to the shareholder value theory, the company should consequently be managed with a view of maximizing the value for its shareholders.[31] At least some of those who support the theory argue that the shareholders' interests should have primacy, since the shareholders are those who have formed and own shares in the

24. *See* § 93 German Stock Corporation Act; Gerner-Beuerle and Schuster, *supra* n. 1, at 8–10. *See also Regentcrest plc v. Cohen* [2001] 2 BCLC 80 and Kershaw, *supra* n. 21, at 47–58.
25. The text under this section is partly based on a revised version of section 3 of my draft article Corporate Sustainability and Profit Maximisation in the Land of Unicorns (7 December 2020) available at https://papers.ssrn.com/abstract_id=3731281.
26. *See Luther v. Luther Co.*, 118 West. 112, 123, 94 N. W. 69 (1903).
27. *Dodge v. Ford Motor Co.*, 204 Mich. 459, 170 N. W. 668 (1919).
28. *See* Milton Friedman, *The Social Responsibility of Business Is to Increase Its Profits*, The New York Times Magazine (13 September 1970), available at https://www.nytimes.com/1970/09/13/archives/a-friedman-doctrine-the-social-responsibility-of-business-is-to.html.
29. *Ibid.*, 1.
30. *Ibid.*, 2–3. It should be noted that Friedman never promoted a short-term focus on the investment. On the contrary he stated: 'it may well be in the long-run interest of a corporation that is a major employer in a small community to devote resources to providing amenities to that community or to improving its government. That may make it easier to attract desirable employees.' (*Ibid.*, 5). *See also* Brian Cheffins, *Stop Blaming Milton Friedman*, ECGI Law Working Paper No 523/2020 (4 June 2020) available at https://ssrn.com/abstract=3552950.
31. *See, e.g.*, Frank H. Easterbrook and Daniel R. Fischel, *The Economic Structure of Corporate Law*, 38 (Harvard University Press 1991); Richard Posner, *Economic Analysis of Law*, 576-583 (Aspen Law & Business 9th ed 2014); Bebchuk and Tallarita, *supra* n. 2, at 16 and Henry Hansmann and Reinier Kraakman, *The End of History of Corporate Law*, 89 Geo. L. J. 745 (2001). Jonathan Macey has recently described the shareholder value principle as a myth and concluded that due to the business judgment rule, it is nothing more than a non-binding norm, not a legally binding principle, *see The Central Role of Myth in Corporate Law*, ECGI Law Working Paper No 519/2020, 22–32 (May 2020).

company.[32] The shareholders' compensation for the provision of risk capital is restricted to the profit distributed, if any, or any return received upon a sale of the shares. Accordingly, their risk is high, typically much higher than bondholders' risk, since bondholders have an agreed, fixed return. At least as long as the company is solvent, the shareholders are furthermore the *residual claimants*. As residual claimants, they have the greatest interest in the outcome of the company's business; if the company is successful, their fortune will increase and if it experiences financial difficulties, they will be the biggest losers.[33] They will consequently have the greatest interest in controlling the management of the company and to decide upon issues that are typically of importance for them, such as the issuance of new shares, amendments of the articles of association, liquidation, merger, and appointment of directors of the company.[34] One important argument supporting the theory is accordingly that it promotes investments.[35]

Even strong supporters of the shareholder value theory, such as Milton Friedman, admit however that not only shareholders' interests but also other stakeholders' interests should be observed to the extent that the value for the shareholders is increased.[36] Furthermore, it is argued that a profitable company will be able to employ more people, pay them a higher salary, and make further investments, including investments in research and development. Therefore, shareholder value is important not only for the shareholders but also for the company's other stakeholders.[37] An important aspect of the shareholder value principle is that it limits the discretion of the

32. *See, e.g.*, Friedman, *supra* n. 28. The question of *ownership* has been challenged by some scholars, who claim that the company is not *owned* by the shareholders. Instead the shareholders merely own the shares and hold a right to vote on certain issues and a right to obtain dividends. They argue that the assets of the company are owned by the company and not by the shareholders, *see, e.g.*, Margaret M. Blair, *Ownership and Control, Rethinking Corporate Governance for the Twenty-First Century*, 5 and 223–225 (Brookings Institute 1995) and Macey, *supra* n. 31, at 9–22. This issue has, as far as I have noted, never been discussed in the Swedish doctrine. The shareholders are normally referred to as the 'owners' and in Swedish they are also called *aktieägare* (Eng. 'shareowners'). In Norway, the Supreme Court has clarified that shareholders are owners in a ruling from 2019 (HR-2019-515-A (Gardemoen Residence), *see also* for Norwegian law Tore Bråthen, *The Myth of Shareholder Ownership – the Norwegian Legal Perspective*, Festschrift in honour of Rolf Skog (Ronald J. Gilson et al. eds, Norstedts Juridik 2021) 231–258, especially at 251.
33. *See, e.g.*, Easterbrook and Fischel, *supra* n. 31, at 36–37. Critical, Blair, *supra* n. 32, Ch. 6 and 7 and Andrew Keay, *Ascertaining the Corporate purpose: An Entity Maximisation and Sustainability Model*, 71 Mod. L. Rev. 663, 668 (2008). *See also* Leo Strine, Jr., *Toward Fair and Sustainable Capitalism*, University of Pennsylvania, Institute for Law and Economy, Research Paper No. 19-39, Harvard John M. Olin Discussion Paper No. 1018 (August 2020).
34. *See* Leo E. Strine, Jr, *The Dangers of Denial: The Need for a Clear-Eyed Understanding of the Power and Accountability Structure Established by the Delaware General Corporation Law*, University of Pennsylvania Law School, Institute for Law and Economics, Research Paper no. 15-08, 6–7 (2016).
35. *See, e.g.*, Stephen M. Bainbridge, *In Defense of the Shareholder Wealth Maximization Norm: A Reply to Professor Green*, 50 Wash. & Lee L. Rev. 1423, 1442 (1993).
36. *See* Friedman, *supra* n. 28, at 5, and Irene L. Fannon, *The Corporate Social Responsibility Movement and Law's Empire: Is There a Conflict?* 58(1) Northern Ireland Legal Quarterly12 (2007).
37. *See* Easterbrook and Fischel, *supra* n. 31, at 38.

directors at least to some extent and provides a single purpose against which the directors' decisions can be evaluated.[38]

The theory of shareholder value has been criticized and accused of promoting short-termism.[39] It has indeed been widely recognized that a short-term focus on the maximum increase of the profit or the share price may be negative for the company's stakeholders and the business. There is however also evidence that short-termism is not necessarily caused by the theory of shareholder value but rather related to other factors such as the imperfectly informed and imperfectly functioning financial markets, the takeover-regime, and the directors' remuneration and compensation packages.[40]

In recent decades, a slightly modified version of shareholder value has been promoted by some scholars and business leaders in reaction to the short-termism, the theory of *enlightened shareholder value*.

The theory of enlightened shareholder value was, *inter alia*, promoted by Michael C. Jensen in 2002,[41] and it was subsequently adopted by the legislator in Section 172 of the UK Companies Act 2006 (CA 2006), which states:

> A director of a company must act in the way he considers, in good faith, would be most likely to promote the success of the company for the benefit of its members as a whole, and in doing so have regard (amongst other matters) to –
>
> (a) the likely consequences of any decision in the long term,
> (b) the interests of the company's employees,
> (c) the need to foster the company's business relationships with suppliers, customers and others,
> (d) the impact of the company's operations on the community and the environment,
> (e) the desirability of the company maintaining a reputation for high standards of business conduct, and
> (f) the need to act fairly as between members of the company.

---

38. *See* Jensen, *supra* n. 2, at 8-21.
39. The problem of short-termism and the imperfectly informed markets are described by, for example, Kent Greenfield, *The Puzzle of Short-Termism*, Boston College Law School Legal Studies Research Paper Series (3 October 2011). *See also* Cheffins, *supra* n. 30; Leo E. Strine, Jr., *Toward Fair and Sustainable Capitalism*, University of Pennsylvania, Inst for Law & Econ Research Paper No. 19-39, Harvard John M. Olin Discussion Paper No. 1018 (3 October 2019); David K. Millon, *Why Is Corporate Management Obsessed With Quarterly Earnings and What Should be Done About It?*, 70 Geo. Wash. L. Rev. 890 (2002); Lawrence E. Mitchell, *Corporate Irresponsibility: America's Newest Export 4-5* (2001); Joseph Fuller and Michael C. Jensen, *Just Say No to Wall Street*, 14(4) J. Appl. Corp. Finance 41–46 (2002) and Beate Sjåfell, *Capitalism, the Sustainability Crisis, and the Limitations of Current Business Governance*, Company Law and Sustainability: Legal Barriers and Opportunities (Beate Sjåfjell and Benjamin J. Richardson eds, Cambridge University Press 2015) 1–13, 2. The problem of short-termism has however been questioned by some scholars, *see, e.g.*, Georg W. Dent, Jr., *Stakeholder Governance: A Bad Idea Getting Worse*, 58 Case W. Res. L. Rev., 1109–1111 (2008) and Mark J. Roe, et al., *The European Commission's Sustainable Corporate Governance Report* (14 October 2020) available at https://ec.europa.eu/info/law/better-regulation/have-your-say/initiatives/12548-Sustainable-corporate-governance/feedback?p_id = 8270916.
40. *See, e.g.*, Millon, *supra* n. 39, at 905–912 and Cheffins highlighting executive pay as a driving factor for short-termism, *see supra* n. 30, at 33–36.
41. *See* Jensen, *supra* n. 2, at 8–21. *See also, e.g.*, Andrew Keay, *The Enlightened Shareholder Value Principle and Corporate Governance* (Routledge 2012).

The theory is based on the recognition that the relationship between a company and its stakeholders is to a large extent mutually beneficial. According to the theory, directors should consequently promote the interests of the shareholders, but in doing so have regard to different stakeholders' interests, ethics, and the long-term effects of the decision.[42] From a theoretical point of view, the difference between shareholder value and enlightened shareholder value is that the latter explicitly *requires* consideration of different stakeholders' interests and the long-term effects of a decision. Considering, however, that there is a business case for corporate sustainability today,[43] which means that such considerations, including the long-term effects of a decision, should in practice be taken into account also when applying the theory of shareholder value, the difference between the theories is in practice limited.[44]

[B] The Stakeholder Theory

In recent years, the debate regarding shareholder value has intensified.[45] A theory that has been promoted by some scholars and practitioners mainly to increase the protection of stakeholders, including the environment, is the *stakeholder theory*. Stakeholder theorists recognize that companies play an important role not only for the shareholders and the economy but also for all stakeholders involved with the company's business.[46]

42. *See* Jensen, *supra* n. 2, at 9.
43. *See, e.g.*, Bebchuk and Tallarita, *supra* n. 2, at 11; Ioannis Ioannou and George Serafeim, *Corporate Sustainability: A Strategy?*, Harvard Business School Accounting and Management Unit, Working Paper 19-065 (1 January 2019); Michael Eugene Porter and Mark R. Kramer, *Strategy and Society: The Link Between Competitive Advantage and Corporate Social Responsibility*, 84(12) Harv. Bus. Rev., 78 (2006) and Gunnar Friede, et al., *ESG and Financial Performance: Aggregated Evidence from More than 2000Empirical Studies*, J. Sustain. Finance Invest., 5(4), 210–233 (15 December 2015). The article combines findings of more than 2,000 academic studies concerning financial performance and ESG. The results show that about 90% of the studies find a non-negative relation between financial performance and ESG and that the large majority of the studies reports a positive correlation. A report from OECD shows however no clear positive link between sustainable finance and performance, *see* OECD Business and Finance Outlook 2020: Sustainable and Resilient Finance, Section 1. Cynthia Williams presents empirical findings relating to corporate sustainability as a business case and provides a number of references, *see* Cynthia A. Williams, *Corporate Social Responsibility and Corporate Governance*, The Oxford Handbook of Corporate Law and Governance (Jeffrey N. Gordon and Wolf-Georg Ringe eds, Oxford University Press 2018) 634–678, 647–650. *See also* Gordon L. Clark, et al., *From the Stockholder to the Stakeholder, How Sustainability Can Drive Financial Outperformance* (5 March 2015), available at https://papers.ssrn.com/abstract_id = 2508281.
44. *See, e.g.*, Bebchuk and Tallarita, *supra* n. 2, at 16.
45. The debate originates out of two articles published in Harv. L. Rev. in the beginning of the 1930s. The first article, which promoted the principle of shareholder value, *Corporate Powers as Powers in Trust*, was published in 1931 by Adolf A. Berle, Professor at Columbia Law School and the second, which promoted the stakeholder theory, was published by a professor at the Harvard Law School, Merrick Dodd Jr., *see Corporate Powers as Powers in Trust*, Harv. L. Rev. 1049–1074 (1931). *See* for a critique of shareholder value also e.g., Edward Freeman, *Managing for Stakeholders*, 9–12 (January 2007), available at http://ssrn.com/abstract = 1186402; Sjåfjell, *supra* n. 2 and Jaap Winter, *Addressing the Crisis of the Modern Corporation: The Duty of Societal Responsibility of the Board* (13 April 2020), available at https://papers.ssrn.com/abstract_id = 3574681.
46. *See, e.g.*, Freeman, *supra* n. 45, at 9–12.

It has been described as being 'an ethical theory about the values of management in relationships with those parties [i.e., the stakeholders], and also a management theory about how to create and manage successful companies'.[47] The stakeholder theorists assert that the company should be operated, not primarily in the interests of the shareholders, but in the interests of all of its stakeholders, without preference for the shareholders. In practice, this means that the management must 'balance' the interests of all stakeholders when taking business decisions.[48]

The stakeholder theory seems at first glance to be perfect when considering how to best promote corporate sustainability, since it allows and in fact requires the directors to take different stakeholders' interests into consideration, even if it will negatively influence the profits of the company. The theory, at least in its more extreme form, requiring the directors to *balance all stakeholders' interests*, raises however some concern.[49] The first problem is that the term *stakeholder* is not clear. The question is who is a stakeholder in the company apart from the apparent ones; shareholders, employees, and creditors?[50] Depending on how the term is defined, the number of stakeholders can be huge in large, global companies. It should also be very hard, if possible, to identify which (hypothetical) interests the different stakeholders have, and there is in addition no guidance on how this balancing, including necessary trade-offs, should be done. The question is how in practice the situation should be handled where several different stakeholders, and even stakeholders within the same group, have conflicting interests. Trade-offs must always be made in conducting business. When applying the theory of shareholder value, this problem with balancing different, conflicting interests does not exist, since the theory clarifies that the shareholders' interest is profit (or value) maximization.[51] In practice, the stakeholder theory also gives the management a lot more discretion than the theory of shareholder value, since there is no single purpose to guide the directors when taking decisions.[52]

[C] The Corporate Purpose

In recent years, some scholars promoting a broader responsibility for companies towards its stakeholders have focused not on this 'balancing-of-stakeholders' interests

47. Williams, *supra* n. 43, at 667.
48. *See* on this, e.g., Freeman, *supra* n. 45, at 13–15. For a critique of the theory, *see* Bebchuk and Tallarita, *supra* n. 2.
49. *See, e.g.*, Bebchuk and Tallarita, *supra* n. 2 and Beate Sjåfjell and Jukka Mähönen, *Corporate Purpose and the Misleading Shareholder vs Stakeholder Dichotomy*, University of Oslo Faculty of Law Legal Studies Research Paper Series No. 2022-43, 13 (21 February 2022).
50. *See* for an illustration of the problem Bebchuk and Tallarita, *supra* n. 2, at 18–21.
51. The board of directors are accordingly not obliged to balance different shareholders' interests when applying the theory of shareholder value, but should instead promote long-term profit (or value) maximization. Difficulties may however arise if a controlling shareholder instructs the board to manage the company with a short-term focus.
52. An additional problem that has been highlighted is that it might reduce the pressure on the governments to take action and propose 'external' legislation protecting stakeholders. *See* regarding this problem, e.g., Bebchuk and Tallarita, *supra* n. 2, at 52–53 and Strine, Jr, *supra* n. 34, at 8.

view, but instead on formulating the *corporate purpose*.[53] As recently outlined by Holger Fleischer, this idea is not new but has early predecessors.[54] As the concept of the corporate purpose is not used in a uniform way, a few words should be mentioned about the concept and its use.

First, there is at least in some jurisdictions[55] a clear difference between the objective of the company, or the company's business field, which might be, for example, to produce and market beverages, and the (ultimate) purpose, which might be, for example, to make profit for distribution to the shareholders.[56] Under Swedish law, the objective (i.e., the business field) of the company must be stipulated in the articles of association, whereas the purpose is regulated in Chapter 3 Section 3 of the Swedish Companies Act (2005:551) (SCA). According to this provision, the purpose is to give profit for distribution to the shareholders, unless another purpose is specified in the articles of association. A similar distinction between the concepts is made under German law.[57]

Second, it should be noted that a discussion regarding the corporate purpose may concern a non-binding *mission statement* or purpose mainly used as a *strategic marketing tool*.[58] One example of such mission statement is Vodafone's purpose: 'Our Purpose is to connect for a better future and our expertise and scale gives us a unique opportunity to drive positive change for society.'[59] Another is Nestlé's purpose: 'Nestlé's purpose is enhancing quality of life and contributing to a healthier future'.[60] Such purposes, or rather mission statements, are not legally binding and enforceable, and they are strictly speaking not related to the duty to act in the company's interest.[61]

Third, the relationship between the corporate purpose and the concept of 'the company's interest' should be clarified since they are inter-related and to some extent

53. *See, e.g.*, Mayer, *supra* n. 2 and *Corporate Purpose: A Concept in Search of Clarification, Data and Evidence*, The ECGI Blog (July 2022), available at https://ecgi.global/blog/corporate-purpose-concept-search-clarification-data-and-evidence.; Edmans, *supra* n. 2; Sjåfjell, *supra* n. 2; Guido Ferranini, *Corporate Purpose and Sustainability*, ECGI Working Paper, Working Paper No 559/2020 (7 December 2020) available at https://ssrn.com/abstract=3753594; Holger Fleischer, *Corporate Purpose: A Management Concept and Its Implications for Company Law*, ECGI Law Working Paper No 561/2021, 7–8 (January 2021). Critical Jill E. Fisch and Steven Davidoff Solomon, *Should Corporations Have a Purpose?*, ECGI Working Paper No 510/2020 (September 2021) available at https://ssrn.com/abstract=3561164. *See* also Rock, *supra* n. 2, at 76; Mark J. Roe, *Corporate Purpose and Corporate Competition*, ECGI Law Working Paper No 601/2021 (13 July 2021), available at http://ssrn.com/abstract_id=3817788; Jill E. Fisch, *Purpose Proposals*, ECGI Law Working Paper No. 638/2022 (4 April 2022) available at https://papers.ssrn.com/abstract_id=4079135 and Kershaw and Schuster, *supra* n. 2, at 4–6.
54. *See* Fleischer, *supra* n. 53, at 7–8.
55. Inter alia, in Sweden, Norway, and Finland (*see* §2.04 [C] *infra*), whereas, for example, Delaware General Corporation Law (DGCL) does not make this distinction.
56. *See, e.g.*, Kershaw and Schuster, *supra* n. 2, at 4–6.
57. *See* for German law, Fleischer, *supra* n. 53, at 16.
58. *See, e.g.*, Kershaw and Schuster, *supra* n. 2, at 8–11.
59. https://www.vodafone.com/about-vodafone, visited on 14 April 2022.
60. https://www.nestle-esar.com/aboutus, visited on 14 April 2022.
61. It is consequently possible also for a Swedish company bound by the statutory profit purpose in Chapter 3 Section 3 SCA to adopt a broad mission statement of the kind outlined above. *See* regarding this question Rock, *supra* n. 2, at 6. *See also* regarding the purpose as a management concept Fleischer, *supra* n. 53, at 3–9.

overlapping. At least in those jurisdictions where the purpose is regulated by law,[62] the corporate purpose may be viewed as a broader concept than the duty to act in the interest of the company insofar as it often binds *the decision-making corporate bodies*, whereas the duty to act in the interest of the company binds primarily *the individual directors,* including the managing director.[63] The function of the corporate purpose is mainly to act as a standard of conduct, or a *guiding star* for the decision-making corporate bodies, and the aim of it is mainly to protect the shareholders' interests of getting a return on the investment and in the end to encourage investments for the benefit of the economy as a whole.[64]

If a company has adopted a legally binding corporate purpose in the articles of association or if the company is bound by a statutory corporate purpose, systematic and teleological aspects suggest that the duty to act in the interest of the company should be interpreted in line with the corporate purpose. Otherwise, the directors would encounter difficulties in applying contravening legal rules in specific situations.

§2.04 'THE INTEREST OF THE COMPANY': A COMPARATIVE OVERVIEW

There has been a strong focus on corporate sustainability and stakeholders' interests within the EU, mainly as a response to the United Nations (UN) Agenda 2030. Accordingly, in 2019 the European Commission adopted the European Green Deal, an ambitious growth agenda that aims to: 'transform the EU into a fair and prosperous society, with a modern, resource-efficient and competitive economy where there are no net emissions of greenhouse gases in 2050 and where economic growth is decoupled from resource use'.[65]

In line with the European Green Deal, the European Commission communicated an initiative in 2020 related to sustainable corporate governance.[66] Based on this initiative, the Commission adopted the proposal for a Directive on Corporate Sustainability Due Diligence (CSDD), the aim of which is to 'foster sustainable and responsible corporate behaviour and to anchor human rights and environmental considerations in companies' operations and corporate governance'.[67] The proposal contains, *inter alia*, a provision regulating directors' duty of care in Article 25. According to this provision directors must, when acting in the interest of the company consider the interest of

62. For example, Chapter 3 Section 3 SCA, Chapter 1 Section 5 of the Finnish Companies Act (624/2006) and § 2-2 (2) the Norwegian lov om allmennaksjeselskaper (LOV-1997-06-13-45).
63. *See, e.g.*, Chapter 1 Section 5 and 8 of the Finnish Companies Act and Skog, *supra* n. 2, at 565.
64. *See, e.g.*, Skog, *supra* n. 2, at 570.
65. The European Green Deal, Brussels, 11.12.2019 COM (2019) 640 final, 2.
66. European Commission Inception Impact Assessment, Ref. Ares (2020)4034032 (30 July 2020). For a summary of the Inception Impact Assessment and the extensive critique *see, e.g.*, Therese Strand, *EU and Sustainable Corporate Governance*, Nordisk Tidsskrift for Selskabsret NTS:3, 1–18 (2021). *See* on the subject also Paul L. Davies et al., *The European Parliament's Draft Directive on Corporate Due Diligence and Corporate Accountability*, Nordisk Tidsskrift for Selskabsret NTS:2, 30–45 (2021).
67. *See* further https://ec.europa.eu/info/business-economy-euro/doing-business-eu/corporate-sustainability-due-diligence_en, visited on 14 April 2022.

climate, the environment, and human rights, including in the short, medium, and long term. The provision is formulated so that it avoids some of the problems with the stakeholder theory, since it limits the number of stakeholders whose interests must be considered.

There has in recent years also been some focus on the duty to act in the interest of the company on a country-specific level in the EU and in Anglo-American jurisdictions, mainly in order to increase the focus on stakeholders' interests, as illustrated in the subsequent section.[68] The section starts with a brief description of Anglo-American law. Thereafter, some jurisdictions in continental Europe are outlined, and finally a brief account is given of the Nordic jurisdictions, with a focus on Swedish law.

[A] Anglo-American Law

The US and UK governance systems are of a one-tier model with relatively strong boards and shareholders that are more dispersed than in continental Europe, with a large proportion of institutional shareholders.[69]

In the US, the principle of shareholder value, as illustrated by the famous case *Dodge v. Ford,* prevailed for many decades.[70] In some later cases a more nuanced approach has, however, been taken. In *Union Pacific Rail-road Co. v. Trustees,* the court accepted a donation to a non-profit association on the grounds that the donation would give the company goodwill and thereby benefit the owners in a long-term perspective.[71] Another case that demonstrates a more nuanced approach is *A.P. Smith Manufacturing Co. v. Barlow,* where a contribution to Princeton University was maintained with the explicit justification that the companies have a responsibility to society.[72]

Today forty-four states in the US have adopted so-called constituency statutes, enabling the consideration of different stakeholders' interests.[73]

Until the adoption of CA 2006, the theory of shareholder value prevailed in the UK.[74] The enlightened shareholder value, which has been outlined in §2.03 [A] above, is however now well established and regulated in Section 172 CA 2006. It has been

---

68. More than fifty countries worldwide have adopted a stakeholder-oriented governance statute, including Italy, Colombia, France, Peru, Rwanda, Uruguay, Ecuador, British Columbia, and Canada, *see* https://www.bcorporation.net/en-us/movement/stakeholder-governance (visited on 14 April 2022).
69. *See* Brian R. Cheffins, *Does Law Matter? The Separation of Ownership and Control in The United Kingdom,* ESRC Centre for Business Research, University of Cambridge Working Paper No. 172, 2–3 (2000) and Paul Davies, *Shareholders in the United Kingdom,* ECGI Working Paper in Law, Working Paper No 280/2015 (2015).
70. *Dodge v. Ford Motor Company,* 204 Mich. 459 (MI 1919). *See also eBay Domestic Holdings, Inc. v. Newmark,* 16 A.3d 1, 8 (Del. Ch. 2010).
71. *Union Pacific Railroad Co. v. Trustees,* 8 Utah 2d 101, 329 P.2d 398 (1958).
72. *A.P. Smith Manufacturing Co. v. Barlow,* 13 N.J. 145, 98 A2d 581.
73. *See* https://www.bcorporation.net/en-us/movement/stakeholder-governance. Critical Bebchuk and Tallarita, *supra* n. 2 and Lucian A. Bebchuk et al., *For Whom Corporate Leaders Bargain,* South. Calif. Law Rev., 94(6), 1467–1560 (2021).
74. *See Gaiman v. National Association for Mental Health* [1971] Ch. 317 and Davies et al., *supra* n. 9, at 275.

accompanied by the UK Stewardship Code of 2020 and the UK Corporate Governance Code 2018, which commit not only companies but also asset managers and asset owners to sustainable long-term investment. The introductory comments in the UK Corporate Governance Code 2018 emphasizes stakeholders' interests and the long-term perspective. Long-term value creation is also emphasized in the first Principle under 1, A.: 'A successful company is led by an effective and entrepreneurial board, whose role is to promote the long-term sustainable success of the company, generating value for shareholders and contributing to wider society'. It is followed by Principle B, which states: 'The board should establish the company's purpose, values and strategy, and satisfy itself that these and its culture are aligned.'[75] Kershaw and Schuster suggest that the purpose referred to concerns a non-binding *mission statement*.[76]

[B] Continental Europe

In continental Europe, the governance structure differs between a one-tier and a two-tier model, with a relatively large number of controlling shareholders.[77]

France adopted the so-called PACTE Law[78] in May 2019, the aim of which is, *inter alia*, to encourage French companies to grow, taking social and environmental aspects into consideration.[79] The reform included a revision of Article 1833 of the Civil Code, which now stipulates: 'The partnership shall be managed in view of its corporate interest taking into consideration the social and environmental stakes of its activity.' This should be compared to the previous wording of Article 1833, where the interest of the partners was clearly emphasized: 'All partnerships shall have a lawful object and shall be created in the common interest of [their] partners'.

One innovation of the French reform, which has gained much attention not least in Europe, is the introduction of a voluntary *raison d'être*, a corporate purpose.[80] A special regulation has also been adopted for French stock corporations, *société anonyme* in Article L 225-35 paragraph 1 and Article L 225-64 paragraph 1 sentence 4 of the Commercial Code. Article L 225-35 paragraph 1 sentence 1 reads:

---

75. David Kershaw and Edmund-Philipp Schuster have in a recent paper discussed this regulation in relation to UK company law, *see* Kershaw and Schuster, *supra* n. 2, at 5 et seq.
76. *Ibid.*
77. *See, e.g.*, Luca Enriques and Paolo F. Volpin, *Corporate Governance Reforms in Continental Europe J. Econ. Perspect.*, 21(1), 117–140 (Winter 2007) and María Gutiérrez-Urtiaga and Maria Isabel Sáez-Lacave, *Europe Faces Problem of Strong Shareholders and Weak Outside Investors*, 7 February 2018, available at https://clsbluesky.law.columbia.edu/2018/02/07/europe-faces-problem-of-strong-shareholders-and-weak-outside-investors/.
78. Law No. 019-486 of 22 May 2019 concerning the growth and transformation of enterprises, known as *Loi PACTE.*
79. *See* https://www.gouvernement.fr/en/pacte-the-action-plan-for-business-growth-and-transformation, visited on 14 April 2022. *See* regarding the French reform Alain Pietrancosta, *Codification in Company Law of General CSR Requirements: Pioneering Recent French Reforms and EU Perspectives*, ECGI Law Working Paper No. 639/2022 (6 June 2022), available at https://papers.ssrn.com/abstract_id=4083398. Pietrancosta analyses the French reform and compares is with the CSDD.
80. Art. 1835 of the Civil Code.

> The board of directors determines the orientations of the company's activity and supervises the implementation, in accordance with its social interest, by considering the social, environmental, cultural and sporting issues of its activity. It also takes into consideration, if applicable, the purpose of the company defined pursuant to Article 1835 of the Civil Code. (Freely translated.)

In addition to the statutory regulation, there are also specific rules governing the duty to act in the interest of the company in the AFEP-MEDEF Code of Corporate Governance for Listed Companies (2020). Section 1, 1.1 stipulates:

> The board of directors performs the tasks conferred by the law and acts at all times in the corporate interest. It endeavours to promote long-term value creation by the company by considering the social and environmental aspects of its activities. If applicable, it proposes any statutory change that it considers appropriate.

Under Italian law, directors have a duty of care pursuant to Articles 2392 and 2476 of the Civil Code and a duty of loyalty, i.e., a duty to promote the interests of the company, avoiding conflicts of interest as specified in Articles 2391 and 2475 of the Civil Code. The corporate purpose is regulated in the Italian Corporate Governance Code 2020. Article 1, Principles I stipulates that: '[t]he board of directors leads the company by pursuing its sustainable success'. Principles IV stipulates that the board shall promote a relevant dialogue with shareholders and other stakeholders. The long-term value creation and sustainable success is also emphasized under Article 1, Recommendations, Item 1.

Under German law, the management board (*Vorstand*) of a public limited liability company (*Aktiengesellschaft*) manages the company under its own responsibility as set forth in Section 76 (1) of the German Stock Corporation Act.[81] The directors are consequently not subordinated to the shareholders. The prevailing view is that the management board as well as the supervisory body (*Aufsichtsrat*) are obliged to act in line with the interest of the enterprise (*Unternehmensinteresse*).[82] The interest of the enterprise is aimed at ensuring the continued existence and the success of the company, which allows consideration of stakeholders' interest to a large extent.[83] Within this framework, it is the task of the management bodies to define the interest of the enterprise.[84] In line with this, the regulation in the German Corporate Governance Code (2019), Principle 1 stipulates: 'The Management Board is responsible for managing the enterprise in its own best interests.' The obligation to act in line with the interest of the enterprise is emphasized in the foreword to the German Corporate Governance Code:

81. AktG, *supra* n. 12.
82. *See, e.g.*, Holger Fleischer, *Zum Inhalt des « Unternehmensintresses » im GmbH-Recht*, GmbHR, 1307–1312, 1309 (2010); Fleischer, *supra* n. 53, at 7–8 and Teubner, *supra* n. 18, at 470–488. Critical Gerard Spindler, *Münchener Kommentar zum Aktiengesetz*, AktG § 76 Rn 67–70 (5th ed. 2019).
83. *See* Jens Koch, *Aktiengesetz*, § 76, Rn 35-35c (16th ed. 2022), and Spindler, *supra* n. 82, at Rn 67–70.
84. *See* Mathias Habersack et al., *GmbHG Großkommentar*, § 52, Rn 260–262 (3d ed 2020) and Koch, *supra* n. 83, at Rn 35a.

> The Code highlights the obligation of Management Boards and Supervisory Boards – in line with the principles of the social market economy – to take into account the interests of the shareholders, the enterprise's workforce and the other groups related to the enterprise (stakeholders) to ensure the continued existence of the enterprise and its sustainable value creation (the enterprise's best interests).[85]

Under Dutch law, the directors must primarily be guided by the interests of the company and the enterprise, which is understood to mean a duty to act in the interest of all stakeholders without preference for the shareholders' interests.[86] The duty is specified in Principle 1.1 Dutch Corporate Governance Code (2016), which states:

> The management board is responsible for the continuity of the company and its affiliated enterprise. The management board focuses on long-term value creation for the company and its affiliated enterprise, and takes into account the stakeholder interests that are relevant in this context.
>
> Asset owners and asset managers holding shares in Dutch listed companies are in addition, since 2019, required to comply (or explain) with the provisions in the Dutch Stewardship Code, the aim of which is to promote, *inter alia*, long-term value creation and corporate culture.[87]

[C] A Nordic Overview with a Focus on Swedish Law

The Swedish corporate governance system is strictly hierarchical with the shareholders at the top, deciding on several important matters such as the election, dismissal and remuneration of directors, instructions to the board of directors, capital increases, distribution of profits, and winding-up.[88] In addition, Chapter 3 Section 3 of the SCA sets forth that the purpose of the company is to make profits for distribution to its members, unless another purpose is stipulated in the articles of association. The theory of shareholder value is also clearly reflected in the Swedish corporate governance code (2020), even though there are some provisions where the aim is to promote sustainability and a long-term focus.[89]

The directors of a Swedish limited liability company are subject to a duty of loyalty and a duty of care.[90] These duties imply, *inter alia*, that the directors must act

85. German Corporate Governance Code 2019, Foreword, item 2.
86. *See, e.g.*, Jaron van Bekkum et al., *Corporate Governance in the Netherlands*, International Congress on Comparative Law, Washington (2010), 7, available at https://papers.ssrn.com/abstract=1507633; ABN AMRO, Supreme Court 13 July 2007, JOR 2007, 178.
87. https://www.eumedion.nl/en/public/knowledgenetwork/best-practices/2018-07-dutch-stewardship-code-final-version.pdf, visited on 14 April 2022.
88. The governance structure in the other Nordic countries is of a similar nature in many aspects *see* further Jesper Lau Hansen, *A Scandinavian Approach to Corporate Governance,* 50 Sc. St. L. 125–142 (2007) and *The Nordic Corporate Governance Model,* Nordic & European Company Law Working Paper No. 14-12 (Per Lekvall, et al. eds, SNS Förlag 2014).
89. *See* regarding shareholder value the foreword, p. 1 and Section I, 1. Sustainability is mainly regulated in Sections 3.1, 9.4 and 10.4.
90. *See, e.g.*, the preparatory works prop. 1975:103, 376 et seq.; the Supreme court ruling NJA 2013 p. 117 and Östberg, *supra* n. 7, at 150 et seq. and 319 et seq.

in line with the interest of the company.[91] Under Swedish law, the interest of the company means the hypothetical interest of all of the shareholders,[92] which under the prevailing view is understood as profit maximization.[93] There is consequently a logic and systematic connection between the duty of loyalty and care and the corporate purpose.

The profit purpose, which has a long history in Sweden,[94] works as a kind of guarantee for the shareholders that they will get a return on their investment, and consequently get paid for their risk-taking, or at least that the governance bodies will work for that.[95] It is a guiding principle for all decision-making bodies, also the general meeting.[96] The governance bodies are consequently not allowed to take decisions that contravene the profit purpose.[97] There is however consensus in the Swedish doctrine and there is case law supporting the opinion that any deviation from the profit purpose must be apparent to be relevant.[98]

There is comprehensive agreement in the Swedish doctrine that the profit purpose does not imply that a short-term perspective must or should be applied. Instead, the focus is rather on the profitable management of the company's business with a long-term perspective.[99] The board of directors' discretion when taking decisions regarding the management of the company is wide. It is accordingly up to the board of directors to decide, as a matter of business judgment, on the strategy of the company and on matters concerning the business. When doing so it must make an overall assessment whether a strategy, or a specific business proposal, is in line with

91. *See* the Supreme court cases NJA 1981 p. 1117; NJA 2013 p. 117 and Östberg, *supra* n. 7, at 153.
92. *See* NJA 1981 p. 1117; NJA 2013 p. 117 and the preparatory works prop. 1997/98:99, 97.
93. *See, e.g.*, Rolf Dotevall, *Aktiebolagsrätt: fördjupning och komparativ belysning*, at 281 (Norstedts Juridik 2015) and Skog, *supra* n. 2, at 567 et seq. In recent years, there has been a debate concerning the interest of the company and the company's purpose among Swedish scholars, *see, e.g.*, Per Lekvall, *On Company Purpose, Directors' Duties and Corporate Sustainability*, Festschrift in honour of Rolf Skog (Ronald J. Gilson et al. eds, Norstedts Juridik 2021), 763–774; Erik Lidman, *The Purpose of the Corporations a Contractarian Perspective*, Festschrift in honour of Rolf Skog (Ronald J. Gilson et al. eds, Norstedts Juridik 2021) 775–792; Sophie Nachemson-Ekwall, *Gör om gör rätt: Synpunkter på Kollegiets vinstfokus i den nya koden för bolagsstyrning 2020*, Tidningen Balans (24 January 2020); Robert Sevenius, *Är ABL redo för ett paradigmskifte?*, 29 September 2015, https://sevenius.se/2015/09/29/ar-abl-redo-for-ett-paradigmskifte/ and Skog, *supra* n. 2 at 563–571.
94. It was introduced as a statutory rule in the Swedish Companies Act 1944, but its importance as a fundamental principle was emphasized already in the preparatory works to the Swedish Companies Act 1895, *see* the preparatory works prop. 1895:6, 117.
95. *See* the preparatory works prop. 2004/05:85, 219; Skog, *supra* n. 2, at 564 and the same author in *Talet om "bolagets intresse" som något mer än aktieägarnas intresse – i vems intresse?* Festskrift till Jan Kleineman (Stefan Lindskog, et al. eds, Jure Förlag 2021) 803–810; Jessica Östberg, *Några tankar kring aktiebolagslagens vinstsyfte*, Vänbok till Anders Lagerstedt (Jan Andersson et al. eds, Jure Förlag 2020) 209–230, 217 and Niklas Arvidsson and Per Samuelsson, *Ett och annat om vinstsyftet, generalklausulen, företagsvärdering och likhetsprincipen*, Festschrift in honour of Rolf Skog (Ronald J. Gilson et al. eds, Norstedts Juridik 2021) 123–136, 124.
96. *See* Skog, *supra* n. 2, at 564 and Östberg, *supra* n. 95, at 217.
97. *See* Skog, *supra* n. 2, at 564 et seq.
98. *See, e.g.*, the Supreme court case NJA 1987 p. 394 and Göran Ohlson, *Vikten av vinst: en studie om syftets betydelse i bolagsstyrning*, 65, 116 (Iustus 2012).
99. *See, e.g.*, Östberg, *supra* n. 95, at 209–230, 220 with further references.

the profit purpose, considering factors, such as the business potential, business risks, and the financial position of the company. Sustainability and stakeholders' interests may and should be promoted to the extent that it is in line with the profit purpose. Should, on the contrary, such activities apparently contravene it, they must not be promoted.[100] If the shareholders disagree with the board, they may practice either 'exit or voice', i.e., either sell their shares, or vote for an instruction to the board or a replacement of the directors.[101]

Under Danish law, it seems to be clear that the board of directors may manage the company with the aim of creating sustainable value, thereby taking different stakeholders' interests into account in order to increase the value of the company. However, they are not obliged to manage the company with a stakeholder-oriented approach.[102] Stakeholders' interests and long-term value creation are emphasized in the Danish Recommendations on Corporate Governance (2020).[103] Section 1, *Principles* stipulates that the management 'must ensure that the company in the short as well as the long term develops in an expedient manner' and that 'the interaction between management and shareholders, as well as with the company's investors and other stakeholders, including society, is well-functioning'. Recommendations relating to the duties of directors are regulated in Section 2. Under *Principles,* it is emphasized that the board of directors shall 'safeguard the company's and the shareholders' interests with care and with due consideration for the investors and other stakeholders.' Recommendation 2.1.1 further stipulates:

> The Committee recommends that the board of directors in support of the company's statutory objects according to its articles of association and the long-term value creation considers the company's purpose and ensures and promotes a good culture and sound values in the company.

Under Norwegian law, the duty to act in the interest of the company has been discussed extensively in recent years, and the trend seems to be towards a more multifaceted, stakeholder-oriented approach, even though there is still some emphasis

100. One exemption from this rule is the provision in Chapter 17 Section 5 SCA regarding gifts for public-benefit purposes.
101. *See* for exit or voice strategies Eleonora Broccardo, et al., *Exit vs. Voice*, Harvard Law School John M. Olin Center Discussion Paper # 1061 (22 April 2022), available at https://ssrn.com/abstract=3671918.
102. *See* regarding Danish law, e.g., Paul Krüger Andersen, *Aktie- og anpartsselskabsret*, 61 et seq. (15th ed. Djøf Forlag 2021) and the same author in *Nye Anbefalinger for god selskabsledelse i Danmark, 2020,* Nordisk Tidsskrift for Selskabsret NTS:1, 95–100, 98 (2021). *See also* Thorbjørn Sofsrud, who means that the interest of the company equals to the interest of the shareholders as residual claimants (*Bestyrelsens beslutning og ansvar – Spørgsmål til bedømmelse af bestyrelsemedlemmers erstatningsansvar*, 233, *Greens Jura* 1999) and Henrik Lando, *Shareholder eller stakeholder value? En retsøkonomisk analyse af loyalitetspligten i aktieselskaber*, NTS 2001:1, 76 et seq. *See* however also Erik Werlauff, *Selskabsret,* 30 et seq. (11th ed. Karnov Group Denmark 2019), who seems to promote a more stakeholder-oriented approach.
103. Paul Krüger Andersen has commented upon the recommendations, *see supra* n. 102, NTS:1 at 95–100.

on the interest of the shareholders.[104] There is a statutory profit purpose – almost identical to the Swedish regulation – in § 2-2 (2) Lov om allmennaksjeselskaper.[105] The duties of directors for listed companies are specified under Section 2 in the Norwegian Code of Practice for Corporate Governance (2021):

> The board of directors should define clear objectives, strategies and risk profiles for the company's business activities such that the company creates value for shareholders in a sustainable manner. When carrying out this work, the board of directors should therefore take into account financial, social and environmental considerations.
>
> Chapter 1 Section 8 of the Finnish Companies Act states that the management must carefully promote the company's interests. According to the preparatory works, this entails a duty of loyalty implying that the management must act in a way that is in line with the company's purpose. The company's purpose, a profit purpose like the Swedish one unless another purpose is stipulated in the articles of association, is regulated in Chapter 1 Section 5 of the Finnish Companies Act.[106] Consequently, the interest of the company is normally understood as the shareholders' interest in (long-term) profit maximization.[107] The duty to act in the shareholders' interest and the profit purpose is further emphasized in the Finnish Corporate Governance Code 2020.[108]

To summarize the Nordic overview, Sweden and Finland have to a large extent maintained a similar, shareholder-oriented view relating to directors' duties and the corporate purpose, whereas Norway and Denmark seem to be moving in the direction of a more stakeholder-oriented approach. It should however be noted that all Nordic jurisdictions provide extensive stakeholder protection via specific statutory rules, such as rules governing employee representation in the boards, employee protection, environmental protection, etc.,[109] and they are also all in the forefront with respect to sustainability, with Sweden in a leading position according to RobecoSAM.[110]

104. *See, e.g.*, the Supreme court rulings Rt-1922-272 (Freja), where the Supreme court accepted a donation to a non-profit organisation and HR-2018-570-A (Ericsson). In the latter ruling, the Supreme court not only stated that a company must observe the interest of the shareholders but also confirmed that it has responsibilities towards its employees, contractors, creditors, and the community and society in general and that securing the company's continuing operations may form part of the company's interest. *See also* the preparatory works Ot.prp. nr. 55 (2005-2006) 114; Rt 2000 p. 2033; Bråthen, *supra* n. 32, at 254–257; Beate Sjåfjell, *Sustainable Companies: Possibilities and Barriers in Norwegian Company Law*, ICCLJ vol. 11, Issue 1, 1 et seq. and Lisa Charlotte Jakobsen, *Vinningsformålet i norsk aksjeselskabsrett*, Nordisk tidsskrift for Selskabsret NTS:2 29–36, 11 et seq. (2018).
105. *See also* § 2-2 (2) Lov om aksjeselskaper LOV-1997-06-13-44.
106. *See* the preparatory works RP 109/2005 rd, 41 et seq.
107. *See* Jukka Mähönen and Seppo Villa, *Aktiebolag I: Allmänna läror*, 404–405 (Alma Talent 2016); Tomas Lindholm and Jakob Storå, *Begreppet corporate benefit i finsk aktiebolags- och insolvensrätt*, 4 JFT, 405–421, 412 (2010).
108. *See* the Finnish Corporate Governance Code 2020, Introduction, item 15 and Section II, Board of Directors.
109. *See* further Per Lekvall (ed.), *The Nordic Corporate Governance Model*, Nordic & European Company Law Working Paper No. 14-12 (2014) https://papers.ssrn.com/abstract_id=2534331.
110. *See, e.g.*, RobecoSAM Country Sustainability Ranking, Update Summer 2021, 5, available at https://www.robeco.com/media/3/2/5/325dd63882d778324dd13ad2122d8ecb_202108-country-sustainability-ranking_tcm17-31263.pdf.

§2.05 INSOLVENT COMPANIES

There are two situations in which the duty to act in the interest of the company requires special considerations: (i) in case of insolvency and (ii) when a takeover is imminent. In this chapter, only the duty under (i) is dealt with.[111]

A company in financial difficulties which is insolvent or close to insolvency is in a complicated situation in terms of business decisions. There may be a hope among the directors and the shareholders that they will be able to turn the loss-making business into a profitable one and a willingness to act accordingly. Conversely, there is a risk that the company, by continuing its operations, will suffer further losses.

In a profitable company, the interests of the company's various stakeholders often coincide, as illustrated in §2.03 [A] above. Thus, all stakeholders usually have an interest in running the business in a way that maintains or preferably increases the company's profit. The shareholders in profitable companies are, as noted earlier, residual claimants.[112] In insolvent companies, however, the situation is different. In many cases, only the creditors are residual claimants, since there is often no equity left and the creditors are the ones who are entitled to payment in front of shareholders from any remaining assets upon liquidation. In that situation, the shareholders may have an interest in taking significantly greater risks than the creditors, as they still have nothing to lose, while the creditors often have an interest in saving what is left. Hence, there is often a conflict of interest between the interests of the shareholders and the creditors.[113]

In line with this, it is accepted in several jurisdictions that in the event of insolvency (or likelihood of insolvency), the duty to act in the company's interest should be understood as a duty to promote primarily the creditors' interests, which would normally require a more risk-aversive management of the business. This is, e.g., the case under Norwegian,[114] Danish,[115] and Anglo-American Law.[116] It should be

111. With respect to takeovers, *see, e.g.*, for Delaware law *Revlon, Inc. v. MacAndrews & Forbes Holdings, Inc.* 506 A.2d 173 (Del. 1986) and *Paramount Communications, Inc. v. Time Inc.*, 571 A.2d 1140 (Del. 1989). Also under English law, the directors are to some extent obliged to observe the shareholders' interest of getting the best price in the event of a takeover offer, *Heron International Ltd v. Lord Grade*, [1986] BCLC 382. *See* however *Re A Company* [1986] B.C.L.C. 382, which notably concerned a small private company, and Davies et al., *supra* n. 9, at 1017–1018.
112. *See* §2.03 [A] *supra*.
113. *See, e.g.*, Davies et al., *supra* n. 9, at 287; Mark Arnold and Marcus Haywood, *Duty to Promote the Success of the Company*, Company Directors: Duties, Liabilities and Remedies (Simon Mortimore QC, ed., 2 ed 2013), 277–285 and Jessica Östberg, *Något om skyldigheten att iaktta bolagets intresse vid insolvens*, Festskrift till Lars Pehrson (Ulf Bernitz et al. eds, Jure Förlag 2016), 455–476.
114. In a high-profile Norwegian court case from 1993 (Rt 1993 s. 1399 'Ytternes'), the Norwegian Supreme Court ruled that the creditors' interest must be observed when the company is insolvent. In a later case, HR-2017-2375-A 'Ulvesund', the Supreme Court imposed on a managing director a duty to inform a supplier about the fact that the company was insolvent.
115. *See, e.g.*, Sofsrud, *supra* n. 102, at 253 et seq.; Werlauff, *supra* n. 102, at 696 et seq.; U. 1998.1137 H, and U. 2010.190 H.
116. *See North American Catholic Educational Programming Foundation, Inc. v. Gheewalla* 930 A.2d 92, 99 (Del. 2007) and *In re Tropicana Entertainment*, LLC, 520 B.R. 455 (Bankr. D. Del 2014).

noted that this understanding of the duty is normally in line with the insolvency regulation and in some countries also with provisions in the criminal act protecting the creditors.

Insolvency and restructuring have in the EU recently been regulated by the Insolvency and Restructuring Directive.[117] Under Chapter 5 Article 19, there is a regulation governing the duties of directors, implying, *inter alia*, that Member States shall ensure that directors have due regard to the interests of creditors, equity holders, and other stakeholders' interests in case of a likelihood of insolvency. Under preamble (70) of the directive, it is emphasized that it is important to ensure that directors may take reasonable business judgment or take reasonable commercial risks, particularly when it would improve the chances of a restructuring of the company. In case of financial difficulties, however, directors should 'take steps to minimize losses and to avoid insolvency.'[118] The preamble (71) clarifies that there is no intention to establish any hierarchy among the different parties whose interests should be considered and that the member states should be able to decide on establishing such a hierarchy.

It should be stressed that the fact that creditors' interests have preference in many jurisdictions in case of likelihood of insolvency, does not mean that the duty is *owed to the creditors* and that creditors may enforce breaches themselves. The duty is instead often *owed to the company*, which means that breaches must be enforced by the company, in case of insolvency normally by the insolvency practitioner. The fact that creditors' interests have preference implies only that the directors must act primarily in their interest, which normally suggests a more risk-averse management of the business.[119]

§2.06 DISCUSSION AND CONCLUSIONS

As discussed earlier, the directors of a limited liability company have a duty to act in the interest of the company, a duty which is related to the duty of loyalty and the duty of care.

The duty implies first that the directors must act in the interest of the *company* and consequently not in, for example, the director's own interest or in the interest of a related party. This negative component of the duty, which is mainly related to the duty of loyalty, is in many jurisdictions well established by statutory law or by case law. It

Under English law, reference is made to the creditors' interest in the regulation in Section 172 (3) CA 2006. That directors have a duty to observe the creditors' interest in insolvency was also confirmed in the case of *Winkworth v. Edward Baron Development Co Ltd*, [1986] 1 WLR 1512, in the relatively recent cases *Bilta (UK) Ltd (In Liquidation) v Nazir* [2015] UKSC 23 and in *Vivendi SA v Richards* [2013] EWHC 3006 (Ch). *See also* Brian R. Cheffins, *Company Law: Theory, Structure and Operation*, 538 et seq. (Oxford University Press 1997).

117. Directive (EU) 2019/1023 of the European Parliament and of the Council of 20 June 2019 on preventive restructuring frameworks, on discharge of debt and disqualifications, and on measures to increase the efficiency of procedures concerning restructuring, insolvency, and discharge of debt, and amending Directive (EU) 2017/1132 (Directive on restructuring and insolvency).
118. A further clarification of the rule is made in the preamble (71).
119. *See* further Arnold and Haywood, *supra* n. 113, at 281–285.

aims at protecting the company and its shareholders from disloyal and damaging behaviour, with the ultimate aim of promoting investments to the benefit of the economy as a whole. This part of the duty is consequently a fundamental part of good corporate governance.

The positive component of the duty, implying that the directors must act (in good faith) to promote the best interests of the company, is not equally straightforward. The question arises how the concept 'the interest of the company' should be understood.

In case of a likelihood of insolvency, when there is often no equity left, the creditors' interests have preference in many jurisdictions. This seems reasonable considering that the board of directors then in reality manages the funds of the creditors. Such an understanding of the duty is also supported by systematic aspects since it is consistent with the insolvency regulation and often also with provisions protecting creditors in the criminal act. A preference for the creditors' interests implies a more risk-averse management of the business. In this respect, the duty may promote good corporate governance at least to some extent.

In other respects, i.e., when the company is solvent, the duty to act in the interest of the company is in some jurisdictions, such as Sweden and Finland, understood as the (hypothetical) interest of all shareholders, which is normally long-term profit (or value) maximization, whereas other jurisdictions, such as Germany and the Netherlands, apply an explicit stakeholder-oriented approach. In case the company is governed by a legally binding purpose, by statute or by a regulation in the articles of association, convincing arguments suggest that the duty should be interpreted in line with such purpose.

Irrespective of the approach taken, *inter alia* the flexibility of the concept, which leaves room for interpretation, in combination with the business judgment rule and the enforcement rules[120] suggest that the function and effect of the duty should not be over-estimated. Furthermore, it should be noted that a broad stakeholder orientation may reduce the governing function and efficiency of the duty, since it gives the board of directors a lot more discretion. A stakeholder-oriented approach should also be more difficult to apply, considering that trade-offs between stakeholders' interests will often be necessary.[121] A shareholder-oriented approach limits the discretion of the board of directors to some extent and is easier to apply, since the shareholders' interest is presumed to be profit maximization. However, there is a risk that it is misinterpreted and that the board of directors focuses on short-term profit (or value) maximization to an extent which is detrimental to the company and its stakeholders (in the long-term).

The debate concerning the duty to promote the interest of the company has intensified in the wake of the increased focus on sustainability and stakeholders' interests worldwide. As the comparative overview has shown, there is a clear trend towards a more stakeholder-oriented regulation in many European and Anglo-American jurisdictions. Some countries, like France and Italy, have adopted statutory,

120. As stated in §2.02, the duty may in many jurisdictions be enforced only by the company, or by shareholders by way of derivative action.
121. Considering this, it seems positive that the number of stakeholders to be considered under Art. 25 of the CDD have been limited to three.

stakeholder-oriented provisions, but in many European jurisdictions a stakeholder-oriented duty has been implemented through regulation in the corporate governance code, i.e., through self-regulation. One advantage with a regulation of the duty in the corporate governance code is that it is normally of a comply or explain nature, which provides flexibility and leaves room for a company to deviate from the rule if the deviation is explained. On the other hand, one disadvantage is that such rules only apply to listed companies, i.e., a minor part of all companies, and another that there are shortcomings with respect to enforcement, which should limit its impact somewhat.[122]

There is one obvious advantage with a specific (soft or hard law) regulation of the duty; it becomes clear that the duty exists, and its meaning may also be clarified. An explicit regulation has consequently an informative and possibly preventive function. The interpretation and application of the duty will be facilitated and misinterpretations of the duty, for example, that it implies a short-term profit maximization, may be reduced.

Considering the convergence in the EU and the trend towards a stakeholder-oriented approach, it should be stressed that even though there are some common principles and similarities between at least the Western corporate governance systems, there are also important differences.[123] The differences are partly a result of differences in, for example, the shareholder and voting structures, the capital markets, the political economy, and social norms.[124] Such differences should be considered when discussing the duty to act in the interest of the company. Any regulation of the duty should be consistent with, *inter alia*, the shareholder structure, the specific governance system (which might, for example, be shareholder-oriented or more board-centric), executive remuneration and the enforcement rules in order for it to be effective and promote good corporate governance.[125] A duty that fits well into one system may consequently not be effective in another legal system, due to differences in any of the above-mentioned aspects.[126] Caution should therefore be taken when discussing and promoting convergence and changes with respect to rules governing directors' duties.[127]

---

122. *See* regarding self-regulation Cheffins, *supra* n. 116, at 364 et seq.

123. *See, e.g.*, Rafael La Porta, et al, *The Economic Consequences of Legal Origins* (November 2007), available at https://ssrn.com/abstract=1028081; Hao Liang and Luc Renneboog, *On the Foundations of Corporate Social Responsibility*, ECGI Finance Working Paper, No 394/2013, available at https://ssrn.com/abstract=2360633; Jesper Lau Hansen, *A Scandinavian Approach to Corporate Governance*, 125–142, 126–128 (2010) available at https://scandinavianlaw.se/pdf/50-8.pdf and Williams, *supra* n. 43, at 662–664. A different categorization is made by Hansmann and Kraakman, *supra* n. 31.

124. *See, e.g.*, Liang and Renneboog, *supra* n. 123; Mark J. Roe and Massimiliano Vatiero, *Corporate Governance and Its Political Economy*, The Oxford Handbook of Corporate Law and Governance (Jeffrey N. Gordon and Wolf-Georg Ringe eds., Oxford University Press 2018) 56–83 and Ronald J. Gilson, *From Corporate Law to Corporate Governance*, The Oxford Handbook of Corporate Law and Governance (Jeffrey N. Gordon and Wolf-Georg Ringe eds., Oxford University Press 2018), 3–27, 9–14.

125. *See, e.g.*, Strine, *supra* n. 34.

126. *See* for an analysis of especially the Swedish corporate governance system Jessica Östberg, *supra* n. 25, at 28–40.

127. *See* Jeffrey. N. Gordon, *Convergence and Persistence in Corporate Law and Governance*, The Oxford Handbook of Corporate Law and Governance (Jeffrey N. Gordon and Wolf-Georg Ringe eds, Oxford University Press 2018), 28–55. Lucian A. Bebchuk and Mark J. Roe, *A Theory of*

Moreover, even if the (positive) duty to act in the interest of the company is specified so that it is consistent with the corporate governance system, it should be kept in mind that the duty works mainly as a guiding principle. It may indeed to some extent promote good corporate governance in this capacity, since it guides the board of directors when taking business decisions, but the business judgment rule and the enforcement rules will, as stated above, often limit its effect in practice. It is therefore important that governments and international organizations, including the EU, consider this when drafting rules to promote good corporate governance.

Path Dependence in Corporate Ownership and Governance, 52 Stan. L. Rev. 127 (1999). Henry Hansmann and Reinier Kraakman are of another opinion and assert that the shareholder value principle should prevail in general, *see supra* n. 31.

CHAPTER 3

A General Corporate Law Duty to Act Sustainably

Beate Sjåfjell[*]

§3.01 INTRODUCTION

My starting point for this chapter is that it is time to get real about corporate sustainability. That means that I am not going to use a lot of space in this chapter to talk about climate change, declared to be code red for humanity,[1] or on the latest research from January 2022, showing that the fifth of the hitherto identified nine planetary boundaries is now exceeded[2] – putting even further stress on the Earth systems on which we depend for this Earth to be relatively safe space for humanity.[3] Nor am I going to elaborate on how many of the global value chains of European businesses are

* I thank the organizers of the January 2022 conference and the editors of the volume, Karsten Engsig Sørensen, Hanne Birkmose, and Mette Neville, for the opportunity and to all participants for inspiring comments and suggestions. This work is based on collaborative research in the EU-funded project Sustainable Market Actors for Responsible Trade (SMART, 2016–2020), and the chapter draws on joint reports and publications flowing from the SMART project. I thank the entire SMART team and especially, in the context of this work, Jukka Mähönen, Tonia Novitz, Clair Gammage, Hanna Ahlström, and Sarah Cornell. For helpful comments to a draft of this chapter, my thanks go to Karsten Engsig Sørensen and Hanne Birkmose, and most of all, for always inspiring and thoughtful insights, to Jukka Mähönen.

1. United Nations, 'UN Meetings Coverage and Press Releases: Secretary-General Calls Latest IPCC Climate Report "Code Red for Humanity", Stressing "Irrefutable" Evidence of Human Influence' (August 2021), https://press.un.org/en/2021/sgsm20847.doc.htm.
2. Linn Persson, et al., *Outside the Safe Operating Space of the Planetary Boundary for Novel Entities* 56(3) Environ. Sci. Technol. (2022). There is also research indicating that a sixth boundary, that of green water (as an element of fresh water), may be breached; Lan Wang-Erlandsson et al., *A Planetary Boundary for Green Water* 3 Nat. Rev. Earth Environ. 1–13 (2022).
3. Johan Rockström, et al., *Planetary Boundaries: Exploring the Safe Operating Space for Humanity* 14(2) Ecology and Society (2009); Will Steffen, et al., *Planetary Boundaries: Guiding Human Development on a Changing Planet* 347 Science (2015) 1259855; Persson et al., *supra* n. 2.

based on destruction of the environment, exploitation of people, and undermining of the economic basis for functioning societies[4] – threatening the overarching goal of sustainability.[5]

In this chapter, I am not going to make the argument for the necessity of the contribution of business to achieve sustainability and how sustainability-oriented legislation is necessary to secure that contribution. That argument is made multiple times elsewhere, by many scholars.[6] Instead, the topic of this chapter responds to the question of how we can use law to ensure this contribution; concretely, how to integrate sustainability into corporate governance. Integrating sustainability into corporate governance is also by the European Commission seen as a prerequisite for securing the contribution of business to sustainability.[7]

I propose that this integration can be done through implementing a general corporate duty to act sustainably, with the corporate board as the key actor. For that we need to go to company law, which is the regulatory infrastructure for decision-making in business, not as a silver bullet – but as a key contribution to the regulatory jigsaw puzzle of sustainability. As all company law scholars who have analysed the sources know, company law gives a broad discretion to corporate boards and by extension senior management in their corporate governance.[8] There is space within the current company law and corporate governance systems to steer businesses in more sustainable directions.[9] This space is, however, taken up by the social norm of shareholder primacy.[10] Company law must take back that space and clarify what the legislative aim

4. Jason Hickel, *The Divide: A Brief Guide to Global Inequality and Its Solutions* (William Heinemann 2017); Mark B. Taylor and Maja van der Velden, *Resistance to Regulation: Failing Sustainability in Product Lifecycles* 11 Sustainability 6526 (2019); Kate Raworth, *A Safe and Just Space for Humanity: Can We Live Within the Doughnut* Oxfam Discussion Papers (2012).
5. The overarching goal of sustainability is in this chapter understood as mitigating pressures on planetary boundaries and securing social foundations for humanity now and for the future – a safe and just space for humanity on this planet, Melissa Leach, Kate Raworth, and Johan Rockström, *Between Social and Planetary Boundaries: Navigating Pathways in the Safe and Just Space for Humanity* World Social Science Report 84–90 (OECD Publishing, 2013). *See* further in §3.02.
6. Including as results of the EU-funded project Sustainable Markets Actors for Responsible Trade, e.g., Beate Sjåfjell, *How Company Law Has Failed Human Rights – and What to Do About It*, Bus. Hum. Rights J. (2020); and *see also* Andrew Johnston, et al., *Corporate Governance for Sustainability*, Corporate Governance for Sustainability (11 December 2019). Available at SSRN: https://ssrn.com/abstract=3502101; Lynn A. Stout, et al., *The Modern Corporation Statement on Company Law*, The Modern Corporation Statement on Company Law (6 October 2016). Available at SSRN: https://ssrn.com/abstract=2848833; Kent Greenfield, *The Failure of Corporate Law: Fundamental Flaws and Progressive Possibilities* (University of Chicago Press 2008); Christopher M. Bruner, *Center-Left Politics and Corporate Governance: What Is the 'Progressive' Agenda?* (2) Brigh Young Univ Law Rev 267-334 (2018).
7. European Commission, Proposal for a Directive of the European Parliament and of The Council on Corporate Sustainability Due Diligence and amending Directive (EU) 2019/1937, COM/2022/71 final (23 February 2022), Explanatory Memorandum, page 1.
8. Beate Sjåfjell, Andrew Johnston, Linn Anker-Sørensen, and David Millon, *Shareholder Primacy: The Main Barrier to Sustainable Companies* in *Company Law and Sustainability: Legal Barriers and Opportunities* 79-147 (Beate Sjåfjell & Benjamin J. Richardson (eds), Cambridge University Press, 2015).
9. *Ibid.*
10. *Ibid.*

is with allowing and encouraging companies to be used as a main form for organising business, and give a principle-based instruction to boards on how to do their jobs in this era, defined by the extreme unsustainabilities resulting from business as usual.[11]

In §3.02, I introduce the concept of sustainable value creation, which already is increasingly being referenced in corporate governance, and suggest that it needs to be interpreted within a research-based concept of sustainability, to make sense. This includes positioning it within the concept of planetary boundaries. In §3.03, drawing on work from two international research projects,[12] I discuss how the concepts of 'sustainable value creation' and 'planetary boundaries' can be used to establish a general duty and thereby integrated into corporate governance, with company law duties of the board at the core.[13] As a follow-up of the EU's Sustainable Corporate Governance initiative, the European Commission in February 2022 presented its proposal for a Corporate Sustainability Due Diligence Directive.[14] With its suggestion for a sustainability-oriented 'duty of care', it is directly relevant to the discussion of a corporate duty to act sustainably. I therefore engage with this proposal to the extent possible within the constraints of space, in this chapter. In §3.04, I turn to due diligence, as a key tool to follow-up on such a general duty, where the proposed Directive is also a part of the analysis. Due diligence is especially relevant at the time of writing, as a core issue in policy-making discussions, influenced by international norm sets, notably the UN Guiding Principles for Business and Human Rights (UNGPs) and the Organisation for Economic Co-operation and Development Guidelines for Multinational Enterprises (OECD Guidelines), developments in domestic legislation, notably the French, German, Norwegian, and Dutch legislative initiatives,[15] and the proposal for a Corporate Sustainability Due Diligence Directive. §3.05 discusses briefly enforcement questions, while §3.06 presents concluding reflections.

§3.02 SUSTAINABLE VALUE CREATION AND PLANETARY BOUNDARIES

In this chapter, the core of the proposal on how to integrate sustainability into corporate governance through company law reform is *sustainable value creation*. Sustainable value creation is an emerging concept, increasingly reflected in corporate governance codes in Europe. Examples include Austrian, German,[16]

11. *Ibid.*
12. Sustainable Companies (2010–2014), https://www.jus.uio.no/ifp/english/research/projects/sustainable-companies/ and SMART (2016-2020), https://www.smart.uio.no/.
13. Austrian Code of Corporate Governance (2021), available at: https://ecgi.global/sites/default/files/codes/documents/austria_corporate-governance-code-012021.pdf.
14. Proposal, *supra* n. 7.
15. *See, e.g.*, Markus Krajewski, Kristel Tonstad, and Franziska. Wohltmann, *Mandatory Human Rights Due Diligence in Germany and Norway: Stepping, or Striding, in the Same Direction?* 6. Bus. Hum. Rights J. 550–58 (2021).
16. German Corporate Governance Code 2022, available at: https://www.dcgk.de//files/dcgk/usercontent/en/download/code/220627_German_Corporate_Governance_Code_2022.pdf.

Belgian,[17] Danish,[18] Norwegian,[19] and Dutch[20] corporate governance code reforms. Rather than profit maximization or maximization of returns for shareholders (which the social norm of shareholder primacy requires), *value creation* is a concept that resonates with business - it is what business sees itself as doing. *Sustainable value creation* is in line with the Zeitgeist of our time as business increasingly recognizes its role as a contributor to the fundamental transformation to sustainability, for the sake of business itself, in light of the increasing financial and corporate risks of unsustainability,[21] and to fulfil its societal role.

To avoid that the concept of sustainable value creation becomes a mechanism of 'sustainability washing' (using references to sustainability to cover over continued unsustainable business) or 'sustainability wishing'[22] (e.g., business goals related to sustainability without clear plans on how to achieve them), the concept must be positioned within a research-based understanding.[23] This entails first that the creation of sustainable value must be interpreted as activity that engages with the goal of securing social foundations for humanity now and for the future, in a way that contributes to mitigating pressures on planetary boundaries.[24] In previous work, including in the project Sustainable Market Actors for Responsible Trade (SMART), we have used the formulation of securing social foundations for humanity now and for the future '*within* planetary boundaries'. Now in 2022, in recognition of the reality of the continuing vast environmental destruction that has led to ever grimmer reports about

17. Belgian Code on Corporate Governance (2020), available at: www.corporategovernancecommittee.be/sites/default/files/generated/files/page/2020_belgian_code_on_corporate_governance.pdf.
18. Danish Recommendations on Corporate Governance (2020), available at: https://corporategovernance.dk/sites/default/files/media/anbefalinger_for_god_selskabsledelse_engelsk.pdf.
19. The Norwegian Code of Practice for Corporate Governance (2021), available at: https://nues.no/eierstyring-og-selskapsledelse-engelsk/.
20. The Dutch Corporate Governance Code (2016), available at: https://www.mccg.nl/download/?id=3367.
21. Patrick. W. Keys, Victor Galaz, Michelle Dyer, et al., *Anthropocene risk* 2 Nature Sustainability 667-73 *(*2019*)*; Gail Whiteman & Amanda Williams, *Systemic Planetary Risks: Implications for Organization Studies* in, *The Routledge Companion to Risk, Crisis and Emergency Management* Ch. 13 (Robert Gephart Jr., C. Chet Miller, Karin. S. Helgesson (eds), Routledge 2019); Beate Sjåfjell, *The Financial Risks of Unsustainability: A Research Agenda University of Oslo Faculty of Law Research Paper No. 2020-18* (2020).
22. Thank you to Sarah Cornell of Stockholm Resilience Centre for coining this apt phrase.
23. This presentation of 'sustainable value' and 'planetary boundaries', draws on and updates the presentation in Beate Sjåfjell and Georgina Tsagas, *Integrating Sustainable Value Creation in Corporate Governance: Company Law, Corporate Governance Codes and the Constitution of the Company* in *Sustainable Value Creation in the European Union: Towards Pathways to a Sustainable Future through Crises*, Ch. 9 (Beate Sjåfjell, Georgina Tsagas, Charlotte Villiers (eds), Cambridge University Press 2022).
24. Raworth, *supra* n. 4; Steffen et al., *supra* n. 3; Persson et al., *supra* n. 2; Leach, et al., *supra* n. 5, at 84–90. *See* further Beate Sjåfjell, Tiina Häyhä, and Sarah Cornell, *A Research-Based Approach to the UN Sustainable Development Goals. A Prerequisite to Sustainable Business*, University of Oslo Faculty of Law Research Paper No. 2020-02, Nordic & European Company Law Working Paper No. 21-12, Available at SSRN: https://ssrn.com/abstract=3526744 or http://dx.doi.org/10.2139/ssrn.3526744.

the extent to which the planetary boundaries are transgressed,[25] I am using rather the terminology of '*mitigating pressures* on planetary boundaries' as a crucial element of sustainable value creation.[26]

Connecting sustainable value creation to the concept of planetary boundaries in this way has potential significance on three interconnected levels: first, it brings to the forefront that there are ecological limits (conversely, that being perceived as 'environmentally friendly' may be totally inadequate) and that transgressing these limits has current and future catastrophic consequences. Second, it highlights the complex interactions between planet-level environmental processes, recognizing, for example, that climate change, however topical (and difficult to mitigate), is only one aspect of the convergence of crises we are heading towards. Third, it continuously reminds us that state-of-the-art natural science must inform our decisions on a work-in-progress-basis, encompassing the uncertainty and complexity of the global challenges. All this is not to say that it is the sole responsibility of business to mitigate pressures on planetary boundaries. The convergence of crises caused by the changing of the climate, the accelerated extinction of species, the pressures on fresh water, soil, and the oceans, and the pollution of the air we breathe, is an international calamity. International institutions, regional and national governments across the world have a duty to act. However, mitigating pressures on planetary boundaries without the contribution of business is not possible. It is therefore necessary to find adequate ways of translating the necessity of action into the governance of business.

This necessity is reflected also in the opening sentences of the explanatory text of the proposed Corporate Sustainability Due Diligence Directive:

> The behaviour of companies across all sectors of the economy is key to succeed in the Union's transition to a climate-neutral and green economy in line with the European Green Deal and in delivering on the UN Sustainable Development Goals, including on its human rights- and environment-related objectives.[27]

Indeed, also securing social foundations for humanity now and for the future requires action on all levels, from international institutions through to the individual business. Engaging with these goals in the governance of business encompasses issues such as fair treatment of employees as well as of workers and local communities across global value chains, with respect for international human rights and core International Labour Organization (ILO) conventions as a minimum, ensuring a 'living wage' and safe working conditions. Further, sustainable business entails supporting democratic political processes and not undermining these through engaging in corporate capture of regulatory processes. It also entails contributing to the economic basis of the societies

25. With just two examples highlighted here: Persson et al., *supra* n. 2; and Wang-Erlandsson, et al., *supra* n. 2; https://doi.org/10.1038/s43017-022-00287-8.
26. My thanks go again to Sarah Cornell, who identified the need for this change in terminology and with whom I developed the new formulation.
27. European Commission, Proposal for a Directive on corporate sustainability due diligence and annex, Explanatory Memorandum 1 (2022).

in which the business interacts by not engaging in so-called aggressive tax planning and outright evasion.[28]

As an intrinsic element of transitioning towards sustainable value creation, the following must be included: participatory aspects of the social foundations,[29] of workers, regardless of their labour law status, and of affected communities, including indigenous peoples and ensuring that all affected are fully involved.[30] And yet, we must avoid merely replacing the 'shareholder' in shareholder primacy with 'stakeholder'.[31] While involving affected communities, trade unions, and civil society is crucial, a mere canvassing of 'stakeholder interests' and giving priority to the ones that make themselves heard the most is insufficient. The backdrop must always be the interconnected complexities and the vulnerability of the often-unrepresented groups (whether invisible workers deep in the global value chains, indigenous communities, or future generations),[32] and the aim of a sustainable future where the pressures on planetary boundaries are successfully mitigated.

§3.03 INTEGRATING SUSTAINABLE VALUE CREATION IN CORPORATE GOVERNANCE

[A] Sustainable Value Creation as Corporate Purpose

Integrating the concepts of 'sustainable value creation' and 'planetary boundaries' into corporate governance can be done by company law setting this out as the overarching purpose of the company, as a basis for a general duty for the company and thereby for its board. Alternatively, we can assume this purpose and go directly to the question of how to set out sustainability as a general duty for the company, integrated into the duties for the board. For several reasons, including that it would be the ultimate push-back by company law against the social norm of shareholder primacy, I would prefer to see such a purpose included in a company law reform, and I outline here how we have suggested that such a purpose could be set up.[33]

Such a proposal, to redefine the overarching purpose of the company, should not be seen as one that dramatically changes the nature of European businesses or their

28. Sjåfjell, *supra* n. 6.
29. Tonia Novitz, *Engagement with Sustainability at the International Labour Organization and Implications for Worker Voice* 159(4) Int. Labour Rev 463-482 (2020). Concerning some of the challenges involved, *see also* Ian Scoones, *The Politics of Sustainability and Development* 41 Annual Review of Environment and Resources 293–319 (2016).
30. As indeed is envisaged by SDG 16.
31. Beate Sjåfjell and Jukka Mähönen, *Corporate Purpose and the Misleading Shareholder vs Stakeholder Dichotomy* University of Oslo Faculty of Law Research Paper No. 2022-43, Available at SSRN: https://ssrn.com/abstract=4039565 or http://dx.doi.org/10.2139/ssrn.4039565. *See also* Marco Ventoruzzo, *On 'Prosperity' by Colin Mayer: Brief Critical Remarks on the (Legal) Relevance of announcing a Multi-Stakeholders 'Corporate Purpose'*, https://iris.unibocconi.it/handle/11565/4037291 (2020).
32. Louis J. Kotzé, *The Anthropocene, Earth System Vulnerability and Socio-ecological Injustice in an Age of Human Rights* 10 Journal of Human Rights and the Environment 62–85 (2019).
33. This Section draws on Beate Sjåfjell, Jukka Mähönen, Tonia A. Novitz, Clair Gammage, and Hanna Ahlström, 'Securing the Future of European Business: SMART Reform Proposals', s. 6.2.1

purpose. It does not take away profit as an intrinsic element of the nature of business or of their value creation. It does not change the differences between various forms of undertakings in the European economy, and how profit is used and distributed in them. For example, cooperatives will still be distinguishable from companies, and multinational enterprises from small and medium-sized enterprises (SMEs). Neither does it challenge the distinction between for-profit and not-for-profit, nor attempt to make all businesses into social enterprises.

What our proposal does do, is to position the value creation of European companies, with profit as an intrinsic element, within the context of the transition to sustainability that we all need to undertake. Today European businesses are at best struggling to be a part of the transition to sustainability, within a globalized economic system that in aggregate appears to value short-term maximization of returns above all else, albeit with local, jurisdictional, and temporal variations. This tension entails that businesses are trying to create value in a sustainable way, while maximization of returns is perceived by many as the overarching purpose, due to the shareholder primacy drive. I therefore propose, drawing on our previous work, that sustainable value creation, including contributing to mitigating pressures on planetary boundaries, is set as the overarching purpose, outlining the scope within which profit will continue to be made. This would give the sustainability-oriented businesses in Europe, of which there undoubtedly are many, the competitive advantage over unsustainable business.

In the SMART proposal, we suggested a text for a reform of European Union (EU) law (specifically of the EU company law directive 2017).[34] I include it below with the revisions based on newer research. Obviously, this can be adapted to a national company law context without being adopted on the EU level first. In our proposal, we suggested that the text of the reform should speak generally of undertakings rather than specifically of companies, which otherwise is the focus of this chapter.

Such an overarching purpose could simply be expressed in the following manner:

> The overarching purpose of the undertaking is to create sustainable value in a manner that contributes to mitigating pressures on planetary boundaries.[35]

Both key concepts should be defined, and we suggested the following definitions in the specific context of the proposed reform:

> … 'planetary boundaries' shall mean the scientifically recognised processes that regulate the stability and resilience of the Earth system within which humanity can continue to develop and thrive for generations to come.
>
> … to create 'sustainable value' shall mean creating value for the undertaking, while respecting the rights of its members, investors, employees, and other

(7 May 2020). University of Oslo Faculty of Law Research Paper No. 2020-11, Nordic & European Company Law Working Paper No. 20-08, Available at SSRN: https://ssrn.com/abstract=3595048.

34. Directive (EU) 2017/1132 of the European Parliament and of the Council of 14 June 2017 relating to certain aspects of company law (Text with EEA relevance), OJ L 169 30.6.2017, p. 46, latest consolidated version available here: https://eur-lex.europa.eu/legal-content/EN/TXT/?uri=CELEX:02017L1132-20190731.
35. *Ibid.*

contractual parties, and promoting good governance, decent work and equality, and the human rights of its workers and affected communities and peoples.[36]

The specific purposes in legislation governing the various forms of undertakings in the Member States may be maintained, with any necessary adjustment to clarify their positioning within the proposed overarching purpose. Similarly, the instruments of constitution, and memorandum and articles of association, could, of course, include a more detailed and individual purpose for the specific undertaking.

[B] Sustainable Value Creation as the Duty of the Company and of the Board

Whether an overarching purpose for business is spelled out in legislation or not – and 'not' is the most likely – a general duty to act sustainably for the company can be established. The crucial point in operationalizing this is to integrate sustainable value creation within the duties of the board.[37] That is what I concentrate on in this section.

[1] Company Law, the Interests of the Company and the Misleading Shareholder vs Stakeholder Dichotomy

Much of the discussion after the Commission launched its Sustainable Corporate Governance Initiative has been constrained within a shareholder versus stakeholder dichotomy, with an understandable confusion as to what this may mean for the company law definition of the interests of the company. Going down the rabbit hole of discussing whether shareholder primacy is preferable to a vague stakeholder concept ignores company law proper; it seems to have been used as a strawman in the discussion, and it is in my view the biggest mistake the European Commission made in its initiative.

Taking a company law point of view, it is clear that the core duty of the board according to company laws across jurisdictions is to promote the interests of the company.[38] The definition of the interests of the company, as a matter of company law,[39] varies across European countries, from the monistic, concentrating on the economic interest, with more or less emphasis on the shareholders, to the pluralistic, including a variety of other involved or affected parties.[40] Company legislation rarely expressly stipulates what is included in the interests of the company. The interpretation

36. *Ibid.*
37. 'Board' can be understood as the administrative or management organ as well as the supervisory organ of the company, depending on the corporate governance system of the individual company.
38. The chapter by Jessica Östberg in this volume takes this starting point but thereafter embarks on a shareholder vs. stakeholder analysis of what the duties entail.
39. I.e., based on proper legal analysis, and not drawing merely on postulates derived on certain law-and-economics doctrines, as we have seen in the shareholder primacy influenced literature; Sjåfjell et al., *supra* n. 8.
40. *Ibid.*

is thereby left to the boards, and in light, *inter alia*, of the business judgment rule, the question of whether the board has interpreted their duty correctly rarely comes to a head in case law.[41] The interests of the company as a company law concept should not be harmonized in EU company law. It only places countries and scholars in different camps, waking up old discussions.[42] Defining the interests of the company should be left to the individual development of the law in each country.

The reform proposal I draw on and present here therefore recognizes the concept of 'interests of the company' in company law and does not propose to harmonize this. Rather it integrates the concept of 'sustainable value creation' in a research- and principle-based manner. The latter reflects our aim to find the balance between proposing rules that are principles-based and open enough to allow for the individual innovative value creation of each business, which characterizes successful market economies, while being firm enough on the framework and the basis.

Our proposed rules on the board therefore start out with clarifying what is well-established in European company law, yet which nevertheless has become clouded through the influence of the shareholder primacy drive, namely that the core duty of the board is to promote the interests of the company.[43] This important step of clarification is included in the proposed Corporate Sustainability Due Diligence Directive Article 25(1), setting out the language of 'when fulfilling their duty to act in the best interest of the company' concerning the corporate board (and more broadly, 'directors').[44]

However, the proposed Due Diligence Directive Article 25(2) continues the sentence by saying that the 'directors' 'when fulfilling their duty to act in the best interest of the company (...) 'shall take into account the consequences of their decisions for sustainability matters, including, where applicable, human rights, climate change and environmental consequences, including in the short, medium and long term'. A reference to 'take into account' is reminiscent of the 'enlightened shareholder value' approach of section 172 of the UK Companies Act, and is not a good starting point.[45] To the contrary, the 'enlightened shareholder value' is an approach that has not contributed to more sustainability-oriented business, and rather continued to facilitate shareholder primacy, as is well-documented in the literature.[46]

---

41. *Ibid.*
42. As we can *see* in Jessica Östberg's contribution to this book.
43. Sjåfjell et al., *supra* n. 8.
44. For a further discussion of this point, *see* Sjåfjell and Mähönen, *supra* n. 31, s. 5.1.
45. It is also one that is employed in the proposal for the Corporate Sustainability Reporting Directive, in its revision of Article 19a, which includes in the suggested reporting duties: 'how the undertaking's business model and strategy take account of the interests of the undertaking's stakeholders and of the impacts of the undertaking on sustainability matters'.
46. *See* among many contributors Charlotte L. Villiers, *Sustainable Companies: Barriers and Possibilities in UK Company Law* 11(1) International and Comparative Corporate Law Journal (2015) University of Oslo Faculty of Law Research Paper No. 2010-03, Available at SSRN: https://ssrn.com/abstract=1712791; Andrew Johnston, *Market-Led Sustainability through Information Disclosure: The UK Approach*, in *Cambridge Handbook of Corporate Law, Corporate Governance and Sustainability* Chapter 15 (Beate Sjåfjell and Christopher M. Bruner (eds), Cambridge University Press, 2019).

[2] Sustainable Value Creation as the Core Connecting Element

Environmental, social, and governance aspects together form the core of sustainable value creation. We can expect to see the concept of sustainable value creation developed further in legislation and through codes and standards, by Member States, business organisations, and front-runner companies. A principle-based formulation of the duty of the board can inspire and form a positively formulated framework for such further development. The sustainability due diligence duty of the board as a key tool, and the guidance developed for this duty, can provide the specificity of which negative sustainability impacts and risks that shall be prevented or mitigated.[47]

The Commission's aim with the proposed Directive, as expressed in the Commission Staff Working Document, is to contribute to the transition to sustainability through fostering sustainable value creation in European companies:

The general objective of this initiative is to better exploit the potential of the single market to contribute to the transition to a sustainable economy, to *foster sustainable value creation* and improve the long-term performance and resilience of EU companies.[48]

Sustainable value creation could have been a useful connecting point between the sustainability goals of the EU and the sustainability efforts of business. It is, however, not mentioned in the proposed Directive or even in its Explanatory Memorandum (as opposed to in the Commission Staff Working Document cited earlier). This is a missed opportunity.

Engaging with sustainable value creation drawing on a research-based concept of sustainability is what the proposal I draw on and present here does. The proposal outlines the boundaries within which the board shall promote the interests of the company, clarifying and redefining the duties of the board. Developing the understanding of what the interests of the specific company entail in a specific instance should remain with the board to define, within the scope of European and national legislation, articles of association, and existing contracts and commitments.

If an overarching purpose is included in a company law reform, as suggested earlier in §3.01, that would of course be the starting point for the formulation of the duty of the board. A reform including the overarching purpose seems highly unlikely at the time of writing. Therefore, I concentrate here on the alternative, namely encompassing such an overarching purpose indirectly through a general duty to act sustainably, integrated into the formulation of the duties of the board.

47. *See* European Parliament, Legal Affairs draft Directive (Sept 2020): 'Recalls that due diligence is primarily a preventative mechanism and that companies should be first and foremost required to identify risks or adverse impacts and adopt policies and measures to address them; highlights that if an undertaking causes or contributes to an adverse impact it should provide for a remedy'.

48. Commission Staff Working Document, February 2022, https://data.consilium.europa.eu/doc/document/ST-6533-2022-ADD-5/en/pdf, s. 4.1. Emphasis in original omitted with emphasis added here to highlight relevance to the text.

[3] Operationalising Sustainable Value Creation as the Duty of the Board

To express a general duty to act sustainably, the duty of the board may be formulated as 'promoting the interests of the company in such a way as to create sustainable value that also contributes to mitigating pressures on planetary boundaries'. The duty should encompass the entire business of the company across global value chains.

The duty should be further specified. This specification can start out by requiring that the board is to ensure the alignment of the business model of the company with this duty and to draw up a strategy that ensures the follow-up of the duty, including the integration into internal control and risk management systems.[49]

Including a duty to assess the business model of the company resonates with the reporting duty according to the so-called Non-Financial Reporting Directive of 2014[50] and further in the 2021 proposal for a revision of the reporting rules through a new Corporate Sustainability Reporting Directive.[51] The proposal for the Corporate Sustainability Due Diligence Directive references the 2014 Directive and the 2021 proposal, with the intention of an alignment. Yet, in the proposal for the Corporate Sustainability Due Diligence Directive, business model and strategy requirements are concentrated in Article 15 on climate change (albeit with the 'transition to a sustainable economy' as a stepping stone), where it is set out that Member States shall ensure that companies shall 'adopt a plan to ensure that the business model and strategy of the company are compatible with the transition to a sustainable economy and with the limiting of global warming to 1.5°C in line with the Paris Agreement'.[52]

The provision goes on to set out a double materiality standard, stating that the plan shall identify the extent to which 'climate change is a risk for, or an impact of, the company's operations'. Where climate change is, or 'should have been', identified as a 'principal risk for, or a principal impact of, the company's operations', the company is to include 'emission reduction objectives' in its plan.[53] This approach, albeit limited to climate in the proposed Directive, resonates with the requirement for drawing up an

49. Sjåfjell, et al., *supra* n. 33, s. 6.2.1.
50. Directive 2014/95/EU amending Directive 2013/34/EU as regards disclosure of non-financial and diversity information by certain large undertakings and groups (OJ L 330, 15.11.2014, pp. 1–9), adding Article 19a to the 2013 Accounting Directive.
51. Proposal for a Directive of the European Parliament and of the Council amending Directive 2013/34/EU, Directive 2004/109/EC, Directive 2006/43/EC and Regulation (EU) No 537/2014, as regards corporate sustainability reporting. *See* further the provisional agreement regarding the Corporate Sustainability Reporting Directive reached by the Council and European Parliament on 30 June 2022, https://www.consilium.europa.eu/en/press/press-releases/2022/06/21/new-rules-on-sustainability-disclosure-provisional-agreement-between-council-and-european-parliament/.
52. Also in the 2021 proposal for the Corporate Sustainability Reporting Directive, climate is given such an emphasis.
53. In the provisional agreement regarding the Corporate Sustainability Reporting Directive reached by the Council and European Parliament on 30 June 2022, the specific reporting requirements on climate are made even more ambitious, *see* https://www.consilium.europa.eu/en/press/press-releases/2022/06/21/new-rules-on-sustainability-disclosure-provisional-agreement-between-council-and-european-parliament/.

ambitious improvement process, which we suggest should be adopted for all sustainability aspects. I return to this below, where I also discuss the proposed Directive's limited and fragmented approach further.

Climate change is a crucial issue. However, mitigating climate change is not synonymous with achieving sustainability; it is not the only planetary boundary which is transgressed, posing threats to humanity. Nor is achieving sustainability possibly without social justice. The complexity and interconnectedness of a research-based concept of sustainability should therefore form the basis for a company law duty to act sustainably. It is not possible to avoid defining sustainability, if the intent is to achieve a level playing field and legal certainty on the path towards securing the contribution of business to sustainability. The concepts of sustainable value creation and planetary boundaries should be explicitly included in the duty of the board, and clearly defined, for example, as we proposed, cited earlier in §3.03[A]. Further specification is needed – and that is what we suggest to include in our reform, cited below. Mitigating pressures on planetary boundaries is not something that easily can be operationalized on the individual company level.[54] It should therefore in a corporate governance context be formulated as a duty to *contribute* to the mitigation, as indicated in §3.02. Again, I draw on our SMART reform proposal, slightly revised here:

> The board shall work to ensure that the operations and activities of the business, including the full life of the products, processes, and services of the business, contribute to global society mitigating pressures planetary boundaries,[55] employing best available knowledge and technology. This entails complying with the most ambitious politically adopted targets at the EU level or relevant Member State level. This further entails protecting and regenerating natural resources and processes. This includes avoiding, or reducing as far as possible, contributions to:
>
> (a) biodiversity loss in all ecosystems, including oceans;
> (b) freshwater pollution and scarcity;
> (c) land system change, including change in regional vegetation;
> (d) greenhouse gas emissions;
> (e) atmospheric aerosol emissions;
> (f) chemical pollution including synthetic organic pollutants, heavy metal compounds, and radioactive materials; and the introduction of novel entities including microplastics and nanomaterials;
> (g) ozone depletion;
> (h) nitrogen and phosphorus pollution; and
> (i) ocean acidification.[56]
>
> Sustainable value creation, however, can be more specifically defined and operationalized on the individual company level:

54. *See, e.g.*, Roland Clift, et al., *The Challenges of Applying Planetary Boundaries as a Basis for Strategic Decision-Making in Companies with Global Supply Chains* 9 Sustainability 279 (2017).
55. For the definition of planetary boundaries in the context of the SMART reform proposal, *see* §3.03[A].
56. Sjåfjell, et al., *supra* n. 33.

The board shall further ensure that the operations and activities of the business, including the full life of the products, processes, and services of the business, creates sustainable value.[57] This entails promoting:

(a) employment and its protection;
(b) a working environment in which dignity, health, and safety are protected, including provision of suitable pay, hours, and holidays;
(c) the acquisition of skills, competencies, and qualifications;
(d) the elimination of discrimination in respect of employment and occupation, regardless of characteristics such as gender, race, age, disability, and migrant status;
(e) freedom of association and the effective recognition of the right to collective bargaining;
(f) consultative processes for engagement with local communities, including indigenous peoples affected by the operations and activities of their business;
(g) inclusion of all affected groups and persons, whether workers, subcontractors, or local or national interest groups and community representatives in due diligence scrutiny; and
(h) responsible tax behaviour.

This further entails avoiding:

(a) child labour and any form of abuse, exploitation, trafficking, and violence against children;
(b) any connection with forced or compulsory labour, modern slavery, and human trafficking;
(c) bypassing any representative government processes or subverting the rule of law, including through corruption;
(d) any form of tax evasion; and
(e) breach of internationally recognized human rights.[58]

In the proposal for duties of the board, we proposed a duty to undertake a stringent sustainability assessment, including employing sustainability due diligence. Items (f) and (g) in the list above, on the consultative process and the inclusion of affected groups and communities, central to effective sustainability due diligence, show how our proposed general duty clearly connects with the key tool of due diligence. I discuss sustainability due diligence in §3.04 below, after first discussing the proposed Directive's limited and limiting approach to sustainability. Thereafter, §3.05 turns to the follow up of the duties in the proposal.

[4] The Proposed Directive's Limiting Approach to Sustainability

The proposed Directive's title of Corporate Sustainability Due Diligence, resonating with the title of the proposed Corporate Sustainability Reporting Directive, indicates that a broad approach to sustainability is taken. However, as we can see in the specification of environmental and human rights issues, this proposed Directive does

57. For the definition of sustainable value in the context of the SMART reform proposal, *see* §3.03[A].
58. *Ibid.*

not draw on any research-based concept of sustainability. The Commission's proposal text does not engage with the planetary boundaries framework, although that would have given a good basis for setting out more ambitious environmental requirements. The proposal document does not define sustainability, despite the term 'sustainability' being used fifty times in the proposal text after the title of the proposed Directive itself. Rather, it narrows 'sustainability' down to those aspects that flow from international environmental and human rights conventions. This shows a Commission on the defensive and out of sync with the EU regulatory system with which its proposal intends to engage and create policy coherence. It is also insufficient in light of a research-based concept of sustainability.

Limiting the 'sustainability matters' to environmental and human rights issues fails to encompass other aspects of the extreme unsustainabilities of our time, notably the undermining of the economic bases of well-functioning societies through illicit financial flows.[59] It is also not in line with the so-called Non-Financial Reporting Directive of 2014, which sets out that companies are to report on 'as a minimum, environmental, social and employee matters, respect for human rights, anti-corruption and bribery matters'.[60] The proposed Corporate Sustainability Due Diligence Directive further limits the scope of its 'sustainability matters' by defining those with reference only to international conventions.[61]

The definition of sustainability aspects in the process leading up to the Commission's proposal were much broader. Environmental aspects were set out in the following way in the suggested wording in the European Parliament, Committee of Legal Affairs draft Directive of September 2020:

- 'environmental risk' means any potential or actual adverse impact that may impair the right to a healthy environment, whether temporarily or permanently, and of whatever magnitude, duration or frequency. These include, but are not limited to, adverse impacts on the climate, the sustainable use of natural resources, and biodiversity and ecosystems. These risks include climate change, air and water pollution, deforestation, loss in biodiversity, and greenhouse emissions.[62]

59. *See* §3.02; and Hickel, *supra* n. 4.
60. Directive 2014/95/EU amending Directive 2013/34/EU as regards disclosure of non-financial and diversity information by certain large undertakings and groups (OJ L 330, 15.11.2014, pp. 1-9), Article 19a. This is followed up in the proposed Corporate Sustainability Reporting Directive 2021, consensus of 2022, which connects its definition of 'sustainability matters' to the 'sustainability factors' in the Sustainable Finance Disclosure Regulation Article 2(24): 'environmental, social and employee matters, respect for human rights, anti-corruption and anti-bribery matters'. https://www.consilium.europa.eu/media/57644/st10835-xx22.pdf
61. *See* the proposed Annex listing the bases for human rights and environmental violations, available at https://ec.europa.eu/info/sites/default/files/1_2_183888_annex_dir_susta_en.pdf.
62. DRAFT REPORT with recommendations to the Commission on corporate due diligence and corporate accountability (2020/2129(INL)), pp. 18-19, available at https://www.europarl.europa.eu/doceo/document/JURI-PR-657191_EN.pdf.

In the final version of the European Parliament resolution of March 2021, we see that it was suggested that the Directive should have an Annex, which broadly should set out:

> a list of types of business-related adverse impacts on the environment, whether temporary or permanent, that are relevant for undertakings. Such impacts should include, but should not be limited to, production of waste, diffuse pollution, and greenhouse emissions that lead to a global warming of more than 1,5°C above pre-industrial levels, deforestation, and any other impact on the climate, air, soil and water quality, the sustainable use of natural resources, biodiversity and ecosystems.[63]

The necessity of policy coherence within the EU legal system is also highlighted in the March 2021 resolution, highlighting that it wishes to 'contribute to the internal coherence of Union legislation and to provide legal certainty', and referring to the Taxonomy Regulation,[64] which in turn repeatedly references EU law on a variety of environmental aspects.

Also, social issues are spelled out broadly in the European Parliament's Legal Affairs Committee Report, not limiting the bases to the international conventions, rather including also rights that flow from 'the European Convention on Human Rights, the European Social Charter, the Charter of Fundamental Rights of the European Union, and national constitutions and laws recognizing or implementing human rights'.[65]

The European Parliament's Legal Affairs Committee Report approach to governance resonates with the approach we took in the SMART project, including also reacting to the undermining of democratic processes as crucial elements.[66]

Followed up in the European Parliament's final resolution of 2021, the broad range of social issues, the interconnections between social and environmental issues as well as the significance of good governance is highlighted. For the latter, an annex is suggested that should set out:

> a list of types of business-related adverse impacts on good governance that are relevant for undertakings. They should include non-compliance with OECD Guidelines for Multinational Enterprises, Chapter VII on Combatting Bribery, Bribe Solicitation and Extortion and the principles of the OECD Convention on Combating Bribery of Foreign Public Officials in International Business Transactions and situations of corruption and bribery where an undertaking exercises undue influence on, or channels undue pecuniary advantages to, public officials to obtain privileges or unfair favourable treatment in breach of the law, and including

63. European Parliament resolution of 10 March 2021 with recommendations to the Commission on corporate due diligence and corporate accountability (2020/2129(INL)), item (23), https://www.europarl.europa.eu/doceo/document/TA-9-2021-0073_EN.html#title2 (23).
64. Regulation (EU) 2020/852 of the European Parliament and of the Council of 18 June 2020 on the establishment of a framework to facilitate sustainable investment, and amending Regulation (EU) 2019/2088.
65. DRAFT REPORT with recommendations to the Commission on corporate due diligence and corporate accountability (2020/2129(INL)), p. 18, available at https://www.europarl.europa.eu/doceo/document/JURI-PR-657191_EN.pdf.
66. *Ibid.*, p. 19.

> situations in which an undertaking becomes improperly involved in local political activities, makes illegal campaign contributions or fails to comply with the applicable tax legislation.[67]

Yet, in the proposal for the Corporate Sustainability Due Diligence Directive, 'bribery', 'corruption' and 'tax' are not even mentioned.

It is understandable, in light of the push-back the Commission was confronted with while preparing the proposal,[68] that the proposal is reticent in both the company law duties it suggests and the way it limits its own concept of sustainability. It is also regrettable.

The important arguments from a perspective that understands business and its challenges, are those of legal certainty and a level playing field. Taking, as the proposed Directive does, the 'enlightened shareholder value' combined with a limited and limiting approach to sustainability is not one that gives a level playing field. It is one that opens up for various ways of 'sustainability washing' and 'sustainability wishing'.

§3.04 SUSTAINABILITY DUE DILIGENCE AS A KEY TO REALIZING THE GENERAL DUTY

Sustainability due diligence as a key tool for the integration of sustainability into corporate governance including risk management, should encompass the business of the company across global value chains.

The aim, as we saw it in the SMART Project, is a due diligence rule that is principle-based enough to be flexible for various types of businesses and future developments, and specific and firm enough on environmental, social, and governance issues that need to be encompassed. Which issues are to be included and on what basis, are fundamental to the success of due diligence as a sustainability tool. The selection of aspects should draw on three sources: (a) international and EU legislative and policy initiatives, (b) sustainability research, and (c) due diligence guidance with which business is already familiar, notably the UNGPs and the OECD Due Diligence Guidance for Responsible Business. Further, it should be based on the recognition that current laws and policies are generally insufficient to ensure social justice and mitigate pressures on planetary boundaries, crucial for a safe and just space for humanity. Taking such a broader approach gives a basis for identifying a combination of key

---

67. European Parliament resolution of 10 March 2021 with recommendations to the Commission on corporate due diligence and corporate accountability (2020/2129(INL)), items (21), (22) and (24), available at https://www.europarl.europa.eu/doceo/document/TA-9-2021-0073_EN.html#title2.
68. Which was twice rejected by the Regulatory Scrutiny Board, in a way that has given rise to the question of whether the Scrutiny Board should be scrutinised, 'MEPs Wolters, Hautala, Aubry and Durand: *The Regulatory Scrutiny Board Still Has Questions to Answer on Due Diligence Delay*, 21 January 2022, https://responsiblebusinessconduct.eu/wp/2022/01/21/meps-wolters-hautala-aubry-and-durand-the-regulatory-scrutiny-board-still-has-questions-to-answer-on-due-diligence-delay/, and 'Big business derails corporate accountability law for human rights abuses and climate crimes', 8 June 2022, https://friendsoftheearth.eu/press-release/big-business-set-to-derail-corporate-accountability-law-for-human-rights-abuses-and-climate-change/.

concepts and a listing of issues similar to those suggested in the general duty of the board in §3.03[B][3], which should be combined with guidance.[69] A smart regulatory mix on several levels is necessary, and the EU is an important actor in that context.

A vast body of international environmental law has been created by the international community that promotes various environmental aspects of sustainability. This cannot be covered here in detail, but it can be noted that the recognition of planetary boundaries is reflected in varying degrees in the environmental body of law, and the planetary boundaries concept has gained interest at national and European levels.[70] Indeed, a mapping of EU secondary legislation shows that the EU has directives and regulations in place for many planetary boundaries related issues (without, however, assessing whether they are sufficient even within Europe); yet a key finding is that:

> Europe has been operating beyond the boundaries for almost all the processes we have analysed. In many cases, EU policy has driven improvements in Europe's own territory, but often at the price of increased impacts elsewhere in the world. For all the boundaries, EU's consumption-based footprint is larger than the production-based (territorial) performance. This indicates that EU has externalized part of its environmental impact and is using natural resources from other countries to maintain its domestic consumption.[71]

In light of the global environmental challenges, also EU's role as a global actor underlines that integrating environmental aspects of sustainability due diligence into the governance of European-based companies is a significant and necessary step.[72]

69. Mandatory guidance from the Commission should outline how the due diligence is to be conducted, and the guidance should be revised every three years, through an open participatory process, integrating expertise, and affected communities, Sjåfjell, et al., *supra* n. 33, s. 6.2.1.
70. For example, comprehensive national studies have been carried out for Sweden, Switzerland, and the Netherlands: Bjørn Nykvist et al., *National Environmental Performance on Planetary Boundaries*, Swedish Environmental Protection Agency, Stockholm, Sweden (2013); Hy Dao et al., *Environmental Limits and Swiss Footprints based on Planetary Boundaries* UNEP/GRID-Geneva and University of Geneva, Geneva, Switzerland (2015); Paul L. Lucas and Harry Wilting, *Using Planetary Boundaries to Support National Implementation of Environment-related Sustainable Development Goals*, PBL Netherlands Environmental Assessment Agency, The Hague, Netherlands (2018). The European Environment Agency commissioned studies to assess the translation of the planetary boundaries framework in the European Union, with key methodologies and findings summarized in Tiina Häyhä, et al., *Operationalizing the Concept of a Safe Operating Space at the EU Level – First Steps and Explorations*, Stockholm Resilience Centre Technical Report, prepared in collaboration with Stockholm Environment Institute (SEI) and PBL Netherlands Environmental Assessment Agency (2018). Stockholm Resilience Centre, Stockholm University, Sweden, available at https://www.sei.org/publications/operationalizing-concept-safe-operating-space-eu/. On the EU level, planetary boundaries are expressly recognized in the EU's Eight Environmental Framework Programme and, for example, in the 2020 Circular Economy Action Plan.
71. Häyhä et al., *ibid.*
72. This should be complemented – as far as possible – with legislative initiatives that ensure that the same rules apply to goods offered to the European market by third country companies. *See* further Eléonora Maitre-Ekern, Mark B. Taylor, and Maja van der Velden, *Towards a Sustainable Circular Economy. SMART Reform Proposals*, University of Oslo Faculty of Law Research Paper No. 2020-12, Nordic & European Company Law Working Paper No. 20-10, Available at SSRN: https://ssrn.com/abstract=3596076.

Encompassing a full range of environmental aspects in sustainability due diligence further resonates with and can draw on 'the basic environmental principles of prevention and precaution'.[73]

In describing an understanding of risk management process that is reminiscent of the due diligence concept, the UN Environment Programme (UNEP) described the *prevention principle* as:

> [A]n overarching aim that gives rise to a multitude of legal mechanisms, including prior assessment of environmental harm, and licensing or authorizations that set out the conditions for operation and the remedial consequences for violation of the conditions. Emission limits and other product or process standards, the use of best available techniques (BAT), and other similar techniques can all be seen as applications of prevention.
>
> Prevention is also linked to the notion of deterrence and the idea that disincentives such as penalties and civil liability will cause actors to take greater care in their behaviour to avoid the increased costs, thus preventing pollution from occurring.[74]

The *precautionary principle* has a basis in EU law as well as on the international level. Article 191(2) of the Treaty on the Functioning of the European Union (TFEU) includes the precautionary principle in its stipulation of environmental principles that the EU shall follow. It is recognized that the scope is much wider than environmental issues in practice, and where 'preliminary objective scientific evaluation' indicates that there are 'reasonable grounds for concern that the potentially dangerous effects on the environment, human, animal or plant health may be inconsistent with the high level of protection chosen for the Community', the precautionary principle should be invoked.[75] The precautionary principle is also listed as Principle 15 of the Rio Declaration among the principles of general rights and obligations of national authorities:

> In order to protect the environment, the precautionary approach should be widely applied by States according to their capabilities. Where there are threats of serious or irreversible damage, lack of full scientific certainty shall not be used as a reason for postponing cost-effective measures to prevent environmental degradation.[76]

The conceptual framework for planetary boundaries itself proposes a strongly precautionary approach, by 'setting the discrete boundary value at the lower and more conservative bound of the uncertainty range'.[77]

Human rights is but one core aspect of social and governance issues. In addition to the range of international conventions, the EU's own objectives and policies on human rights, social and governance issues, the UNGPs and the OECD Guidelines

---

73. Lise Smit et al., for the European Commission, *Study on Due Diligence Requirements through the Supply Chain*, 180, final report, 20 February 2020, https://op.europa.eu/sv/publication-detail/-/publication/8ba0a8fd-4c83-11ea-b8b7-01aa75ed71a1/language-en.
74. *Ibid.*, at 182–183.
75. European Commission, *Communication from the Commission on the Precautionary Principle*, (COM/2000/0001 final) (2000).
76. UN General Assembly, *The Rio Declaration on Environment and Development*, A/CONF.151/26 (Vol. I) (1992).
77. *See* Rockström et al., *supra* n. 3.

show the breadth of issues.[78] As opposed to what the proposed Corporate Sustainability Due Diligence Directive does, we see including anti-corruption and fair taxation in the due diligence as necessary elements of sustainability due diligence. This is reflected in our inclusion of these issues in the general duty of the board.

That anti-corruption is a crucial governance issue is explained, *inter alia*, in the OECD Guidelines for Multinational Enterprises:

> Bribery and corruption are damaging to democratic institutions and the governance of corporations. They discourage investment and distort international competitive conditions. In particular, the diversion of funds through corrupt practices undermines attempts by citizens to achieve higher levels of economic, social and environmental welfare, and it impedes efforts to reduce poverty. Enterprises have an important role to play in combating these practices.[79]

This is also an area where due diligence is already established:

> Anti-corruption laws often require due diligence through the supply chain, and failure to exercise this could be a criminal offence, also exposing individual directors to criminal liability. For example, the US Foreign Corrupt Practices Act and the UK Bribery Act 2010 provide for due diligence as a defence to liability.[80]

Corruption and bribery are included in OECD Guidelines for Multinational Enterprises and the OECD Due Diligence Guidance, with the former setting out that enterprises should:

> Develop and adopt adequate internal controls, ethics and compliance programmes or measures for preventing and detecting bribery, developed on the basis of a risk assessment addressing the individual circumstances of an enterprise, in particular the bribery risks facing the enterprise (such as its geographical and industrial sector of operation). These internal controls, ethics and compliance programmes or measures should include a system of financial and accounting procedures, including a system of internal controls, reasonably designed to ensure the maintenance of fair and accurate books, records, and accounts, to ensure that they cannot be used for the purpose of bribing or hiding bribery. Such individual circumstances and bribery risks should be regularly monitored and re-assessed as necessary to ensure the enterprise's internal controls, ethics and compliance programme or measures are adapted and continue to be effective, and to mitigate the risk of enterprises becoming complicit in bribery, bribe solicitation and extortion.[81]

---

78. As we see also in the proposed Corporate Sustainability Reporting Directive 2021, consensus of 2022, which connects its definition of 'sustainability matters' to the 'sustainability factors' in the Sustainable Finance Disclosure Regulation Article 2(24): 'environmental, social and employee matters, respect for human rights, anti-corruption and anti-bribery matters'. https://www.consilium.europa.eu/media/57644/st10835-xx22.pdf
79. OECD Guidelines for Multinational Enterprises, Chapter VII. Combating Bribery, Bribe Solicitation and Extortion, Commentary, Item 74.
80. Smit et al., *supra* n. 73, at 172.
81. OECD Guidelines for Multinational Enterprises, Chapter VII. Combating Bribery, Bribe Solicitation and Extortion.

Taxation is not included in the OECD Due Diligence Guidance. Rather, it merely refers to the OECD Guidelines, which state that 'enterprises should comply with both the letter and spirit of the tax laws and regulations of the countries in which they operate'.[82] However, in a comprehensive sustainability due diligence, taxation issues should be included because of their significance for the businesses themselves in terms, *inter alia*, of the corporate and financial risks of being involved in illegal tax evasion and also in – from a responsible business perspective – illegitimate tax avoidance.

Taking a broad and inclusive approach to sustainability resonates with the EU Treaty provision dealing with the relationship between the EU and the international community, where the EU expresses that it shall 'foster the sustainable economic, social and environmental development of developing countries, with the primary aim of eradicating poverty',[83] reinforced in the EU's development cooperation with developing countries under Article 208 TFEU. Policy coherence for development (PCD) is set out as an EU legal norm in Article 208 TFEU, requiring that any area of EU law and policy must not work against developmental policies, resonating with the sustainability aim of 'leaving no-one behind'.[84]

A full list of due diligence aspects should be drawn up in a revised version of the proposed Directive. As an intrinsic element of sustainability due diligence should be the participation of workers, regardless of their labour law status,[85] and of affected communities, including indigenous peoples and ensuring that all affected are fully involved.[86] This is an embedded aspect of good due diligence, for which there is ample guidance. Further, what the board is meant to do with the results of the due diligence also needs to be clearly set out, to consistently integrate sustainability into corporate governance. The proposed Directive's approach here is insufficient.[87]

The due diligence process should be sufficiently specified to also serve as guidance for the board in following up their duty to create sustainable value including contributing to mitigating pressures on planetary boundaries.

I draw again here on the SMART proposals, where we suggested that it should be set out clearly in the law that:

> ... the board shall identify ongoing negative sustainability impacts and principal risks of future negative sustainability impacts, and select relevant quantitative and qualitative Key Performance Indicators.

82. OECD Guidelines for Multinational Enterprises, Chapter XI Taxation.
83. Article 21(2)(d) and (f) TEU, cited in §3.02.
84. Clair Gammage, *The EU's Evolving Commitment to Promoting Sustainability in Its External Actions: Policy (In)Coherence for Development?* SMART working paper on file with current authors, University of Oslo (2020). *See also* UN General Assembly, *General Assembly Resolution 70/1. Transforming Our World: The 2030 Agenda for Sustainable Development*, A/RES/70/1, (25 September 2015), www.undocs.org/A/RES/70/1.
85. Novitz, *supra* n. 29. Concerning some of the challenges involved, *see also* Scoones, *supra* n. 29, 293–319.
86. As indeed is envisaged by SDG 16.
87. *See, e.g.*, G. Dusepulchre, S. Feierabend, and M. Neglia, *Europe Can Do Better – How EU Policy Makers Can Strengthen the Corporate Sustainability due Diligence Directive*, June 2022, FIDH N°794a, https://www.fidh.org/IMG/pdf/duediligence.pdf.

> In its identification and management of principal risks, the board shall be guided by the precautionary principle. For the purposes of this paragraph, 'precautionary principle' entails that where there are threats of serious or irreversible damage to nature or to humans, avoidance or mitigation of possible harm must be undertaken also in cases of scientific uncertainty.[88]

Also the follow-up needs to be clearly expressed in the law:

> Where the negative impacts or risks thereof are caused by lack of legal compliance, the board must ensure that this is rectified as soon as possible. For other issues, a system for an ambitious continuous improvement process must be put into place.[89]

In the proposed Directive, the duty to draw up a plan is fragmented. As mentioned earlier in §3.03[B][3], climate change is given more emphasis in the proposed Directive' Article 15, with a requirement for a plan for how to ensure that the business model and the strategy of the company 'are compatible with the transition to a sustainable economy and with the limiting of global warming to 1.5 °C in line with the Paris Agreement'. [90] Ironically this requirement is not explicitly connected to the due diligence duties, with reference being given rather to 'information reasonably available to the company' (Article 15(1)). In Article 7(2)(a), there is a more openly formulated requirement for a prevention action plan ('where necessary due to the nature or complexity of the measures required for prevention, develop and implement a prevention action plan, with reasonable and clearly defined timelines for action and qualitative and quantitative indicators for measuring improvement'), while Article 8 requires corrective action when necessary. With the emphasis given to climate change, there is a risk that plans for preventing or correcting issues related to other sustainability matters, will not be followed up as they should. If the proposed Directive is adopted as set out now, we may therefore see a further limitation in the follow-up of the proposed Directive's already limiting approach to sustainability.

Clear rules on an ambitious continuous improvement process for all sustainability aspects based on sustainability due diligence is a crucial element and can provide the basis for reliable and relevant reporting, which is not the case today. Sustainability due diligence, with a satisfactory basis, properly mandated and enforced, would give the basis for identifying and mitigating financial and business risks of unsustainability (forward-looking risk management), for starting the transition towards sustainable business (strategy; business model choice; decision-making) and provide a basis for meaningful reporting (which would facilitate sustainable finance, sustainable public procurement, etc.). It is, in other words, a crucial step towards a sustainable future.

88. Sjåfjell et al., *supra* n. 33, s. 6.2.1.
89. *Ibid.*
90. The requirement for drawing up a plan according to Article 15 is also given more emphasis than the general reference to sustainability issues in the consensus for the Corporate Sustainability Reporting Directive, *see, e.g.*, suggested new Article 19a(2)(iii) in the 2022 consensus.

§3.05 LEGAL CERTAINTY, LEVEL PLAYING FIELD AND AVOIDING 'SUSTAINABILITY WISHING'

The proposed Corporate Sustainability Due Diligence Directive aims to put into place mandatory and harmonised sustainability due diligence rules in the European Economic Area, in recognition of the insufficiency of voluntary action by business and the regulatory chaos that business faces in its cross-border activities.[91] As regards the scope of the proposal, rather than employing a threshold as is often done in EU policy-making, including in the proposed Corporate Sustainability Due Diligence Directive, we suggested in the SMART reform proposals that the proposals should include companies of all sizes, and drawing on the experience from the field of auditing, we suggested that the duties of the board should be proportional and adapted to the scale and complexity of the undertaking.[92]

To finally start taking people and the environment as seriously as financial issues have been taken for decades, a legislative reform should include external verification and auditing. According to our SMART proposal, EU rules should provide for external verification that the due diligence process is undertaken in accordance with the rules, and annual reporting on this should be audited.[93] The consensus on the Corporate Sustainability Reporting Directive is now moving in this direction.[94]

We also proposed a set of possible enforcement mechanisms, both private and public.[95] Together this would provide a good basis for legal certainty for the board that it is following this up as it should and a level playing field in the sense that it would know that other undertakings would be subject to the same rules.

The proposed Corporate Sustainability Due Diligence Directive goes some way in encompassing such issues, by setting up civil liability rules and a system for EU-wide supervision. However, there are weaknesses in the proposal that need to be rectified in the further work.[96]

As a minimum and as a form of public enforcement that would be easy to put into place, we suggested in the SMART report that the submission of corporate documents relevant to the general duty and the due diligence should be a prerequisite for the continued validity of the registration of an undertaking. These documents should include:

---

91. As explained in the Explanatory Memorandum of the Directive proposal, pp. 1–3.
92. *Ibid.*
93. Sjåfjell et al., *supra* n. 33, s. 6.2.3.
94. Proposed Corporate Sustainability Reporting Directive 2021, consensus of 2022, notably Article 34(1)(2)(aa).
95. Sjåfjell et al., *supra* n. 33, Sections 6.2.4–6-2.5.
96. *See, e.g.*, International Federation of Human Rights, 'Corporate Accountability: EU Must Not Squander Historic Opportunity to Tackle Environmental Crisis, Human Rights Abuses', 23 Feb 2022, https://www.fidh.org/en/issues/globalisation-human-rights/business-and-human-rights/corporate-accountability-eu-must-not-squander-historic-opportunity-to; Finance Watch, 'Commission Bends to Lobby Pressure on Sustainable Corporate Governance', 23 Feb 2022, https://www.finance-watch.org/press-release/eu-commission-bends-to-lobby-pressure-watering-down-proposals-on-directors-duties-and-remuneration-mandatory-corporate-sustainability-due-diligence-is-welcome-but-too-limited-in-scope/.

(a) the strategy (valid until resubmitted);
(b) the externally assured documentation of the sustainability assessment and the sustainability due diligence (at a minimum assured every three years);
(c) financial statements (annually); and
(d) the audited management report (annually).[97]

This entails that lack of submission of any of these documents will lead to sanctions and eventually, in case of continued non-compliance, the winding-up of the undertaking, or dissolution. This is comparable to the consequence for nullity of a company in present Article 12(2) of the Company Law Directive 2017, and as such a well-established company law enforcement. It is unclear what the effect will be of the proposed requirement in the Corporate Sustainability Due Diligence Directive for Member States to put into place sanctions (Article 20).

We proposed a European supervisory element in our SMART report.[98] It is positive that the proposed Directive includes a provision on a European Supervisory Network (Article 21) with specifications of the supervisory authorities in the Member States.

In the SMART project, we suggested that a new European supervisory authority should be able to bring public interest proceedings against undertakings that are not following up their EU company law duties as implemented national legislative acts. Filling a gap in the European supervisory system, we suggested that this supervisory authority should have the competence to enforce the full scope of EU company law duties. As a minimum, the supervisory authority should be given the mandate of enforcing the sustainability duties. We also proposed that affected parties, including across global value chains of European undertakings, should have the possibility of bringing complaints in before the supervisory authority. We said that the supervisory authority should have the right to require information and documentation from European undertakings, make public statements, and issue fines to non-compliant undertakings. This would provide a channel for dealing with complaints from, for example, workers in global value chains of European undertakings, without them having to resort to a lawsuit against the European undertaking.[99]

It is encouraging that the proposed Directive sets out in Article 18 that each Member States must designate a supervisory authority that is to have 'adequate powers and resources to carry out the tasks assigned to them under this Directive, including the power to request information and carry out investigations related to compliance with the obligations set out in this Directive' (Article 18(1)). The proposed Directive sets out that the supervisory authority 'may initiate an investigation on its own motion or as a result of substantiated concerns' (Article 18(2)). As there is no jurisdictional limitation to the proposed provision in Article 19 that 'natural and legal persons' can put forward such substantiated concerns, this should ensure that affected persons across global value chains would be able to use such a channel. With the specification of sanctions

97. Sjåfjell et al., *supra* n. 33, s. 6.2.5.1.
98. *Ibid.*, s. 6.2.5.
99. *Ibid.*

that the supervisory authority as a minimum should have the power to put in place (cessation of infringements; the abstention from any repetition of the relevant conduct and, where appropriate, remedial action; pecuniary sanctions; and interim measures to avoid the risk of severe and irreparable harm, Article 18(5)), it is clear that the Commission has intended for the proposed Directive to have teeth.[100]

As for civil liability, this already exists, in an unpredictable manner, with lack of legal certainty for businesses, their decision-makers, and those affected by business. This is evidenced by the international trend of lawsuits against businesses for harms committed in their global value chains.[101] Putting into place a good system for civil liability is therefore not only a possible approach to ensuring enforcement of sustainability duties. It is also crucial to ensure a level playing field for business and legal certainty for all involved. We propose that this should be linked to the duty to undertake a sustainability due diligence, which should be a duty for the undertaking – and to make it effective and ensure follow-up – a duty for the board, as I have outlined earlier. If the sustainability due diligence has not been carried out in accordance with EU law and harm has occurred, there should be a presumption of liability for the undertaking and its board members. Conversely, if due diligence has been carried out and assured by external experts as proposed as a duty, this may serve as a defence for the undertaking and its board. This would increase the legal certainty for European business, while providing better access to justice for affected workers and communities.[102]

The proposed Directive's civil liability rules risk undermining due diligence as a key tool for integrating sustainability in corporate governance, by allowing for the delegation of responsibility from the company through contractual provisions and limiting too strongly the possibilities for bringing corporate decision-makers to

100. Such a follow-up would be a stronger option (with fines as sanctions) compared to the more limited possibility that is now available through the extra-judicial system of National Contact Points institutionalized through and as an enforcement of the OECD Guidelines for Multinational Enterprises, OECD Watch, 'National Contact Points (NCPs)' *OECD Watch*, www.oecdwatch.org/oecd-ncps/national-contact-points-ncps/. The impact of the OECD National Contact Point system is limited through the types of businesses it concerns as well as through the non-judicial nature of the system, the low number of complaints, and even lower number of cases in which remedy actually has been granted, D.C. Rare, J. Wilde Ramsing, K.M.G Genovese, and V. Sandjojo, *OECD watchdog calls for reform of failing complaint system*, regarding the report Remedy Remains, *OECD Watch*, 15 June 2015, at www.oecdwatch.org/news-en/oecd-watchdog-calls-for-reform-of-failing-complaint-system.

101. *See* European Coalition for Corporate Justice, *Suing Goliath: An Analysis of Civil Cases Against EU Companies for Overseas Human Rights and Environmental Abuses* (28 September 2021), https://corporatejustice.org/publications/suing-goliath/; Mark B Taylor, *Litigating Sustainability – Towards a Taxonomy of Counter-Corporate Litigation*, University of Oslo Faculty of Law Research Paper No. 2020-08 www.ssrn.com/abstract = 3530768; Carol Liao, *Regulation by Litigation on the Path to Sustainable Corporations*, in *Innovating Business for Sustainability: Regulatory Approaches in the Anthropocene* Ch. 11 (Beate Sjåfjell, Carol Liao, and Aikaterini Argyrou (eds), Edward Elgar Publishing, 2022).

102. Sjåfjell, et al., *supra* n. 33, s. 6.2.5.3.

court.[103] As Lise Smit and Claire Bright point out, it is important that due diligence does not act as a safe harbour, meaning that affected parties cannot file a lawsuit against the undertaking or its board if some kind of due diligence has been carried out nor must it devolve into a box-ticking exercise.[104] There is a danger that the proposed Directive's limitation in Article 22(2)(1) indeed would become a rather too efficient 'safe harbour', undermining the potential that a well-formulated due diligence regime could have. This may be further exacerbated through the broad and unspecified mandate to the Member States in Article 26(2) to ensure that 'directors' follow up on the due diligence requirement. Of course, compliance with a thoughtfully formulated mandatory sustainability due diligence regime should serve as a defence for the company and its board. However, it is important that it is not set out in manner that undermines the willingness to undertake due diligence and follow properly up on the results.

§3.06 CONCLUDING REFLECTIONS

Business is increasingly realizing the significance of moving towards sustainability and asking for mandatory rules to give them a level playing field and legal certainty. It is time to put aside ideological differences and concentrate on how to get into place the regulatory infrastructure that business and the world needs. The work with the Commission's proposal for a Corporate Sustainability Due Diligence Directive has unfortunately gone from being one that focused primarily on integrating sustainability into corporate governance with due diligence as a key tool, to concentrating on due diligence and adding a company law 'duty of care' in the due diligence context. There are positive elements in the proposed Directive, showing also that the Commission has meant for the rules to be enforceable and enforced - and not another gateway to sustainability washing and wishing. However, with such a narrowly formulated corporate sustainability due diligence and a company law duty of care as an add-on, the proposed Directive does not provide a satisfactory framework for further development neither on jurisdictional nor on corporate level. The result is one that is satisfying neither from a sustainability-oriented perspective nor from the perspective of business. It is also doubtful whether the proposed due diligence process will give decision-makers in business - and those affected by business - the legal certainty they require.

The research-based proposals presented in this chapter draw on commonly agreed sustainability goals and sustainability science, thereby increasing legal certainty for business in the sense that it will become clearer what the boundaries of legitimate business activities are. The emerging recognition of risks as unsustainability are an important driver for change and possibly what will bring consensus in the end for

103. *See, e.g., Position Paper: Corporate Sustainability Due Diligence Directive Must Be Strengthened by EU Policymakers*, 16 June 2022, https://www.business-humanrights.org/en/latest-news/position-paper-corporate-sustainability-due-diligence-directive-must-be-strengthened-by-eu-policymakers/.

104. Lise Smit and Claire Bright, *The Concept of a 'Safe Harbor' and Mandatory Human Rights Due Diligence*, 1 CEDIS Working Papers (December 2020) www.cedis.fd.unl.pt/wp-content/uploads/2020/12/CEDIS_working-paper_the-concept-of-safe-harbour.pdf.

change also in the area of company law. With the tools and processes along the lines of those that we proposed in the SMART Project, risk management would be improved, as would legal certainty in the sense of better knowing the extent of the vulnerabilities of the business. Sustainability due diligence would further act as a defence if claims are made against the company, for wrong-doings that have happened despite the best efforts of the company to avoid harm.

Reforming company law is not a silver bullet – a whole jigsaw puzzle of sustainability needs to be put into place. But reforming company law is a key element; a necessary albeit not sufficient condition. I have concentrated in this chapter on how sustainability can be integrated into corporate governance through company law reform. In other work in the SMART project, we engaged with a number of other important areas, as do other scholars. Policy coherence for sustainability should be a guiding star for further work, rather than path-dependency and the influence of vested interests.

CHAPTER 4

Managerial Procedural Rules

Karsten Engsig Sørensen

§4.01 INTRODUCTION

Efforts to promote good corporate governance has primarily focussed on detailing what task and duties the directors have, how the management should be structured (hereinafter structural rules, which deals in particular with the composition of the board and committee structures), and how the right incentive can be ensured through remuneration policies. Less focus was placed on how the management best makes decisions and solves the tasks required of them. For rules concerning the 'internal management', the law has been reluctant to interfere.[1] The assumption seems to have been that these procedural aspects are better addressed by management itself by the adoption of company specific code of conducts or should be regulated in the articles of association of the company and therefore ultimately to be decided by the shareholders.

This reluctance to regulate procedural aspects of management is in stark contrast to how both company law and corporate governance codes focus on the procedures applicable when shareholders make decisions in general meetings. There are extensive rules on which decisions should be presented to the shareholders, how the meeting is called, how the shareholders are informed, how the meeting including the voting is to be conducted, etc. European Union (EU) law has also addressed this issue with detailed rules on how shareholders should be involved in deciding on corporate transactions such as mergers, divisions, takeovers, and conversions.[2] For listed companies,

1. Paul L. Davies, Sarah Worthington & Christopher Hare, *Gower Principles of Modern Company Law*, 243 (Sweet & Maxwell 11th ed. 2021). The statement is made in relation to UK law, but it seems as appropriate for most other jurisdictions.
2. *See* the Codified Company Law Directive, Council Directive 2017/1132 of 14 June 2017 relating to certain aspects of company law (Text with EEA relevance) OJ L 169, 30.6.2017 with later amendments (hereinafter CCLD).

shareholders' involvement in takeovers is also regulated, and furthermore several important aspects of the conduct of general meetings are harmonised.[3]

However, the importance of the procedural aspects of management for corporate governance has been recognised for a long time. The 1992 report of the Cadbury Committee – which launched the European corporate governance movement – mainly focussed on structural aspects and remuneration. It did, however, acknowledge the importance of procedural rules for good corporate governance, as it stated that '[t]he effectiveness of a board is buttressed by its structure and procedures'.[4] The report then, *inter alia*, points out the importance of meeting regularly, with due notice, supported by the necessary paperwork, and by keeping a record of the conclusions of the meeting.[5] Thus, the report acknowledges that these basic procedural aspects are important for the effectiveness of the board, even though there were no specific recommendations on the issue.

This reluctance to regulate procedural aspects of management has evaporated with time. As more and more structural elements of management have been detailed in codes and law, it is logical to turn from how to 'set the players' to how 'the game is played'. This development is supported by the realisation in behaviour economics that management processes are important for achieving effective boards.[6] Even with the right composition, the management as a group may make less than optimal decisions if the directors are pressured for time, ill informed, biased, or not involved at all. When studying processes in boards, these need not be dictated by procedural rules but may also be dictated by customs, and what is considered prudent by the chair. But it seems clear that board processes may be dictated or influenced by procedural rules, and therefore it should be considered what role law (or codes) play for how boards operate.[7]

An additional factor that has spurred this development towards more procedural rules is the fact that the sustainability agenda has become part of the corporate

3. *See* the Takeover Directive, Council Directive 2004/25 of 21 April 2004 on takeover bids (Text with EEA relevance), *OJ L 142/12, 30.4.2004* and the Shareholder Rights Directive, Council Directive (EU) 2007/36 of 11 July 2007 on the exercise of certain rights of shareholders in listed companies, OJ L 184, 14.7.2007 with later amendment.
4. *See* para. 4.21 of the *Report of the Committee on the Financial Aspects of Corporate Governance*, 1 December 1992.
5. *See ibid.* para. 4.23.
6. *See also* Terry McNulty, *Process Matters: Understanding Board Behavior and Effectiveness* in *The Oxford Handbook of Corporate Governance* 163–176 (Douglas Michael Wright, Donald S. Siegel, Kevin Keasey and Igor Filatotchev eds, OUP 2013), arguing the board process is more important in ensuring board performance and effects than board structure or composition. Similarly, Sydney Finkelstein and Ann C. Mooney, *Not the usual suspects: How to use board process to make boards better*, 17 Acad. Manag. Exe., 3, 101–113 (2003), which concludes on page 112 that it 'seems clear that board process likely has a very real and important impact on overall board effectiveness and even firm performance.' Zhu Yikun, *The Legal Regulation of Irrational Elements in the Operation of Board of Directors*, 38:2 Soc. Sci. China, 95–113 (2017), not only points out the importance of addressing processes but also insists that this must go hand in hand with structural measures.
7. *See also* Yikun, *ibid.*

governance debate.[8] The many soft law instruments that have been adopted to promote sustainable business are often focussed on processes.[9] For instance, the UN Guiding Principles on Business and Human Rights list a number of Foundational Principles and Operational Principles, where the latter in some detail addresses several procedural aspects. Therefore, when considering if and how sustainability may be integrated in corporate governance it is natural to consider procedural solutions.

Even though there are different arguments in favour of embracing procedural rules, it is also clear that these may not solve all problems and may even have a negative effect. Therefore, to estimate the potential of managerial procedural rules to promote good corporate governance, a closer examination of the positive and negative effects of this regulatory instrument is required. This chapter aims to provide an overview over these effects.

After having outlined the existing procedural rules and their purposes in §4.02, §4.03 discuss the possible benefits and disadvantages of adopting such rules. §4.04 try to tease out some overall conclusions about what potential procedural rules have as an instrument of corporate governance.

§4.02 DIFFERENT TYPES OF PROCEDURAL RULES

In the context of this chapter, procedural rules are rules that address or recommend how the management should approach the tasks that they have been given. It may be rules governing how the management makes (certain) decisions or how they should solve tasks allotted to them such as the duty to supervise different aspects of the company. This covers a range of issues and a delamination is necessary. The focus is on listed companies,[10] and even though the chapter try to trace the development by using examples of national codes and law,[11] the focus is on outlining how EU has over time addressed this aspect. Both hard law and soft law measures are covered.

Procedural rules are often part of recommendations or regulations that aim to enforce specific duties of the management or part of a structural initiative. For instance,

8. This is clearly seen by the ongoing discussion of sustainable corporate governance in the EU, but the development to integrate sustainability (or CSR) in corporate governance goes back several years in the national corporate governance codes, *see* Daniel Szabo and Karsten Engsig Sørensen, *Integrating Corporate Social Responsibility in Corporate Governance Codes in the EU*, Eur. Bus. L Rev, 781–828 (2013).
9. Similarly, Iris H.-Y. Chiu, *Unpacking the Reforms in Europe and UK Relating to Mandatory Disclosure in Corporate Social Responsibility: Instituting a Hybrid Governance Model to Change Corporate Behaviour?* Eur. Comp. Law, 193–208, at 201 (2017).
10. Non-listed companies are a very inhomogeneous group where it would be very difficult to formulate procedural rules that make sense in all companies. Therefore, listed companies are those most likely to be subject to procedural rules, although banks seem to be even more targeted by such rules, *see also* Iris H-Y Chiu and Anna Donovan, *A new milestone in corporate regulation: procedural legislation, standards of transnational corporate behavior and lessons from financial regulation and anti-bribery regulation*, J. Corp. L. Stud. 427–467 (2017).
11. The focus is on Danish, French, German, and UK law and corporate governance practices.

a duty to manage risks are coupled with some specification as to how it should be done, or the setting up of a committee is coupled with specification of how the committee should be involved in specific decisions. Even where procedural rules have such an ancillary character, they are interesting in the present context as they are an add-on that could have been omitted as these procedural aspects could have been left for the management themselves to decide.

Procedural rules exist in many forms, but for the purpose of this chapter they are broken down into rules that focus on divisions of competences, rules that details how the management should proceed when they address their duties, and finally rules that details how the management should disseminate the result of their efforts.

Management is organised differently in different jurisdictions, and in particular it varies whether a one-tier and two-tier board structure is used. Consequently, procedural rules may be focussed on different organs in different jurisdictions. These differences should of course be kept in mind for those intending to regulate procedural aspects, but in this chapter these differences are not exploited. I therefore in the following sections use examples of procedural rules applicable to different organs. When the nature of the organ is less important, I just refer to the board and the individual member of management as directors.

[A] Allocation of Tasks and Competence to Make Decisions

Rules stipulating or recommending which corporate organ (or person(s)) should address a specific decision or task may be qualified as a procedural rule. Such rules determine where the procedure leading to these decisions or solving these tasks should be initiated or take place. Such rules are a natural companion to structural measures, as they aim to ensure that the board(s) and committees are given the role intended.

There is a long tradition in company law for specifying that certain decisions should be taken (or approved) by the shareholders. Such rules are also found in EU law, for instance, in relation to capital maintenance, and decisions involving corporate transactions such as mergers, divisions, or conversions must be presented to the shareholders at the general meeting.[12]

There are also rules allocating decisions or tasks to the board. EU law provides a few examples of this. In some cases, it is left for the Member State to allocate the competence to either the shareholders or the management,[13] and there are examples where the management is allocated specific tasks in preparing decisions that are

12. *See* CCLD Arts 60 (acquisition of own shares) 64(3) (financial assistance),68(1) (increase of capital), 73 (reduction in the capital), 86h (conversion), 93 (merger), 126 (cross-border merger), 139 (division), 160h (cross-border division). Under the Shareholder Rights Directive, Directive 2007/36/EC as amended, Art. 9a requires that the shareholders in listed companies should decide on the remuneration policy and according to Art. 9b(4), the general meeting has the right to hold an advisory vote on the remuneration report.
13. *See* Art. 9c(4) of the Shareholder Rights Directive, as amended, *supra* n. 3.

ultimately to be taken by the shareholders.[14] There are also rules allocating responsibility to the board and this in practice will also mean that competence is allocated.[15]

Sometimes there are recommendations or rules addressing how tasks should be allocated within management. This is normally the case in jurisdictions with two-tier systems where different solutions have been adopted as to the role the different organs should have in the management.[16] But there are also examples where tasks are divided within a management organ. Thus, there are plenty of examples where codes recommend the introduction of different committees and in doing so allocate specific tasks to these committees.[17] At the EU level, the European Commission has recommended setting up of nomination committees, remuneration committees, and audit committees and in doing so have indicated the tasks that these committees should as a minimum handle.[18] The audit committee has been obligatory for public-interest entities, and the minimum task that should be allocated to this committee is defined by the Statutory Audit Directive.[19]

In addition to these examples where decisions or tasks are allocated to a specific body, there are also examples of recommendations for the companies to ensure that

14. *See,* for instance, the task of preparing a conversion plan and the report on its consequences (Arts 86d and 86e), and the similar tasks in relation to mergers (Arts 91 and 95), cross-border mergers (Arts 122 and 124), divisions (Arts 137 and 141), and cross-border divisions (Arts 160d and 160e). *See also* the report to be preferred by the board of the offeree company according to Art. 9(4) of the Takeover Directive, *supra n. 3.*
15. Art. 64(2) of the CCLD stipulates that the board (referred to as either the administrative or management body of the company) is responsible for ensuring that any financial assistance given should be at fair market conditions. Art. 33 of the Accounting Directive, Council Directive 2013/34 of 26 June 2013 on the annual financial statements, consolidated financial statements and related reports of certain types of undertakings, amending Directive 2006/43/EC of the European Parliament and of the Council and repealing Council Directives 78/660/EEC and 83/349/EEC Text with EEA relevance, *OJ L 182, 29.6.2013*, require the Member States to ensure that the management collectively has the duty to ensure that the annual accounts and annual report (and consolidated ditto) are drawn up and published as required by the directive. Finally, *see* the Shareholder Rights Directive, *supra* n. 3 Art. 9b(5) on the collective responsibility of the directors to draw up and publish the remuneration report. A duty to ensure that, *inter alia*, the main management organs are responsible for the information given in a prospectus flow from Art. 11 of Regulation (EU) No. 2017/1129 of 14 June 2017 on the prospectus to be published when securities are offered to the public or admitted to trading on a regulated market, and repealing Directive 2003/71/EC Text with EEA relevance, *OJ L 168, 30.6.2017*. Finally, the recent proposal for a directive on Corporate Sustainability Due Diligence in Art. 26 suggests that the directors of a company should be responsible for putting in place and overseeing the due diligence actions required by the directive.
16. *See,* for instance, the regulation of competences for the executive directors and supervisory board in German law according to German Public Companies Act § 76, § 84, and § 111, Danish Companies Act §§ 114–118 and the French two-tier system in Arts L. 225–64 and L. 225-68 of the Commercial Code.
17. The committees may not be delegated the right to make a decision, but only given the task of preparing decisions for the full board. The Commission, however, suggested that some tasks may be delegated to the committees, *see* Recital 10 of the Commission Recommendation of 15 February 2005 on the role of non-executive directors in listed companies and on the committees of the (supervisory) board, 2005/162/EC.
18. *Ibid.*
19. *See* Council Directive 2006/43 of 17 May 2006 on statutory audits of annual accounts and consolidated accounts, amending Council Directives 78/660/EEC and 83/349/EEC and repealing Council Directive 84/253/EEC (Text with EEA relevance), *OJ L 157, 9.6.2006*, Art. 41(2)–(3).

there is a clear allocation of competences, without specifying how this should be carried out. Already the Cadbury Report recommended that companies make a clear division of competences.[20]

These rules seem to serve different purposes.

One obvious purpose is to ensure *objective decisions* by allocating the decision to a body that is not likely to be affected by a conflict of interest. Thus, in many jurisdictions the remuneration of the management is not allocated to the managers themselves but a different body.[21] The revised Shareholders Rights Directive similarly requires that the shareholders in listed companies should have a binding vote on the remuneration policy of the company and an advisory vote on the remuneration report.[22] Allocation of competences may also serve the purpose of ensuring that the decision is not left to the shareholders due to their lack of objectivity. This explains why the administrative or management body of the company under EU law is responsible for ensuring that any financial assistance given should be at fair market conditions.[23] It also explains why dividends in some jurisdictions can only be distributed to the extent that it is approved by the board.[24] Setting up committees may also aim to ensure more objective decisions, by ensuring that independent directors are sitting on these committees.[25]

Distribution of competences also seem to be serving the purpose of *distributing influence*. This may hinder that one corporate organ becomes too dominant by ensuring a certain checks-and-balance. This seems to be a feature of the German two-tier system where competences are clearly divided between the executive management and the supervisory board.[26] Also, some national corporate governance codes indicate that the purpose is to distribute power among the members of the management, at least to the extent that the power of the chair is often constrained by excluding him or her from committees or from chairing committees.[27] Also the division of powers between the board and the general meeting may have this effect as it seems that the

20. Similar recommendations are found in the Danish Recommendations on Corporate Governance, 2 December 2020 (hereinafter Danish CG code), recommendation 2.1.4, French Corporate Governance Code of Listed Companies, January 2020 (hereinafter French CG code), recommendation 1.9 and The UK Corporate Governance Code, July 2018 (hereinafter UK CG code), provision 14.
21. Thus, in Germany and Denmark the remuneration of the executive management is decided by either the supervisory board (Aufsichtsrat) or the full board of directors (bestyrelse), *see* German Public Companies Act § 87(1) and Danish Companies Act § 111, which specifies that the board recruits the executive management, which also means they decide his or her salary.
22. *See* Arts 9a and 9b(4) of Council Directive 2017/828 of 17 May 2017 amending Directive 2007/36/EC as regards the encouragement of long-term shareholder engagement (Text with EEA relevance), *OJ L 132, 20.5.2017.*
23. *See* Art. 64(2) of the CCLD.
24. This is the case in Denmark, *see* Danish Companies Act § 180(1). According to German law, the management may restrict the distribution of part of the profits, *see* German Public Companies Act § 58.
25. *See* recital 12 and 13, *supra* n. 17.
26. *See Michael Hoffmann-Becking ed., Münchener Handbuch des Gesellschaftsrechts, Band 4,* 308–310 (5th ed. C.H.Beck 2020).
27. *See,* for instance, UK CG code, provision 24 and the German Corporate governance Code, 16 December 2019 (hereinafter German CG code), recommendation D.4.

board will tread more careful if the decision needs their shareholders' approval or even just their advisory opinion.[28]

The purpose of such rules may also be to ensure that the persons making decisions or handling tasks have a specific competence and thus make the decisions more *professional*.[29] For those reasons, it may be recommended – or required – that members of a committee have a specific expertise.[30]

The rules allocating competence to the general meeting will often serve the purpose of allowing the shareholders to *protect their individual rights*. This is the reason why shareholders need to accept certain transactions often with a qualified majority.[31] If a decision is allocated to the board, then it ensures that the board will be involved in a decision or that the decision is only delegated with the express consent from the board. It may be going too far to say that the rules protect the directors' right to participate in the management of the company, but it may protect the interest of those who have elected them.[32]

Finally, the purpose of such rules may be to *allocate responsibly*. Allocating competence will also indicate that the body or persons granted competence will be responsible for the decision or task. It may be that the competence cannot be delegated and thus the responsibility may not be escaped. Even if delegation is possible, it will require a positive act to do so, and furthermore the delegation must be prudent, i.e., to a competent organ or person, and there may still be a need to supervise how the delegated power is exercised. Rules allocating competence thus makes it easier for the company and its stakeholders to hold the management accountable. The fact that allocation of competences also allocates responsibility may be one of the reasons for several corporate governance codes to propose that listed companies adopt a plan for

28. *See* the impact assessment prepared for the revised Shareholder Rights Directive, SWD (2014) 127, at 60: 'Boards will be less inclined to enter into problematic related party transactions if they know their shareholder will have a say on this.' The same effect is shown for the say on pay rules in Germany by Tobias H. Tröger and Uwe Walz, *Does Say on Pay Matter? Evidence from Germany*, ECFL Rev. 381–414 (2019).
29. *See* recital 12 and 13 of the Recommendation, *supra* n. 17. For the obligatory audit committee, the intension is to minimise risks and enhance the quality of financial reporting.
30. Expertise in finance and accounting is mentioned as desirable for the audit committee, *see* recital 16 and para 11.2 of the Recommendation, *supra* n. 17 and in the Statutory Audit Directive, Art. 41(1) it is required that at least one member of the audit committee shall be independent and have competence in accounting and/or auditing. *See also* the recommendation in the German CG code, recommendation D.2 that committees are formed by members with relevant specialist expertise and recommendation D.4 that the chair of the audit committee shall have special knowledge and experience in applying accounting principles and internal control procedures and familiar with audits.
31. Recital 69 of the CCLD. *See* the examples mentioned *supra* n. 12 above.
32. Even though directors may be elected by a class of shareholders (or the employees), they will normally not be expected to act as a nominee for these. Even so, if it is clear that directors elected by employees or a class of shareholders are kept out of influence this will not be acceptable, and therefore rules allocating competence may be said to protect the interest of the nominator. In several jurisdictions, it is agreed that even if delegation of tasks is allowed delegations may not be used to exclude one or more directors from the decision-making process, *see* for the UK, William Willson, *Directors' Decision-making and Delegation* in *Company Directors*, ch. 5, at 133 (Simon Mortimore ed., 2017) and for Denmark, Paul Krüger Andersen, Aktie- og anpartsselskabsret 355 (15th ed. Jurist og Økonomiforbundets Forlag, 2021).

a clear division of competences.[33] Another reason is to that such a plan will make it less likely that some tasks are not handled at all.

[B] How to Make a Decision or Solve a Task

There are a variety of rules that regulate either how decisions should be made or how tasks should be solved. They include basic rules for conducting board meetings, rules on the role of committees, rules on disqualification of directors, what information should be available, consultations, etc. Some rules have general application whereas others only concern specific decisions made by the board. It is impossible to list all these rules, and therefore in the following sections, their different purposes are explained coupled with examples of the types of rules that serve different purposes.

Most of these rules have the purpose of ensuring *better and more objective decisions*. But it is possible also to point out other purposes that some of them pursue.

Thus, many procedural rules aim to ensure that all directors may *participate on an equal basis*. This is normally the aim of rules that ensures that the basic procedural rules are laid down by the board themselves (often termed code of conducts), including rules on calling meetings, due notice, agenda, access to information, etc. As mentioned already in the Cadbury Report, the importance of such rules was highlighted.[34] Company law in some jurisdictions may require[35] or recommend[36] that the board adopts such rules. In addition, there may be rules in company law that regulate quorum and whether it is possible to send a substitute or use power of attorney.[37] Also there are examples where national law provides rules for holding board meetings in writing or online.[38] In addition, there are several examples of codes that recommend that the board agrees on such procedural rules for different types of tasks, including internal and external audit functions and risk management.[39] The underlying assumption seems to be that by setting procedures in advance everyone will make it easier for everyone involved to participate.

Other procedural rules allow the board to cope with *conflicts of interests*. Often national law provides that directors who have conflict of interest either cannot

33. *See* Danish CG code, recommendation 2.1.4, French CG Code, recommendation 1.9, and UK CG Code, provision 14.
34. *See supra* n. 4.
35. *See*, for instance, the Danish Companies Act § 130. The act does dictate what should be in the code of conduct but does suggest a number of issues to be included: composition of the board, the division of responsibilities, supervision of the executive board's day-to-day management, the keeping of books, minutes, etc., any written and electronic meetings, the duty of confidentiality, alternate members, accounting control, signing of audit records, and provisions to ensure that there is the requisite basis for auditing. The code of conduct will therefore also deal with issues that goes beyond the basic procedural rules of the board.
36. *See* German CG code, recommendation D.1. In the UK the Model Articles have several rules on procedural aspects of how the board works, and will this work as an incentive to adopt such rules in the articles of associations, *see* Willson *supra* n. 32.
37. *See*, for instance, the German Public Companies Act §§ 107–108 and the Danish Companies Act § 124.
38. *See*, for instance, Danish law § 125 and German Public Companies Act § 108(4).
39. *See*, for instance, the UK CG codes, principles M and O.

participate in the decision,[40] that the decision must be taken by the board,[41] that directors need to disclose their conflict of interest,[42] that the general meeting is informed and asked to approve the decision,[43] or national law applies several of these requirements.[44] There are few examples of this in EU law, but the revised Shareholder Rights Directive allows Member States to choose whether it is the general meeting or the administrative or supervisory body that approves related party transactions, but they need to ensure that there are procedures in place that 'prevent the related party from taking advantages of its position…'. If the transaction involves a director or shareholder, then that person (or company) should not take part in the approval or vote.[45]

In addition, the purpose of such rules may be to *improve the basis for decision-making.*[46] There may be rules on how directors may access information about the company. These could, for instance, be rules that stipulate when the director should be presented with the necessary information,[47] or rules stipulating who it is that are responsible for providing the necessary information.[48] Other codes recommend that directors or committees may have direct access to information from the company, for instance, through the company secretary[49] or principal managers.[50]

Some procedural rules focus on ensuring a better basis for decision by encouraging or requiring stakeholder consultations. Several codes recommend that there should be an ongoing dialogue and interactions with stakeholders.[51] Other rules recommend or require consultation for specific decisions. There are plenty of examples in labour law where consultation of workers is required for certain decisions, *see,* for instance, Directive 2001/23/EC on transfer of undertakings and the work council established according to Directive 2009/38/EC. This duty for consultation is now embedded in company law through the Codified Company Law Directive (CCLD).[52] In

40. *See* Danish Companies Act § 131, the French Commercial Code L. 225-40, and UK Companies Act s. 175(6).
41. *See,* for instance, German Public Companies Act §§ 114–115 on contracts with and the grant of credit to supervisory board members.
42. *See* German CG code recommendation E.1 and E.2 and UK Companies Act s. 177.
43. *See* French Commercial Code L. 225-40 on decision to enter into a transaction with a director.
44. *See,* for instance, the French Commercial Code L. 225-38 et seq. For a comparative discussion of the different approaches to conflict of interests. *see* Paul L. Davies & Klaus J. Hopt, *Corporate Boards in Europe: Accountability and Convergence,* Am. J. Compar. L, 301–376 at 349–355 (2013).
45. *See* Council Directive 2017/828 *supra* n. 22 Art. 4. The Directive does provide that the Member State may allow a shareholder who is a related party to vote given certain conditions are complied with.
46. *See also* Jens-Henrich Binder, *'Proceduralisierung' und Corporate Governance,* Zeitschrift für Unternehmens- und Gesellschaftsrecht 745–788 at 764. (2007).
47. *See,* for instance, the French CG code, recommendation 12 and the German CG code, principles 15–16.
48. Normally the chair will be tasked with this job, *see,* for instance, UK CG code, Principle F or the executive management, *see* the German Public Companies Act § 90 and the German CG code, principles 15–16, or both. *See* French Commercial Code Art. L225-35.
49. *See* UK CG code, provision 16.
50. French CG code, recommendation 15.3.
51. *See,* for instance, Danish CG code, recommendation 1.1.1.
52. *See* Arts 86k, 126c, 145, and 160k.

the proposed directive on corporate sustainability due diligence, there are also rules suggesting that stakeholders should be consulted at different levels of implementation of a due diligence policy.[53] Finally, it should be mentioned that an indirect way of ensuring that the board considers stakeholders' interest is to ask them to prepare a report on their position. Thus, the board is required to make a report on the effect the transaction (a takeover, a conversion, a division, or cross-border merger) has on other stakeholders than shareholders, and it seems likely that this requirement will require the board to consider the interests of these stakeholders and maybe even consult with these.[54] A similar effect may be expected from the recommendation in the UK Corporate Governance Code that companies should describe how the interest of other key stakeholders has been considered during the board's discussions and decision-making.[55]

Certain decisions may benefit from input from experts. Some jurisdictions recommend that committees may contact experts or request studies from experts,[56] but it is more common to suggest or require such expert input in certain decisions or tasks. This may be the case for related party transactions or other significant transactions where the board either should or must involve experts.[57] Codes recommending that the board performs regular self-evaluations may also recommend that this sometimes takes place with the participation of external experts.[58]

Finally, processes may be *designed to favour a particular outcome*. Thus, consulting certain stakeholders may aim to promote decisions that take their interest into account.[59] Similarly, the Commission has made a proposal for a directive to improve the gender balance among directors of listed companies, where it proposes a partial harmonisation of the process for selecting candidates for appointment or election to the post of directors that aim to ensure that more women are hired.[60] Of course, it would be simpler just to stipulate what decision the board should take, but procedures may

53. *See* COM(2022) 71 final, Art. 7(2)(a), Art. 8(3)(b), and Art. 26(1).
54. *See* Takeover Directive, *supra* n. 3, Art. 9(5) and the requirement for the transaction plan and accompanying report that should be prepared according to CCLD, Arts 86d-86e (conversions), Arts 122 and 124 (cross-border mergers), and Arts 160d-160e (cross-border divisions).
55. *See* UK CG code, para. 5.
56. *See* French CG code para. 15.3.
57. In the revised Shareholder Rights Directive, *supra* n. 22 the option of having a report assessing whether the transaction is fair and reasonable is suggested, but not required, *see* Art. 9c(3). The provision does not specify who should make the report, but an expert is the obvious choice. In France, it is recommended that the board may seek expert opinions to assess transactions concerning at least half of the company's assets, *see* the French CG code, para. 5.3.
58. *See* French CG code, recommendation 10.3 and UK CG code, provision 21.
59. How it affects the outcome is more debatable. The study performed for the Commission by EY entitled 'Study on directors' duties and sustainable corporate governance', July 2020, at 132, assumed that such consultation would favour more long-termed outcome, but they are also citing empirical research that points to other outcomes such as more effective communication, improved efficiency leading to competitive advantages, and fewer conflicts.
60. *See* Art. 4a of the proposal presented by the Council Presidency on 31 May 2017, 9496/17, Interinstitutional file 2012/0299 (COD). The Council and the European Parliament has reached an agreement on the text of the directive in 2022, but it has not been adopted when the manuscript for this chapter was submitted.

have a nudging effect that in some cases may be preferable over the more paternalistic approach that substantial law constitutes.[61]

[C] Transparency Rules as a Procedural Rule or Catalyst for Such

Transparency may either be part of a procedure and/or have the effect of promoting the formulation of procedures. Each of these types of rules are examined briefly below, again focussing on the purpose they may serve.

Often some form of transparency is the last step in a procedure. For instance, the minutes of board meetings need to be disclosed to all members of the directors and kept by the board. The purpose of these rules is to ensure that all directors agree with what has been decided, but the minutes may also later help establish what has been decided and thus keeps the board *accountable for their decisions*. There are a few other examples where a decision has to be made more widely public, but one example of such rules is the duty to disclose material transactions with related parties.[62] The aim of these rules is to allow shareholders, creditors, employees, and other interested parties to be informed of potential impacts that such transactions may have on the value of the company.[63] Thus disclosure allows them to safeguard their own interests, and where appropriate hold the board accountable for their decision to approve the transaction.

There are several examples where the board is required to publish their procedures. Sometimes such disclosure is only recommended, but due to the comply or explain-principle this will often *prompt that the board formulates such procedure*. Even though such disclosure requirement may not indicate how these procedures should look, there will often be best practice rules that have the effect that such procedures become more uniform.[64] This type of regulation has been termed as indirect procedural regulation.[65] Such disclosure rules may take different forms. There are examples of codes that recommend that processes for different tasks or decisions are published.[66]

---

61. *See also* Marina B. Madsen, *Behavioural Economics in European Corporate Governance – Much Ado about Nudging*, 32:2 Eur. Bus. Law Rev. 295–316 (2021).
62. *See* Art. 9c(2) of the revised Shareholder Rights Directive *supra* n. 22.
63. *See* recital 44 of the Directive, *ibid.*
64. Thus, the comply or explain-principle may have the effect of box-ticking and thus ensuring at least formal compliance with the corporate governance codes reported on, *see also* Konstantinos Sergakis, *Deconstruction and Reconstruction of the 'Comply or Explain' Principle in EU Capital Markets*, Account. Econ. Law: Conviv. 233–288, at 269–70 (2015). A similar harmonising effect have been suggested in other areas such a non-financial reporting, *see* Gregory Jackson, Julia Bartosch, Emma Aventlsyan, Daniel Kiderman and Jette Steen Knudsen, *Mandatory Non-financial Disclosure and Its Influence on CSR: An International Comparison*, J. Bus. Ethics 162, 323–342 (2020) and risk management reporting, *see* Luca Enriques and Dirk Zetzsche, *The Risky Business of Regulating Risk Management in Listed Companies* 10:3 ECFL Rev. 271–303, at 292–294 (2013).
65. Chiu, *supra* n. 9 193–208, at. 200.
66. *See*, for instance, the UK CG code that recommends disclosure of the recruitment process used by nomination committees, para. 23. A more general requirement to publish the internal code of conduct adopted by the board is found in the French CG code, para. 2.2. *See also* the German CG

But such disclosure rules may also be found in hard law.[67] An example of a – vague – requirement to report on procedures is found in the Accounting Directive, Directive 2013/34/EC, Article 20 according to which the corporate governance statement should include reporting on the main feature of internal control and management systems and the operation of the management and supervisory bodies and their committees. This obligation should also include procedural aspects. Another example is the rules on non-financial reporting found in Article 19a and 29a of the Accounting Directive as amended according to which large public-interest entities should report on their policies relating to environment, social and employment matters, etc., including their due diligence processes, the outcome of these policies, and principal risks which are likely to cause adverse effects and how these risks are managed. In particular, the reference to due diligences processes[68] and how risks are managed[69] encourages companies to report on procedures they have in place and are therefore likely to help generate such procedures. It should be recalled that there is no duty to have such procedures (or policies), and therefore the companies may choose to forego of such procedures. But according to the comply or explain-principle, the company will then need to report this fact, which may seem a less attractive option. Alternatively, there could be a duty to set up procedures and instead of regulating in detail how these should look, the companies may be required to report on the procedure they have adopted. This is the solution chosen by the Commission in their recent proposal for a directive on corporate sustainability due diligence.[70] However, the duty to conduct a due diligence process is coupled with some minimum requirements that need to be included in these processes.

§4.03 THE PROS AND CONS OF PROCEDURAL RULES AS A TRIGGER OF GOOD GOVERNANCE

As explained earlier, procedural rules may help to promote good corporate governance in different ways. Overall, they aim to induce management to act in a way that is better informed, more professional, more efficient, and objective.[71] As one of the aims of promoting good corporate governance is to promote high performing, effective boards

code, recommendation D.1 that not only recommends that the supervisory board adopt its own rules of procedure but also publish these on the company's website.

67. An example is found in Danish law where state enterprises must disclose code of conduct, *see* Danish Companies Act § 130(3).
68. The Commission have published guidelines on non-financial reporting (OJ 2017 C 251/1), and here the purpose of due diligence processes is explained as: 'Due diligence processes relate to policies, to risk management and to outcomes. Due diligence processes are undertaken by a company to ensure that it delivers against a concrete objective (e.g., to ensure that carbon emissions are below a certain level or that supply chains are free from trafficking in human beings). They help identify, prevent and mitigate existing and potential adverse impacts.' (at 12).
69. According to the guidelines, *ibid.*, the companies should, *inter alia*, explain the processes used to identify and assess such risks, at 12.
70. *See* COM(2022) 71 final.
71. Whether they have this effect in practice is difficult to verify, as there are few empirical studies addressing this. However, there is interdisciplinary research that supports the assumption that

to challenge executive management,[72] it seems that procedural rules could be one of the instruments applied. More recently, the Commission has focused on embedding sustainability in corporate governance, and here it also seems that procedural rules may offer some solutions. Thus, in the public consultation on institutional investors' and asset managers' duties regarding sustainability, a majority of the respondents seems to favour solutions whereby sustainability factors are integrated in the investment decision process, and less keen on more structural solutions, solutions addressing remuneration or reporting.[73] Many of the proposals offered for promoting sustainable corporate governance in listed companies also have a procedural character.[74]

But procedural solutions are not the only way to promote good corporate governance as the solution may alternatively be to specify the duties of directors, make structural arrangements, change the rules on remunerations, etc. Therefore, it is necessary to consider why and when procedural rules may be the better regulatory alternative and of course examining when such rules may prove to be problematic.

[A] Possible Advantages by Using Procedural Solutions

The increased use of procedural rules may in part be justified by the need to *strengthen the corporate governance measures that are already in place*. Thus, for instance, structural rules may ensure more competent and diversified boards but this will not matter if it is not ensured that the (whole) board is involved in making decisions and solving those tasks where these features are beneficial. This may be achieved by procedural rules.[75] Procedural rules may also support the enforcement of the duties imposed on directors. This is especially true for duties that are vague (even soft law)[76] and therefore otherwise difficult to enforce.[77] This could be a duty to take account of

procedural requirements may impact corporate decision-making and culture and ensure more effective boards, *see* further references in McNulty *supra* n. 6 and Chiu and Donovan *supra* n. 10, at 461–466.

72. *See* the Green Paper entitled *The EU Corporate governance framework prepared by the Commission*, COM(2011) 164 final, 3.
73. *See* the Feedback Statement from 24 May 2018 prepared by the Commission entitled*: Public Consultation on Institutional Investors' and Asset Managers' Duties regarding Sustainability*, at 12.
74. At the moment, the Commission is only committed to proposing rules on mandatory due diligence, which has clearly a procedural element. The Ernst & Young report prepared for the Commission entitled: Study on directors' duties and sustainable corporate governance, July 2020, includes a number of proposals that focus less on procedural element. It has been argued that procedural rules should be preferred to a larger extent in this area, *see* Florian Möslein and Karsten Engsig Sørensen, *Sustainable Corporate Governance: A Way Forward*, Eur. Comp. L. 7-14 (2021).
75. *See also supra* s. §4.02[A].
76. The procedural rules promoted by the duty to report on non-financial matters is thus intending to promote soft law and not hard law.
77. *See* Cary Coglianese & David Lazer, *Management-Based Regulation: Prescribing Private Management to Achieve Public Goals*, Law & Soc'y Rev 691–730 (2003); Chiu, *supra*, n. 9, at 197, and Florian Möslein & Karsten Engsig Sørensen, *Nudging for Corporate Long-termism and Sustainability? Regulatory Instruments from a Comparative and Functional Perspective*, Colum. J. Eur. L. 391–454, 444 (2018).

certain stakeholders' interests. Such a duty is hard to specify and consequently also hard to enforce. Instead, procedures may ensure that it becomes more likely that the board considers their interest, for instance, by asking the board to report on how it is done or by requiring it to consult stakeholders about their opinion. It will be easier to enforce procedural rules (although this is not without problems, *see* next section) than enforcing a vague duty, and it will also be easier for the board to comply with a procedure than complying with a vague duty. If the procedure is conductive to achieving the right result, then procedural rules may help enforce substantive duties.

Procedural rules may not only make it easier for those who are directors but also *inspire confidence in the company's stakeholders*. Thus, clear and transparent procedures may convince investors that the tasks assigned to the board are taken seriously. This is particularly the case when the procedure is published which explains why it is often recommended that the recruitment procedures for directors and risk management procedures are published. But it must also be assumed that stakeholders benefit from the disclosure of non-financial information, including those parts that deal with procedures.[78] Also procedural requirements laid down in law or codes may have the effect of inspiring confidence. For instance, the right to be consulted on certain decisions is likely to give employees the impression that their interests are taken into account.

Often the choice will be between setting procedural rules or leaving it to the companies to decide how to make decisions or solve tasks. It may *save time and cost* if such procedures are either dictated or recommended as the companies will not have to invent their own solutions then. Such benefits may especially be at hand when a best practice has evolved for solving tasks or decisions.

For some problems, the procedural solutions do not only seem to be preferable but the only solution. This is the case for problems of conflicts of interests. There is a structural solution to these problems as persons likely to have conflicts of interests may be barred from the management. But such a solution will often be too heavy-handed, as it will also exclude persons that only in some cases may enter a conflict of interests.[79] The better alternative is to ensure that the procedural solutions are in place to cope with such problems.

Procedural rules may have a role in *preventing some of the risk associated with decision-making in groups*. Normally it must be assumed that decisions taken in groups are better than decisions taken by individuals since the group may benefit from more

78. Thus, the Directive identifies not only shareholders (or investors) but also other stakeholders as the addressees for the non-financial report, *see* Recital 3 and 4 of Council Directive 2014/95 of 22 October 2014 amending Directive 2013/34/EU as regards disclosure of non-financial and diversity information by certain large undertakings and groups *Text with EEA relevance, OJ L 330, 15.11.2014*. The effect it may have on shareholders and other stakeholders is more debatable, *see* Möslein & Sørensen *ibid.*, at 420–422.
79. Of course, there may be exceptions. For instance, in Germany no one can be a member of both the executive board and the supervisory board, as this would cause obvious conflict of interest, *see* German Public Companies Act § 105.

diverse and qualified input and by having advantages in information processing.[80] This may help the group to overcome some of the biases that individuals face, such as bounded rationality, bounded perception. But behavioural economics also indicate that group dynamics may result in less than optimal decisions. Thus, groups may be inclined to spend more time on examining information that two or more directors share than information that only one director brings, and the group may suffer from confirmation bias, and search for information that confirms prior held beliefs.[81] These potential pitfalls may be prevented if procedural rules ensure that expert or stakeholders give input to the decision. There is also a risk that groups end up making extreme decisions due to 'groupthink'. This happens when groups are eager to seek consensus and overestimates the capabilities of the group. Groupthink is more likely to happen when the groups are insulated and working in a way that makes it likely that decisions are being taken too quickly.[82] The risks associated with groupthink may be reduced by procedural rules, that may ensure that more opinions are presented to the board and ensure that decision making is allowed to proceed in a pace that is conductive to contemplation.[83]

Finally, there may be *advantages in harmonising* procedural rules at European level. If indeed procedural rules may help enforcing substantive rules and/or may boost stakeholders confidence, then the European capital market may benefit from having such common rules in place.[84] In addition, it is often pointed out that to the extent that procedural rules impose costs, see the comments on this below, the need to ensure a level playing field also favours harmonisation of rules.[85] Finally, if Member States develop their own procedures the fragmentation that is the result hereof will make it difficult for those companies that need to comply with several diverging sets of

80. *See* Jaap Winter, *A Behavioral Perspective on Corporate Law and Corporate Governance* in *The Oxford Handbook of Corporate Law and Governance* 159–183 at 167 (Jeffry N. Gordon & Wolf-Georg Ringe eds. Oxford University Press 2018).
81. *Ibid.*, at 168.
82. *See* Irving Lester Janis, *Groupthink: Psychological Studies of Policy Decisions and Fiascoes* (Houghton Mifflin 2nd ed. 1983).
83. *See* McNulty *supra* n. 6 and Julia Redenius-Hövermann, *Behavioural Economics, Neoroeconomics, and Corporate Law*, in *Advances in Corporate Governance: Comparative Perspectives*, Ch. 12 269–291 (Helmut K. Anheier & Theodor Baums, OUP eds. 2020).
   It has also been suggested that groupthink may be avoided by designating one director as devil's advocate, *see* Carsten Gerner-Beuerle & Michael Schillig, *Comparative Company Law* 318 (OUP 2019); *See* Finkelstein and Mooney *supra* n. 6.
84. The consultation on the Sustainable corporate governance initiative showed that a majority of the respondents were in favour of an EU framework for due diligence, and the main reason was that harmonisation avoids fragmentation, creates awareness of the negative impacts of companies, and may effectively contribute to a more sustainable development. *See* the document, *Sustainable corporate governance initiative: Summary report – public consultation*, at 8.
85. The level playing field argument plays a prominent role in the incept impact assessment in the sustainable corporate governance initiative presented by the Commission on 30 July 2020, Ares(2020)4034032. In the consultation undertaken by the Commission, *Sustainable corporate governance initiative: Summary report – public consultation*, 75.5% of the respondents pointed to benefits of harmonisation of due diligence procedures may level the playing field, at 4. Consequently, it is hardly surprising that the argument is prominent in the proposed directive on corporate sustainability due diligence, *see* COM(2022) 71 final, at 3, 11, and 13.

procedures.[86] But as explained below, harmonisation in this area can also be complicated due to the cultural differences that exists.

[B] Potential Negative Effect of Procedural Solutions

It will be difficult to design procedural rules that work in companies of different sizes, engage in different activities and from different jurisdictions. Even designing common rules for all listed companies in a jurisdiction may be difficult. This problem is articulated in the French corporate governance code, para. 2.2:

> The wide diversity of listed corporations does not allow formal and identical forms of organisation and operation to be imposed for all Boards of Directors. The organisation of the Board's work, and likewise its membership, must be suited to the shareholder make-up, to the size and nature of each firm's business, and to the particular circumstances facing it. Each Board is the best judge of this, and its foremost responsibility is to adopt the mode of organisation and operation that enable it to carry out its tasks in the best possible manner. Its organisation and operation are described in the internal rules that it has drawn up, which are published in part or in full on the company's website or in the report on corporate governance.

Making common procedural rules across jurisdictions and culture will present additional problems. Not only are the board structures different but there may also be existing institutions in place that allow for stakeholder involvement, such as worker participation rules. Cultural differences may also make harmonisation difficult. What may work in one jurisdiction seems overly formal and rigid in other cultures. As national corporate governance codes have already introduced several procedural rules, different ways of making decision or solving task may have become entranced, and difficult to change.[87]

Procedural rules may *inflict costs* on the companies, for instance, if they involve hiring experts, or they may simply just take up more time than the decision or task would otherwise do. If the procedures do not improve corporate governance, these costs will not be justified. Even in the circumstances that the procedures are likely to improve the decision, there must be a balance between the cost and the importance of the decision or task regulated.

Even if the procedural rules work, they may not be optimal, and (some) companies will benefit from adopting their own procedures. However, if procedural rules exist (either as hard law or best practices), the boards may be *less inclined to adopt their own rules*.[88] This reluctance to develop different rules may also prevent companies from developing better procedures and adopting new procedures to address

86. This risk flowing from fragmentation has been pointed out as one of the reasons for harmonising the rules on due diligence processes, *see* the proposed directive, COM(2022) 71 final, at 3 and 11.
87. However, research indicates that using solutions from foreign codes is common and therefore such legal transplants may often not be a problem. *See* Carsten Gerner-Beuerle, *Diffusion of regulatory innovations: The case of corporate governance codes*, J Inst. Eco. 271–303 (2017).
88. *See also* Jaap Winter, *Towards a Duty of Societal Responsibility of the Board*, Eur. Comp. L 192–200, 193 (2020).

new conditions or challenges. Setting procedural rules may therefore have a static effect.[89] This effect is likely to be most prominent for hard law procedural rules but also procedures found in soft law may have this effect if the soft law is accepted as best practice.

There is also the risk that procedural rules may not contribute to the enforcement of substantive rules but may instead *deflect the focus from the substantial rules*. If there are detailed procedures in place, then boards are likely to follow these assuming that in doing so they will comply with the norm that the procedures are intending to enforce, and in doing so they may lose track of this norm. The effect is sometimes called excessive proceduralisation or form over substance.[90]

There may also be elements of the procedural rules that may pose problems. Getting different input when making decisions will normally be a good thing, but there may be a risk of *information overload* if the board is presented with too much input. Procedures should also balance the need to take appropriate steps and the need to make decisions without undue delay. Also, it should be ensured that procedures do not allow any *holdout problems*, for instance, by allowing stakeholders or board members to unduly delay decisions.[91]

Finally, it may be *difficult to enforce procedural rules*, and this may make it more difficult to ensure that they have the intended effect. Breach of procedural rules may not necessarily invalidate the decision taken by the board. The conditions for invalidations differ from jurisdiction to jurisdiction, but if the decision in its substance does not infringe company law, it will often only be invalidated in the case of severe procedural deficiencies.[92] This may be the case if the breach of procedures has affected the outcome of the decision,[93] fraud is involved,[94] or if the procedural rules breached

89. Binder, *supra* n. 46, at 785 and Enriques and Zetzsche *supra* n. 64.
90. *See* Chiu, *supra* n. 9 at 198 and Enriques and Zetzsche, *supra* n. 64, at 294. The German term 'Bürokratisierung' has been used for the same phenomena, *see* Binder *supra* n. 46.
91. *See* the critique of the consultation and grievance mechanism foreseen in the Parliament draft for a directive on due diligence presented by European Company Law Experts Group, *The European Parliament's Draft Directive on Corporate Due Diligence and Corporate Accountability*, Nordic Journal of Company Law 2021:4 30–45, at 41–42.
92. In the UK, the remedy of rescission is used for contracts entered into in breach of the self-dealing rule, *see* also Davies, Worthington & Hare, *supra* n. 1. The conditions for this seem relatively generous, *see* UK Companies Act sec. 195 and 213.
93. Thus, in Danish law a breach of the duty not to participate in a decision where a director has a conflict of interest will only be invalid if the breach has impacted the outcome of the decision, *see* for Danish law, Peer Schaumburg-Müller & Erik Werlauff, *Selskabsloven med kommentarer* 792 (DJØF Forlag 2020). *See also* Paul Krüger Andersen, *supra* n. 32, at 355, who assumes that if a decision is taken without the sufficient majority or the required number of directors present (quorum) according to § 124 of the Danish Companies Act, the decision will be invalid if the decision had been different if all formalities had been complied with.
94. *See*, for instance, France law in relation to the procedural aspects of related party transactions, Grossi/Poracchia/Raynouard, *France*, in *Company Laws of the EU* 67-68 (Andrea Vicari & Alexander Schall eds. 2020). Also, in several jurisdictions infringement of procedural rules that have the aim of keeping particular directors from participating in decision-making will cause the decision to be invalid, *see* Willson, *supra* n. 32, at 133 and for Denmark Andersen *supra* n. 32, at 355.

has an essential impact on the company and/or its stakeholders.[95] Even if there is such a severe deficiency, the decision may be invalid for the company, but not necessarily vis-à-vis relating third parties who have contracted with the persons authorised to represent the company.[96] If there is a violation of procedural rules, then it will often also be difficult to claim damages. The requirement of causation will make it necessary to prove that the decision adopted if the procedure had been complied with would have been different, and that the different decision would have caused a smaller or no loss.[97] In particular for procedural rules adopted by the company for their internal use (code of conduct etc.), it may be difficult to pursue a claim for damages.[98]

There are, however, ways to overcome some of these enforcement problems. One solution could be to shift the burden of proof in favour of the plaintiff, if it can be shown that the board did not comply with procedural rules. Such a solution is proposed in the Commission's proposal for a directive on corporate sustainability due diligence, where companies that have complied with the specific due diligence steps will not be liable for damages, unless it was unreasonable to assume that the steps would be adequate.[99]

A different solution may be to allow for a more thorough review of decisions where there has been a breach of procedures. This is sometimes the effect of the business judgment rules that apply in many jurisdictions.[100] Normally decisions taken by the board which involves business decisions will not be scrutinised to the same degree as other decisions. In many jurisdictions, an exception is made, *inter alia*, if the board has failed to secure the necessary information before making the decisions. Such 'procedural' failure will trigger a more intense review of the decision by the courts.[101]

Another solution will be to have public enforcement. Even though infringement of certain procedural rules may be subject to fines, it will often be difficult to enforce such rules.[102] The recent proposal for a directive on corporate sustainability due

95. In German law, it seems that decisions will be invalidated if the breach of procedural rules are significant (absoluten Verfahrensfehler), for instance, because the procedural rule is indispensable (unversichtbare Verfahrensvorschriften), *see* further Hoffmann-Becking, *supra* n. 26, at 648. In France entering into an agreement with a director in violation of the procedures can only be cancelled if the agreement has prejudicial consequences for the company, *see* Art. L. 225-42 and Pierre-Henri Conac, *France* in *Comparative Corporate Governance*, 463 (Andreas M. Fleckner & Klaus Hopt eds., CUP 2013).
96. Thus, CCLD Art. 9(2).
97. Consequently, liability for damages will often not be available even though procedural requirements are not complied with, *see* for German law further Hoffmann-Becking, *supra* n. 26, at 527, and Danish law, Peer Schaumburg-Müller & Erik Werlauff, *Selskabsloven med kommentarer* 792 (2020).
98. Thus, the Danish Supreme Court has held that non-compliance with internal rules will not cause liability unless it is proven that the specific deviation from the rules was tortious, *see* the Danish Supreme Court decision in UfR 2019.1907 H. It may be easier to establish a liability if the internal rules have been published, *see*, for instance, Thorbjørn Sofsrud, *Bestyrelsens beslutning og ansvar* 207–208 (DJØF Forlag 1999).
99. *See* COM(2022) 71 final, Art. 22(2).
100. *See* the comparative overview in Carsten Gerner-Beuerle *et al.*, *Study on Directors' Duties and Liability* 108–118 (2013), http://eprints.lse.ac.uk/50438/.
101. *See* further on the German business judgment rule in German Public Companies Act § 93(1) and Binder, *supra* n. 46, 750–753.
102. Even though a broad range of company law rules are sanctioned with fines according to the Danish Companies Act § 367 – including several procedural rules – there are very few attempts

diligence aims to make public enforcement more likely, *inter alia*, by providing for a complaint mechanism.[103]

It may also enhance enforcement if the company's auditor is required to ensure that procedures are complied with. The rules on non-financial reporting require that the auditor should have a role in their enforcement. However, the Member State should only ensure that the auditor checks the existence of the non-financial statement or, if so, provided for by the Member State law, the existence of the separate report prepared using national, EU, or international frameworks.[104] Thus, neither it is foreseen that the auditor performs a consistency check of the statement nor it is foreseen that the auditor should test that the company is actually acting according to the procedures described. However, in the proposal for a directive on sustainability reporting, it is proposed to give the auditor a slightly more prominent role. This includes that the statutory auditor must perform a limited assurance engagement on a company's sustainability reporting, including 'on the process carried out by the company to identify the information reported'.[105] Given that only a limited assurance engagement is required, this will not require the auditor to make a detailed review of what procedures the company actually uses. But it may be a first step towards a more comprehensive assessment.[106]

Finally, procedural rules may affect how the court and authorities review corporate behaviour. The presence of such procedural rules may make it more likely that the review will focus on the process rather than the substance as checking the procedural requirement will often be easier than testing whether a decision harms stakeholders or is transacted at arm's length conditions. Given that procedural rules are likely to ensure decisions that complies with company law, this, however, will be acceptable.[107]

§4.04 CONCLUSIONS

There are good arguments that procedural rules may – if used correctly – be used to promote good corporate governance. It may provide for better informed and more objective decisions and may help to enforce duties that are otherwise elusive and

to enforce this. It seems that in the UK and Germany criminal sanctions are seldom used as sanctions for infringements of such rules, *see* Poelzig/Bärnreuther, *Germany*, in *Company Laws of the EU*, at 321–322 (Andrea Vicari and Alexander Schall eds, Beck/Hart 2020). Criminal sanctions seem to play a more important rule in France, *See*, Beuerle & Schilling *supra* n. 83, at 720, although not necessarily for breaches of procedural rules, *see* Ledouble, *France* in Andrea Vicari and Alexander Schall et al., *ibid.* at 104.

103. *See* COM(2022) 71 final, Arts 17–21.
104. *See* Art. 19a(5) *supra* n. 15.
105. *See* COM(2021) 189, Art. 1(10) and Art. 3(12).
106. Thus, according to recital 53 of the proposal the Commission intends to work towards a more comprehensive assessment. A first step will be that the Commission adopts assurance standards for the more far-reaching *reasonable* assurance of sustainability reporting, which will allow companies voluntarily to opt for the more comprehensive solution.
107. For a discussion of substantive versus procedural fairness in relation to related parties' transactions. *See* Alessio M. Pacces, *Procedural and Substantive Review of Related Party Transactions* in *The Law and Finance of Related Party Transactions* 181–217 (Luca Enriques & Tobias H. Tröger eds., CUP 2019).

therefore difficult to enforce. At the same time, it is clear that procedural rules may not be a solution in all cases as they may potentially have more negative effect than positive. Therefore, it is necessary to use this instrument with care. This requires that any initiative is assessed on its own, and one should be careful to make general statements. With that reservation, a few general observations will be attempted.

At present procedural rules exist as both hard law and soft law and in both national law and EU law. In EU, the first procedural rules were suggested as recommendations but in recent years there have been some examples of hard law rules and more seem to come. We also see some hybrid solutions where disclosure requirements are ensured through hard law and include a duty to report on procedural soft law rules.

Hard law solutions seem justified when there are important interests that need to be protected and this is best achieved with procedural rules. This would be the case for conflict of interest within the board, when it is necessary to protect the interests of the company, shareholders, or other stakeholders. Hard law may be adopted either with a compulsory template for the procedure or as a duty for companies to adopt a procedure. The latter solutions may be combined with some minimum requirements that procedures must fulfil (as in the proposal for a directive on corporate sustainability due diligence), or it may be a duty to adopt procedures without any minimum requirement but only an indication of the purpose they should serve. Hard law with a compulsory template may be difficult to fit to companies of different sizes or activities. Therefore, they should only be used either where there is a recognised best practice or when the choice is between procedural rules and substantive rules, and the former offers the best solutions. Otherwise, the more flexible solution of having scope for individually designed procedures is likely to cause fewer problems as these may be designed to accommodate the needs of the individual companies. A hard law solution that allows the companies to develop their own rules (maybe restrained by some minimum requirements) may be coupled with requirements that the rules adopted should be disclosed. This solution helps enforcing the requirement to adopt rules but is also likely – in time – to lead to more or less uniform rules.

However, soft law solutions as well as the hybrid solutions mentioned earlier will provide a better solution in other cases. This may be the case when it is assumed that procedural rules may provide for better corporate governance by improving how the board makes decision or handle tasks or by helping to avoid some of the potential problems based on behavioural economics. Again, this can be done with or without a template on how the procedural rules should look. Whether such templates should be suggested will normally depend on whether a best practice has evolved or not and depend on the likelihood that the template can be used successfully by most companies or not. If there are no practices yet, a solution could be to require disclosure of the rules adopted and thus encourage the development of best practices.

CHAPTER 5

Corporate Governance Codes

*Matteo Gargantini & Michele Siri**

§5.01 CORPORATE GOVERNANCE AND SOFT LAW

This chapter analyses the role of corporate governance codes (CGCs) in shaping the regulatory framework for listed companies, with specific regard to board organisation and duties. CGCs rely on soft law and self-regulation, which distinguish them from traditional company law measures. These regulatory strategies have comparative advantages and disadvantages, which this chapter explains in light of the main characteristics of CGCs and the matters they address. In more detail, the chapter explains how soft law (§5.01) and self-regulation (§5.02) work in CGCs. It also analyses the most typical provisions of CGCs and how these adjust to the needs of specific listed companies (§5.03). It then explains the role of the 'comply or explain' (CoE) principle in fostering better corporate governance practices (§5.04) and highlights the effect of formal and informal enforcement of CGC provisions (§5.05). Some reflections on the current state and the future of CGCs conclude the chapter (§5.06).

[A] Soft Law in CGCs

Ever since its inception in its currently dominating form,[1] the development of soft law in the field of corporate governance has revolved around a combination of two

* While the chapter is the result of common reflections, §§5.01, 5.03, and 5.05 shall be attributed to Matteo Gargantini, and §§5.02, 5.04, and 5.06 to Michele Siri.
1. The most influential CGC in this regard has been the UK Cadbury Code, adopted in 1992 (Committee on the Financial Aspects of Corporate Governance, Cadbury Report); for a description of its origins and its impact, *see* Donald Nordberg, *Corporate Governance. Principle and Issues*, 93–101 (SAGE 2011). Other countries had already adopted CGCs before 1992, however: *see* Ruth Aguilera & Alvaro Cuervo-Cazurra, *Codes of Good Governance*, 17 Corp. Governance. An Int'l Rev. 376 (2009) (referring to the US, Hong Kong, and Ireland).

elements: (i) the definition of standards against which companies can benchmark their governance system; (ii) a duty to disclose the result of such benchmarking exercise under a CoE principle. Strictly speaking, only the first element is a matter of soft law, while the transparency obligation, albeit ancillary, is a hard-law measure that strengthens the effectiveness of the standards in their role as yardsticks. We consider soft law in this section, and the CoE mechanism in §5.04.

Soft law is the most typical feature of CGCs, but drawing a clear-cut dividing line between it and traditional company law is more difficult than it appears at first sight. The reason is that there are intermediate stages that separate traditional hard law – and the command-and-control approach it reflects – and non-binding rules that only set forth general standards.[2]

Recourse to soft law in certain areas of corporate governance is regularly justified by the high level of variance of corporate entities' features, even within the subset of listed companies alone. This explains the impossibility of designing efficient rules for all the addressees and, therefore, the need to allow for deviations from the pre-defined legal model. Indeed, the nature of the soft-law provisions in CGCs is that of best practices reflecting the state of the art in corporate governance. This goes hand in hand with the understanding that not all companies are expected to comply with all CGC standards.

However, traditional statutory law has tools at its disposal that could meet this need for flexibility, which leaves the question concerning the comparative advantages of soft law partially unanswered. Company law often adopts default rules that reflect what most market participants can be expected to adopt spontaneously, as this reduces transaction costs that repeated bargaining would entail.[3] Default provisions that define best practices allow companies to opt out whenever they do not find such standards suitable to their specific characteristics.

To be sure, default rules may not be as flexible as expected due to the costs companies incur when departing from them. For instance, default rules allow companies to rely on the interpretations provided by case law – which hardly exists for provisions tailored at the charter level – and to take advantage of the updating activity lawmakers perform on those provisions.[4] These factors may discourage deviations from default rules, making them quite sticky. However, enabling rules (or menu rules, when they offer multiple options) do not necessarily display these features and can therefore be more similar to soft-law measures. What does then characterise CGC provisions?

2. Junhai Liu, *Globalisation of Corporate Governance Depends on Both Soft Law and Hard Law*, in *Corporate Governance Codes for the 21st Century. International Perspectives and Critical Analyses* 276 (Jean du Plessis & Chee Keong Low eds., Springer 2017) (analysing different criteria to distinguish soft law and hard law).
3. Frank H. Easterbrook & Daniel R. Fischel, *The Economic Structure of Corporate Law*, 34–37 (Harvard University Press 1991).
4. Reinier Kraakman et al., *The Anatomy of Corporate Law. A Comparative and Functional Approach* 20 (Oxford Univ. Press 2017).

Besides the use of self-regulation, which, however, equally comes in different fashions,[5] a defining feature of soft law in CGCs - compared to default or enabling rules in traditional company law - seems to lie with the regime for the decisions to adhere to the benchmark defined in the standards. Contracting around default or enabling rules requires, in most company laws, a formal decision, often through a provision in the articles of association or a charter amendment.[6] This is not the case with CGC standards, whose implementation is typically left to a decision by the board or by its executive members and, therefore, is subject to lighter procedural and formal requirements.[7] This flexibility is particularly suitable to decisions on matters that do not lend themselves to a once-and-for-all assessment. It is no coincidence that CGCs typically deal with matters that may only be addressed with general standards.

The definition of independent directors is a case in point, as independence can be a remarkably elusive concept. In the European Union (EU), the Commission Recommendation on the role of non-executive directors recommended already in 2005 that Member States define the framework for non-executive board members - including independence requirements - either through a CoE approach or through legislation.[8] The question arises, therefore, which of the two systems is more suitable in this regard.

In some EU jurisdictions, hard-law provisions define certain independence requirements, but capturing all the relevant ties that may prevent a director from being independent is usually impossible. Even in these jurisdictions, therefore, soft-law measures are often in place, as well, to define stricter standards of independence. These standards can be deviated from when the specific circumstances of the case so suggest, thus reducing the risk of false positives and false negatives simultaneously.[9] This regulatory technique better reflects the intractable nature of independence when the assessment goes beyond clear impediments (such as having an executive role),[10] in line with an 'I know it when I see it' approach.[11] The decision to opt-in or opt-out independence criteria may be case-specific, as every director has unique features that may require adaptation of the standard, subject to disclosure. This is an advantage that

5. *See infra* §5.02.
6. Kraakman et al., *supra* n. 4, 18–20 (listing examples from various jurisdictions where choices on default or enabling rules occur through charter provisions).
7. Iain MacNeil & Xiao Li, *'Complay or Explain': Market Discipline and Non-compliance with the Combined Code*, 14 Corporate Governance: An International Review 486 (2006), 493. For a theoretical analysis of the procedural rule accompanying optional regimes, *see* Ian Ayres, *Regulating Opt-Out: An Economic Theory of Altering Rules*, 121 Yale Law Journal 2032 (2012).
8. §§1.1 and 1.3.2 Recommendation 2005/162/EC.
9. *See, e.g.*, regarding Italy, Marco Ventoruzzo et al., *Comparative Corporate Law* 259–261 (West Academic 2015) (noting that the Italian mandatory provision on director independence - Article 148(3) Consolidated Law on Finance - falls short of providing bright-line guidance despite its intentions, thus creating legal uncertainty, and highlighting the stricter requirements in the Italian CGC).
10. Lisa Fairfax, *The Elusive Quest for Director Independence*, in *Research Handbook on the Economics of Corporate Law* 170–178 (Claire Hill & Brett McDonnell eds., Edward Elgar 2012) (drawing a distinction between the bright-line test for independence under the Sarbanes-Oxley Act and listing standards, on the one hand, and the more calibrated situational approach by the Delaware courts, on the other hand).
11. §13.2 Recommendation 2005/162/EC (allowing case-by-case assessment of independence).

CGCs retain even when compared to contractible company law provisions, which typically require formalised decisions that are difficult to adjust over time.

[B] Relationship Between Soft Law and Hard Law

Despite their structural differences, soft and hard law are not, however, independent silos that operate in isolation. To begin with, hard law has of course priority over soft law, and therefore drives the interpretation of CGC recommendations. As we shall see, some CGCs even reproduce generally applicable company law provisions, next to their recommendations subject to CoE mechanisms. This is a way to ensure that companies apply soft-law measures in a way that is compatible with mandatory provisions.

It is harder to tell whether a reciprocal influence also exists, so that CGCs may play a role in the interpretation of corporate law. The question seems to be particularly relevant for directors' duties – including those concerning the organisation of the board, of its internal committees, and of the internal controls. While such influence may be remarkable on day-to-day managerial practices, whether it can lead to shaping the interpretation of directors' liability before a court is a different matter.

In principle, CGCs might play this role in two different ways. The first one relates to the ability of CGCs to provide, in and of themselves, authoritative interpretations of directors' duties and of their implications in specific cases, such as related-party transactions, the consideration to pay to stakeholder interests, and the organisation of the board. The second way a recommendation may shape directors' liability is through the declaration of compliance with the CGC by the company. In this case, the question is not so much whether that recommendation fleshes out some implications of fiduciary duties. The point is, instead, whether that specific company and its directors can be held liable for breaching a commitment they took through their declaration of compliance.

As regards the first setting, the opinion among scholars seems to be that CGC recommendations have overall a limited role in shaping directors' liability. Based on the analysis of national case law, the understanding is that CGCs do not typically provide an autonomous basis for liability[12] – a logical conclusion, if one considers that some key CGC provisions can be rather vague as they refer to general standards and that causation and damage may be difficult to demonstrate.[13] In some jurisdictions, CGCs are regarded as a source of information to consider when trying to grasp the substance of mandatory provisions, a role that has been compared to that of case law. When this happens, courts are however reluctant to consider CGCs as an autonomous basis for liability unless the articles of associations incorporate them by reference.[14]

12. Eddy Wymeersch, *European Corporate Governance Codes and Their Effectiveness*, in *Boards and Shareholders in European Listed Companies* 98–101 (Massimo Belcredi & Guido Ferrarini eds., Cambridge Univ. Press 2013), (regarding the Netherlands); Pierre-Henri Conac, *Public Versus Private Enforcement in Corporate Governance*, in *Comparative Corporate Governance* 417 (Afra Afsharipour & Martin Gelter eds., Edward Elgar 2021).
13. Conac, *ibid.*
14. *Ibid.*

Rather, CGCs may be invoked in support of interpretations that would most likely hold on the basis of legal provisions alone.[15]

As we mentioned, there is another way CGCs might influence, in theory, directors' liability, namely through the declaration of adoption and application of a relevant recommendation. In this case, liability would originate because of investor reliance on a company's statement. Once again, this seems to be a weak legal basis for liability, however. In most jurisdictions, fiduciary duties are grounded in legal provisions, and a declaration by the company concerning the standard of behaviour adopted by corporate directors would hardly seem able to have an equivalent effect. In principle, only a strong form of detrimental reliance would seem to lead to such a conclusion but, even in countries where this doctrine exists, a declaration alone would unlikely provide a solid basis to claim a breach of fiduciary duties.

Rather, liability might arise in a similar context – not so much out of the violation of a self-imposed duty, but rather – from the misleading effects of a false declaration of compliance with CGC provisions or an untrue explanation justifying departure from those provisions. In this case, the legal basis for liability would be the rules mandating CoE principle. We therefore explore this form of liability and its limitations below.[16]

The earlier examples show that soft and hard law can cooperate with variable intensity. The two can also compete to some extent, however. It is no mystery that CGCs are, in part, an attempt to pre-empt hard-law developments that could affect corporate governance more than recommendations of best practices.[17] For this reason, low levels of compliance with CGC provisions on delicate matters often raise concerns about the risks that more intrusive company law measures may address those corporate governance issues in the future.[18] And, indeed, experience shows that this may be the case, relevant examples being directors' remuneration, gender diversity, and related-party transactions.[19]

[C] Subjection to CGCs and Compliance

The soft-law quality of CGCs can manifest itself at different levels. Intuitively, the non-mandatory nature of CGCs means, in the first place, that companies are free to deviate from the recommendation that the soft-law provision brings about. As a matter of fact, however, this can mean different things. Sometimes, the soft-law nature of a CGC goes as far as to involve the very fact that a company is free to decide whether to consider that CGC as a term of reference for its organisation and practice. In other cases, the company is made subject to a CGC by a binding provision, but it can then

15. *See* Wymeersch, *supra* n. 12, 101.
16. *See infra* §5.04.
17. David Kershaw, *Corporate Law and Self-Regulation*, 5, LSE Legal Studies Working Paper No. 5/2015, available at https://papers.ssrn.com/sol3/papers.cfm?abstract_id=2574201.
18. Cadbury Report, *Supra* n. 1, §1.10.
19. Wymeersch *supra* n. 12, 69, 119 (on remuneration). *See* Art. 9c Directive 2007/36/EC (for related-party transactions) and Commission Proposal for a Directive on improving the gender balance among non-executive directors of companies listed on stock exchanges (COM/2012/0614 final), 14 November 2012.

freely decide whether to align with its recommendations. The difference between the two situations lies in the fact that, when the CGC applies, deviations from its recommendations normally require an explanation (CoE principle).[20] Therefore, a distinction should always be drawn between the subjection of a company to a CGC and the actual alignment of that company's governance to the provisions of such CGC. For the sake of clarity, we use the expressions 'adoption' or 'applicability' of a CGC when hinting at the fact that a company is subject to a certain CGC and therefore refers to it as a benchmark for its corporate governance.[21]

The adoption of a CGC – and, therefore, its applicability to a company – may originate from different acts, all of which determine a formal connection between the company and the code. Sometimes, listing rules may make such reference, so that the listed company commits to adopt the CGC by asking to be admitted to listing on a market subject to those listing rules. In other cases, which are however rather exceptional, the law itself may prescribe which code a company must adopt and, therefore, refer to on a CoE basis.[22]

More frequently, companies are bound to adopt a code of their choice. When this is the case, the question may arise as to what corporate body is competent for deciding on the adoption of a CGC by the company. In most cases, this body is the board of directors, but the answer may depend on the specific matter at stake and inevitably involves national company law rules that allocate powers among corporate bodies. To be sure, one should always distinguish between the overall commitment to adopt a CGC, which may lie with one body, from the actual alignment of the corporate organisation to one or more provisions of such CGC, which may be in the remit of a different body.

This distinction between adoption and compliance also shows that the decision to make the company subject to a specific CGC – when this is not mandated – does not entail a commitment to align to all its provisions. With the exceptions we show, the baseline scenario is one where companies that are (or have declared to be) subject to a CGC are allowed to deviate from one or more of its provisions, provided that they disclose this choice and the reasons underlying it.[23] When pointing to the decision (not) to align with a provision, we refer to the (lack of) 'implementation' or 'application' or 'compliance' with the CGC.

[D] Beyond Recommendations: CGCs and Their Provisions

Due to their soft-law nature, the typical provisions in CGCs take the form of recommendations. Some CGCs, however, adopt a broader array of provisions, which display

20. On the CoE principle, *see infra* §5.04.
21. For this taxonomy, *see* Wymeersch, *supra* n. 12, 71.
22. *See* Wymeersch, *supra* n. 12, 101, referring to the corporate governance recommendations by the Portuguese CMVM. More recently, however, a more traditional CGC was adopted (Portuguese CGC 2010). After some coexistence between the two instruments, the CGC took then the prevalence as the CMVM committed, in March 2016, to discontinue the publication of its own recommendations (Portuguese CGC 2020, 34).
23. *See infra* §5.04.

different levels of flexibility and have various consequences on disclosure. We analyse these provisions below, starting from the tools that adopt a lighter touch and then moving on to the provisions that, due to their content or nature, set more stringent limits on corporate discretion.[24]

The first deviation from the typical recommendations occurs when CGCs contain statements that do not require disclosure when companies deviate from their contents. These statements have various labels, such as 'suggestions'[25] or 'guidance'[26] and can be distinguished from traditional recommendations in different ways. For instance, they may appear in specific sections of the CGC, such as those providing more detailed explanations or highlighting further implications of recommendations. Sometimes, they can be placed in a separate document, which is however connected to the main CGC through cross-references that encourage reading the CGC – and its recommendations – together with the guidance provided in the separate document.[27] The most notable example is the United Kingdom (UK) CGC, which is sided by the UK Guidance on Board Effectiveness. This latter is meant to support the application of the main CGC by directors, who are encouraged to refer to the Guidance alongside the CGC.[28] The two documents also display an identical structure, which strengthens their connection and makes them not that different from CGCs that include both traditional recommendations and softer suggestions.[29]

In other cases, verbal tenses drive the distinction between recommendations and suggestions instead. This is the case with the German CGC, where the indicative case or a modal verb such as 'must' or 'shall' qualifies recommendations, while the modal verb 'should' identifies mere suggestions not subject to the CoE mechanism.[30]

The contents of these 'suggestions' (or comparable statements) are various. Sometimes, the duty to justify a deviation from a best practice under a CoE mechanism may put companies in an uneasy situation, when explaining a deviation may prove problematic. The German CDC, for instance, suggests that the supervisory board chair be available to discuss with investors issues related to the activity of that board, 'within reasonable limits'.[31] A suggestion of this kind may be suitable in some circumstances, but whether direct contacts with investors are advisable clearly depends on the specific topic addressed, as this may be sensitive for strategic reasons that are not easy to reveal.

---

24. *See* Gregor Bachmann, *Disclosure of Corporate Governance by Codes*, in *Transparency of Stock Corporations in Europe* 66 (Vassilios Tountopoulos & Rüdiger Veil eds., Hart Publishing 2019).
25. German CGC: Regierungskommission Deutscher Corporate Governance Kodex, German Corporate Governance Code (2019), 2, available at https://www.dcgk.de (last accessed 15 April 2022).
26. UK CGC: FRC (Financial Reporting Council), UK Corporate Governance Code (2018), 3, available at https://www.frc.org.uk (last accessed 15 April 2022), (referring to the UK Guidance on Board Effectiveness).
27. *Ibid.*, 1.
28. *Ibid.*
29. *Ibid.* ('The structure of the Guidance follows the structure of the Code').
30. German CGC, *supra* n. 25, 2.
31. German CGC, *supra* n. 25, 5.

In other contexts, the use of suggestions rather than recommendations seems to reflect the understanding that the variety of the circumstances in which companies operate prevents certain conducts from qualifying as generally applicable best practices. For instance, it is uncertain whether the ideal duration of the general meeting should lie – as the German CGC suggests[32] – between four and six hours, as this is issuer-specific and highly dependent on the complexity of the deliberations and the number of participating shareholders.

Next to mere suggestions, the second kind of deviation from the traditional recommendations is high-level statements of a more general nature that are typically labelled as 'principles'. However, due to the essential role of these principles in good corporate governance, all companies are expected to comply with them. At the same time, and partially because of their ability to apply to all listed companies, principles are typically quite broad in their formulation. For this reason, proper assessment of their implementation requires disclosure that goes beyond a mere declaration of compliance, as we shall see.[33]

Among the CGCs that include principles of this kind are the UK and the Italian ones. For instance, best practices that appear in those CGCs as principles are the need for the board to define the company's strategies and its governance and internal control systems, and to promote dialogue with shareholders and stakeholders.[34]

Finally, not all the provisions in CGCs have innovative content. Sometimes, they simply reproduce company law provisions that would apply to the addressee companies in any event.[35] This is not necessarily a window-dressing exercise to foster compliance rates. Rather, juxtaposing mandatory provisions from national company law and recommendations on best practices can facilitate the application of these latter. Reading recommendations against mandatory provisions fosters interpretations of best practices that are consistent with baseline company law requirements, and may even support a specific interpretation of company law rules. To some extent, this dynamic completes the other one, described earlier, that explains the influence of CGC recommendations on the interpretation of mandatory provisions, and of general standards in particular.

§5.02 CGCs AND SELF-REGULATION

While soft law defines the intensity of the command that provisions bring about, self-regulation refers to the procedure through which those provisions are shaped. Self-regulation and soft law often come together, but they do not coincide. Self-regulatory procedures may lead to binding provisions when their legal basis provides so, and government-led rulemaking may deliver soft-law measures instead.

32. *Ibid.*
33. *See infra* §5.04.
34. UK CGC, *supra* n. 26, §§B, C; Italian CGC: Comitato Corporate Governance, Corporate Governance Code (2020), available at https://www.borsaitaliana.it/comitato-corporate-governance (last accessed 15 April 2022), §§II, III, IV.
35. Kershaw, *supra* n. 17, 33, providing examples from the German and the Austrian CGCs.

Elements of self-regulation may manifest themselves with different intensities at each stage of the rulemaking procedure - initiative, drafting, and approval. As to the initiative, self-regulation by market participants may develop spontaneously, but it may also originate from a request by the law.[36] As to the drafting process, the level of involvement of market participants may vary from being little more than the ordinary representation mechanisms that characterise policymaking in a democratic context, to full delegation of regulatory powers. In between lies a broad array of intermediate participation mechanisms, which may range from light forms of involvement through the provision of advice to much more intense rulemaking powers giving the CGC addressees - or their representatives - complete control over the process.[37] The appointment of the members of the rulemaking committees and public consultations among stakeholders also calibrate the intensity of self-regulation. Finally, public or quasi-public regulatory authorities may play a role in the final stage of the self-regulatory process, as is the case when formal approval is required before the official release of the CGC. For instance, this may be the case with the recognition of the CGC by a regulated market, which performs the function of a quality label on CGCs.

In its various forms and intensity, self-regulation is considered particularly suitable when traditional top-down regulation may be prone to severe regulatory failures. Knowledge problems - the regulatory failures which mirror the market failure of asymmetric information[38] - are often mentioned among the reasons for self-regulation.[39] Market participants may be more informed than traditional policymakers on how to best shape corporate governance, and on the state of the art in that field.

When self-regulation supports a sense of belonging among the relevant constituencies, alignment to best practices may be high due to the perception of legitimacy that supports recommendations. In this regard, drafters of CGCs always need to strike a delicate balance between two needs. If CGCs have to identify best practices and foster genuine progress in corporate governance, then they must contain standards that are not too widespread and do not therefore lend themselves to window-dressing. Self-regulation is, indeed, a form of regulation. After all, the CoE principle rests on the assumption that deviations from the CGC standards are physiological, and full compliance with a CGC already in the initial years of its application would cast doubts on its effectiveness. However, CGC standards tailored to a small number of top-performing companies may clash with the idea that self-regulation draws its legitimacy from peer pressure through recognition of sufficiently widespread practices. In this case, self-regulation would weaken its reflexive elements.[40]

36. Kershaw, *supra* n. 17, 3 (referring to 'endogenous self-regulation' as opposed to 'forced self-regulation' - or 'market-controlled regulation').
37. *See* in general Robert Baldwin et al., *Understanding Regulation: Theory, Strategy, and Practice* 138–139 and 146–147 (Oxford Univ. Press 2011).
38. Thomas Lambert, *How to Regulate. A Guide for Policymakers* 195 (Cambridge Univ. Press 2017).
39. Baldwin et al., *supra* n. 37, 139.
40. On the connection between the players of self-regulation and its outcome, *see* Jeroen Veldman, *Self-Regulation in International Corporate Governance Codes*, in *Corporate Governance Codes for the 21st Century. International Perspectives and Critical Analyses* 85–88 (Jean du Plessis & Chee Keong Low eds., Springer 2017).

[A] Self-Regulation in Practice

CGCs display some variety as regards their self-regulatory nature. For instance, the German CGC is prepared by an ad hoc Commission (*Regierungskommission Deutscher Corporate Governance Kodex*), which was set up by the Federal Minister of Justice in 2001.[41] The Commission includes not only representatives of German listed companies (selected from both managing and supervisory boards) but also stakeholders such as 'institutional and retail investors, academics (economics, jurisprudence), auditors and a trade union federation.'[42] The Commission is also committed to involving all capital market participants and the public at large in its activities, particularly through periodical conferences and open consultations.[43]

In the UK, the code is prepared by the Financial Reporting Council (FRC), led by a Board appointed by the Department for Business, Energy and Industrial Strategy (BEIS).[44] The background of the Board members is diverse, ranging from regulation and supervision to the financial industry and from consultancy to auditing. This composition shows that the members' expertise supports a private-minded approach to the preparation of recommendations, as does the regular dialogue between the FRC and the market.[45]

As to France, the preparation of the main CGC (the Afep-Medef Code – hereinafter also 'French CGC') takes place under the responsibility of the two French associations representing listed companies (Afep) and employers (Medef) and therefore perfectly reflects the self-regulatory nature of that tool. The drafting process reflects inputs from other constituencies, as well.[46] The French Financial Conduct Authority (*Autorité des marchés financiers* – AMF) also has an influence on the process, as the drafting of the CGC takes into account areas that the Authority proposed for consideration to the two associations.[47]

In Italy, the CGC is prepared by an ad hoc Corporate Governance Committee jointly promoted by the main associations of issuers, employers, and institutional investors, together with the Italian Stock Exchange. Besides the representatives of the promoting entities, the Committee also includes actual or former directors of some listed companies.[48] There are no formal public consultations, although the Committee

41. Peter Hommelhoff, *Corporate Governance: Directors' Duties, Financial Reporting and Liability – Remarks from a German Perspective*, in *Perspectives in Company Law and Financial Regulation* 266–267 (Michel Tison et al., eds., Cambridge Univ. Press 2009).
42. Regierungskommission Deutscher Corporate Governance Kodex, Commission, https://www.dcgk.de (last accessed 15 April 2022).
43. *Ibid.*
44. *See* FRC, About the FRC, https://www.frc.org.uk (last accessed 15 April 2022).
45. Wymeersch, *supra* n. 12, 114.
46. French CGC: Afep and Medef, Corporate Governance Code of Listed Corporation (2018) – Consultation, available at https://consultation.codeafepmedef.fr (last accessed 15 April 2022).
47. *Ibid.*
48. Comitato Corporate Governance, Comitato (2022), https://www.borsaitaliana.it/comitato-corporate-governance (last accessed 15 April 2022).

has frequent informal interactions with listed companies and relies on a panel of corporate law experts who provide supporting advice.[49]

[B] Convergence in CGCs and Supranational Code

Self-regulation is not a distinguishing feature of collections of corporate governance principles that are prepared by supranational organisations, instead. Typically, these collections of best practices do not address companies directly, but rather target national policymakers – including those involved in self-regulation on corporate governance matters – and, for this reason, do not qualify as CGCs in our analysis. The most famous set of principles is the collection jointly prepared by the Group of Twenty (G20) and the Organisation for Economic Co-operation and Development (OECD),[50] other notable examples being those drafted by the International Corporate Governance Network (ICGN) and the Commonwealth Association for Corporate Governance (CACG).[51]

These collections address most of the topics that traditional CGCs also tackle, but they do so in more general terms, as required by their supranational nature.[52] Most notably, the OECD collection, which is the most prominent among them, has been historically influenced by the UK CGC – notoriously a pioneer in applying soft law to corporate governance.[53] For the purpose of our analysis, this influence is relevant because it strengthens a feature that characterises CGCs around the world, namely the tendency to foster approximation of corporate governance practices along the lines of the UK (and United States (US)) model.[54] According to many observers, this has been the case even when local market conditions would have suggested a more cautious approach due to the strong link between some best practices originating from the UK and specific features of that system such as unitary (one-tier) boards and dispersed ownership.[55] For instance, one can think of the influence these two characteristics have on the appointment of directors and, therefore, on the role and functioning of

49. *Ibid.*, 1; Comitato Corporate Governance, Publication of the New Corporate Governance Code (2020), https://www.borsaitaliana.it/comitato-corporate-governance (last accessed 15 April 2022), 1.
50. OECD Principles: OECD, G20/OECD Principles of Corporate Governance (Paris: OECD Publishing, 2015).
51. ICGN Principles: International Corporate Governance Network, Global Governance Principles (2021), available at https://www.icgn.org (last accessed 15 April 2022); CACG Principles: Commonwealth Association for Corporate Governance, Principles for Corporate Governance in the Commonwealth. Towards global competitiveness and economic accountability (1999), available at https://ecgi.org (last accessed 15 April 2022).
52. Andrew Keay, *An Analytical Study of Board Accountability in Transnational Codes of Corporate Governance*, in *Corporate Governance Codes for the 21st Century. International Perspectives and Critical Analyses*, 125 (Jean du Plessis & Chee Keong Low eds., Springer 2017).
53. Nordberg, *supra* n.1, 109.
54. Umakanth Varottil, *Proliferation of Corporate Governance Codes in the Backdrop of Divergent Ownership Structure*, 24 Competition & Change 471, 474 (2020).
55. Andrew Johnston, *EC Regulation of Corporate Governance* 343–345 (CUP 2009) (on unitary boards); Iain MacNeil & Irene-Marié Esser, *The Emergence of 'Comply or Explain' as a Global Model for Corporate Governance Codes*, 33 Eur. Bus. Law Rev. 1, 21–22 (2022) (on ownership patterns).

nomination committees, one of the typical governance devices recommended by the UK CGC since its inception.[56]

The intensity of convergence in governance practices through CGCs and its drivers - and, therefore, the dynamics that lead self-regulators to align - have been subject to extensive literature whose results can only be mentioned here. Besides supranational CGCs, other factors that are normally considered to come into play include elements that are both endogenous and exogenous to national systems. Among the endogenous factors is the need to improve the efficiency of governance systems that lag behind the state of the art in their ability to protect investors.[57] The desire to imitate practices from countries with higher reputation, even when this may not lead to substantive improvements, also strengthens such trend.[58] Among the exogenous factors, large institutional investors may be familiar with certain practices they tend to consider as proxies of good governance and may therefore be more inclined to invest in companies that display those practices.[59]

§5.03 THE CONTENTS OF CGCs

In this section, we provide a synthetic overview of some of the most typical contents of CGCs. While we cannot go into the details of CGC provisions, we aim to give an outline of the governance tools CGCs mostly rely upon when defining best practices. We first address CGC provisions that refer to listed companies in general. We then address how CGCs adjust to reflect the needs of specific companies.

[A] Main Provisions in CGCs

Since their very inception, the main concerns of CGCs have been board structure and composition. The most salient feature in this regard is the requirement that independent members be present within the board in a sufficient number, which is normally understood as half of the seats as a minimum.[60] Independence is typically defined in the negative, as it comes from the absence of relationships with the company and its related parties that could compromise the ability of directors to take decisions free from conflicting influences. This is meant to ensure that directors act in the interest of the company and of all its shareholders (and stakeholders, according to some opinions).

---

56. Kershaw, *supra* n. 17, §4.30; *see* today UK CGC, *supra* n. 26, §17.
57. Ruth Aguilera & Alvaro Cuervo-Cazurra, *Codes of Good Governance Worldwide: What Is the Trigger?*, 25 Organ. Stud. 415, 422–426 (2004).
58. Kershaw, *supra* n. 17, 19.
59. Aguilera & Cuervo-Cazurra, *supra* n. 57, 426–427.
60. UK CGC, *supra* n. 26, §11; German CGC, *supra* n. 25, §C.7 (with reference to shareholder representatives in the supervisory board); French CGC, *supra* n. 46, §9.3; Italian CGC, *supra* n. 34, §5; Dutch CGC: Monitoring Committee Corporate Governance Code, The Dutch Corporate Governance Code (2016), available at https://www.mccg.nl (last accessed 15 April 2022), §2.1.7 (with reference to the supervisory board).

The standard relationships that determine the loss of independence include executive roles (so that independent directors are always a subset of non-executive directors), performance-based remuneration, ownership of a stake in the company's capital that allows exerting a significant influence, as well as family, employment, and business relationships.[61] Serving as a board member for long periods is also often considered to prevent independence due to the risk of capture.[62]

In most CGCs, non-executive and independent directors have a key role in selecting and monitoring executive directors. To ensure the effectiveness of independent directors, CGCs often recommend the appointment of a senior (or lead) independent director who facilitates the interactions with the other directors and the shareholders. Another strategy recommends convening ad hoc meetings open to independent directors alone,[63] so that these can more easily share their views and coordinate how to voice their possible discontent. Some CGCs also recommend[64] or suggest[65] appointing a lead independent director when the roles of chairperson and chief executive officer coincide - while other CGCs deem the separation of the two roles as a best practice. [66]

In more recent years, CGCs have also started to pay more attention to gender balance within boards, increasingly in combination with other criteria of diversity such as social and ethnic backgrounds.[67] These provisions may improve corporate governance because they help reduce groupthink within boards, but they have not traditionally been supported by reference quotas. The tools CGCs adopt to foster these objectives are, rather, disclosure[68] or the definition of ad hoc policies by the board, with the support of the nomination committee.[69] The absence of quotas and the very nature of recommendations on diversity as soft law have reduced the ability of CGCs to achieve significant results,[70] and they have induced national and EU policymakers to step in with hard-law proposals.

Board composition - particularly as regards independence - is also a key ingredient to making directors' role more effective through the creation of internal committees, which support the board in the performance of its critical functions. This

61. UK CGC, *supra* n. 26, §10; German CGC, *supra* n. 25, §C.7; French CGC, *supra* n. 46, §9.5; Italian CGC, *supra* n. 34, §7; Dutch CGC, *supra* n. 60, §2.1.8.
62. For instance, the UK and the Italian CGCs set a nine-year threshold (UK CGC, *supra* n. 26, §10, Italian CGC, *supra* n. 34, §7); for Germany and France, the limit is twelve years (German CGC, *Supra* n. 25, §C.7; French CGC, *supra* n. 46, §9.5).
63. UK CGC *supra* n. 26, §§12, 13; Italian CGC, *supra* n. 34, §13.
64. Italian CGC *supra* n. 34, §13.
65. French CGC, *supra* n. 46, §3.2.
66. UK CGC, *supra* n. 26, §9 (allowing for deviations subject to shareholder consultation and disclosure of the reasons for the coincidence of roles).
67. UK CGC, *supra* n. 26, §J; Italian CGC, *supra* n. 34, §VII.
68. UK CGC, *supra* n. 26, §23.
69. German CGC, *supra* n. 25, §C.1; French CGC, *supra* n. 46, §7; Dutch CGC, *supra* n. 60, §2.1.6.
70. Heike Mensi-Klarbach et al., *The Carrot or the Stick: Self-Regulation for Gender-Diverse Boards via Codes of Good Governance*, 170 J. Bus. Ethics 577 (2021) (on the Austrian system, but with generally applicable results).

support may involve a consultative role on specific matters, but it typically results in the competence to submit proposals for approval by the plenum. All the most important CGCs recommend the creation of three committees. With variable labels, these are the nomination committee, the remuneration committee, and the audit committee.

Nomination committees are in charge of the assessment of the overall composition of the board. They normally identify potential candidates the board can submit to shareholder approval and may also prepare succession plans for the executives. Remuneration committees support the definition of compensation policies by the board (followed up in turn by shareholder say on pay - Article 9a Directive 2007/36/EC on shareholder rights) and assess the effectiveness of such policies over time. Audit committees monitor the proper functioning of key company functions such as financial reporting systems, risk management, and internal controls. They also play a role in the selection of the auditors (as required under Article 39(6) Directive 2006/43/EC on statutory audit).

The composition of board committees heavily relies, as we mentioned, on independent and other non-executive directors. The recommended proportions change depending on the CGC and, within each CGC, from committee to committee. Sometimes, CGCs top up on legal provisions by recommending stricter independence requirements or a higher percentage of independent directors.[71] This is the case with audit committees, which in the EU must include non-executive directors alone, the majority of which shall be independent (Article 39(1) Directive 2006/43/EC on statutory audit). Most CGCs recommend a majority of independent members also for nomination and remuneration committees,[72] some of them going as far as to suggest that all members be independent.[73] The presence of executives is often considered a deviation from best practices, although this requirement tends to relax in most CGCs for nomination committees.[74]

While structural elements such as board composition and organisation are typical matters for CGCs, other areas have not always received equal attention or have been subject to less homogeneous approaches. This is the case with directors' duties, and in particular with the duty of care. A common explanation is that the very nature of such duty is hardly compatible with the *ex ante* identification of generally applicable best practices, dependent as it is on the need to consider all the circumstances of the specific

71. *See, e.g.*, French CGC, *supra* n. 46, §16 (recommending two-thirds of independent members). *See also* §24 UK CGC, *supra* n. 26, (recommending that all members be independent).
72. UK CGC, *supra* n. 26, §17 (for nomination committees); French CGC, *supra* n. 46, §§17–18; Italian CGC, *supra* n. 34, §§19 and 25; Dutch CGC, *supra* n. 60, §2.3.4.
73. UK CGC, *supra* n. 26, §32 (for remuneration committees).
74. UK CGC, *supra* n. 26, §17; German CGC, *supra* n. 25, §D.5; Italian CGC, *supra* n. 34, §19; Dutch CGC, *supra* n. 60, §2.3.4 (which applies the same standard to remuneration committees). *See* however French CGC, *supra* n. 46, §§17–18 (recommending both nomination and remuneration committees comprise only non-executive members).

decisions directors have to make.[75] Against this backdrop, however, CGCs increasingly display provisions that address some specific elements of the duty of care. The procedural elements of that duty are, of course, natural candidates, as reflected, for instance, in the recommendation that directors keep their knowledge up to date and allocate sufficient time to carry out their duties.[76]

In addition to these general provisions, CGC may also focus on the duty of care in specific settings. One could mention the role of the UK Takeover Code in shaping directors' passivity obligations pending takeovers but, to confine the analysis to generally applicable CGCs, the role of sustainability is perhaps the best case in point. Most CGCs include provisions on the consideration directors should pay to stakeholder interests as a way to ensure the long-term sustainability of companies.[77] It is however debated whether CGCs can deliver effective results in this area,[78] as it appears that best practices are defined in generic terms, possibly with the exception of provisions on transparency.[79] For instance, very few CGCs recommend the creation of an ad hoc committee for Corporate Social Responsibility (CSR)-related matters.[80] Sustainability is also at the core of dedicated collections of principles and guidelines prepared by international organisations, including, once again, the OECD.[81] Remarkably, the effectiveness of such collections is also called into question.[82]

CGCs traditionally paid more attention to directors' duty of loyalty instead, particularly regarding conflicts of interest and related-party (including intra-group) transactions. This is hardly surprising considering the role of independent directors in CGC and their ability to assess conflicted transactions with fewer biases than their peers. However, while many CGCs retain recommendations on these prongs of fiduciary duties, it is hard to define the remaining provisions as the state of the art on such matters. As we mentioned, this is one of the areas where hard law stepped in out of an unsatisfactory assessment of the results of CGCs.[83]

---

75. *See, e.g.*, MacNeil & Li, *supra* n. 7, 487; Hommelhoff *supra* n. 41, 269.
76. *See, e.g.*, UK CGC, *supra* n. 26, §H; German CGC, *supra* n. 25, §12; French CGC, *supra* n. 46, §19.1; Italian CGC, *supra* n. 34, §XII; Dutch CGC, *supra* n. 60, §2.4.
77. *See* Michele Siri & Shanshan Zhu, *Integrating Sustainability in EU Corporate Governance Codes*, in *Sustainable Finance in Europe* 201–210 (Danny Busch et al. eds., Palgrave Macmillan 2021).
78. For a sceptical view *see* Beate Sjåfjell, *When the Solution Becomes the Problem: The Triple Failure of Corporate Governance Codes*, in *Corporate Governance Codes for the 21st Century. International Perspectives and Critical Analyses* 32, 48 (Jean du Plessis & Chee Keong Low eds., Springer 2017); for a more optimistic view *see* Guido Ferrarini et al., *The EU Sustainable Governance Consultation and the Missing Link to Soft Law*, 9–16, ECGI Law Working Paper N° 576/2021, https://www.ecgi.org (last accessed 15 April 2022).
79. Daniel Gargely Szabó & Karsten Engsis Sørensen, *Integrating Corporate Social Responsibility in Corporate Governance Codes in the EU*, 24 Eur. Bus. Law Rev. 781, 794–797 (2013).
80. Middlenext CGC: Middlenext, Code de gouvernement d'entreprise, Cahier n°14 (2021), available at https://www.middlenext.com (last accessed 15 April 2022), §R8 (on this code *see infra* §5.03[B]).
81. OECD Guidelines: OECD, Guidelines for Multinational Enterprises (2011), available at http://mneguidelines.oecd.org (last accessed 15 April 2022); UN Guiding Principles: United Nations, Guiding Principles on Business and Human Rights (2011), available at https://www.ohchr.org (last accessed 15 April 2022).
82. *See* Sjåfjell, *supra* n. 78, 34–35; Ferrarini et al., *supra* n. 78, 13–16.
83. *See supra* §5.01[B].

[B] Sectoral CGCs

The typical CGCs address listed companies alone, and all listed companies with little differentiations. In principle, the soft-law nature of traditional CGCs should provide enough flexibility to accommodate a variety of needs. If 'one size does not fit all' in corporate governance, companies that, for any reason, display features that suggest departing from a CGC provision can freely do that, provided they explain the reasons to do so. However, this is not necessarily the case in practice,[84] as deviations from CGC best practices are less common than theory predicts.[85] In addition, when the reasons to deviate are based on elements that are common to a large number of companies, it may be efficient to codify specific best practices such companies can use as guidance. Among the variables that determine the codification of specific recommendations, three are worth considering here – company's size, company's ownership, and the performance of banking activity.

As some governance devices may be cumbersome for small listed companies, some CGCs adjust their provisions to make them lighter when they apply to such entities. For instance, CGCs may reduce the recommended size of internal committees to make sure they fit within smaller boards,[86] or may waive the provision that independent directors hold regular separate meetings.[87] Ad hoc CGCs also exist that address small companies, such as the French Middlenext code. Among the distinguishing features of this CGC is the absence of a general best practice supporting the creation of board committees. This is replaced by a recommendation that boards evaluate whether the characteristics of the company, such as the size of the board and the activities performed, suggest the creation of internal committees.[88]

Small listed companies are also more likely to have concentrated ownership, in particular when family-owned, and CGCs addressing small and medium-sized enterprises (SMEs) may therefore factor capital structure in their corporate governance formulas.[89] However, some generally-applicable CGCs also include differentiated provisions for companies with concentrated ownership, considering the specific nature of the agency problems this creates.[90] For instance, specific recommendations may set a lower percentage of independent directors within the board[91] or relax the suggestion to create nomination committees.[92]

Yet other agency problems arise within banks. It is now a well-established understanding that bank corporate governance is special and, therefore, generally

84. David Walker et al., *A Review of Corporate Governance in UK Banks and Other Financial Industry Entities. Final Recommendations*, 31 (for banks) (2009), https://www.ecgi.org (last accessed 15 April 2022).
85. *See infra* §5.04[C].
86. UK CGC, *supra* n. 26, §§24, 32 (for remuneration and audit committees).
87. Italian CGC, *supra* n. 34, §5.
88. Middlenext CGC, *supra* n. 80, §R7.
89. *Ibid.*, 9.
90. Varottil, *supra* n. 54, 478.
91. Italian CGC, *supra* n. 34 §5; Middlenext, *supra* n. 80, §R3.
92. Italian CGC, *supra* n. 34 §16.

applicable best practices may not be advisable for banks.[93] The main reasons for this are the heightened market failures stemming from high leverage in banks' balance sheets and intense problems of asymmetric information and rational apathy that afflict depositors.[94] In this context, the traditional shareholder-oriented approach to corporate governance – although receding in the last years due to the increasing consideration paid to environmental, social, and governance (ESG) factors[95] – does not sit well with the downsides of excessive risk-taking it may determine on banks.

Despite banks' special features, CGCs addressing banks alone are not as widespread as their equivalents dedicated to listed companies. One remarkable example is the Dutch Banking Code (Code Banken) adopted by the Netherlands Bankers' Association (NVB). The Banking Code recommends all banks, subject to a CoE principle, pay due consideration to the interests of all stakeholders involved in the banking activity.[96] Among the implications of this principle, three are worth mentioning in more detail. First, all members of the supervisory board and of the executive board should be aware of the role of their bank in society[97] and shall take into account the interests of stakeholders in light of the societal, socio-economic, and political cultures of the markets where the bank operates.[98] Second, both boards shall always make sure that the bank treats its customers with due care,[99] which also involves the adoption of the product approval process[100] – remarkably, product governance appeared in EU financial and banking law only more recently.[101] Third, the Code Banken puts a strong emphasis on risks, their sources and their management. In particular, it requires the definition (by the executive board) and the approval (by the supervisory board) of the bank's risk appetite, and defines procedural and substantive requirements for remuneration policies, mindful of the impact these can have on risk appetite.[102] Once again, the Code Banken recommendations predated hard-law measures that now adopt the same approach.[103]

93. *See, e.g.*, John Armour et al., *Principles of Financial Regulation* 372–380 (Oxford Univ. Press 2016).
94. For an analysis of agency problems as a combination of asymmetric information and negative externalities *see* Lambert, *supra* n. 38, 97.
95. *See supra* §5.03[A].
96. Code Banken: NVB (Nederlandse Vereniging van Banken), Code Banken (2010), available at https://www.nvb.nl (last accessed 15 April 2022), 2.
97. *Ibid.*, §§2.1.3 and 3.1.2, for the two boards respectively.
98. *Ibid.*, §§2.1.5 and 3.2.1.
99. *Ibid.*, §§2.1.8 and 3.2.2.
100. *Ibid.*, §4.5.
101. *See* Art. 16(3) Directive 2014/65/EU (MiFID II) for financial instruments and EBA (2016) for retail banking products. On the connections between corporate governance and product governance *see* Court of Justice of the European Union, C-911/19, FBF, 15 July 2021, ECLI:EU:C:2021:599.
102. Code Banken, *supra* n. 96, §§4.1 and 6.
103. *See* Arts 76 and 88 as well as Arts 92 to 95 Directive 2013/36/EU (CRD) for the board responsibilities concerning risks and executive compensation respectively.

§5.04 THE 'COMPLY OR EXPLAIN' PRINCIPLE

Since its appearance along with the UK Cadbury Code of 1992, the CoE principle has accompanied the development of CGCs across the world. Underlying the principle is the intuition that the soft-law nature of CGCs should not result in any lack of accountability as to their implementation. On the contrary, the ability of CGC to incentivise compliance with best practices rests on the assumption that market mechanisms are a crucial driving force for good governance. The decisions (not) to adopt a CGC and (not) to implement one or more of its provisions are free, but they remain subject to market scrutiny. This requires that such decisions be made available to the public of investors – and stakeholders more broadly – through ad hoc 'corporate governance statements.'

[A] The Nature of the Principle

As one can easily tell, CoE relies on an approach that is comparable to that of the Efficient Capital Market Hypothesis (ECMH), as it is equally based on the understanding that information can drive market participants' decisions to trade or vote and that those decisions will have an influence on market prices. In turn, the ability of market prices to reflect the available information also makes them a disciplining tool for directors and managers. Investors unsatisfied with a company's corporate governance would discount this assessment – under the assumption that corporate governance matters[104] – from the expected cash flows of shares (or other relevant securities).[105] They may therefore vote with their feet, thus contributing to depressing the share price, or engage with the board to voice their discontent and possibly trigger a change.

Despite its supporting role relating to best corporate governance practices, CoE is mandatory in nature and does not partake of the soft-law quality of CGCs. Traditionally, CoE has had its most common legal basis in the listing rules of regulated markets or listing authorities,[106] but it has more recently been embedded into statutory law provisions. In the EU, listed companies are subject to a CoE obligation under (national provisions implementing) the financial reporting regime (Article 20 Directive 2013/34/EU on annual and consolidated financial statements – Accounting Directive). For the purpose of CoE, 'listed companies' under Article 20 Accounting Directive are EEA-based companies having their transferable securities admitted to trading on a regulated market of any Member State (Article 2(1)(a) Accounting Directive; Article 4(1)(21) Directive 2014/65/EU – MiFID II). Therefore, other companies that qualify as 'public-interest entities' under the same regime, such as banks, are not subject to this

104. The evidence on this matter is mixed (*see* already Sanjai Bhagat & Bernard Black, *The Uncertain Relationship between Board Composition and Firm Performance*, 54 The Bus. Law. 921 (1999); more recently, Ronald Gilson & Jeffrey Gordon, *Board 3.0: An Introduction*, 74 The Bus. Law. 351 (2019)), but for the purpose of this chapter, we can assume that the effect of good corporate governance on prices is beneficial (MacNeil & Esser, *supra* n. 55, 2, 13).
105. On the scope of application of CGCs *see infra*, in this section (§5.04[A]).
106. For the UK, the source is the FCA Handbook (Listing Rules 9.8.6.R(6)).

harmonised EU framework for CoE and will apply relevant national provisions alone, if any. Member States also have the option to limit the EU CoE regime to issuers of shares alone, thus essentially excluding companies issuing listed bonds from its scope of application.[107]

[B] 'Comply or Explain' and Applicability of CGCs

In more detail, the EU CoE regime makes listed companies subject to two sets of disclosure duties concerning CGCs. The first one relates to the applicability of the CGC. Listed companies must specify the CGC (if any) to which they are subject or which they may have voluntarily decided to adopt (Article 20(1)(a)). This alternative shows that the applicability of CGCs may come in different fashions, depending on the room left to the issuer's choice. To some extent, different regimes concerning issuer choice also determine the competitive setting for CGCs. Mandatory reference to a specific set of best practices can stifle competition among self-regulatory bodies and reduce the ability of the market for soft law to provide CGCs that are tailored to the specific needs of certain types of companies.

In practice, this kind of competition may develop more easily at the national level because CGCs tend to be country-specific as their recommendations are often closely connected to local company law provisions.[108] A look at national rules shows some differences in this regard. Sometimes, the applicability of a specific CGC may be linked to mandatory law provisions, as is the case in the Netherlands. The Dutch CGC is considered a mandatory reference for corporate governance statements of Dutch listed companies, which can also decide to adopt other CGCs in addition to it.[109] Similar provisions may be found in listing rules defined by listing authorities or by regulated markets themselves. For instance, the Listing Rules of the UK FCA adopt the UK CGC as the term of reference for the CoE duties for all primary listings in that country.[110] In other countries, listed companies may have more leeway to decide their CGC, at least on the books. In Italy, for instance, neither the law nor the listing rules of the main stock exchange mandate the applicability of the Italian CGC,[111] although listing rules refer to that CGC as a yardstick for some specific purposes.[112]

107. However, Member States cannot opt-out of the EU regime for companies having their bonds admitted to trading on a regulated market and shares admitted to trading on an MTF (Art 20(4) Accounting Directive).
108. *See supra* §5.01[B].
109. Arts 2 and 3 Besluit inhoud bestuursverslag (23 December 2004, as amended).
110. UK Listing Rules 9.8.6.R(6).
111. *See* in particular Art. 123-II(2)(a) Consolidated Law on finance (CLF) (leaving listed companies freedom to determine their CGC).
112. For instance, all companies applying for admission to listing shall inform the operator of the stock exchange whether they comply with the best practice of the Italian CGC (Section IA.1.1.11 Instructions accompanying the Rules of the markets organised and managed by Borsa Italiana S.p.A.). Some of those best practices are mandatory to access specific segments of the market (for the STAR segment, *see* Art. 2.2.3 Rules of the markets organised and managed by Borsa Italiana S.p.A.)

When listed companies have leeway and opt not to be subject to any CGC, the Accounting Directive completes the first prong of the CoE regime by mandating the publication of a justification for such choice (Article 20(1)(b)).

[C] 'Comply or Explain' and Recommendations

The second prong of the CoE regime, which defines the essence of the principle, applies when listed companies refer to a CGC, whether because of choice or because they are bound to it. In such case, those companies have to provide twofold information relating to (i) which parts of the CGC they depart from and (ii) the reasons for doing so (Article 20(1)(b) Accounting Directive).

Depending on the applicable company law and the CGC provisions, the corporate body that takes responsibility for the corporate governance report and the accuracy of the CoE statement may vary.[113] In systems based on one-tier governance systems, the board will normally have this role.[114] In two-tier governance systems, responsibility is often upon the management and the supervisory board jointly – this is the case, in particular, with Germany and the Netherlands.[115]

It is also worth noting that, in the Accounting Directive, the CoE principle attaching to CGCs is part of a broader set of information concerning corporate governance, which listed companies provide through their corporate governance statements.[116] In this context, whether the origin of the governance practice subject to disclosure is to be found in a CGC is not particularly salient. Listed companies have to provide the market with a complete picture of the corporate governance practices they apply 'over and above the requirements of national law', even when these are not originating from CGCs (Article 20(1)(a)(iii) Accounting Directive).[117] What remains typical of CoE is, therefore, its ability to focus on negative information, which sheds light on the distance, if any, between the corporate governance practice of the company and the standards delineated in the applicable CGC.

The essence of CoE excludes that disclosure is needed, beyond a declaration of compliance, in case of full implementation of the CGC best practices. However, mere declarations of compliance are often considered unable to convey a meaningful message on the actual quality of corporate governance. The reasons for this lack of trust are manifold, but most of them can be directly or indirectly connected to a strong preference for compliance that market mechanisms tend to determine.

113. As to the substantive decisions concerning applicability and compliance with CGCs, *see supra* §5.01[C].
114. In France, this responsibility lied originally with the chair of the board, but it is now upon the entire board (Conac, *supra* n. 12, 415).
115. *See* respectively Hommelhoff *supra* n. 41, 267, and Dutch CGC, *supra* n. 60, 11.
116. The corporate governance statement is part of the management report under the default regime, but Member States may allow listed companies to publish it separately, whether as an autonomous report to be published together with the management report or in an online document to which the management report shall refer (Article 20(2)). The allocation of CoE statements in one document or the other is neutral from the point of view of the audit regime (*see infra* §5.05).
117. Bachmann, *supra* n. 24, 63.

Overall, enhanced attention to the 'comply' part of CoE seems to result from reduced consideration for the 'explain' component. From the investor side, carefully reading and assessing explanations provided in corporate governance statements postulates efforts that are not required for declarations of compliance, which easily lead to a box-ticking approach,[118] especially when the company's financial performance is satisfying.[119] These incentives inevitably influence the supply side of governance statements, as issuers may feel forced to comply with best practices that they do not deem suitable to their specific conditions, despite the flexibility the CoE principle should ensure.

It is difficult to tell how much dynamics affecting the supply and demand of corporate governance statements can explain why the compliance rate with each individual CGC provision[120] has been traditionally very high, especially for larger firms.[121] This evidence seems to contradict the very nature of 'best' – as opposed to merely 'good' or 'ordinary' – practices of CGC recommendations.[122] To some extent, CGCs may be a victim of the tendency to move the most demanding but effective best practices, which easily receive a smaller level of compliance,[123] to hard law. The shifting content of CGCs towards practices that are easier to implement can therefore make compliance equally easier. However, scholars and policymakers also believe that the trend towards very high compliance levels may stem from a tendency to declare formal compliance even when this does not correspond to a thorough engagement with the principle underlying the relevant CGC provisions.[124]

[D] Towards 'Comply and Explain'?

Mindful of the risk of formalistic implementation of CGC provisions, EU policymakers have recommended that listed companies which align their conduct and organisation to codified best practices go beyond a mere declaration of compliance. Rather, they should 'describe how they have applied' the best practices that are 'of most importance for shareholders' (§4 Commission Recommendation 2014/208/EU on the quality of corporate governance reporting (CoE)). The scope of this recommendation is inevitably subject to an individual assessment of what is more important for investors, but its

118. Konstantinos Sergakis, *Deconstruction and Reconstruction of the 'Comply or Explain' Principle in EU Capital Markets*, 5 Journal of Accounting, Economics, and Law: A Convivium 233 (2015), 237–238, 256, 269–271.
119. MacNeil & Li, *supra* n. 7, 492–493.
120. Compliance with the entire set of CGC best practice inevitably scores lower because it calculates cumulated non-compliance with each provision. For a distinction, *see* MacNeil & Li, *supra* n. 7, 488–489.
121. For smaller firms, Sergakis, *supra* n. 118, 259.
122. A high level of compliance is a common feature among CGCs. *See, e.g.*, Kershaw, *supra* n. 17, 32.
123. This is the case with remuneration policies (Wymeersch *supra* n. 12, 68). *See also supra* §5.01[B].
124. Marcello Bianchi et al., *Comply or Explain? Investor Protection Through Corporate Governance Codes*, 11–12, ECGI Finance Working Paper N° 278/2010, https://www.ecgi.org (last accessed 15 April 2022); Sergakis, *supra* n. 118, 258–259.

contents are rather straightforward in that listed companies should enable investors to get a 'good understanding of the manner in which the company is governed' (§5). This requires the corporate governance statement to be 'clear, accurate and comprehensive', and to specify how 'the company's specific characteristics and situation, such as size, company structure or ownership' influence the way that company has implemented the best practices of the CGC (§5).[125]

As one can see, these recommendations go well beyond a traditional CoE mechanism and rather hint toward a 'comply *and* explain' system. The reason is that, in the Accounting Directive and in the Commission Recommendation, CoE and the reference it entails to CGCs are just a part – although an important one – of a broader description of corporate governance. Such description is meant to be self-standing, so that CGCs represent a term of reference, and not just a collection of best practices to be incorporated by reference.

Also pushing towards a 'comply *and* explain' approach on governance matters is the content of some CGCs, especially when reflected in the (mandatory) rules requiring corporate disclosure. As we have seen, CGCs sometimes include provisions – normally labelled as 'principles'[126] – that listed companies are expected to comply with when they adopt a CGC. When this is the case, implementation of such provision is not voluntary in nature, and what companies shall do is to make sure their corporate structure and conduct reflect those principles. The most notable example in this regard is the Listing Rules adopted by the UK FCA, which require such disclosure to be provided in a way that enables shareholders to evaluate *how* the company has applied the principles of the UK CGC (Section 9.8.6.R(5) UK Listing Rules). These statements are sometimes referred to as 'apply and explain', to distinguish them from the traditional CoE that applies to recommendations.[127]

[E] Addressing the Quality of Disclosure

The essence of CoE lies in the explanations due in case of deviations from CGC recommendations. Next to the high compliance rate with CGCs, scholars often highlight widespread recourse to superficial explanations for such deviations,[128] for instance, through mere reference to a generic impossibility of complying with the relevant best practice.[129] The Commission Recommendation invites companies to go beyond a mere declaration of non-compliance in their corporate governance statements. They should specify in what manner they departed from the relevant recommendation and the reason for such discrepancy. Moreover, they should explain how

125. Renato Mangano, *Improving the Quality of the Comply or Explain Approach and Introducing Self-Monitoring Through Online Feedbacks*, 14 ECFL Rev. 435, 443–445 (2017).
126. *See supra* §5.01[D].
127. MacNeil & Li, *supra* n. 7, 488; MacNeil & Esser, *supra* n. 55, 17.
128. Veldman, *supra* n. 40, 78.
129. Sergakis, *supra* n. 118, 270–271.

they took the decision not to comply with the CGC provision.[130] Finally, companies should clarify the measures they are considering to address the departure, in particular by complying in the future or by adopting alternative governance measures that achieve the same objectives underlying the CGC recommendations or, in any case, contribute to good corporate governance (§8 Commission Recommendation).

As self-regulation is a recursive exercise,[131] drafters of CGCs often take into account listed companies' explanations for non-compliance and may react by amending the codification of best practices. To name just one example,[132] the Italian CGC has long recommended timely provision of draft deliberations and supporting materials to the board. This best practice has received a relatively low level of compliance, often accompanied by justifications referring to the need to ensure confidentiality. For this reason, the last version of the Italian CGC specifies that confidentiality issues should be managed without affecting the timely access of information by the board (Article 3).

Self-regulatory initiatives have also strived to improve the quality of disclosure. Besides *ex post* strategies that pertain to enforcement in a broad sense, which we address in the next section, the efforts towards standardisation of corporate governance statements are worth mentioning here. Various market participants such as CGC committees, operators of regulated markets, or associations of stakeholders have devised templates that listed companies can adopt when preparing their reports. These templates may concern some of the most salient recommendations, such as those on board composition and director independence or remuneration,[133] or they may cover the entire set of best practices within CGCs.[134] Either way, these templates may nudge companies into better disclosure, as it may be harder to remain silent when a template asks for an explanation. In addition, standardisation facilitates comparability, which may also lead to better disclosure (or higher compliance rates) because it helps spot outliers, thus supporting market discipline.

§5.05 MONITORING AND ENFORCING CGCs

Adoption and implementation of CGCs have long involved complex questions concerning the best strategies to ensure their effectiveness. In this regard, a distinction should always be drawn between different forms of enforcement, which tend to correspond to the diverse nature of the provisions involved. A first form of enforcement addresses the quality of corporate governance as such and mainly takes place with informal tools even when it enrols the drafters of CGCs or financial supervisors. This kind of enforcement uses CGCs as a reference point and may lead to a reaction when enforcers

130. *See* supra, in this section, on the corporate body competent for the decision (not) to comply with CGC provisions.
131. *See supra* §5.02.
132. Assonime & Emittenti Titoli, *Corporate Governance in Italy: The Implementation of the Italian Corporate Governance Code (2021)*, Note e Studi 4/2022), 38–39, https://www.assonime.it (last accessed 15 April 2022).
133. *See, e.g.*, the tables in the French CGC, *supra* n. 46 (appendix 2, 3, and 4).
134. *See* Borsa Italiana, *Format per la relazione sul governo societario e gli assetti proprietari* (2019), https://www.borsaitaliana.it/comitato-corporate-governance (last accessed 15 April 2022).

believe a listed company should comply with CGC best practices or, in any case, improve its governance. In this case, the soft-law nature of CGCs goes hand in hand with the informal mechanisms that oversee the implementation of best practices and the persuasiveness of explanations for non-compliance.[135] These informal mechanisms rely on an assessment of the merit of CoE and may include, when they involve shareholders or other stakeholders, traditional tools based on exit or voice such as the threat to sell shares (or even bonds), negative votes at the general meeting, or direct engagement.

Informal enforcement tools hinge upon the reliability of corporate disclosure due under the CoE principle, as this is the prerequisite for the assessment of companies' governance. However, the ability of market-based mechanisms alone to reach a sufficient level of trust in corporate statements is subject to the same market failures – such as asymmetric information and agency problems – that afflict corporate disclosure in general, with the additional feature that governance statements inevitably involve more pervasive value judgment than traditional financial disclosure.

Hence, enforcement tools for CGCs also rely on more formalised strategies, in addition to the informal ones mentioned earlier. However, formal enforcement plays a smaller role than in other areas of mandatory disclosure. In the EU, disclosure due under the CoE principle is part of the management report,[136] but it is subject to a carve-out from the generally applicable auditing rules. Under the general requirement, auditors express an opinion on the consistency of the management report with the corresponding financial statements as well as on its conformity with the applicable rules (Article 20(1)(a) Accounting Directive). Most importantly, they state whether the management report contains any 'material misstatement' they could identify 'in the light of the knowledge and understanding of the undertaking and its environment obtained in the course of the audit' (Article 20(1)(b) Accounting Directive). Remarkably, this kind of opinion does not apply to the statements concerning compliance with CGCs and the explanations of deviations from its best practices. When CoE is at stake, auditors only verify that the information required was provided (Article 20(3) Accounting Directive).

Formal enforcement of the contents of corporate governance statements is, instead, an exception. Ideally, litigation and sanctions should be grounded on the misleading effects of a false declaration of compliance with CGC provisions or an untrue explanation justifying departure from those provisions. In this case, the main hindrances to redress would seem to be the subjective nature of the assessments underlying those declarations and explanations. For civil liability, the weak link between a false statement and financial damage would also be an issue.[137]

Bridging the gap between informal and formal enforcement are various forms of intermediate monitoring systems aimed at motivating companies to comply with CGCs

135. On the limitations of formal public enforcement tool in this fields, *see* Conac, *supra* n. 12, 423–425.
136. *See supra* §5.04[C] for some qualifications, which do not affect the regime described in this section.
137. Conac, *supra* n. 12, 417.

or to improve the quality of their explanation in case of departure from their provisions (§11 Commission Recommendation on CoE). Strategies in this regard vary considerably from one country to another for both the allocation of the monitoring tasks and the outcome of the monitoring process.

Entities that support monitoring through some forms of centralised scrutiny are quite common.[138] This is far from surprising if one considers that such tasks are subject to economies of scale, due to the specialisation required, and positive externalities, as the assessment of the quality performed by one market participant easily benefits all the others. Depending on the country, monitoring functions can be performed by the same body in charge of preparing the code,[139] by ad hoc entities,[140] by issuers' or investors' associations,[141] by regulated markets,[142] by financial supervisors,[143] or by some of them simultaneously.

Irrespective of the entity in charge of the monitoring process, the outcome of the procedure never involves formal measures, in line with the soft nature of descriptions concerning corporate governance mechanisms - unless, of course, the corporate governance statement displays blatantly false information. The typical outcome of the process takes the form of a report that provides an overarching analysis of the level of implementation of CGCs and their recommendations, and on the quality of the explanations included in the corporate governance statements. At the supranational level, the OECD also runs a monitoring exercise concerning corporate governance of a large number of countries worldwide, with a focus on the implementation of its G20/OECD Principles.[144]

Sometimes, national reports may include the name of the companies whose statements are deemed unsatisfactory, thus triggering a 'name and shame' effect that gives more teeth to the monitoring exercise.[145] More often, the relevant body addresses

138. For a survey *see* Wymeersch, *supra* n. 12, 120–122; Sergakis, *supra* n. 118, 272–274; Conac, *supra* n. 12, 419–422.
139. For the UK, *see* FRC, *Review of Corporate Governance Reporting*, November 2021, available at https://www.frc.org.uk (last accessed 15 April 2022); for Italy, Comitato Corporate Governance, *Relazione 2021 sull'evoluzione della corporate governance delle società quotate* (2021), https://www.borsaitaliana.it/comitato-corporate-governance (last accessed 15 April 2022).
140. For the Netherlands, *see* Monitoring Commissie Corporate Governance Code, *Rapport monitoring boekjaar 2020* (2021), https://www.mccg.nl/de-commissie (last accessed 15 April 2022); for France, *see* High Committee for Corporate Governance, *Annual Report (2021)*, available at https://hcge.fr (last accessed 15 April 2022).
141. For Italy, *see* Assonime & Emittenti Titoli, *Corporate Governance in Italy: The Implementation of the Italian Corporate Governance Code (2021)*, Note e Studi 4/2022, https://www.assonime.it (last accessed 15 April 2022).
142. This is the case with Luxembourg (Conac, *supra* n. 12, 418).
143. For France, *see* AMF, *Rapport 2021 sur le gouvernement d'entreprise et la rémunération des dirigeants des sociétes cotées* (2021), https://www.amf-france.org (last accessed 15 April 2022); for Italy, *see* Consob, *Report on Corporate Governance of Italian Listed Companies* (2021), https://www.consob.it (last accessed 15 April 2021).
144. OECD, *Corporate Governance Factbook 2021* (OECD Publishing 2021).
145. *See* Wymeersch, *supra* n. 12, 123 (referring to Portugal); Conac, *supra* n. 12, 421 (for France).

such companies with individual requests for additional information[146] or with confidential letters that point out the shortcomings identified and invite adjustment through moral suasion.[147]

§5.06 CONCLUSION: WHAT ROLE AND WHAT FUTURE FOR CGCs?

This chapter has analysed the nature and the functioning of CGCs. It has highlighted the various forms CGC provisions may take and has explained the effects these forms have on their ability to shape issuer corporate governance and, potentially, issuer liability.

As the chapter has shown, CGCs have played an important role in developing corporate governance during the last decades. They have been able to record best practices effectively and foster their adoption by an increasing number of companies. In so doing, they have been a powerful tool that reduced transaction costs for issuers and investors alike, as they have offered a benchmark to which both parties could refer.

To be sure, scholars believe that declarations of compliance with CGCs are often perfunctory, and that investors have weak incentives to inquire whether issuer statements in this regard correspond to an actual improvement in governance practices. However, CGCs seem to have the merit of keeping the attention on corporate governance high and facilitating shared reflections on the relative best practices.

But what is the current role of CGCs, regardless of their historical merits? And what can be expected from CGCs in the future? All in all, the ability of CGCs to pioneer best practices seems to have slowly faded.[148] To be sure, CGCs have been able to identify new areas where corporate governance could develop, as is the case with gender balance and diversity, as well as, more recently, sustainability and the role of stakeholders. However, the analysis above shows that, even in these cases, CGCs have often reflected a defensive attitude that has not been able to prevent more pervasive measures from policymakers through traditional regulatory tools.

Consequently, the ability of self-regulation to breed new ideas appeared compromised in recent years, and the revision of existing CGCs has mostly been limited to a fine-tuning exercise. This does not mean that self-regulation has become unworthy, but it surely shows that lawmakers and regulators are increasingly having a more proactive role in corporate governance, thus inevitably taking away space from CGCs.

This increased proactivity of hard law could be witnessed in matters such as directors' remuneration, related-party transactions, shareholder rights and engagement, and it is now evident in board diversity and corporate sustainability. All these developments make CGCs a less-salient source of corporate governance rules than in the past.

146. As is the case with the French High Committee for Corporate Governance (Sergakis, *supra* n. 118, 274).
147. For Italy, *supra* n. 139, 9.
148. Brian Cheffins & Bobby Reddy, *Thirty Years and Done – Time to Abolish the UK Corporate Governance Code*, ECGI Law Working Paper N° 654/2022, https://www.ecgi.org (last accessed 15 July 2022).

Against this reduced faith in self-regulation, CGCs would seem to retain utility in their ability to support the implementation of company law rules or listing requirements in ways that maximise the effectiveness of corporate governance, possibly beyond what formalistic compliance with mandatory provisions would allow. In this regard, they may further lose traction as collections of innovative principles, but they can retain a crucial role in the interpretation of legal and regulatory provisions and in supporting alignment with the spirit of legal provisions.

CHAPTER 6

Reporting as a Corporate Governance Instrument

Charlotte Villiers

§6.01 INTRODUCTION

The European Commission website states that the purpose of European Union (EU) rules on company law and corporate governance is:[1] to enable businesses to be set up and to carry out operations anywhere in the EU; to provide protection for shareholders and other parties with a particular interest in companies, such as employees and creditors; to make business more efficient, competitive, and sustainable in the long term; and to encourage businesses based in different EU countries to cooperate with each other. Company reporting, auditing, and transparency rules 'complement this legal framework'.[2] This tells us that the reporting requirements should assist companies to carry out their EU-wide business activities and cooperate with each other. Such transparency should also help to protect the shareholders and other stakeholders and increase the efficiency and sustainability of business activities. Another dedicated European Commission web page focuses specifically upon *Company Reporting* and states that 'companies operating in the EU should disclose certain information about their finances and how they operate in reports for transparency purposes'.[3] That web page identifies specific categories of reporting: financial reporting, corporate sustainability reporting, transparency requirements for listed companies, and public country by country reporting. Together these web pages confirm that reporting is an important

---

1. European Commission Website: *Company Law and Corporate Governance: EU Rules in this Area*, https://ec.europa.eu/info/business-economy-euro/doing-business-eu/company-law-and-corporate-governance_en.
2. *Ibid.*
3. European Commission Website: *Company Reporting*, https://ec.europa.eu/info/business-economy-euro/company-reporting-and-auditing/company-reporting_en.

part of the EU's approach to regulating corporate activities and shaping the corporate governance framework across the EU.

This chapter explores how and to what extent reporting and reporting requirements help to shape corporate governance inside corporations operating within the EU and the corporate governance framework around them. In §6.02, the chapter tracks the broader EU policy developments connected to company law and corporate governance, highlighting the developing EU policy shifts – from harmonization towards re-shaping the legal and regulatory frameworks within the global economy. The 'four freedoms' (movement of workers, goods, services, and capital) were at the heart of the harmonization efforts and as these have been consolidated, the EU has moved towards encouraging stewardship and responsible business. This part shows how such shifts have also resulted in a broadening focus from protecting shareholders and strengthening their rights towards a more sustainable value creation approach that sees both shareholders and stakeholders as important. This tracking exercise may help to explain the developments in the reporting regime described and mapped onto those EU policy shifts in §6.03 of the chapter. Section 6.04 considers how the evolving reporting requirements are instrumental for corporate governance as they support or even influence corporate governance practices and structures and how the more recent reporting developments may lead to more extensive changes to those practices and structures. Section 6.05 identifies outstanding challenges for establishing an effective reporting regime that will contribute to the broader corporate governance goals. The chapter concludes with some predictions about the future of reporting and how the reporting framework might be a trigger for further structural and behavioural changes to corporate governance across the EU.

The argument presented is that the earlier focus of EU legislators upon harmonization of financial reporting largely mirrored support for a shareholder primacy approach to company law and corporate governance, seeking to protect shareholders' interests and increasingly encouraging greater levels of shareholder engagement. The EU has also sought to champion stakeholder value, corporate social responsibility (CSR) and, more lately, sustainable value creation. As this aspect of EU policy has strengthened, there has been a change in the development of reporting regulation, with greater focus on non-financial and sustainability reporting. The financial dimension remains central but is more fully embraced within the sustainability goals and aims to establish a culture built on trust. This shift towards sustainable finance, sustainable value creation and trust is also likely to generate important changes in boardrooms, requiring different expertise in the composition of the boardroom membership, as well as introducing mechanisms for more meaningful participation in decision-making by shareholders and other stakeholders, improving the verification of claims and statements made by corporations and ensuring the possibility of effective enforcement by external regulators.

§6.02 EU COMPANY LAW AND CORPORATE GOVERNANCE: FROM CONSOLIDATION AND HARMONIZATION TO RE-SHAPING THE DYNAMICS OF THE FRAMEWORK

The EU company law and corporate governance framework, launched with the first European Economic Community (EEC) company law harmonization directive in 1968,[4] started as a project to harmonize the laws of the different Member States[5] based on freedom of establishment under what is now Article 50.2(g) of the Treaty of the Functioning of the European Union (TFEU).[6] That harmonization project continued until the early 2000s. The main purpose was to make business and cooperation activities across the EU easier and more efficient for the EU economy. The early reporting and disclosure directives were an important part of this harmonization project. They also highlighted the need for a flexible approach so that different national traditions and legal approaches would still be respected. Thus, Member States and companies trading throughout Europe were granted options to choose the provisions which best suited their needs and practices. As more states joined and the EU grew, these options and differences came to be more extensively accommodated so that directives evolved into being no more than 'framework'[7] directives. Really, the harmonization project itself went through different phases – or generations[8] – as the character of the EU changed through its growth and changing political economy with a 'reflexive' approach to developing regulation at EU level.[9] Gelter and Reif, for example, describe two broad 'waves' of company law harmonization.[10] The first wave covered the mainstream company laws, but this did not achieve complete uniformity – the Directives attempted to harmonize board structures and legal capital, pushing for a more Germanic style of company law, but the UK remained largely resistant to those efforts. The second wave, focused on the capital markets, and was driven by the liberal market economies in which shareholder primacy and financialized capital featured strongly.[11] Thus, for Gelter and Reif 'the UK model became the driving force for harmonization' and 'in areas such as takeover law and financial reporting, EU law

4. First Council Directive 1968/151/ECC of 9 March 1968 on coordination of the safeguards which, for the protection of the interests of members and others, are required by Member States of companies within the meaning of the second paragraph of Article 58 of the Treaty, with a view to making such safeguards equivalent throughout the Community, O.J. 1968, L 65/8.
5. *See, e.g.*, Jan Wouters, *European Company Law: Quo vadis?* 37(2) CML Rev., 257–307 (2000).
6. Note also the relevance of Art. 352 TFEU (adopting the appropriate measures needed to attain one of the objectives set out in the Treaties when they have not provided the necessary powers) and Art. 63 TFEU (free movement of capital), Art. 114 TFEU (approximation of national laws) (2015).
7. Emilia Korkea-aho, *Legal Interpretation of EU Framework Directives: A Soft Law Approach* 40(1) *Eur. L. Rev.*, 70–88.
8. *See, e.g.*, Charlotte Villiers, *European Company Law: Towards Democracy?* 28–51 (Ashgate/Dartmouth 1998); Joseph A. McCahery and Erik P. M. Vermeulen, *The Changing Landscape of EU Company Law* (TILEC Discussion Paper Series; Vol. 2004, No. 023).
9. *See* Simon F. Deakin, *Reflexive Governance and European Company Law* 15(2) *Eur. L. J.* 224–245 (2009).
10. Martin Gelter and Alexandra M. Reif, *What Is Dead May Never Die: The UK's Influence on EU Company Law* 40 *Fordham Int'l L.J.* 1413, 1416 (2017).
11. *Ibid.*

generally adopted UK models emphasizing transparency and shareholder choice.'[12] For Horn, the period since 1989 was one in which a 'renewed impetus for market integration reinforced the shift towards a considerably less mandatory and harmonised company law.'[13]

A further harmonization phase, given the amount of freedom it granted to Member States through use of 'framework' directives,[14] might really be called a *non*-harmonization stage. In that time, EU company law development went beyond harmonization towards new company law innovations, including a Regulation for a European supranational corporate form, the *Societas Europea* in 2001. Corporate governance also came more fully into focus for the European legislators after the beginning of the new millennium, following the highly publicized demise of the United States (US) corporation, Enron, as well as others such as Royal Ahold, and appreciating the potential effect of similar corporate failures in a globalized trading context. An action plan called *Modernising Company Law and Enhancing Corporate Governance in the European Union: A Plan to Move Forward* was published on 21 May 2003 highlighting the goal of modernizing company law and corporate governance following publication of a set of reports by a High Level Group of Company Law Experts in 2002 and 2003.[15] The Action Plan emphasized the contribution that well-managed companies and good corporate governance could make to efficiency and competitiveness of business throughout the EU and to strengthening shareholders' rights and third parties' protection.[16] The need to improve investors' confidence after a wave of corporate governance scandals and to protect pension investments was confirmed. The priorities were: to accommodate the needs of enterprises and reduce the red tape burden for them through a plan to simplify, clarify, and reduce legislation,[17] to protect shareholders and creditors, and to enhance cross border mobility for corporations.[18]

---

12. *Ibid.*
13. Laura Horn, *Corporate Governance in Crisis? The Politics of EU Corporate Governance Regulation*, 18(1) Eur. L. J. 93, (2012).
14. Villiers, *supra* n. 8, at 28–52.
15. European Commission, *Communication. Action Plan. Modernising Company Law and Enhancing Corporate Governance in the European Union - A Plan to Move Forward*, Brussels (21.5.2003), COM(2003) 284 final. *See also, A Modern Regulatory Framework for Company Law in Europe*, Report of the High Level Group of Company Law Experts, European Commission, Brussels, 4 November 2002.
    High Level Group Report II, Ch. II. 3: *Disclosure of Information as a Regulatory Tool* and Ch. VIII.2: *General Rules for Enterprises (transparency for all legal persons with limited liability).*
16. Action Plan, *ibid.*, at 3, 8–9.
17. *See, e.g.*, Speech 06/720 of Charlie McCreevy to the European Parliament JURI Committee (Committee on Legal Affairs), *Europe - Succeeding Together*, Presidency Programme 1 January to 30 June 2007, at 8 (21 November 2006).
    http://www.eu2007.de/includes/Downloads/Praesidentschaftsprogramm/EUPresidencyProgrammejfinal.pdf
    discussed in Daniela Weber-Rey, *Effects of the Better Regulation Approach on European Company Law and Corporate Governance*, ECFL Rev., 4(3), 370–416 (2007). *See also* Enriques, Luca. *EU Corporate Law: Time for Cutting Red Tape*, 9 Eur. Company L., 172 (2012).
18. Carlos Gorriz, *EU Company Law: Past, Present and...Future?*, Global Jurist 8 (2018).

Protection of shareholders' rights, reinforced by the growing reach of capital markets law into the realm of company law,[19] was advanced as a goal after the global financial crisis of 2007–8, and shareholder engagement became a further priority after that time as a major step forward for EU level corporate governance regulation. This focus on protecting shareholders came at the expense of other stakeholders such as employees and workers, who were left to rely on social policy and labour law for the protection of their interests.[20] The shareholder focus was reinforced in December 2012 with the publication of the Action Plan: *European Company Law and Corporate Governance; A Modern Legal Framework for More Engaged Shareholders and Sustainable Companies* which included increasing transparency as a key plan of action, encouraging shareholder engagement, and investor-related transparency.[21] This period marked 'a shift from a legislative programme centred on company law harmonisation towards a regulatory approach based on minimum requirements and mutual recognition, increasingly geared at adjusting the governance of corporations to the demands of liberalised capital markets.'[22] Horn indeed observes 'shifts from industrial democracy' to a 'shareholder democracy', and 'from harmonisation to marketisation'[23] just as Birch and Mykhnenko discerned a shift towards financialization.[24]

Parallel to these changes, CSR also became, globally, an important part of company law debate, taking hold more strongly during the 2000s. Even in the 1970s, Milton Friedman's suggestion that directors should not pursue social responsibility[25] was not universally accepted.[26] A literature on CSR was germinated.[27] In the US, following the establishment of a 'progressive' corporate law movement during the final decade of the twentieth century, research explored more fully the concept of CSR[28] and, despite the existence of different understandings,[29] CSR became influential in

19. Horn, *supra* n. 13.
20. *Ibid.*
21. Gorriz, *supra* n. 18, at 10–14.
22. Horn, *supra* n. 13.
23. *Ibid.*, at 92.
24. Kean Birch, Vlad Mykhnenko, *Lisbonizing versus Financializing Europe? The Lisbon Agenda and the (un)Making of the European Knowledge-Based Economy* 32(1) Environment and Planning C: Government and Policy 108–128 (2014).
25. Milton Friedman, *The Social Responsibility of Business Is to Increase Its Profits*, The New York Times Magazine, 13 Sept. 1970: 32–3, 124–6.
26. *See, e.g.*, Keith Davis, *The Case for and against Business Assumption of Social Responsibilities* 16(2) Acad. Manage. J. 312–22 (1973).
27. Indeed, one can go back earlier to the famous debate between Berle and Dodd in the US legal literature, during the 1930s. Archie B. Carroll (Ed.) *Managing Corporate Social Responsibility* (Boston: Little, Brown 1977); Archie B. Carroll *A Three-dimensional Conceptual Model of Corporate Social Performance* 4 Acad. Manage. Rev. 497–505 (1979); Archie B. Carroll, *Corporate Social Responsibility: Evolution of a Definitional Construct* 38(3) Business and society 268–295 (1999).
28. *See, e.g.*, Carroll, *supra* n. 27, and David Vogel *The Market for Virtue: The Potential and Limits of Corporate Social Responsibility* (Brookings 2006).
29. *See, e.g.*, Alexander Dahlsrud, *How Corporate Social Responsibility Is Defined: An Analysis of 37 Definitions*, 15 Corp. Soc. Resp. Envtl. Mgnt. 4–5 (2008).

international and EU level debates and policy development.[30] Indeed, as international institutions pursued policies based on CSR by creating (usually voluntary) CSR business standards, such as the United Nations (UN) Global Compact created in 1999,[31] so too did the EU.[32]

The European Commission set out its thinking about CSR in a Green Paper in 2001. It established a Multistakeholder Forum, and in 2006 it published a new policy emphasizing support for a business-lead initiative called the European Alliance for CSR. Not only building on that earlier work and progress made towards business acceptance of the importance of CSR but also recognizing continued limitations and challenges, the Commission addressed CSR again in a Communication on a renewed strategy for CSR in 2011, with a new definition and a new agenda aimed at retaining the EU's global influence over CSR-related practices and reducing the risk of too much cost-inducing divergence of approaches, as well as better aligning the EU's and international approaches to CSR.[33] Already, the Organisation for Economic Co-operation and Development (OECD) had produced its own Guidelines for Multinational Enterprises, and there were in place at the international level a UN Global Compact which incorporated ten principles related to CSR, and an ISO Standard 26000 Guidance Standard on Social Responsibility, as well as an International Labour Organization (ILO) Tri-partite Declaration of Principles Concerning Multinational Enterprises and Social Policy. The UN's Guiding Principles on Business and Human Rights, alongside those other international initiatives, were the drivers for the pledge in the Green Paper, for the European Commission to 'identify ways to promote responsible business conduct in its future policy initiatives towards more inclusive and sustainable recovery and growth in third countries.'[34]

By 2010, sustainability in company law and corporate governance was also a topic of interest, potentially more demanding than CSR. Sjafjell's research team was beginning to set an agenda for debate and for implementation,[35] and that work has

30. Lawrence E. Mitchell *Progressive Corporate Law* (Routledge 2019); David Millon, *Theories of the Corporation*, Duke LJ 201 (1990).
31. *See also* UN Guiding principles on Business and Human Rights 2011 and OECD Guidelines for Multinational Enterprises.
32. *See, e.g.*, European Commission, *Green Paper, Promoting a European Framework for Corporate Social Responsibility*, Brussels, 18.7.2001 COM(2001) 366 final; European Commission, *Communication, A Renewed EU Strategy 2011–14 for Corporate Social Responsibility*, Brussels, 25.10.2011 COM(2011) 681 final; Daniel Kindermann, *Corporate Social Responsibility in the EU, 1993–2013: Institutional Ambiguity, Economic Crises, Business Legitimacy and Bureaucratic Politics* 51 J. Common Market Stud. 702 (2013).
33. *See, e.g.*, European Commission, *supra* n. 32; and European Commission, *supra* n. 32.
34. European Commission, *Communication. A Renewed EU Strategy 2011–14 for Corporate Social Responsibility*. COM(2011) 681 final, Part 4.8.
35. Beate Sjåfjell, *If Not Now, When? European Company Law in a Sustainable Development Perspective* 7(5) Eur. L. J. 187–194 (2010); Beate Sjåfjell and Benjamin J. Richardson, *The Future of Company Law and Sustainability* in Beate Sjåfjell and Benjamin J. Richardson (Eds.), *Company Law and Sustainability: Legal Barriers and Opportunities*, 312–340 (Cambridge: Cambridge University Press 2015).

carried on through the last decade as a leading inspiration behind the current policies at EU level. Thus, more recently we have witnessed a transition from harmonizing company law to developing company law and corporate governance as a route towards sustainable business practices and value creation. This is evident in the current EU Green Deal,[36] the sustainable finance initiative,[37] and the sustainable corporate governance initiative[38] discussed below.

This evolution highlights a shift in emphasis from shareholders towards sustainability with potential for a change of focus onto different issues. The shareholder primacy versus stakeholder value debate, in which the interests of different stakeholders beyond those of the shareholders became relevant, developed further later in the last decade to include also a focus on sustainability.[39] Moreover, many shareholders are also looking beyond financial performance and are increasingly concerned with the financial risks of unsustainability as well as their potential to contribute towards a just transition to sustainability through their investments. A responsible investment approach has emerged for the shareholding and investing community.[40]

In conclusion, it is possible to witness policy changes and development of parallel policies at the EU level. Financialization occurred globally, especially from the early 1970s[41] and the EU was a major player, with policies that sought to protect shareholders interests and increase their engagement as key corporate governance actors. This reflected the theoretical grounding widely recognized for corporate governance: the principal-agent relationship between managers and shareholders.[42] Yet, alongside this lasting feature, the EU policy-makers, since the beginning of the twenty-first century, have sought to embed CSR and stakeholder value into legal and regulatory instruments. Now sustainable value creation has become the driver of legal developments alongside a will to achieve a culture of trust between corporate directors and their shareholders and stakeholders. The frequently simultaneous development of these parallel policies and objectives could generate tensions and misunderstandings and possible contradictions and complexities in the legal and regulatory instruments that are introduced. This can be observed in the reporting instruments that have been continually expanded over time. These are explored in the next section.

---

36. European Commission, *Communication on the European Green Deal*, COM(2019) 640 final.
37. European Commission, *Action Plan: Financing Sustainable Growth*, COM(2018) 97 final.
38. *See* European Commission, *Roadmap* (July 2020) and *Consultation on Sustainable Corporate Governance* (October 2020), https://ec.europa.eu/info/law/better-regulation/have-your-say/initiatives/12548-Sustainable-corporate-governance_en.
39. Charlotte Villiers, Beate Sjåfjell, and Georgina Tsagas, *Pathways Towards Sustainable Value Creation in the EU* in Beate Sjåfjell, Georgina Tsagas, and Charlotte Villiers (eds), *Sustainable Value Creation in the EU: Towards Pathways to a Sustainable Future through Crises* (Cambridge University Press, forthcoming 2022).
40. UN PRI, impact investing are growing investment strategies: *see, e.g.*, Mark Anthony Camilleri, *The Market for Socially Responsible Investing: A Review of the Developments* 17:3 *Soc. Resp. J. l* 412–428 (2020).
41. *See* Sahil Jai Dutta *Financialisation – A Primer* (Transnational Institute, updated 2018) https://www.tni.org/files/publication-downloads/financialisation-primer-sept2018-web.pdf.
42. *See, e.g.*, Deakin, *supra* n. 9, at p. 244.

§6.03 HOW THIS BROAD DEVELOPMENT IS REFLECTED IN THE REPORTING INSTRUMENTS

As the company law and corporate governance reporting requirements have been developed at EU level and in the Member States, their scope has broadened over time, and they also reflect the policy developments described earlier. This part describes the expansion from financial to non-financial (now 'sustainable') reporting and shows how these two major categories of reporting have been influenced by economic and political developments since company law harmonization was begun in 1968.

For financial reporting, the role of the EU was largely to harmonize the rules that already existed in Member States, and so the EU followed existing financial reporting frameworks. Thus, for many years, all limited liability companies have had to prepare financial statements (and consolidated statements) that provide a true and fair view of their financial position. Perhaps recognizing also the extent to which the contemporary phase of globalization picked up after the fall of the Soviet Union and further again as the internet and e-commerce became widely used,[43] creating global competition for European companies in the financial markets,[44] the EU 'introduced rules to promote the convergence of accounting standards at global level and to ensure consistent and comparable financial reporting across the EU.'[45] The EU has been a key player in pushing listed companies towards preparing their consolidated financial statements in accordance with the international financial reporting standards (IFRS), a single set of international standards.[46] In the non-financial reporting and sustainability reporting arenas, the EU has adopted a 'norm entrepreneur'[47] role, leading the development of the rules to be adopted in the Member States pushing certain large companies 'to disclose information on the way they operate and manage social and environmental challenges' and for such reporting to help 'investors, civil society organisations, consumers, policy makers and other stakeholders to evaluate the non-financial performance of large companies' and encourage those companies 'to develop a responsible approach to business.'[48]

---

43. *See, e.g.*, Jan Nederveen Pieterse, *Periodizing Globalization: Histories of Globalization* 6(2) New Global Studies (2012); Antimo Verde, *Globalization: Definition and Phases* in *Is Globalisation Doomed?* 3-12 (Palgrave Macmillan 2017); George Ritzer and Paul Dean *Globalization: A Basic Text* (John Wiley & Sons 2015), especially Ch. 2.
44. *See, e.g.*, Regulation (EC) No 1606/2002 of the European Parliament and of the Council of 19 July 2002 on the application of international accounting standards, OJ L 243, 11.9.2002, pp. 1–4, preamble, para. 4.
45. European Commission, *Financial Reporting*, https://ec.europa.eu/info/business-economy-euro/company-reporting-and-auditing/company-reporting/financial-reporting_en.
46. Regulation (EC) No 1606/2002 of the European Parliament and of the Council of 19 July 2002 on the application of international accounting standards, OJ L 243, 11.9.2002, pp. 1–4; and *see* Commission Regulation (EC) No 1126/2008 of 3 November 2008 adopting certain international accounting standards in accordance with Regulation (EC) No 1606/2002 of the European Parliament and of the Council (Text with EEA relevance), OJ L 320, 29.11.2008, pp. 1–481.
47. *See, e.g.*, Martha Finnemore and Kathryn Sikkink, *International Norm Dynamics and Political Change*, 52(4) International Organization 887–91 (1998).
48. European Commission, *Corporate Sustainability Reporting*, https://ec.europa.eu/info/business-economy-euro/company-reporting-and-auditing/company-reporting/corporate-sustainability-reporting_en.

At the EU level, the path towards sustainability and sustainable development[49] means seeking economic growth in correspondence with the UN's Sustainable Development Goals, with 'fair outcomes for all of humanity' and 'ensuring that humans don't consume more resources than the Earth has to offer'.[50] For businesses, shareholders are still given a central role even as this focus has shifted towards a sustainable development agenda.[51] These shifts in focus have determined the direction of corporate reporting not only with a fast-growing emphasis upon the non-financial information but also with an eye to seeing such information from a financial materiality perspective as well as a societal and environmental impact perspective.[52] Integrated reporting, primarily understood as a tool for financial stakeholders,[53] is also supported as a mechanism for connecting non-financial information with a firm's financial performance,[54] but the relationship between this still voluntary reporting approach and the legislative developments in the EU remains complex and unclear.[55]

[A] Financial Reporting and Disclosure Requirements in the Earlier Directives

Reporting and disclosure has traditionally been seen as an important feature of company law.[56] Portugal appears to have introduced accounting rules during the

49. The European Commission describes sustainable development as 'development that meets the needs of current generations without compromising the ability of future generations to meet theirs'. *A Sustainable Europe by 2030*, 30 January 2019, https://ec.europa.eu/info/publications/reflection-paper-towards-sustainable-europe-2030_en.
50. This definition provided in: European Commission, *European Reflection Paper: Towards a Sustainable Europe by 2030* (January 2019) https://ec.europa.eu/info/sites/default/files/rp_sustainable_europe_30-01_en_web.pdf at 3.
51. *Ibid.*, at 26.
52. The 'double materiality' requirement introduced in the 2014 Non-Financial Reporting Directive. Directive 2014/95/EU of the European Parliament and of the Council of 22 October 2014 amending Directive 2013/34/EU as regards disclosure of non-financial and diversity information by certain large undertakings and groups Text with EEA relevance, OJ L 330, 15.11.2014, at 1-9.
53. Dinh Tami, Anna Husmann, and Gaia Melloni, *The Role of Non-financial Performance Indicators and Integrated Reporting in Achieving Sustainable Value Creation* (European Parliament, 24 September 2021), at 40.
54. Communication from the Commission – Guidelines on non-financial reporting (methodology for reporting non-financial information) C/2017/4234, OJ C 215, 5.7.2017, pp. 1-20 interpreted by the CEO of the International Integrated Reporting Council as reflecting the principles of integrated reporting, 'recognising our key concept of connectivity, "the importance of linkages and inter-relations of information (connectivity), whether it is between different aspects of non-financial information or between financial and non-financial information."': Richard Howitt, *Encouraging' New EU Guidelines for Integrated Reporting by European Businesses* (11 July 2017) https://www.integratedreporting.org/news/business-review-europe-encouraging-new-eu-guidelines-for-integrated-reporting-by-european-businesses/.
55. *See also* David Monciardini, John Dumay, and Lucia Biondi, *'IR' and EU Law. Competing, Converging or Complementary Regulatory Frameworks?* Paper presented at the conference, Life-cycle based management and reporting for sustainable business, Oslo, Norway, 29-30 November 2016.
56. L. Sealy, *The Disclosure Philosophy and Company Law Reform*, 2 The Company Lawyer 51-6 (1981).

eighteenth century and France early in the seventeenth century, with the so-called Savary Code, and adopted in Napoleon's Code de Commerce in 1809, features of which inspired the laws adopted in other European countries such as Belgium and Germany.[57] In the UK, accounting requirements laid out in the Joint Stock Companies Act 1844 and the Limited Liability Act 1856 required companies to keep 'proper books of account' and to balance them annually. The directors were required to present a 'full and fair' balance sheet at each annual meeting of shareholders, and the shareholders were required to appoint auditors to report on whether the balance sheet met the legal requirements. An accountancy profession grew from the mid-nineteenth century, alongside the development of the railways, and the accountants helped to develop accounting standards that continue still to be used and built upon today.[58] Other drivers of a reporting regime in the early days of company law included the rise of stock markets, and companies were required to provide financial information to the stock exchanges perhaps as a way of building trust with the shareholders, and for the purpose of taxation.[59] Gulin et al. identify this as the first European harmonization phase.[60]

After the European Community was established and as it grew, different accounting and reporting approaches could be identified. Countries with 'strong reporting' such as the UK, catered particularly for shareholders, whilst countries with 'weak reporting' focused more on reporting for the benefit of creditors.[61] By the time accounting harmonization Directives were being created, the UK had joined the then EEC to become a Member State. Gulin et al. would call this the second accounting harmonization phase.[62] It was also regarded as the second of four 'generations' of company law harmonization directives, in which discretion was granted to Member States or companies to select from different options in their preparation and presentation of their accounts.[63] The fourth company law harmonization Directive[64] coordinated the national requirements for the presentation of and content of annual accounts and reports, valuation methods, and their publication relating to certain limited liability companies. The seventh company law harmonization Directive[65] coordinated

57. *See* Danimir Gulin, Spajić Ferdo, Vesna Vašiček, and Žager Lajoš, *History of Accounting Regulation in the Europe and Its Effects on the Accounting Regulation in Croatia* (2004) https://citeseerx.ist.psu.edu/viewdoc/download?doi=10.1.1.544.8685&rep=rep1&type=pdf.
58. Christopher J. Napier, *The History of Financial Reporting in the UK* in Gary Previts, Peter Walton, and Peter Wolnizer (eds) *A Global History of Accounting, Financial Reporting and Public Policy* (Bingley: Emerald 2010), at. 243–273.
59. *Ibid.*
60. Gulin et al., *supra* n. 57.
61. Michele Bertoni and Bruno De Rosa, *The Evolution of Financial Reporting for Private Entities in the European Union* (2010). *Available at SSRN 1536065.*
62. Gulin, et al., *supra n. 57.*
63. *See* Charlotte Villiers, *supra* n. 8, who discusses the four generations which show the directives giving increasingly more freedom to the Member States to design their own legal implementations of the requirements or principles laid out in the relevant directives.
64. Fourth Council Directive 78/660/EEC of 25 July 1978 based on Article 54 (3) (g) of the Treaty on the annual accounts of certain types of companies, OJ L 222, 14.8.1978, pp. 11–31.
65. Seventh Council Directive 83/349/EEC of 13 June 1983 based on the Article 54 (3) (g) of the Treaty on consolidated accounts, OJ L 193, 18.7.1983, pp. 1–17.

the accounting requirements for the consolidated accounts and reports of companies belonging to a group. A true harmonization was not fully achieved, differences in accounting and measurement practices and approaches remained,[66] and accounts were still difficult to compare across the European market. The accounting directives were later repealed and replaced, under the European Commission's 'better regulation' programme,[67] by an umbrella re-cast accounting directive in 2013[68] to provide a single legal framework for single and consolidated accounts of EU undertakings.[69] The aim of the 2013 directive, like its predecessors, was still to harmonize national requirements for the presentation and content of annual or consolidated financial statements (usually comprising the balance sheet, profit and loss account, and notes to the financial statements) and management reports, and the measurement basis used for preparing financial statements, their audit and publication.

The European Commission signalled adherence to international accounting standards in its communication, published in November 1995, *Accounting Harmonisation: A New Strategy Vis-à-vis International Harmonisation,*[70] and later introduced a Regulation in 2002[71] to require that listed companies prepare their consolidated accounts in accordance with IFRS which would provide a common accounting language used in more than 100 countries. The EU adopted the IFRS in a further Regulation in 2008.[72] The goal was to ensure that consolidated accounts would be more understandable and comparable across international boundaries. Whilst these would become compulsory for consolidated accounts, EU countries and non-listed companies could choose to extend them for use in preparing their annual financial statements.

Having largely completed legislating on the financial reporting requirements (though the reforming accounting directive came later in 2013), the Action Plan of

66. Peter Joos and Mark Lang, *The Effects of Accounting Diversity: Evidence from the European Union* 32 Journal of Accounting Research, 141–168 (1994); and Christopher Nobes, *The True and Fair View: Impact on and of the Fourth Directive* (1993) Working paper, University of Reading.
67. This aimed to reduce the administrative burden for small and medium-sized companies.
68. Directive 2013/34/EU of the European Parliament and of the Council of 26 June 2013 on the annual financial statements, consolidated financial statements, and related reports of certain types of undertakings, amending Directive 2006/43/EC of the European Parliament and of the Council and repealing Council Directives 78/660/EEC and 83/349/EEC Text with EEA relevance, OJ L 182, 29.6.2013, pp. 19–76.
69. Covering not just private and public limited liability companies with but also unlimited companies and limited or other partnerships in which all members have limited liability.
70. COM(95) 508 final.
71. Regulation (EC) No 1606/2002 of the European Parliament and of the Council of 19 July 2002 on the application of international accounting standards, OJ L 243, 11.9.2002, pp. 1–4.
72. Commission Regulation (EC) No 1126/2008 of 3 November 2008 adopting certain international accounting standards in accordance with Regulation (EC) No 1606/2002 of the European Parliament and of the Council (Text with EEA relevance), OJ L 320, 29.11.2008, pp. 1–481. *See* R. Ball, *International Financial Reporting Standards (IFRS): Pros and Cons for Investors*, 36(1) Accounting and business research 5–27 (2006); and more recently: David Cairns, *Financial Reporting in Europe: Future Challenges*, 12(2) Accounting in Europe 187–196 (2015).

2003[73] included recommendations for transparency relating to corporate governance issues with a proposal for a requirement of an annual corporate governance statement for listed companies. The Action Plan proposed the outline of a new Directive that would require listed companies to publish a coherent and descriptive annual statement covering the key elements of their corporate governance structure and practices[74] and a Recommendation to require disclosure on executive remuneration.[75] The Action Plan also introduced plans for institutional investors to make certain disclosures: (a) their investment policy and their policy with respect to the exercise of voting rights in companies in which they invest; (b) and to disclose to their beneficial holders at their request how these rights have been used in a particular case.[76] These requirements would seek to encourage institutional investors to develop their own corporate governance and engage more effectively with their investee companies.

Shareholders' rights and engagement were a further priority identified in the Action Plan and this meant electronic facilitation of attendance at and democratic participation in shareholders' meetings, with the provision of relevant information about their rights.[77] The Transparency Directive of 2004[78] aimed to improve information given to investors about issuers of securities admitted to trading on a regulated market, located or operating in an EU country. The now consolidated Directive[79] requires publication of periodic financial information and continuous information concerning the possession of significant percentages of voting rights. Directive 2013/50/EU[80] sought, *inter alia*, to harmonize the different rules applicable to the management report. Thus Article 19 of the Accounting Directive made clear that an undertaking or group must provide a fair review of the development and performance of its business. The review (management report) was required to provide a 'balanced and comprehensive analysis of the development and performance of the undertaking's

73. European Commission, *supra* n. 15. *See also*, Report of the High Level Group of Company Law Experts, *supra* n. 15. High Level Group Report II, ch. II.3: *Disclosure of Information as a Regulatory Tool* and ch. VIII.2: *General Rules for Enterprises (transparency for all legal persons with limited liability)*.
74. Action Plan, *supra* n. 37 at 12–13.
75. *Ibid.*, at 16.
76. *Ibid.*, at 13.
77. *Ibid.*, at 14.
78. Directive 2004/109/EC of the European Parliament and of the Council of 15 December 2004 on the harmonisation of transparency requirements in relation to information about issuers whose securities are admitted to trading on a regulated market and amending Directive 2001/34/EC, OJ L 390, 31.12.2004, at 38–57.
79. *Ibid.*, at 38.
80. Directive 2013/50/EU of the European Parliament and of the Council of 22 October 2013 amending Directive 2004/109/EC of the European Parliament and of the Council on the harmonisation of transparency requirements in relation to information about issuers whose securities are admitted to trading on a regulated market, Directive 2003/71/EC of the European Parliament and of the Council on the prospectus to be published when securities are offered to the public or admitted to trading and Commission Directive 2007/14/EC laying down detailed rules for the implementation of certain provisions of Directive 2004/109/EC Text with EEA relevance, OJ L 294, 6.11.2013, at 13–27.

business and of its position, consistent with the size and complexity of the business'. The Directive laid out similar requirements for a consolidated management report.[81]

The main purpose of the management report is to provide a narrative covering the financial results and prospects – forward-looking information and qualitative information enabling recipients to forecast the entity's future earnings potential, and to assess the management's strategies and plans for the business and any material risks.

[B] Non-financial Information Requirements

Moving towards non-financial information requirements at the EU level, a 2006 Directive,[82] amending the accounting Directives again, and pursuing the goals laid out in the 2003 Action Plan, introduced a requirement for listed companies to publish a corporate governance statement as part of their accounts which 'should at least provide shareholders with easily accessible key information about the corporate governance practices actually applied, including a description of the main features of any existing risk management systems and internal controls in relation to the financial reporting process.'[83] The Directive stated that shareholders should be given information about the operation of the shareholder meeting and its key powers and a description of the shareholders' rights and how they can exercise those rights as well as information about the composition and operation of the administrative, management, and supervisory bodies and their committees.[84]

The European Commission moved beyond financial and narrative reporting as part of its renewed strategy for CSR in 2011,[85] and its Green Paper declared an intention to develop legislation to improve disclosure of social and environmental information by all organizations, including companies, civil society organizations, and public authorities. Such information should 'facilitate engagement with stakeholders and the identification of material sustainability risks' as well as contribute to improving accountability and 'building public trust in enterprises.'[86]

---

81. Art. 29.
82. Directive 2006/46/EC of the European Parliament and of the Council of 14 June 2006 amending Council Directives 78/660/EEC on the annual accounts of certain types of companies, 83/349/EEC on consolidated accounts, 86/635/EEC on the annual accounts and consolidated accounts of banks and other financial institutions and 91/674/EEC on the annual accounts and consolidated accounts of insurance undertakings (Text with EEA relevance), OJ L 224, 16.8.2006, at 1–7.
83. Preamble, para. 10.
84. Art. 7.
85. European Commission, *supra* n. 34.
86. *Ibid.*, part 4.5. Re-iterating findings in the European Commission document, 'Single Market Act – Twelve levers to boost growth and strengthen confidence – 'Working together to create new growth', adopted on 13 April 2011, in which the Commission identified 'the need to raise to a similarly high level across all Member States the transparency of the social and environmental information provided by undertakings in all sectors.' *See also* European Parliament Resolutions of 6 February 2013: 'Corporate Social Responsibility: accountable, transparent and responsible business behaviour and sustainable growth' and 'Corporate Social Responsibility: promoting societys interests and a route to sustainable and inclusive recovery'.

The European Commission's 2012 Action Plan on company law and corporate governance[87] largely centred on encouraging transparency and dialogue predominantly with companies and their investors and shareholders, and it did not add anything to its views on CSR expressed in the 2011 Green Paper. It did, however, contain plans for further disclosures on boardroom diversity and on non-financial risks. This laid the ground for the landmark Non-Financial Reporting Directive of 2014[88] (NFRD) which endorsed this focus on non-financial risks and observed that 'disclosure of non-financial information is vital for managing change towards a sustainable global economy by combining long-term profitability with social justice and environmental protection.'[89] The NFRD also sought to enhance the consistency and comparability of non-financial information disclosed by large undertakings throughout the EU.

The NFRD introduced a requirement for certain large undertakings (companies with more than 500 employees, covering approximately 6,000 large companies and groups across the EU, including listed companies, banks, insurance companies, and other companies designated by national authorities as public interest entities) to include in their management reports a non-financial statement containing information relating to environmental matters, social and employee-related matters, respect for human rights, anti-corruption and bribery matters.[90] The NFRD also stipulated a requirement for reporting on non-financial key performance indicators relevant to the particular business. Following a 'comply or explain' approach, where the undertaking does not pursue policies relating to one or more of those matters, the non-financial statement was required to provide a clear and reasoned explanation for not doing so.

In June 2017, the European Commission published a set of guidelines[91] to help companies disclose environmental and social information in compliance with the NFRD. The Guidelines Communication and the Commission's Press Release[92] prioritized the business case for non-financial reporting, rather than supporting sustainability goals: 'Transparent companies perform better over time, enjoy lower financing costs, attract and retain talented employees and are ultimately more successful. Well-informed business and investment decisions have much better chances to succeed.'[93] The Guidelines Communication[94] specifically states that information needs to be *stakeholder* oriented, and companies should focus on *stakeholders as a group*,

87. European Commission, *Communication, Action Plan: European Company Law and Corporate Governance—A Modern Legal Framework for More Engaged Shareholders and Sustainable Companies*, COM(2012) 740 final.
88. Directive 2014/95/EU, *supra* n. 52.
89. *Ibid. See* Preamble, para. 3.
90. New Article 19a of the Accounting Directive (2013/34/EU) as amended by Directive 2014/95/EU.
91. European Commission, *supra* n. 54.
92. European Commission, *Commission Takes Further Steps to Enhance Business Transparency on Social and Environmental Matters* (26 June 2017)https://ec.europa.eu/commission/presscorner/detail/en/IP_17_1702.
93. *Ibid.*
94. European Commission, *supra* n. 54.

rather than on the needs and preferences of individual or atypical stakeholders.[95] In June 2019, the European Commission published further supplementary guidelines focusing on reporting climate-related information.[96]

[C] The EU's Sustainable Finance Initiative and Sustainable Corporate Governance Initiative

The NFRD is currently undergoing a transformation. As part of its European Green Deal[97] and Sustainable Finance Action Plan[98] and in furtherance of the UN Sustainable Development Goals,[99] on 21 April 2021, the European Commission adopted a proposal for a Corporate Sustainability Reporting Directive (CSRD) to amend and rename the NFRD. The shift in terminology from non-financial information to sustainability information (to reflect that such information does have financial relevance), highlights the aim to obtain better data from companies about the sustainability risks they are exposed to, and their own impact on people and the environment, to make companies more accountable and to improve the reliability, comparability, and relevance of the information provided by companies on their sustainability risks, opportunities, and impacts. The proposed CSRD aims also to tackle the 'lack of precision in the current requirements, and the large number of private standards and frameworks in existence',[100] that 'make it difficult for companies to know exactly what information they should report.'[101] The goal is to 'bring clarity and certainty on what sustainability information to report, and make it easier for preparers to get the information they need for reporting purposes from their own business partners.'[102]

The proposed CSRD extends the scope to all large companies and all companies listed on regulated markets (except listed micro-enterprises), requires the audit (assurance) of reported information, and requires companies to digitally 'tag' the reported information, to make it machine readable and feeds into the European single access point envisaged in the capital markets union action plan.

The proposed CSRD will build on and revise the requirements set out in the NFRD, in order to make sustainability reporting requirements more consistent with the broader sustainable finance legal framework, including the Sustainable Financial

95. C215/01 2017 Guidelines at 3.5 'Stakeholder-oriented' (emphasis added).
96. European Commission, *Guidelines on Reporting on Climate-related Information* (17 June 2019) https://ec.europa.eu/finance/docs/policy/190618-climate-related-information-reporting-guidelines_en.pdf.
97. European Commission, *supra* n. 36.
98. European Commission, *supra* n. 37.
99. These are a core part of the UN General Assembly's global sustainable development framework: The 2030 Agenda for Sustainable Development (the '2030 Agenda').
100. Proposal for a Directive amending Directive 2013/34/EU, Directive 2004/109/EC, Directive 2006/43/EC and Regulation (EU) No 537/2014, as regards corporate sustainability reporting. COM/2021/189 final.
101. *Ibid.*
102. *Ibid.*

Disclosure Regulation[103] and the Regulation on the establishment of a framework to facilitate sustainable investment (the Taxonomy Regulation),[104] and to align in with the objectives of the European Green Deal. The Taxonomy Regulation contains a classification system for identifying what may be regarded as environmentally sustainable economic activities, with the aim of scaling up sustainable investments and tackling the greenwashing of 'sustainable' financial products.

As part of the sustainable corporate governance initiative, and as noted earlier, taking into account the existence of the United Nations Guiding Principles (UNGPs) and OECD initiatives, the European Commission has proposed a new corporate duty for human rights and environmental due diligence,[105] requiring companies to take measures to address their adverse sustainability impacts, such as harm in their own operations and in their value chain by identifying and preventing relevant risks and mitigating negative impacts (due diligence duty). In addition, the plan includes a reform of directors' duties, to include sustainability matters in directors' acts that 'take into account all stakeholders' interests which are relevant for the long-term sustainability of the firm, or which belong to those affected by it (employees, environment, other stakeholders affected by the business, etc.)' and to integrate stakeholders' interests into the corporate strategy. At this date, it is difficult to comment in a concrete way on what will be the final outcome, since the proposal is still under consideration.

Section 6.03 has shown that the reporting framework has been developed in line with shifting EU policies. The earlier, financial reporting requirements were part of the company law harmonization project, largely confirming settled corporate governance arrangements. As the EU developed CSR and stakeholder-oriented policies, it became more proactive and its sustainable finance and corporate governance initiatives show the EU to be pioneering new legal innovations. These developments have given rise to new legislation around reporting that is no longer just about harmonization but requires new reports and processes to be delivered by larger undertakings, within the financial and non-financial sectors. The next section considers how these legislative changes may be significant for corporate governance structures and practices. How might reporting be seen as an instrument of corporate governance?

§6.04 REPORTING AS AN INSTRUMENT OF CORPORATE GOVERNANCE

Typical dictionary definitions of the word 'instrument' include: an item of measuring equipment; a tool or device for performing a particular task; or a way of causing or

103. Regulation (EU) 2019/2089 of the European Parliament and of the Council of 27 November 2019 amending Regulation (EU) 2016/1011 as regards EU Climate Transition Benchmarks, EU Paris-aligned Benchmarks and sustainability-related disclosures for benchmarks. OJ L 317, 9.12.2019, at 17.
104. Regulation (EU) 2020/852 of the European Parliament and of the Council of 18 June 2020 on the establishment of a framework to facilitate sustainable investment, and amending Regulation (EU) 2019/2088. OJ L 198, 22.6.2020, at 13.
105. Proposal for a Directive of the European Parliament and of the Council on Corporate Sustainability Due Diligence and Amending Directive (EU) 2019/1937, COM/2022/71 final, 23.02.2022.

achieving something.[106] Considering these definitions, reporting can be viewed as instrumental, first, as a process for measuring corporate and managerial behaviours and impacts and reporting on them, second as a mechanism of corporate governance which requires an account from the managers to the stakeholders of decisions made and of the company's position, and third as a mechanism for corporate governance, to bring about or achieve particular corporate governance goals. Most reporting requirements underline management accountability, particularly to the shareholders.[107] Thus, managers must at least show how they have used the corporate assets in their efforts to secure shareholder wealth maximization[108] corresponding with the principal-agent model of corporate governance. Within the EU, some Member States hold on to an entity model of the corporation in which a range of different interests are given attention, but overall, the EU has shown a drift towards 'implicitly accepting the social norm of shareholder primacy'[109] reflected in much of the reporting framework, which concentrates on either financial reporting which is of concern to the shareholders or non-financial reporting which highlights the financial risks connected to non-financial impacts, again of interest to the shareholders. However, the recent shift towards *sustainability* reporting and sustainable value creation under the EU's Green Deal initiative, whilst connecting the financial and the non-financial, also includes a proposal for a directive on environmental and human rights due diligence and a change in directors' duties to include a requirement to pursue a sustainable business strategy. This shift looks beyond the shareholders' wealth maximization goals and may also require structural corporate governance changes and different management and corporate behaviours. This part of the chapter explores these ways in which the reporting framework might be an instrument of corporate governance.

[A] Financial Reporting

The development of a sophisticated financial reporting framework could be said to have supported and cemented the shareholder primacy approach, so dominant over the last fifty years. Sikka and Stittle observe in this way a 'current system of financial reporting which reinforces the shareholder primacy model of governance and has played a key role in manufacturing short-term shareholder returns and hollowing out companies'[110] and 'stakeholder concerns are treated as externalities and largely

106. *See, e.g.*, Cambridge University dictionary definition, https://dictionary.cambridge.org/dictionary/english/instrument.
107. *See, e.g.*, Ans Kolk, *Sustainability, Accountability and Corporate Governance: Exploring Multinationals' Reporting Practices*, 17(1) Business Strategy and the Environment 1–15 (2008).
108. *See, e.g.*, Directive 2013/34/EU, Preamble, para. 3.
109. Andrew Johnston and Beate Sjåfjell, *The EU's Approach to Environmentally Sustainable Business: Can Disclosure Overcome the Failings of Shareholder Primacy?* in Marjan Peeters and Mariolina Eliantonio (eds), *Research Handbook on EU Environmental Law* (Edward Elgar 2020).
110. Prem Sikka and John Stittle, *Debunking the Myth of Shareholder Ownership of Companies: Some Implications for Corporate Governance and Financial Reporting*, (2019) Critical Perspective on Accounting Vol 63: 101992.

ignored.'[111] They tell us also that 'corporate laws and financial reporting rules emphasise that directors should give a truthful account of material costs incurred in pursuit of shareholder wealth maximisation.'[112] The balance sheet, the income statement (the profit and loss account), and the cash flow statement are of central importance, as they provide a snapshot of the company's financial position at a given time, upon which the shareholders will make their investment decisions. The focus on fair value and mark to market accounting connects to shareholder primacy by encouraging management to focus on short-term consumption to be derived from earnings creation rather than on long-term productive potential. Hence fair value accounting and shareholder primacy became 'natural bedfellows'.[113]

Financial reports also put 'gatekeepers' under the spotlight, drawing attention to the role and qualities of auditors as corporate governance actors, who contribute by checking and providing assurance and verification of the financial reports. Indeed, a recent consultation by the European Commission highlights the connection between the 'three pillars' of reporting which include audit, corporate governance, and supervision, and these operate to underpin the quality and reliability of corporate reporting.[114] Reporting therefore brings collective board responsibilities into view, especially systems of control, prevention of risks of fraud, going concern and quality of audit of corporate reports, as well as auditor independence, firm rotation, provision of non-audit services, and transparency rules.[115] In addition, the reporting framework requires some focus on the role of the external supervisory authorities, the external regulators.[116] Thus, as an instrument of corporate governance, reporting is a catalyst for developing corporate governance arrangements and structures for the purpose of steering management behaviours and actions, at least towards the corporation's financial success.

[B] Non-financial Reporting

As the financial reporting is closely tied to shareholder primacy, the non-financial reporting has also exhibited a shareholder-oriented focus, but perhaps one that is closer to the concept of '*enlightened* shareholder value' – shareholders first but recognizing the importance of the corporation's relationships with other stakeholders and taking

111. *Ibid.*
112. *Ibid.*
113. Colin Mayer, Anette Mikes, and Sudhir Rama Murthy, *Responsible Business Theory and Accounting*, Said Business School, University of Oxford (19 September 2021) https://www.sbs.ox.ac.uk/sites/default/files/2021-09/Paper%201.%20Responsible%20Business%20Theory%20and%20Accounting.pdf at 14.
114. European Commission, *Consultation Document, Strengthening of the Quality of Corporate Reporting and its Enforcement* (November 2021) https://ec.europa.eu/info/sites/default/files/business_economy_euro/banking_and_finance/documents/2021-corporate-reporting-consultation-document_en.pdf.
115. *Ibid.*
116. *Ibid.*

into account their interests as relevant for promoting the shareholders' interests.[117] The purpose of corporate governance under this enlightened shareholder perspective is expressed in the UK's corporate governance code as 'to facilitate effective, entrepreneurial and prudent management that can deliver the long-term success of the company.'[118] Thus, for Meyer et al., non-financial reporting, or narrative reporting, 'constitute a form of performance measurement and supplementary reporting, not a reformulation of corporate financial accounting.... They are still carrying the managerialist spirit of enlightened shareholder value in suggesting ways of incorporating the interests of the environment and society in a form that enhances rather than detracts from financial performance.'[119] Shareholders are, indeed, the main targeted recipients of the financial and non-financial accounts with the expectation that they will use them to exercise their so-called exit, voice or loyalty responses,[120] either by selling their shares or by holding managers to account by challenging them and exercising their votes.[121]

These reporting requirements reinforce corporate governance structures that are shaped to reflect the principal-agent model; reporting as an instrument *of* and *for* corporate governance. Such reporting may be considered a procedural mechanism[122] providing support for corporate governance, giving the principals (the shareholders) an opportunity to monitor and respond to the reported actions of their agents (the managers). Thus, shareholder meetings, especially the annual general meetings, give to shareholders a chance to put questions to the board and vote to appoint or dismiss board directors and to reappoint or remove from office the auditors who would have overseen the presentation of the accounts.

Whilst not itself necessarily initiating structural changes, the reporting framework provides a starting point for possible further corporate governance developments, inviting attention to management behaviours, remuneration and rewards, and boardroom composition. The process of internal reporting could itself lead boardrooms and managers to reflect on their own behaviours and the policies and decisions they adopt. For example, accounting information and the internal management report, sometimes referred to as a performance report, should provide boardrooms with the information around key performance indicators they need to make appropriate decisions[123] though it remains unclear how and to what extent managers use these reports.[124] The public-facing reports, including the strategic report (or non-financial narrative report), corporate governance report, remuneration report, could increase

117. Meyer, Mikes, and Rama, *supra* n. 113, at 6–7, and 23.
118. Financial Reporting Council, *UK Corporate Governance Code 2018.*
119. Meyer, Mikes, and Rama, *supra* n. 113, at 23.
120. Albert O. Hirschman, *Exit, Voice and Loyalty* (Perlego 1970).
121. *See, e.g.*, Directive (EU) 2017/828 of the European Parliament and of the Council of 17 May 2017 amending Directive 2007/36/EC as regards the encouragement of long-term shareholder engagement (Text with EEA relevance) OJ L 132, 20.5.2017.
122. Florian Möslein and Karsten Engsig Sørensen, *Sustainable Corporate Governance: A Way Forward*, Law Working Paper 583/2021, ECGI.
123. CIMA, *Performance Reporting to Boards: A Guide to Good Practice* (undated).
124. Matthew Hall, *Accounting Information and Managerial Work* 35:3 Accounting, Organizations and Society 301–315 (2010).

directors' accountability to shareholders for their decisions and show how their remuneration is linked to their performance.[125] These reports appear not to have always produced the required results. For example, remuneration reports have not generally reined in executive pay levels. To the contrary, they may have helped to ratchet such pay upwards as they encourage a competitive awareness of the 'going rate' for the job[126] and more importantly, they rely on shareholder engagement to vote effectively to control the pay policies and amounts which may not always be forthcoming.[127] Such reports could also be catalysts for changes to be made in the boardrooms. For example, fears about boardroom 'groupthink' contributing to corporate failures, especially in the aftermath of the financial crisis, as well as requirements to report on matters such as remuneration policy and payments, pay ratios, and gender balance, might lead, for example, to efforts to improve remuneration policies or to diversify boardroom membership, predominantly in terms of gender. At EU level, a draft directive was proposed in 2012[128] with discussions ongoing and still in progress.[129]

As discussed earlier, reporting has expanded significantly to reflect the growing recognition of CSR and long-term value creation as important goals for company law and corporate governance. As much of this information is not required to be formally audited, its capacity to instigate significant structural corporate governance changes will most likely remain minimal. The softer approach in EU legislation to non-financial reporting could, for example, provide a partial explanation for the slow progress in achieving gender parity of boardroom membership. The NFRD, requires relevant companies to disclose information about their diversity policy regarding their administrative, management, and supervisory bodies, but if no such diversity policy exists, they merely have to make a statement explaining why this is the case. Such information does not have to be assured or audited.[130] This soft reporting approach might have contributed in part also to the painfully slow progress of the proposed directive on gender quotas through the legislative process since it was first presented in 2012, although there are signs of these efforts finally having a positive outcome perhaps during 2022, at the same time as we see efforts to reinforce non-financial reporting to

125. This was the reasoning behind remuneration reporting requirements introduced in the UK following publication of the *Greenbury Report* (Gee Publishing 1995).
126. Charlotte Villiers, *Executive Pay: A Socially Oriented Distributive Justice Framework* 37(5) The Company Lawyer 139–154 (2016).
127. Jingchen Zhao and Zhihui Li, *The Regulatory Framework of Executive Remuneration: Contribution from Shareholder Activism and Board Accountability*, 15(2) Hastings Bus. L.J. 203–252 (2019).
128. European Commission, *Proposal for a Directive on Improving the Gender Balance Among Non-executive Directors of Companies Listed on Stock Exchanges and Related Measures*, COM/2012/0614 final - 2012/0299(COD).
129. Rosamund Shreeves and Ülla Jurviste, *Legislative Train: Gender Balance on Boards* European Parliament (April 2022) https://www.europarl.europa.eu/legislative-train/theme-area-of-justice-and-fundamental-rights/file-gender-balance-on-boards.
130. *See* NFRD, *supra* n. 52, preamble, para. 16 and Article 19a(6). Member States may opt to require verification of such information by an independent assurance provider.

become sustainability reporting and with a requirement that such information will be independently assured.[131]

[C] The Sustainability Initiative

The advent of the CSRD, the Taxonomy Regulation, and the proposed due diligence directive signals a more expansive and demanding sustainability reporting framework than has been the case previously, with greater influence on the corporate governance system both inside and outside the corporations covered.

Much of the required information in this latest sweep of reporting requirements is technically difficult, not least information focusing on greenhouse gas emissions and other climate-change matters, with challenges relating to targets, measurement, and mitigation. Such reporting demands may call for different expertise within the boardroom going well beyond financial literacy, perhaps requiring directors also to have scientific knowledge and training in ethics so they may understand the business impacts relating to climate change, environmental protection, and the just transition towards a 'net-zero' emissions economy. Given the plans for environmental and human rights due diligence in supply chains, board members may also require an understanding of human rights issues. Under the due diligence proposals, companies will have to show that they have made efforts to expunge or minimize and mitigate environmental or human rights risks throughout their supply chain processes. This will demand a knowledge and understanding of these aspects of the business and is likely to require changes in boardroom membership. Heindrick and Struggles recently published a report to this effect in which they observed a potential competency gap as combined climate-change knowledge and board-relevant business experience is not widely present; fifty per cent of all board members expressed concerns with the level of reporting they receive on climate-change progress; sixty-nine per cent said climate-change knowledge is not a formal requirement for joining their board, and climate-change knowledge is not included in their board's competency matrix; sixty-five per cent said that knowledge of climate change is not a formal requirement in CEO selection; and seventy-five per cent of boards believe climate change is important to companies' success, yet few board governance measures link executive performance to climate-change goals.[132] In order to meet the growing regulatory and stakeholder demands around climate-change issues, the Report recommends that boardrooms

---

131. *See* CSRD proposal, stating a preference to require all companies within the scope to *see*k limited assurance for reported sustainability information, while including an option to move towards a reasonable assurance requirement at a later stage (expressed in impact assessment of the proposal) and Article 1(10) requires the statutory auditor to perform a limited assurance engagement on a company's sustainability reporting, including on the compliance of the sustainability reporting with the reporting standards, on the process carried out by the company to identify the information reported pursuant to the standards, on the mark-up of sustainability reporting, and on the indicators reported pursuant to Article 8 of the Taxonomy Regulation.
132. Heidrick & Struggles and the INSEAD Corporate Governance Centre, *Changing the Climate in the Boardroom* (December 2021).

should consider adding more climate-change voices with relevant expertise to the boardroom; create board chair accountability on the processes and dynamics that support advancing climate change; anchor climate-change strategy in social and organizational purpose, and connect it to specific operations; integrate climate-change objectives into executive compensation and search strategies, especially for the CEO; build climate-related disclosures with the same rigour required of financial disclosures.[133] Similar expertise will also be required of auditors and independent assurance providers as more sustainability disclosures are required, alongside efforts to create global standards and improvements around enforcement, monitoring, governance and controls, and assurance.[134]

If sustainability reporting is designed to build trust in the corporate governance system and between companies and society,[135] this might also demand a different style of boardroom leadership. The competitive, short-term profit maximization orientation will have to give way to a more patient capitalism, looking to the longer term and with boardrooms focusing more on relationship-building, compassion, and servant-leadership.[136] A more participatory system may be required, giving the chance for stakeholders beyond just the shareholders and investors to contribute and be involved in the decision-making processes. A broad understanding of sustainability recognizes the interests of all those affected by corporate activities including future generations. This turn towards sustainability may bring with it opportunities for those other stakeholders to exercise their voice and express their needs and demands,[137] just as the shareholder community has been able to do in pursuit of their financial interests.

§6.05 CHALLENGES AND HOW TO RESPOND

The evolving reporting framework has grown to be significantly more expansive than when it was first legislated upon in the EEC during the 1970s, reflecting the widening aims of company law and corporate governance system, going beyond wealth maximization towards sustainable value creation. At the EU level, this area of business regulation has proven difficult to harmonize fully. As noted earlier, still significant differences remain among the Member States who display an eagerness to protect their own accounting and regulatory traditions. It is a considerable challenge to accommodate the different economic models across the large EU region. Consequently, the EU legislation offers options for different ways of reporting, leading to a continued lack of

133. *Ibid.*
134. Natasha Spencer-Jolliffe, *Audit Committees Must Take Climate Change a Lot More Seriously*, Accountancy Age (December 2021). *See also* in the UK, Client Earth, *Auditing and Climate Change – The Role of the FRC* (15 December 2021)https://www.clientearth.org/media/viaafrcy/clientearth-letter-to-frc-on-audit-15-december-2021-_redacted.pdf.
135. As suggested in the CSRD proposal, context of the proposal setting out reasons for the proposal.
136. *See, e.g.*, Charlotte Villiers, *Boardroom Culture – An Argument for Compassion* 2 EBL Rev. 253–278 (2019).
137. Matthew Johnson, Friederike Redlbacher, and Stefan Schaltegger, *Stakeholder Engagement for Corporate Sustainability: A Comparative Analysis of B2C and B2B Companies* 25(4) Corporate Social Responsibility and Environmental Management, 659–673 (2018).

comparability of company reports throughout the EU.[138] This has been alleviated with EU adoption of IFRS as a universally applicable body of accounting standards. Until a more universal standardization of reporting requirements and accounting standards becomes available for non-financial or sustainability reporting, problems of lack of comparability and conceptual difficulties will remain.[139] Moreover, the comply or explain principle has become a feature of EU non-financial reporting legislation as exhibited in the NFRD. Whilst this principle provides flexibility, it also potentially undermines the need for meaningful and reliable reporting, allowing for companies simply to explain their reasons for not pursuing policies on matters covered by the Directive. Indeed, the Commission Action Plan of 2012 noted the presentation of poor-quality reporting of corporate governance stemming from the comply or explain component.[140] Reporting quality may also suffer from a continued lack of clarity around concepts such as materiality.[141] In turn, these problems could impede the monitoring and accountability dimension of reporting.

The above discussion has revealed that success levels for reporting are not consistent: reporting seems to be effective for some issues – financial reporting and sustainability – but for other issues – such as boardroom gender and remuneration – reporting has had little impact. These differences may arise as result of the design of the reporting requirements. Thus, for example, the remuneration reporting has increasingly been tied to the so-called say on pay granted to shareholders.[142] For it to be effective, though, that reporting requires buy-in from the shareholders. Over the years that has not always been so forthcoming. The granting of an advisory, rather than a binding vote, in the earlier years of the say-on-pay legislation could have limited its impact, but shareholders might simply not be so concerned about this issue.[143] It is noticeable, by contrast, that shareholders care about their financial return and they are increasingly interested in climate and sustainability issues, possibly because they carry significant risks for their investments.[144] This interest, together with a hardening up and audit requirements for such reporting, might ensure it has greater impact and success.

---

138. *See, e.g.*, Georgina Tsagas and Charlotte Villiers, *Why 'Less Is More' in Non-financial Reporting Initiatives – Concrete Steps Towards Sustainability* 10(2) Account. Eco. & L.: A Convivium (2020).
139. Rebecca Hansford, AFME calls for more consistent ESG Reporting Requirements to help deliver Europe's Sustainable Finance ambitions, (AFME 4 April 2021), https://www.afme.eu/news/press-releases/detail/AFME-calls-for-more-consistent-ESG-Reporting-Requirements-to-help-deliver-Europes-Sustainable-Finance-ambitions.
140. European Commission, *supra* n. 87.
141. Josef Baumüller and Michaela-Maria Schaffhauser-Linzatti, *In Search of Materiality for Nonfinancial Information – Reporting Requirements of the Directive 2014/95/EU*, 26(4) NachhaltigkeitsManagementForum| Sustainability Management Forum 101–111 (2018, December).
142. Betty (H.T.) Wu, Iain MacNeil, and Katarzyna Chalaczkiewicz-Ladna, *Say on Pay' Regulations and Director Remuneration: Evidence from the UK in the Past Two Decades*, 20:2 J. Corp. L. Stud. 541–577 (2020).
143. *See* Carsten Gerner-Beuerle and Tom Kirchmaier, *Say on Pay: Do Shareholders Care?* Finance Working Paper N° 579/2018, ECGI.
144. Ben Warren, *Why Investors Are Putting Sustainability at the Top of the Agenda*, (EY 19 May 2020), https://www.ey.com/en_gl/power-utilities/why-investors-are-putting-sustainability-at-the-top-of-the-agenda.

How hard should the requirements be? Should a principles-based or a rules-based reporting regime be adopted? Reporting regulation that is either too soft or too hard and inflexible may be problematic. Voluntary, softer requirements tend to result in greenwashing and lack of comparability of reports, thereby reducing their potential value. Similarly, requirements that are too vague may encourage creative accounting.[145] Likewise, reporting requirements that are too hard or too inflexible may be burdensome and ignore different companies' unique features and challenges and so might encourage 'aggressive accounting'.[146] Offering some flexibility at least recognizes the unique circumstances of each company.

Evolving and new reporting requirements have been 'added through a patchwork of laws, regulations, standards, codes, guidance and stock exchange listing requirements.'[147] This has expanded reporting topics[148] to create an intricate and detailed reporting framework that gives rise to the challenge of complexity. Such complexity has potential for misunderstandings, provides opportunity for hiding harmful or dishonest behaviours, and may result in inadequate accountability, a high-cost burden, and information overload.[149] Unlike with financial reporting, for which IFRS are widely used, a fully adopted set of universal non-financial reporting standards has not yet been achieved for sustainability reporting, though efforts are now being made in that direction.[150] These flaws could limit the value or contribution of reporting as a corporate governance instrument. A rationalization and clarification of the rules must be a starting point to enhance their potential benefit for corporate governance. Nevertheless, it is not difficult to predict that, alongside the reporting initiatives being developed, the due diligence measures will create an additional complex layer to an already complex sustainable business regulatory landscape. The result might be what has been described as a 'plurality of law-making mechanisms, and the complex landscape featuring the legal centre, the legal periphery and the social environments of law'.[151]

Steps towards a verification and assurance process for all reporting, financial and non-financial, signalled in the CSRD proposal, may help to strengthen the reliability of

145. Branka Remenarić Ivana Kenfelja and Ivo Mijoč, *Creative Accounting-motives, Techniques and Possibilities of Prevention*, 31(1) Ekonomski vjesnik, 193–199 (2018).
146. Denton L. Collins, William R. Pasewark, and Mark E. Riley, *Financial Reporting Outcomes under Rules-Based and Principles-Based Accounting Standards*, 26(4) Accounting Horizons, 681–705 (2012).
147. Monciardini, Dumay, and Biondi, *supra* n. 55, at 2.
148. Rachel Chambers and Anil Yilmaz-Vastardis, *The New EU Rules on Non-Financial Reporting: Potential Impacts on Access to Remedy*, 10 Hum. Rts. & Int'l Legal Discourse 18 (2016).
149. *See* further, Charlotte Villiers, *New Directions in Sustainability Reporting and Due Diligence in the EU – the Problem of Complexity*, EJRR (forthcoming).
150. Non-financial reporting Standards, ERD (February 2021),https://ert.eu/wp-content/uploads/2021/05/ERT_Expert-paper_NFRS-FINAL.pdf.
151. Radu Mares, *Business and Human Rights After Ruggie: Foundations, the Art of Simplification and the Imperative of Cumulative Progress* in Radu Mares (ed.), *The UN Guiding Principles on Business and Human Rights – Foundations and Implementation* (Martinus Nijhoff Publishers, Leiden, Boston 2012), at 27, citing Andreas Fischer-Lescano and Gunther Teubner, *Regime-Collisions: The Vain Search for Legal Unity in the Fragmentation of Global Law*, 25 Michigan Journal of International Law 1004 (2004).

the reporting process as a measurement of behaviours and impacts and as a basis for dialogue with stakeholders. Currently, it is predominantly financial reports that are subject to auditor verification, but a significant area of reporting remains open to misinformation and distrust. Of course, as verification becomes a requirement across the spectrum of the reporting framework, significant changes and demands will arise for the corporate governance gate keepers, not least the accountants and auditors. More scientific climate-change related information will demand of auditors, as well as boardroom members, greater education and expertise in those non-financial reporting topics, involving effort and cost. Similarly, the proposed due diligence legislation will require a greater knowledge of procedures and compliance and will very likely increase compliance costs for the relevant corporations. Against those costs of adapting though, there are also major financial risks arising from non-compliance and continuation of unsustainable behaviours.

§6.06 CONCLUSION AND FUTURE PREDICTIONS

Overall, the evolution of the reporting framework, at EU level and beyond, mirrors an expansion of the scope and remit of corporate governance and a shift from merely harmonizing to creating and shaping the corporate governance agenda and framework, including the reporting requirements. The EU provisions, within a global trade setting, are likely to have global reach, especially where corporations are operating their business through global supply chains or with multinational or transnational structures. This expansion of remit and reach has arguably resulted in a framework that is too complex, risking an ineffective expansion into sustainable value creation in which the regulators and gatekeepers could lose direction. Success may then depend on activism of the relevant stakeholders to ensure that companies stay on course to meet the sustainability goals and move towards a just transition.

There is need for some simplification and standardization of the non-financial sustainability reporting, but this must be balanced against a necessity for the EU laws to be robust and resilient and adaptable to change.

A central concern is to establish clarity in the relationship between the shareholders' interests and the needs and interests of the wider stakeholders and societal needs. Whilst financial investors are increasingly understanding that they face financial risks in unsustainable practices of their investee companies, the growth of sustainability reporting demands that they do not just 'talk a good story', but that they actively contribute towards a more sustainable business culture through their investments and their engagement with boardrooms.[152] The growth of this reporting also implies that the interests of the wider stakeholders are important.[153] If that is the case,

152. Herman Bril, Georg Kell, and Andreas Rasche, *Sustainable Investing: A Path to a New Horizon* in Herman Bril, Georg Kell, and Andreas Rasche (eds.). *Sustainable Investing: A Path to a New Horizon* (Routledge: London/New York 2021), at 1–14.
153. Irene M. Herremans, Jamal A. Nazari, and Fareshteh Mahmoudian, *Stakeholder Relationships, Engagement, and Sustainability Reporting*, 138(3) J. Bus. Ethics 417–435 (2016).

they too must be given greater opportunities to participate in the corporate decisions and strategies being pursued.

Ultimately, the reporting framework could be described as a reflection of the existing corporate governance values and goals, with potential also to be a stepping-stone towards more radical structural changes both inside and outside the corporations operating within the EU. Whilst reporting and transparency might be regarded as a more liberal regulatory approach that provides the corporate actors with space to tell their own financial and sustainability stories, it may also be an instrumental platform for closer scrutiny and for protecting and strengthening the participation opportunities of constituents beyond just those of managers and shareholders.

Part II Indirect Regulation of Corporate Governance

CHAPTER 7

Composition of Boards

Jessica Schmidt

§7.01 INTRODUCTION

The board or boards play(s) an essential role in corporate governance. A key factor for whether a board can fulfil its functions properly and effectively is its composition. Over the years, different European Union (EU) initiatives have addressed various aspects of board composition. This chapter sets out how EU law addresses board composition,[1] assesses the pros and cons of the different initiatives, and explores areas for potential future legislation.

§7.02 BOARD SYSTEMS

[A] The Proposal for a Fifth Company Law Directive: A Failed Attempt at Harmonisation

The board systems in the EU are not harmonised. In 1972, the European Commission (Commission) presented a proposal for a Fifth Company Law Directive,[2] which stipulated in Article 2(1) that public limited companies shall have a management organ and a supervisory organ (two-tier system). But this mandatory limitation to a two-tier system was widely criticised as too restrictive.[3] Against this background, the second

1. This chapter is limited to general rules for all companies or listed companies as well as special rules for CRD IV/CRR institutions and investment firms. Other special rules (e.g., for the insurance sector or for AIF or UCITS) have been deliberately omitted.
2. Proposal for a fifth directive on the structure of sociétés anonymes, COM(72) 887.
3. *See, e.g.*, Thomas Conlon, *Industrial Democracy and EEC Company Law: A Review of the Draft Fifth Directive*, (1975) 24 ICLQ 348, 358; *see* on this issue also Hans Jürgen Sonnenberger, *Die Organisation der Aktiengesellschaften im Gemeinsamen Markt*, AG 1974, 1 et seq.

proposal of 1983[4] continued to require a two-tier system on principle but allowed Member States to offer 'their' companies a choice between a two-tier structure with a supervisory and a management board or a one-tier structure with a single administrative board (Article 2(1)). The third and fourth proposals (1990/1991)[5] contained the same rules. Ultimately though, the project of a Fifth Company Law Directive failed due to irreconcilable differences regarding employee co-determination.[6]

§7.03 STATUS QUO IN THE MEMBER STATES

Today, there are basically three types of board systems existing in the Member States: The one-tier system, the two-tier system, and the Nordic hybrid system; some Member States even give companies the right to choose between different systems.[7]

The two-tier system (dualistic system) is characterised by a personal and functional separation of management board and supervisory board.[8] It is, for example, mandatory for *Aktiengesellschaften* (public limited companies) in Germany and Austria. The management board is responsible for managing the company under its own responsibility.[9] The supervisory board appoints and removes the members of the management board[10] and supervises the work of the management board.[11]

In the one-tier system (monistic system), there is only a (unitary) administrative board which exercises both the management and the supervisory function; its members are elected by the general meeting.[12] Examples for countries with a one-tier system are especially the United Kingdom (UK)[13] (which, of course, is no longer an EU Member State) and Ireland.[14] However, since both UK and Irish law nowadays

4. Amended proposal for a fifth directive founded on Art. 54(3)(g) of the EEC Treaty concerning the structure of public limited companies and the powers and obligations of their organs, COM(83) 185.
5. Second amendment to the proposal for a Fifth Council Directive based on Art. 54 of the EEC Treaty concerning the structure of public limited companies and the powers and obligations of their organs, COM(90) 629; Third amendment to the proposal for a Fifth Council Directive based on Art. 54 of the EEC Treaty concerning the structure of public limited companies and the powers and obligations of their organs, COM(91) 372.
6. *See* Marcus Lutter, Walter Bayer, and Jessica Schmidt, *Europäisches Unternehmens-und Kapitalmarktrecht* (6th ed. 2018), 9.47 with further references.
7. For an overview of the various systems in the different Member States, *see* Paul Davies, Klaus J. Hopt, Richard Nowak, Gerard van Solinge (eds)., *Corporate Boards in Law and Practice* (Oxford University Press 2013); Carsten Gerner-Beuerle, Philipp Paech, and Edmund Philipp Schuster, *Study on Directors' Duties and Liabilities*, April 2013 (< https://ssrn.com/abstract = 3886382 >).
8. *See* only Klaus J. Hopt and Patrick Leyens, *Board Models in Europe – Recent Developments of Internal Corporate Governance Structures in Germany, the United Kingdom, France, and Italy*, ECFR, 135, 141 (2004).
9. Cf. § 76(1) AktG (Germany), § 70(1) AktG (Austria).
10. Cf. § 84 AktG (Germany), § 75 AktG (Austria).
11. Cf. § 111(1) AktG (Germany), § 95(1) AktG (Austria).
12. *See* only Gerner-Beuerle, Paech, and Schuster, *supra* n. 7, at 7; Klaus J. Hopt, *Vergleichende Corporate Governance*, ZHR 175 (2011) 444, 467.
13. *See* only Hopt and Leyens, *supra* n. 8, at 149 et seq.
14. *See* Brian Hutchinson, *Keane on Company Law*, chapter 27 (5th ed., Bloomsbury Professional 2017).

differentiate between executive and non-executive directors, one can observe a convergence of the one-tier and two-tier system.[15]

In the Nordic Member States, there is a kind of hybrid system:[16] There is a board of directors (the members of which are appointed by the general meeting) and a management board (the members of which are appointed by the board of directors). The management board deals with the day-to-day running of the company. In addition, the system is characterised by a strict hierarchy: The general meeting may give instructions to the board of directors, which in turn may give instructions to the management board. In contrast to the two-tier system, a manager may serve as a director (Figure 7.1).

Figure 7.1 Board Systems

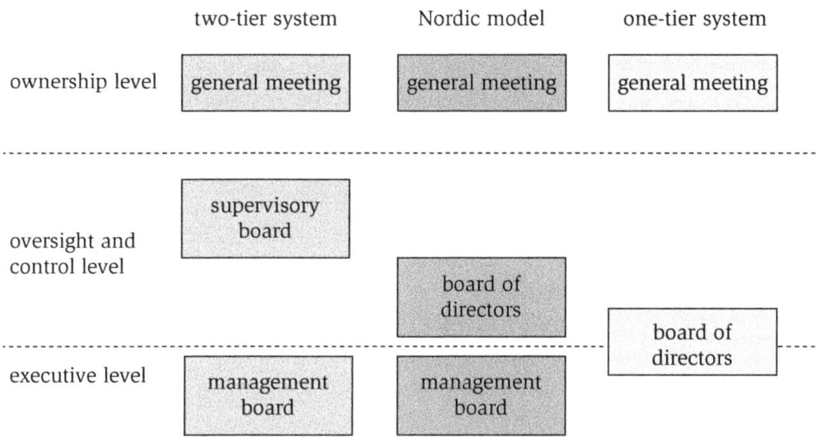

Finally, there are Member States which offer their companies a choice between different systems. In France, for example, a *société anonyme (SA)* may choose between a one-tier system[17] and a two-tier system.[18] In Italy, a *società par azioni* (S.p.A.) may even choose one of three different systems.[19]

15. *See, e.g.*, Paul Davies, *Struktur der Unternehmensführung in Großbritannien und Deutschland: Konvergenz oder fortbestehende Divergenz?*, ZGR 268, 292 (2001); Hopt and Leyens, *supra* n. 8, at 160 et seq.
16. *See* in more detail: Jesper Lau Hansen, *The Nordic Corporate Governance Model – A European Model?*, in *Perspectives in Company Law and Financial Regulation: Essays in Honour of Eddy Wymeersch* (Michel Tison, Hans de Wulf, Christoph van der Elst, Reinhard Steennot eds., Cambridge University Press 2009), 145, 152 et seq.; *The Nordic Corporate Governance Model* (Per Lekvall ed., SNS Förlag 2014), 22 et seq.
17. Art. L225-17 C.com. et seq.
18. Art. L225-57 C.com. et seq.
19. *See* on this, *e.g.*, Federico Ghezzi and Corrado Malberti, *The Two-tier Model and The One-tier Model of Corporate Governance in the Italian Reform of Corporate Law*, ECFR 1, 9 et seq. (2008).

[A] SE and SCE: Freedom of Choice

Article 38 of the Regulation on the Statute for a European Company (SE)[20] (SE-Regulation – SER) offers SEs a choice between a one-tier system with an administrative organ or a two-tier system with a management organ and a supervisory organ. Recital 14 sentence 2 SER explains that this freedom of choice was granted in light of the different board systems existing in the Member States.

In fact, the first drafts for the SER of 1970/1975 had only provided for a two-tier system.[21] During the 1970s and 1980s, the pros and cons of the one-tier system and the two-tier system were vividly debated.[22] After the second proposal for a fifth directive had allowed Member States to offer 'their' companies a choice between the one-tier and the two-tier system (*see supra* §7.02[A]), the 1989 SER proposal[23] went one step further by generally allowing all SEs to freely choose between a one-tier and a two-tier system.

The final version retains this freedom of choice between a one-tier system and a two-tier system (Article 38 SER). In addition, it allows Member States to provide that a managing director or managing directors shall be responsible for the day-to-day management (Article 39(1) 2 SER for the two-tier system, Article 43(1) 2 SER for the one-tier system).[24] This option was included upon request of Sweden to ensure that the Swedish board system was also possible for a Swedish SE.[25]

For many Member States, the freedom of choice between the one-tier system and the two-tier system offered to SEs was downright 'revolutionary'.[26] It is widely considered as one of the most important advantages of the SE as compared to the national company forms of many Member States.[27]

The Regulation on the Statute for a European Cooperative Society (SCE)[28] (SCER) copied the model of the SER: SCEs also have a choice between a one tier system and a two-tier system (Article 36 SCER).

20. Council Regulation (EC) No 2157/2001 of 8 October 2001 on the Statute for a European Company (SE), OJ 2001 L 294/1.
21. *See* COM(70) 600, Arts 62–82; COM(75) 150, Arts 62–82.
22. *See, e.g.*, Thomas Raiser, *Führungsstruktur und Mitbestimmung in der Europäischen Aktiengesellschaft nach dem Verordnungsvorschlag der Kommission vom 25. August 1989*, in *Festschrift für Ernst Steindorff zum 70. Geburtstag am 13. März 1990* (Jürgen F. Baur, Klaus J. Hopt, and K. Peter Mailänders eds, Walter de Gruyter1989), 201, 203 et seq. with further references.
23. COM(89) 268, Arts 61–80.
24. Art. 39(1) 2 SER uses the words 'current management', whereas Art. 41(1)2 uses the words 'day-to-day management'. This is apparently an unfortunate drafting error and does not imply any difference in terms of substance.
25. *See* Lutter, Bayer and J. Schmidt, *supra* n. 6, 45.92, 45.117 with further references.
26. *See* especially from a German perspective: Peter Hommelhoff, *Einige Bemerkungen zur Organisationsverfassung der Europäischen Aktiengesellschaft*, AG 2001, 279, 282.
27. *See* Lutter, Bayer, and Schmidt, *supra* n. 6, 45.94 with further references.
28. Council Regulation (EC) No 1435/2003 of 22 July 2003 on the Statute for a European Cooperative Society (SCE), OJ 2003, L 207/1.

[B] EU Rule Requiring a Freedom of Choice Also for National Companies?

Based upon a recommendation of the High Level Group,[29] the Commission's 2003 Action Plan had included the introduction of a choice between a one-tier and a two-tier system for all listed companies in the EU as one of its priorities.[30] However, after only 38% of stakeholders approved of this in the course of the consultation, this objective was not actively pursued.[31]

In 2011, the Reflection group floated the idea again, wholeheartedly recommending giving more choice for companies to decide their governance structure.[32] But the Commission did not include this point in the 2012 Action Plan[33] and has also not put it on the agenda in another context since then.

This is regrettable. After all, on the basis of empirical studies, it is increasingly recognised that neither of the two systems is generally superior,[34] but that this ultimately depends on the individual circumstances of the specific company in question.[35] Moreover, the experiences with a freedom of choice between different governance systems have been very positive – both in the Member States offering such choice and in case of the SE. Many experts have long advocated an EU rule requiring such freedom of choice for all companies in the EU,[36] and the European Parliament also expressly called for it in a resolution of 2006.[37] The European Model Company Act (EMCA) also offers a freedom of choice between a one-tier system and a two-tier system, but it also allows hybrid models.[38]

§7.04 APPOINTMENT AND REMOVAL OF DIRECTORS

In light of the different governance systems, EU law has not harmonised the rules on appointment and removal of directors. There are, of course, provisions on the

29. Report of the High Level Group of Company Law Experts on a modern regulatory framework for company law in Europe (2002) (< https://ecgi.global/sites/default/files/report_en.pdf >), III.9.
30. *Modernising Company Law and Enhancing Corporate Governance in the European Union – A Plan to Move Forward,* COM(2003) 284, 3.1.3 and Annex I.
31. Lutter, Bayer, and Schmidt, *supra* n. 6, 13.28.
32. Report of the Reflection Group on the future of EU company law (2011) (< https://www.ilf-frankfurt.de/fileadmin/_migrated/content_uploads/ILF_WP_126.pdf >), 3.3.1.
33. *Action Plan: European Company Law and Corporate Governance – A Modern Legal Framework for More Engaged Shareholders and Sustainable Companies,* COM(2012) 740.
34. *See* Lutter, Bayer, and Schmidt, *supra* n. 6, 45.94 with further references.
35. Jessica Schmidt, *SE and SCE: Two New European Company Forms – and More to Come,* 27 Co Law 99, 103 (2006); Klaus J. Hopt, *Board oder Vorstand und Aufsichtsrat?,* EuZW 201, 202 (2016).
36. *See, e.g.*, Mathias Habersack, *Das Aktiengesetz und das Europäische Recht,* ZIP 445, 450 (2006); Klaus J. Hopt and Patrick Leyens, *The Structure of the Board of Directors: Boards and Governance Strategies in the US, the UK and Germany,* ECGI Law WP point 567/2021, p. 44; Lutter, Bayer and J. Schmidt, *supra* n. 6, 13.30 with further references.
37. European Parliament resolution on recent developments and prospects in relation to company law, P6_TA(2006)0295, point 26.
38. European Model Company Act (EMCA), chapter 8, available at < https://ssrn.com/abstract=2929348 > .

appointment of the members of the management and supervisory board as well as the management board of SEs[39] and SCEs,[40] but not companies governed by the national law of the Member States.

However, this question is at least addressed partially in Recommendation 2005/162/EC.[41] Its point 10 sentence 1 provides that non-executive and supervisory directors should be appointed for specified terms subject to individual re-election, at maximum intervals to be determined at national level with a view to enabling both the necessary development of experience and sufficiently frequent reconfirmation of their position. Sentence 2 adds that it should be possible to remove them, but their removal should not be easier than for an executive or managing director.

In addition, there are certain rules and recommendations regarding a special nomination committee; *see* in more detail *infra* §7.07.

[A] Balance of Executive and Non-executive Directors

As a general principle of good corporate governance, it is necessary to provide for an effective and independent supervisory function.[42] The supervisory function, whether consisting of non-executive directors or a separate supervisory board, has the essential task of reviewing the performance of the executive in order to ensure that it works effectively in the interest of the company.[43] Moreover, it is crucial in order to ensure sound corporate governance that the supervisory function takes the lead in cases where there is a conflict of interest between the interests of the executive and the company (e.g., directors' pay, related party transactions, or takeovers).[44] An effective supervisory function requires a sufficient number of individuals who are sufficiently qualified and independent to be up to these tasks.

Hence, point 3.1 in Recommendation 2005/162/EC advises that the administrative, managerial, and supervisory bodies of listed companies include in total an appropriate balance of executive/managing and non-executive/supervisory directors so that no individual or small group of individuals can dominate decision-making on the part of these bodies. In addition, point 4 of Recommendation 2005/162/EC provides that a sufficient number of independent, non-executive, or supervisory directors should be elected to the (supervisory) board of the listed companies to ensure that any material conflict of interest involving directors will be properly dealt with. The issue of independence is looked at in more detail *infra* §7.06[D].

39. Art. 39(2), 40(2), 43(3) SER.
40. Art. 37(2), 39(2), 42(3) SCER.
41. Commission Recommendation 2005/162/EC of 15 February 2005 on the role of non-executive or supervisory directors of listed companies and on the committees of the (supervisory) board, OJ 2005, L 52/51.
42. Cf. recital 8 Recommendation 2005/162/EC.
43. *See* Report of the Committee on the Financial Aspects of Corporate Governance (Cadbury Report 1992) 4.5.
44. *Ibid.*, at 4.6.

However, given that EU law does not harmonise the board systems, the European legislator has so far refrained from laying down any binding rules in this regard.

[B] Chairman

Irrespective of the governance system, the chairman of the board usually plays a pivotal role. In a one-tier system, the chairman of the board is often at the same time also the chief executive officer (CEO). The pros and cons of such a CEO duality have been controversially discussed in academic literature for decades.[45] On the one hand, CEO duality can be problematic both in terms of the chairman possessing the necessary objectivity as well as in terms of the chairman potentially wielding excessive power. On the other hand, CEO duality also has evident benefits: a unified leadership and faster decision-making. Similar issues arise if the CEO immediately becomes chairman of the board afterwards.

In the two-tier system, correspondent questions materialise if the chairman of the management board immediately becomes chairman of the supervisory board afterwards.[46] On the one hand, this may lead to conflicts of interests; on the other hand, the person already knows the company 'inside out' and so can fulfil the supervisory function much better than someone coming from 'outside'.

Against this background, the Commission refrained from a general prohibition of either CEO duality or the chairman of the management board immediately becoming chairman of the supervisory board. Point 3.2 in Recommendation 2005/162/EC only provides as 'best practice' that this should be accompanied with information on any safeguards put in place. The 2011 Green Paper considered to make the separation of *chairman of the board* and *CEO* mandatory; but this was never implemented.[47]

However, the European legislator has implemented stricter standards for CRD IV[48]/CRR[49]-institutions (i.e., credit institutions and systemic investment

45. For a concise overview of the debate with many further references *see* Rebeca García-Ramos and Belén Díaz Díaz, *Chief Executive Officer (CEO Duality), in Encyclopedia of Sustainable Management* (Samuel Idowu, René Schmidpeter, Nicholas Capaldi, Liangrong Zu, Mara Del Baldo, Rute Abreu eds, Springer 2020).
46. *See* in detail, *e.g.*, Patrick Velte, *Wechsel vom Vorstand in den Aufsichtsrat mit oder ohne Cooling Off als „gute" Corporate Governance?*, WM 537 (2012).
47. Green Paper. The EU Corporate Governance Framework, COM(2011) 164, 1.
48. Directive 2013/36/EU of the European Parliament and of the Council of 26 June 2013 on access to the activity of credit institutions and the prudential supervision of credit institutions, amending Directive 2002/87/EC and repealing Directives 2006/48/EC and 2006/49/EC, OJ 2013, L 176/338; last amended by Directive (EU) 2021/338 of the European Parliament and of the Council of 16 February 2021 amending Directive 2014/65/EU as regards information requirements, product governance, and position limits, and Directives 2013/36/EU and (EU) 2019/878 as regards their application to investment firms, to help the recovery from the COVID-19 crisis, OJ 2021, L 68/14.
49. Regulation (EU) No 575/2013 of the European Parliament and of the Council of 26 June 2013 on prudential requirements for credit institutions and amending Regulation (EU) No 648/2012, OJ 2013, L 176/1; last amended by Regulation (EU) 2021/558 of the European Parliament and of the

firms)[50]: Article 88(1) subparagraph 2 lit. e CRD IV provides that the chairman of the management body[51] in its supervisory function of an institution must not exercise simultaneously the functions of a CEO within the same institution, unless justified by the institution and authorised by competent authorities. The proposal for CRD VI now even envisages to prohibit the chairman of the management board in its supervisory function of an institution from exercising simultaneously the functions of a CEO within the same institution.[52] Pursuant to Article 9(1) subparagraph 1 MiFID II, Article 88(1) subparagraph 2 lit. e CRD IV also applies to other investment firms.

§7.05 PROFILE OF THE BOARD MEMBERS

[A] Unfit Persons (Disqualified Directors)

The basic question which persons can be directors of companies has so far not been harmonised. This leads to the problem that persons who have been disqualified as a director in one Member State then go on to become director in another Member State ('disqualification arbitrage').

But there have been several attempts to harmonise the rules on director's disqualification, i.e., on which persons are disqualified from being a director. The Commission had already proposed a harmonisation in its 2003 Action Plan.[53] After this met with a lot of criticism, the Reflection Group had recommended to at least increase transparency in this respect in its 2011 report.[54] Harmonisation was then again considered in the run-up to the 2019 Restructuring Directive, but it was ultimately not included into the directive.[55]

The entire issue is extremely controversial due to the rather different systems and approaches in the various Member States. Some Member States (e.g., Ireland)[56] have central disqualification registers which make information about disqualified directors

---

Council of 31 March 2021 amending Regulation (EU) No 575/2013 as regards adjustments to the securitisation framework to support the economic recovery in response to the COVID-19 crisis, OJ 2021, L 116/25.

50. Pursuant to Art. 3(1) point 3 CRD IV in conjunction with Art. 4(1) point 3 CRR, institutions are credit institutions and systemic investment firms.
51. Pursuant to the definition in Art. 3(1) point 7 CRD IV, 'management body' means an institution's body or bodies, which are appointed in accordance with national law, which are empowered to set the institution's strategy, objectives and overall direction, and which oversee and monitor management decision-making, and include the persons who effectively direct the business of the institution.
52. COM(2021) 663, Art. 88(1) subparagraph 2 lit. e.
53. COM(2003) 284, 3.1.3.
54. Report of the Reflection Group (n. 31), 2.8.3.
55. Directive (EU) 2019/1023 of the European Parliament and of the Council of 20 June 2019 on preventive restructuring frameworks, on discharge of debt and disqualifications, and on measures to increase the efficiency of procedures concerning restructuring, insolvency, and discharge of debt, and amending Directive (EU) 2017/1132 (Directive on restructuring and insolvency), OJ 2019, L 172/18.
56. <https://core.cro.ie/>.

publicly available. Others (e.g., France)[57] have central disqualification registers which are only accessible by courts and/or administrative authorities, but not by the public. But there are also Member States such as Germany which do not have any central disqualification register at all.[58] In addition, a number of Member States have concerns regarding data protection if disqualification data is shared with authorities from other Member States or made public. Moreover, the reasons for which a person can be disqualified vary significantly from Member State to Member State.

The Commission proposal for a Digitalisation Directive of 2018 suggested a pure transparency solution coupled with a Member State option to refuse the appointment of a person disqualified in another Member State.[59] Yet, the Digitalisation Directive (DigiD)[60] ultimately went one step further: Article 13i Company Law Directive (CLD)[61] not only covers exchange of information via the Business Registers Information System (BRIS) but also addresses the reasons for disqualification themselves. Article 13i(1) 1 CLD now expressly requires Member States to have rules on disqualification of directors. Pursuant to Article 13i(1) 2 CLD, those rules shall include providing for the possibility to take into account any disqualification that is in force, or information relevant for disqualification, in another Member State. Yet, 'take into account' does not mean that a disqualification in one Member State must necessarily lead also to a disqualification in another Member State.[62] Recital 23 sentence 8 DigiD emphasises that Member States should not be obliged to recognise disqualifications in force in other Member States. Naturally though, 'taking into account' disqualifications from other Member States requires knowing that they exist. Hence, Article 13i(3)-(5) CLD provides for an exchange of information via BRIS; details are governed by Regulation (EU) 2021/1042.[63]

---

57. Fichier National des Interdits de Gérer (FNIG).
58. In Germany, potential directors have to give an assurance that they are not disqualified when they are registered in the companies register (cf. § 37(2) AktG, § 8(3) GmbHG); if the register court has specific doubts, it may request information from the German Bundeszentralregister (Federal Central Criminal Register) or the Gewerbezentralregister (central commercial register).
59. COM(2018) 239 (Art. 13h).
60. Directive (EU) 2019/1151 of the European Parliament and of the Council of 20 June 2019 amending Directive (EU) 2017/1132 as regards the use of digital tools and processes in company law, OJ 2019, L 186/80.
61. Directive (EU) 2017/1132 of the European Parliament and of the Council of 14 June 2017 relating to certain aspects of company law, OJ 2017, L 169/46; last amended by Regulation (EU) 2021/23 of the European Parliament and of the Council of 16 December 2020 on a framework for the recovery and resolution of central counterparties and amending Regulations (EU) No 1095/2010, (EU) No 648/2012, (EU) No 600/2014, (EU) No 806/2014, and (EU) 2015/2365 and Directives 2002/47/EC, 2004/25/EC, 2007/36/EC, 2014/59/EU, and (EU) 2017/1132, OJ 2021, L 22/1.
62. Jessica Schmidt, *DiRUG-RefE: Ein Digitalisierungs-Ruck für das deutsche Gesellschafts- und Registerrecht*, ZIP 112, 120 (2021).
63. Commission Implementing Regulation (EU) 2021/1042 of 18 June 2021 laying down rules for the application of Directive (EU) 2017/1132 of the European Parliament and of the Council as regards technical specifications and procedures for the system of interconnection of registers and repealing Commission Implementing Regulation (EU) 2020/2244, OJ 2021, L 225/7.

These new rules in the DigiD are certainly a major step ahead. They at least create a common EU minimum standard.[64] However, the problem of 'disqualification arbitrage' can only be really resolved by a harmonisation of the reasons for disqualification, coupled with a duty to recognise disqualifications from other Member States; this remains an important desideratum.[65]

[B] Qualification

To ensure that a company is managed properly, it is essential that the directors are sufficiently qualified for their positions. However, ultimately, the qualification necessary will to a large extent depend on the individual company's activities, size, and environment.[66] EU rules and recommendations have taken this into account.

§7.06 GENERAL REQUIREMENTS FOR DIRECTORS

[A] Listed Companies

Recommendation 2005/162/EC deliberately refrained from setting out specific qualification requirements for each individual board member.[67] However, point 11.1 in Recommendation 2005/162/EC provides that the board should be composed of members who, as a whole, have the required diversity of knowledge, judgment, and experience to complete their tasks properly; with a view to this, the (supervisory) board should determine its desired composition relating to the company's structure and activities and evaluate it periodically. Point 11.3 adds that all new members of the (supervisory) board should be offered a tailored induction programme covering to the extent necessary their responsibilities and the company's organisation and activities and that the (supervisory) board should conduct an annual review to identify areas where directors need to update their skills and knowledge.

In order to enable the market and the public to assess the appropriateness of the board member's competences, point 11.4 of Recommendation 2005/162/EC requires transparency: The competences of a new director should be disclosed when his appointment is proposed; moreover, the (supervisory) board should disclose every year a profile of the board's composition and information on the particular competences of the individual directors. Today, this is complemented by the information

64. Schmidt, *supra* n. 62, at 120.
65. Walter Bayer and Jessica Schmidt, *BB-Gesetzgebungs- und Rechtsprechungsreport zum Europäischen Unternehmensrecht 2018/19 – Teil I: Company Law Package*, BB 2019, 1922, 1924; Schmidt, *supra* n. 62, at 120; *see also* Segismundo Álvarez Royo-Villanova, *Proposal Regarding the Use of Digital Tools and Processes in Company Law: The Practioner's perspective*, ECFR 149, 174 (2019).
66. *See also* recital 16 sentence 1 Recommendation 2005/162/EC.
67. Cf. Recital 16 Recommendation 2005/162/EC.

required in the corporate governance statement pursuant to Article 20 EU Accounting Directive.[68]

[B] CRD IV/CRR Institutions and Other Investment Firms

As regards CRD IV/CRR institutions,[69] the European legislator felt it necessary to lay down binding rules to ensure a sound management of risks.[70] Article 91(1) 1 CRD IV provides that members of the management body are at all times of sufficiently good repute and possess sufficient knowledge, skills, and experience to perform their duties. Article 91(7) CRD IV provides that the management body shall possess adequate collective knowledge, skills, and experience to be able to understand the institution's activities, including the main risks and that the overall composition of the management body shall reflect an adequately broad range of experience. This is further fleshed out by EBA and ESMA guidelines.[71]

Pursuant to Article 9(1) subparagraph 1 MiFID II, these rules also apply to other investment firms.

In addition, the Investment Firms Directive (IFD)[72] lays down special rules for investment holding companies and mixed financial holding companies: Pursuant to Article 52 IFD, Member States shall require that the members of the management body of such companies are of sufficiently good repute and possess sufficient knowledge, skills, and experience to effectively perform their duties, taking into account the specific role of an investment holding company or mixed financial holding company.

[1] Special Requirements for Members of the Audit Committee

Special rules apply to the members of the audit committee. In light of huge accounting scandals, some specific knowledge was deemed to be indispensable here.[73] Hence, point 11.2 in Recommendation 2005/162/EC provided that members of the audit

68. Directive 2013/34/EU of the European Parliament and of the Council of 26 June 2013 on the annual financial statements, consolidated financial statements, and related reports of certain types of undertakings, amending Directive 2006/43/EC of the European Parliament and of the Council and repealing Council Directives 78/660/EEC and 83/349/EEC, OJ 2013, L 182/19; last amended by Directive (EU) 2021/2101 of the European Parliament and of the Council of 24 November 2021 amending Directive 2013/34/EU as regards disclosure of income tax information by certain undertakings and branches, OJ 2021, L 429/1.
69. As regards the term 'institutions' within the meaning of CRD IV, *see supra* n. 48.
70. Cf. recital 54 sentence 1 CRD IV.
71. Joint ESMA and EBA Guidelines on the assessment of the suitability of members of the management body, EBA/GL/2021/06, ESMA35-36-2319. *See* on them in more detail Malte Wundenberg in *Europäisches und Deutsches Kapitalmarktrecht* (Rüdiger Veil ed., 3rd ed. 2010), § 34 para. 42 et seq.
72. Directive (EU) 2019/2034 of the European Parliament and of the Council of 27 November 2019 on the prudential supervision of investment firms and amending Directives 2002/87/EC, 2009/65/EC, 2011/61/EU, 2013/36/EU, 2014/59/EU, and 2014/65/EU, OJ 2019, L 314/64.
73. Cf. recital 16 sentence 2 Recommendation 2005/162/EC.

committee of listed companies should, collectively, have a recent and relevant background in and experience of finance and accounting for listed companies appropriate to the company's activities.

The Statutory Audit Directive (SAD)[74] then introduced hard and fast rules for the audit committee of public interest entities (PIE).[75] Originally Article 41(1), subparagraph 1, sentence 3 SAD, had only required that at least one member of the audit committee shall be independent[76] and shall have competence in accounting and/or auditing (independent financial expert). However, Directive 2014/56/EC[77] tightened the standards significantly in order to reinforce the independence and technical competence of the audit committee.[78] Article 39(1), subparagraph 2 SAD, continues to require that at least one member of the audit committee shall have competence in accounting and/or auditing (financial expert). Moreover, pursuant to Article 39(1), subparagraph 3 SAD, the committee members as a whole shall have competence relevant to the sector in which the audited entity is operating. Interestingly though, it is no longer necessary that the financial expert is independent; however, according to Article 39(1) subparagraph 4 sentences 1 and 2 SAD, a majority of the members of the audit committee and its chairman shall be independent of the audited entity.

[2] Special Requirements for Members of the Remuneration Committee

In order to strengthen the role of remuneration committees,[79] EU law also sets out special requirements for their members. Point 7.1 in Recommendation 2009/385/EC[80] recommends that at least one of the members of the remuneration committee of listed companies should have knowledge of and experience in the field of remuneration policy (remuneration expert).

For CRD IV/CRR institutions,[81] the European legislator considered it expedient to impose binding rules: Article 95(1) 2 CRD IV provides that the remuneration committee shall be constituted in such a way as to enable it to exercise competent and independent judgment on remuneration policies and practices and the incentives created for managing risk, capital, and liquidity.

---

74. Directive 2006/43/EC of the European Parliament and of the Council of 17 May 2006 on statutory audits of annual accounts and consolidated accounts, amending Council Directives 78/660/EEC and 83/349/EEC and repealing Council Directive 84/253/EEC, OJ 2006, L 157/87; last amended by Directive 2014/56/EU of the European Parliament and of the Council of 16 April 2014 amending Directive 2006/43/EC on statutory audits of annual accounts and consolidated accounts, OJ 2014, L 158/196.
75. Defined in Art. 2, point 13 Statutory Audit Directive.
76. Independence is discussed in detail *infra* §7.06[D].
77. Directive 2014/56/EU of the European Parliament and of the Council of 16 April 2014 amending Directive 2006/43/EC on statutory audits of annual accounts and consolidated accounts, OJ 2014, L 158/196.
78. Cf. recital 24 sentence 2 Directive 2014/56/EU.
79. Cf. recital 11 sentence 2 Recommendation 2009/385/EC.
80. Commission Recommendation 2009/385/EC of 30 April 2009 complementing Recommendations 2004/913/EC and 2005/162/EC as regards the regime for the remuneration of directors of listed companies, OJ 2009, L 120/28.
81. As regards the term 'institutions' within the meaning of CRD IV, *supra* n. 48.

[C] Sufficient Time

A further essential element of good corporate governance is that directors devote sufficient time to their duties.[82] Hence, point 12.1 of Recommendation 2005/162/EC specifically spells out not only that each director should devote to his duties the necessary time and attention but also that each director should undertake to limit the number of his other professional commitments (in particular, any directorships held in other companies) to such an extent that the proper performance of duties is assured. Point 12.2 also recommends transparency in this respect. The 2011 Green Paper considered to impose general limits on the number of mandates.[83]

However, so far EU law only sets out binding limits on the number of mandates for significant CRD IV/CRR institutions[84] in Article 91(3)-(6) CRD IV: Members of the management body shall not hold more than either one executive directorship with two non-executive directorships or four non-executive directorships (Article 91(3) sentence 2 CRD IV).[85] However, the competent authorities may authorise members of the management body to hold one additional non-executive directorship (Article 91(6) CRD IV). In addition, Article 91(2) CRD IV provides that all members of the management body of all CRD IV/CRR institutions[86] shall commit sufficient time to perform their functions in the institution. Details are governed by paragraphs 39 et seq. of the ESMA/EBA guidelines.[87]

Pursuant to Article 9(1) subparagraph 1 MiFID II, Article 91(3)-(5) CRD IV also apply to other investment firms. However, competent authorities may also authorise members of the management body to hold one additional non-executive directorship (Article 9(2) subparagraph 1 MiFID II).

In addition, both CRD IV/CRR institutions (Article 435(2)(a) CRR) and other investment firms (Article 48(a) IFR) shall (at least) annually disclose the number of directorships held by members of the management body.

[D] Independence

The presence of independent representatives on the board, capable of challenging the decisions of management, is widely considered as a means of protecting the interests of shareholders and other stakeholders.[88] However, a board consisting exclusively of

82. Cf. recital 17 sentence 1 Recommendation 2005/162/EC.
83. COM(2011) 164, 1.2.
84. As regards the term 'institutions' within the meaning of CRD IV, *see supra* n. 48.
85. According to Art. 91(3) 2, (5) CRD IV, directorships in organisations which do not pursue predominantly commercial objectives and directorship as representative of a Member State shall not count. Moreover, according to Art. 91(4) CRD IV, certain directorships within a group shall count as a single directorship.
86. As regards the term 'institutions' within the meaning of CRD IV, *see supra* n. 48.
87. ESMA/EBA guidelines, *supra* n. 71.
88. Cf. recital 7 sentence 1 Recommendation 2005/162/EC.

independent directors carries the risk of insufficient knowledge of the business of the company.[89]

Against this background, Recommendation 2005/162/EC put particular emphasis on the independence of the directors, but deliberately refrained from setting out strict independence quotas. Instead, its point 4 only provides that a sufficient number of independent non-executive or supervisory directors should be elected to the (supervisory) board of companies to ensure that any material conflict of interest involving directors will be properly dealt with.

In the absence of any common understanding of what independence precisely entails, Recommendation 2005/162/EC deliberately limited itself to providing a 'general objective'.[90] Pursuant to point 13.1 in Recommendation 2005/162/EC, a director should be considered to be independent only if he or she is free of any business, family or other relationship, with the company, its controlling shareholder or the management of either, that creates a conflict of interest such as to impair his judgement. Annex II of Recommendation 2005/162/EC contains a list of criteria to be used to assess independence; but in light of the complexity of the issue, this list is non-exhaustive and Member States should only take it into account as guidance (cf. point 13.2, sentence 1 of Recommendation 2005/162/EC). In addition, the criteria should be tailored to the national context (Annex II point 1 sentence 4 of Recommendation 2005/162/EC). Moreover, point 13.2 sentence 2 Recommendation 2005/162/EC emphasises that determination of what constitutes independence is fundamentally an issue for the (supervisory) board itself to determine. In this context, the board should generally apply the criteria laid down at national level but may deviate from them in light of special circumstances (point 13.2, sentence 3 of Recommendation 2005/162/EC). Point 13.3 provides for complementary transparency, both ad hoc when a new director is appointed and annually. Ultimately, Recommendation 2005/162/EC thus applies a 'comply or explain' approach: The framework established by the Recommendation and national rules implementing it is not binding, but deviations have to be publicly justified.[91]

However, as already mentioned there are binding independence requirements for the audit committee of PIE (*see supra* §7.06[B][1]).

For CRD IV/CRR institutions,[92] the ESMA/EBA guidelines[93] set out further requirements as regards independence.

89. Succinctly Michael Hoffmann-Becking, *Unabhängigkeit im Aufsichtsrat*, NZG 2014, 801, 809: 'Übertriebene Unabhängigkeit führt [...] zu Inkompetenz.' ('Excessive independence leads to [...] incompetence.').
90. Cf. recital 18 sentence 3 Recommendation 2005/162/EC.
91. *See* Lutter, Bayer, and Schmidt, *supra* n. 6, 13.52.
92. As regards the term 'institutions' within the meaning of CRD IV, *see supra* n. 48.
93. ESMA/EBA guidelines, *supra* n. 71, para. 80, 87 et seq.

[E] Diversity

[1] Diversity in General

Both the 2010 Green Paper[94] and the 2011 Green Paper[95] had considered to establish rules on professional, international, and gender diversity in order to further enhance corporate governance by ensuring a broad spectrum of competences. However, so far, the European legislator has not implemented general rules regarding diversity on the boards of companies and there is also no Commission recommendation in this respect. But Article 20(1) sentence 2 lit. g EU Accounting Directive,[96] which was introduced in 2014 by the NRFD,[97] requires PIE to include a description of the diversity policy applied in relation to the undertaking's administrative, management, and supervisory bodies into their corporate governance statement.

Moreover, binding rules as regards diversity have been implemented for CRD IV/CRR institutions.[98] Here, it was of special importance for the European legislator that, to facilitate independent opinions and critical challenges, management bodies should be sufficiently diverse as regards age, gender, geographical provenance, and educational and professional background to present a variety of views and experiences.[99] Hence, in case of significant institutions, Article 88(2) subparagraph 2 lit. a CRD IV requires the nomination committee to evaluate, *inter alia*, diversity of the management body[100] when choosing candidates. Pursuant to Article 91(10) CRD IV, all institutions and their respective nomination committees shall engage a broad set of qualities and competences when recruiting members to the management body and for that purpose put in place a policy promoting diversity on the management body; pursuant to Article 9(1) subparagraph 1 MiFID II, this also applies to other investment firms. These rules are fleshed out further by paragraphs 102 et seq. of the ESMA/EBA guidelines.[101] According to Article 435(2)(c) CRR, institutions shall at least annually disclose their diversity policy; Article 48(b) IFR[102] requires the same for other investment firms.

94. COM(2010) 284, 5.1.
95. COM(2011) 164, 1.1.
96. *Supra* n. 47.
97. Directive 2014/95/EU of the European Parliament and of the Council of 22 October 2014 amending Directive 2013/34/EU as regards disclosure of non-financial and diversity information by certain large undertakings and groups, OJ 2014, L 330/1.
98. As regards the term 'institutions' within the meaning of CRD IV, *see supra* n. 48.
99. Cf. recital 60 sentence 3 CRD IV.
100. With regard to the meaning of the term 'management body', *see supra* n. 48.
101. ESMA/EBA guidelines, *supra* n. 71.
102. Regulation (EU) 2019/2033 of the European Parliament and of the Council of 27 November 2019 on the prudential requirements of investment firms and amending Regulations (EU) No 1093/2010, (EU) No 575/2013, (EU) No 600/2014, and (EU) No 806/2014, OJ 2019, L 314/1.

[2] In Particular: Gender Diversity

Since the beginning of the 2000s, EU and EEA Member States started to introduce gender quotas (e.g., Norway,[103] France,[104] Belgium,[105] and Italy[106]) or at least gender targets into their national laws (e.g., Spain[107]); others at least included recommendations into their corporate governance codes (e.g., Finland,[108] Sweden,[109] and Germany[110] [which included a quota into its national law in 2015[111]]).

The rationale for such rules is threefold: First, they are seen as an instrument to ensure gender equality.[112] Second, in economic terms, they are seen as a tool to ensure

103. Norway introduced a quota of 40% in 2006, § 6-11a Allmennaksjeloven.
104. In France, there is a quota of 20% for listed companies and large companies since 2014, since 2017 it is 40% (Loi point 2011-103 du 27 janvier 2011 relative à la représentation équilibrée des femmes et des hommes au sein des conseils d'administration et de surveillance et à l'égalité professionnelle, JORF point 23 du 28 janvier 2011, p. 1680). Pursuant to the Loi Rixain (Loi point 2021-1774 du 24 décembre 2021 visant à accélérer l'égalité économique et professionnelle, JORF point 300 du 26 décembre 2021), from 1 March 2026, there will be a quota of 30% of all *l'instance dirigeante* for all companies which have had at least 1000 employees for the past three years; from 1 March 2029 the quota will be 40%.
105. The Loi modifiant la loi du 21 mars 1991 portant réforme de certaines entreprises publiques économiques, le Code des sociétés et la loi du 19 avril 2002 relative à la rationalisation du fonctionnement et la gestion de la Loterie Nationale afin de garantir la présence des femmes dans le conseil d'administration des entreprises publiques autonomes, des sociétés cotées et de la Loterie Nationale (Moniteur Belge 14.9.2011, 59600) introduced a quote of 1/3 for listed companies (originally Art. 518bis(1) Code des Sociétés, since 2019: Art. 7:86 Code des sociétés et des associations).
106. Legge 12 luglio 2011, n. 120 Modifiche al testo unico delle disposizioni in materia di intermediazione finanziaria, di cui al decreto legislativo 24 febbraio 1998, n. 58, concernenti la parita' di accesso agli organi di amministrazione e di controllo delle societa' quotate in mercati regolamentati (GU Serie Generale n.174 del 28-7-2011) introduced a quota of 1/3 which applied from 2015. Legge 27 dicembre 2019, n. 160 (GU Serie Generale n.304 del 30-12-2019 - Suppl. Ordinario n. 45) increased the quota to 40%.
107. Art. 75 Ley Orgánica 3/2007, de 22 de marzo, para la igualdad efectiva de mujeres y hombres, BOE núm. 71, de 23/03/2007 provides that certain large undertakings shall endeavour to include a number of women on their board of directors that allows for a balance of men and women by 2015.
108. *See* on this Ina Anne Frost and Leena Linnainmaa, *Corporate Governance: Frauen im Aufsichtsrat – Können wir von unseren skandinavischen Nachbarn lernen?*, AG 601, 607 f (2007).
109. *Ibid.*, at 606.
110. 5.1.2 sentence 2, 5.4.1(2) DCGK 2010.
111. In 2015, the FüPoG (Gesetz für die gleichberechtigte Teilhabe von Frauen und Männern an Führungspositionen in der Privatwirt-schaft und im öffentlichen Dienst v. 24.4.2015, BGBl. I, 642) introduced mandatory gender quotas and targets; these were amended in 2021 by the FüPoG II (Gesetz zur Ergänzung und Änderung der Regelungen für die gleichberechtigte Teilhabe von Frauen an Füh-rungspositionen in der Privatwirtschaft und im öffentlichen Dienst v. 7.8.2021, BGBl. I, 3311). Inter alia, there is a quota of 30% for the supervisory board of AG and KGaA which are listed and subject to co-determination (§ 96(2) 1 AktG, for KGaA in conjunction with § 278(3) AktG). Moreover, if the management board of AG or KGaA which is both listed and subject to parity codetermination consists of more than three persons, at least one man and one woman must be a member of the management board (§ 76(3a) AktG, for KGaA in conjunction with § 278(3) AktG). In addition, there are rules on gender targets for certain types of companies (*see* § 76(4) AktG, §§ 36, 52(2) GmbHG, 9(3), (4) GenG).
112. *See, e.g.*, political agreement on the Gender Balance Directive, document 9880/22 ADD 1, recital 1; with respect to German law: Explanatory Notes to the government draft of the FüPoG, BT-Drs. 18/3784, at 40.

that companies draw upon the pool of highly trained and qualified women.[113] Third, in terms of corporate governance, it is widely considered that the presence of women on boards improves corporate governance because team performance and the quality of decision-making are enhanced due to a more diverse and collective mind-set incorporating a wider range of perspectives and therefore reaching more balanced decisions.[114]

However, in particular rules imposing 'hard quotas' have also been subject to severe criticism. Especially where quotas are not subject to candidates of both genders being equally qualified, there are good arguments to doubt whether they are compatible with EU law and national (constitutional) law.[115] Moreover, there are concerns that quotas for women on boards lead to discrimination of qualified men and to not sufficiently qualified women being appointed as board members. In addition, there is also the problem that women on boards may be respected less because there will be a perception that they have only gained their position because of their gender.

The Commission had already announced in 2010 that it also wanted to introduce EU rules on gender quotas.[116] In 2012, it presented a proposal for a directive on gender balance among non-executive directors of listed companies.[117] But debates in the European Parliament and the Council soon reached a deadlock. In the meantime, Article 88(2) subparagraph 2 lit. a CRD IV required the nomination committee of significant CRD IV/CRR institutions[118] to decide on a target for the representation of the under-represented gender in the management body and prepare a policy on how to increase the number of the under-represented gender in the management body in order to meet that target. Pursuant to Article 9(1) subparagraph 1 MiFID II, this also applies to other investment firms.

Finally, after very controversial discussions for almost ten years and significant modifications, an agreement on the directive on gender balance on boards was reached in trilogue negotiations in June 2022.[119] Although this political agreement[120] is subject to formal approval by the European Parliament and by the Council, one may assume that the final text of the Directive will (almost) identical it. Hence, the following overviews is based on the political agreement.

The directive applies only to listed companies with registered office in a Member State whose shares are admitted to trading on a regulated market in one or more

113. *See*, e.g., political agreement on the Gender Balance Directive, *ibid.*, recital 10 sentences 1-4; with respect to German law: Explanatory Notes to the government draft of the FüPoG, *Ibid.*, at 42.
114. *See, e.g.*, political agreement on the Gender Balance Directive, *ibid.*, recital 1 sentences 5-6; with respect to German law: Explanatory Notes to the government draft of the FüPoG, *ibid.*
115. *See, e.g.*, Tim Drygala, *Harte Quote, weiche Quote und die Organpflichten von Vorstand und Aufsichtsrat*, NZG 2015, 1129 et seq.; Mathias Habersack and Jens Kersten, *Chancengleiche Teilhabe an Führungspositionen in der Privatwirtschaft - Gesellschaftsrechtliche Dimensionen und verfassungsrechtliche Anforderungen*, BB 2819 ff. et seq. (2014).
116. COM(2010) 491, 3.
117. COM(2012) 614.
118. As regards the term 'institutions' within the meaning of CRD IV, *see supra* n. 48.
119. IP/22/3478.
120. Text: document 9880/22 ADD 1.

Member States (Article 1, 2(1)). SMEs are excluded (Article 2(8), 3). It establishes only minimum standards (Article 7).

Pursuant to Article 4(1), Member States shall ensure that listed companies are subject to either of the following objectives to be reached by 30 June 2026: (a) members of the under-represented sex hold at least 40% of non-executive director positions; or (b) members of the under-represented sex hold at least 33% of all director positions, including both executive and non-executive directors. Listed companies which are not subject to (b) shall set out individual quantitative objectives in view of improving gender-balanced representation of both sexes among executive directors (Article 4(1a)). Article 4a lays down comprehensive rules on the means to attain the objectives – some of which seem rather impracticable.[121] Article 5 sets out far-reaching reporting obligations.

However, Article 8a allows Member States to suspend the application of Article 4a and Article 4(1a) in certain cases: First, where members of the under-represented sex hold at least 30% of the total number of all non-executive director positions or at least 25% of the total number of all director positions in listed companies (Article 8a(1)(a)). Second, where national legislation requires corresponding quotas; effective, proportionate, and dissuasive enforcement measures apply in case of non-compliance; and all listed companies not covered by such national legislation set individual quantitative objectives for all director positions (Article 8a(1)(b), 'German rule').

Regarding sanctions, the directive limits itself to establishing a framework (*see* Article 6(1)).

After almost a decade of negotiations, the directive only achieves a minimum harmonisation of gender balance on boards of listed companies.[122] Moreover, if one takes a closer look, it becomes immediately obvious that the directive leaves Member States a broad leeway.[123] At least with respect to the rather impracticable rules on the means to reach the objectives laid down in Article 4a, this is a positive thing.[124] Whether such gender quotas are generally a sensible means to achieve real gender equality in terms of equal opportunities is an entirely different question.[125]

§7.07 BOARD COMMITTEES

To make board work more efficiently, it is generally recommended to set up special committees, especially in areas which are particularly sensitive or prone to conflicts of

121. With good reasons and in detail: ECLE, *Gender Balance Broom Wagon – The Resurrection of the Commission Proposal on Improving the Gender Balance among Board Members*, OBLB 11 March 2022.
122. Jessica Schmidt, *BB-Gesetzgebungs- und Rechtsprechungsreport zum Europäischen Unternehmensrecht 2021/22*, BB 2022, 1859, 1864.
123. *Ibid.*
124. *Ibid.*
125. *Ibid.*

interests.[126] Work in smaller committees, especially if they consist of persons specialised in the relevant field, is generally more efficient than in the plenum; moreover, in case of sensitive issues, it is easier to ensure confidentiality within the committee.[127]

[A] Listed Companies

The creation of committees is one of the key points of Recommendation 2005/162/EC. Point 5, sentence 2 in Recommendation 2005/162/EC advises the creation of nomination, remuneration, and audit committees within the (supervisory) board of listed companies – of course only where that board plays a role in the areas of nomination, remuneration, and audit under national law. However, in the interest of flexibility, point 7.1, sentence 2 in Recommendation 2005/162/EC expressly allows companies to group the functions as they *see* fit and create fewer than three committees. Moreover, in companies where the (supervisory) board is small, the function assigned to the three committees may be performed by the (supervisory) board as a whole, provided that it meets the composition requirements advocated for the committees and that adequate information is provided in this respect (point 7.2, sentence 1 in Recommendation 2005/162/EC).

According to the concept of Recommendation 2005/162/EC, the nomination, remuneration, and audit committee should generally only have an advisory function (cf. recital 10 sentence 3 and point 6.1, sentence 2 in Recommendation 2005/162/EC). However, the (supervisory) board should not be precluded from delegating part of its decision-making powers to committees when it considers it appropriate and when this is permissible under national law (cf. recital 10, sentence 4 and point 6.2, sentence 2 in Recommendation 2005/162/EC.). The Recommendation also explicitly emphasises that even in case of a delegation, the (supervisory) board remains fully responsible for the decisions taken in its field of competence (cf. recital 10 sentence 4, point 6.1 sentence 3 Recommendation 2005/162/EC). Moreover, it advises that any delegation of decision-making power should be explicitly declared, properly described, and made public in a fully transparent way (point 6.2, sentence 2 in Recommendation 2005/162/EC).

Composition, role and operation of the nomination, remuneration and audit committee are further specified in Annex I of Recommendation 2005/162/EC. All committees should normally be composed of at least three members, and in companies with small (supervisory) boards, two members are sufficient (Annex I, point 1.1 of Recommendation 2005/162/EC). The majority of the members of the committees should be independent;[128] in addition, the remuneration and audit committee should be composed exclusively, the nomination committee should at least have a majority of

126. Cf. G20/OECD Principles of Corporate Governance, 2015, VI.E.2; Report of the High Level Group of Company Law Experts on a modern regulatory framework for company law in Europe, 4.11.2002 (<https://ecgi.global/sites/default/files/report_en.pdf>), III.4.1a; recital 9 sentence 1 Recommendation 2005/162/EC.
127. *See, e.g.*, Jens Koch, *Aktiengesetz* (16th ed. C.H. Beck 2022), § 107 para. 24.
128. On independence *see supra* §7.06[D].

non-executive or supervisory directors (Annex I point 2.1, paragraph 2, point 3.1, paragraph 2, point 4.1 of Recommendation 2005/162/EC). The exact mandate of each committee created should be described in the terms of reference drawn up by the (supervisory) board (Annex I, point 1.3 of Recommendation 2005/162/EC). But Annex I, points 2.2, 3.2, and 4.2 of Recommendation 2005/162/EC set out a minimum catalogue of tasks of the three committees.

Section III of Recommendation 2009/385/EC added further recommendations on the creation, composition, role, and operation of the remuneration committee.

[B] Public Interest Entities

In order to enhance effective internal control and the quality of financial reporting,[129] the 2006 SAD[130] introduced a requirement for PIE[131] to establish an audit committee. The rules were significantly tightened by Directive 2014/56/EU[132] in order to reinforce the independence and technical competence of the audit committee.

Pursuant to the general rule in Article 39(1) sentence 1 SAD, each PIE shall have an audit committee. However, there are a number of exceptions. Article 39(2) SAD lays down to cases where Member States may provide that the functions assigned to the audit committee may be performed by the administrative or supervisory body as a whole: on the one hand, in case of PIE which meet the criteria set out in Article 2(1)(f), (t) Prospectus Directive[133] (Article 2(f) Prospectus Regulation),[134] i.e., SMEs; on the other hand, where an audit committee forms part of the administrative body or of the supervisory body of the audited entity. Moreover, Article 39(3) SAD permits Member States to decide that certain PIEs are not required to have an audit committee. In addition, according to Article 39(4) SAD, Member States may require or allow PIEs not to have an audit committee provided that it has a body or bodies performing equivalent functions to an audit committee.

Article 39(6) SAD sets out a (non-exhaustive) catalogue of tasks of the audit committee. Moreover, as already explained (*see supra* §7.06[B][1]), Article 39(1) SAD also lays down requirements regarding the composition of the audit committee.

129. Cf. recital 24 sentence 1 SAD.
130. *Supra* n. 74.
131. Defined in Art. 2 point 13 SAD.
132. *Supra* n. 77.
133. Directive 2003/71/EC of the European Parliament and of the Council of 4 November 2003 on the prospectus to be published when securities are offered to the public or admitted to trading and amending Directive 2001/34/EC, OJ 2003, L 345/64.
134. Regulation (EU) 2017/1129 of the European Parliament and of the Council of 14 June 2017 on the prospectus to be published when securities are offered to the public or admitted to trading on a regulated market, and repealing Directive 2003/71/EC, OJ 2017, L 168/12; last amended by Regulation (EU) 2021/337 of the European Parliament and of the Council of 16 February 2021 amending Regulation (EU) 2017/1129 as regards the EU Recovery prospectus and targeted adjustments for financial intermediaries and Directive 2004/109/EC as regards the use of the single electronic reporting format for annual financial reports, to support the recovery from the COVID-19 crisis, OJ 2021, L 68/1.

[C] CRD IV Institutions and Other Investment Firms

After the financial crisis, point 6.4, 8(a) Recommendation 2009/384/EC[135] sets out additional recommendations on the creation, role, composition, and tasks of the remuneration committee. In 2010, CRD III[136] made a remuneration committee mandatory for significant credit institutions and laid down requirements relating to its precise composition (Annex V point 24 Directive 2006/48/EC[137] as amended by CRD III). This was then (without any significant changes) included into Article 95 CRD IV, which today applies to all CRD IV/CRR institutions, i.e., credit institutions and systemic investment firms. Details are specified in the EBA guidelines on sound remuneration policies.[138]

Moreover, following up on contemplations in the 2010 Green Paper,[139] the CRD IV also lays down mandatory rules on the establishment, composition, and role of a nomination committee (Article 88(2) CRD IV) and of a risk committee (Article 76(3), (4) CRD IV). The establishment of a risk committee and of a remuneration committee is also required for other investment firms (Article 28(4), 33(1) IFD).[140] Moreover, other investment firms shall also establish a nomination committee (Article 9(1) subparagraph 1 MiFID II, Article 88(2) CRD IV).

§7.08 CONCLUSION

In light of the various board systems in the Member States and the fact that early attempts at harmonising them ended in failure, EU law has so far not established a general framework as regards board composition of companies governed by the national laws of the Member States.

Instead, the European legislator has so far relied on targeted harmonisation of selected issues, leading to a kind of 'mosaic harmonisation'. The various harmonisation measures were often initiated in light of scandals (e.g., accounting scandals) or crisis situations (e.g., the 2007/2008 financial crisis), but sometimes also by political motivations (e.g., the directive on gender balance on boards). Moreover, the EU legislator has clearly focused on companies which are most important economically and financially: listed companies and companies in the financial sector. Hence, most

135. Commission Recommendation 2009/384/EC of 30 April 2009 on remuneration policies in the financial sector, OJ 2009, L 120/22.
136. Directive 2010/76/EU of the European Parliament and of the Council of 24 November 2010 amending Directives 2006/48/EC and 2006/49/EC as regards capital requirements for the trading book and for re-securitisations, and the supervisory review of remuneration policies, OJ 2010, L 329/3.
137. Directive 2006/48/EC of the European Parliament and of the Council of 14 June 2006 relating to the taking up and pursuit of the business of credit institutions, OJ 2006, L
138. EBA, Guidelines on sound remuneration policies under Arts 74(3) and 75(2) of Directive 2013/36/EU and disclosures under Art. 450 of Regulation (EU) No 575/2013, EBA/GL/2005/22.
139. Cf. COM(2010) 284, 5.1.
140. However, small investment firms within the meaning of Art. 32(4)(a) IFD are excepted.

stringent rules have deliberately been set for CRD IV/CRR institutions (i.e., credit institutions and systemic investment firms).

The various rules and recommendations also focus on different aspects in order to improve corporate governance. On the one hand, there are rules and recommendations addressing the profile of the individual board members (e.g., qualification, fitness, independence) which aim at ensuring that the company is governed by sufficiently capable persons. On the other hand, there are rules and recommendations focussing on the functioning of the board as a whole (e.g., rules on committees, requirements as regards a certain number of independent directors); their goal is to ensure that the board as a whole works smoothly and efficiently.

However, there seems to be growing tendency to instrumentalise rules on board composition for extrinsic purposes which are not - or at least not exclusively - aimed at addressing traditional corporate governance issues. One example is the recent Gender Balance Directive. Moreover, against the background of the current focus on sustainable corporate governance, there are discussions on whether and in what way sustainability could or should be reflected in board composition.

Will and should EU law strive for more harmonisation in the area of board composition? This is ultimately a very political question. Yet one may ask whether it would not be time to abandon the current 'piecemeal' approach and strive for a more streamlined and coherent framework.

CHAPTER 8

Boards in Small- and Medium-Sized Companies?

Mette Neville

§8.01 INTRODUCTION

The discussion of corporate governance, including new instruments and new agendas, primarily focuses on listed companies, leaving a more limited focus on corporate governance instruments in small- and medium-sized enterprises (SMEs). However, SMEs[1] are the backbone of many economies[2] and an engine for economic growth all over the world. In 2021, they represented 99.8% of businesses, employed 66.2% of employees, and generated approximately 53% of the value added in Europe. Between 2012 and 2017, they created 85% of all new jobs. Therefore, it is of great socio-economic importance that SMEs are properly governed so that their full potential is released. From a business perspective, governance is more significant than ever if SMEs are to be able to stay relevant or even grow in times where the business environment is constantly changing due to crises like COVID-19 and megatrends like digitalisation and sustainability. Areas where studies show that most SMEs lack behind large enterprises. Hence corporate governance in SMEs warrants attention. This chapter discusses whether SMEs should have a board of directors (board) and which role the board should play to enhance good corporate governance. To address this, the corporate governance problems in SMEs need first to be identified as they are very different from those in listed companies (§8.02). Next, it must be analysed whether a

1. There are no universal definitions of SMEs. Typically, a mix of quantitative criteria are used to define SMEs. According to the definition setup by the European Commission (EU Recommendation 2003/361), SMEs are firms with less than 250 employees, while not exceeding a turnover of EUR 50 million or EUR 43 million in the balance sheet.
2. Cf. Europe SBA Fact Sheet 2021 https://single-market-economy.ec.europa.eu/smes/sme-strategy/sme-performance-review_en#paragraph_885.

board can help overcome these problems (§8.03). Some of the problems linked to the board as a corporate governance mechanism are identified in §8.04, and finally it is discussed whether there is a need for regulatory instruments to strengthen the role of the board in SMEs, either through changes in company law through special corporate governance codes for SMEs or through other measures (§8.05). §8.06 concludes.

§8.02 CORPORATE GOVERNANCE IN SMEs

There is no universal definition of Corporate Governance as the approach to corporate governance has evolved over time. In this chapter, corporate governance is defined as the set of principles and practices by which the enterprise is directed and controlled, for example the various mechanisms defining and influencing the power and decisions of the chief executive officer (CEO), ownership structures, board of directors, finance, and reporting systems, etc.[3] It also relates to the regulatory framework for SMEs and their board, for example, Company Law, codes of conduct, etc.

When trying to address whether SMEs should have a board, it requires an understanding of whether a board has potential to enhance good governance in SMEs. To answer this, the most relevant governance problems in SMEs must be identified. This is not necessarily easy as the problems are not only different from those in large companies but SMEs are also a very heterogeneous group of enterprises. Consequently, the corporate governance problems and requirements may differ due to a variety of factors[4] such as the ownership structure, type of ownership, size, life circle stage,[5,6]

3. Cf., Jonas Gabrielsson, Morten Huse, & Carl Åberg, *Corporate Governance in Small and Medium Sized Enterprises*, in *Advances in Corporate Governance: Comparative Perspectives*, 83 (Helmut K. Anheier & Theodor Baums, eds, Oxford University Press 2020). The definition is close to the original Cadbury definition from 1992.
4. Morten Huse, *Corporate Governance: Understanding Important Contingencies*, 4 (2) Corporate Governance & Control, 41–50 (2005), Mette Neville, *The Many Roles of Boards in SMEs*, in *Board of Directors in European Companies: Reshaping and Harmonising Their Organisations and Duties*, 179–217 (Hanne S. Birkmose, Karsten Engsig Sørensen & Mette Neville eds, Kluwer Law International 2013).
5. Several organisational lifecycle models (OLC) have been developed to interpret and predict the course of business development stages. *See* for a review Marek Matejun & Zdenek Mikolás, *Small Business Life Circle: Statics and Dynamics*, 9 (6) Engineering Management in Production and Services 48–58 (2017). They give a holistic approach to how the company's development from small to large goes through different phases, which make different demands on the board, the managing director, and the organisation. The life circle models have been criticised, e.g., because they see the development of an enterprise as a linear process. A dynamic life circle approach has to acknowledge, that SMEs do not follow a linear process, but rather can be seen as dynamic networks of belief systems, relationships, and organising principles that enable them to navigate and adapt to changing conditions. Coral Ingley, Wafa Khlif, & Lotfi Karouri, *SME Growth Trajectories, Transitions and Board Role Portfolios: A Critical Review and Integrative Model*, 35 (6) Int. Small Bus. J. 729–750 (2017). A new version of the OLC model move focus to the environment to anticipate the need for organisational adaptation, focussing on a process where the 'engine' is the changes associated with the variety and uncertainty of the environment. *See* Luigi Mosca, Martine Gianecchini & Diego Campagnolo, *Organizational Life Cycle Models: A Design Perspective*, 10 (3) J. Organ. Des. 18 (2021).
6. Also, other contextual factors such as type of ownership, industry, national, geographical, and cultural differences are contextual factors which has influence on the governance issues of the company, cf. Huse, *supra* n. 4, at 41–50.

and what kind of external pressure the companies are exposed to. External pressure may, e.g., be in the form of not only a crisis like COVID-19 or the war in Ukraine but also other radical changes in the SMEs' business environment, e.g., due to major agendas such as sustainability or the exponential development in digital technologies.[7] This means that it is probably not possible to determine a singular best way of defining the role of the board. The board's role and the governance structures must be based on the different internal and external factors that influence corporate governance in SMEs. From the outset, it must therefore also be flagged that it is outside the scope of this chapter to identify the corporate governance problems from a full contingency perspective.[8] Instead, the problems are elucidated based on one of the most important context factors and by applying a major default approach.

One of the most important contextual factors is the *ownership and management structure.*[9] The corporate governance theory originates from agency theory, which addresses the specific problems that arise in companies with an ownership and management structure characterised by dispersed ownership and centralised management. The central problem is the conflicting interests of owners and managers, which can arise when managers (agents) manage a company on behalf of the owners (principals). The objective in agency theory is to reduce agency costs by imposing internal controls where boards should act as watchdogs to align the managers' interests with the shareholders' interests.[10]

In SMEs, the governance structure looks very different. SMEs are typically closely held with one or a few owners. A survey of Danish public and private limited companies from 2015[11] shows that approximately 75% of Danish private limited companies only have one shareholder.[12] In addition, there is usually a complete or partial overlap between the owners and the company's management as 81.5% of all both public and private limited companies are owner managed. A consequence of this typical ownership and management structure is that the owner-manager is not subordinate to the board since the owner-manager elects the board. The owner, therefore, in practice has the authority to overrule board decisions and dismiss board members. Thus, contrary to the premise of company law, the board in owner-managed companies cannot in practice react to managerial deficits by replacing the owner-manager. This means that the varying motivations of owner-managers may influence

7. Mette Neville, *Corporate Governance and Strategic Change in SMEs in a Digital Age – the Board as a Digital Catalyst?* In *Festschrift in Honour of Rolf Skog* 963–991 (Ronald J. Gilson et al. eds, Norsteds Juridik 2021).
8. Morten Huse et al., *Power Shift, Strategic Change and Board Roles in SMEs: A Portfolio Approach,* ECMLG 2016 – Proceedings of the 12th European Conference on Management 88–98 (2016).
9. Neville, *supra* n. 4, at 179–217 and Carsten Fode & Mette Neville, SMV-bestyrelsen. Hele vejen rundt (Karnov 2018); Huse, *supra* n. 4, at 41–50; Gabrielsson et al., *supra* n. 3, at 83.
10. Shaker A. Zahra & John A. Pearce, *Boards of Directors and Corporate Financial Performance: A Review and Integrative Model,* 15 J Manage 291–334 (1989); Eugene F. Fama & Michael C. Jensen, Separation *of Ownership and Control,* 26 (2) J Law Econ 301–325 (1983).
11. Morten Bennedsen & Kasper M. Nielsen, *Ejerledelse i Danmark* (2015). https://www.cbs.dk/files/cbs.dk/ejerledelse_i_danmark_rapport.pdf. *See also* Niels Westergård-Nielsen (ed.), *Danske bestyrelser og deres medlemmer - hvem bestemmer i danske selskaber?* (Center for Corporate Governance. Copenhagen Business School 2020)
12. And 67% of all private and public limited companies, *Ibid.*, at 11 (Westergaard-Nielsen).

the boards' role in SMEs[13] and the SME-boards' prospect of for example making strategic decisions to strengthen the company.[14] If the balance of power over strategic decisions falls primarily to the owner-manager, then the board has limited options to influence the actual shaping of company strategies and future performance.[15] Literature[16] further states that the results from strategic choices and performance levels of organisations can be viewed as reflections of the values and cognitive bases of powerful actors in the company.[17] In the many companies that are owner-managed, the owner-manager is the company's most important resource. In literature, SMEs are sometimes described as an extension of the owner-manager, where the owner-manager's goal is also the company's goal.[18]

[A] Agency Problems in SMEs

Due to the above-mentioned prevalent ownership and management structure, most SMEs do not have a traditional agent-principal problem. However, ownership structures are not necessarily static. A new ongoing research project 'Ownership Dynamics'[19] shows that approximately one-fourth of the responding SME owners during their ownership expanded their circle of shareholders, for example in the form of a new active co-owner, a capital fund, or employees or next generation as part of a succession process.[20] If the number of shareholders increases, then agency problems can arise and minority shareholders who are not part of management have an interest in monitoring

13. Neville, *supra* n. 7.
14. Olof Brunninge, Mattias Nordquist, & Johan Wirklund, *Corporate Governance and Strategic Change in SMEs: The Effects of Ownership in SMEs: The Effect of Ownership, Board Composition and Top Management Teams*, 29 Small Bus. Econ 295, 298 (2007).
15. Literature states that in small privately owned companies, the founder/owner-manager's close control over the board generally works against board empowerment, John L. Ward & James L., *A Survey of Board Practices*, 1 (3) Fam. Bus. Rev, 289–308 (1988); Morten Huse, *Board Composition in Small Enterprises*, 2 (4) Entrepreneurship & Regional Development 363–374 (1990).
16. Brunninge et al., *supra* n. 14, at 295–308; Mikko Mustakallio, Errko Autio, & Shaker A. Zahra, *Relational and Contractual Governance in Family Firms: Effects on Strategic Decision Making*, 15 Fam. Bus. Rev. 205–222 (2002); Donald C. Hambrick & Phyllis A. Mason, *Upper Echelons: The Organization as a Reflection of Its Top Managers* 9(2) Academy of Management Review 193–206 (1984).
17. Brunninge et al., *supra* n. 14, at 298, pointed out that empirically investigating such linkages may be of both practical and scholarly importance.
18. Calvin Wang, Elizabeth A. Walker, & Janice Redmond, *Explaining the Lack of Strategy Planning in SMEs: The Importance of Owner Motivation*, 12 (1) Int. J. Organ. Behav. 1–16 and 431–446 (2007); Mark R. LeCournu, Richard G.P. McMahon, David M. Forsaith, & Anthony M.J. Stanger, *The Small Enterprise Financial Objective Function: An Exploratory Study*, 34 (3) Small Bus 1–16 (1996); Neville, *supra* n. 7, 963–991.
19. *See* Marina B. Madsen, Mette Neville, Hanna Almlöf, & Kajsa Haag, *Ejerskabsdynamik i SMV'er – Et svensk/dansk projekt om problemer og løsninger ved ændringer i ejerkredsen*, Nordisk Tidsskrift for selskabsret, 74–96 (2019:4).
20. And if the owner-manager is being replaced with an external director, some of the more classic agent-principal problems may arise, cf., e.g., Marc-Phillippe Weller, *Corporate Governance in geschlossesenen Gesellschaften: Status Quo und Anforderungen*, 41 (2–3) ZGR: Zeitschrift für Unternehmens- und Gesellschaftsrecht 386–417 (2012).

majority shareholder and the CEO/owner-manager's behaviour.[21] Also conflicts pose a corporate governance problem.[22] As shareholders are often part of the management and/or board,[23] conflicts will directly affect the management of the company calls for both minority protection rules and regulatory solutions to conflicts,[24] cf. Hanna Almlöf's contribution to this book. Such conflicts also affect the role of boards in SMEs.

[B] Corporate Governance Problems Linked to the Internal Operations of the Company

Even though the agency problems are typically reduced in SMEs as most SMEs are owned by a single shareholder, the size, ownership, and management structures of SMEs often, however, give rise to other corporate governance challenges. These are frequently linked to the internal operations and can negatively influence the SMEs' ability to adapt to a changing business context.[25] As pointed out by Brunninge et al. (2007),[26] irrespective of whether adverse environmental conditions or new opportunities call for strategic change, such change is often difficult for SME managers to accomplish.[27] The owner-manager is frequently the main decision-maker and the epicentre of everything in the company,[28] but he or she may lack the necessary management competences[29] and an organisation that possesses all relevant competences.[30] Equally, a financial focus is important, but is often limited[31] in SMEs, which

21. *See* Karsten Engsig Sørensen & Mette Neville, *Interessentskabslignende anpartsselskaber*, in *Selskabers organisation* (Paul Krüger Andersen ed. DJØF Forlag 1997).
22. A not yet published survey conducted as part of the ongoing project 'Ownership Dynamics' showed that in 58% of SMEs subsequent disagreements had arisen between the owners, and in 25% of all the companies the conflicts were serious. Typical conflict themes were power relations, strategy for the company, work effort, risk profile, return requirements, etc.
23. Bennedsen & Nielsen, *supra* n. 11. *See also* Westergård-Nielsen, *supra* n. 11.
24. *See* Mette Neville, *Shareholder Conflicts in Small and Medium Sized Companies*, in *Shareholder Conflicts* (Paul Krüger Andersen, Nis Jul Clausen, & Rolf Skog eds, DJØF Forlag 2006); Mette Neville, *A Statutory Buy-Out Right in SMEs – An Important Corporate Governance Mechanism and Minority Protection?* in *Company Law and SMEs* (Karsten Engsig Sørensen, & Mette Neville eds, Thomson Reuters 2010); Hanna Almlöf's contribution to this book; Weller, *supra* n. 20, at 386–417.
25. *See* Neville, *supra* n. 7, at 963–991.
26. Brunninge, et al., *supra* n. 14, at 295–308.
27. Carl Kampel, *Why Privately Held and Family-Owned Businesses Should Have Independent Boards of Directors*, 28 Financial Executive 18 (2012); Gabrielsson, et al., *supra* n. 3, 83.
28. Neville, *supra* n. 7, at 963–991.
29. Tammi S. Feltham, Glen D. Feltham, & James L. Barnett, *The Dependence of Family Businesses on a Single Decision-maker*, 43 *J. Small Bus.* 1–15 (2005).
30. David J. Storey, *Optimism and Chance: The Elephants in the Entrepreneurship Room*, 29 (4) Int. Small Bus. J. 303–323 (2011).
31. E.g., simple company periodic reports, budgets, performance indicators, and risk management are often limited or even lacking, cf. Kuldeep Singh & Deepa Pillai, *Corporate Governance in Small and Medium Enterprises: A Review*, 22 (1) Corporate Governance: International Journal of Business in Society 23–41 (2022); Gabrielsson, et al., *supra* n. 3, 94. From the European Commission, there is a strong focus on risk management as a central part of the corporate governance instrument in SMEs. EU Directive 2019/1023 Council directive (EU) 2019/1023 of 20 June 2019 on preventive restructuring frameworks, on discharge of debt and disqualifications, and on measures to increase the efficiency of procedures concerning restructuring, insolvency,

can have serious consequences for the viability and the growth of the company. For example, an overview over the strategic room for manoeuvring is difficult to obtain.

A deficient financial overview can also make it difficult to obtain financing from banks or external investors.[32]

These internal governance problems are potential threats to the viability and growth of SMEs. Furthermore, a fast-changing business environment increases complexity and the need for a strategic and financial focus, managerial skills, etc.[33] A growth project carried out by *Vidensforum*[34] over a period of three years offered the participating SMEs the use of a specifically devised growth model.[35] The result showed positive effect on the growth in EBITDA[36] and the financial robustness of the SMEs[37] from the enhanced governance through a stronger focus on strategic business development,[38] manager and organisational behaviour,[39] and cash flow parameters. This means that a board can create value by focussing on the strategic development, the organisation, and cash flow parameters of the company.

§8.03 THE BOARD AS A CATALYST FOR GOOD CORPORATE GOVERNANCE IN SMEs?

SMEs are a heterogeneous group but looking at SMEs from a major default approach, there is a need to improve the internal governance of SMEs, both in relation to the financial control and especially the strategic focus of the business. In SMEs with

---

and discharge of debt, and amending Directive (EU) 2017/1132 (Directive on restructuring and insolvency OJ L 172/18 26.6.2019, commonly known as the Insolvency Directive, has been introduced to ensure that risks can be identified sufficiently early that they can be avoided or dealt with. It deals with how to create suitable corporate governance structures that can help maintain the viability of SMEs.

32. Raisal Ismail & Arun Kumar Tarofder, *Corporate Governance Structure and Firm Performance in Small and Medium-sized Enterprises (SMEs) in Sri Lanka: A Path to Access the Credit*, 12 (1) J. Man. 28–37 (2015); Singh & Pillai, *supra* n. 31, at 23–41; Gabrielsson, et al., *supra* n. 3, at 94. Financing has since long been identified as one of the primary challenges in creating growth in SMEs, and several initiatives have been launched at EU level.
33. Jonas Gabrielsson & Morten Huse, *Outside Directors in SME Boards: A Call for Theoretical Reflections*, 1 (1) Corporate Board: Role, Duties & Composition, 28–37 (2005).
34. The research is financed by a consortium between Centre for SME, Aarhus BSS, a large banking organisation (Nykredit) and a large accounting organisation (PWC).
35. To start with, the businesses were screened with a view to establishing their business model, strengths, and weaknesses. Thereafter, there were sparring sessions to exchange ideas with the owner-manager every quarter, quarterly learning modules for all the participants on, for example, innovation, including business model innovation, pricing policy and segmentation, leadership, strategy, making use of a board of directors, etc.
36. Generally, larger impact on EBITDA than on turnover is revealed.
37. The research material revealed for example, that 32% of the research participants had used all trinity antecedents. The growth in EBITDA ranged from +27% to +31%. In comparison, the 27% of the research participants, who had not used any of the trinity antecedents, had a growth in turnover, which ranged from + 99% to -23% and growth in EBITDA ranged from +143% to -47%. A more detailed insight will be published in near future.
38. *See* Alexander Osterwalder & Yves Pigneur, *Business Model Generation* (Wiley 2010).
39. Jolande Jacobi, *The Psychology of C.G. Jung* (Yale University Press 1973); Kim S. Cameron, & Robert E. Quinn, *Diagnosing and Changing Organizational Culture – Based on the Competing Values Framework* (Wiley 2011).

multiple owners, there may also be a need to address the agency problems described in §8.02[A].

[A] The Role of the Board: Straight from the Horse's Mouth

Boards and owner-managers in SMEs respectively both emphasise the strategic role of the board when asked to assess, what they consider to be the most important role of the board, cf. for example a small 2022-survey among the participants of the Programme for SME-boards offered by Aarhus University (Table 8.1).[40]

Table 8.1 How Would You Describe the Primary Function of the Board? Remember Your Answer Should Specifically Reflect the Board of Which You Are a Member

To exercise top-level control function	30%
To initiate and embed the strategy	34%
To strengthen the management efficacy in the company	30%
To be sparring partner for the management	64%
To be sparring partner for the owner/owners	32%
To be an ambassador for the company	4%
To contribute with specific knowledge in a number of areas which is lacking in the company	43%
To ensure management executes decisions made	21%
To ensure the organisation is adapting in accordance with the development of the company	21%

If owner-managers were asked the same questions,[41] Nykredit/Neville 2010 showed that 53% found the strategic role most important.[42] Thus, both the board members themselves and the owner-managers see the board having a strategic and an advisory role and less of a control function.

[B] The Potential for Boards in SMEs: A Theoretical Perspective

Competences, strategy, and financial overview are identified as some of the key corporate governance issues in SMEs. Thus, the board role is closely linked to enterprise governance defined by the International Federation of Accountants (IFAC), as 'the set of responsibilities and practices exercised by the board and executive management with the goal of providing strategic direction, ensuring that objectives are

40. Up to three ticks.
41. It is important to note, that the owner managers asked all had a board with external board members.
42. This is in line with for example Anita Van Gils, *Management and Governance in Dutch SMEs*, 23(5) Eur. Manag. J. 583–589 (2005).

achieved, ascertaining that risks are managed appropriately and verifying that the organization's resources are used responsibly'. Notably, this should be adjusted to SMEs.[43] Putting it in a board theoretical perspective, this approach to the role of the board is found in the resource-based board theories, where the board is regarded as an important human capital resource.[44] A board with experienced board members, with the right competences, can help overcome an internal lack of competences in the company,[45] and add value to strategic decision-making by advising the owner-manager and ensuring a more professional and less-intuitive process.[46] Boards are also seen as having an important external role. According to the resource dependence theory, the board members have an external function linking the firm to its external environment, for example through networking.[47] However, just as an agency perspective on the role of boards is too narrow, a one-sided application of the resource approach to the board is also too narrow. Even though the agency problems are reduced in SMEs, §8.02[A] shows that different types of agency problems can arise in SMEs, for example minority protection issues. From a board-role perspective, the board must make sure that decisions made by the board are in the interest of the company and not only the majority shareholder. The board also has an important role when conflicts arise between shareholders, mitigating in conflicts between shareholders, cf. above.[48] As all shareholders are often members of the board, the external members frequently have an important role in mitigating conflicts.[49] So instead of discussing the role of boards as a

43. IFAC, *Enterprise Governance – Getting the Balance Right* (2004).
44. Jay Barney, *Firm Resources and Sustained Competitive Advantage*, 17 J. Manage 99–120 (1991); C.K. Prahalad & Gary Hamel, *The Core Competence of the Corporation*, Harv. Bus. Rev., 79–91 (1990); David J. Teece, Gary Pisano, & Amy Shuen, *Dynamic Capabilities and Strategic Management*, 18(7) Strateg. Manag. J. 509–533 (1997); Jeroen Van den Heuvel, AnitaVan Gils, & Wim Voordeckers, *Board Roles in Small and Medium Sized Family Businesses: Performance and Importance*, 14(5) CGIR 467–485 (2006); Mustakallio, et al., *supra* n. 16, at 205–222. For a detailed review of the theoretical basis for the advisory role of the board, *see* Yannick Bammens, Wim Voordecker, & Anita Van Gils, *Board of Directors in Family Businesses: A Literature Review and Research Agenda*, 13 Int. J. Man. Rev. 134–152 (2011). Equally, stewardship theory is based on the assumption that the role of boards is to facilitate and empower the top management team (TMT) in the area of strategy. The stewardship approach, in contrast to the agency theory, regards the management, including the board of directors as stewards of the owners. Thus, board members and the executives are not inclined to indulge in opportunistic behaviour, but rather to pursue the interests of the owners. The board of directors should therefore not be too controlling but instead focus on being supportive by empowering the CEO and act as mentor. According to the stewardship theory, the board and the CEO practise shared decision-making.
45. Richard Castaldi & Max S. Wortman Jr., *Boards of Directors in Small Corporations: An Untapped Resource*, 9 (2) American Journal of Small Business 1–10 (1984).
46. Howard H. Stevenson & David E. Gumpert, *The Heart of Entrepreneurship*, 64 (2) Harv. Bus. Rev., 85–94 (1985); Castaldi & Wortman Jr., *ibid.*, at 10.
47. Jeffry Pfeffer & Gerald Salancik, *The External Control of Organisations: A Resource Dependence Perspective* (Stanford University Press 1978); Zahra & Pearce, *supra* n. 10 291–334; Odd J. Borch & Morten Huse, *Informal Strategic Networks and Boards of Directors*, 18 (1) Entrepreneurship: Theory and Practice 23–36 (1993).
48. Fode & Neville *supra* n. 9, chapter 6.
49. Neville, *supra* n. 4, at 217.

choice between the two approaches, they should be combined to apply a multi-theoretical approach.[50]

This means that a properly functioning board has the *potential* to enhance good governance in SMEs if these tasks are directly assigned either to the board through provisions in the Companies Act or by the board's management mandate being so broad that they can take on the role (and do it cf. below). Typically, company legislation stipulates the governance structure, the division of tasks between the various company bodies, as well as fundamental principles guiding the decision-making of the board (i.e., the fiduciary duties). The pattern is less clear when it comes to specific positive duties such as the strategic role of the board and its financial oversight duty. In some jurisdictions, the legislation is detailed, while Company Law in other jurisdictions contains a generally formulated management mandate or in some cases do not contain separate provisions on the board's management duties. Denmark is an example of a jurisdiction where company legislation directly establishes that the board has a strategic responsibility. § 115 in the Danish Companies Act specifies that the board is responsible for the *overall and strategic management of the company*, just as it must ensure a sound organisation.[51] An example of a provision stipulating a broad management duty is the Swedish Companies Act, Chapter 8, § 4, which instructs that the board is responsible for the company's organisation and the management of the company's affairs. The concept of 'the management of the company's affairs' is not detailed in the Swedish Companies Act, the reason for which is said to be that the conditions may vary from company to company.[52] Similar broad management provisions are found in other jurisdictions. In some jurisdictions such as the United Kingdom (UK), the Companies Act does not contain provisions on the more specific duties of the board besides the fundamental principles. This is due to a tradition where the UK has relied heavily on corporate governance being dealt with privately rather than through public code or legislation. [53] It was, for example, only with the corporate reform in 2001 that the fundamental principles of the work of the board were codified. On the more specific duties, the UK still refers to contractual freedom. Table A part 2(3) contains a

50. Gabrielsson & Huse, *supra* n. 33, at 28–37; Van den Heuvel, et al. *supra* n. 44, at 467–485 (2006); and Amy J. Hillman & Thomas Dalziel, *Boards of directors and firm performance: integrating agency and resource dependence perspectives*, 28 Academy Management Review 383–396 (2003); Blanca Arosa, Txomin Iturralde & Amaia Maseda, *Outsiders on the board of directors and firm performance: Evidence from Spanish non-listed family firms*, 1 (4) J. Fam. Bus. Strategy 236–245; Catarine M. Daily, Dan R. Dalton & Albert Canalla, *Corporate Governance: Decades of dialogue and data*, 28 Academy of Management Review 379 (2003); Gavin J. Nicholson & Geoffrey Kiel, *Can Directors Impact Performance? A Case-Based Test of Three Theories of Corporate Governance*. 15 (4) CGIR, 585–608 (2007).
51. On the role of boards and board work in practice, *see* Fode & Neville, *supra* n. 9; and Zahra & Pearce, *supra* n. 10.
52. Prop. 1997/98: 99. p. 78.
53. Corporate regulation has been based upon a notion of the company as a private organisation and has accordingly had remarkably little to say of mandatory nature, about either structure or the proper role of boards or their individual members. What is said is usually been put forward as default rules subject to contractual exclusion or variation by the parties, cf. John De Lacy, *The Reform of United Kingdom Company Law*, 149 et seq. (2002).

default provision according to which 'Subject to the articles, the directors are responsible for the management of the company's business, for which purpose they may exercise all the powers of the company.' Finally, in some jurisdictions where a two-tier system is applied, the supervisory board is not allowed to take an active strategic role. The main task of the supervisory board is to supervise and exercise control over the finances and the management board. The management board handles the over-all management, including the strategic planning and decision-making. In the German version of the two-tier system, the management board is given much power as the supervisory board is not allowed to instruct the management board specifically.[54] The board typically has a control function, including controlling the firm's financial performance, monitoring the firm's strategies, and the performance of the management. However, again it differs how directly this follows from company legislation. The two-tier system like the German example is insufficient in fulfilling the needs of SMEs. However, only few SMEs use the German public limited company as company form, and the management structure is often more flexible for private limited companies. In company law the management structures vary, but regardless of the management system applied, there is a common tendency across most jurisdictions that there is more flexibility in relation to the choice of governance system in the types of private limited companies, which target SMEs, than in public limited companies. This is exemplified by the German GmbH, the Dutch BV,[55] the Belgian BV,[56] the Danish ApS, and the Swedish Privata Bolag.[57] Hence, it is often possible to have a company be led by a single managing director, typically with the option[58] of electing either a supervisory board (two tier) and/or a board according to the one-tier model. In Denmark, e.g., neither there is requirement that a board has to be set up nor are there specific requirements on the composition, if a board is set up.As can be seen from the above discussions, there is much to suggest that the board has the *potential* to enhance good governance in SMEs, as both the control and strategic role is in many jurisdictions are part of the duties or the broad management mandate for the board. However, the

54. However, differences apart, there is also a strong trend towards convergence in practical ways of board organisation, cf. Poul Davies, Klaus J. Hopt, Richard Nowak, & Gerard van Solinge (eds), *Corporate Boards in European Law: A Comparative Analysis* (Oxford University Press 2013). *See also* Georg Ringe, *German versus Nordic Board Models: Form, Function, and Convergence*, 65 (1) Nordic Journal of Business 27–40 (2016), http://njb.fi/wp-content/uploads/2016/03/Ringe.pdf.
55. The board of directors in a Dutch limited liability company (*besloten vennootschap*, 'BV' or *naamloze vennootschap*, 'NV') may consist of only one managing director.
56. A private limited liability company in principle consists of a one-tier structure made up of one or more directors. In the case of a public limited liability company, it is possible (but not common) to choose between a one-tier structure (consisting of a board of directors or a sole director) or a two-tier structure (consisting of a supervisory board and a management board).
57. In Sweden and Denmark, a dual governance structure is only required in public limited companies. In the private limited companies, there is only a requirement for one management body. In Sweden, the default has been maintained that it is the board of directors (board) that is mandatory, while in Denmark it is the management board (CEO).
58. However, this can also be mandatory if the company fulfils different conditions. For example, if the GmbH is subject to German Co-Determination Law (*Mitbestimmung*), the implementation of a supervisory board is mandatory following some listed ratios.

question is whether boards also take on that role in practice and create the expected value. Here there are both good and bad news, cf. the following sections.

[C] The Good and the Bad News on the Value Creation of Boards

[1] The Good News

The question of whether a board creates value has preoccupied researchers for a long time. Scholars working with the link between boards and the performance of the company have most frequently focused on the question of whether external board members[59] enhance the performance of the company. The results have been ambiguous,[60] but nevertheless the opinion has prevailed that SMEs can benefit from external board members.[61] The good news is that a new Danish study[62] shows that the election of new board members and especially the election of new *external* members is associated with growth in productivity in Danish companies. An important finding is that the greatest growth in productivity is seen in small companies. Interestingly, it is stated that this is probably because external members constitute an important resource in SMEs. Hence, the board can contribute to the company's expertise and ability to make investments, which can increase revenue and efficiency.[63] Other – but older – Danish studies[64] show that having a board results in an increased focus on some of the factors that are considered important with a view to running a healthy business, e.g., risk management and strategy.

[2] The Bad News

The sections above indicate that boards not only have the potential to create value in the form of better governance in SMEs but that they also often in practice do create value. However, the news is not all good. The bad news is that there also seem to be various challenges. First, most SMEs do not have a board (§8.03[C][2][a]). Even if the SME has a board, the value creation may be challenged by issues linked to the composition of the board (§8.03[C][2][b]) to lack of competences (§8.03[C][2][c]) and

59. There are wide differences between how different studies define 'external board members'. In a Survey by *Nykredit/Neville* (2010), external board members were defined as those who are neither owners nor family members of owners.
60. Cf. Nicholson & Kiel, *supra* n. 50, at 585–608; Dan R. Dalton, Catherine M. Daily, Travis S. Certo, & Rungpen Roengpitya, *Meta-analyses of Financial Performance and Equity: Fusion or Confusion?* 46 Academy of Management Review 13–26 (2003); Dan R. Dalton, Catherine M. Daily, Allan E. Ellstrand, & Jonathan L. Johnson, *Meta-analytic Reviews of Board Composition, Leadership Structure and Financial Performance,* 19 (3) Strateg. Manag. J. 269–290 (1998).
61. Catherine M. Daily and Dan R. Dalton, *Board of Directors Leadership and Structure: Control and Performance Implications*, 1 J. Financ. Econ. 55–64 (1993); Morten Huse, *Researching the Dynamics of Board-stakeholder Relations*, 31 Long Range Planning 218–226 (1998); Borch & Huse, *supra* n. 47, at 23–36.
62. *See* Westergård-Nielsen, *supra* n. 11.
63. *Ibid.*
64. *See* Neville, *supra* n. 4, *at* 179–217.

to how boards work in practice (§8.03[C][2][d]). Finally, as pointed out earlier in §8.02, the value creation of the board may be challenged by factors linked to the owner's (manager's) motivations and behaviour.

[a] The Absence of Boards in SMEs

In most SMEs, there is no question at all about whether and how the board can create value, as they simply do not have a board. Company Law often only requires a board in public limited companies, whereas it is typically voluntary in private limited companies. In the one-tier systems only a board is required, and this may consist of the managing director. In Denmark, it is left to the shareholders in private limited companies (anpartsselskaber), whether they want to set up a board or not. Danish figures show that only 10% (2016 figures) of Danish private limited companies have a board, and studies also show, that micro-enterprises and owner-managed SMEs have the lowest board-rate. This may be explained by the fact that as ownership is not separated from the control, the need for a board is seemingly quite small (agency theory).[65] However, it can also be explained by the fact that many owner-managers are driven by the urge for self-determination, which speaks against establishing a board. Many founders and owner-managers reject the idea of a board, as they conceive that a board will mean the loss of control over their company.[66] The fact that most SMEs, if possible, choose not to establish a board raises the question of whether there is a need to strengthen the use of boards of directors through a requirement to have a board also in private limited companies (§8.05).

[b] Internal Board Members

Different studies, cf. above, and theory indicate that the value creation of the board is to a large extent connected with the presence of external board members. However, various studies, for example the study by Westergård-Nielsen et al., show that only 36%-40% of Danish board members are external members.[67] Companies that are owner-managed have the lowest proportion of external members, namely 31%. The study does unfortunately not say anything about how many SMEs have entirely internal boards, as the survey only shows the total number of external board members in relation to the total number of board members. However, older Danish studies have shown that one-third of private limited company SMEs have entirely internal boards.[68]

---

65. *See* Westergård-Nielsen *supra* n. 11, at 31 et seq. Fama & Jensen describe closely held companies as small, non-complex organisations, and they consider boards and risk management systems to be excessive in relation to SMEs, Eugene F. Fama & Michael C. Jensen, *Separation of Ownership and Control*, 26 (2) J of Law & Econ. 301-325 (1983).
66. Fode & Neville, *supra* n. 9, at 22 et seq; Coral Ingley, Lotfi Karoui, & Wafa Khlif, *Power Shift, Strategic Change and Board Roles in SMEs: A Portfolio Approach*, ECMLG 2016 – Proceedings of the 12th European Conference on Management, 88 (2016).
67. Defined as not being family members, co-owners, or representative for a parent company, or employees.
68. Nykredit/Neville, Ejerlederanalysen 2011.

If external members are a prerequisite for the board to create value, then the question is what can be done to increase the number of external members (*see* §8.05).

[c] *Lack of the Right Competences*

Encouragingly, many SMEs have external board members, but external members as such is, however, not enough. It is important that the professional competences reflect the company's strategic direction and the challenges that the board faces. In SMEs, it should also include the external board members complementing the competences of the managing director and the organisation. Clearly, the board of directors should not be involved in day-to-day operations, but there may be a need for close sparring where the organisation and the owner-manager are weak in terms of competence. The changing business environment and new agendas such as digitalisation and green transition challenge SME boards. Two questionnaire surveys from 2018/2019[69] and from 2020/2021[70] showed that the major challenges relating to the board's work with digitalisation was (1) lack of knowledge of the new digital technologies, (2) ability to analyse where digitalisation can create the greatest value, and (3) the lack of competences within the organisation. Without the right competences, it is difficult to fulfil the strategic role of the board, and the surveys illustrate that the board composition with traditional competences such as law, finance, and general strategic competences may have to be reconsidered. However, as SMEs have small boards, there is a limit to how many different competences can be represented. Therefore, new ways of adding competences must be considered. In an ongoing project 'The SME-board as a Digital Catalyst',[71] three models for digital competence development in SME boards were implemented in thirty-seven SME-boards over a two-year period. One group of boards were supplemented with a new board member with digital competences matched with the need of the company. A second group was offered a board educational programme (six days) with focus on digitalisation,[72] and the last group were matched with an external consultant. Of the thirty-seven participating companies, a subset of twenty SME-boards is until now evaluated and ranged on a scale[73] inspired by Nadler's system for board involvement.[74] Nadler's levels of board involvement are not directly applicable since they are not targeting SME boards.[75] As can be seen from Table 8.2, the

69. *SMV-bestyrelsen i en digital tidsalder*, https://mgmt.au.dk/fileadmin/SMVbestyrelsenIenDigitalTidsalder_Rapport.pdf
70. *Krise som digital driver i SMV-bestyrelser* https://mgmt.au.dk/fileadmin/MGMT/Subsites/Centre/SMV/Reports/Digital-Katalysator-2021-Rapport-170x240mm_Indholdssider_08.pdf
71. The research conducted is financed by Industrial Foundation, a geographically anchored business association with no influence on research conducted. Centre for SMEs at Aarhus BSS owns the project, but the project is managed as a cooperation with DTU (Technical University of Denmark) and Gejst Studio.
72. At the Danish Technical University (DTU).
73. In accordance with their own statements during in depth-interview. Thanks to Jeanette Brogaard at the Centre for SMEs for her valuable contribution to analysing data.
74. David A. Nadler, *Building Better Boards*, 82(5), Harv. Bus. Rev. 102–11 (2004).
75. For example, Nadler assumes that the board has the power to replace management. This is, however, not the case with owner-managed companies.

interventions meant that the boards participating in the project are now more actively involved in the strategic work than before.

Table 8.2 The Boards Level of Strategic Involvement in Digitalisation

	At the Time of Entry in the Project	*At the End of the Project Period*
The Passive Board No or very limited focus and involvement in the digitalisation of the company. DigitaliSation is not integrated in the strategic work of the board.	9	3
The Certifying Board Awareness of the importance of digitalisation, but digitalisation is only to a limited extent part of the strategic considerations of the board. Digitalisation is initiated by the CEO. Stays informed about the digital initiatives initiated by the CEO. Rarely challenges the decisions on digital initiatives made by the CEO.	7	2
The Engaged Board Provides insight and support to the CEO/management team on the digitalisation of the company at a strategic level. Conducts useful, two-way discussions about key decisions on digitalisation facing the company. Seeks out sufficient expertise on digitalisation to add value to decisions.	2	6
The Intervening Board Becomes intensely involved in decision-making around digitalisation. Frequent contact and discussions with the CEO or management team about digitalisation.	2	9
The Operating Board Very close to and sometimes involved in the implementation process. Fills gaps in management expertise.		

Source: In the project 'The SME Board as a Digital Catalyst'.

It should be emphasised that the table is not a grading system. Nonetheless, if boards are passive in terms of addressing digitalisation, they will face difficulties in meeting Danish company law requirements regarding the board's overall responsibility for the general and strategic management of the company. Whether the board's role should be certifying, engaged, or intervening remains an open question. It depends on several factors, including how digital the management and the organisation is.

As mentioned, Table 8.2 shows the development in twenty of the thirty-seven participating boards. The analysis of the last seventeen companies will be analysed in the autumn 2022, and it will also be analysed how the different interventions worked in practice and what results were achieved.

[d] *The Traditional Board Work May Be Challenged*

To fulfil all tasks at a level that creates value, the board must have a strong focus on the planning of the board's work. It is common to use planning tools such as the annual cycle, the rules of procedure, well-thought-out agendas, etc., to ensure efficiency.[76] A new Danish Survey by Board Partner[77] indicates that many boards lack the necessary professional approach to board work. However, one may question whether planning is sufficient[78] or whether the board also needs new ways and tools to facilitate its strategic work. A survey 'Krise som digital driver i SMV-bestyrelser' (2021) shows that boards need to be more agile and develop and execute faster than before. The responding board members point at the need to have a better overview, be closer to the core business and collaborate more with the owner-manager/CEO.[79] This challenges the traditional approach to board work with four to six meetings annually. All in all, it seems that board work in SMEs needs revision if boards are to be able to create the necessary value in the future.[80]

§8.04 PAVING THE WAY FOR BOARDS IN SMEs?

This chapter has so far provided an overview of some of the corporate governance challenges and also explained why the board may be the organisational unit that has the greatest potential to enhance the level of corporate governance in SMEs. However, there are also several challenges to the board's value creation. Briefly summarised challenges are:

- many SMEs do not have a board;
- SME boards are often composed of purely internal board members;
- board members, including the external ones, often lack the right competences;

76. Fode & Neville, *supra* n. 9, at 451 et seq.
77. From Board Partner, https://boardpartner.dk/vaerktoejer/bestyrelsesrapporten-2022/.
78. Mette Neville, *Fremtidens SMV-bestyrelse - værdiskabelse i en turbulent verden* in *Festskrift for Rolf Doteval* (Maria Karlsson-Tuula, Annika H. Persson, & Patrik Lindskoug eds, Juristförlaget i Lund 2020).
79. Neville, *supra*, n. 7.
80. *Ibid.*; and the survey, *Krise som digital driver i SMV-bestyrelser (2021), https://mgmt.au.dk/fileadmin/MGMT/Subsites/Centre/SMV/Reports/Digital-Katalysator-2021-Rapport-170x240mm_Indholdssider_08.pdf.*

- the board's way of working is often not sufficiently professional and is partly challenged by a changing world; and finally
- the ownership can create barriers that obstruct the board's strategic work.

The question is whether it is possible to meet some of these challenges through various regulatory measures, for example, by introducing a board requirement in the form of hard law or through default rules or recommendations in soft law.

[A] Hard Law Instruments

A primary source of corporate governance instruments is the company laws of individual jurisdictions, which determine the board as an internal mechanism of corporate governance. A proper legal framework may help enhance the desired role of the board. The differences between the rules governing boards in different jurisdictions make it difficult to discuss concrete legal solutions regarding strengthening the role of boards. However, at a more general level, it can be discussed whether the flexibility concerning the governance structure should be reduced by hard-law provisions with the aim to enhance the role of boards as a corporate governance mechanism.

Fundamentally, one should consider whether it is a legislative task to try to force SMEs into better corporate governance to unleash their growth potential. Research demonstrates that owner-managers run a business for many different reasons, but growth and financial outcome is rarely the most important parameter.[81] This raises the question, whether one should not respect that SMEs are private economic entities where there are no market considerations. In relation to the application of hard-law regulation, this should then focus on introducing provisions that protect creditors and minority shareholders.

In addition, the value creation of the board is extremely difficult to regulate through hard law, as value-creating board work is a puzzle consisting of many pieces, none of which can be dispensed with. Focusing on the internal role of boards, the puzzle includes for example pieces as illustrated in Table 8.3.

81. Fode & Neville, *supra* n. 9, at 22 et seq., Wang, et al., *supra* n. 18, at 1–16 and 431–446; C. Gray, *Growth Orientation and the Small Firm*, in *Small Enterprise Development Policy and Practice in Action* (Kevin Caley, Elizabeth Chell, Francis Chittenden, & Colin Mason eds, Sage Publications 1992); Storey, *supra* n. 30, at 303–323; Panikkos Poutziouris, *The Strategic Orientation of Owner-managers of Small Ventures: Evidence from the UK Small Business Economy*, 9 (5) International Journal of Entrepreneurial Behaviour & Research 185–214 (2003).

Table 8.3 Factors That Influence The Board's Value Creation

The establishment of a board	External – and maybe independent – members	The right competences	Good ownership
Effective board work	Dynamic board work	Good collaboration with the owner-manager	Strategic and financial focus

Source: Author's own

The specific contents of each piece in practice also depends on the specific company's governance challenges. Looking at each piece individually, it is of course possible to introduce a legal requirement for a board in SMEs. This would reduce the flexibility that has otherwise been a fundamental principle in many company laws where private limited companies should be allowed the discretion to voluntarily adopt their own governance structure and shape other internal mechanisms that reflect how they want to organise their business relationship. SMEs as a group span from companies with a single owner and perhaps only one employee, for example, who make websites, to companies with up to 250 employees in the form, for example, of an innovative production company with export activities. The requirement of a board would pose burden and cost on very small and simple companies, whereas the production business in all likelihood would benefit from a board. That means, that it is probably necessary to introduce conditions, which must be met, before a board is required. It is very difficult to decide on the right conditions. It could be obvious to link these to size and maybe exempt micro businesses from a requirement for a board. However, business complexity is not always linked to size, and according to new Danish research, the value creation of the boards with external members seems to be greater in smaller companies than in larger companies.[82] So even though at first sight it may be tempting to introduce a legal requirement for a board, it is more difficult in practice. The decision must be based on more research and analyses of consequences. Maybe, a mentor or an advisory board could be an important first step towards a board in small SMEs, when the complexity grows.

As indicated by studies, the real value creation is linked to the presence of external board members, but most company laws set very few rules relating to the composition of the board in private limited companies. Consequently, many SMEs choose to establish internal boards. Thus, it may be tempting to introduce a legal requirement for outside and maybe independent board members. In SMEs, however, it must be stressed that competence is more important than independence.[83] In addition, it is difficult to decide what proportion of board members should be external, as this may differ from company to company. If a hard-law solution should apply in

82. Westergård-Nielsen, *supra* n. 11.
83. Code Buysse: Corporate Governance for non-listed enterprises.

companies where there is no market considerations and typically no traditional agency-linked problems, one must make sure, that it enhances the governance and in turn leads to value creation. Therefore, further studies should be carried out to create a solid and valid basis for the decision. One hypothesis is that the value creation may depend on whether the other pieces in the board puzzle are met, for example that the board has the right competences, is actively involved, and conducts the board work in an effective manner and that the board collaborates in a dynamic way both internally and with the management board.[84] For example, if the owner-manager does not want the involvement of the board or is forced to have an unwanted board with external board members, he or she can easily side-track the board. Examples of potential side-tracking could be denying the board the necessary information or not involving the board in the decision-making processes. It should also be taken into consideration that too strict and stringent hard-law provisions could hamper corporate entrepreneurship by imposing disproportionate burdens and costs on small companies.[85] As many owner-managers appear sceptical towards boards, it may be an option to consider the inclusion of alternatives in company law, such as advisory boards. It may not be the perfect solution but could be an important first step for improving the governance in SMEs, as it can provide competences and advice, but without exposing the owner-managers to the control they wish to avoid.

[B] Soft-Law Instruments: One Size Does Not Fit All SMEs

An alternative to hard-law solutions may also be soft-law solutions in the form of codes of conduct, which may be more appropriate. Codes of conduct have originally focused on listed companies and are often based on a comply or explain principle, making it possible for the market to decide, whether the corporate governance behaviour of the individual company is appropriate. However, in recognition that, e.g., different ownership structures entail special corporate governance challenges, and one size therefore does not fit all, several codes of conduct have been developed for different types of companies and ownership structures. In Denmark, for example, corporate governance codes have been developed for boards in listed companies, boards of business foundations, democratic companies like cooperatives, etc., which also means that corporate governance codes have spread from listed companies to larger unlisted companies. The question is whether codes could also provide a useful framework for improving corporate governance in unlisted SMEs?

The European Commission raised the question in the Greenbook on European Corporate Governance COM(2011) 164:2: 'Should any corporate governance measures be taken at EU level for unlisted companies? Should the EU focus on promoting

84. Finally, one needs to consider the organisations' ability to perform.
85. Joshua Aboi & Charles K.D. Adjasi, *Corporate Governance and Small and Medium Enterprises Sector: Theory and Implications*, 7 (2) Corporate Governance 111-122 (2007); Mette Neville & Karsten Engsig Sørensen, *Promoting Entrepreneurship – The New Company Law Agenda*, 15(4) Bus. Organ. Law. Rev. 545-584 (2014).

development and application of voluntary codes for non-listed companies?' Approximately 70% of the respondents spoke out against it. Many of the traditional corporate governance mechanisms, for example, were viewed as being too expensive and inappropriate for SMEs. Another argument was that since owners of non-listed companies are typically much closer to their companies, more long-term and more involved than the typical owners of listed companies, governance guidelines for unlisted companies should not be prescribed at EU level.[86] Moreover, one could argue, that a unified code for SMEs would have to take into consideration the diversity of legal frameworks in different countries, different corporate cultures, and first and foremost the diversity of SMEs in size, ownership structure, etc. The European Commission subsequently abandoned the idea of a code for unlisted companies. However, national corporate governance codes may be an alternative, as they do not have to take the diversity of legal frameworks in different countries and different corporate cultures into account. This means that it may be possible to formulate appropriate recommendations although a number of important prerequisites to be considered remain.

First, a code of conduct should not just be a 'simplified' version of corporate governance practices recommended for listed companies, as the governance problems in SMEs are very different from those in listed companies. Second, for SMEs to benefit from corporate governance codes, it should offer solutions that are fitting, which requires that they both address the relevant governance problems and offer appropriate solutions. But the governance problems and solutions are not only different from those found in listed companies. As mentioned earlier, SMEs as a group is very heterogeneous and the governance problems also differ within the group, for example depending on their size, ownership structure, development stage, culture, etc. A uniform code would result in recommendations at a very general level thus not giving real advice to SMEs and risking that the code would be burdensome and costly for SMEs rather than creating the desired value. When it comes to advising SMEs on corporate governance, there is no one-size-fits-all solution. SMEs are highly diverse, and this diversity needs to be considered.[87]

[1] Tailormade Codes: The Way Forward?

National and international organisations have drawn up different codes of conduct with a focus on unlisted companies.[88] Interestingly, from the point of view of this

86. *See*, for example, ACCA No. https://www.accaglobal.com/gb/en/technical-activities/technical-resources-search/2011/july/eu-framework.html and https://safe-frankfurt.de/fileadmin/user_upload/editor_common/Policy_Center/Boecking_Gros_Comment_Green_Paper_CG_Framework.pdf.
87. ACCA, *Governance for All: The Implementation Challenge for SMEs* (2015).
88. *See*, for instance, in Belgium the Buysse Code – Corporate governance recommendations for non-listed enterprises (http://www.codebuysse.be/downloads/CodeBuysse_EN.pdf); in Finland, the Central Chambers of Commerce initiative Improving corporate governance of unlisted companies (http://www.keskuskauppakamari.fi/content/download/19529/421972); in the UK, Corporate Governance Guidance and Principles for Unlisted Companies in the UK, Institute of Directors (http://www.iod.com/MainWebsite/Resources/Document/corp_gov_guidance_

contribution, most codes contain recommendations for the establishment of boards. Recommendations also include, for example, the introduction of external board members and regard this as a solution to the governance problems linked to limited resources and skills in SMEs, cf. §8.02. Also, the work process of boards is often a central focus of attention in the codes.[89] Most codes aim at ensuring the accountability of SMEs and contribute to building trust within the main stakeholder group and help investors manage their risk (external focus). Some codes, however, also focus more specifically on operations as a governance problem. In view of owner-mangers' scepticism towards boards, cf. §8.02, it is surprising that the establishment of an advisory board is not mentioned as an alternative to a board.

Some codes are characterised by being simplified codes for listed companies,[90] but there seems to be a tendency towards recognising that SMEs are not just smaller listed companies[91] and taking the diversity of SMEs into consideration. An example is the pan European initiative by ecoDa, The European Voice of Directors, 'Corporate Governance Guidance and Principles for Unlisted Companies in Europe'. It presents fourteen principles of good governance that are based on a 'dynamic phased approach', which considers the degree of openness, size, complexity, and level of maturity of individual enterprises. The guideline makes a distinction between a basic framework that applies to all companies, including the small companies with simple organisational structures. The guideline also contains more sophisticated recommendations for larger SMEs with more complex organisations. However, the recommendations are still relatively broad so as to apply to a wide range of companies.[92] A differentiated approach is also taken in the Belgium 'Code Buysse: Corporate Governance for Non-listed Enterprises',[93] which takes three differentiating factors into consideration; the shareholding structure of non-listed enterprises, the growth phase in which the enterprise finds itself, and the special relationship between the owners and the board. The code is divided into a general chapter, which applies to all unlisted companies and covers topics such as vision and mission, the judicious use of outside advisors, active

---

and_principles_for_unlisted_companies_in_the_uk_final_1011.pdf). Also in other parts of the world, similar initiatives have been taken, for example *The Corporate Governance Code For Small and Medium Enterprises: Building the Foundations for Growth and Sustainability in Dubai* (SME Dubai and Hawkamah 2011), *The Corporate Governance Code For Small and Medium Enterprises: Building the Foundations for Growth and Sustainability* and *Guidelines on Corporate Governance for SMEs in Hong Kong* (Hong Kong Institute of Directors 2014).

89. *See also* Gabrielsson, et al., *supra* n. 3, at 83.
90. The Finnish code 'Improving Corporate Governance of Unlisted Companies' by the Central Chamber of Commerce is a good example of this. For example, it does not take the very different ownerships structures into account, and the recommendations build on the assumption that the board may appoint and dismiss the managing director. The codes contain recommendations on almost same topics as for listed companies, but in a simplified form.
91. *See* on a differentiated approach for example Weller, *supra* n. 20, at 386–417; Gabrielsson, et al., *supra* n. 3, at 83; Joseph A. McCahery & Erik P.M. Vermeulen, *Corporate Governance of Non-listed Companies*, 210 et seq. (Oxford University Press 2008).
92. Cf. Vladislava Ryabota, Alexey Volynets, Axel Kravatzky, and Helen Carrington, *IFC Corporate Governance Knowledge Publication*, Iss. 43. Private Sector Opinion, 2–16, (2019) and *IFC SME Governance Guidebook* (2019); Weller, *supra* n. 20; McCahery & Vermeulen, *ibid. See* https://ecoda.eu/wp-content/uploads/2019/08/GUIDANCE_-_2010_CG_for_Unlisted_-_EU.pdf.
93. The code also contains specific recommendations for family enterprises – Family governance.

boards of directors, including the task and composition of the board, evaluation, etc., a high-performance (senior) management, involved shareholders, external audit, and shareholder agreement. Chapter II is aimed at family enterprises: Family governance focussing on special governance instruments such as family forum, meetings and charter, succession, and conflicts. Finally, chapter III contains basic recommendations for sound entrepreneurship and is aimed specifically at the entrepreneur him- or herself. Special focus is on the relationship with the company's stakeholders, like banks, suppliers, customers, and personnel, etc., judicious use of outside advisors and the government as partner. A Code with an even more differentiated approach is the relatively new International Finance Corporation's (IFC's) Growth matrix for SMEs, which relies on the life circle approach to governance in SMEs, analysing stages of SME growth from start-up to maturity, and identifying the various opportunities and challenges associated with each stage. Four stages are identified and defined as Start-up, Active growth, Organisational development, and Business expansion. Governance guidance is developed specifically to address these different phases[94] and thereby gradually implementing governance where solutions are coherent with one another as well as with prevailing state-specific business practices, challenges, and objectives.[95] The guide covers five areas of governance across the different stages of development: (1) Culture and Commitment to Good Governance; (2) Decision-Making and Strategic Oversight, 3) Risk Governance and Internal Control, 4) Disclosure, and Transparency and 5) Ownership.

For each stage, a set of specific recommendations is presented.

Some countries have chosen to develop separate codes for specific ownership structures. In Italy,[96] Switzerland, and Germany,[97] for example, a code of conduct for family firms has been developed. One of the recommendations is that, after the initial establishment stage, all companies should be led by a board to encourage fair and balanced weighing of decisions and to reduce the risks associated with the potential deficiencies of the sole director' capabilities. To facilitate proper operation, the Code proposes that the board be composed of a minimum of three members up to a maximum of nine, depending on the size, with the task, e.g., to identify the elements of the medium to long-term strategy; assessment of the adequacy of the company's organisational, administrative, and accounting structure; and to make resolutions on the operations of the company when they are significant at strategic, capital, or financial level.[98]

---

94. It should be noted that the analysis and recommendations are not science based but based on practical experience.
95. Cf. Ryabota, et al., *supra* n. 92, at 2–16 and IFC, *SME Governance Guidebook* (2019).
96. Italian Corporate Governance Principles for Unlisted Family-Controlled Companies (2017).
97. The German Code, Governance Kodex für Familieunternehmen, has its main focus on the code on how to best ensure the influence of the family. Alexander Koeberle Schmid, Karsten Schween, & Peter May, *Governance Kodex für Familienunternehmen in der Praxis – Ergebnisse einer Studie über Familienverfassungen*, 41 Betriebs-Berater 2499–2506 (2011); and critically towards the second edition from 2010 Weller, *supra* n. 20, at 397.
98. A list of all corporate codes including those aimed at SMEs can be found at the homepage of ECGI, https://ecgi.global/content/codes-0

These few examples illustrate a growing acknowledgement that corporate governance is important in SMEs and that one size does not fit all, and therefore a more tailormade approach is necessary to target the diversity of SMEs. But even though a differentiated approach is presented, the recommendations will still often be too broad. For example, IFC recognises that all the characteristics described in the stages will not hold true across all economies, sectors, or types of SMEs.

Taking the path of codes to enhance good governance and strengthen the role of boards is a delicate balance between, on the one hand, finding the necessary level of differentiation and, on the other hand, avoiding a blurred and scattered picture of corporate governance. Too many codes for SMEs could lead to inconvenience and confusion, and as pointed out by Organisation for Economic Co-operation and Development (OECD), overshoot the target of promoting good governance, and hamper the creation of a corporate governance culture through raising awareness and training,[99] cf. below §8.04[B][4].

[2] The Target Audience for the Codes of Conduct

Another relevant question is who the target audience for the codes is. Traditionally, corporate governance codes have been aimed at the board, but if one looks at the challenges listed in §8.02, this is too narrow an approach. Often SMEs do not have boards and if they do, they are often not composed in an appropriate way. These problems are not remedied by a code addressed at the boards. There is a need for owner-managers to gain insight into the value of establishing good governance structures and management behaviours. It requires owner-managers to know what it takes to run a business so that it is competitive, and how to ensure that its position in the market is constantly secured and perhaps strengthened in order that the business can grow. In addition, the owner-manager must identify the blind spots and understand that the board can contribute to strengthening the management layer in the company. The next step is for the owner-managers to be able to make an appropriate competence clarification and recruit the board members with the right competence, chemistry, and cultural match. After this, expectations must be aligned between the board and the owner-manager, and the owner-manager must realise what it takes for his or her part for the board to be able to create value. Recommendations for shareholders and owner-managers should therefore be part of a corporate governance code for SMEs, or codes should be prepared for the board and shareholders / owner-managers, respectively. The need to address the shareholders/founder/owner-manager does not make a code for boards superfluous. It could contain recommendations not only in relation to their tasks and how the work is best organised but also in relation to the special characteristics that apply to SMEs according to ownership structures and related issues, owner-managers' very different motivations and values, etc. Finally, the speed with which SMEs' business environments may change calls for completely new approaches to the work.

---

99. OECD, *Corporate Governance of Non-Listed Companies in Emerging Markets*, 14 (2005).

[3] Comply or Explain

If a code of conduct is introduced, should then the principle of comply or explain be introduced? Arguments against are that there are not the same marked considerations in SMEs as in listed companies, since SMEs in contrast to listed companies, do not rely on the open capital market. Second, as already mentioned, SMEs present a heterogenous group, so if the recommendations are to enhance governance, they must be tailormade.

If tailormade codes are deemed more appropriate and therefore more are developed, then the comply or explain principle may not be applicable, as it will be difficult to decide which codes it should be linked to. Instead, the solution may be to let SMEs decide themselves the extent to which they follow these recommendations and how much transparency they provide. Instead of trying to enforce good governance, codes could function as an inspiration and provide guidelines on how good governance structures and behaviour can be achieved.[100] A 'market pressure' could be created through banks and potential investors reviewing compliance with relevant codes. This mechanism is already on the rise with governance and e.g., the use of external boards applied as a measure by banks when looking at credit ratings.

[4] Codes of Conduct: A Stand-Alone Solution?

With a differentiated approach to corporate governance codes, codes may enhance good governance by offering tailormade advice on good governance for boards and for owner-managers. However, the question is whether codes can stand alone. A recommendation is one thing, another is how to put the recommendations into best practice, going from theory to practice. Several research projects anchored at the Centre for SMEs[101] – for example, *Vidensforum* mentioned above – show how difficult it is to keep focus and work with the fundamental issues such as strategy, organisational development, and financial overview etc. Both due to lack of competences and due to daily operations steeling time and focus. Incidentally, this is also why a board is needed. However, when it comes to the establishment of a board, owner-managers may, as mentioned, be reluctant towards the establishment of a board with external members due to fear of losing control and giving up some decision-making power. Often there is also scepticism as to whether a board can in fact create value. Next, even if they recognise the value of a board, owner-managers still find it difficult to generate a competency clarification, to find the right board members, and to use the board properly once composed.

This raises the question whether training and education should supplement codes. Many different action-based research projects at the Centre for SMEs give an indication. Here, owner-managers have reviewed development and growth processes

100. UK and France recommend that companies that adopt the code should be expected to comply with the recommendations.
101. A research centre at Aarhus BSS focusing on growth and development in SMEs, https://mgmt.au.dk/smv.

over periods from two to four years and a combination of new knowledge, tools tailormade for SMEs, and ongoing sparring from a 'mini-board' actually enhances governance, creates value, and more robustness. The same conclusion is reached by IFC who has supplemented their code with a Guidebook that founders, leaders, and their advisers can use to better understand their experience. It presents good governance practices with examples, templates, tools, and an overall process for how to arrive at a practical action plan. In addition, courses with real life training are held.

§8.05 CONCLUSION

Both theory and empirical studies point at the board as an organisational unit that has great potential to enhance the level of corporate governance in SMEs. However, as pointed out, there are also several challenges to the board's value creation, for example that many SMEs use the flexible regulation of the management structure granted by company law, to not establish a board. Furthermore, in SMEs where a board is established, this frequently does not include elected external board members. Many boards do not plan the board work in an efficient way and do not possess the right competences, and even if a professional, working board with the right competences is established, ownership behaviour may hinder the value creation of the board.

As SMEs are the backbone of the economy, the enhancement of corporate governance is in the interest of society, which leads to a discussion whether it is possible to strengthen the role of boards as a corporate governance mechanism in SMEs through hard-law or soft-law provisions. However, strengthening the role of boards is not an easy task partly because of the diversity of SMEs. The role of the board depends on factors like ownership structure and type, size of the SME, the stage of growth, contingency factors surrounding the business, industry, culture. etc. This may make hard-law initiatives an inappropriate and insufficient solution. Mandatory, hard-law solutions are only suitable where it is possible to reduce the flexibility of company legislation regarding the management structures of SMEs through hard-law initiatives. For example, to force SMEs to have a board and maybe also introduce stricter rules on the composition of the board as well as more explicit duties of the board. However, hard law solutions must necessarily include mandatory provisions where infringement can be established and sanctioned. This means that in relation to the role of the board, one can, through statutory provisions, require that a board is established and set certain types of requirements for its composition. Since, as a group, SMEs span from sole proprietorships to companies with 250 employees and across companies of widely varying complexity, such solutions require careful consideration of when a SME should have a board. If one removes a basic flexibility in the law, there should be research-based arguments to support this, including when and how a board adds value that exceeds the burden and the costs, it will entail. Even if it were possible to target the right companies and introduce a requirement of a board, the question remains whether a coercive solution is appropriate. As the contribution shows, a board does not create value in itself. Value-creating board work is a puzzle with many pieces, which must fit together, and some of the pieces cover conditions that cannot be remedied through hard law. The duties of the board can be specified in the Companies Act, but the value depends on how these are handled in practice. Finally, there is the fundamental issue of the typical ownership and management structure of SME. If an owner-manager does not want a value-creating board, then the board's governance enhancing role can be obstructed through the composition, lack of involvement, and side-tracking. Thus, strengthening the role of boards will probably have to start somewhere else, namely with the owner-manager, who must realise that they have a governance problem, and that the board can help solve it. The next step is for the owner-managers to be able to make an appropriate competence clarification and recruit board members with the right competence, chemistry, and cultural match. After this, expectations must be aligned between the board and the owner-manager. It is a comprehensive process that is difficult to shortcut. One can, however, consider whether, through codes aimed at SMEs, one can increase insight into these matters and thus help to change their behaviour, for example, increasingly set up boards. One could also consider whether company law and/or codes should offer alternatives such as advisory boards, that could help enhance good governance without threatening the power of the owner-manager. As governance problems can vary greatly depending, among other, on the ownership structure of the company or the type of life cycle, codes must have a differentiated approach and the same applies to codes that address the boards. Some countries such as Belgium and organisations such ecoDa and IFC have taken the first steps towards a differentiated approach. Taking the path of codes to enhance good governance and strengthen the role of boards is a delicate balance between, on the one hand, hitting the necessary level of differentiation and, on the other hand, avoiding a blurred and scattered picture of corporate governance. As pointed out, codes will probably not provide the full solution but must be supplemented by educational activities aimed at entrepreneurs, owner-managers, as well as boards.

A complicated and long journey lies ahead for the political system, researchers, and advisers in the various jurisdictions if we really want to strengthen the board's role as a corporate governance enhancing mechanism in SMEs.

CHAPTER 9

Remuneration and Shareholdings of Directors

Christoph Van der Elst

Directors' pay is a pivotal issue in corporate governance. Even before corporate governance became a fashionable topic in the 1990s, remuneration was on the research agenda of companies, academics, and policy makers, and it stayed ever after. In the first part of this chapter, I address how remuneration is being used as an instrument of corporate governance during the different waves of interests in directors' pay. In the pre-corporate governance era, compensation was embedded in the managerialist governance approach of companies: management followed a stakeholder interest approach, and pay was largely tied to supply and demand of managerial services and expertise of running large companies. Later in the twentieth century, the shareholder wealth maximization perspective took root and compensation packages were used as an instrument for increasing shareholder wealth. Corporate governance codes largely supported this approach. Due to managerial power, directors' pay continued to increase and the say-on-pay mechanism must now mitigate exaggerated compensation. In the meantime, compensation is more frequently being used as an instrument to tie pay to sustainability goals.

An important component of directors' pay are shares of the company. Most executive directors' remuneration contracts do contain long-term incentive schemes, which include (options on) (restricted) shares in many different forms and colours according to the jurisdiction preferences, industry characteristics, company specificities, and executive director's requests. All corporate governance codes contain many detailed and lengthy provisions on how the remuneration package with bonuses, long-term incentive schemes, and shareholdings of executive directors should be structured. However, little is known of the recommendations for non-executive directors of acquiring and holding shares in the company and the related corporate practices. In the second part of this chapter, I address this issue. The first section studies the legal framework of the director as a shareholder. Next, the best practices of the compensation of the non-executive directors in different corporate governance codes are investigated. The second part of section two analyses the practices of acquiring and holding shares of non-executive directors in four jurisdictions of which the corporate governance code contains different provisions for the remuneration of non-executive directors. The last part of the chapter provides in a conclusion.

§9.01 DIRECTORS' COMPENSATION AS A GOVERNANCE INSTRUMENT

[A] Compensation in the Pre-corporate Governance Era: From Managerialism to Shareholder Wealth

'The directors of such companies, however, being the managers rather of other people's money than of their own, it cannot well be expected that they should watch over it with the same anxious vigilance with which the partners in a private copartnery frequently watch over their own'.[1] This famous quote of Adam Smith illustrates the agency conflict between the board of directors of a company and its shareholders. Directors of companies hold the residual rights of control and are expected to possess more expertise than the shareholders. However, it can also result in inefficient director-enriching actions which lowers the return of the company. One mechanism overcoming this agency problem is incentivizing contracts inducing the directors to act in the interest of the company. During the era of the principal-agency theory preceding the corporate governance heydays, compensation policies had to give directors the incentives to select and execute corporate strategies that pursued long-term growth of the company.

Overall and as far as compensation data are available, companies practiced a *bonus* to well-performing executive directors aligning the interests of the involved parties. Murphy showed that when larger companies emerged in the early days of the twentieth century, there was a shift from owner-managers to managerial directors without equity stakes for which alternative remuneration schedules were developed with bonuses tied to company revenues.[2] The data support the thesis that the interest of the company included the interest of different stakeholder groups, on equal footing.[3] 'Stockholders have no special priority; they are entitled to a fair return on their investment, but profits above a "fair" level are an economic sin'.[4] Consequently, compensation packages had to take into account the skills and expertise of the managers running the ever-increasing companies rather than shareholder wealth

1. Adam Smith, *An Inquiry into the Nature and Causes of the Wealth of Nations*, 310 (T. Nelson and Sons, London 1852).
2. Kevin Murphy, *Executive Compensation: Where We Are, and How We Got There*, in *Handbook of Economics of Finance* 250 (George M. Constantinides, Milton Harris, Rene M. Stulz eds., Elsevier 2013).
3. An extensive overview of the developments from managerialism towards shareholder wealth maximization can be found in James Park, *From Managers to Markets: Valuation and Shareholder Wealth Maximization*, 47 J. Corp. L. 2, 435–484 (2022).
4. Wilbert Moore, *The Conduct of the Corporation* 9 (Random House, 1962).

maximization. Since the 1930s, information on executive pay had to be disclosed and more studies were investigating the relationship between corporate performance and executive pay. It led to the finding that the pay-to-performance remained similar from the 1930s to the 1980s.[5] Even more remarkable, Frydman and Saks showed that the sensitivity of changes in wealth to corporate performance was stable since the 1950s to the 1980s with a plunge in the 1970s.

In the 1980s, performance related pay became the economic talk of the town and the shareholder wealth maximization idea took root. However, using compensation for the alignment between the interests of directors and management and shareholder wealth was encountering many hurdles. Various reports showed that the size of the company, often measured by sales was the dominant criterion affecting executive compensation, questioning the effects of corporate performance. Murphy was among the first to criticize these views as he successfully argued that the studies omitted important parts of the pay package including stock options, deferred compensation, and stock awards and ignored the performance effects of the different parts of the remuneration package.[6] Nevertheless, making use of remuneration data stretching over the 1960s to the early 1980s and the shareholder returns, he confirmed that sales growth is an important determinant of executive compensation. Testing the self-serving management hypothesis, whereby managers were maximizing their own welfare which would be opposite to the interest of the shareholders, Benston studied the effects of shareholder returns and wealth effects of executive directors in conglomerates.[7] He noted that while the relative holdings of directors in those companies is very limited, the effects of shareholder returns can be considerable. Benston argued that the widespread belief in the self-serving management hypothesis should be taken with much caution and that the (direct and indirect) shareholdings induce directors to act in the interest of the shareholders. Jensen and Murphy expanded the studies of Murphy and Benston with an empirical assessment of both the incentives of the compensation packages in the contract with the chief executive officer (CEO) as well as the effects of stock ownership of CEO's.[8] The study confirms Bentson's findings of the performance incentives that come from ownership of shares. All their indicators show that sensitivity of the compensation to the shareholder wealth is decreasing. Pay-performance sensitivity was nine times higher in the 1930s compared to the 1970s to mid-1980s. Importantly, the study shows that remuneration was already an important corporate governance (alignment) instrument before it became embedded in the corporate governance discussion.

5. Carola Frydman and Raven Saks, *Executive Compensation: A New View from a Long-Term Perspective, 1936–2005*, 23 Rev. Financ. Stud. 5, 2100 (2010).
6. Kevin Murphy, *Corporate Performance and Managerial Remuneration – An Empirical Analysis*, 7 J. Account. Econ., 11–42 (1985).
7. George Benston, *The Self-Serving Management Hypothesis – Some Evidence*, 7 J. Account. Econ., 67–84 (1985).
8. Michael Jensen and Kevin Murphy, *Performance Pay and Top-Management Incentives*, 98 J. Political Econ. 2, 225–64 (1990).

[B] Compensation in the Early Corporate Governance Days: Pay for Shareholder Return

In the 1990s and (only) after the publication of the first corporate governance codes, director compensation became to be seen as a pivotal instrument of good corporate governance. The first corporate governance code, the Cadbury Code was hesitant in identifying compensation as a corporate governance instrument when emphasizing appropriate disclosure of the remuneration packages and referring to the shareholders' requests 'that the remuneration of directors should be both fair and competitive'.[9] Similarly, in the first Dutch and French corporate governance codes, compensation was not immediately addressed as a corporate governance instrument. The Dutch 1997 Peters report referred to an employee stock option plan strengthening the 'involvement in the company over the long term', but it did not specify that these plans must be considered, while the French Vienot I report stressed only that the remuneration committee can be charged with providing recommendations of the remuneration levels and occasionally stock option plans.[10] The focus lied on the role, composition, and functioning of the board of directors.

After a hesitant start, all codes soon considered compensation as an ideal instrument for the *alignment of the interests of directors and shareholders*. The 1995 United Kingdom (UK) Greenbury Code reads in Best Practice C4: 'The performance related elements of remuneration should be designed to align the interests of Directors and shareholders and to give Directors keen incentives to perform at the highest levels.' The Greenbury Best Practices C5 and C6 empower the remuneration committee to consider the eligibility of the director for an annual bonus and a long-term incentive scheme. For executive directors, a common remuneration package includes, according to section 6.14 of the Greenbury Code, a basic salary, benefits in kind, annual bonus, share options, other long-term incentive schemes, and pension rights. The Greenbury Committee considered an annual bonus as a valuable instrument of management, reflecting company performance against targets. The Committee was flexible vis-à-vis long-term incentive schemes with options of which the exercise price could be set at the share price of the granting date or up to 15% below.[11] These schemes 'give Directors a personal financial interest in seeing the share price rise, thus helping to align the interests of Directors and shareholders. In principle, they enable Directors to build up holdings of shares in the company.'[12] Rewarding directors with a predetermined number of shares depending on 'challenging performance criteria' are considered a valuable alternative. All directors should be encouraged to acquire and retain significant shareholding in the company for enforcing the alignment of the interests of both

9. The Committee on the Financial Aspects of Corporate Governance, *Report*, 4.44 (GEE December 1992).
10. Committee on Corporate Governance, *Recommendations on Corporate Governance in the Netherlands*, 4.6 (Amsterdam, 1997); C.N.P.F. and A.F.E.P, *The Boards of Directors of Listed Companies in France*, 20 (Paris, 10 July 1995).
11. Study Group chaired by Sir Richard Greenbury, *Directors' Remuneration*, 6.24 (GEE 17 July 1995).
12. *Ibid.*, 6.27.

directors and shareholders.[13] Similarly, the Dutch Tabaksblat Code of 2003 acknowledged the remuneration of the management board as an important corporate governance instrument, although recognizing next to the 'share price performance' also its relationship with the interests of the company:

> The remuneration structure, including severance pay, is such that it promotes the interests of the company in the medium and long term, does not encourage management board members to act in their own interests and neglect the interests of the company and does not 'reward' failing board members upon termination of their employment. The level and structure of remuneration shall be determined in the light of, among other things, the results, the share price performance and other developments relevant to the company.[14]

In the United States (US), compensation and especially stock options were considered the pivotal instruments for increasing firm value. Share option plans were common practice, and consequently CEOs pay tripled in the 1990s due to the explosion in the use of stock options. Since the mid-90s, stock options became the single largest compensation component of CEOs of S&P 500 firms and by the end of the decade those options accounted for more than half of the compensation.[15] Also, and as a result, the (executive) directors were significant shareholders in the company. Overall, the contingency of CEO-compensation on the achievement of performance goals is common practice. A study of Bebchuk and Tallarita showed that in 2021 the mean part of the performance related compensation of the S&P 100 companies CEOs exceeds 85%, the median being 91%.[16]

[C] Compensation as an Imperfect Corporate Governance Instrument: Managerial Power and Risk-Taking

Noticing these continuously increasing pay packages, Bebchuk and Fried argued in the early years of the new millennium that these compensation packages are to be considered as part of the agency conflict.[17] These scholars show the managerial influence of the remuneration package in the direction of favouring the executive director. The introduction of equity-based compensation did not replace the cash compensation. Executive directors received pay increases in option plans, which were, at best, only partially a result of the directors' own performance. Market and sector trends influenced executive pay, and directors could easily reap those windfalls. Pay

---

13. *Ibid.* 6.41.
14. Corporate Governance Committee, *The Dutch Corporate Governance Code*, Principle II.2 Remuneration (Amsterdam, December 2003).
15. Murphy, *Supra* n. 2, 274–5.
16. Five companies do not provide performance related pay, all others offer more than two-third of the total compensation as performance-based compensation. Lucian Bebchuk and Roberto Tallarita, *The Perils and Questionable Promise of ESG-Based Compensation*, 48 J. Corp. L., Forthcoming (2022).
17. Lucian Bebchuk and Jesse Fried, *Executive Compensation as an Agency Problem*, 17 J. Econ. Perspect. 3, 71–92 (2003); and Lucian Bebchuk and Jesse Fried, *Pay Without Performance* (Harvard University Press, Cambridge 2004).

consultants helped to structure the compensation packages in the advantage of the newly hired executive directors. Research showed that practices of vesting terms of three to five years for the equity component did not filter the 'luck' component, and adequate refining the impact of macro-economic factors in compensation packages is advisable.[18]

Later in the first decade of the new millennium, the role of risk in compensation packages became a hotly debated issue. Especially in financial institutions, the remuneration packages were seen as one of the contributors of the financial crisis at the end of the first decade.[19] Bonuses of directors and other key personnel of (large) (financial) institutions were designed to enhance risk-taking behaviour. The Financial Stability Board issued standards addressing a pay package that incorporates the risk exposure of the firm.[20] Thereto a significant portion of the compensation should be variable, substantially deferred for at least three years and in the event of negative contributions, the unvested portions should be clawed back. The risk component was acknowledged in the European Capital Requirements Directive III.[21] The remuneration policy of the financial institution must address:

> The measurement of performance used to calculate variable remuneration components or pools of variable remuneration components includes an adjustment for all types of current and future risks and takes into account the cost of the capital and the liquidity required. The allocation of the variable remuneration components within the credit institution shall also take into account all types of current and future risks.[22]

In the meantime, claw back provisions, especially when the company needs to file a restatement, became common practice in the US compensation practice.[23]

---

18. Lars Oxelheim, Clas Wihlborg, and Jianhua Zhang, *How to Avoid Compensating the CEO for Luck: The Case of Macroeconomic Fluctuations* in *Research Handbook on Executive Pay*, 159–182 (Randall Thomas and Jennifer Hill eds., Edward Elgar, Cheltenham 2015).
19. European Commission, Green Paper – Corporate Governance in Financial Institutions and Remuneration Policies, 11 (Brussels, COM2010 284 Final, 2 June 2010). David Walker, *A Review of Corporate Governance in UK Banks and Other Financial Industry Entities – Final Recommendations* (London, 26 November 2009).
20. Financial Stability Board, *FSB Principles for Sound Compensation Practices*, 3 (Basel, 25 September 2009).
21. Directive 2010/76/EU of the European Parliament and of the Council of 24 November 2010 amending Directives 2006/48/EC and 2006/49/EC as regards capital requirements for the trading book and for re-securitisations, and the supervisory review of remuneration policies, OJ L 329, 14.12.2010. This Directive is abolished but similar requirements are to be found in article 94 of Directive 2013/36/EU of the European Parliament and of the Council of 26 June 2013 on access to the activity of credit institutions and the prudential supervision of credit institutions and investment firms, amending Directive 2002/87/EC and repealing Directives 2006/48/EC and 2006/49/EC, OJ L 176 27.6.2013.
22. *See* Art. 94 Directive 2013/36/EU of the European Parliament and of the Council of 26 June 2013 on access to the activity of credit institutions and the prudential supervision of credit institutions and investment firms, amending Directive 2002/87/EC and repealing Directives 2006/48/EC and 2006/49/EC, OJ L 176 27.6.2013.
23. Shearman and Sterling, *Corporate Governance & Executive Compensation Survey 2021*, 59–62 (Shearman & Sterling LLP 2021).

[D] Say on Pay and Remuneration Policies: Shareholders Holding the Reins of Remuneration

At the start of the corporate governance era, a participative role of the shareholders in executive directors' compensation packages was not considered as best practice. The Cadbury Code stated explicit:

> The Committee has received proposals for giving shareholders the opportunity to determine matters such as directors' pay at general meetings but does not see how these suggestions could be made workable. A director's remuneration is not a matter which can be sensibly reduced to a vote for or against; were the vote to go against a particular remuneration package, the board would still have to determine the remuneration of the director concerned. In addition, there are such practical considerations as the need to agree directors' remuneration on appointment.[24]

However, soon afterwards, the involvement of the shareholders became a leading best practice. Already in 2002, the UK introduced a mandatory non-binding say-on-pay vote through the Directors' Remuneration Report (DRR) Regulations 2002.[25] The European response followed soon with the 2003 *Modernising Company Law and Enhancing Corporate Governance in the European Union – A Plan to Move Forward*. The European Commission considered the participation of the shareholders key in the issuance of share and share option schemes.[26] Only one year later, the Commission's recommendation added that a 'remuneration statement should be submitted to the annual general meeting of shareholders for a vote'.[27] The example of the UK regulations woke up many jurisdictions that started experimenting with many different forms of say-on-pay systems. In the Netherlands, the Dutch legislator introduced in 2004 a division of powers for remuneration policy and the remuneration packages. The remuneration policy of listed Dutch companies must always be adopted by the general meeting of shareholders. It is common practice that the supervisory board in a two-tier board structure is empowered to determine this individual remuneration package of the executive board members.[28]

24. The Committee on the Financial Aspects of Corporate Governance, *Report*, 4.43 (GEE December 1992).
25. The original version of the regulation can be found (21 March 2022), https://www.legislation.gov.uk/uksi/2002/1986/regulation/3/made.
26. European Commission, *Modernising Company Law and Enhancing Corporate Governance in the European Union - A Plan to Move Forward* (Brussels, COM (2003) 284 final, 21 May 2003).
27. Art. 4.2 of Commission Recommendation of 14 December 2004 fostering an appropriate regime for the remuneration of directors of listed companies OJ L 385 29.12.2004. In 2007 a study of the European Commission found that only a few Member States followed the recommendation of the European Commission of providing a shareholder vote on the remuneration policy (Commission Staff, *Report on the Application by Member States of the EU of the Commission Recommendation on Directors' Remuneration*, SEC(2007) 1022 (Brussels, 13 July 2007)). The European Commission confirmed its viewpoints in Commission Recommendation of 30 April 2009 complementing Recommendations 2004/913/EC and 2005/162/EC as regards the regime for the remuneration of directors of listed companies, OJ L 120, 15.5.2009, 28.
28. Christoph Van der Elst and Anne Lafarre, *Shareholder Voice on Executive Pay: A Decade of Dutch Say on Pay*, 18 European Business Organization Law Review, 56–58 (2017).

In the US, the advisory say on pay vote for top executives' compensation was embedded in corporate life by section 951 of the Dodd-Frank Act.[29] According to the SEC's final rule related to this section, a separate shareholder advisory vote must be provided to the shareholders for approving the compensation of the CEO, the chief financial officer (CFO), and the three most highly compensated executive officers other than the CEO and CFO. Further, shareholders of American companies also regularly vote on the frequency of the say-on-pay vote.

Many other countries introduced other kinds of a say-on-pay vote.[30] Australian companies make use of the two-strike rule. Shareholders of listed companies can 'spill the board' if the company remuneration report receives a negative reception at two consecutive annual general meetings (AGMs) of more than 25% of the votes. The company must organize another general meeting with an agenda containing a resolution to hold fresh elections for directors, not being the managing director.[31]

The European Union (EU) harmonized the say-on-pay system in the Member States in the Shareholder Rights Directive II (SRD II). Shareholders should be offered a binding vote on the remuneration policy at least every four years and a yearly advisory vote on the remuneration report.[32] The SRD II provides guidelines as to the content of the remuneration policy and the remuneration report. Currently, there is mixed evidence as to the effects of these say-on-pay votes.[33]

Another mechanism in the 'fight' against badly composed pay packages,[34] next to the say on pay and accompanying frequency say on pay vote in the US, is the ratio of

29. Dodd-Frank Wall Street Reform and Consumer Protection Act, Pub. L. 111–203, H.R. 4173 (July 2010) (the 'Dodd-Frank Act'). Randall Thomas and Christoph Van der Elst, *Say on Pay Around the World*, 92 Washington University Law Review 671–673 (2015).
30. *See* for an overview Christoph Van der Elst, *Shareholder Engagement and Corporate Voting in Action: The Comparative Perspective* in *Shareholder Engagement and Voting*, 501–536 (Harpreet Kaur, Chao Xi, Christoph Van der Elst, and Anne Lafarre eds., Cambridge University Press 2022).
31. Art. 250V Australian Companies Act.
32. There are exceptions possible, like an advisory vote for the remuneration policy. Article 9b and 9a of Directive (EU) 2017/828 of the European Parliament and of the Council of 17 May 2017 amending Directive 2007/36/EC as regards the encouragement of long-term shareholder engagement, OJ L 132, 20.5.2017. Christoph Van der Elst and Anne Lafarre, *Article 9a and 9b: Say on Pay*, in *The Shareholder Rights Directive II: A Commentary*, 250–284 (Hanne Birkmose and Konstantinos Sergakis eds., Edward Elgar 2021).
33. *See, e.g.*, Jie Cai and Ralph Walkling, *Shareholders' Say on Pay: Does It Create Value*, 46 J. Financ. Quant. Anal. 2, 299–339 (2011); Fabrizio Ferri and David Maber, *Say on Pay Votes and CEO Compensation: Evidence from the UK*, 17 Review of Finance, 527–563 (2013); Gregorio Sanchez-Marin, Gabriel Lozano-Reina, Samuel Baixauli-Soler, and Maria Ernacion Lucas-Perez, *Say on Pay Effectiveness, Corporate Governance Mechanisms, and CEO Compensation Alignment*, 20 Business Research Quarterly, 226–239 (2017).
34. Institute for Policy Studies, *Executive Excess 2013: Bailed Out, Booted, and Busted*, 8 (IPS 2013) (25 March 2022), https://ips-dc.org/wp-content/uploads/2013/08/EE13-FINAL.pdf: 'Of the 500 slots on the highest-paid lists, 38 percent were held by CEOs who led firms that were bailed out or crashed in the 2008 financial crisis, wound up getting fired, or had to pay settlements or fines related to fraud charges'. Dittmann, Maug, and Zhang have shown that restrictions of executive pay packages are difficult to be structured and may have many negative consequences, depending on the restrictive technique being used (Ingolf Dittmann, Ernst Maug, and Dan Zhang, *Restricting CEO Pay*, 17 J. Corp. Finance 1200–1220 (2011).

the total compensation of the CEO to that of a median employee of that company.[35] Ratios of more than 900 to 1 are frequently found in the US.[36] The UK also requires listed companies with more than 250 employees to justify the pay packages of the CEO through the annual disclosure of the ratio of their CEO's pay to the median, lower quartile, and upper quartile pay of their UK employees,[37] but other jurisdictions did not follow in a similar way for disclosing pay ratios like they did for say on pay.

[E] Compensation as an Instrument for Sustainability

A recent remuneration trend which gained ground after the enactment of the International Treaty on Climate Change (Paris Agreement 2015)[38] is the inclusion of environmental, social, and governance (ESG) criteria in remuneration packages of executive directors.[39] According to CGLytics, only 3% of the companies included ESG criteria in a key performance indicator (KPI) in remuneration packages in 2008, increasing to 19% in 2013 and 27% in 2018.[40] The 'social' criterion was the first that was incorporated in the compensation package. Overall, the effect of these KPIs remains limited as in 2018 those ESG-measures accounted for less than 15% of the bonus. In 2020, already 45% of the UK Footsie 100 companies included at least one ESG-measure in their remuneration package, 37% in the annual bonus, and 19% in their long-term incentive scheme.[41] The energy industry is taking the lead. All companies in this industry include ESG measures, predominantly environmental criteria. In other industries, a social criterion is the most common. A similar increase of the use of ESG metrics

35. Section 953(b) Dodd-Frank Wall Street Reform and Consumer Protection Act, Pub. L. 111-203, H.R. 4173 (July 2010) (the 'Dodd-Frank Act').
36. The Shearman and Sterling annual reviews of corporate governance practices found in nine (2021) and in six (2020) of the largest 100 companies exceeding this threshold (Shearman and Sterling, *Corporate Governance & Executive Compensation Survey 2021 and 2020* (25 March 2022), https://www.shearman.com/perspectives/2021/11/19th-annual-corporate-governance-executive-compensation--the-survey and https://www.shearman.com/perspectives/2020/09/corpgovsurvey2020/shearman-releases-18th-annual-corporate-governance-and-executive-compensation-survey.
37. Arts 19A to 19G of Schedule 8 of the remuneration report added by The Companies (Miscellaneous Reporting) Regulation 2018 (25 March 2022) https://www.legislation.gov.uk/uksi/2018/860/regulation/17/made.
38. For an overview of this agreement, *see* https://unfccc.int/process-and-meetings/the-paris-agreement/the-paris-agreement (25 March 2022).
39. Kristen Sullivan and Maureen Bujno, Incorporating ESG Measures into Executive Compensation Plans, Harvard Law School Forum on Corporate Governance (24 May 2021), https://corpgov.law.harvard.edu/2021/05/24/incorporating-esg-measures-into-executive-compensation-plans/. Conversely, there are indications that corporate social responsibility (CSR) performance of companies also affect the structure of the compensation package. Companies with better CSR performance results pay their CEO a higher portion of equity-based compensation (Khondkar Karim, Eunju Lee, and Sanghuyn Suh, *Corporate Social Responsibility and CEO Compensation Structure*, 40 Advances in Accounting, 27-41 (2018)).
40. FTI Consulting and CGLytics, *ESG and Executive Remuneration – Disconnect or Growing Convergence*, 15 October 2019 (26 March 2022), https://corpgov.law.harvard.edu/2019/10/15/esg-and-executive-remuneration-disconnect-or-growing-convergence/.
41. Some companies included ESG measures in both compensation elements. PWC and London Business School, *Paying Well by Paying for Good*, 14 (2021).

in compensation plans is to be found in the US. Almost 70% of the S&P 500 companies include these metrics in the incentive plan in 2022.[42]

Some studies point at the positive effects of the inclusion of non-financial criteria in executive remuneration policies: firm innovation increased significantly with the inclusion of corporate social responsibility (CSR) criteria.[43] However, this rapid shift towards ESG-related compensation plans does not come without criticism. Bebchuk and Tallarita examine the ESG-incentives in the S&P 100 companies and show that the ESG-incentive mechanisms tie the pay to a (too) limited number of ESG-dimensions, which can even be harmful for stakeholder welfare. Next, the arrangements cannot easily be monitored by third parties. The scholars conclude that this new compensation development serves the interest of the executives and not the stakeholders.[44] Kay is more nuanced.[45] As her survey shows, there is an overwhelming support of different stakeholder classes for using ESG-compensation metrics, with careful monitoring, compensation can help reaching out towards a better-balanced stakeholder approach of US companies.

Recently, the European Commission promoted ESG criteria to the legislative level. In Article 15 of the proposal for a Directive of the European Parliament and of the Council on Corporate Sustainability Due Diligence and amending Directive (EU) 2019/1937, the Commission wants to oblige companies combatting climate change and setting variable remuneration considering the fulfilment of companies in that respect.[46]

[F] Compensation Levels

Notwithstanding the many regulatory interventions in setting remuneration, the total compensation of (executive) directors is almost always on the rise. Further, while many best practices in corporate governance codes have a similar approach of setting directors' remuneration, compensation packages seem to differ significantly between countries, with the total compensation being the highest in the US. Murphy pointed at the insignificance of the differences between pay packages of US CEOs and those in other countries, 'but rather reflects tighter links between CEO pay and shareholder

42. PayGovernance, *ESG Incentives: Intended to Improve Corporate and Societal, Environmental, and Social Outcomes* 10 May 2022 (25 May 2022), https://www.paygovernance.com/viewpoints/esg-incentives-intended-to-improve-corporate-and-societal-environmental-and-social-outcomes.
43. Albert Tsang, Kun Tracy Wang, Simeng Liu, and Li Yu, *Integration Corporate Social Responsibility Criteria into Executive Compensation and Firm Innovation: International Evidence*, 70 J. Corp. Finance 102070 (2021).
44. Bebchuk and Tallarita, *supra* n. 16.
45. Ira Kay, *The Perils and Questionable Promise of ESG-Based Compensation: A Response to Bebchuk and Tallarita* 27 April 2022 (25 May 2022) https://corpgov.law.harvard.edu/2022/04/27/the-perils-and-promise-of-esg-based-compensation-a-response-to-bebchuk-and-tallarita/.
46. Art. 15 of the proposal for a Directive of the European Parliament and of the Council on Corporate Sustainability Due Diligence and amending Directive (EU) 2019/1937, 23 February 2022 (COM (2022) 71 Final). For the financial industry, this requirement already exists (*see* article 5 of Regulation (EU) 2019/2088 of the European Parliament and of the Council of 27 November 2019 on sustainability-related disclosures in the financial services sector, OJ L 317, 9.12.2019.

performance in US firms'.[47] In seventeen out of twenty-two countries, the CEO pay package has grown between 1997 and 2005 with an average growth rate of 8%.[48] In the 2010s, more moderate pay increases resumed, resulting in median pay packages of more than USD 12 million for S&P 500 CEOs in 2020, almost three times as high as the package for a median Russell 3000 company of USD 4.5 million.[49] Edmans, Gabaix, and Jenter add to these findings the size of the median compensation package of non-CEO executives showing similar developments over time but at a significant lower level, with a median of USD 1.7 million in 1992 growing to USD 4.4 million in 2000, lowered to USD 3.5 million in 2008 and returning to USD 4.1 million in 2014.[50] For the smaller companies, the development of the total compensation of executive non-CEOs was much flatter with a median growing from USD 0.7 million in 1992 to USD 1.2 million in 2014.

Non-executive directors play, obviously, in a totally different league regarding compensation. According to a 2019 study by Korn Ferry, the median pay for a non-executive director of a European listed company was EUR 70,000 in 2018, varying from a low of only EUR 20,000 in Austria to a generous EUR 207,800 in Switzerland, the only country with a median exceeding EUR 100,000.[51]

These levels of compensation do not differ dramatically from those of outside directors of American companies. The annual cash compensation of an American director accrued to USD 107,500 in 2018, and the average director receiving an additional retainer and meeting fee for taking part in a committee of the board. The major difference between the US and Europe lies in the recurring stock compensation. Almost all outside directors in the US receive this kind of compensation, with a median value of USD 150,000.[52] Approximately 94% of the American companies have either stock ownership guidelines or retention requirements, and the median guideline value for non-executive directors reaches USD 500,000. The difference between European and American companies regarding the retainer of shares and stock ownership in the company questions the best practice of shareholdings for non-executive and

---

47. Murphy, *supra n.* 2.
48. Marc Goergen and Luc Renneboog, *Managerial Compensation*, 17 J. Corp. Finance 1068–1077 (2011).
49. Semler Brossy and the Conference Board, *CEO and Executive Compensation Practices in the Russell 3000 and S&P 500*, 5 (Conference Board Inc., October 2021). *See* for similar findings between 1992 and 2014, Alex Edmans, Xavier Gabaix, and David Jenter, *Executive Compensation: A Survey of Theory and Evidence*, in *The Handbook of the Economics of Corporate Governance*, 390 (Benjamin E. Hermalin, Michael S. Weisbach eds., Elsevier 2017).
50. Alex Edmans, Xavier Gabaix, and David Jenter, *Executive Compensation: A Survey of Theory and Evidence*, in *The Handbook of the Economics of Corporate Governance*, 391 (Benjamin E. Hermalin and Michael S. Weisbach eds., Elsevier 2017).
51. Korn Ferry, *Non-Executive Directors in Europe 2019*, 7 (Korn Ferry).
52. Willis Towers Watson, *Executive Compensation Bulletin*, 2 (Willis Towers Watson, 6 September 2018). The median director pay in 2020 topped USD 203,000 according to the NACD report (Pearl Meyer, *2020–2021 Director Compensation Report*, 15 NACD, Arlington, 2021). For comparability with the European data, the numbers of 2018 Willis Towers Watson study have been presented in the body of the chapter.

independent directors. In the next section, I study the best practices for non-executive and independent directors of holding and acquiring shares in the company.

§9.02 THE NON-EXECUTIVE DIRECTOR AND REMUNERATION IN SHARES

An important component of many directors' pay packages is equity-based compensation. Granting (restricted) stock to executive managers and directors can motivate them to think and act like an 'owner' of the company. Further, it turns directors into shareholders and entitles them to all shareholder rights. (Non-executive) director ownership positively affects corporate performance,[53] and it improves monitoring over financial reporting.[54] The question whether a non-executive director needs to be a shareholder for holding the reins efficiently is commonly positively answered in the US. According to Warren Buffet, the chairman of the board of Berkshire Hathway Inc., there is little doubt that effective directors invest and hold shares in which they are a director. In his letter to the shareholders accompanying the annual report over 2019,[55] he wrote:

> Not long ago, I looked at the proxy material of a large American company and found that *eight* directors had never purchased a share of the company's stock *using their own money*. [...] This particular company had long been a laggard, but the directors were doing wonderfully. Paid-with-my-own-money ownership, of course, does *not* create wisdom or ensure business smarts. Nevertheless, I feel better when directors of our portfolio companies have had the experience of purchasing shares with their savings, rather than simply having been the recipients of grants.

Buffet follows the American common practices. According to Skadden, Arps, Slate, Meagher, and Flom, American companies make use of stock ownership guidelines for directors.[56] The director must acquire and hold a meaningful number of shares. This stake should be accumulated within three to five years after the first appointment. The meaningful number is equal to a multiple of the annual cash compensation. The multiple varies commonly between three to five times this compensation.[57]

This view is not unanimously shared. According to others, stock-owning directors show more myopic behaviour booting the short-term stock price, and directors'

53. Sanjai Bahagat and Brian Bolton, *Director Ownership, Governance, and Performance*, 48 J. Financ. Quant. Anal. 1, 105–135 (2013).
54. Amanda Bree Josefy, *An Examination of Director Stock Ownership Requirements* (Texas A&M University, 2016) (24 May 2022), https://oaktrust.library.tamu.edu/bitstream/handle/1969.1/156916/JOSEFY-DISSERTATION-2016.pdf;sequence = 1.
55. Warren Buffett, *Letter to the Shareholders of Berkshire Hathaway Inc.* (22 February 2020).
56. Skadden, Arps, Slate, Meagher, and Flom LLP and Affiliates, *2021 Compensation Committee Handbook*, 101 (15 April 2022) https://www.skadden.com/insights/publications/2021/02/2021-compensation-committee-handbook.
57. According to the former report ISS recommends a multiple of four.

ownership can negatively affect their independence and objectivity.[58] Further, director ownership hinders the monitoring of excess CEO compensation.[59]

The number of studies assessing the effects of acquiring and holding shares as a non-executive director is limited, and its effects are not unambiguous. Whether this component of pay is to be considered as a good corporate governance practice or a legal requirement is not been studied intensively. The next sections address this underexposed topic.

[A] The Regulatory Framework

In many jurisdictions, concentrated ownership is a corporate characteristic. According to a recent Organisation for Economic Co-operation and Development (OECD) corporate governance report, in thirty-three out of forty-five countries, more than 20% of the stock exchange listed companies have one shareholder owning more than 50% of the shares; in twelve countries, more than half of the companies have a majority shareholder; and in twenty-seven countries, the three largest shareholders own more than 50% of the shares.[60] Often, these shareholders are combining their ownership with a board position, either as an executive or as a non-executive. Warren Buffett serves as an example of this type of shareholder-director owning more than 38% of the high voting class A stock of Berkshire Hathaway Inc. according to the proxy statement 2021. However, many non-executive directors are elected by the general meeting of shareholders for their specific expertise and not for their shareholdings. Do these directors have to hold or acquire shares for effective governance or are shareholdings impairing their independence? This question is not answered in all jurisdictions in a similar way. I discuss whether the law provides in requirements for directors to hold or to acquire shares (§9.02[A][1]). Next, I study the best practices regarding the position of the non-executive director as shareholder in corporate governance codes (§9.02[A][2]). Section 9.02[B] analyses the practices of director's ownership in four countries with different best governance practices.

[1] The Director-Shareholder in the Law

In some jurisdictions, the former companies' acts considered that a director must be a shareholder. In France, the Companies Act of 1867 stated:

> Directors must own a number of shares determined by the articles of association. These shares serve the purpose of covering all management actions, even those

58. Jacob Rose, Cheri Mazza, Carolyn Norman, and Anna Rose, *The Influence of Director Stock Ownership and Board Discussion Transparency on Financial Reporting Quality*, 38 Account, Organizations and Society 5, 397–405 (2013).
59. Amanda Bree Josefy, An Examination of Director Stock Ownership Requirements (Texas A&M University, 2016) (24 May 2022), https://oaktrust.library.tamu.edu/bitstream/handle/1969.1/156916/JOSEFY-DISSERTATION-2016.pdf;sequence = 1.
60. OECD, *Corporate Governance Factbook 2021*, 26 (2021) (1 April 2022), https://www.oecd.org/corporate/corporategovernance-factbook.htm.

> that would be exclusively personal to one of the directors. They are nominative, inalienable, stamped with a stamp indicating inalienability, and deposited in the social fund.[61]

This ownership requirement was maintained in Article 95 of the Companies Act 1966 and even sanctioned. If a director did not own the required number of shares on the day of the appointment or ceases to own this number of shares during the term, then the director was deemed to have resigned from office if the director had not regularized it within three months. The scheme of this guarantee stock was abolished in 1988, and (only) in 2008 the system has reversed: only if the articles of the company require the director to acquire and to hold shares, the director must be a shareholder.[62] Many French companies still have this requirement in their articles of association but mostly with a very modest threshold.[63] A similar requirement was enacted in Article 47 of the Belgian companies act of 18 May 1873. First, different from the French requirement was that the director of a Belgian company must assign a number of shares as a guarantee of the management of the company. The director did not have to be a shareholder, if a shareholder was willing to provide in the guarantee in favour of the director. Second, the Belgian law provided in two thresholds. If the director had been identified by name in the articles of association, the director must deposit 2% of the shares as a guarantee. If the general meeting elected the director, then the latter must (have) deposit(ed) the number of shares as identified in the articles of association. The legislators in both France and Belgium were not worried that the interests of the directors were not aligned with the interests of the shareholders, but they wanted to address the issue of the directors' adequate management of the company. It is most obvious in the Belgian Companies Act of 1873 as the law did not retain the requirement of the director of (personally) being a shareholder.

Some other jurisdictions discussed the director's requirement of being a shareholder. When preparing the modernization of the Danish Companies Act, it was proposed in 1942 to introduce the requirement for directors to hold shares, but this proposal was rejected.[64] This proposal followed the idea of guaranteeing the good management of the company. The UK Companies Act 1948 did not require the director to hold shares but explicitly provided how the director must obtain shares in case the company provided in the articles of association this requirement:[65]

61. Art. 26 of the Law of 24 July 1867 on Companies: 'Les administrateurs doivent être propriétaires d'un nombre d'actions déterminé par les statuts. Ces actions sont affectées en totalité à la garantie de tous les actes de la gestion, même de ceux qui seraient exclusivement personnel à l'un des administrateurs. Elles sont nominatives, inaliénables, frappées d'un timbre indiquant l'inaliénabilité, et déposées dans la caisse sociale'.
62. Law n° 2008-776 of 4 August 2008 on the modernization of the economy, OJ 181, 5 August 2008.
63. It is not uncommon to stipulate in the articles of association that the director must own one share.
64. H. O. Jensen, *Træk af den danske Aktierets Udvikling i det syttende og attende Aarhundrede*, UfR Online 2-3 (U.1944B.221, 2016). My thanks go to Julie Nielsen for research assistance regarding these former Danish legal developments.
65. A common practice in former times (Susan McLaughlin, *Unlocking Company Law*, 230 (Routledge, Oxon, 2013)

> It shall be the duty of every director who is by the articles of the company required to hold a specified share qualification, and who is not already qualified, of directors, to obtain his qualification within two months after his appointment, or such shorter time as may be fixed by the articles. [...] The office of director of a company shall be vacated if the director does not within two months from the date of his appointment, or within such shorter time as may be fixed by the articles, obtain his qualification, or if after the expiration of the said period or shorter time he ceases at any time to hold his qualification.[66]

With its rule on the holder of the share warrant, it has some resemblances with the former Belgian system. The UK Companies Act 2006 is no longer explicitly providing consequences for directors who fail to meet the requirements of the articles of association.[67]

In some other jurisdictions, there are specific shareholder requirements for directors. For example, in the US, to qualify as a director of a national bank[68] or its controlling entity, the director must be the owner of shareholders' equity with a value of USD 1,000.[69]

Requirements of memberships served the requisite of good management of the company rather than aligning the interests of the directors with the wealth maximization of the shareholders.

[2] Corporate Governance Best Practices

In current times, most of the jurisdictions do not provide legal requirements for directors to hold shares. Whether corporate governance codes consider the holding and/or acquisition of shares of non-executive directors as a best practice, I study next. The first corporate governance code, the UK Cadbury Code stresses the independent position of the non-executive directors and was vague in providing best practices related to shareholdings of directors: 'This means that apart from their directors' fees and *shareholdings*, they should be independent of management and free from any business or other relationship which could material interfere with the exercise of their independent judgement.'[70] The fees of the director should be reflecting the time commitment. Non-executive directors should not participate in a share option scheme and not be pensionable by the company.[71]

The code recognized the holding of shares but does not provide in best practices related to the acquisition of shares, the holding of a certain number of shares, or the payment of the director's fee in shares. The 1995 Greenbury Code advised in a further alignment of the interest of the shareholders and those of the directors, stating that (all)

66. Section 182 UK Companies Act 1948. A similar provision can be found in section 291 UK CA 1985.
67. Obviously, under the Companies Act 2006, the director that fails to hold the shares as required in the articles of association of the company, (s)he is in breach with section 171 CA 2006.
68. A national bank in the US is a commercial bank chartered by the US Treasury.
69. 12 CFR § 7.2005 – Ownership of stock necessary to qualify as director of a national bank.
70. The Committee on the Financial Aspects of Corporate Governance, *Report*, 4.12 (GEE December 1992).
71. *Ibid.*, 4.13.

directors are encouraged 'to acquire and retain significant shareholdings in their company so as to reinforce alignment of the interests of Directors and shareholders',[72] a clear position considering shares as an important governance instrument. In the 1998 Hampel Code, the committee considered that remuneration in shares can be a useful method for paying the non-executive directors, although it does not need to be a universal practice and the committee did not want to provide in guidelines identifying what proportion of the fee should be paid in shares.[73] None of the later editions of the UK Corporate Governance Code explicitly changed these approaches. In the current Code, the remuneration of the non-executive directors should reflect the time commitments and responsibilities of the role of the non-executive director.[74] There should not be share options or other performance-related elements included in the remuneration package, but the Code does not overrule the previous recommendations of share-based remuneration or holding shares. The Code only notes that when determining the independence of the director, the board must consider whether the director has or has had in the last three years a material business relationship with the company which includes the relationship as a shareholder.[75] The Code also refers to the articles of association for setting the remuneration of the non-executive directors, while the current Companies Act 2006 no longer provides in the mandatory rule of the consequences of a breach of the articles of association of the company of holdings of shares, like the Companies Act 1948 prescribed.[76]

The 2004 Belgian Corporate Governance Code approached the remuneration of the non-executive directors in a negative way. Those directors 'should not be entitled to performance-related remuneration such as bonuses, stock related long-term incentive schemes, fringe benefits or pension benefits.'[77] The approach allowed to take appropriately into account the – at that moment – mandatory rule that every director can always, without any cause or reason, be dismissed. Specific remuneration schemes could be a hindrance when applying this rule to the extent that companies could be confronted with extra costs when dismissing a director that go against the general principle of this '*ad nutum*' dismissal. The 2019 Companies Code abolished the principle of the '*ad nutum*' dismissal[78] but made explicit that an independent director cannot receive any kind of performance-related fee, and a contract with a non-executive, non-independent director containing any kind of variable remuneration is conditional on the approval of the general meeting of shareholders.[79] The 2020 Belgian Code on Corporate Governance expanded the remuneration policies that companies must take into consideration. First, it entered the rule that the remuneration should

72. Study Group chaired by Sir Richard Greenbury, *Directors' Remuneration*, 6.41 (GEE 17 July 1995).
73. Committee on Corporate Governance, *Final Report*, 4.8 (GEE January 1998).
74. Financial Reporting Council, *The UK Corporate Governance Code*, Provision 34 (Financial Reporting Council Limited, London, July 2018).
75. *Ibid.*, Provision 10.
76. *See* Buffett, *supra* n. 55.
77. Corporate Governance Committee, *Belgian Code on Corporate Governance*, Provision 7.4 (Brussels, 2004).
78. The Belgian Company Code changed the principle of 'ad nutum' dismissal into a default regime.
79. Article 7:92 Belgian Company Code.

reflect the responsibilities and the time commitment of the non-executive director, a provision that resembles the UK best practice. Further, the Code added that 'non-executive board member should receive part of their remuneration in the form of shares in the company. These shares should be held until at least one year after the non-executive board member leaves the board and at least three years after the moment of award.'[80] Share-based payments are to be considered fixed remuneration when granting the shares is provided upfront as a well-identified number of shares, even if the stock price fluctuates, and independent from any performance-related criterion.[81] Performance-related remuneration or stock options cannot be considered as a good corporate governance practice.[82] These provisions raise several questions such as how the company can state its compliance with the Code when a director ends its membership and has no longer any relationship with the company but should hold on to the shares.

It was shown that the French law required the directors to hold shares in the company until 2008. The system was largely eroded as the number of shares that a director must hold had to be determined in the articles of association, and many companies introduced in their articles a very low threshold. The first French corporate governance codes do not contain any other specific requirements for the remuneration of the non-executive directors. However, in the current French Corporate Code of Listed Corporations, the director must be a shareholder: 'the director should personally be a shareholder and, by virtue of the provisions in the by-laws or the internal rules, hold a minimum number of shares that is *significant* in relation to the compensation awarded to them. If he or she does not hold these shares when assuming office, he or she should use his or her compensation to acquire them'.[83] The remuneration should consider the attendance of the director, the responsibilities and time commitment, and the participation in specialized committees or specific functions like being chair of the board.[84] It is up to the board of directors to decide on the significance of this ownership in relation to the total remuneration of the director.

The corporate governance practices in the Netherlands were developed in another direction. In the first Dutch Corporate Governance Code of 1997, it was recommended that the members of the supervisory board do receive neither any performance related pay nor stock options, and if a member holds shares in the company, it 'should be for long-term investment'.[85] It was not further explained what this long-term investment entails. From 2003 onwards, every edition of the Dutch

80. Corporate Governance Committee, *Belgian Code on Corporate Governance*, Provision 7.6 (Brussels, 2019).
81. Thomas Douillet, *La gouvernance des rémunerations des dirigeants dans les sociétés cotées – le point après le code des sociétés et des associations, le code de gouvernance 2020 et la loi droit des actionnaires II*, Revue de Droit Social 580–639, 607 (2020); Jan van Gysegem and Wim Devos, *De Corporate Governance Wet: eerste indicaties van de gevolgen in de praktijk van de bepalingen inzake variabele verloning en vertrek-vergoedingen*, 8 Oriëntatie 4, 224 (2011).
82. *Supra* n. 77, Provision 7.4 and 7.6.
83. Afep-Medef, *Corporate Governance Code of Listed Corporations*, Provision 20 (Paris, 2020).
84. *Ibid.*, 21.
85. Committee on Corporate Governance, *Recommendations on Corporate Governance in the Netherlands – Forty Recommendations*, Provision 2.12 (25 June 1997).

Corporate Governance Code – 2003, 2008, 2016, and the draft 2022 edition – explicitly states that 'the remuneration of the supervisory board members should reflect the time spent and the responsibilities of their role ... may not be awarded remuneration in the form of shares and/or rights to shares ...and... shares held by a supervisory board member in the company on whose supervisory board they serve should be long-term investments.'[86] The board member should be remunerated in a way that it 'promotes an adequate performance of their role',[87] but shares should not be a part of the compensation.

In short, these jurisdictions show that the best practices of the compensation and position of the non-executive director as shareholder differ substantially. A French non-executive director should acquire and hold a significant number of shares which is since 2020 also seen as a best practice in Belgium. In both countries, the acquisition of shares should follow from the remuneration of the director. The older UK Codes had a similar approach, but more recently this remuneration practice is less pronounced. Receiving compensation in shares is considered a bad practice in the Netherlands. A Dutch (supervisory) board member can own shares as a long-term investment, but a director without shares is considered all but problematic.

[B] The Non-executive Director and Remuneration in Shares: Governance Practices

[1] Framework of the Study

Assessing the practices and effects of the corporate governance codes on shareholdings of non-executive directors, I study the evolution of the shareholdings and compensation of non-executive directors in listed real estate investment trusts in the aforementioned four countries, Belgium, France, the UK, and the Netherlands. The countries were selected based on the differences and developments of their best remuneration practices. Belgium started to recommend non-executive directors to hold and to invest (part of their remuneration) in shares in the Corporate Governance Code 2020. The Dutch corporate governance code recommends the company not to award non-executive directors (and supervisory board members) in (options of) shares, and in case this type of director is a shareholder, then the ownership must be considered as a long-term investment. The UK practices hold the middle between Belgium and the Netherlands. The non-executive directors should not be paid in share options or performance-related elements, but the holding of shares is considered appropriate if the position as shareholder does not result in a material business relationship. Finally, French best practice includes that the non-executive director is a shareholder of the company and acquires shares with the compensation (s)he receives as a board

86. Provision 3.3.1, 3.3.2, and 3.3.3 of the draft 2022 Dutch Corporate Governance Code (unchanged from the 2016 Code).
87. Monitoring Committee Corporate Governance Code, *The Dutch Corporate Governance Code*, Principle 3.3 (8 December 2016).

member. How these different recommendations affect the holding and acquisition of shares of the non-executive directors is studied in this section.

For comparability reasons, I made use of companies in one industry, the real estate. The Euronext IEIF REIT Europe index, which, at the start of 2022, contained forty-seven listed real estate companies in seven European countries, was used to select the companies in the four countries in this assessment. I selected seven Belgian companies for investigating the developments of acquisitions of shares before and after the introduction of the 2020 Corporate Governance Code. The Netherlands has only three representative companies in the REIT index, but I added one other Dutch REIT company, Wereldhave.[88] For the UK and France, I randomly selected five companies of each country. For France, I added a sixth French company Unibail-Rodamco-WE, which has French, Dutch, and Australian roots. This company has a two-tier board structure, like one of the other French companies, in that way balancing the different board structures of the selected French companies.

For each of the companies, I identified all the non-executive directors or, for the Dutch and some French companies, the members of the supervisory board in the period from 2017 to 2021, and for each of these directors their ownership of shares. Table 9.1 provides an overview of the number of companies, the number of directors, the number of director-years, and the number of observations. A substantial number of non-executive directors left the board between 2017 and 2021 and similarly a considerable number was newly elected. Non-executive director turnover was the highest in the UK where only 25% of the directors have been board member over the five consecutive years. In Belgium, the turnover was the lowest: 62% of the non-executive board members stayed as member of the board between 2017 and 2021. Dutch and French non-executives were in the middle of Belgium and the UK with 42% and 49% of the non-executives being member of the board in all five years. Consequently, the number of director-years of observations is lower than the number of directors multiplied with the number of years. Finally, the annual report of Belgian companies does not always disclose whether the non-executive directors are also shareholder and how many shares the non-executive director holds.[89] Since 2020, this lack of information was remedied. It explains the lower number of total observations for the Belgian companies. The regular changes of non-executive directors in the board questions whether any kind of recommendation – either to acquire shares and hold shares or the opposite – could significantly affect their (independent) opinion.

88. This company is added providing a better balance in the number of companies of the different jurisdictions. The size of Wereldhave is close to that one that is requested for becoming part of the REIT index.
89. I also have controlled the database of the transactions in financial instruments of the issuer (in accordance with Article 19 of the Market Abuse Regulation (EU) No. 596/2014), which the Belgian regulator FSMA, pursuant to Art. 25, §2, of the Law of 2 August 2002 on the supervision of the financial sector and on financial services, discloses on its website. This database did not provide any transaction information of the directors of the companies for which the annual report does not contain the shareholdings in the period 2017–2019.

Table 9.1 Overview of the Sample of Companies and Director Observations

	Companies	*Directors*	*Dir.* Years*	*Observ.*
Belgium	7	61	248	187
France	6	65	246	246
Netherlands	4	24	87	87
UK	5	54	167	167
All	22	206	748	687

Source: own research based on the annual report of the REITs.

[2] Frequency of Non-executive Director Shareholdings

Figure 9.1 provides an overview of the non-executive directors' holdings of shares in the real estate investment trust industry. All French directors and as good as all UK directors hold shares in the company. The few non-executive directors of UK companies that do not hold shares were recently elected. In the consecutive year, the annual reports show that those directors were building up a share stake. Developments take place in Belgian companies. From 2017 to 2019, less than 30% of the non-executive directors hold shares in their company. This relative number increased to 36% in 2020 and even to 43% in 2021. The 2020 Belgian Code on Corporate Governance was published in early 2019 and came into effect in 2020. Consequently, directors and their companies had a reasonable period to comply with the new best practice, but compliance remained modest. Some companies consider it an unnecessary provision. At the other end of the spectrum are the directors of Dutch companies. Only 10% to 15% of the supervisory board members of the Dutch REITs in this sample hold shares in the company.

Overall, there is a significant effect of the best practices on the behaviour of non-executive directors as to the holding of shares. In France and the UK, holding shares is since many years considered an extension of a directorship. In Belgium, this new best practice will take time to get embedded in corporate governance. The Dutch findings support the opposite best practice.

Figure 9.1 Number of Non-Executive Directors Holding Shares in the Company

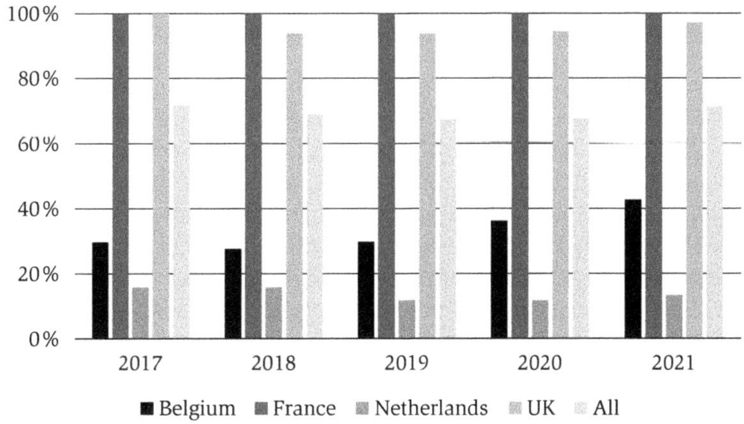

Source: Own research based on the annual report of the REITs.

[3] Evolution of Shareholdings of Non-executive Directors

In some of the jurisdictions, directors do not immediately have to comply with the best practice of holding shares and are granted an acquisition period. Especially in France and Belgium, part of the remuneration can be provided in shares. In the latter country, this component of remuneration should continue for the time the non-executive director remains a member of the board. It results in four different approaches. Since 2020, Belgian directors should yearly increase their shareholdings in the company. The French directors should already from the start own a significant number of shares or start acquiring the shares from the first year of the election. In the UK, it depends on the remuneration practices of the company whether the non-executive director should be a shareholder and increase its shareholdings regularly, while in the Netherlands, shareholdings should be the exception to the rule.

The results of the study largely confirm these hypotheses, Belgium being the exception. First, in French companies, the candidate for a board membership hold shares when the general meeting elects the director. Only a minority of directors further increases its shareholdings. Their shareholdings remain largely unchanged after the election to the board and rarely the director decreases its stake. The next section addresses the question whether the shareholdings can be considered significant. In the UK, it is a common practice that a candidate for the board of directors has acquired shares and further develops its shareholdings during the term of the directorship. As the current UK Code is silent, but refers to the articles of association, it is common (in our sample) that the articles provide in a minimum threshold of shareholding for non-executive directors. For example, Land Securities states:

> Non-executive Directors are expected to meet a minimum shareholding requirement of 100% of the relevant annual fee within three years of appointment to the Board. The shareholding requirements are considered met once the Non-executive Director has obtained the required holding value and, provided those shares are retained, no adjustment is required due to movements in the share price.[90]

The evolution of the Dutch ownership of shares of supervisory board members supports the best practices of the Dutch Code. Most of the directors do not own shares (Figure 9.1), and only rarely does the supervisory director acquire shares during the term as board member (Table 9.2). For Belgium, it is expected that since 2020, non-executive directors start to yearly acquire shares in the company, but the results do not confirm this hypothesis. A large majority of the non-executives do not change their shareholdings, and less than half of the directors hold shares in the company in 2021 (Figure 9.1), resulting in a common practice opposite to the best practice in the Belgian Code on Corporate Governance.[91] Only a few directors increased their holdings, especially in one company that amended its corporate governance practices in 2016 supporting the directors' acquisition of shares in line with, but long before, the amendment of the Belgian Code in 2020.

Table 9.2 Developments of the Shareholdings of Non-executive Directors (Increase/Decrease/Unchanged Holdings)

	2017–2018 (in %)	*2018–2019 (in %)*	*2019–2020 (in %)*	*2020–2021 (in %)*
Belgium	17/0/83	11/0/89	22/5/73	13/2/85
France	19/5/76	14/2/84	31/4/65	22/9/69
The Netherlands	0/0/100	0/0/100	0/0/100	7/0/93
UK	42/16/42	33/0/67	41/0/59	34/0/66
All	21/5/74	16/1/83	27/3/70	20/4/76

Source: Own research based on the annual report of the REITs.

[4] Size of the Shareholdings of Non-executive Directors

The French Corporate Governance Code recommends the non-executive directors to hold a *significant* number of shares in the company. The current UK Code does not provide in a similar requirement, but it was recommended in the former Code. The

90. Land Securities, *Annual Report 2021*, 125.
91. This finding confirms a VBO-Guberna study of the compliance of companies with the Belgian Corporate Governance Code 2020. According to the study, only 11% of the companies partially compensates their non-executive directors in shares. In the group of the largest companies, already 41% remunerates in shares, but none of the smaller companies provides shares to their non-executive directors as part of their pay (Guberna-VBO, *Studierapport – Naleving van de Belgische Corporate Governance Code 2020*, 12 (2021)). Many companies explain why they do not complain with this best practice.

Belgian Code does not specify the size of the shareholdings but contain the recommendation of a yearly acquisition of shares while the Dutch Code does not recommend acquisitions or holdings of shares.

As there are major differences in the total number of shares that companies issued, I calculated the value of the shareholdings of each director at the end of each year (and converted the UK values into Euro). In case a director does not hold any shares, the value of the stake is 0.

In France it regularly occurs that a legal entity, holding a substantial number of shares is elected as a board member.[92] As these observations significantly influence the average value, these non-executive directors have been excluded in Table 9.3.[93] Also one non-executive director of a significant shareholder in a UK company was excluded.[94]

Table 9.3 provides the results of this analysis. The average shareholdings of a non-executive director in the real estate investments trust varies between EUR 75,000 and EUR 110,000 in the period from 2017 to 2021. These averages hide significant differences as the median values ranged from EUR 8,000 to EUR 18,000 due to the large number of non-executive directors that do not hold any shares and a few non-executive directors that hold share packages exceeding a value of EUR 1 million.

The French Code recommends the holding of a *significant* number of shares in relation to the compensation. Overall, the average value of the shareholdings is rather modest and varies between EUR 21,000 and EUR 35,000.[95] The median value of the shareholdings remains for every year even under EUR 16,200. As the average yearly total remuneration of the non-executive director of French companies in 2019 and 2020 approached EUR 50,000, it can be doubted that the average shareholding complies with the French best practice. This is different for the UK companies. The average value of the shareholdings of non-executive directors of UK REIT companies fluctuates significantly between EUR 158,000 in 2019 and EUR 671,000 in 2021, with medians varying from EUR 71,000 to EUR 135,000, both set of numbers show the significance of the shareholdings. With an average overall remuneration of EUR 127,000 in 2019 and 2020, many non-executive directors hold an investment in the company that exceeds their annual remuneration. In Belgium, the average value of the shareholdings increased significantly in 2019 and remained at this high level in the follow up years. This is due to a few independent directors that hold and increased their stakes in the company. Overall, the majority of the directors do not hold shares in the company, and the median value of the shareholdings of a non-executive director in Belgian REITs is nil. A similar finding is noted for the supervisory board members of Dutch companies. Only a few members of the Dutch supervisory board hold shares in the company, and since 2019 only one director's shareholdings exceeded a value of EUR 100,000. In

92. The legal entity is represented by a natural person.
93. In many cases, the value of the shareholding exceeded EUR 100 mio.
94. The disclosure of the director holdings referred to the shareholdings of the significant shareholder.
95. In 2018, we excluded the shareholdings of one director of Unibail-Rodamco-WE as this non-executive director had an Australian background. Including his holdings in the 2018 would increase the average almost 4 times to more than EUR 76.000.

recent years, and contrary to the (value of the) shareholdings of non-executive directors in Belgian, the value of the board members of Dutch companies decreased to amounts between EUR 10,000 and EUR 15,000.

Table 9.3 Average Value of the Shareholdings of a Non-Executive Director (in EUR)[96]

	2017	*2018*	*2019*	*2020*	*2021*
Belgium	10,602	10,658	113,576	113,360	163,176
France	32,933	21,305	35,066	23,231	21,918
Netherlands	39,533	27,343	13,198	11,197	14,160
UK	335,741	254,457	158,111	428,033	670,639
All	108,444	99,459	84,271	75,430	106,110
N	122	124	129	144	139

Source: own research based on the annual report of the REITs

[5] Company Performance and Shareholding of the Non-executive Directors

The shareholdings of non-executive directors, and especially independent directors should not impair their judgment but as a former UK code stated it can be encouraged 'to reinforce alignment of the interests'.[97] Thereto, I also have related the shareholdings of the non-executive directors to the total shareholder return. I assessed for each of the companies in the sample the total shareholder return as the stock price evolution over the year and the distributed dividend to the stock price at the start of the year, and averaged over the different years. As a proxy for the shareholdings of the non-executive directors, I used the average relative number of non-executive directors that hold shares in the company. The result of this analysis is presented in Figure 9.2. When more non-executive directors hold larger shareholdings in the company, it could be expected that the board is putting more emphasis on the financial return of the shareholders. It should result in observations that go from the lower left in the figure to the higher right side. The results do not confirm this hypothesis. The highest total shareholder returns of more than 20% are found in some companies with low levels of non-executive directors' holdings of shares as well as at high levels. Low and negative total shareholder returns can be found in companies where all non-executive directors hold shares as well as in companies were none or one of the non-executive directors hold shares. While the number of observations is too limited to generalize the findings, there is an indication that neither a best practice to recommend the acquisition and

96. The value of the shareholdings of directors in UK companies have been converted in Euro.
97. Study Group chaired by Sir Richard Greenbury, *Directors' Remuneration*, 6.41 (GEE 17 July 1995).

holding of shares nor a recommendation to refrain non-executive directors from acquiring shares should be considered as good corporate governance, *from a shareholder return perspective.*

Figure 9.2 The Relationship of the Total Shareholder Return to the Number of Non-executive Directors Holding Shares

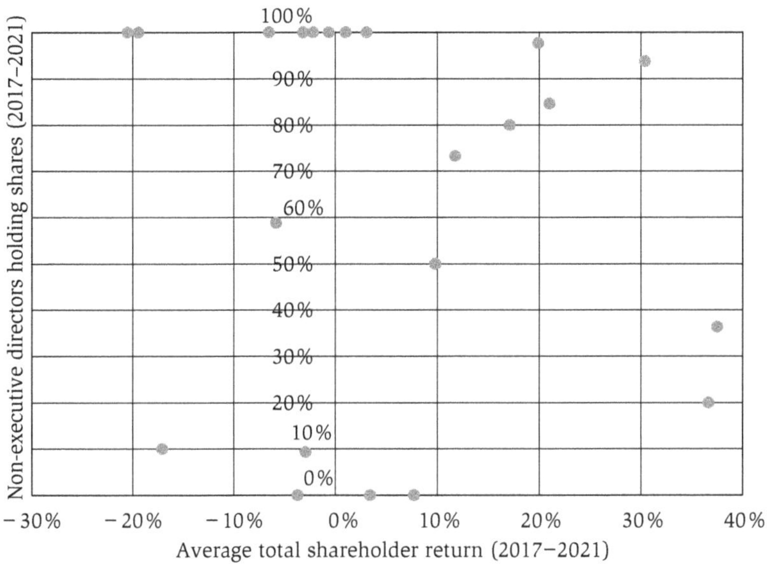

Source: Own research based on the annual report of the REITs, share prices of Euronext and LSE.

§9.03 CONCLUSION

The remuneration and the optimization of the remuneration package of the board and executive management plays a key role in company management, even long before the term corporate governance entered the corporate arena. Since the start of the corporate governance discussions, compensation belongs to the key instruments for shaping a good corporate environment. For a long time, compensation was approached as a solution for agency conflicts and in particular aligning the interests of executive board members and management with shareholder wealth, in more recent times it started to be seen as a problematic area of governance. In all corporate governance codes that have been issued since the 1990s, the remuneration of the board and top executives takes a major part of the recommendations, especially, the alignment of the remuneration of the management and the directors with the interests of the company, the shareholders, and the stakeholders. Share and share options are as good as always instruments used to reach out to good corporate governance for executive board members.

The remuneration of non-executive directors is less of an issue. At first sight, it looks as if good corporate governance includes a fixed fee for the non-executive director, share options or performance-related compensation are bad governance practice, and holding shares is tolerated. In a more detailed study, I found that the best practices differ for non-executive directors from jurisdiction to jurisdiction. Some jurisdictions recommend a fixed fee which include (partial) payment in shares, while others recommend a significant holding of shares for non-executive director, and some codes do not want companies to pay non-executive board members in shares and refrain from recommending any holding of shares.

These best practices affect the behaviour of companies. The Dutch Corporate Governance Code considers it a bad practice to award non-executive directors (and supervisory board members) in (options of) shares, and only a limited number of supervisory board members hold shares. The opposite practice can be found in France where all non-executive directors hold shares. The French code considers a significant shareholding of a non-executive director as a best practice. However, while all directors own shares, most non-executive directors hold only a modest number of shares which more than likely fails to meet the standard of the French code of a 'significant' stake. Non-executive directors in the UK, another country where approximately all directors hold shares, build up *significant* shareholdings. Recent UK codes do not explicitly recommend it but leave it to the company to develop an appropriate practice. Finally, the Belgian best practice significantly changed in 2020. Currently, non-executive directors should be partially compensated in shares. However, corporate practice is unruly. Less than half of the non-executive directors hold shares, and only a few are compensated partially in shares. Finally, there is some preliminary evidence that shareholdings of non-executive directors have no direct effect on the total shareholder return of the company.

It is surprising that the *best governance practice* of acquiring and holding shares in the company as a non-executive director is differently approached in different jurisdictions. Corporate governance environments in many countries are, regarding this corporate governance feature, similar and it is hard to explain why best practices are divergent. Consequently, it is less surprising to find that companies approach these 'best practices' in different ways. In the absence of convincing arguments related to recommending or dissuading non-executive directors in acquiring or holding shares, I make a plea for a 'best practice' of developing a company specific policy for non-executive directors' remuneration which the shareholders will regularly assess when voting for this remuneration policy. In this policy, the company establishes how it will remunerate their non-executive directors and whether the directors must acquire and hold shares.

CHAPTER 10

The Future Role of the General Meeting

Bastiaan Kemp[*]

§10.01 INTRODUCTION[1]

Shareholders play a crucial role in the governance of listed companies. One of the characteristics of the modern company is that shareholders have important control rights[2] over the company, such as the right to appoint and dismiss board members, to amend the articles of association, to approve decisions that change the capital structure of the company, and to approve important decisions by the management board. The shareholders exercise these rights through 'their' corporate body; the general meeting of shareholders.

Although the general meeting has played an important role in the modern company law form since the incorporation of the first modern companies in the seventeenth century,[3] the role of the general meeting in listed companies is changing. This is the result of two developments. First, it plays a less-prominent role as an instrument for information and dialogue with bilateral meetings or investor calls with

* The author would like to thank all participants at the (virtual) conference in Aarhus on 26 January 2022 for their valuable feedback to the presentation.

1. Parts of this contribution build on earlier work by the author as recently published in: Bastiaan Kemp, *Naar een werkbaar en realistisch model voor stakeholder governance en de rol van aandeelhouders daarin* (inaugural lecture Maastricht), Maandblad voor Ondernemingsrecht (2022); Bastiaan Kemp, *Developments in Stakeholder Governance: Lessons from the Netherlands* (editorial), 3 European Company Law (2022); Adriaan F.M. Dorresteijn et al., *European Corporate Law*, (Wolters Kluwer 2022), Chapter 6, par. IV (The management and control of companies under national law).
2. When referring to control rights, I refer to rights that grant control over the company. This can be, for instance, not only the right to manage the day-to-day operations of the company or to amend the articles of association but also a right that grants a measure of control over another corporate body, such as an instruction right or the right to appoint and dismiss board members.
3. Ella Gepken-Jager, Gerard van Solinge, & Levinus Timmerman (ed.), *VOC 1602–2002, 400 Years of Company Law* (Kluwer Law International 2005).

institutional shareholders becoming more important and frequent. Second, there is a growing concern about how companies act towards and as part of society, also considering the major challenges our society is facing. There seems to be more support for the argument that companies are acting to the detriment of stakeholders and are in part to blame for creating a situation in which there is a too steep trade-off between material wealth and social order. As part of the effort to face these challenges, there has been more focus on the company form, its purpose and whose interests the company should serve.[4] An important part of the debate on this second question is the prominent position of shareholders in corporate governance – and by extension the control rights allocated to the general meeting of shareholders. What should be the role of the general meeting of shareholders in listed companies in this changing corporate governance landscape?

In this contribution, I focus on this question and a potential answer based on law and economics theories, in particular agency theory. When doing so, I apply two assumptions:

(1) company law should be focused on value creation for stakeholders, independent of whether this also serves the shareholders. This can be referred to as pluralistic stakeholderism;[5] and
(2) there is currently no alternative corporate body, such as a general meeting of stakeholders, that can realistically be implemented to fulfil a monitoring role within the company instead of the general meeting of shareholders. As a result, the general meeting of shareholders and the board are the relevant corporate bodies within the corporate governance framework.[6]

These assumptions are widely discussed in literature, and there are those that would (absolutely) not agree with these assumptions. Their views are briefly discussed, but ultimately for the purpose of this contribution I do not elaborately 'defend' these assumptions because the purpose of the contribution is to address the challenges that arise if national company law applies these assumptions.

§10.02 THE DECISION-MAKING FUNCTION UNDER SIEGE

The general meeting of shareholders is a mandatory corporate body under most company laws and fulfils several functions.[7] One of these functions is the decision-making function. Most of the collective rights of the shareholders, such as the right to

4. *See*, §10.03 for more detail.
5. *See*, for this term, Lucian Arye Bebchuk & Roberto Tallarita, *The Illusory Promise of Stakeholder Governance*, 106 Cornell L. Rev. 19 (2020).
6. *See*, §10.03 [B] [5] *infra*.
7. *See*, Anne Lafarre, *The AGM in Europe: Theory and Practice of Shareholder Behaviour* (Emerald Publishing 2017), 7 *et seq.*; Therese Strand, *The Owners and the Power: Insights from Annual General Meetings*, PhD series No. 25.2012 (2012), 13; Rebecca Strätling, *General Meetings: A Dispensable Tool for Corporate Governance of Listed Companies?* 11 Corporate Governance: An International Review 74–82; 74 (2003); Dorresteijn, *supra* n. 1, p. 168-172.

appoint and dismiss the directors, amend the articles of association and issue instructions, are exercised through the general meeting. To ensure that the shareholders can properly exercise these collective rights, it is important that shareholders are able to gain access to a general meeting. The more difficult it is to gain access to a general meeting, the more difficult it is for shareholders to exercise their rights and to monitor and control the board. The main option other than to exercise their rights through the general meeting is 'to vote with their feet'. There have been several initiatives in recent years to enable shareholders to play a more active role within the company by removing barriers to exercising shareholder rights, such as the introduction and then recasting of the Shareholder Rights Directive, which provides for minimum harmonization regarding certain rights of shareholders relating to the general meeting.[8]

The decision-making function of the general meeting embodies the prominent position that shareholders hold in the corporate governance framework. However, the legitimacy of the control rights that are allocated to shareholders and that shareholders can unilaterally exercise through the general meeting can be questioned as part of the broader discussion whether the company should – as far as company law concerns – be focused on serving the interests of shareholders. If companies are required to focus more on the interests of (all) stakeholders and less on shareholder interests, then this inevitably raises the question whether shareholders should retain influential control rights.

[A] International Development Towards More Pluralistic Stakeholderism

Discussions about which interests the company should serve, and by extension how company law should be organized as a legal framework, are in full swing in the international arena. In this discussion, there seems be to a trend of pluralistic stakeholderism gaining a certain popularity over the shareholder model.[9] A prominent example is the Business Round Table (BRT), an association of chief executive officers (CEOs) of leading United States (US) companies, that made headlines in August 2019 when it replaced its earlier statement for shareholder value[10] with a new 'Statement on the Purpose of the Corporation'. This renewed statement argues that companies should be run in the interests of all stakeholders.[11] Reactions to this statement varied. Some commentators were enthusiastic, but at the same time there was criticism from, for

8. *See*, Hanne Søndergaard Birkmose & Konstantinos Sergakis, *The Shareholder Rights Directive II: A Commentary* (Edward Elgar 2021).
9. In the words of Wachtell lawyers Lipton, Rosenblum & Cain: '*In hindsight, 2019 may come to be viewed as a watershed year in the evolution of corporate governance. After years of growing alarm about endemic short-termism, the sustainability and competitiveness of businesses over a long-term horizon, and the role of corporate policies in contributing to socioeconomic inequality, there has been an emerging consensus that the prevailing corporate governance system is broken*' (Martin Lipton et al., *Thoughts for Boards of Directors in 2020*, Harvard Law School Forum on Corporate Governance (10 December 2019)).
10. Business Roundtable, *Statement on Corporate Governance 3–4* (September 1997), www.ralphgomory.com/wp-content/uploads/2018/05/Business-Roundtable-1997.pdf.
11. Business Roundtable, *Statement on the Purpose of Corporation* (19 August 2019).

example, the Council of Institutional Investors, which feared a dangerous coup.[12] Certain academics also reacted sceptically, using words such as 'empty' and 'old rhetoric'.[13] Bebchuk and Tallarita took it a step further and wrote a series of papers in which they – in essence – argue that the statement does not lead to an actual reorientation of boards and that focusing more on stakeholderism is counterproductive to safeguarding the interests of stakeholders.[14] Despite the criticism, the BRT's statement is not an isolated incident. Earlier, in 2018, CEO of Blackrock Larry Fink had said that companies should not only perform financially but also make a positive contribution to society. The role of the company has also received significant attention in US politics in recent years, with proposals from US Senators Elizabeth Warren, Bernie Sanders, and Marco Rubio.[15] In addition, the World Economic Forum issued a statement that the purpose of the company should be to connect with all stakeholders, and that the creation of value should not only serve shareholders but also all stakeholders.[16]

There are similar developments taking place on the other side of the Atlantic. One example is the project of the British Academy called the 'Future of the Corporation'. This project, led by Colin Mayer, focuses on corporate purpose and a renewed contract between companies and society.[17] In addition, in July 2020, the European Commission published a report entitled 'Study on Directors' Duties and Sustainable Corporate Governance' by EY.[18] This report points out the negative short-term focus in European corporate governance and was received with severe criticism.[19] Following the publication of the report, the European Commission responded in July 2020 with an

12. Council of Institutional Investors, *Council of Institutional Investors Responds to Business Roundtable Statement on Corporate Purpose* (19 August 2019).
13. Jesse Fried, *The Roundtable's Stakeholderism Rhetoric Is Empty, Thankfully*, Harvard Law School Forum on Corporate Governance (22 November 2019); Luca Enriques, *The Business Roundtable CEOs' Statement: Same Old, Same Old, Promarket* (9 September 2019).
14. Bebchuk & Tallarita, *supra* n. 5; Lucian Arye Bebchuk et al., *For Whom Corporate Leaders Bargain*, 94 S. Cal. L. Rev. 1467 (2021); Lucian Arye Bebchuk & Roberto Tallarita, *Will Corporations Deliver Value to All Stakeholders?*, 75 Vand. L. Rev. 1031 (2021).
15. Section 3348, Accountable Capitalism Act, 115th Cong. (2018), para. 4. *See* for further information: *Empowering Workers Through Accountable Capitalism*, elizabethwarren.com (2020), https://elizabethwarren.com/plans/accountable-capitalism; *Corporate accountability and democracy*, berniesaunders.com, https://berniesanders.com/issues/corporate-accountability-and-democracy/; Marco Rubio, *American Investment in the 21st Century: Project for Strong Labor Markets and National Development* (15 May 2019), www.rubio.senate.gov/public/_cache/files/94fcb79e-eedd-4496-a262-7091647563e6/B68DE3EF858700E482305C9ED26AEC72.5.14.2019.-final-project-report-american-investment.pdf.
16. Davos Manifesto 2020: World Economic Forum, *The Universal Purpose of a Company in the Fourth Industrial Revolution* (2 December 2019).
17. www.thebritishacademy.ac.uk/programmes/future-of-the-corporation/.
18. *Study on Directors' Duties and Sustainable Corporate Governance* (July 2020), op.europa.eu.
19. Jesse M. Fried & Charles C.Y. Wang, *Short-termism, Shareholder Payouts, and Investment in the EU* (ECGI Law Working Paper, nr. 544/2020), (October 2020); Mark J. Roe et al., *The European Commission's Sustainable Corporate Governance Report: A Critique* (ECGI Law Working Paper, nr. 553/2020) (November 2020); Mark J. Roe et al., *The EY Sustainable Corporate Governance Report's Major Flaws: Discussion and Analysis* (2020), https://ec.europa.eu/info/law/better-regulation/have-your-say/initiatives/12548-Sustainable-corporate-governance/F594640; The

Inception Impact Statement, in which it largely supported the report's findings.[20] Despite the criticism of the report, the European Parliament issued a similar statement in a resolution of 17 December 2020, in which it considered, *inter alia*, that 'the duty of care of directors towards their company should be defined not only in relation to short-term profit maximization by way of shares, but also sustainability concerns' and 'directors' duties cannot be misconstrued as amounting solely to the short-term maximization of shareholder value, but must instead include the long-term interest of the company and wider societal interests, as well as that of employees and other relevant stakeholders'.[21] Subsequently, in early 2021, the European Commission held a consultation on the 'sustainable corporate governance' initiative, which again appears to be heavily based on the aforementioned EY report.

§10.03 THE *RAISON D'ETRE* OF THE COMPANY AND HOW TO MAXIMIZE ITS VALUE

When considering the role of the general meeting and – by extension – the shareholders within corporate governance against the background of the development as set out in §10.02[A], a distinction can be made between two questions:

(1) by whom and for what purpose is the company as a legal instrument created?
(2) how should company law be structured to ensure that companies achieve this purpose as successfully as possible?

[A] The Purpose of the Company as a Legal Instrument

Companies play an important role in our economy. There is a considerable amount of literature about the history and 'invention' of the company as a legal instrument to promote entrepreneurship.[22] What is particularly relevant for the first question above, is the awareness that the company is an instrument made available by society to its users. The prevailing view is that the modern company has five core characteristics:

(1) legal personality;
(2) limited liability;

European Law Experts Group, *A Critique of the Study on Directors' Duties and Sustainable Corporate Governance Prepared by Ernst & Young for the European Commission*, Oxford Business Law Blog (9 December 2020).

20. *Inception Impact Statement* (30 July 2020), https://ec.europa.eu/info/law/better-regulation/have-your-say/initiatives/12548-Sustainable-corporate-governance.
21. European Parliament resolution of 17 December 2020 on sustainable corporate governance (2020/2137(INI)) OJ C, C/445, 29.10.2021.
22. *See*, for good overviews: Andreas Martin Fleckner, *Antike Kapitalvereinigungen: ein Beitrag zu den konzeptionellen und historischen Grundlagen der Aktiengesellschaft* (Böhlau 2010); Harwell Wells (ed.), *Research Handbook on the History of Corporate and Company Law* (Edward Elgar 2018); Gepken-Jager et al. (ed.), *supra* n. 3; Matthijs de Jongh, *Tussen societas en universitas. De beursvennootschap en haar aandeelhouders in historisch perspectief* (IVOR nr. 94; diss. Rotterdam) (2014).

(3) transferability of shares;
(4) delegated management with a governance structure; and
(5) economic ownership by the shareholder.[23]

These characteristics play an important role in the success of the company as a legal instrument. Because the company has legal personality, it is considered an actual person in many respects. In addition, limited liability makes it easier for shareholders to invest risk bearing capital[24] and to transfer shares.[25] The company-form can, in part because of the system of representation and the fact that companies can hold shares in each other and thus form groups, achieve this on a large scale. This makes it possible to create and maintain sizeable enterprises through companies. Without the legislator granting legal personality to the corporate form, this would be difficult to achieve on the same scale. Both aspects are essential for the proper functioning of the company within the (global) economy.

The company however does not have these characteristics by chance; it has them because the legislator – and by extension society – confers them on companies through a legal system. In addition, companies benefit from social resources made available by society, such as well-trained employees and infrastructure.[26] Companies only receive these privileges if it is of benefit to society at large and not just to those who wield the instrument of the company. In other words, society provides the entrepreneur with the legal instrument and the means to increase social welfare for both society and the entrepreneur.[27] This is where the concept of the license to operate originates from; society giving the entrepreneur a 'licence' to do business with his company.[28] From this it follows that all stakeholders in the company have an interest in the company as a legal instrument for generating social welfare, and therefore companies must create welfare at the bottom line.[29]

---

23. John Armour et al., *What Is Corporate Law?*, in Reinier H. Kraakman et al., *The Anatomy of Corporate Law. A Comparative and Functional Approach* (OUP 2017), p. 5 et seq. *See also*: Robert C. Clark, *Corporate Law* (Little, Brown 1986), 2 et seq.
24. Richard Allen Posner, *Economic Analysis of the Law* (2014), p. 432.
25. Stephen M. Bainbridge & Matthew Todd Henderson, *Limited Liability: A Legal and Economic Analysis* (Edward Elgar 2016), 44 et seq.
26. *See*, Nien-hê Hsieh et al, *The Social Purpose of Corporations*, 6(s1) Journal of the British Academy 58 (2018).
27. A. Jan A.J. Eijsbouts & Bastiaan Kemp, *Over maatschappelijk verantwoord ondernemen, waardecreatie, ondernemingsrecht en vennootschappelijk belang*, TvOB 5 (2012), 122.
28. *See*, Thomas Donaldson, *Corporations and Morality* (Prentice-Hall 1982); Thomas Donaldson & Thomas W. Dunfee, *Ties That Bind: A Social Contracts Approach to Business Ethics* (Harvard Business Review Press 1999).
29. Patrick Bolton, Marco Becht, & Alisa Roell, *Corporate Governance and Control*, in George M. Constantinides, Milton Harris & René Stulz, *Handbook of the Economics of Finance* 1 (Elsevier 2003), 1-109; Michael Magill, Martine Quinzil, & Jean-Charles Rochet, *A Theory of the Stakeholder Corporation*, 83 Econometrica 1685 (2015). *See also*, Ronald J. Gilson, *From Corporate Law to Corporate Governance*, in Jeffrey N. Gordon & Wolf-Georg F. Ringe, *Oxford Handbook of Corporate Law and Governance* (OUP 2018), 17, 24.

[B] What Corporate Governance Maximizes the Purpose of the Company

Assuming that the company should ultimately create social welfare, the second question is how the governance of a company should be organized in order to do this as successfully as possible. On this question, there are more fundamental differences. In summary, a distinction can be made between two main doctrines,[30] each with a number of sub-doctrines. The main doctrines are (a) the shareholder model and (b) the stakeholder model/pluralistic stakeholderism.[31] Although many supporters of both doctrines take the view that the company should create social welfare, they have a very different view on which governance structure should be used to best achieve this welfare.

[1] The Shareholder Model

Supporters of the shareholder model argue that social welfare can best be created by regulating in company law that the company and, by extension, the board should focus on shareholder interests and that control rights should in principle be allocated to shareholders through the general meeting because the shareholders are the residual claimant of the company, meaning that the shareholders bear the risk for the company's success or failure.[32] The underlying reason for the qualification of the shareholders as residual claimants is that the company should be conceived as a 'nexus of contracts' between the various stakeholders of the company.[33] Starting point in this nexus of contracts is the freedom of the parties to the contract to structure the company in the way they see fit, with (national) company law providing a 'template' for the division of power of the company. This template is, however, never complete because parties cannot foresee all circumstances that could arise within the company, and it is not efficient or possible to provide for all circumstances in the written governance of the company, such as the law, the articles of association, and bylaws. As a result, a party should be assigned the residual power to resolve unforeseen issues. Under the shareholder model, the shareholders are considered the appropriate stakeholder to in principle assign this residual power to because shareholders are in a different 'normative relationship' to the company than other stakeholders, such as employees, creditors, and suppliers.[34] The main difference being that the latter stakeholders have a more or less fixed relationship with a set return, whereas shareholders are incentivized

30. Several other models have been identified in the international literature, such as the manager-oriented model, the labour-oriented model, and the state-oriented model (*see*, Henry Hansmann & Reinier H. Kraakman, *The End of History of Corporate Law*, 89 Geo. L.J. (2001)).
31. I should note that different authors also have different ideas about what exactly these doctrines mean and that there is no such thing as 'the' shareholder model and 'the' stakeholder model. Nevertheless, for the purpose of this contribution, I treat these doctrines somewhat generic.
32. Frank H. Easterbrook & Daniel R. Fischel, *The Economic Structure of Corporate Law* (Harvard University Press 1991), 67–68.
33. Michael Cole Jensen & William H. Meckling, *The Theory of the Firm: Managerial Behaviour, Agency Costs, and Ownership Structure*, 3.4 J. Financ. Econ. 305–360 (1976). The reference to contracts should be understood in a normative sense, not in the civil law sense.
34. Easterbrook & Fischel, *supra* n. 32, 67–68.

to maximize shareholder value and therefore their return on investment. Moreover, shareholders are most incentivized to avoid negative results for the company, as shareholders are last in line and will receive nothing if the company performs poorly. Therefore, shareholders have the correct incentives to exercise discretionary power in such a way that their interest is maximized.[35] The interests of stakeholders should be protected not through company law, but other public and private law regulations.[36]

[2] Optimal Allocation of Control Rights and the Principal Costs Theory

Although under the shareholder model, shareholders are the appropriate stakeholder to assign the residual power, that does not necessarily mean that all control rights should be allocated to the general meeting. First, shareholders are generally less competent to take decisions within the company, which is one of the reasons they delegate part of their control over the company to more competent directors. Second, it is more costly to have shareholders take all decisions, since in that case the company will need to call a general meeting, and shareholders need to be properly informed to take adequate decisions. Delegating part of the powers over the company to the board is a way of reducing these costs.[37] Shareholders only retain crucial control rights in order to monitor the board to whom they delegated a significant part of the control over the company.

In their principal costs theory,[38] Goshen and Squire provide an interesting overview of what considerations are relevant when determining to delegate control with the aim of keeping the total 'control costs' as low as possible. Control costs are the costs associated with the exercise of control over the company by the shareholders and the directors. For both parties, the shareholders and directors, these costs can be divided into competence costs, which are agent competence costs and principal competence costs, and conflict costs, which are agent conflict costs and principal conflict costs. Competence costs are the costs associated with making honest mistakes. These costs are higher when the person exercising control has less expertise and information, and these costs will decrease when this person is better informed and/or improves his expertise. The costs can also be reduced by transferring control to someone who has more expertise, which is one of the reasons why shareholders delegate a significant part of the control over the company to the board.[39] The directors have more expertise and are better informed about the functioning of the company. So, in principle, delegating control by shareholders to the board reduces the competence costs as part of the control costs. However, at the same time, delegating control

35. *Ibid.*, 68.
36. Luca Enriques et al., *The Basic Governance Structure: Minority Shareholders and Non-Shareholder Constituencies*, in Kraakman et al., *supra* n. 23, 93.
37. Clark, *supra* n. 23, 23–24.
38. Zohar Goshen & Richard Squire, *Principal Costs: A New Theory for Corporate Law and Governance*, 117 Colum. L. Rev. 767 (2017).
39. *Ibid.*, p. 786; Lynn Stout, *The Economic Nature of the Corporation*, in Francesco Parisi (ed.), *The Oxford Handbook of Law and Economics. Volume II: Private and Commercial law* (OUP 2017), 341.

introduces classic agency costs. Because the shareholders delegate powers to a better-informed board, the directors have an incentive to act opportunistically in their own interests rather than in the interests of the shareholders, whereas, with a view to value maximization, it is desirable that directors focus entirely on the shareholders' interests. Goshen and Squire refer to these costs as agent conflict costs.[40] Besides agent conflict costs, there are principal conflict costs. These costs are the result of shareholders putting their own private interests above the objective interests of the joint shareholders.[41] This can be the result of a different investment horizon,[42] empty voting,[43] and competing interests of the shareholder.[44] Reducing principal costs increases agent costs and vice versa. Assuming that parties want to be efficient and therefore consider minimal control costs to be important, the optimal governance for a specific company is where the sum of the principal and agent costs is as low as possible.[45]

[3] Criticism of the Shareholder Model

The shareholder model was the internationally dominant doctrine for several decennia,[46] but it has also received criticism. For example, it is questioned whether the shareholder is actually the residual claimant, or that there are also other stakeholders who – to a certain extent – can be identified as such.[47] It is also pointed out that shareholders – certainly in listed companies – sometimes are not residual claimants at all,[48] such as in case of securities lending or when the company is in severe financial difficulties. In addition, there is the criticism that the shareholder model involves a too sharp trade-off between material prosperity and social order. The argument is that, in addition to material prosperity, people also attach great importance to social order. To overcome this criticism, some have suggested nuances to the traditional shareholder

40. Ibid., 793–794.
41. *Ibid.*, 791–792. The argument that there is such a thing as an objectified shareholder interest has also been criticised. *See, e.g.*, Stephen M. Bainbridge, *Director Primacy and Shareholder Disempowerment*, 119 Harv. L. Rev. 1745 (2006), note 54; Lynn Stout, *The Shareholder Value Myth* (Berrett-Koehler 2012) 9.
42. Jose-Miguel Gaspar et al., *Shareholder Investment Horizons and the Market for Corporate Control*, 76 J. Financ. Econ. 135, 138 (2005).
43. Henry T.C. Hu & Bernard Black, *The New Vote Buying: Empty Voting and Hidden (Morphable) Ownership*, 79 S. Cal. L. Rev. 811, 816–817, 894 (2006).
44. Think of the shareholder who is also a creditor or employee of the company.
45. Goshen & Squire, *supra* n. 38, 796.
46. *See* Hansmann & Kraakman, *supra* n. 30.
47. Kent Greenfield, *The Failure of Corporate Law: Fundamental Flaws and Progressive Possibilities* (University of Chicago Press 2006); Tamara Belinfanti & Lynn Stout, *Contested Visions: The Value of Systems Theory for Corporate Law*, 166 U. Pa. L. Rev. 591 et seq (2018); Stout, *supra* n. 41, 39 et seq.; Bernard S. Black, *Corporate Law and Residual Claimants*, Stanford Law and Economics Olin Working Paper No. 217 (2001); Margaret M. Blair, *Ownership and Control: Rethinking Corporate Governance for the Twenty-First Century* (1995).
48. Michael C. Schouten, *The Decoupling of Voting and Economic Ownership* (Wolters Kluwer 2012).

model. Perhaps best known is the enlightened shareholder value model,[49] as included in section 172(1) of the 2006 UK Companies Act. Under this model, shareholder value must be pursued in the long term, and it is explicitly recognized that it is important, to this end, to look after the interests of other stakeholders in the company. The relationship between the company and its stakeholders is to some extent mutually beneficial. Another influential view is that of Hart and Zingales on shareholder 'welfare' maximization.[50] They argue that while companies should focus on the interests of shareholders, they should maximize shareholder welfare rather than market value. By this, the authors mean the fact that shareholders will not only find the monetary value of their shares important but also have social and ethical concerns that can (and should) be addressed.

[4] Stakeholder Model/Stakeholderism

Opposite to the shareholder model is the stakeholder model. Although there are different views on what this model entails, I focus on the fact that in this model the company – and by extension the company's board – should not focus on the interests of a single stakeholder, such as the shareholder, but on the interests of multiple stakeholders in the company. This has also been referred to as pluralistic stakeholderism.[51]

The appeal of the stakeholder model is that it is close(r) to the view that the company exists to promote social welfare by serving the interests of all stakeholders. It also fits the ideal that it is more fair to promote the interests of all stakeholders in the company, rather than just the interests of one stakeholder, and that there should be a less steep trade-off between material prosperity and social order. This model therefore reinforces more than the shareholder model, the social legitimacy of the company as a legal entity created by society,[52] which plays such an important role in our economy.

[5] Challenges of the Stakeholder Model

Although the stakeholder model is attractive from the perspective of justifying the corporate form and its privileges, at the same time it poses a number of corporate governance challenges, two of which I discuss here. First, the stakeholder model requires the board to determine who the stakeholders are. If the board manages to do that, then it must determine what the interest of these stakeholders is and weigh it against the interests of other stakeholders. But who are the stakeholders of the company? Generally speaking, this is someone whose interests are affected by the

49. Michael Cole Jensen, *Value Maximization, Stakeholder Theory, and the Corporate Objective Function*, 12 Bus. Ethics Q. 235–256 (2002).
50. Oliver Hart & Luigi Zingales, *Companies Should Maximize Shareholder Welfare Not Market Value*, 2(2) J. Law Finance Account. 247–274 (2017).
51. *See*, for this term: Bebchuk & Tallarita, *supra* n. 5.
52. Gilson, *supra* n. 29, 17; R. Edward Freeman, *Strategic Management: A Stakeholder Approach* (CUP 1984) 45.

decisions taken within the company.[53] This is a very broad and ambiguous concept,[54] and it will not always be easy for the board to determine what the relevant interests are and with whom the board should communicate about these interests.[55] Certain interests are relatively easy to identify, such as shareholders, employees, suppliers, and buyers/consumers. It becomes more difficult where it concerns broader societal interests. Moreover, the answer to the question of how relevant these interests are, can change (rapidly) on the basis of social and political developments. Equally difficult is the question to what extent companies should take into account the interests of, for example, partners in the supply chain. Are they also a stakeholder that the board should consider, and if so, in what way? Even more difficult is the question whether the interests of future stakeholders, such as future employees, should be taken into account.

If the board has determined which stakeholders the company has at any given time, then these interests must be weighed by the board in the performance of its duties. This is not easy either. How should the company's board determine what weight should be given to a particular interest? Should it try to express the interests of all stakeholders in monetary terms? Is that even possible? In practice it is difficult, if not impossible, to create a precise framework for weighing the interests at the company. This can be 'solved' by simply not making this framework precise,[56] but leave the determination with the board, which – under most circumstances – enjoy a certain degree of discretion. This autonomy, however, is regarded as problematic, which introduces the second challenge.

An essential aspect of company law is the question how to effectively monitor the board and avoid self-dealing by directors. How can it be ensured that the directors serve the interests of the company and not their own interests? The shareholder model tries to address this by imposing on directors the task of focusing on the interests of the shareholders, giving the shareholders control rights enabling them to monitor the board and intervene if necessary, and aligning the interests of directors with those of the shareholders where possible.[57] The idea is that the shareholder will exercise his control rights efficiently because he has an intrinsic interest in doing so.

In the stakeholder model, it is more difficult to ensure effective monitoring. The board should focus on the interests of all stakeholders in the company and has a certain discretion when determining and weighing the relevant interests. Who can under those circumstances monitor the board? The shareholders are not an obvious choice, since

53. Bebchuk & Tallarita, *supra* n. 5, 23; Freeman, *supra* n. 52, 25.
54. In the US, a number of states have introduced so-called constituency statutes, in which a number of stakeholders are explicitly named. For an overview of this, *see* Bebchuk & Tallarita, *supra* n. 5, 22; Kathleen Hale, *Corporate Law and Stakeholders: Moving Beyond Stakeholder Statutes*, 45 Ariz. L. Rev. 823 (2003).
55. *See also*, Andrew R. Keay, *Stakeholder Theory in Corporate Law: Has It Got What It Takes?*, 9 Rich. J. Global L. & Bus. 249 (2010).
56. Collin Mayer, *Shareholderism Versus Stakeholderism – A Misconceived Contradiction. A Comment on 'The Illusory Promise of Stakeholder Governance' by Lucian Bebchuk and Roberto Tallarita*, European Corporate Governance Institute – Law Working Paper No. 522/2020.
57. *See also*, the various legal strategies as described in John Armour, Henry Hansmann, & Reinier H. Kraakman, *Agency Problems and Legal Strategies*, in Kraakman et al., *supra* n. 23, 29–45.

they will mainly focus on their own interests, and for other specific stakeholders essentially the same problem applies. Certain authors have proposed the establishment of a 'general meeting of stakeholders', in which all or the most important stakeholders are represented.[58] In practice, stakeholder representation is to a limited extent already applied in jurisdictions where employees have the right to nominate or appoint members of the supervisory board and have certain rights of consent.[59] Introducing a formal 'meeting of stakeholders' is, however, a significant step and raises complex questions, who and how certain stakeholders, such as the environment and local community, are represented. And if a representative meeting can be established, how will the decision-making process be shaped? It seems to me that it is difficult, if not impossible, to give a proper answer to these questions and to arrive at corporate governance that is workable for companies.

[6] The Role of the Company's Own Interest

A slightly different variant from the earlier challenges is that the company focuses on the interest of the company itself, which lies in realizing value for the benefit of all stakeholders by focusing on those interests.[60] In some jurisdictions, including the Netherlands and Germany, the company's interest is to a certain extent framed as an autonomous interest, separate from the interests of individual stakeholders.[61] In the Netherlands, the Supreme Court ruled that the interest of the company - which is the norm that directors should serve - should in case the company has an affiliated enterprise be explained as 'promoting the continued success of this enterprise'.[62] The question could be raised whether qualifying the company's interest in such a manner can help (partly) overcome the challenges I described earlier. Qualifying the company's interest as an autonomous interest provides for more guidance as to what interest the company and by extension the board should serve. The company's own interest as a single metric can be further strengthened by putting more emphasis on the purpose of the company.[63] This should not be focused on the more abstract purpose of the

58. For such a proposal in a Dutch context, *see*, recently Samuel B. Garcia Nelen, *De participantenvennootschap: gedachten over een mogelijke nieuwe rechtsvorm*, MvO 3–4 (2021) 120–128.
59. Germany is the classic example for employee participation through appointment rights in the *Aufsichtrat*. *See*, on this Alexander Schall, *Stock Corporations: Corporate Governance* in Andrea Vicari & Alexander Schall (ed.), *Company Laws of the EU* (C.H. Beck, Hart, Nomos 2020), 284–285. Similarly, in the Netherlands the works council under certain circumstances also has a binding nomination right for one-third of the members of the supervisory board. *See* Van Bekkum, Hijink, Schouten, and Winter, *Corporate Governance in the Netherlands*, in Andreas M. Fleckner & Klaus Jürgen Hopt, *Comparative Corporate Governance. A Functional and International Analysis* (CUP 2013).
60. Klaus Jürgen Hopt, *Comparative Corporate Governance: The State of the Art and International Regulation*, in Fleckner & Hopt, *supra* n. 59, 42–43.
61. Steins Bisschop, Roelink, and Kemp, *The Netherlands*, in Vicari & Shall (ed.), *supra* n. 59, 1312; Schall, *supra* n. 59, 264 et seq.
62. Dutch Supreme Court 4 April 2014, *NJ* 2014/286.
63. There has been a lot of interest in corporate purpose in recent years. For a helpful overview, *see* Jill E. Fisch & Steven Davidoff Solomon, *Should Corporations Have a Purpose?*, 99 Texas Law Review (2021).

company, such as making profit, but more on what an individual company wants to achieve. Making a profit can be one of the consequences of the company pursuing its objective.[64]

At the same time, even with more focus on the own interest of the company, it remains a challenge to shape 'the' interest of the company and use this to strengthen the monitoring function. Moreover, the company cannot be viewed completely separate from its stakeholders. If a decision has to be made to a certain investment, then the board will have to determine whether that investment contributes to achieving its purpose. In doing so, the board will have to weigh, at least indirectly, the impact this investment will have on the company and thus on the interests of the stakeholders involved.[65] What will this investment do for turnover, profits, employment, the environment, and society? These questions continue to play a role and, in order to come to an answer, the board must weigh the interests involved. Formulating an 'own' interest of the company and a clear goal may therefore reduce the challenges, but it certainly does not remove them.

§10.04 PARADOX OF THE CURRENT DIVISION OF POWER IN PLURALISTIC STAKEHOLDERISM AND HOW TO UNWIND IT

As discussed earlier, there has been a shift in the perception as to what the company and company law should focus on, with more emphasis being placed on the interests of stakeholders. However, when this extents to a responsibility for the board to serve the interests of all stakeholders instead of the interests of shareholders, while at the same time keeping in place the current corporate governance framework in which important control rights are allocated to the general meeting of shareholders, this creates a paradox. After all, the board must serve different interests than the corporate body that monitors it and determines whether directors are appointed, suspended, and dismissed, that approves important board decisions and approves the annual accounts. It could be argued that this leads to a situation in which directors will de facto still mainly be concerned with the shareholders because their own 'survival' in the company depends on how the shareholders' value their performance. Given that the alternatives to the current corporate governance framework with a board and general meeting, such as introducing a general meeting of stakeholders, do not seem to be practical,[66] it seems prudent to explore how corporate governance, including the functioning of the general meeting and the division of powers, can be structured such that it limits the potential negative effects of shareholders monitoring the board within broadly the current corporate governance framework.

64. This is the way Colin Mayer puts the commitment to purpose in his book, *Prosperity: Better Business Makes the Greater Good* (OUP 2018).
65. For a similar view, *see* Samuel B. Garcia Nelen, *De beursvennootschap, corporate governance en strategie* (Wolters Kluwer 2020) 182.
66. *See*, §10.3[B][5].

[A] A First Fundamental Question: What Interest Should the General Meeting of Shareholders Be Focused On?

Bearing in mind the assumptions around pluralistic stakeholderism and retaining the current corporate governance framework with a board and general meeting, a first question is which interests the general meeting and shareholders should promote. In summary, the following considerations are relevant. If shareholders through the general meeting are allowed to focus on the shareholder's interest, it is obvious, in view of the aforementioned assumptions, that the role of the general meeting has to be marginal in order to insulate the board and the company. After all, shareholders will not be primarily focusing on the company's interest, but on their own interest. In that case, allocating far-reaching controlling rights to the general meeting would be diametrically opposed to the idea that the company should serve the interests of the company and by doing so successfully increase social welfare. The marginalization of the role of the general meeting however also severely weakens the monitoring function of the shareholders, which would then have to be compensated by – for example – more far-reaching possibilities for courts to review the behaviour of the board at the request of stakeholders. If it is determined that shareholders have a duty to serve the interests of all stakeholders, similar to the board, then it is not always necessary to marginalize the role of the general meeting. In that case, the focus could be on how to ensure that shareholders will actually focus on serving these interests by making informed decisions about how to exercise the control rights allocated to the general meeting. The question then is how shareholders, through the general meeting, can be incentivized to let the company's interests prevail over their own interests.

[B] Who Is the Principal in Pluralistic Stakeholderism?

There is a significant body of literature on the application of the principal-agent theory in company law,[67] with the most prominent being the relationship between the shareholders as principals and the directors as agents. However, this principal-agent relationship is difficult to apply in pluralistic stakeholderism. After all, the starting point in this relationship is that the shareholder is the principal, while this starting point is not accepted under pluralistic stakeholderism. The principal-agent theory, insofar as it pertains to the relationship between the board and the general meeting, also relies heavily on aligning the interests of directors to the interests of the shareholders, while this is precisely what should be avoided under pluralistic stakeholderism. But if the shareholders are not the principals, then who is?

67. Traditionally, three principal-agent problems are identified in company law, being: (i) the conflict between the shareholders (principals) and the directors (the agents), (ii) the conflict between the minority shareholders (principals) and the majority shareholders (agents), and (iii) the conflict between the shareholders (agents) and the other parties contracting with the firm (principals). *See* Kraakman et al., *supra* n. 23, 30.

I believe that – as part of pluralistic stakeholderism – it is possible to identify two principal-agent relationships:

(1) the relationship between the company and the corporate bodies and their members, where the company is the principal and the corporate bodies and their members are the agents; and
(2) the relationship between those involved in the company and its business (the stakeholders) and the company bodies and their members, where these stakeholders are the principals and the company bodies and their members are the agents.

It is, certainly in the first principal-agent relationship, not a very strict application of the principal-agent theory, but rather the application of the underlying thoughts. This theory is based on the principal delegating control over decisions to the agent and retaining a certain degree of control over the agent himself.[68] The principal determines the ultimate goal and the general strategy.[69] With the company as principal, these concepts do not apply because the company is a legal fiction and cannot exert proactive control over the agents.[70] Where there is a parallel with the principal-agent theory, is that the power to make decisions that affect the interest of the company is delegated to the corporate bodies, and they should exercise their powers in the interest of the company.[71] This delegation also inherently holds the risk that the person to whom that control is delegated will act primarily in his own interest rather than in – here – the corporate interest. These are, in essence, the agent conflict costs as described by Goshen and Squire,[72] and strategies to limit these costs are – to a certain extent – also helpful when thinking about the two principal-agent relationships mentioned earlier.

Identifying the company as the principal under the first principal-agent relationship has many consequences. The most prominent is that all parties to whom control rights are granted (or delegated) over the company should be regarded as agents and should therefore act in the interest of the company as principal.[73] This standard of conduct therefore also applies to the general meeting and the shareholders as agents, to whom control rights over the company are delegated. This leads to another

68. *See*, Eric Andrew Posner, *Agency Models in Law and Economics*, John M. Olin Program in Law and Economics Working Paper No. 92, 2000; John Winsor Pratt & Richard Jay Zeckhauser, *Principals and Agents: An Overview*, in John W. Pratt & Richard J. Zeckhauser (ed.), *Principals and Agents: The Structure of Business* (Harvard Business School Press 1991) 1–35.
69. Robert C. Clark, *Agency Costs Versus Fiduciary Duties*, *in* Pratt & Zeckhauser (ed.), *supra* n. 68, 56.
70. It is however possible to create standards on the basis of which directors and shareholders are required to focus on the interest of the company and can – to the extent necessary – be corrected (*see* Kraakman et al., *supra* n. 23, 31).
71. Beate Sjåfjell, *Redefining Agency Theory to Internalize Environmental Product Externalities: A Tentative Proposal Based on Life Cycle Thinking*, in Eleonore Maitre-Ekern, Carl Dalhammar, & Hans Christian Bugge (ed.), *Preventing Environmental Damage from Products* (CUP 2018) 101 et seq.; Sofie Cools, *The Dividing Line Between Shareholder Democracy and Board Autonomy: Inherent Conflict of Interest as Normative Criterion*, 11(2) Eur. Co. Financ. Law Rev. 271 (2014).
72. Goshen & Squire, *supra* n. 38, 793 et seq.
73. This is similar to the position taken by Sjåfjell, *supra* n. 71, 111.

interesting insight, namely that the agent conflict costs, as described in §10.03[B][2], also arise when the general meeting exercises control rights, similar to when the board exercises those rights. To the extent that national law confers control rights to the general meeting, this will therefore lead to agency conflict costs. These costs will further increase when national law allows the shareholders to serve their own interests, as it does in many jurisdictions, because this actually allows the shareholders to create these agency conflict costs when exercising control rights through the general meeting. From this perspective, this is an undesirable and costly freedom granted to shareholders. This insight can also lead to the conclusion that, from a policy perspective, it is quite conceivable to approach the reduction of agency conflict costs created by shareholders with similar legal strategies as those developed for directors, including rules that regulate the behaviour of shareholders in the form of fiduciary duties and limit the shareholders' freedom to make certain decisions.[74]

The qualification of all stakeholders in the company as principals under a second principal-agent relationship also has certain consequences. A difference with the first principal-agent relationship is that for this principal-agent theory it is possible to – at least in theory – identify stakeholders who could have the power to determine the ultimate goal and the general strategy of the company. At the same time, it will be difficult to turn this theory into practice. After all, it would mean that all stakeholders would have to be identified and be able to consult each other. In practice, the information and coordination costs are (yet) too high to achieve a reasonable working model.[75] However, this second principal-agent relationship does offer a legal argument for creating a duty of the corporate bodies and their members towards all stakeholders as principals. To ensure that the corporate bodies and their members adhere to this duty, the principals must have some form of monitoring rights over the agents. As in many principal-agent relationships, there is information asymmetry and coordination costs between the principals and the agents,[76] which are particularly high in this principal-agent relationship because of significant diversity between stakeholders and the difficulty in identifying them. As a result, it is difficult for the stakeholders as principals to effectively monitor the corporate bodies and their members as agents for their responsibilities without incurring excessive costs.[77] In practice, these high costs result in more control being delegated to the agents, where these costs are incurred to a lesser extent.[78] In order to reduce information asymmetry and improve the monitoring function and thereby reduce costs as far as possible, certain strategies could be adopted around disclosure of information by the company, such as additional disclosure on the effect decisions have on stakeholders, setting up meetings to strengthen the dialogue between company and stakeholders, etc.

74. *See* for more detail on these strategies: Kraakman et al., *supra* n. 23, 31 et seq.
75. *See* for these challenges §10.03[B][5].
76. Pratt & Zeckhauser, *supra* n. 68, 3.
77. Kraakman et al., *supra* n. 23, 29.
78. *See* more broadly on the relationship between monitoring costs and delegating control: Easterbrook & Fischel, *supra* n. 32, 66–67.

[C] Instruments to Reduce Agency Conflict Costs and Agency Competence Costs under These Two Principal-Agent Relationships

Identifying the abovementioned principal-agent relationships in pluralistic stakeholderism immediately raises the question which legal instruments could be used to regulate these relationships to reduce overall control costs. This question can be considered from many different perspectives, but within the limits of this contribution I attempt to develop two perspectives:

(1) the role of enforceable standards of behaviour versus control rights; and
(2) the potential of mandatory cooperation between the corporate bodies of the company.

[1] Enforceable Standards of Behaviour Versus Control Rights

When considering company law, a distinction can be made between enforceable standards of conduct and control rights.[79] A standard of conduct states how the corporate bodies and their members should conduct themselves. This can be a generally prescribed standard of conduct, such as promoting the company's interests and acting reasonable and fair, but it can also be a specific standard of conduct that applies to the exercise of a particular control right. An enforceable standard of conduct may ensure that the corporate body and its members can actually be forced to act according to the standard of conduct rather than in their own interests. This correction can take place not only through (1) the exercise of a right of control by another corporate body[80] but also through (2) intervention by the public supervisory authority or (3) because a stakeholder - including the company itself - requests the court to intervene.

Allocating control rights to the general meeting of shareholders as a correction mechanism is more effective in a shareholder model than in pluralistic stakeholderism. In the shareholder model, these rights are granted to the shareholders so they can ensure that the directors act in the interest of the shareholders and, if necessary, correct the behaviour of directors. If the control right is structured such that the shareholders themselves take important decisions, this is also effective because the shareholder is intrinsically motivated to promote its own interests and will decide accordingly - or so

79. This is in some ways similar to the distinction made in the Anatomy of Corporate Law between rules and standards (Kraakman et al., *supra* n. 23, 32), but different in the sense that the control rights are focused on allocating the decision-making power over a certain topic to a specific corporate body, whereas standards of conduct determine in what way the corporate body should act. These standards can focus on not only how the corporate body should act in general but also how it should act when exercising a very specific control rights. *See*, for example, the dividend distributions on the Dutch private limited liability company, as discussed in para. §10.04[B][2].
80. For instance, when a corporate body (or its members) is granted the right to exercise control over another body or over certain decisions. This allows the corporate body with the right of control to monitor the other corporate body and its members and, where necessary, correct them.

it is argued.[81] This is different under pluralistic stakeholderism. There, too, these rights can and are granted to shareholders, but shareholders are not intrinsically motivated to promote the interests of all stakeholders. Granting control rights to shareholders in the stakeholder model therefore does not reduce agent conflict costs, but rather shifts these costs from one agent (the directors) to another (the shareholders). Because there are no alternative corporate bodies to monitor the board in the interest of the company and its stakeholders, it is more difficult to structure the monitoring function in pluralistic stakeholderism in a way that the control rights are allocated to the principals. In the first principal-agent relationship, the company is the principal and, as a legal fiction, cannot exercise control rights itself. In the second principal-agent relationship, the joint stakeholders are the principals. However, as set out earlier, it is difficult to identify all of these principals,[82] let alone ensure that they can all be represented. The coordination costs are therefore too high, which argues in favour of delegating control rights to agents.[83]

Based on this observation, I would argue that under pluralistic stakeholderism, more than under the shareholder model, the focus should be on enforceable standards of behaviour rather than on control rights for other corporate bodies. Standards of conduct can require corporate bodies and their members to promote certain interests, such as the corporate interest or the interests of the joint stakeholders. This is a legal strategy aimed at the first principal-agent relationship. In addition, standards of conduct may impose a duty of care, for example, that company bodies and their members must act with due care in relation to the interests of all stakeholders. This is a legal strategy aimed at the second principal-agent relationship.

Standards of conduct cannot be prescribed without engagement and – at least to an extent and potentially subject to certain threshold – must be enforceable, so that corporate bodies and their members have an incentive to comply with these standards. To ensure that standards of conduct are enforceable, stakeholders need to have access to courts in order to enforce standards. But what type of litigation instruments could be useful? This depends on national law, but inspiration could be taken from procedures on specialized business courts, such as the Dutch Enterprise Chamber before which certain stakeholders in the company can initiate so-called inquiry proceedings.[84] In inquiry proceedings, the claimant has to request the Enterprise Chamber to order an investigation into the policy and affairs of the company, which can include acts of both the directors and the shareholders.[85] After the court-appointed investigator has performed its investigation, parties can request the Enterprise Chamber to rule that mismanagement took place and order certain measures to be taken, such as the dismissal of directors, temporarily transfer shares to a trustee, or the dissolution of the company. This type of proceedings can be a useful tool to enforce standards of conduct.

81. In practice however, shareholders do not always have the same interests and are not necessarily always focused on the 'objective' interests of the joint shareholders.
82. *Study on Directors' Duties and Sustainable Corporate Governance*, July 2020, op.europa.eu, p. 5.
83. Kraakman et al., *supra* n. 23, 30.
84. *See* Van Bekkum et al., *supra* n. 59, 694–696.
85. Parties can also request the Enterprise Chamber to order interim relief, for instance, in order to break a deadlock within the board or general meeting (art. 2:239a DCC).

At the same time, there are several challenges to this system. First, courts – even specialized ones – will probably not be the most competent to fully scrutinize business decisions.[86] With most judges realizing this limitation, they will almost instinctively try to limit their review to procedural steps and obvious abuse / self-dealing and otherwise defer to the business judgment of the directors. Second, allocating rights to stakeholders to challenge the behaviour of corporate bodies and their members in court could open the floodgates to more litigation by special interest groups. To avoid this, it could be considered using preliminary procedures to determine to what extent the claims brought have merit, for instance, as is the case in many national laws for derivative claims by (minority) shareholders, while at the same time providing adequate reimbursement of actual legal costs for the claimant if the claim is considered to have (potential) merit.[87]

Another possibility is to see which legal strategies can be used to bring the interests of agents into line with those of the principal. In this respect, the first principal-agent relationship is particularly important. Allowing these interests to align can be done, for example, by organizing the remuneration of the board in this way. In the second principal-agent relationship, there is no principal with a relatively unambiguous interest, but several principals with divergent interests. There it is much more difficult to let the interests coincide. A serious challenge is to develop legal strategies that allow the interests of shareholders to coincide with the interests of the company, even if these interests are less incompatible as they may seem. After all, the interests of shareholders and the company often overlap in practice; the enlightened shareholder value model is based on this line of thinking, and it also underlines the EU Shareholder Rights Directive II, as can be seen from recital 14 of this Directive, and various Stewardship Codes.[88] It is especially important to think about this in situations where this is potentially not the case and the agent conflict costs are potentially high, such as in dividend distributions, share repurchases, and takeovers.

[2] Cooperation and How Cooperation Can Be Shaped: Back to the Idea of Governance Costs

In contrast to the shareholder model, under pluralistic stakeholderism there is no clear principal to whom certain control rights over the companies can be allocated. As a result, the legal strategy of reducing agency conflict costs by assigning control rights to the principal cannot be effectively applied. However, I believe there is a legal strategy relating to control rights, namely mandatory cooperation between the corporate bodies. The concept in essence entails that by forcing cooperation when exercising certain control rights, the corporate bodies (and their members) are forced to reach

86. John Edward Parkinson, *Corporate Power and Responsibility: Issues in the Theory of Company Law* (Clarendon Press 1993), p. 86.
87. *See* Carsten Gerner-Beuerle & Michael A. Schillig, *Comparative Company Law* (OUP 2019) 698, 711; Dorresteijn et al., *supra* n. 1, pp. 180–182.
88. *See,* for instance, the Dutch Stewardship Code: https://www.eumedion.nl/themas/Stewardship.html.

compromises, as a result of which they cannot solely serve their own interests. Although it does not directly force the corporate bodies to serve the interests of all stakeholders, it does create a form of interconnectedness between the corporate bodies within the company, whereby the corporate bodies 'control' each other when exercising control rights. Control rights that must be exercised jointly are already common practice in some jurisdictions. Also here, inspiration can be obtained from Dutch law. An example is dividend distribution rules for the Dutch private company.[89] Under this provision, the general meeting in principle resolves whether to make a distribution, but that resolution remains without effect unless and until the board approves this resolution. Because of this provision, a distribution will only take place if the board and general meeting are in agreement. A similar cooperation mechanism can be found in many oligarchic clauses for Dutch companies.[90] An oligarchic clause is a provision in the articles of association whereby the power of an individual shareholder or the general meeting is limited by determining that exercising that power (1) is partly dependent on another corporate body or third party or (2) is subject to a higher threshold. There are many different forms of oligarchic clauses, but these include in any case (a) clauses that remove the right of initiative from the general meeting and provide it to another corporate body or third party, and (b) clauses that link a right of prior or subsequent approval of another corporate body to the implementation of a resolution by the general meeting. These categories of oligarchic clauses can also be combined.[91] To illustrate: the shareholder has the power to amend the articles of association,[92] but in Dutch listed companies the articles of association generally determine that the board has to take the initiative to amend the articles and the supervisory board needs to approve that proposed resolutions. As a result, the articles of association of the company can effectively only be amended if all corporate bodies cooperate and thus agree with each other.[93] These oligarchic clauses are used by a significant majority of Dutch listed companies.

A comparable proposal is made by Garcia Nelen. He proposes that only negative control rights (approval rights) should be allocated to the general meeting.[94] The idea behind his proposal is that the board in principle has primacy when it comes to initiating policy, strategy, and other matters that fall within the remit of the board. Although GarciaNelen and I have broadly the same intention, I am not advocating the complete abolition of the shareholders' right of initiative because this would unnecessarily limit the possibilities for the corporate bodies to monitor each other. Shareholders must be able to raise issues in the same way as the board, in order for shareholders to be able to initiate a dialogue and to resolve in the general meeting whether or not to

89. Art. 2:216 (1), (2) DCC.
90. Bastiaan Kemp & A. Sebastian Renshof, *The Limited Power to Appoint and Dismiss Management Board Members in Dutch Listed Companies*, 17(2) Eur. Co. Law (2020).
91. *Ibid.*, 38.
92. Art. 2:121 (1) DCC.
93. *See* for more detail: Bastiaan Kemp, Philippe L. Hezer, & A. Sebastian Renshof, *Limiting Shareholder Power in Dutch Listed Companies*, Oxford Business Law Blog: www.law.ox.ac.uk/business-law-blog/blog/2020/05/limiting-shareholder-power-dutch-listed-companies.
94. Garcia Nelen, *supra* n. 65, 385.

approve certain proposals. As long as cooperation is mandatory and thereby limits the possibilities for agents to act in their own interest, it is ensured that the shareholders cannot pursue solely their own interests. Such mandatory cooperation can be achieved, for example, by stating that in most cases shareholder proposals must be approved by the board before the general meeting can pass a resolution. It should at the same time be recognized that an exception to this system is required in case of control rights that affect the directors themselves, such as the power to appoint, suspend, or dismiss directors. For those cases, it could be considered to raise the threshold for exercising these control rights (the majority requirement and/or quorum) in the case of a resolution at the initiative of the shareholders, rather than requiring cooperation between the board and the general meeting.[95]

Starting from the concept that mandatory cooperation between corporate bodies can strengthen corporate governance and limit agency costs, what is an effective way of shaping the division of powers? Here, too, law and economics theories can offer valuable insights, where I take inspiration from the principal costs theory by Goshen and Squire as discussed earlier. They assume that the total control costs consist of four quadrants (*see* Table 10.1).[96]

Table 10.1 Overview Total Control Costs

	Competence Costs	*Conflict Costs*
Principal	*Principal competence costs*: these costs arise from, for example, a lack of expertise, information and high coordination costs on the part of the principal	*Principal conflict costs*: these costs result from lack of incentives to act in the interest of the collective interests of the collective principals, such as – in the case of shareholders – rational apathy, empty voting and different investment horizons
Agent	*Agent competence costs*: these costs arise from, for example, a lack of expertise, competence and information	*Agent conflict costs*: these are the classic agency costs, arising from acting in the agent's own interest rather than in the principal's interest

Although this theory builds on the shareholder as principal and the directors as agents, it also offers insights for shaping mandatory cooperation between the agents in the first principal-agent relationship. It clarifies, for example, that allocating control rights to a particular agent within the company, such as directors, supervisory directors, and shareholders leads to certain costs. Those costs vary depending on which agent is granted certain control rights. An effective corporate governance aims to minimize the costs that arise from a particular allocation of powers. Consider the following theoretical and abstract example: suppose, as a starting point, that the

95. Kemp & Renshof, *supra* n. 90.
96. Goshen & Squire, *supra* n. 38, 795.

shareholders have 100% (full) control over the company. If the shareholders transfer 1% control to the directors, this will result, as a fictional example, in a saving of 100 control costs. However, this delegation also creates new control costs of 50 because allocating control rights to the board also generates competence costs and conflict costs. In this fictional case, the shift of competences is efficient because it would lower the total control costs by 50. How much control can/should be transferred within a specific company depends on the characteristic of the specific company and its actors, including:

(1) Competence: how competent are the directors and shareholders?[97] One of the reasons that control over the company is partly delegated to the board is because these directors are often more competent than shareholders when it comes to decisions affecting the company.[98] However, the precise division of competences will depend on the specific competences of the board and the general meeting. In particular for shareholders, the differences can be significant. Private equity investors will generally be more competent, especially concerning certain aspects of the company, than a private retail investor. From the point of view of competencies, it is therefore arguable that the general meeting should have more control over the company when the shareholder is highly competent than when the shareholders have a low competence.
(2) Complexity: closely related to competence is the complexity of the decision. Not every decision is equally complex. A low-competent decision maker can more easily take a decision on a less-complex issue, whereas a good decision on complex issues requires more competence. As a result, it is generally advisable to link complex decisions to a highly competent corporate body. More simple decision can be linked to a low-competent corporate body. Again, in general terms, the distinction between the board and the general meeting is relatively easy to make. Shareholders will generally be less able to take a complex decision because they lack the necessary information and competence and the fact that they do not want to incur costs to compensate for this. The directors, on the other hand, are more likely to have the necessary information and competence. Here again, however, it is important what type of shareholder the company has: a highly competent shareholder will generally be better able to take good complex decisions than a less-competent shareholder. If exercising control rights consists of taking several steps, then the complexity of the decision and the competence of the agent can also be taken into account within that series of steps. An example is the amendment of articles of association and the oligarchic clauses as already briefly described earlier. Deciding exactly how the articles of association should be amended is a more complex decision than deciding whether the

97. *Ibid.*, 785.
98. Donald J. Smythe, *Shareholder Democracy and the Economic Purpose of the Corporation*, 63 Wash. Lee Law Rev. 1407, 1409 (2006).

proposed amendment should be adopted (yes or no). For this reason, in a listed company with dispersed ownership it could be better to allocate the right of initiative to a high competent body (the board) and the 'yes-no' decision to a low competent body (the general meeting).

(3) Information: closely related to competence and complexity is supply of information. To what extent does the agent have sufficient information to take decisions and, if he does not have this information, what is needed to ensure that this information is made available and what are the costs of obtaining and processing this information?? Again, when taking decisions in the company, the general meeting will generally have less access to information than the board. In addition, shareholders will be less inclined to incur the costs of processing large amounts of information to ensure that they are adequately informed, certainly in the case of dispersed share ownership. Moreover, the question is to what extent information can be freely shared with shareholders, given that the information can also include sensitive information that could fall in the hands of competitors.

(4) Coordination costs: there are costs associated with exercising control rights. These costs are almost always higher when the control rights are exercised through the general meeting because their position generally means that they have an information deficit, there is often a considerable number of shareholders, and a general meeting must be convened and held to take the decision.[99] The more dispersed the ownership of the shares in the company, the higher these costs become because each individual shareholder who wants to participate in the general meeting has to incur these costs.[100] The costs are generally lower if the decision is taken by the board, where there is also more flexibility regarding the manner and timing of the decision-making.

Each of these circumstances can provide insights on how to structure mandatory cooperation between corporate bodies within the company. First, it argues in favour of a flexible company law that can be organized on the basis of competencies, complexity of decisions, information allocation, and coordination costs. Second, default rules can be used to organize company law in a way that will in most cases lead to an efficient allocation of control rights, which would then require the founders or - later - the shareholders and board members to deviate from. In case of listed companies, this would include a significant delegation of control rights to the board because they are better able to decide what is in the company's interests. This is indeed also the default rule in most jurisdictions, where directors have significant control over the company and its day-to-day management, and shareholders only retain the most important control rights, such as the power to appoint and dismiss board members, amend the articles of association, and approve the most important board decision. In case of mandatory cooperation between the corporate bodies of the company, the right of

99. Cools, *supra* n. 71, 272.
100. Goshen & Squire, *supra* n. 38, 786.

initiative for complex decisions will more often be allocated to the board, whereas less-complex decisions can be resolved by the general meeting. If the coordination costs for a corporate body are significant, this provides an additional incentive to allocate only the most important decisions to that corporate body.

§10.05 CONCLUSION

At the start of this contribution, the question was raised what the role of the general meeting should be in the changing corporate governance landscape. After discussing how this landscape is changing, what the main doctrines are on how to maximize the purpose of the company and looking at the shareholders – and by extension the general meeting – as agents of the company and of the joint stakeholders, several thoughts about the answer to this question can be shared.

First, it seems sensible to keep the general meeting of shareholders in place and not replace it by a general meeting of stakeholders. Although a general meeting of stakeholders could theoretically provide for a corporate body in which the stakeholders as principals can be represented, the challenges and costs related to implementing such a meeting seems to be (at least for now) insurmountable. Therefore, a general meeting of shareholders can play a key role in monitoring the board and avoiding that directors serve primarily their own interests instead of the interests of the company. Second, given that shareholders could be qualified as agents of the company and its stakeholders, I would argue in favour of changing the role of the general meeting in the sense that the corporate body and its members should have a duty to focus on the interests of the company and its stakeholders instead of having the freedom to act in their own interests. To ensure that shareholders actually adhere to this duty and to avoid that shareholders act in their own interests, two mechanisms could be considered, namely (i) creating or enhancing the possibility for stakeholders to enforce this duty through the courts and (ii) instating a system of mandatory cooperation between the corporate bodies when exercising control rights, so as to force these corporate bodies to reach compromises.

These insights do not give a full answer to the question what the role of the general meeting in a more pluralistic company law should be. It does however – I hope – provide food for thought on how to deal with this, and thereby fulfils its purpose.

CHAPTER 11
Empowering Minority Shareholders

Hanna Almlöf[*]

§11.01 INTRODUCTION

The limited company is an extraordinary legal invention. Its charm is based on legal personality and limited liability, combined with a flexible ownership construction with units (shares) that can be traded individually without affecting the business as such. This makes the company independent of its owners and potentially able to outlive its shareholders in eternally. However, the main usage of the limited company is not for this reason. Most companies are small- and medium-sized enterprises (SMEs) and closely held, i.e., run by a few numbers of owners who are also managers and active in the day-to-day business.[1] This makes the company indeed dependent on its shareholders and on a functional collaboration between them. It also means that conflicts among the shareholders can pose a serious corporate governance problem in SMEs, as they affect the management of the company, due to the overlap of roles.

The purpose of this chapter is to evaluate if company law regulation is in need of new instruments to enhance good governance when tacking shareholder conflicts in SMEs. For this purpose, I first need to explore statutory and contractual regulation and its function in situations where there is a disagreement or a conflict between controlling and minority shareholders in owner-managed SMEs. This discussion is divided into three phases: before an individual becomes a minority shareholder, during the co-ownership, and when a conflict has arisen leading to a collapse of the collaboration.

---

* This study has been enabled through generous financial support by the Ragnar Söderberg Foundation, Jan Wallander and Tom Hedelius Foundation, and Tore Browaldh Foundation. Special thanks to my fellow team members of the Ownership Dynamics research project in Sweden and Denmark. Also, many thanks to Assistant Professor Britta Behrendt Jonsson, who have read and commented early drafts of the chapter and helped me with German sources.

1. *See, e.g.*, Brian Robert Cheffins, *Company Law: Theory, Structure, and Operation* 48–49 (Clarendon 1997).

In each of these phases, statutory or contractual regulation can empower the minority shareholder. The analysis will, however, show that traditional shareholder protection rules can increase the conflict rather than solve it and hereby hinder the company to run properly. Consequently, I discuss three instruments on how to empower minority shareholders in SME-conflicts while also promoting good governance.

The chapter is organized in sections as follows: In §11.02, a theoretical background to the tension between minority and controlling shareholder(s) is introduced, and how ownership issues inevitably affect management and board work in closely held companies. In §11.03, the origins of disagreements or conflicts in SMEs are explained based on diverse interests and a combination of financial and non-financial goals. Section 11.04 starts with an overview of regulatory techniques used by the legislature to protect minority shareholders. Regulatory tools discussed in the chapter include procedural safeguards, disclosure, mandatory prohibitions, standard based review, and statutory exit rights. I continue the section by discussing how conflicts in SMEs are, or fail to be, prevented, counteracted, or solved by these regulatory techniques also taking into consideration contractual aspects such as bargaining power. As a response to identified regulatory shortfalls, three instruments to help overcome shareholder conflicts as a corporate governance problem are analysed and suggestions on how to regulate this in the companies act or by contractual means are put forward in §11.05. The chapter ends with concluding remarks including some suggestion for future research avenues.

§11.02 THE CORPORATE GOVERNANCE DILEMMA IN SMEs

SMEs represent 99% of all businesses in the European Union (EU) and are often referred to as the backbone of Europe's economy.[2] According to the EU definition, SMEs are enterprises which employ fewer than 250 persons and which have an annual turnover not exceeding EUR 50 million, and/or an annual balance sheet total not exceeding EUR 43 million.[3] Notably, the EU definition says nothing about the ownership structure of these firms, and such data is much harder to collect. However, studies show that most limited companies have only one shareholder. Among companies with several owners, two shareholders are most common, followed by three to four shareholders, and five or more shareholders are actually quite rare.[4] Further, in a typical SME, the shareholders are also engaged in the daily business activities.[5] For these firms, with an overlap of roles between shareholders, board members, and managers, I use the term owner-managed companies.

2. https://ec.europa.eu/growth/smes_en.
3. *See* Commission Recommendation of 6 May 2003 concerning the definition of micro, small and medium-sized enterprises.
4. *See, e.g.*, Nykredit, *Ejerlederanalysen 2018*, 5; Morten Bennedsen & Kasper Meisner Nielsen, *Ejerledelse i Danmark – Rapport 1: Ejerledelse – baggrund og udbredelse* (Center for Ejerledede Virksomheder, Copenhagen Business School 2015).
5. *Ibid.*, p. 34 which report an overlap of 84% in Danish private limited liability companies (anpartsselskaber).

Corporate governance is the overall system of rules, norms, processes, and practices to manage and control a business entity. The essence of corporate governance mechanisms is to address divergence of interests between involved parties. The dominating theory to describe the governance mechanism of a limited company is agency theory as developed by Jensen & Meckling. They defined a principal-agent relationship: 'as a contract under which one or more persons (the principal(s)) engage another person (the agent) to perform some service on their behalf which involves some decision making authority to the agent'[6] In the 'modern firm', as defined by Berle & Means in 1932,[7] the shareholders are the principal and the managers are its agent, and the agency costs origin from the risk of suboptimal decisions or opportunistic behaviour taken by the agent.

However, Jensen & Meckling have also shown that agency cost appears in all type of collaborations: businesses, public bodies, cooperatives, universities, etc. as well as in collaborations between equal parties.[8] Consequently, more than one principal-agent relationship can be identified in limited companies. Three agency problems are commonly addressed in company law, with the first relationship between owners and managers.[9] The second principal-agent relationship lies among shareholders where the shareholder(s) with decision-making power is the agent for all shareholders. In other words, minority shareholders are the principals relying on the controlling shareholder(s).[10] Finally, the third agency problem, which will not be further developed in this chapter, is between the company and creditors or other outside stakeholders.[11]

In owner-managed companies, the first agency problem could be non-existent if there is a full overlap between shareholders and managers in the firm.[12] However, even if full overlap is not the case, the agency costs are typically lower in small firms as the principals and agents are few and visible for each other resulting in, e.g., low-monitoring costs.[13] The opposite could however be the case for the second agency

6. *See* Michael C. Jensen & William H. Meckling, *Theory of the Firm: Managerial Behavior, Agency Costs and Ownership Structure,* 3 (4) J, Financ. Econ. 305, 308 (1976).
7. *See* Adolf Augustus Berle & Gardiner Coit Means, *The Modern Corporation and Private Property* (9th ed., Harcourt 1932).
8. Jensen & Meckling, *supra* n. 6, at 309.
9. *See, e.g.*, John Armour, Henry Hansmann, & Reinier H. Kraakman, *Agency Problems and Legal Stategies*, in *The Anatomy of Corporate Law: a comparative and functional approach*, 29–31 (Reinier H. Kraakman, et al. eds, Oxford University Press, 2017).
10. In family business literature, this relationship is sometimes called principal-principal. *See, e.g.*, Sanjay Goel, Iiro Jussila, & Tuuli Ikäheimonen, *Governance in Family Firms: a Review and Research Agenda,* in *The Sage Handbook of Family Business*, 239–240 (Leif Melin, et al. eds, SAGE Publications, 2014).
11. *See, e.g.*, Jonathan R. Macey, *Corporate Law and Corporate Governance – A Contractual Perspective*, J. Corp. Law 187 (1992/93).
12. *See, e.g.*, Guido Corbetta & Carlo Salvato, *Self-Serving or Self-Actualizing? Models of Man and Agency Costs in Different Types of Family Firms – A Commentary on 'Comparing the Agency Costs of Family and Non-Family Firms: Conseptual Issues and Exploratory Evidence'*, 28 (4) Entrepreneurship Theory and Practice, 360 (2004). *See also*, Mette Neville, *Conflicts in Small and Medium-sized Enterprises*, in *Shareholder Conflicts*, 89–90 (Paul Krüger Andersen, et al. eds, Thomson Reuters 2006).
13. *See* Frank H. Easterbrook & Daniel R. Fischel, *Close Corporations and Agency Costs*, 38 (2) Stanf. Law Rev. 271, 274 (1986).

problem. Conflicting interests and opinions which in companies with dispersed ownership could lie between the shareholders and managers would instead typically lie between controlling owners and minority shareholders.[14] In addition, the close relationship between owners, and consequently between owners and managers, can both be an advantage and handicap for the business, i.e., it can both reduce transaction costs and be the source for them.[15] Due to the overlap of roles in owner-managed firm, disagreements or conflict among the owner are likely to affect both strategic decision and the daily management of the company. Therefore, shareholder conflicts become a corporate governance problem. Worse case scenarios include deadlocks, oppression, and possible liquidation of the company. Hence, in closely held companies, ownership issues become business issues, as the overlap of roles make it close to impossible to separate the two spheres.

Overall, the essence of corporate governance is to address divergence of interests between agents and principals, and in closely held businesses this is often divergence of interests between the majority and the minority shareholders. Corporate governance instruments can both be statutory, i.e., provided by law, or contractual. Before discussing such instruments in §11.04 and §11.05, let us examine some typical origins of disagreements or conflict in SMEs.

§11.03 DISAGREEMENTS AND CONFLICTS IN SMEs

Owner-managed firms are dependent on a functional and fruitful collaboration between shareholders. The shareholders are often key employees, and full-time dedication in the firm is sometimes regulated in a shareholders' agreement or simply a tacit assumption for the collaboration. However, just as the business is being put to the test during its lifetime, so are the shareholders. In difficult times, such as regression or any financial restraints for the company, even minor disagreements might become vital. When each individual is important, every opinion matters.

One characteristic of closely held businesses that increases this complexity is diversified goals. Research shows that an important part of the ownership logic of closely held businesses, including family firms, is the combination of both economic and non-economic goals. Goals are an embedded part of the owners' idiosyncratic

14. *See, e.g.*, Mette Neville, *Corporate Governance i mindre og mellemstore virksomheder*, in *Corporate Governance i Danmark: Om god selskabsledelse i et dansk og internationalt perspektiv*, 221, fn 14; James J. Chrisman, Jess Huan Chua, & Reginald A. Litz, *Comparing the Agency Costs of Family Firms and Non-Family Firms – Conceptual Issues and Exploratory Evidence*, 28 (4) Entrepreneurship Theory and Practice 339 (2004); Øyvind Bøhren, *Eierne, styret og ledelsen: corporate governance i Norge* 50 (Fagbokforlaget, 2011); Daniel Stattin, *Aktieägares rätt till information*, in *Aktieägares rättigheter* 49 (Carl Svernlöv ed., Stockholm Centre for Commercial Law, Iustus, 2009).
15. *See, e.g.*, Mette Neville, *A Statutory Buy-Out Right in SMEs – an Important Corporate Governance Mechanism and Minority Protection?*, in *Company law and SMEs* 251 (Mette Neville & Karsten Engsig Sørensen eds, Thomson Reuters, 2010).

vision.[16] For example, reputation and social status are important aspects of running the business.[17] Studies have also shown that owner-managers uphold good relations with co-owners and/or family members as a goal itself, as well as responsibility towards employees and the local community.[18] The latter is often explained by the fact that the owners are resident where the business is situated, they are known in town and are often involved in a set of local activities.

Based in empirical studies, Neville concludes that owner-managers primary motivation often is freedom and autonomy.[19] In a Danish survey from 2010, owner-managers listed reasons for running their company. The most common answers were to work within their interest, to be autonomous, and to pursue their entrepreneurial vision. Only 3.3% answered that high salary and dividend was their main reason to pursue business, and merely 3.8% stated economic gain by selling the shares as their main goal.[20] Similar results are found in a Finnish survey from 2002, where the three most common reasons of the respondents were (1) to be among the top three companies in the main business, (2) to provide financial independence to the owning family and, (3) to maximize profitability.[21] High dividend came as number eight on the list of ten fixed alternatives, and to sell the firm when opportunity arises came absolute last. Mustakallio et al. use this data to study corporate governance structures of Finnish family firms. They conclude that family firms need to develop governance structures that promote cohesion and shared vision among owners and reduce harmful conflict. When it comes to non-financial goals, implementation of social control mechanisms that promote social interaction and the formation of a shared vision is crucial.[22]

Considering all possible combinations of both financial and different non-financial goals, it is easy to understand that a joint vision of the business is difficult to uphold. In particular, if the majority and minority shareholders enter the business with different perspectives, it is hard to imagine a complete consensus. For example, imagine a second-generation family business owner with majority vote who is aiming to let the third generation enter the company, while the minority shareholder is a key

16. The notion is used by Zohar Goshen & Assaf Hamdani, *Corporate Control and the Regulation of Controlling Shareholders*, in *The Law and Finance of Related Party Transactions* 28 (Luca Enriques & Tobias Tröger eds, Cambridge University Press 2019) to capture an entrepreneur's business idea or their method for pursuing it.
17. Cf. Ronald J. Gilson, *Controlling Shareholders and Corporate Governance: Complicating the Comparative Taxonomy*, 119 (6) Harv. Law Rev. 1663–1664 (2006) who discuss non-pecuniary private benefits of control.
18. *See* Ethel Brundin, Emilia Florin Samuelsson, & Leif Melin, *Family Ownership Logic: Framing the Core Characteristics of Family Business*, 20 (1) J.Manag Organ. Vol. 6 (2014), Theme 4.
19. *See* Mette Neville, *Corporate Governance and Strategic Change in SMEs in a Digital Age – the Board as a Digital Catalyst?*, in *Festskrift till Rolf Skog* 978 (Ronald J. Gilson, et al. eds, Norstedts Juridik 2021).
20. *See* Nykredit, *Ejerlederanalyse 2010 – Potentiale for vækst i ejerledede virksomheder* 26 (2010). *See also*, Neville, *supra* n. 15, at 252–258.
21. *See* Mikko Mustakallio, *Contractual and Relational Governance in Family Firms – Effects on Strategy Decision-Making Quality and Firm Performance* 166 (Helsinki University of Technology, Institute of Strategy and International Business, 2002).
22. *See* Mikko Mustakallio, Erkko Autio, & Shaker A. Zahra, *Relational and Contractual Governance in Family Firms: Effects on Strategic Decision Making*, 15(3) Fam. Bus. Rev. 205 (2002).

employee who was once offered some shares mainly as a sign of appreciation and as incitement to stay with the company. Or imagine the minority shareholder in such family business as a local investment firm.

When conflicts occur, the complexity can be increased by the personal relationship between owners because both the professional and personal spheres are affected simultaneously.[23] A disagreement might, for example, result in a deadlock where investments or strategic decisions are blocked by one shareholder, perhaps based on a so-called consensus clause in a shareholders' agreement. This would paralyse board work. Studies by Neville indicate that disagreements on daily management issues and on future investments for growth are typical grounds for deadlocks, as well as disagreements and disappointments on how much time and effort a co-owner puts into the business.[24] Deadlocks are particularly cumbersome in companies owned 50:50, i.e., to equal share by two parties. Another consequence of disagreements could be that the minority shareholder is not re-elected as a member of the board at the general meeting, i.e., by the controlling owners.[25] By such resolution, the minority shareholders will lose not only his/her influence over the business but also the main channel for information. This will result in further information asymmetry between the parties, and the minority shareholder could struggle with lack of transparency leading to lack of trust.

If the disagreement or conflict is severe or long lasting, then the final solution would be to end the collaboration. However, the minority often finds it difficult or even impossible to sell the shares to anyone beside the controlling shareholder(s), who might not be so willing to negotiate a deal that would benefit both parties. Shares in closely held companies are normally illiquid for two reasons. First, there is no open market for the shares. Personal relationship, such as family ties or friendship, is the primary foundation of the co-ownership. This limits the pool of potential buyers significantly to individuals who are willing to enter that particular ownership constellation while also being accepted by current owners.[26] In reality, this often mean that only current co-owners are potential buyers. Alternatively, all shares must be sold at the same time, or the share must be redeemed by the company, *see infra* on shareholder exits. Second, the shares are often subject to transfer restrictions in the articles of association or in shareholders' agreements. The purpose of such regulation is to control ownership transfers and avoid unwanted new shareholders. In sum, a minority shareholder has few alternatives in shareholder conflicts other than relying on the tools for minority protection offered by the legislature or negotiate with the controlling shareholder(s) on the terms for leaving the collaboration.

23. *See, e.g.*, Neville, *supra* n. 12, at 91–92; Manfred F.R. Kets de Vries, *The Dynamics of Family Controlled Firms: The Good and the Bad News*, 21 (3) Organizational Dynamics 61–62 (1993).
24. *See* Mette Neville, *Konfliktløsning*, in *Den nye selskabslov* 212 (Mette Neville & Karsten Engsig Sørensen eds, Jurist- og Økonomforbundet 2009).
25. Cf. Manne Airaksinen, *Conflicts between Shareholders and How to Solve them in the Legislation*, in Shareholder Conflicts 249–250 (Paul Krüger Andersen, et al. eds, Thomson Reuters, 2006).
26. *See also*, Susanne Kalss, *The Transfer of Shares of Private Companies*, 1 (3) ECFR 347–349 (2004).

§11.04 REGULATION ON CONFLICTS

[A] Introducing Regulatory Techniques for Minority Protection

Minority protection provisions comes in many forms, for example as mandatory or defaults, rules or standards and with aim to function *ex ante* or *ex post*. This subsection provides a general overview of some alternative regulatory techniques used for minority protection in company law.[27] In the subsequent subsections, I discuss how these regulatory techniques are used to prevent, counteract, or solve shareholders' conflicts in SMEs.

As a first alternative, the legislature can protect minority shareholders by procedural safeguards. In first-hand, such safeguards come in form or requirements of special majority or supermajority approval at the general meeting. The strictest regime will require consensus among shareholders. This is very seldom demanded by the companies act but could be stipulated in a shareholders' agreement or in the articles of association. An alternative could be approval by all shareholders who are negatively affected by the decision. A procedural safeguard discussed in the context of related party transactions is majority-of-the-minority approvals. This means that a transaction between the company and, e.g., a controlling shareholder is allowed if the majority of the disinterested shareholders approve.[28] Another safeguard to allow such transaction would be upon approval by independent directors or by an external evaluator guaranteeing that the terms of the transaction are made on arms-length, e.g., by a so-called fairness opinion.[29] The advantage of procedural safeguards is that they are clear rules with high level of predictability. Since the assessment is on formalities, it does not necessitate advanced *ex post* review. The downside of the regulatory technique is that its efficiency is highly dependent on the access to information.

A second regulatory technique to protect minority shareholders is therefore to counteract information asymmetry. Disclosure provisions, most intensively regulated by the financial reporting standards, are frequently used to protect creditors, investors, and shareholders. However, information is also provided though the general meeting and enforced by shareholders' right to pose questions. In some legislations, a minority shareholder also has the right to information outside the general meeting. One such opportunity is discussed *infra*. Information can also be upheld by other means. Two examples are by appointing a separate (minority) auditor to participate in the audit or by applying for an examiner to perform a special examination of the company's management and accounts during a specific period. Commonly, these measures to access information are granted to a minority of certain size, for example holding at least 10% of the shares in the company. The function of disclosure provisions is primarily to make sure that minority shareholders have the opportunity to make informed decisions

27. One example of a regulatory techniques not regarded in this chapter is the usage of independent directors as it mainly targets other companies than SMEs.
28. *See, e.g.*, Luca Enriques, *Related Party Transactions: Policy Options and Real-World Challenges (with a Critique of the European Commission Proposal)*, 16 (1) EBOR 15–18 (2015).
29. *Ibid.*, at 22–23.

and have enough information to utilize any other rights given to them. They can also have some deterrent effect. However, any disclosure rule is subject to a cost-benefit analysis, as the cost of collecting, systematising, and providing the information is often borne by the company no matter if the information is used or needed in the individual case.

A third regulatory alternative is to prohibit actions which typically will harm minority shareholders. An example of such mandatory regulation is found in the Swedish Companies Act[30] which prohibit companies to provide loans or offer security for loans to a related party. This kind of regulation is nowadays rather rare from a European perspective to tackle related party transaction.[31] The prohibition is however not explicitly motivated as a minority protection rule but mainly for tax reasons.[32] For this purpose, unlawful loans provided by the company are not only void but any person who intentionally or through gross negligence violates these rules also faces the risk of fines or a term of imprisonment of a maximum of one year. Thus, the prohibition is supplemented with a criminal sanction. Mandatory prohibitions would normally carry the benefit of clear rules that are easy to grasp and apply.[33] When combined with efficient sanctions, such rules can have strong deterrent effect. However, the scope of a clear rule is always with limits, carrying the risk of other harmful actions falling outside the scope, underinclusion, and that parties tries to circumvent the rule.[34] Further, a mandatory provision leaves no room to assess if a particular action in a given situation is not harmful for the minority shareholder, or indeed beneficial for the company at large. Thus, mandatory prohibitions also bear risk of overinclusion.

As a fourth alternative, the legislature can protect minority shareholders by standard based review provisions. Equal treatment of shares, and of shareholders, is a predominant norm in most companies acts. In alignment with the directors general duty of loyalty to act in the interest of the company, avoiding conflict of interest, principles of reasonableness or fairness, etc. they form standards which allows shareholders to request for *ex post* review of resolutions, decisions, and transactions. Standards are utmost important in a legal system as their open endings compensate for humans bounded rationality and consequently for the legislature's limitation to foresee all contingencies.[35] Disadvantages of such catch-all standards include lack of predictability, risk of inconsistencies in interpretation and application, and that *ex post* review risk to be time consuming and thereby costly.[36]

Fifth and finally, any minority protection provision, but particularly *ex post* reviews, are dependent on shareholders' right to bring suit. This includes the right to

30. Aktiebolagslag (2005:551).
31. For example, the EU Shareholders rights directive (Directive (EU) 2017/828) rely on disclosure in combination with a procedural safeguard, in some members states with demand of a so-called fairness opinion by an external examiner.
32. *See* Government bill Prop. 1973:93, at 90–95 and Government bill Prop. 2004/05:85, at 426–428.
33. *See, e.g.*, Cheffins, *supra* n. 1, at 277–278.
34. *See, e.g.*, Louis Kaplow, *Rules versus Standards: An Economic Analysis*, 42 Duke Law J. 588–596 (1992); Isaac Ehrlich & Richard Allen Posner, *An Economic Analysis of Legal Rulemaking*, 3 (1) J. Leg. Stud. 267–269 (1974).
35. *See* Herbert Lionel Adolphus Hart, *The Concept of Law* 125 (Clarendon, 1961).
36. *See* Cheffins, *supra* n. 1, at 282–285.

bring proceedings against a resolution adopted at general meetings and the right to suit for damages. An important aspect of these rights is if the minority shareholder can take actions in the company's name against board members, managers, auditors, or other parties against whom the company may have cause of action. Another important aspect is if this right can be exercised individually or requires shareholdings above a certain size, e.g., one-tenth of all shares or votes.

Against this general background, let us look at contractual and legislative tools which aim to prevent, counteract, or solve conflicts in SMEs. The discussion is divided into three phases; upon the entry of a minority shareholder, during the co-ownership, and when the collaboration has collapsed.

[B] Phase 1: Entry

Easterbrook and Fischel have argued that potential investors are in little need of legal protection as they enter as shareholders freely, and that the price mechanism on the market will constitute accurate protection.[37] Professional actors on the market will evaluate companies and provide an adequate price of the shares. Non-professional investors act on the same market and will benefit from the analysis. The mechanism is supported by disclosure rules, including the prospectus regulation which aim to provide investors with necessary information in a harmonized format.[38] The purpose of prospectus is to enable investors to make an informed assessment of the company and the transferable securities that are being offered or admitted to trading.

Noteworthy, these arguments are aimed at public and listed firms. In contrast, shares in closely held SMEs lack open market and for this reason, there is no functional price mechanism. However, other argument can be forwarded supporting that potential shareholders, also in SMEs, are able to assess their investment and make informative decisions. As a starting point, joining a company as a shareholder is based on free will. For this reason, individuals ought to be able to negotiate essential terms of the co-ownership before joining. We also know that the relationship among shareholders in SMEs are based on close connections in form of, e.g., family ties or friendship. Therefore, it can also be assumed that the average shareholder entering a business has a good dialogue with current owners. Further, when current owners have interest in expanding the owner group, for example to attract new capital, it is also in their interest to offer shares on transparent and reasonable terms. Hence, it must be presumed that an entering shareholder has good chances to assess the benefits and risks of becoming a co-owner in an SME, and that the parties can use contractual regulation to balance their interests.

---

37. *See* Frank H. Easterbrook & Daniel R. Fischel, *The Corporate Contract*, 89 (7) Columbia Law Rev. 1430–1431 (1989). The same argument is found among other scholars. *See, e.g.*, Macey, *supra* n. 11, at 189. Cf. the distinction between *informed* and *uninformed investors* by Jeffrey N. Gordon, *The Mandatory Structure of Corporate Law*, 89 (7) Colum. L. Rev. 1557–1562 (1989).
38. Harmonized in the EU by Directive 2003/71/EC of the European Parliament and of the Council of 4 November 2003 on the prospectus to be published when securities are offered to the public or admitted to trading and amending Directive 2001/34/EC.

However, the following examples can illustrate situations when the free and informed choice of an entering shareholder can be questioned. When a partner, colleague, or employee is offered shares in a business, it can be a sign of trust and appreciation. The person offered a minority position might feel gratitude, be honoured, and flattered. To question the terms of the co-ownership can be perceived as ungrateful, and an employee who says no to become a co-owner might feel unwelcome to stay on his/her position. Current owner(s) have the ultimate power to accept the new owner, creating the possibility for a take-it-or-leave-it deal. Hence, in some situations, the future minority shareholder lacks bargaining power. The opposite situation can also be the case. In the event of a venture capitalist or business angel entering the company, the investor might dictate the terms of the investment leaving no space for negotiation for the current owner(s). Research also indicates that parties in many situations fail to align expectation,[39] which could be a sign of no negotiations at the entry phase. A second situation when a future minority shareholder experience low bargaining power is when the shares are given to him/her, through a gift, will, or inheritance. A significant number of closely held companies are family firms, and among family members shares are not always sold on market price. Even if a beneficiary has the right to say no to an asset, feelings of letting the family down or of being ungrateful might be a hinder.

Two examples from interviews with owner-managers that we have met in the Ownership Dynamics project[40] can illustrate the problem. In one case, the founder of a consultancy firm regularly hired two external consultants. At one point in time, the business needed to move from a rented facility to a new building. The move was costly as it included purchase of new equipment. The two external consultants were offered shares in the company, but the founder left no room for negotiation. This was most evident when the founder unilaterally changed the terms of the investment several times during process. The parties failed to align expectations, which became apparent rather soon after the co-ownership started. The new owners, who worked fulltime in the company, sought to develop the business, but the founder who used the business as a part time job had no such interest. The disagreement was not solved at the time for the interview.

In the second case, an employee was offered to buy shares in the company by the three current owners. All three of them were closing in on retirement, but the new co-owner was roughly ten years younger. The entry took place after almost no negotiation. Soon after the entry, the new co-owner started to feel trapped as a minority shareholder. The old owners saw no need to invest time or the yearly profit to develop the business. Being close to retirement, they instead aimed to cash out. The conflict arose quickly, and hard words were exchanged. After the interview, the minority shareholder told me that the majority owners finally agreed to repurchase his shares, and he left the business both as owner and employee.

---

39. *See* Marina Bitsch Madsen, Mette Neville, Hanna Almlöf, & Kajsa Haag, *Ejerskabsdynamik i SMV'er – Et svensk/dansk projekt om problemer og løsninger ved ændringer i ejerkredsen*, Nordisk Tidsskrift for Selskabsret 79 (2019:4).
40. This research project, started in 2018, is a Danish-Swedish collaboration. *See also*, *ibid*.

In sum, upon an entry of a new co-owner, i.e., in the first phase, both statutory and contractual instruments are used to prevent the upcoming of future disagreements and conflicts. Two instruments seem relevant. The first is to enable entering shareholders to make an informed decision. The regulatory technique with disclosure provisions is important in this aspect, but the close connection between co-owners of closely held SMEs work in the same direction. Second, the interests of the parties need to be aligned, but in this aspect the legislature falls short. Instead, communication is essential to construct a joint vision and common goals, but imbalance in bargaining power complicates this process which calls for other mechanisms.

[C] Phase 2: During

Once the co-ownership has been established, the shareholders need to stay on good foot with each other for a fruitful cooperation. A disagreement or conflict could jeopardize the collaboration, or even the company. In this second phase, all rules protecting minority shareholders together set the playing field of the joint ownership. Hence, the different regulatory techniques presented *supra* in §11.04[A] are combined to hopefully form an effective minority protection. However, two strategies are particularly important to counteract escalation of disagreements and conflicts and both of them relate to access to information.

First, as mentioned in §11.03, the shareholders in SMEs are often active in the everyday business and function as key employees as well as managers. Sometimes this is regulated in a shareholders' agreement, both the expectation to work fulltime in the company, and the right to be a member of the board. Such agreement deviates from the typical majority rule that otherwise dominate company law.[41] Hence, instead of allowing the controlling(s) to appoint all board members, the contract allows the minority to be represented, either in person or by electing one or several members. Corresponding rules can be included in the article of association. In the Danish report from 2015, it was noticed that *anpartsselskap* with more than one shareholder often choose to have a board, which is a voluntary company organ, and the researchers conclude that this indicates that in practise the board is, among other things, utilized to give minority shareholders voice against controlling owners.[42] The foundation of these contractual strategies must be assumed to be that the collaboration is based on personal relations and mutual trust. Trust in its turn is dependent on transparency, and a position in the board is a main channel for information. Enriques et al. hold: 'Even if they select a fraction of the board, a minority can benefit from access to information, and, in some cases, the opportunity to form coalitions with independent directors'.[43]

41. Occasionally, company law stipulates the default right to appoint minority directors.
42. *See* Bennedsen & Nielsen, *supra* n. 4, at 27.
43. *See* Luca Enriques, Henry Hansmann, Reinier H. Kraakman, & Mariana Pargendler, *The Basic Governance Structure: Minority Shareholders and Non-Shareholder Constituencies*, in *The Anatomy of Corporate Law: a comparative and functional approach* 80 (Reinier H. Kraakman, et al. eds, Oxford University Press, 2017).

Second, the legislature also recognizes that access to information is a key aspect in the relationship among shareholders. Disclosure provisions come in many forms. One interesting example is found in the Swedish Companies Act. In Chapter 7, Section 36, we find a special right to information for shareholder in companies with no more than ten shareholders.[44] This rule is an add-on to the individual right to pose questions at the general meeting. The Swedish legislature has found that shareholders in closely held companies are in particular need of information to be able to exercise any other minority rights that are given to them.[45] Posing questions at the general meeting is simply not enough. Therefore, the rule in Chapter 7, Section 36 entitles the minority to review accounts and other documents which relate to the company's operations, to the extent necessary for the shareholder to be able to assess (1) the company's financial position and results at any time of the year, or (2) a particular matter which is to be addressed at the general meeting. The information should be provided by the board,[46] making it impossible for potential non-shareholding board members to stay out of the disagreement. The purpose of the rule is to strengthen the individual shareholder's position and bargaining power by counteracting information asymmetry.[47] In literature, it is argued that such information can prevent or resolve conflicts, but it is otherwise essential for being able to put forward any critique of the management and in the long run to equip the minority with evidence needed to bring actions against board members, managers, or the company.[48]

In a recent study, I have conducted in-depth interviews with legal advisors and used this data in combination with the scarce case law from the lower courts of Sweden to investigate how this rule is used.[49] My conclusion is that the rule is beautiful in theory but hopeless in practice for a minority shareholder in need. The information is often accessed too late to be of any practical use. The company, and the majority shareholder(s), may delay the process, and the sanctions are too vague and too slow to help the situation. Even more cumbersome, the right to information is often used as a weapon in an already ongoing conflict between majority and minority shareholders. In this fight, both parties play rough: the majority stonewall, and delay while the minority shareholders use different minority rights to defend themselves such as calling for extra general meetings or special examination. Sometimes, these minority rights are used

44. The rule was introduced in the companies act early 1980s by Government bill Prop. 1979/80:143, at 103, 106, and 179, but it was originally presented in a suggested but never adopted act for a new corporate form for SMEs in Swedish Government Official Reports SOU 1978:66.
45. *See* Swedish Government Official Reports SOU 1978:66, at 128–129.
46. After a questionable ruling in a court of appeal in 2009, it appears uncertain if the respondent in such litigation should be the company or the individual board members. *See* Urban Båvestam, *Några frågor kring den särskilda insynsrätten enligt 7 kap. 36 § aktiebolagslagen*, in *Vänbok till Anders Lagerstedt – Studier i associationsrätt och förmögenhetsrätt* 49–52 (Jan Andersson, et al. eds, Jure 2020).
47. Cf. Stattin, *supra* n. 14, at 49.
48. *See* Torsten Sandström, *Svensk aktiebolagsrätt* 209–210 (7th ed. Wolters Kluwer, 2020); Sten Andersson, Svante Johansson, & Rolf Skog, *Aktiebolagslagen: en kommentar*, (JUNO version 16, Norstedts Juridik 2021).
49. *See* Hanna Almlöf, *Insynsrätt i ägarledda aktiebolag*, in *Festskrift Rolf Dotevall* 12–36 (Marie Karlsson-Tuula, et al. eds, Juristförlaget i Lund 2021).

solely to put pressure on the controlling shareholder(s) to place a bid on the minority shares. Some advisors use the notion of abuse of minority rights in this context. Hence, my study provides some evidence that the right to information sometimes backfires and nurture the conflict, instead of resolving it.[50]

To summarize the second phase, we see that both contractual and legislative corporate governance instruments are used to ensure the minority a right to insight and information. Transparency is essential to nurture trust between parties. One evidence of this is that parties often include consensus clauses in shareholders' agreements, i.e., a list of decisions which requires unanimity by all shareholders.[51] Such clauses bear risk of deadlocks but are often motivated by the business owners as the only realistic path for a successful collaboration. If one shareholder holding majority vote would exclude other co-owners from important decisions and use his/her voting power to overrule them, it would itself be the source of conflict. Similarly, as indicated in this section, once a minority shareholder puts a statutory right to information to proper use, it is a sign of an already ongoing conflict which hardly can be solved with additional information. Hence, in the second phase minority rights to insight and information works poorly to counteract escalation of disagreements and could in fact even aggregate an already ongoing conflict. The need to end the collaboration then becomes inevitable. This also means that rights to insight and information, as well as contracted veto rights and other provisions protecting the minority, such as the norm of equal treatment, mainly function to prevent the upcoming of disagreements or conflicts during the second phase,[52] just as aligning interests as discussed in the first phase but is of no help if their preventative function fails.

[D] Phase 3: Exit

If disagreements or conflicts occur, the parties might find a way to mediate without the interference of legal advisors or litigation. However, as has been shown *supra* in §11.04[C] with the in-depth interview study with legal advisors, once a minority shareholder starts putting his/her contractual or statutory rights to use, transparency and trust has most likely already been lost leaving very little room for a functional collaboration. The only realistic solution would then be to end the co-ownership.[53] However, the minority often finds it difficult or even impossible to sell the shares to anyone beside the controlling shareholder(s) leading to unwanted lock-in effects, *see supra* §11.03. This can create a conflict or aggravate an ongoing conflict between the owners.[54] Consequently, the third and final phase addressed in this chapter includes shareholder exits to solve the disagreement or conflict.

50. Cf. Mathias Dahlerup Krarup, *Interessekonflikter i små og mellemstore selskaber* 101–102 (Djøf Forlag 2019), who makes a similar conclusion concerning the right for special examination.
51. *See, e.g.*, Neville, *supra* n. 24, at 215–216.
52. Cf. Krarup, *supra* n. 50, at 37–38.
53. *See* Almlöf, *supra* n. 49, at 34–36.
54. *See, e.g.*, Klaus Ulrich Schmolke, *Expulsion and Valuation Clauses – Freedom of Contract vs. Legal Paternalism in German Partnership and Close Corporation Law*, 9 (3) ECFR 388 (2012).

Countries seem to deal with the question of shareholder exits very differently in their companies acts. The Swedish legislature, for example, provides a very narrow application of exit alternatives, mainly focusing on situations of clear and long-termed abuse of power by the controlling shareholder, also requiring a breach of law or the articles of associations, and that the situation bears a risk of continuous oppression.[55] With this regulatory technique, the parties are strongly encouraged to regulate exits in shareholders agreements, as the legislation is of very little help in conflict situations. An analysis of the Swedish regulation of exits is presented in a separate study.[56] A slightly less strict regulation is found in Norway, which since the end of 1990s includes severe and long-termed disagreement between the shareholders on the running of the business as a ground for requesting exit or to buy out a shareholder.[57] The rules are, however, not meant to be used lightly, but they are considered as a safety valve in the most severe cases when a continuous collaboration appear as unthinkable.[58]

Another regulatory strategy is represented by the German legislature. Shareholders in a Gesellschaft mit beschränkter Haftung (GmbH) may request an exit of the company on so-called important grounds – 'aus wichtigem Grund'.[59] This is an un-codified mandatory rule, which work both ways, i.e., it can both give the company the right to exclude a shareholder (a buy-out right) and a shareholder the right to exit (a right to withdrawal).[60] When assessing if an important ground is present, all circumstances must be taken into consideration, and decisive factors can either be with the exiting shareholder, the company or any co-owner, particularly controlling shareholders. Examples of important grounds include situations in which a shareholder makes the achievement of the company purpose impossible or acts in a way that makes his/her remaining in the company appear intolerable and hence the trust between shareholders have been lost.[61] Examples also include serious or repeated violation of shareholder obligations and reputation-damaging effects on the company.[62] Exit on important ground is only permissible as a last resort, but it is always seen as a less dramatic solution compared to an action for dissolution.[63]

In the Netherlands, we find another legal strategy to shareholder exits. Similar to the German regulation, specific reasons for the exit are set up, but in this case, the rules are codified. The Dutch Companies Act both grants shareholders the right to withdraw from the company in cases of minority oppression, and the right for co-owners to buy

55. Similar regulation is found in Denmark, *see, e.g.*, Krarup, *supra* n. 50, at 46.
56. *See* Hanna Almlöf, *Regulation of Shareholder Exits in Closely Held Companies – Reflections from Sweden*, 19 (2) ECFR 175–202 (2022).
57. Norwegian Companies Act, Ch. 4, ss 24 and 25; Norwegian Government Official Reports NOU 1996:3, at 109–111.
58. *See* Tore Bråthen, *Selskapsrett* 129–132 (6th ed. Gyldendal, Focus Forlag, 2019).
59. *See* Hartmut Wicke, *Gesetz betreffend die Gesellschaften mit beschränkter Haftung (GmbHG)*, Anh. § 34: Austritt und Ausschließung eines Gesellschafters, Rn. 10 (C.H. Beck, 4. Auflage 2020).
60. *See, e.g.*, BGH NJW 1999, 3779; OLG Köln, NZG 1999, 1222.
61. *See* Holger Altmeppen & Günter H. Roth, *Gesetz betreffend die Gesellschaften mit beschränkter Haftung – GmbHG* § 60 Rn. 80 (C.H. Beck, 10. Auflage 2021).
62. *Ibid.*, § 60 Rn. 82.
63. *See* Wicke *supra* n. 59, Anh. § 34: Austritt und Ausschließung eines Gesellschafters, Rn. 12.

out an individual shareholder based on that person's harmful conduct towards the company or other shareholders.[64] In both situations, the same value principle to set the price for the shares is used, and upon a decision by the court, the shares shall be transferred and the compensation paid within two weeks.[65]

The exit regulations of Germany and the Netherlands provide examples on important grounds for dissolving a harmful or dysfunctional collaboration among shareholders. In German company law, the shareholders have the possibility to include additional grounds for exits in their articles of association, but they may not limit the scope of the general standard.[66] For example, the shareholders may include an ordinary right of termination without particular reason. Such general exit right without cause, familiar to partnership law, is also chosen by the Italian legislature. According to Article 2473, Section 2 of the Italian Civil Code any member of a Società a Responsabilità Limitata (S.r.l.) is entitled to exit at any moment, with a notice of at least 180 days or another time period stipulated in the articles of association, not exceeding one year.[67] Further, any member has the right to exit in a number of given situations stipulated in the Article 2473, Section 1; i.e., when the member did not agree (1) with the decision to change the company's object or type, (2) on a merger or division, (3) on the revocation of a decision for the company's winding-up, (4) on the transfer of seat abroad, and (5) on the execution of operations involving a significant modification of the company's object or a significant modification of the administrative or financial rights belonging to single members.[68] In addition, members can add any other exit ground in the articles of association, and if any such ground is removed from the articles, then it itself constitute a ground for exit.

As shown, the regulatory strategy to enable shareholder exits varies from country to country. Sweden, as well as Denmark, represents a strict regime, which has been criticized. Neville argues that an exit at will could be a key corporate governance mechanism for promoting effective management, as it allows the minority to put pressure on the management, and if not respected, the minority shareholder can choose to leave.[69] Andersson concludes that only with a proper exit right, minority shareholders are placed in a bargaining position where they can achieve either renewed grounds for trust, loyalty, and long-term commitment between the parties or an exit on fair terms.[70] Both authors stress the importance of carefully drafting such

64. The Dutch Civil Code, Art. 2:343 and Art. 2:336. For an in-depth analysis, *see* Paul de Vries, *Exit rights of minority shareholders in a private limited company*, Ch. 6 in particular (Kluwer 2010).
65. *See* Samantha Renssen, *Extra ordinary corporate transactions. Liquidation and winding up*, in *Company laws of the EU: a handbook* 1438–1440 (Andrea Vicari & Alexander Schall eds, C.H. Beck 2020).
66. *See* Wicke, *supra* n. 59, Anh. § 34: Austritt und Ausschließung eines Gesellschafters, Rn. 10.
67. According to de Vries, *supra* n. 64, at 14, most of the Italian private limited companies are set up for a fixed term, for which this exit right at will does not apply.
68. Cf. Danish Companies Act, ss 110, 286, 306, and 318k which entitle a down voted minority to request redemption of shares in specific situations. *See* Krarup, *supra* n. 50, at 42–43.
69. *See* Neville, *supra* n. 15, at 289.
70. *See* Jan Andersson, *Minority shareholder protection in SMEs: a question of information ex post and bargaining power ex ante?*, in *Company law and SMEs* 204 (Mette Neville & Karsten Engsig Sørensen eds, Thomson Reuters 2010).

right to minimize the risk of opportunistic behaviour by minority shareholders and avoid financial instability and possible obstruction of the company. In sum, exit rights are essential in SMEs as an important corporate governance instrument to empower minority shareholders.

§11.05 NEW INSTRUMENTS TO TACKLE SHAREHOLDER CONFLICTS

[A] Beyond Current Regulation

In closely held companies, disagreements or conflict will inevitably affect the business. For example, it might be impossible to separate an ownership conflict from the board work, as the two are intertwined due to the overlap of roles. Shareholder conflicts, thus, pose a corporate governance problem. After reviewing the three phases in §11.04, it is now possible to deepen the discussion and identify new, or at least less recognized, instruments to prevent, counteract, or solve disagreements or conflicts in SMEs. In this section, I discuss instruments to align shareholders' interests, to entitle a minority shareholder a position on the board, and to enable shareholder exits. To enrich the discussion with new elements, these mechanisms are viewed outside the described phases and with reflection on possible changes in the companies act.

[B] New Instrument to Promote Aligned Interests

A key element to prevent disagreements or conflicts is to properly align interests of the parties upon entry on a minority shareholder. Legal advisors I have interviewed in research projects often stress that the process before signing a shareholders' agreement is utterly important, and often more important than the final document. The process includes communication on topics such as the aim of undertaking business together, future plans, expectations, and assumptions for the collaboration. The research performed by Mustakallio et al., *see* §11.03, adds a dimension to this. They argue that companies need corporate governance structures throughout the joint ownership that promote cohesion and shared vision among owners. This can include arenas that promote social interaction with the aim to form a shared vision, which could reduce harmful conflict.

In management literature, arenas for shareholders' interaction outside the company organs are discussed and often put forward as important governance tools. Such arenas include shareholders' meeting; or for family-controlled firms, family assembly, family council, or family office.[71] The choice of arena depends on, e.g., the size of the business, the number of owners, whether the business is a family firm, and the degree of involvement of family members. Arenas can both be formal, informal and of hybrid

71. *See, e.g.*, Miguel Angel Gallo & Denise Kenyon-Rouvinez, *The Importance of Family and Business Governance*, in *Family Business: Key Issues* 45–57 (Denise Kenyon-Rouvinez & John L. Ward eds, Palgrave Macmillan 2005); EcoDa, the European Confederation of Directors' Associations, *Corporate Governance Guidance and Principles for Unlisted Companies in Europe* (2010).

character, with complementary purposes.[72] One main purpose could be to separate business issues, which normally should be dealt with in the boardroom, from ownership issues, which requires a separate forum. The discussions can and are often encouraged to lead to documents, in which the parties put their agreements in wording. Such documents can be legally binding contracts but are often indented as non-binding arrangements.

Alternative shareholders' arenas are seldom discussed in legal literature, and to my knowledge never acknowledged by the legislatures. However, a legal analysis of so-called family constitutions, as a possible output from a family council or alike, has been provided by Fleischer. He concludes that these documents are 'chameleon-like regulatory instruments' with various purposes and levels of obligation, which makes it impossible to collectively classify them as legally binding or not.[73] Fleischer suggest that a family constitution can be seen as a linked contract to other documents such as the articles of association and shareholders' agreement, allowing for the creation of duties of care, loyalty, and cooperation among individuals that are not bound by a single contractual agreement, but are part of the same contractual group.[74] Hence, the process of creating a family constitution not only assist the shareholders to align their interests but a family constitution can also be used as aid to interpret the article of association and other agreements between shareholders with the purpose to counteract any escalation of potential disagreements or conflicts.

Against this background, it is possible to discuss the role of the board relating to formal and informal shareholders' arenas. The board is often seen as the company organ that takes strategic decisions about the future of the business, e.g., by formulating the company's vision and mission.[75] As a subordinate decision-taking body to the general meeting, which is the starting point in the Nordic Corporate governance model, such strategic work must take directions from the owners into account. In cases where shareholders in SMEs fail to provide a joint vision of the business, it could be argued that the board should assist the owners in this matter and promote a process where the owners meet and discuss.[76] As soon as the board is composed by other individuals than solely shareholders, this function is both feasible in theory and desirable in practice.

In sum, aligning the interest of shareholders is crucial not only at the beginning but also throughout the co-ownership, i.e., both in phase 1 and phase 2. A seldom regarded corporate governance instrument to achieve this is found in formal or informal arenas outside the traditional company organs. The challenge for business

72. *See* Mattias Nordqvist, *Understanding Strategy Processes in Family Firms: Exploring the Roles of Actors and Arenas*, 30 (1) Int. Small Bus. J. 36 (2012) who argue that too strong reliance on formal arenas may have a negative impact on the flexibility and speed of decision-making, while too much strategic work channelled to informal arenas can lead to the exclusion of individuals from being allowed to influence the strategy process.
73. *See* Holger Fleischer, *Family Firms and Family Constitutions: A Legal Primer*, 15 (1) Eur. Comp. L. 16 (2018).
74. *Ibid.*, at 18.
75. For a recent discussion on the boards strategic work, *see* Neville, *supra* n. 19, at 969–974 and 976–977.
76. This is, e.g., argued by Carsten Fode & Mette Neville, *SMV-bestyrelsen – hele vejen rundt: Bestyrelsesarbejde i små og mellemstore virksomheder* 168–170 (Karnov Group 2018).

owners and their advisors is to identify a relevant and appropriate arena in each specific case and define its function as a corporate governance, a family governance, and/or an ownership governance tool. The board can be active in this process and take on a guiding and supporting role. Consequently, the instrument discussed in this section consists of both the arena itself and the board's role to support its function. The challenge for legal scholars is to recognize the importance of such arenas and assess the legal bindingness of any imperative document coming out of it. Fleischer provide an excellent example of this and could be an inspiration for others. Comparative analysis in these matters would be particularly beneficial.

[C] New Instrument to Ensure Minority Insight

A main legislative tool to counteract disagreements or conflicts is shareholders' right to information and insight. This tool is based on the logic that information equals transparency, which in turn is essential to promote trust. And reversed, lack of transparency can lead to mistrust. Therefore, companies acts include provisions which entitle current or entering shareholders the right to information and the responsibility to provide such information is placed on the board. However, as has been shown and argued *supra* in §11.04[C], this legal strategy does not always fulfil the function to counteract escalation of conflicts.

A common contractual regulation to promote trust is to give minority shareholders the right to be a member of the board or appoint one. When such regulation is included in shareholders' agreements, a disagreement or conflict can result in the controlling shareholder(s) not honouring the contract. The advantage of such action by the controlling shareholder(s) is that the conflict formally can be placed outside the boardroom as the minority no longer holds a seat. The problem for the minority might be that that is it! The sanctions of the contract are not strong enough to avoid these situations and as illustrated in §11.04[C], a statutory extensive right to information does not help either.

A relevant question could therefore be what if the right to a chair in the boardroom was stipulated in the companies act or the articles of association?[77] Initially, it should be recognized that such statutory rule should never be mandatory, as it for sure does not fit all SMEs. It should not even be a default rule without the empirical evidence that this is the preferred rule for most SMEs and therefore correspond to the hypothetical bargaining model that can be employed to select default provisions.[78] It could however be an opt-in alternative that the shareholders enact by inserting a provision in their articles of association. Such opt-in possibility could have a signalling

77. In the discussion here, I am using Nordic company law as my starting point, as this is the legal framework that I am most familiar with.
78. *See, e.g.*, Ian Ayres & Robert Gertner, *Filling Gaps in Incomplete Contracts: An Economic Theory of Default Rules*, 99 Yale Law J. 91–95 (1989); David Charny, *Hypothetical Bargains: The Normative Structure of Contract Interpretation*, 89 (7) Mich. Law Rev. 1821 (1991).

effect, encouraging more parties to choose this alternative.[79] Even in absence of such a provision in the articles, a proactive court might, based on the behaviour of the shareholders, argue that this opt-in rule in fact is applicable in the relationship between shareholders. Hence, if the parties since the beginning of the co-ownership or during a significant period of time have acted in accordance with the opt-in rule, it could be regarded as applicable without formally being inserted in the articles of associations.

Regulating a minority shareholder's right to be a member of the board in the article of associations carries significant risk because it makes it impossible to isolate a shareholder conflict, so it does not affect the governance of the company. For this reason, I imagine that many legal scholar and advisors would dissuade such solution. However, on the topic of regulation shareholder conflicts, I see one major positive effect from this kind of regulation. As argued *supra* in §11.03, a consequence of a disagreement among shareholders could be that the minority shareholder is not re-elected as a member of the board. Hence, this could be a clear sign of a collapsed co-ownership. However, from the analysis in §11.04[D] of different exit regulations, losing one's seat in the boardroom does not normally constitute an exit ground, while breach of the article of associations may.[80] Therefore, in situations where the mutual trust between shareholders have been manifested by a joint right to be part of the board, and this trust is lost, the legislature could consider including this as a potential ground for minority shareholders to withdraw from the company. If such statutory exit right would be the only remedy to this opt-in rule, controlling shareholder(s) can still banish the minority shareholder from the board but this would trigger the minority's right to withdraw. This constitutes a new instrument to save the company from harmful conflicts for legislatures to consider. Another possible consequence of empowering a minority shareholder with a statutory exit right is that it increases his or her bargaining power in the boardroom. This allows the minority shareholder to put pressure on the controlling owner(s) to promote good governance.[81] For example, it might make the board focus more on the strategic issues, business opportunities, growth potential, development of products or services to stay relevant on the market, etc.

[D] New Instrument to Enable Shareholder Exits

Regulatory strategies to enable shareholder exits varies across countries, which has been shown *supra* in §11.04[D]. As been pointed out by others before me, a too strict regime is not in the interest of SMEs.[82] Arguments for an exit right at will, similar to the

79. Cf. Henry Hansmann, *Corporation and Contract*, 8 (1) Am. Law Econ. Rev. 12 (2006); Ian Ayres, *Regulating Opt-Out: An Economic Theory of Altering Rules*, 121 Yale Law J. 4–5 (2012).
80. As seen in §11.04[D], e.g., both Germany and Italy allow shareholders to include additional grounds for shareholder exits in the articles.
81. *See* Neville, *supra* n. 15, at 289.
82. *See, e.g.*, Andersson, *supra* n. 70, at 204–206; Neville, *supra* n. 15, at 289–293.

Italian regime, has been put forward[83] but also rejected,[84] and in literature, suggestions on how to regulate for exits in shareholders' agreements to compensate for the lack of legislative solutions have been presented.[85]

A less highlighted difference between the national exit regulations, which I wish to address in this section, is how the exit is executed. Two main alternatives exist; either someone must acquire the shares from the exiting shareholder or the shares must be redeemed by the company. The question is which of these two alternatives is preferable from a corporate governance perspective.

From the exiting shareholder's point of view, it might be irrelevant from whom the compensation is paid. For the other shareholders, it might be both a question of how to finance the withdrawal or buy out and a question of whether the balance of power among remaining owners can be kept. If the shares from the exiting shareholder are acquired by only one out of several shareholders, the exit will be followed by a redistribution of power. One reason for such result could be that some shareholders lack the resources needed. By using the company's resources, unwanted redistributions of power could be avoided. Capital that otherwise can be used for dividend may be utilized for redemption of shares. In legal regimes with minimum capital requirement in the companies act, or if stipulated in the articles of association, the compensation might deem a reduction of share capital, perhaps with a necessary restoration of the same, to prevent it falling below the stipulated threshold. For the given reasons, redemption of shares may be the first-hand alternative to enable a shareholder exit, but this requires that the company has the financial resources needed. When drafting exit rights, either in the companies act, in articles of associations, or in shareholders' agreements, one must therefore consider which alternative should come in first hand, or if there is a choice to be made between the alternatives.

In the Dutch regulation, it is the co-owners who on the courts order must acquire the shares of a shareholder who ask for his/her withdrawal. The same applies when a shareholder is bought out.[86] However, a shareholder may start exit proceedings against the company in certain situation, when the reprehensible action was taken by a company organ, but this appears less common.[87] The Italian regulation stipulates that the compensation to the exiting shareholder should in first hand come from the remaining shareholders, who should acquire the shares proportionally to their current holdings.[88] Alternatively, if unanimously agreed by the shareholders, a third party may acquire the shares. As a second-hand alternative, the compensation should be paid by the company using free reserves or, if no free reserve is present, by reducing the share capital. Lastly, if compensation is not possible based on these two alternatives, the company must be dissolved. In both Germany and Norway, a shareholder who wish to exit target his/her request towards the company. In Germany, the GmbH may then

83. *See* Harm-Jan de Kluiver, *Private Ordering and Buy-Out Remedies Within Private Company Law: Towards a New Balance Between Fairness and Welfare?*, 8 (1) EBOR 103 (2007).
84. *See* de Vries, *supra* n. 64, at 18.
85. *See* Krarup, *supra n. 50*, ch. 7.
86. *See* Renssen, *supra* n. 65 at 1438–1440.
87. *See* de Vries, *supra* n. 64, at 295–298.
88. The Italian Civil Code Art. 2473, s. 4.

choose either to redeem the shares using free reserves,[89] to acquire the shares, or to let other co-owners or a third party acquire the sharers.[90] If the company lacks necessary free reserves to compensate the exiting shareholder, and if no other buyer accepts to acquire the shares, the only solution left is to wind up the company.[91] In Norway, the rules on share buyback or on reduction of share capital must be considered, but if the company appoints someone else who is willing to acquire the shares, the exiting shareholder must accept this and cannot demand that the companies reserves are used instead.[92]

The difference in regulatory solutions presented here gives us reason to analyse the decisions needed to enable the exit from a corporate governance perspective. On the one hand, the decision to reduce the share capital or to redeem shares to give compensation to an individual shareholder are fundamental for the company and normally requires a resolution by the general meeting. For example, in the Netherlands, such solution must both be supported in the article of association and requires a resolution by the general meeting.[93] On the other hand, the board is given the main responsibility to provide financial oversight and to protect the company's assets. The board must therefore approve and execute any usage of the company resources for this purpose. Problem arises, of course, when most assets are tied and the company face liquidity problems. At the same time, a destructive relationship may have negative spill-over effects on the company and in worst case scenario jeopardize the business as such. Therefore, it might be in the company's interest, and arguably part of the duty of the board to enable the exit.[94] Consequently, if the company face a destructive conflict among co-owners, company law could impose a duty on the board to use the company's assets to end the harmful relationship.

Notably, in closely held companies, the board might be composed of, or dominated by, the controlling shareholder(s) who are part in the conflict. Knowing that the minority shareholder has few alternatives to exit the business by other means, the board members might argue that the company lack the resources needed for the compensation. One alternative could be to entitle a shareholder, who requests exit on important grounds, to demand that capital that otherwise could be used for dividend is used as exit compensation without the approval by the general meeting or a decision by the board. This would mean that a minority shareholder, based on his/her right to withdrawal may seize free reserves without the interference of co-owners. So far, I have neither noticed this solution in national exit regulation nor discussed in the literature that I have studied.

In sum, exit solutions for minority shareholders are an essential tool to solve disagreements or conflicts in SMEs. There are many reasons for a default statutory redemption clause in the companies act, making the parties less dependent on costly

89. *See* Wicke, *supra* n. 59, Anh. § 34: Austritt und Ausschließung eines Gesellschafters, Rn. 13.
90. *See* Christian Kersting (Ulrich Noack, et al. eds, Gesetz betreffend die Gesellschaften mit beschränkter Haftung: GmbHG, C.H.Beck 2022), Anhang nach § 34 Rn 24.
91. *Ibid.*, Anhang nach § 34 Rn 25.
92. *See* Bråthen, *supra* n. 58, at 130.
93. *See* de Vries, *supra* n. 64, at 297.
94. *See* Fode & Neville, *supra* n. 76, at 179.

contractual solutions in shareholders' agreements. When drafting such rule, many arguments can be forwarded why redemption of shares should be the first-hand alternative and consequently why the company should be the counterparty in such process or litigation. However, if the company lacks the financial resources needed, the duty to acquire the shares must be placed on the remaining shareholders. Alternatively, upon the request to exit, the company can choose how to execute the exit.

§11.06 CONCLUDING REMARKS

In this chapter, I have argued that conflicts cause corporate governance problems in SMEs, and that they often origin from diverse interests and a combination of financial and non-financial goals among shareholders. The chapter have explored three possible new instruments and their functions to enhance good governance in owner-managed SMEs in situation where there is a disagreement or a conflict between controlling and minority shareholders. These instruments aim to either prevent or solve shareholders' conflicts. First, the usage of formal and informal areas outside the company's decision-taking organs should be considered. This is not a task for the legislature, but the board can be active in the process and guide and support the shareholders to find appropriate arenas to align their interests with the purpose to prevent conflicts. Second, the legislature should consider an opt-in rule in the companies act on minority shareholder's right to insight and information by being a member of the board. The purpose is twofold. Insight and information aim to prevent conflicts, but when this function fails, it instead allows the minority shareholder to withdraw from the company. Such exit right can put pressure on the controlling shareholder(s) to enhance good governance. Lastly, the minority shareholder's right to exit the collaboration have been discussed, and arguments for why redemption of shares should be the first-hand solution to finance the exit have been forwarded. Redemption of shares will put financial restraints on the business but can avoid deadlocks and other harmful effect that will hinder the company to be run properly.

As always, a study comes with limitations. While this study has touched upon comparative elements, more could be done. Suggestions for future research avenues therefore include more comparative studies on shareholder exits and the role of the board in shareholders conflicts. If possible, such study should benefit from an empirical approach such as an interview or case study. Also, conflicts in mutual co-ownerships, i.e., companies owned to equal share by two parties (50:50) have not been considered in this study. Another related topic not considered in this chapter is the range from destructive to productive (value-creating) shareholder conflicts.

CHAPTER 12
Regulating Institutional Shareholders

Iris H.-Y. Chiu

§12.01 INTRODUCTION

The corporate governance roles of institutional shareholders have been the subject of policy reform in the European Union (EU) since the early 2000s, reflected in the Shareholders' Rights Directive 2007,[1] subsequently in the amended Directive in 2017.[2] This chapter charts the nature of policy development and argues that the tenets of EU policy are shifting from perceiving institutional shareholders within their 'agency' relationship with corporate management to one of institutions having a key 'representative capacity' to discipline corporate behaviour. The policy that focuses on institutions' agency-based relationship in corporate governance tends to be inward-looking, leaving the purposes of corporate governance to be privately determined. However, a policy that regards institutions as being able to exercise useful influence over investee companies in order to shape corporate purpose or behaviour may be more externally-facing, as institutions' influence is seen as contributing towards purposes or outcomes that are more *socially beneficial.*

The shift from institutions' agency-based corporate governance role to one of 'representative capacity' can be discerned from certain policy changes and reform but is at the same time not unequivocally clear. Policy reforms for institutional shareholders seem to be shifting from a framing based on corporate law to one based on capital markets regulation. Regulative forms of framing are more closely related to mobilising

1. Council Directive 2007/36/EC of 11 July 2007 on the exercise of certain rights of shareholders in listed companies OJ L 184, 14.7.2007.
2. Council Directive (EU) 2017/828 of 17 May 2017 amending Directive 2007/36/EC as regards the encouragement of long-term shareholder engagement OJ L 132, 20.5.2017.

institutions' 'representative capacity', while facilitative forms of framing, under corporate law, relate more pertinently to endorsing the agency-based position of institutions. In particular, the EU's sustainable finance agenda[3] has driven substantial legislative reform, including regulating institutional investors in terms of their investment management purposes and conduct. Although this regulatory agenda does not explicitly refer to institutions' corporate governance roles, there are implications for recalibration of institutions' relationships with their investee companies. The sustainable finance agenda may play the most significant role yet in relation to the agenda for 'regulating institutional investors' as such. Nevertheless, the argument made is not that there is a binary between institutions' roles framed in corporate law and their roles framed in capital markets regulation. Indeed, we argue that policy-makers seem to be treading a path that aims at the integration or hybridity of institutions' incentive-based purposes in the 'agency-based' paradigm and the wider socially-beneficial purposes in the 'representative capacity' paradigm. Whether such premises can be ideologically and practically reconciled is however open to question.

§12.02 discusses the 'agency-based' framing of institutions' corporate governance roles, drawn largely from the Shareholders' Rights Directive 2007. It charts the development towards the amended Directive 2017 reflecting the move towards conceiving the 'representative capacity' of institutions in the aftermath of the global financial crisis 2007–2009. In this Section, we pose the question whether the agency-based and 'representative capacity' conceptions of the institutional shareholder can be reconciled. We argue that legal framing treads uneasily in this question. §12.03 discusses whether institutions' private interests can be integrated with socially-beneficial purposes pursued by policy-makers. We explain legal framing in EU reforms and posit that what policy-makers are seeking is a 'trickle-down' theory of institutions' private corporate governance interests and roles, so that institutions' exercise of their roles based on the 'agency-based' paradigm can at the same time also achieve social benefit. We discuss not only where such alignment may be found but also where chasms and gaps remain. §12.04 discusses the rise in regulative means to steer institutions' corporate governance roles, effectively regulating institutions' 'representative capacity' so that their incentives are steered towards a form of investment management conduct that secures social good as a priority. There seem hints of such an approach, in particular in the EU's sustainable finance agenda. However, the signals are mixed. On the whole, we perceive a mixed landscape in EU policy which requires greater clarification.

One point of clarification is that this chapter does not take a normative stance on the 'agency-based' or 'representative capacity' approach in framing institutions' roles. This question implicates theoretical and political economy conceptions of institutions in corporate governance relationships, such as whether shareholder or stakeholder primacy is subscribed to, and to what extent corporate governance should be regarded as a private web of relationships for a for-profit purpose or should embed 'bargains'

3. https://ec.europa.eu/info/business-economy-euro/banking-and-finance/sustainable-finance_en showcasing regulatory reforms for investment intermediary disclosure, investment product design, marketing and corporate disclosure.

and 'negotiations' of public interest or social character. These underlying underpinnings remain a subject matter for debate in corporate governance policy, although some[4] argue that the leaning in EU policy is clearly towards stakeholder and pluralist systems of corporate governance reflecting many Member States' political economies and 'coordinated market economy' systems.[5] In this manner, accommodating the shift towards regulating institutional shareholders may be seen as not incompatible with Member States' political and legal fabric. The normative question, however, deserves extended and dedicated treatment which is beyond the chapter's scope and focus. §12.05 provides a short conclusion to the chapter.

§12.02 THE FRAMING OF INSTITUTIONAL SHAREHOLDERS' ROLES IN EU POLICY

In the 2007 Shareholders' Rights Directive, EU policy focused on the weakness of institutions' corporate governance roles and the need to ensure that they are sufficiently unhindered to exercise such roles meaningfully. This policy dated back to the European Commission's communication in 2003,[6] addressing the need to modernise company law to the extent that could be harmonised in the EU. Further, the corporate scandals at that time formed the backdrop to the reforms, though largely emanating from the United States (US), i.e., the fall of Enron in 2001.[7] That episode highlighted the tragedy of capital markets being obscured from the real financial state of Enron disguised by aggressive and complex accounting practices. Although the EU did not see the need for similar reforms to the ensuing US Sarbanes-Oxley Act 2002, the United Kingdom (UK) embarked on a study on the state of internal control within companies,[8] while the EU considered the need to ensure that shareholders' monitoring roles, principally in decision-making and voting at general meetings, should be as unhindered as possible.

The Shareholders' Rights Directive 2007 made significant improvements to harmonise shareholders' access to information concerning general meetings, and to remove impediments to shareholders' participation and to vote. Commentators[9]

4. Massimo Belcredi and Guido Ferranini, *Corporate Boards, Incentive Pay and Shareholder Activism in Europe: Main Issues and Policy Perspectives* ch. 1 (Massimo Belcredi and Guido Ferranini eds, Cambridge: CUP 2013); Steve Sauerwald, J. (Hans) Van Oosterhout and Marc Van Essen, *Expressive Shareholder Democracy: A Multilevel Study of Shareholder Dissent in 15 Western European Countries* 53 J. Mgmt. Stud. 520 (2016).
5. Peter A Hall and David Soskice, *An Introduction to Varieties of Capitalism* ch. 1 (Peter A Hall and David Soskice eds, OUP 2001).
6. Communication from the Commission to the Council and the European Parliament - Modernising Company Law and Enhancing Corporate Governance in the European Union - A Plan to Move Forward.
7. Belcredi and Ferranini, *supra* n. 4.
8. Financial Reporting Council, *Internal Control: Revised Guidance for Directors on the Combined Code* (2005), also known as the 'Turnbull Report 2005', https://www.frc.org.uk/getattachment/fe1ba51a-578d-4467-a00c-f287825aced9/Revised-Turnbull-Guidance-October-2005.pdf.
9. Caspar Rose, *The New European Shareholder Rights Directive: Removing Barriers and Creating Opportunities for More Shareholder Activism and Democracy* 16 J. Mgmt. & Governance 269 (2012); Dirk A Zetzsche, *Shareholder Passivity, Cross-Border Voting and the Shareholder Rights*

pointed out that cross-border ownership of European company shares had been rising, and there was a significant need to facilitate shareholders' monitoring roles, especially through the ease of cross-border voting. The Directive provides for ease of access to notices of general meetings in good time,[10] with a minimum stipulated twenty-one days from the day of notice to when the meeting can be held.[11] Share blocking, a practice that some Member States instituted, is abolished and harmonised by a requirement of a maximum of thirty days from which shareholder identification procedures could start to be undertaken by the company.[12] Electronic participation at general meetings must be facilitated,[13] procedures for voting must be clearly specified,[14] and postal votes in advance must also be facilitated.[15] Proxy voting is to be enabled, subject to some legitimate restrictions by Member States.[16] A general rule to treat shareholders equally and fairly has also been instituted,[17] more concretely fleshed out in shareholders' rights to put items on the general meeting agenda[18] and to ask questions.[19] These are intended to provide a level playing field as well as clear opportunities and channels for shareholders to call management to accountability, therefore effectively exercising their monitoring roles.[20]

However, it has also been pointed out that the provisions do not interfere with Member States' characterisation of who a shareholder is, for the purposes of exercising the Directive's rights.[21] In the UK, the 'no look-through' rule accords the legally-registered shareholder, oftentimes the depositary or custodian holding share registration certificates, with the incidents of shareholder rights. The Directive does not go further to accord rights to beneficial shareholders.[22] The Directive arguably goes some way towards reducing the transaction costs of exercising shareholder rights at general meetings and facilitating shareholder access to a slate of harmonised rights such as

---

Directive 8 J. Corp. L. Stud. 289 (2008); Fidy Xiangxin Hong, *Protection of Shareholders' Rights at EU Level: How Far Does It Go?* 3 Eur. Co. L. 124 (2009).

10. Art. 5 includes the need to provide sufficient information on procedures for attendance, voting, and exercise of shareholder rights as well as comments on draft resolutions to inform shareholders adequately.
11. *Ibid.*
12. Art. 7.
13. Art. 8.
14. Art. 5.
15. Art. 12.
16. Arts 10–11.
17. Art. 4.
18. Arts 6.
19. Art. 9.
20. Hong, *supra* n.9; Vanessa Knapp, *The Requirements of the Shareholders' Rights Directive* 9 ERA Forum 377 (2008).
21. Anthony Hainsworth, *The Shareholder Rights Directive and the Challenge of Re-enfranchising Beneficial Shareholders* 1 L. & Fin. Mkt Rev. 11 (2007); Zetzsche, *supra* n. 9.
22. Eva Micheler, *Intermediated Securities from the Perspective of Investors: Problems, Quick Fixes and Long-term Solutions* ch. 12, 237–258 (Louise Gullifer and Jennifer Payne eds, Oxford: Hart Publishing, 2019); Law Commission, *Intermediated Securities: Who Owns Your Shares? A Scoping Paper* (Nov 2020), https://s3-eu-west-2.amazonaws.com/lawcom-prod-storage-11jsxou24uy7q/uploads/2020/11/Law-Commission-Intermediated-Securities-Scoping-Paper-1.pdf; para. 2.18-2.34 on challenges for asset owners in pooled funds to instruct their wishes. For benefits of the intermediated shareholder system, for example, para. 2.91, *ibid*.

introducing items on the agenda and submitting questions, but whether these rights will be significantly used would depend on the incentives of financial intermediaries who are legally registered as shareholders. Custodians and depositary institutions have been known to be passive,[23] and other financial intermediaries such as asset managers have been criticised to suffer from passivity due to the demands of general meeting attendance and voting for many portfolio companies,[24] as well as the pressures of conflicts of interest where asset managers maintain business relationships with the companies they invest in.[25]

Commentators point out the success of the Directive as surveys from Eurosif indicate greater levels of voting engagement by institutions after the introduction of the Directive.[26] In this manner, the Directive has to an extent successfully addressed the market failure of shareholders' market discipline, caused by the fragmentation of different procedures in Member States, some of them fraught with obstacles for the exercise of shareholder rights. Hence, despite what is perceived regarding institutions' poor incentives to engage with their corporate governance roles, the Directive has made a difference. Empirical research[27] shows a rise in shareholders' tabling of proposals on the agenda and exercising voice. What in sum the Directive has achieved is to introduce procedural facilitation and modernisation, in order to enable institutions' own incentives in exercising their corporate governance roles. The underpinning premises for the Directive are the 'agency-based' paradigm for corporate governance, where shareholders are regarded as the primary monitors of corporate management,[28] due to their residual claimant interests.[29] The removal of hindrances to such monitoring is therefore to promote good corporate governance, where shareholders are not artificially disempowered due to archaic laws or procedures in Member States. The Directive is therefore consistent with the framing in corporate law that leaves what is to be achieved by good corporate governance to be privately determined between shareholders and the management they call to account.

23. Zetzsche, *supra* n. 9.
24. For example, 'Fund houses back the boss too often', *Financial Times* (17 May 2015); 'Beyond the Rubber Stamp: Fund Managers and the Stewardship Dilemma', *Financial Times* (2 April 2015). Earlier literature *see* Marc Goergen and Luc Renneboog, *Strong Managers and Passive Institutional Investors in the UK* (1998) at http://ssrn.com/abstract=137068; Marc Goergen, Luc Renneboog and Chendi Zhang, *Do UK Institutional Shareholders Monitor Their Investee Firms?* (2007) at http://ssrn.com/abstract_id=1124406.
25. CB Ingley and NT van der Walt, *Corporate Governance, Institutional Investors and Conflicts of Interest* 12 Corp. Governance 534 (2004); for a US perspective, Jennifer S Taub, *Able but Not Willing: The Failure of Mutual Fund Advisers to Advocate for Shareholders' Rights* 34 J. Corp. L. 102 (2009).
26. Cristina Ungureanu, *Engagement of Institutional Shareholders* ch. 13 (Danny Busch, Guido Ferrarini, Gerard van Solinge eds, Oxford: OUP 2019).
27. Luc Renneboog and Peter Szilagyi, *Shareholder Engagement at European General Meetings* ch. 7 (Massimo Belcredi and Guido Ferranini eds, Cambridge: CUP 2013).
28. Michael C Jensen and William H Meckling, *Theory of the Firm: Managerial Behavior, Agency Costs and Ownership Structure* 3 J. Fin. Econ. 305 (1976).
29. Armen A Alchian and Harold Demsetz, *Production, Information Costs and Economic Organisation* 62 Am. Econ. Rev. 777 (1972).

The dominantly agency-based paradigm for conceiving shareholders' rights and their mobilisation seems to have shifted with the amendment Directive in 2017. The context for the 2017 Directive was the global financial crisis 2007–9 which saw a number of significant banks nearing failure in the EU, UK, and US. Although the mainstream view of the crisis[30] was that key weaknesses lay in bank risk management[31] and there were regulatory failures and gaps in setting standards for these[32] and in supervisory monitoring,[33] it was also queried whether poor bank risk management could in part be attributed to sub-optimal senior management and Board oversight. In the UK, the Walker Review was commissioned to look into the corporate governance aspects surrounding the near-failures of banks in the UK.[34] The Review found many aspects of bank board governance as well as shareholders' roles that were lacking and sub-optimal. 'Poor' corporate governance was not the key reason for the near-failures of banks during the global financial crisis,[35] and indeed many banks had 'good' corporate governance structures compliant with the UK's Corporate Governance Code for listed companies.[36] However, what was lacking was an effective form of corporate governance for bank risk management that would require different standards from those in the Corporate Governance Code generally applicable to the corporate sector. In this manner, the structures of corporate governance were still a contributory factor to poor bank risk management. Hence, bank corporate governance underwent specific regulatory reform in EU financial regulation.[37] In this tide of reform,[38] the Commission

30. Howard Davies, *The Financial Crisis - Who Is to Blame* (London: Polity Press 2010).
31. Hans J Blommestein, Lex Hoogduin, and JJW Peeters, *Uncertainty and Risk Management after the Great Moderation: The Role of Risk (Mis)Management by Financial Institutions* (28th SUERF Colloquium, Utrecht, The Netherlands, 3-4 September 2009) http://papers.ssrn.com/sol3/papers.cfm?abstract_id = 1489826; Gilles Bénéplanc and Jean-Charles Rochet, *Risk Management in Turbulent Times* (New York: Oxford University Press 2011); Michel Crouhy, *Risk Management Failures During the Financial Crisis* (Robert W Kolb ed., New Jersey: John Wiley 2010). Iris H-Y Chiu, *The Legal Framework for Internal Control in Banks and Financial Institutions* ch. 3 (Oxford: Hart, 2015), argues that the embrace of shareholder primacy and wealth maximisation for banks in a competitive landscape has affected the nature of bank risk management to be pro-business.
32. The standards in Basel II left too much discretion for internal risk modelling and ultimately were gamed by bankers to minimise risk provisions, Chris Terry, *The New Basel Capital Accord: A Major Advance at a Turbulent Time* (ANU Press 2009), https://press-files.anu.edu.au/downloads/press/p88211/mobile/ch02s06.html.
33. Such as the poor regulatory supervision revealed for Northern Rock and Halifax Bank of Scotland, Financial Services Authority, *The Failure of Northern Rock, A Lessons Learnt Review* (2008), https://www.fca.org.uk/publication/corporate/fsa-nr-report.pdf; Prudential Regulation Authority and Financial Conduct Authority: *The Failure of HBOS* (2015) at https://www.bankofengland.co.uk/-/media/boe/files/prudential-regulation/publication/hbos-complete-report.
34. David Walker, *A Review of Corporate Governance in UK Banks and Other Financial Industry Entities: Final Recommendations* (26 November 2009), http://webarchive.nationalarchives.gov.uk/+/http://www.hm-treasury.gov.uk/d/walker_review_261109.pdf.
35. Emilios Avgouleas and Jay Cullen, *Market Discipline and EU Corporate Governance Reform in the Banking Sector: Merits, Fallacies, and Cognitive Boundaries* 41 J. L. & Soc'y 28 (2014).
36. Brian R Cheffins, *Did Corporate Governance 'Fail' During the 2008 Stock Market Meltdown? The Case of the S&P 500* 65 Bus. Law. 1 (2009).
37. Arts 76, 88, Capital Requirements Council Directive 2013/36/EU of 26 June 2013 on access to the activity of credit institutions and the prudential supervision of credit institutions and investment firms, amending Directive 2002/87/EC and repealing Directives 2006/48/EC and 2006/49/EC,

also considered aspects of corporate governance that should be reformed for harmonised EU policy.[39]

In particular, the Commission considered institutional shareholders' roles in a similar manner to the expectations articulated in the UK's Walker Review.[40] The Walker Review opined that institutional shareholders should have played a more engaged role in order to question bank management and to hold them to account. In this light, the UK's Institutional Shareholders' Committee introduced a self-regulatory set of Principles of Responsibilities in 2010[41] in order to show voluntary efforts in improving shareholders' corporate governance behaviour. This became the basis for the Financial Reporting Council's introduction of the first Stewardship Code for institutional shareholders to sign up to, on a comply-or-explain basis. The first Stewardship Code contained seven principles which revolved around institutions having policies and implementing engagement with their investee companies, including voting, informal engagement, escalation of engagement, and collective engagement. They also needed to disclose how they managed conflicts of interest in carrying out their engagement roles.[42]

Although the Stewardship Code applied more generally to institutional shareholders' conduct in relation to their investee companies, it was inspired significantly by the Walker Review and the diagnosis of the malaises surrounding large, complex banks that were virtually unmonitored by shareholders or regulators. Spotlight was shone upon institutional shareholders who had remained passive and had a record of frequently voting with management.[43] It was queried in particular whether institutional shareholders behaved in an excessively short-termist manner and exacerbated the tendencies of short-term profit-seeking by risk-taking banks.[44] The UK government turned its attention to the issue of institutional shareholders' short-termist behaviour

---

OJ L 176, 27.6.2003. *Also see* international endorsement of corporate governance reforms for banks and financial institutions, G-30, *Towards Effective Governance in Financial Institutions* (2012) at http://www.group30.org/rpt_64.shtml.

38. Laura Horn, *Corporate Governance in Crisis? The Politics of EU Corporate Governance Regulation* 18 Eu. L. J. 83 (2012).
39. European Commission, *Green Paper on The EU Corporate Governance Framework* COM(2011) 164 final.
40. Walker, *supra* n.34.
41. *See* p1, FRC, *Revisions to the UK Stewardship Code Consultation Document* (April 2012), https://www.frc.org.uk/getattachment/69188de6-3dcf-46ab-afd9-050886ef0c5d/-;.aspx.
42. Iris H-Y Chiu, *Turning Institutional Investors into 'Stewards'- Exploring the Meaning and Objectives in 'Stewardship'* 66 Current Legal Probs. 443 (2013).
43. Walker, *supra* n.34, para. 5.7.
44. Ing-Haw Cheng, Harrison G Hong, and Jose A Scheinkman, *Yesterday's Heroes: Compensation and Creative Risk-Taking* (NBER Working Paper July 2010), http://papers.ssrn.com/sol3/papers.cfm?abstract_id=1502762, arguing that shareholder short-termist incentives facilitated excessive risk-taking by banks during the global financial crisis. Andrea Beltratti and René M Stultz, *Why Did Some Banks Perform Better during the Credit Crisis? A Cross-Country Study of the Impact of Governance and Regulation* (NBER Working Paper July 2009), http://papers.ssrn.com/sol3/papers.cfm?abstract_id=1433502, also suggests that banks in shareholder-friendly jurisdictions performed the worst during the crisis; Reint Gropp and Matthias Köhler, *Bank Owners or Bank Managers: Who Is Keen on Risk? Evidence from the Financial Crisis* (January 2010) European Business School Research Paper No 10-02, http://ssrn.com/abstract=1555663.

and their sub-optimal influence on corporations. This led to the government's commissioning of the Kay Review[45] to examine the role of institutional monitoring.

The Review concluded that institutions were undertaking short-termist investment strategies that would ultimately affect the long-term well-being of the corporate sector to serve social and economic good.[46] In this manner, the Kay Review framed market and corporate short-termism as malaises pitted against the optimal goal of long-termism and recommended that changes in institutional ownership behaviour would be key to reversing the unhealthy trend. The Review in particular recommended that institutional shareholders should be more engaged as monitors of their investee companies for long-term economic well-being, and such engagement should be of a type that is specific and involves strategic and governance matters at companies. The Review suggested that such behaviour could be incentivised, in terms of lowering the barriers and cost to collective engagement,[47] as well as potentially legalised, in terms of reviewing the fiduciary law that governs investment management.[48] Finally, institutions were admonished to emulate Warren Buffett's investment ethos of more concentrated holdings in smaller numbers of companies in order to monitor and engage effectively.[49] Hence, the 'issuer-specific' form of shareholder engagement[50] became perceived as optimal shareholder behaviour. This envisages institutional shareholders to 'go alongside' in order to monitor management, raise critical questions, and exert a benign influence. However, Gomstian[51] raises scepticism that the conclusion is rightly drawn that active shareholder engagement would result in long-termist portfolio management, ultimately to better investment and corporate performance, in the absence of clear empirical findings.

The policy recommendations in the Kay Review, although not immediately implemented by the UK government, formed the basis for 'long-termism' to become cemented as a policy rhetoric underlying the public and social expectations of institutional shareholders' 'stewardship' behaviour. The developments in the UK have arguably[52] been influential for the Commission who similarly views shareholder engagement as an important reform in order to mobilise institutions' 'long-termist' behaviour[53] where consistent with their investment horizons.

45. John Kay, *The Kay Review of UK Equity Markets and Long-term Decision Making* (Final Report, July 2012), https://assets.publishing.service.gov.uk/government/uploads/system/uploads/attachment_data/file/253454/bis-12-917-kay-review-of-equity-markets-final-report.pdf.
46. Paras 5.16ff, *ibid.*
47. Paras 7.2–7.7, p51, *ibid.*
48. *See* Recommendation 9, p13; Art. 9 from paras 9.1–9.25, *ibid.*
49. Para. 7.28, p55, *ibid.*
50. Bobby V Reddy, *The Emperor's New Code? Time to Re-Evaluate the Nature of Stewardship Engagement Under the UK's Stewardship Code* (2021), https://ssrn.com/abstract=3773156.
51. Suren Gomstian, *Transparency of Asset Managers* ch. 8 (Hanne S Birkmose and Konstantinos Sergakis eds, Cheltenham: Edward Elgar, 2021).
52. Corrado Malberti, *The Proposed Directive on the Encouragement of Long-term Shareholder Engagement in European Listed Companies: A Critical Appraisal* ch. 3 (PM Vasudev and Susan Watson eds, Cheltenham: Edward Elgar, 2017).
53. Deirdre Ahern, *The Mythical Value of Voice and Stewardship in the EU Directive on Long-term Shareholder Engagement: Rights Do Not an Engaged Shareholder Make* 20 Cambridge Y.B. Eur.

The resulting EU reforms in the amended Shareholders' Rights Directive 2017 are arguably of a character that goes beyond the facilitative, agency-based approach taken in 2007 to enable shareholders to effectively assume their corporate governance roles. As §12.03 discusses in greater detail, provisions introduced in relation to institutional shareholder engagement and the transparency of their arrangements with asset managers are both enabling and regulative. These provisions facilitate institutional shareholder engagement as a 'total' phenomenon including informal conduct and formal conduct, such as voting. However, they also embed an expectation[54] that shareholder engagement contributes to optimal investment management conduct, particularly as regards an orientation towards medium to long-termism. The 2017 Directive further provides for increased shareholder powers in relation to shareholder approval of executive pay policies[55] and potential monitoring of related-party transactions,[56] although these ultimately fall short of being harmonised across the EU. It may be argued that the reforms towards boosting shareholders' powers and engagement reflect a mixed character in terms of policy expectations for institutional shareholders. Do these reforms reflect the Commission's response to 'agency-based' problems, such as the opacity of related-party transactions and executive remuneration being on the rise and potentially out of control? Are they to be regarded as powers implicitly subject to the 'regulative' effects of the policy encouragement in favour of long-termism are expected to be exercised for broader purposes?

It is less clear that the reforms in the 2017 Directive merely support an agency-based conception of institutional shareholders' roles. The policy rhetoric surrounding the long-termist roles of institutions in engaging with their investee companies, including in relation to non-financial or 'environmental, social or governance' (ESG) issues[57] supports the perception that there are expectations for institutions in relation to their 'socially-facing' dimension. Their corporate governance roles are not merely supported as exercises of private power as such. Institutions, as stewards of many beneficiary citizens' savings, such as in occupational pension schemes, need to see themselves in a 'representative' capacity in their corporate governance roles, so that their investments are not only duly monitored but investee companies are also subject to influences reflecting an 'enlightened'[58] ethos towards corporate well-being in the long-term. However, can it be argued that such 'representative capacity' is an over-reading of the 2017 Directive, and it is at best only implicit? Can it be argued that the 2017 Directive does not depart from the agency-based paradigm for institutions'

Legal Stud. 88 (2018); Hanne S Birkmose and Konstantinos Sergakis, *SRDII- Political Ambitions and Regulatory Rationale* (Birkmose and Sergakis 2021), paras 1.01–1.10.

54. Dionysia Katelouzou, *Shareholder Stewardship: A Case of (Re)Embedding the Institutional Investors and the Corporation?* ch. 41 (Beate Sjåfjell and Christopher M. Bruner eds, Cambridge: CUP 2019).
55. Arts 9a, 9b, Directive 2017/828.
56. Art. 9c, *ibid*; more detailed discussion in Sec. C.
57. Art. 3g, *ibid*.
58. The enlightened shareholder value approach was first endorsed in the UK as providing for a form of shareholder primacy that is nevertheless socially-conscious and beneficial, Andrew Keay, *The Enlightened Shareholder Value Principle and Corporate Governance* chs 3, 4 (Oxford: Routledge 2013).

corporate governance roles, as what policy-makers are seeking is to motivate institutions incentives, but in a manner that is also aligned with wider social good? In this way, there is an assumption that institutions' desire to address agency problems, such as in related-party transactions, executive pay, and general engagement with investee companies, would at the same time benefit social good, bringing about sound corporate behaviour and ultimate well-being for the corporate sector in the long-term. Such an interpretation of the policy intentions of the 2017 Directive would be more akin to a 'trickle-down' approach – where the 2017 reforms are not treated as an attempt to 'regulate' institutional shareholders, but only as steers to capture the hybrid or integrated benefits of addressing corporate governance agency problems and public interest at the same time.

§12.03 proceeds to discuss the 'trickle-down' approach for framing the 2017 reforms and to what this perspective can be sustained. We then discuss in §12.04 whether this position is changed by reforms to regulate institutions' sustainable finance investment conduct.[59]

§12.03 ALIGNING INSTITUTIONS' AGENCY-BASED INCENTIVES IN THEIR SHAREHOLDER BEHAVIOUR WITH SOCIAL GOOD?

It is arguable that the 2017 reforms dealing with shareholder powers in monitoring executive pay and related-party transactions clearly reflect an agency-based foundation for treating shareholders' corporate governance roles. For executive pay, rise in the levels of executive pay[60] could be a way of wealth transfer to benefit their private interests, whether or not the performance of the company warrants such reward levels.

59. Regulation (EU) 2019/2088 of the European Parliament and of the Council of 27 November 2019 on sustainability–related disclosures in the financial services sector; also forthcoming regulatory changes in: Commission Delegated Directive amending Directive 2010/43/EU as regards the sustainability risks and sustainability factors to be taken into account for Undertakings for Collective Investment in Transferable Securities (UCITS); Commission Delegated Regulation amending Delegated Regulation (EU) No 231/2013 as regards the sustainability risks and sustainability factors to be taken into account by Alternative Investment Fund Managers; Commission Delegated Regulation amending Delegated Regulations (EU) 2017/2358 and (EU) 2017/2359 as regards the integration of sustainability factors, risks, and preferences into the product oversight and governance requirements for insurance undertakings and insurance distributors and into the rules on conduct of business and investment advice for insurance-based investment products; Commission Delegated Directive amending Delegated Directive (EU) 2017/593 as regards the integration of sustainability factors into the product governance obligations; Commission Delegated Regulation amending Delegated Regulation (EU) 2015/35 as regards the integration of sustainability risks in the governance of insurance and reinsurance undertakings; Commission Delegated Regulation amending Delegated Regulation (EU) 2017/565 as regards the integration of sustainability factors, risks and preferences into certain organisational requirements and operating conditions for investment firms. These are a draft package dated 21 April 2021, https://ec.europa.eu/info/publications/210421-sustainable-finance-communication_en.

60. Christoph van der Elst, *Shareholders Holding the Reins on Remuneration: The European Say on Pay* 14 Eur. Co. L. 114 (2017).

Pay without performance can be a severe agency problem,[61] and shareholders would have an interest in monitoring how corporate wealth is distributed to executives. However, the concern with executive pay in the Directive was also influenced by the backdrop of the global financial crisis.

In the aftermath of the crisis, policy-makers accepted that financial sector remuneration had given rise to perverse incentives for uncontrolled risk-taking at some banks.[62] The structure of financial sector remuneration, particularly high bonuses, has given rise to a number of perverse incentives[63] on the part of financial sector employees and management towards short-termism and excessive risk-taking, impacting on institution and wider financial sector stability. Further, there is also the issue of the sheer size of remuneration packages, which has become a source of social discontent.[64] Financial sector remuneration structures have also been linked to mis-selling and other forms of adverse conduct.[65] Hence, regulators, coordinated under the Financial Stability Board embarked on introducing remuneration regulation reforms for the financial sector. The regulation of financial sector remuneration in the EU and UK developed in two stages. First, the 2010 amendments made to the Capital Requirements Directive 2006 introduced a general principle of aligning remuneration policies to sound and effective risk management[66] and provided some prescriptive detail on the composition of remuneration.[67] Subsequently, the recast Capital Requirements Directive 2013[68] was enacted and the Directive preserved much of the Remuneration Code but added tighter controls over the composition of financial sector remuneration, especially in relation to the reward of bonuses and introduced a bonus cap of twice the amount of fixed remuneration.[69] The financial sector reforms introduced regulative framing for remuneration based on public interest, i.e., financial and systemic stability that could be threatened by financial sector employees' perverse behaviour incentivised by remuneration structures. Such reforms extend beyond senior executives to 'material risk-takers', a much larger range of responsible persons in financial firms.[70]

---

61. Lucian Bebchuk and Jesse M Fried, *Pay without Performance: The Unfulfilled Promise of Executive Compensation* (Mass: Harvard University Press, 2006).
62. Financial Stability Board, *The FSB Principles for Sound Compensation Practices and Their Implementation Standards* (April 2009), https://www.fsb.org/wp-content/uploads/r_0904b.pdf; FSB, 'Thematic Review on Compensation: Peer Review Report' (30 March 2010) http://www.financialstabilityboard.org/publications/r_100330a.pdf.
63. Markus K Brunnermeier et al., *The Fundamental Principles of Financial Regulation* (Geneva Reports on the World Economy, London: Centre for Economic Policy Research 2009); Bernard S Sharfman, *How the Strong Negotiating Position of Wall Street Employees Impacts the Corporate Governance of Financial Firms* 5 Va. Bus. & L. Rev. 350 (2011).
64. Alan Dignam refers to 'snarky' social language surrounding bankers' pay, *Understanding the Financial Crisis: Pay, Risk and Responsibility in the 21st Century* ('Current Legal Problems' lecture at Bentham House, University College, London, 4 November 2010).
65. FCA, *Commercial Insurance Intermediaries - Conflicts of Interest and Intermediary Remuneration: Report on the Thematic Project* (May 2014), p.6ff; FCA, *Risks to Customers from Financial Incentives: Final Guidance* (Jan 2013), p.13ff.
66. Capital Requirements Directive 2010, Art. 22(1).
67. Capital Requirements Directive 2010, Annex V, para. 11.
68. CRD IV Directive 2013/36/EU, Arts 92–95.
69. Art. 94, *ibid.*
70. Commission Delegated Regulation 2016/861/EU amended in 2020.

Can it be argued that the 2017 Directive has adopted explicit shareholder monitoring of executive pay for similar reasons of public interest in order to leverage upon institutions' 'representative capacity' to monitor senior management behaviour and how they are incentivised by remuneration structures? However, the same prudential stability needs are not applicable to the corporate sector generally. Hence it is surmised that the momentum of post-crisis reforms paved the way for policy-makers to deal with a long-running agency problem of excessive executive pay.[71] This is reflected in the leadership taken in the US to introduce a minimum three-yearly say on pay, i.e., a shareholders' advisory vote on the highest executive compensation packages. It can be argued that international regulatory attention to executive remuneration[72] was generally galvanised by post-crisis reforms, although the premises underpinning corporate governance reforms generally, as opposed to financial sector regulatory reforms, are different. The UK introduced a binding three-yearly shareholders' vote on executive pay policies with a yearly advisory vote on shareholders' approval of policy implementation.[73] The Directive ultimately introduced a mandatory shareholders' vote for the company's remuneration policy for directors, and although Member States may be able to implement this as advisory,[74] remuneration can only be paid in accordance with a policy put to the general meeting.[75] The remuneration policy should be put to a vote at least every four years or where there is a material change.[76]

It is queried whether the Directive's say-on-pay provisions are based on the agency problem or public-interest concerns. As prudential stability needs are not generally applicable to the public sector, it is queried what public-interest concerns would shareholders' say-on-pay address? One interpretation is that shareholders are empowered to monitor executive pay in a representative capacity due to rising social discontent regarding the pay disparity between executives and other employees. The Directive requires the remuneration policy to explain how pay and employment conditions of other employees have been taken into account. However, despite the hint of mixed messages, there is much more in the Directive drawing attention to the agency problem and ensuring that pay is made for performance.[77] Empirical research in the US shows shareholders voting mainly with pay for performance in mind, sending signals

71. Stephen F O'Byrne, *Say on Pay: Is It Needed? Does It Work?* (Harvard Corporate Governance Forum, 25 January 2018), https://corpgov.law.harvard.edu/2018/01/25/say-on-pay-is-it-needed-does-it-work/ arguing for the agency basis for say on pay.
72. Roberto Barotini, Stefano Bozzi, Guido Ferranini, and Maria-Cristina Ungureanu, *Directors' Remuneration Before and After the Crisis: Measuring the Impact of Reforms in Europe* ch. 6 (Massimo Belcredi and Guido Ferranini eds, Cambridge: CUP 2013); *Also*, SEC, *Say on Pay and Golden Parachute Votes*, https://www.sec.gov/files/sayonpay.pdf.
73. Sec. 439A, UK Companies Act 2006 as amended.
74. Detailed discussion Christoph van der Elst and Anne Lafarre, *Article 9A and 9B: Say on Pay* ch. 11 (Birkmose and Sergakis 2021).
75. Art. 9a, Directive 2017/828/EU.
76. *Ibid.*
77. On what more should be done in the reform to re-orient pay towards the benefit of the company as a whole, Aino Asplund, *Who Should Say on Pay and for the Sake of Whom in a Listed Company?* 12 Eur. Co. L. 286 (2015).

regarding the agency-based underpinnings.[78] Further, observed levels of pay disparity remain in the EU, and say on pay has had negligible effect upon pay ratcheting in the corporate sector.[79] Lafarre[80] argues that this may be because an ordinary majority to pass the remuneration policy may be too low a threshold and fails to reflect significant levels of dissent at general meetings. In this manner, we may be cautious to have expectations that shareholder powers pursuant to 'say on pay', for example, is a way of mobilising institutions' 'representative capacity' to influence corporate behaviour in line with broader social expectations.

Next, it may be argued that the 2017 Directive's provisions on monitoring related-party transactions reflect the intentions of EU policy-makers to boost shareholder monitoring powers. However, the end result remains incomplete.

Much of the European corporate sector, unlike the listed sector in the UK, feature concentrated ownership structures instead of dispersed ownership. Hence, opportunities for controlling shareholders to tunnel corporate wealth or carry out expropriation are a key concern for minority and other stakeholders of the company.[81] Enriques[82] argues that these incentives on the part of controlling shareholders are not always extractive and harmful, but it may be in the interest of the EU to be able to send policy signals that show commitment to protect minority shareholders in order to build up strong capital markets.[83] In this manner, reforms providing for controls over related-party transactions would be a close and important proxy in monitoring the agency problem on the part of controlling shareholders.[84]

The 2017 Directive is arguably a product of compromise which watered down the Commission's original proposals[85] that situate shareholders at the heart of monitoring related-party transactions. The Commission's original proposals comprised of shareholder control over material related-party transactions defined as exceeding 1% of the company's assets. Shareholder control would be exercised by a majority of the minority shareholders not associated with the controlling shareholder. Further an

78. Vicente Cunãt, Mireia Gine, and Maria Guadalupe, *Say Pays! Shareholder Voice and Firm Performance* Rev. of Fin. 1799 (2016).
79. Katarzyna Chalaczkiewicz-Ladna, *Failed Reform of Say on Pay in the UK? The Future of Shareholder Engagement with Executive Pay* 40 Co. Law. 47 (2019); Jörn Obermann, Patrick Velte, *Determinants and Consequences of Executive Compensation-Related Shareholder Activism and Say-On-Pay Votes: A Literature Review and Research Agenda* 40 J. Accounting Literature 116 (2018).
80. Anne Lafarre, *Consequences of Significant Minority Shareholder Revolt over Executive Pay* 16 Eur. Co. L. 114 (2019).
81. Alperen Afsin Gözlügöl, *The Political Economy of the Related Party Transactions Regulation in the Shareholders' Rights Directive II* 39 Y.B. Eur. L. 497 (2020); Belcredi and Ferranini (2013), *supra* n. 4. *See also* wider concerns, Kyoung-Soo Yoon and Yangsoo Jin, *Related Party Transactions, Agency Problem, and Exclusive Effects* 51 Eur. J. L. & Econ. 1 (2021).
82. Luca Enriques, *Related Party Transactions: Policy Options and Real-World Challenges (with a Critique of the European Commission Proposal)* 16 Eur. Bus. Org. L. Rev. 1 (2015).
83. Rafael La Porta, Florencio Lopez-De-Silanes, Andrei Shleifer, *What Works in Securities Laws* 61 J. Fin. 1 (2006).
84. Nick Hallemeesch, *Self-dealing by Controlling Shareholders: Improving Minority Protection in the Light of Article 9c SRD* Eur. Co. & Fin. L. Rev. 197 (2018).
85. Gözlügöl, *supra* n. 81; Andreas Engert and Tim Florstedt, *Which Related Party Transactions Should Be Subject to Ex Ante Review? Evidence from Germany* 20 J. Cor. L. Stud. 263 (2020).

independent third-party valuation opinion should be provided to show that the related-party transaction has been assured. The Directive ultimately provided for Member States to opt for general meeting approval of related-party transactions or Board approval. The third-party valuation is optional and the definition of what is 'material' is left to Member States with some guidance on financial thresholds. The Directive provides for the immediate public announcement of the conclusion of material related-party transactions with salient details. The *ex post* announcement may be seen to be relevant for market discipline even though *ex ante* discipline has been made more flexible and unharmonized in the Directive.[86] It is opined that the final shape of the Directive has been due to fierce business lobbying.[87] Institutional shareholders had supported a stronger monitoring role as such the approval of the general meeting with a majority of minority shareholders unassociated with the controlling shareholder.

The reform for controlling related-party transactions is quite clearly framed in the agency paradigm as what is important is some form of control, both *ex ante* and *ex post,* for such transactions. However, as pointed out by Bianchi and Miliê, the point seems not to be about empowering shareholders as such, as a broader range of stakeholders is recognised for monitoring purposes.[88] This may show that policy-makers are not necessarily keen on placing institutional shareholders in representative monitoring position for the good of the company and other stakeholders as a whole.[89] But this may also reflect the generally more pluralist corporate governance ideologies in the EU.

Finally, it may be queried if the Directive's provisions on institutional shareholder engagement and the management of investment assets for a long-term horizon are regulative in nature and reflect policy-makers' attempt to steer institutions' corporate governance as well as their investment management conduct according to public policy goals (Articles 3g to 3j). In other words, even if the provisions discussed so far are based on the same old agency-based paradigm for institutions' corporate governance roles, it may be queried if Articles 3g to 3j are in the same vein.

Article 3g of the 2017 Directive requires that institutions should publicly disclose their engagement policy with investee companies or explain in reasoned and clear terms why they choose not to have one. Further, institutions should also publicly disclose the annual implementation of their engagement policy and their voting behaviour. It may be argued that, based on the 'comply-or-explain' framework for institutions to have an engagement policy or to implement engagement or voting, this provision is merely soft law and works within the agency-based paradigm. Institutions remain at discretion to determine if issuer engagement and voting works within their

86. Irene CP Groenland, *Related Party Transactions in the Revised Shareholders' Rights Directive: The EU Perspective and Implementation in National Law* 16 Eur. Co. L. 44 (2019).
87. Gözlügöl, *supra* n. 81.
88. Marcello Bianchi and Mateja Miliê, *Article 9C: Transparency and Approval of Related Party Transactions* para. 12.28 (Birkmose and Sergakis 2021).
89. Kristin Reynisson, *Related Party Transactions: Analysis of Proposed Article 9c of Shareholders' Rights Directive* 5 Eur. Co. L. 175 (2016).

private interests.[90] Further, the lack of a firm hardening of a duty to vote is reflected in the soft law in Article 3i governing proxy advisers. Proxy advisers under Article 3i are to disclose a code of conduct they adhere to in relation to how they generate their advice and voting policies, as well as their management of conflicts of interest, or else explain how they carry out their roles and activities. The key proxy advisers in the industry subscribe to the Best Practice Principles,[91] an industry code of conduct, and are hence self-regulating. As voting remains largely a self-regulatory exercise, it may be argued that Article 3g has not taken any definitive regulative step in relation to investment intermediaries' corporate governance roles.

However, a 'comply or explain' approach nevertheless reflects the optimal choice preferred by policy-makers (the standards for compliance),[92] and this implicitly gives rise to 'normification' of the tenet of shareholder engagement,[93] which, as discussed in §12.02, has, after the global financial crisis, been framed in terms of being undertaken in 'representative capacity' and for the public good of securing corporate sector well-being and stability. Further, the UK Financial Conduct Authority has transposed Article 3g into the regulation for investment firms and funds, albeit retaining the 'comply or explain' character, showing that the regulative nature of the provision, in terms of normative expectations of investment management conduct, is recognised.[94] In sum however, it remains ambiguous whether Article 3g conveys normative signals, as being soft law, it does not convey a clear regulative steer.[95]

It can be argued that Articles 3h and 3j are more regulative in character. Article 3h governs institutions' public transparency on their arrangements with asset managers, on key matters that may be regarded to be in public interest. One relates to institutions' mandates to asset managers incentivising a long-termist investment management approach. The other relates to incentivising asset managers to monitor investee companies in relation to medium and long-term financial and non-financial performance. In particular, institutions should monitor incentives, such as remuneration and performance evaluation of asset managements, as well as practices in portfolio turnover, which can be associated with short-termist investment management behaviour. Article 3j deals with asset managers' corresponding transparency to institutions in relation to the matters in Article 3h in order to assist institutions in forming views for the purposes of public transparency under Article 3h.

---

90. Lorraine E Talbot, *Polanyi's Embeddedness and Shareholder Stewardship: A Contextual Analysis of Current Anglo-American Perspectives on Corporate Governance* 62 N. Ireland Legal Q. 451 (2011).
91. https://bppgrp.info/.
92. Characterising comply-or-explain as comply-or-else, observed in relation to the UK Corporate Governance Code, *see* Marc T Moore, '*Whispering Sweet Nothings*': *The Limitations of Informal Conformance in UK Corporate Governance* 9 J. Cor. L. Stud. 35 (2009).
93. Katelouzou, *supra* n. 54; Iris H-Y Chiu and Dionysia Katelouzou, *From Shareholder Stewardship to Shareholder Duties: Is the Time Ripe?* ch. 7 (Hanne Søndergard Birkmose ed., Alphen aan den Rijn: Wolters Kluwer International, 2016).
94. Financial Conduct Authority FCA Handbook, COBS 2.2B.1; SYSC 3.4.
95. Hanne S Birkmose, *European Challenges for Institutional Shareholder Engagement: Is Mandatory Disclosure the Way Forward?* Eur. Co. & Fin. L. Rev. 214 (2014); Marina Madsen, *Nudging Institutional Shareholders* 32 Eur. Bus. L. Rev. 295 (2021).

The explicit policy preference for investment management conduct based on having a long-term view of corporate performance is arguably a regulative steer. Left to market forces, investment intermediaries can *rationally* choose short-term trading-based strategies for their portfolios, especially if they are so incentivised by remuneration or performance structures.[96] The policy preference for long-termism reflects post-crisis sentiments in relation to the normative social good of a stable and well-performing corporate sector, aligned with the sentiments expressed in the UK's Walker and Kay Reviews discussed earlier. In this manner, the mandatory disclosure regulation may not merely be regarded as a market-based regulation that allows institutions to monitor their asset managers.[97] Public transparency is intended to attract broader regulatory and stakeholder scrutiny in terms of institutions' roles in shaping financial allocations, market behaviour, and the relations between economy and society.

Further, although the Directive is not explicit with regard to what 'non-financial matters' means, reference to Article 3g may shed light upon the nature of non-financial matters in Article 3h, as relating to 'environmental, social and governance' matters. These may be of broader concern to society and stakeholders.

In this way, the mandatory disclosure regulation for institutions embeds[98] normative and public-interest based expectations for institutions' monitoring of their mandates with asset managers, steering towards concern for long-termism and non-financial as well as financial performance of investee companies. This is arguably a regulative provision that seeks to establish, in implicit terms, institutions' 'representative capacity' in their investment management conduct to secure purposes of greater good. Again, in the UK, Article 3h is transposed as a matter of financial regulation – as regulative obligations for investment firms and funds regulated by the Financial Conduct Authority,[99] and occupational pension schemes overseen by the Department of Work and Pensions and Pensions Regulator.[100] Such transposition reinforces the regulative nature of the provision. However, it can be argued that such a framing is still at best ambiguous due to the wrapper of disclosure regulation which is fundamentally market-facing. It would be envisaged that institutions' beneficiaries are the chief sources of discipline for institutions, while institutions themselves would discipline and monitor their asset managers. However, the inertia of beneficiaries and the collective action problem is likely to deter meaningful discipline for institutions, and it remains uncertain if the financial regulatory transposition in the UK means much in terms of regulatory and broader social oversight.

It remains ambiguous that Articles 3g to 3j of the 2017 Directive have clearly departed from an agency-based paradigm in framing institutions' and asset managers'

96. Roger Barker and Iris H-Y Chiu, *Investment Management and Corporate Governance* ch. 2 (Cheltenham: Edward Elgar 2017).
97. However, public disclosure can be interpreted as chiefly for beneficiaries' interests, *see* Birkmose and Sergakis (2021), ch. 7.
98. Katelouzou, *supra* n. 54.
99. FCA Handbook SYSC 3.4.9.
100. Regulation 2(3)(d), The Occupational Pension Schemes (Investment) Regulations 2005, as inserted by The Occupational Pension Schemes (Investment and Disclosure) (Amendment) Regulations 2019, reg. 2.

corporate governance relations. The comply-or-explain regime for engagement and voting policies, as well as the market-facing orientation of mandatory disclosure tend to reflect deference for institutions' management of their investment conduct as a private matter, including their corporate governance relations, although policy rhetoric nudges towards certain expectations, such as long-termism, issuer engagement, and non-financial considerations. We do not consider the 2017 Directive as sufficiently having given rise to a new framing of institutions acting in 'representative capacity' for wider social good. Empirical research shows that shareholder expression has been largely made in relation to agency-based interests, such as pay for performance, anti-takeover practices,[101] and shareholders' rights.[102] It would require much clearer regulative framing for an era of 'regulating institutional investors' to arise,[103] in order to steer institutional shareholders to act in certain ways. We have earlier argued[104] that such framing is most likely to be based on financial regulation, and arguably, some radical steps have been taken forward by the EU in relation to the regulatory initiatives for sustainable finance. The next section discusses how financial regulation more broadly provides a basis for locating the regulation of institutional shareholders and critically reflects on what sustainable finance regulation has achieved in this regard.

§12.04 REGULATING INSTITUTIONAL SHAREHOLDERS: INITIATIVES FROM SUSTAINABLE FINANCE REGULATION

It has been argued elsewhere that setting norms for the conduct of institutional shareholders' corporate governance roles should not be situated within the legal framework for company law and corporate governance. These frameworks generally provide for the private and relational nature of corporate constituents' relationships inter se[105] and may not cater optimally for public policy steers. The realm of securities or financial regulation may be more appropriate for locating the 'normification' of aspects of investment institutions' conduct, whether relating to their customer relations, ongoing portfolio management, or assuming their corporate governance roles.[106] In this light, this section explores what is achieved by the EU's sustainable finance reforms which represent a significant step towards the regulation of investment management conduct. In regulating investment management conduct, these reforms

---

101. Renneboog and Szilagyi, *supra* n. 27.
102. Christoph van der Elst and Anne Lafarre, *Shareholder Stewardship in the Netherlands: The Role of Institutional Investors in a Stakeholder Oriented Jurisdiction* (ECGI Working Paper 2020), https://ecgi.global/sites/default/files/working_papers/documents/final_2.pdf.
103. Iris H-Y Chiu and Dionysia Katelouzou, *Making a Case for Regulating Institutional Shareholders' Corporate Governance Roles* J. Bus. L. 67 (2018).
104. *Ibid.*
105. Reinier Kraakman, John Armour, Paul Davies, Luca Enriques, Henry Hansmann, Gerard Hertig, Klaus Hopt, Hideki Kanda, Mariana Pargendler, Wolf-Georg Ringe, and Edward Rock, *The Anatomy of Corporate Law* (Oxford: OUP 2017, 3rd ed.), chapters 1–8 on the functional aspects of corporate law catering to the key constituents of the corporation. Chapter 9 explicitly refers to securities regulation as having a different objective and scope in relation to being market regulation, and covered as a companion topic rather than as a subset of corporate law.
106. Chiu and Katelouzou, *supra* n. 103; ch. 3, Barker and Chiu, *supra* n. 96.

would also compel investment intermediaries to monitor and evaluate their investee companies' sustainability footprints and performance in certain ways, therefore having the potential to transform institutional shareholders' corporate governance roles for the purposes of sustainable objectives. The sustainable finance reforms offer some insights into how policy goals provide direction towards an agenda for 'regulating institutional shareholders'.

Policy reforms to regulate investment management conduct may be attributed to the investment intermediaries' market failure in internalising the costs of their sustainability footprint and in pricing the benefits of pro-sustainability investments. Empirical research has pointed out the persistent lack of counting sustainability cost in terms of financiers' valuation of their assets, in particular, the cost of stranded assets in due course.[107] Stranded assets are assets that would be forced to be written down or made obsolete due to unsustainable characteristics, such as high carbon footprint or polluting characteristics. In allocating investments to portfolio companies, it is queried if investment intermediaries effectively interrogate companies' data regarding stranded assets or assets under transition in order to value their investments accurately. Further, investment intermediaries may suffer from the behavioural tendency to underweight the long-termist nature of such valuations,[108] not to mention that such valuations are still being developed in terms of accounting metrics.[109] The EU's sustainable finance reforms for the investment management sector can be warranted on the basis of observed market failures in their valuation practices that would in due course be adverse to beneficiaries.

The Sustainable Disclosure Regulation 2019[110] now introduces certain 'baseline' duties for investment firms and funds so that sustainability cost would be internalised in their investment management. These apply whether or not investment intermediaries engage with the universe of 'socially responsible investing' (SRI)[111] or ESG

107. Bob Buhr, *Assessing the Sources of Stranded Asset Risk: A Proposed Framework* 7 J. Sustainable Fin. & Inv. 37 (2017); Jemma Green & Peter Newman, *Disruptive Innovation, Stranded Assets and Forecasting: The Rise and Rise of Renewable Energy* 7 J. Sust. Fin. &Inv. 169 (2017); John Byrd & Elizabeth S. Cooperman, *Investors and Stranded Asset Risk: Evidence from Shareholder Responses to Carbon Capture and Sequestration (CCS) Events* 8 J. Sust. Fin. & Inv. 185 (2018).

108. Nicholas Silver, *Blindness to Risk: Why Institutional Investors Ignore the Risk of Stranded Assets* 7 J. Sust. Fin. & Inv. 99 (2017); Jakob Thomä and Hugues Chenet, *Transition Risks and Market Failure: A Theoretical Discourse on Why Financial Models and Economic Agents May Misprice Risk Related to the Transition to a Low-Carbon Economy* 7 J. Sus. Fin. & Inv. 82 (2017).

109. Dan Esty and Todd Cort, *The Data Challenges that Remain* ch. 9 (Cary Kronsinsky and Sophie Purdom eds, Routledge Earthscan, 2017); Johan Frishammar and Vinit Parida, *Circular Business Model Transformation: A Roadmap for Incumbent Firms* 61 Cal. Mgmt Rev. 5 (2019); Robert Sroufe, *Integration and Organizational Change Towards Sustainability* 162 Journal of Cleaner Production 315 (2017); Francisco Szekely and Zahir Dossa, *Beyond the Triple Bottom Line: Eight Steps toward a Sustainable Business Model* ch. 6 (Mass: MIT Press, 2017).

110. Regulation 2019/2088/EU.

111. Magnus Jansson and Anders Biel, *Investment Institutions' Beliefs About and Attitudes Toward Socially Responsible Investment (SRI): A Comparison Between SRI and Non-SRI Management* 22 Sustainable Development 33 (2014); Peer Osthoff, *What Matters to SRI Investors?* ch. 54 (Tessa Hebb, James P. Hawley, Andreas G. F. Hoepner, Agnes L. Neher, David Wood eds, Oxford: Routledge 2015) on SRI catering for investors whose primary focus is on investment performance and are merely seeking an alignment with socially responsible aspects. *Also see* Christin Nitsche and Michael Schröder, *Are SRI Funds Conventional Funds in Disguise Or Do They Live*

funds.[112] First, the Regulation compels all financial markets participants who engage in portfolio management or fund management (whether as mainstream pension or collective investment schemes, or alternative investments funds)[113] to make mandatory disclosure of how they integrate sustainability risks in their investment decision-making.[114] 'Sustainability risk' is defined as 'environmental, social or governance event or condition that, if it occurs, could cause an actual or a potential material negative impact on the value of the investment'.[115] Such a definition adopts a 'single materiality' approach of treating sustainability risk as salient only if it materially affects investment performance. At a baseline, this is not novel and consistent with the interpretation of fiduciary duty in private investment management.[116] It may even be argued that this baseline duty pertains only to disclosure and does not change the nature of the financially-focused duty of fiduciary investment management. Policy-makers in the EU have responded by clarifying that the baseline duty is not merely a duty of disclosure but also a duty to integrate sustainability risks as such, in the governance and risk management of investment intermediaries.[117] In this way, the

Up to Their Name? ch. 19 (Sabri Boubaker, Douglas Cumming, and Duc Khuong Nguyen eds, Cheltenham: Edward Elgar, 2018) arguing that many SRI investment funds do not differ significantly from conventional ones.

112. An investment strategy that views non-financial aspects as chiefly risks to be managed for financial performance, Rajna Gibson Brandon and Philipp Krüger, *The Sustainability Footprint of Institutional Investors* (ECGI Working Paper 2018) at https://ssrn.com/abstract=2918926; Gunnar Friede, Timo Busch and Alexander Bassen, *ESG and Financial Performance: Aggregated Evidence from More Than 2000 Empirical Studies* 5 J. Sustainable Fin. & Inv. 210 (2015); Heather Hachigian and Sarah M. McGill, *Reframing the Governance Challenge for Sustainable Investment* 2 J. Sustainable Fin. & Inv. 166 (2012); Ick Jin, *Is ESG a Systematic Risk Factor for US Equity Mutual Funds?* 8 J. Sust. Fin. & Inv. 72 (2018); N. C. Ashwin Kumar, Camille Smith, Leïla Badis, Nan Wang, Paz Ambrosy, and Rodrigo Tavares, *ESG Factors and Risk-Adjusted Performance: A New Quantitative Model* 6 J. Sustainable Fin. & Inv. 292 (2016). Dana Brakman Reiser and Anne Tucker, *Buyer Beware: Variation and Opacity in ESG and ESG Index Funds* 41 Cardozo L Rev 1921 (2020) shows that ESG funds do not differ much from conventional funds.
113. Regulation 2019/2088, Art. 2.
114. *Ibid*, Art. 3.
115. *Ibid*, Art. 2(22).
116. Freshfields Bruckhaus Deringer, *A Legal Framework for the Integration of Environmental, Social and Governance Issues into Institutional Investment* (Report for the UNEP Finance Initiative, 2005), https://www.unepfi.org/fileadmin/documents/freshfields_legal_resp_20051123.pdf; UNEPFI, *Fiduciary Duty in the 21st Century* (2019), https://www.unepfi.org/wordpress/wp-content/uploads/2019/10/Fiduciary-duty-21st-century-final-report.pdf; Sarah Barker, Mark Baker-Jones, Emilie Barton, & Emma Fagan, *Climate Change and the Fiduciary Duties of Pension Fund Trustees – Lessons from the Australian Law* 6 J. Sustainable Fin. & Inv. 211 (2016); Benjamin Richardson, *From Fiduciary Duties to Fiduciary Relationships for Socially Responsible Investing: Responding to The Will of Beneficiaries* 1 J. Sustainable Fin. & Inv. 5 (2011).
117. Commission Delegated Regulation to amend the Alternative Investment Fund Managers Directive, https://ec.europa.eu/finance/docs/level-2-measures/aifmd-delegated-act-2021-2615_en.pdf (21 April 2021); Commission Delegated Directive to amend the UCITs Directive, https://ec.europa.eu/finance/docs/level-2-measures/ucits-directive-delegated-act-2021-2617_en.pdf (21 April 2021); Commission Delegated Directive to amend the Markets in Financial Instruments Directive, https://ec.europa.eu/finance/docs/level-2-measures/mifid-2-delegated-act-2021-2612_en.pdf (21 April 2021).

achievement in this legalisation is that all mainstream investment intermediaries are at least bound to consider material sustainability issues in their investment management, and it is no longer a discretionary matter, such as for funds that opt to be labelled as SRI or ESG. However, it may be argued that the baseline duty is not terribly potent, as enforcement is likely to come from market discipline, relying on mandatory disclosure by investment intermediaries. It is challenging for regulators to undertake clear enforcement actions regarding how firms integrate sustainability risks into their governance and risk-management processes. This aspect is meta-regulatory in nature[118] and allows firms a certain scope of open-endedness for implementation within their systems, processes, and culture.

Next, investment intermediaries of a certain scale, defined as having 500 employees or above, or being a parent company of such an undertaking,[119] are mandated to account for principal adverse sustainability impacts (applying from 30 June 2021). This applies whether or not such financial services providers engage with sustainably-labelled products. They must account for any adverse impact of their investment decision-making processes on sustainability objectives, how adverse impacts are discovered, and what due diligence policies are deployed.[120] Smaller providers are able to declare that they do not consider adverse sustainability impacts in their investment decision-making process but must clearly explain why and whether this practice cuts across all their products.[121] This means that smaller providers are subject to the broad duty to integrate sustainability risks as discussed earlier but not specifically to the prescribed mandatory disclosures of due diligence policies and measurement of adverse sustainability impact imposed on larger investment intermediaries. In this manner, larger investment intermediaries are imposed with an obligation that is more socially-facing in nature, i.e., to account for sustainability cost *as such*. The type and nature of principal adverse impact that will be disclosed are based on double materiality, i.e., these are measured in terms of their impact upon not only investment performance but also sustainability performance.[122]

It is arguable that the imposition of 'principal adverse impact' mandatory disclosure on large investment firms and funds represents a firm regulatory steer to compel such firms and funds to count sustainability cost as such, and these asset managers would likely in turn put pressure on portfolio companies to measure and disclose the same, therefore producing a virtuous circle of influence for behavioural change. Of course, that also assumes the virtuous circle is incentivised, i.e., that the asset owner recipients of large firms or funds' disclosure treat such disclosures as being influential for their allocation decisions. There is increasing evidence that asset

118. Christine Parker, *The Open Corporation* (Cambridge: CUP 2000). Discussion on the opaque and unsupervised nature of meta-regulation, Julia Black, *Paradoxes and Failures: 'New Governance' Techniques and the Financial Crisis* 75 Mod. L. Rev. 1037 (2012).
119. Arts 4(3), (4), Regulation 2019/2088.
120. Art. 4(1)(a), *ibid.*
121. Art. 4(1)(b), *ibid.*
122. European Securities and Markets Authority's draft technical standards as of 23 April 2020, at https://www.esma.europa.eu/press-news/esma-news/esas-consult-environmental-social-and-governance-disclosure-rules.

owners, such as pension funds[123] and pro-social individuals value the avoidance of adverse sustainable impact in their investment allocations.[124] However, this is not necessarily the case with many conventional institutions,[125] and investment beneficiaries have highly heterogenous preferences.[126] Further, there is the issue of whether corporations are able to produce such measurements for investor use, and in this respect, the EU is undertaking reform to comprehensively introduce sustainability disclosures for all corporations.[127] But it remains uncertain to what extent these reforms would produce the standardised and user-friendly metrics for sustainability that investors need.[128] Nevertheless, many large investment firms or funds targeted under the Regulation are likely to be the largest global asset managers, a number of whom are passive managers, such as Vanguard and the world's largest exchange-traded fund provider, Blackrock. These have been observed to be already involved in engagement with corporate issuers on common issues across portfolios, such as sustainability or ESG issues.[129] Hence, the EU reforms may be regarded as facilitating this process which is already underway and do not impose radically new expectations that may run the risk of falling short.

The above reforms seem proportionate for smaller fund intermediaries who can declare that they are agnostic to adverse sustainability impact. But the reforms nevertheless drive a bifurcation, suggesting that smaller firms can elect to be principally 'private-facing' and potentially 'exempt', subject to their explanation, from a

123. George Apostolakis, Gert Van Dijk, Robert J Blomme, Frido Kraanen, & Athanasios P. Papadopoulos, *Predicting Pension Beneficiaries' Behaviour When Offered a Socially Responsible and Impact Investment Portfolio* 8 J. Sustainable Fin. & Inv. 213 (2018); Anett Wins and Bernhard Zwergel, *Comparing Those Who Do, Might and Will Not Invest in Sustainable Funds: A Survey Among German Retail Fund Investors* 9 Bus. Rsch 51 (2016); Lei Delsen & Alex Lehr, *Value Matters or Values Matter? An Analysis of Heterogeneity in Preferences for Sustainable Investments* 9 J Sustainable Fin. & Inv. 240 (2019).
124. Manuel Ammann, Christopher Bauer, Sebastian Fischer, Philipp Müller, *The Impact of the Morningstar Sustainability Rating on Mutual Fund Flows* (2018), https://ssrn.com/abstract=3068724.
125. Magnus Jans Jansson and Anders Biel, *Investment Institutions' Beliefs About and Attitudes Toward Socially Responsible Investment (SRI): A Comparison Between SRI and Non-SRI Management* 22 Sustainable Development 33 (2014); Federica Ielasi and Monica Rossolini, *Responsible or Thematic? The True Nature of Sustainability-Themed Mutual Funds* 11 Sustainability J. 3304 (2019).
126. George Apostolakis, Frido Kraanen, and Gert van Dijk, *Pension Beneficiaries' and Fund Managers' Perceptions of Responsible Investment: A Focus Group Study*16 Cor. Gov. 1 (2016); also prosocial individual investors remain a minority, *see* Charlotte Christiansen, Thomas Jansson, Malene Kallestrup-Lamb, and Vicke Noren, *Who Are the Socially Responsible Mutual Fund Investors?* (2019) at http://ssrn.com/abstract=3128432.
127. European Commission, *Communication from the Commission to the European Parliament, the Council, the European Economic and Social Committee and the Committee of the Regions: EU Taxonomy, Corporate Sustainability Reporting, Sustainability Preferences and Fiduciary Duties: Directing finance towards the European Green Deal* (21 April 2021), https://ec.europa.eu/finance/docs/law/210421-sustainable-finance-communication_en.pdf.
128. Iris H-Y Chiu, *The EU Sustainable Finance Agenda- Developing Governance for Double Materiality in Sustainability Metrics* 23 Eur. Bus. Org. L. Rev. 87 (2022).
129. Virginia Harper Ho, *From Public Policy to Materiality: Non-Financial Reporting, Shareholder Engagement, and Rule 14a-8's Ordinary Business Exception* 76 Wash & Lee L. Rev. 1231 (2019); Suren Gomstian, *Voting Engagement by Large Institutional Shareholders* 45 J. Cor. L. 659 (2020).

scope of socially-facing accountability imposed on larger firms. There is a large sector of investment firms that are medium sized and employ under 500 employees. Hence it is questioned as to whether the EU's legalisation has achieved much in terms of steering investment management conduct towards double materiality. Nevertheless, it may be argued that the reforms recognise the potential systemic impact of large investment firms' or funds' stewardship actions, and their leadership may in time provide isomorphic pressures for smaller firms in demonstrating to their clients how sustainability cost can be counted in investment management.

Our analysis so far is nuanced regarding the achievements in the EU's sustainable finance reforms to mobilise institutional shareholders' monitoring of investee companies for sustainability cost. Market discipline remains key to the enforcement and meaningfulness of disclosure obligations, and it remains to be seen if large investment firms wield sufficient monitoring influence over their portfolio corporations. It may be argued that investment intermediaries may exercise their discipline on corporations in the following manner: corporations whose sustainability performance is weak or difficult to ascertain could be excluded from investment intermediaries' fund products, due to the legal risk for disclosure compliance that investment intermediaries need to make. In this manner, the regulative steer can incentivise a form of market discipline that translates into a force for change for corporations that wish to remain attractive on securities markets. However, investment intermediaries may not take such an approach. Investment firms 'integrating' material sustainability risks can do so in various 'balancing' manners not excluding the recognition of sustainability risks. Further, a market-based approach in the reforms means that investment entities would only be moved by their perception of market appetite and impact on fund flows. If asset owners or retail investors are 'sticky' or do not translate their pro-sustainability appetites to significant market reactions, mainstream investment intermediaries would be steered by market perceptions. It is hardly conceivable that investment intermediaries see their compliance obligations as triggering a sense of 'representative capacity' for monitoring corporate sustainability.

Finally, we briefly offer some views as to the other aspect of the EU sustainable finance reforms, which is the building up of a market for sustainable finance.[130] The reforms provide extensively for how actively and passively managed investment products that are labelled as sustainable, in particular, environmentally sustainable, need to meet positive sustainable outcomes on a double materiality basis.[131] Certain environmentally sustainable investment products are tied to prescribed scientifically determined outcomes under the Taxonomy Regulation 2020,[132] while a Social Taxonomy is being developed for investment products intending to achieve social development outcomes.[133] The Taxonomy reforms and prescription for double materiality in

130. Iris H-Y Chiu, *Building a Single Market for Sustainable Finance in the EU- Mixed Implications and the Missing Link of Digitalisation*, 18(5) Eur. Co. & Fin. L. Rev. 181 (2022).
131. Art. 2, Regulation 2019/2088 on the definition of sustainability objective.
132. Regulation 2020/852.
133. Social Taxonomy envisaged by the Commission, https://ec.europa.eu/info/sites/default/files/business_economy_euro/banking_and_finance/documents/finance-events-210226-presentation-social-taxonomy_en.pdf.

performance are meant to prevent greenwashing[134] and can compel institutions to scrutinise their allocational decisions and engage with portfolio companies. However, whether the virtuous circle of sustainable investment and stewardship can be attained depends very much on market appetite for sustainably-labelled investment products as superior to current 'SRI' or 'ESG' offerings. If the market increasingly cares for double materiality and allocates to the EU's sustainably-labelled investment products, a market-led sea change can occur. However, it is expected that the regulatory obligations underlying sustainably-labelled investment products may translate into increased cost of offering, and it remains uncertain if the market would still settle for lower 'SRI' or 'ESG' labels that could be less expensive. Such lower labelled products are not outlawed in the EU's sustainable finance reforms[135] but have had a chequered record in terms of securing change in corporate behaviour.[136]

As we perceive regulatory steers in building up the market for sustainable finance to be predominantly based on incentivising market forces, the nature of such regulatory reform is arguably facilitative in nature. Ultimate conduct changes depend on how the voice of the demand side is exercised to shape investment product design and supply.

§12.05 CONCLUSION

EU policy-makers have turned their attention to the positions and normative roles of shareholders, especially institutional shareholders during the last two decades. Policy reform based on facilitating the exercise of shareholder power without extensive harmonisation was first intended to help shareholders overcome obstacles in their corporate governance roles, such market failures not having been addressed in many Member States. After the global financial crisis, more policy thinking was mobilised in relation to the normative roles of institutional shareholders, in terms of how their monitoring roles in corporate governance could be more broadly beneficial to economy and society. This resulted in the articulation of 'stewardship' for institutional investors in the UK and influenced the EU level reforms that sought to encourage more institutional shareholder engagement with their investee companies, and for institutions to adopt long-termist investment management strategies and conduct. These EU level reforms are however pitched delicately between the continued framing of institutions acting in their natural 'agency-based' self-interest and the roles that would meet normative expectations in terms of long-termism and issuer monitoring. This

134. Unregulated 'greenwashing'? ESG investing is under the microscope as the money rolls in' (CNBC News, 14 October 2020), https://www.cnbc.com/2020/10/14/esg-investing-meaning-is-under-the-microscope-as-the-money-rolls-in.html.
135. Art. 7, Taxonomy Regulation 2020.
136. SRI funds may actively field proposals and voice at portfolio companies, Erwin Eding and Bert Scholtens, *Corporate Social Responsibility and Shareholder Proposals* 24 Cor. Soc. Resp. & Env't Mgmt. 648 (2017); US: Jody Grewal, George Serafeim, and Aaron Yoon, *Shareholder Activism on Sustainability Issues* Harvard Business School Working Paper, 2016, but passive ESG funds may not be much different from conventional ones, Jacquelyn Humphrey, *Socially Responsible Screening in Mutual Funds* ch. 51 (Hebb et al., 2015); Nitsche and Schröder (2018).

ambiguity is not really resolved, and policy-makers remain keen to introduce more regulative steers for institutions, particularly within the agenda for regulating sustainable finance. The more overt adoption of financial regulation as the paradigm for regulating institutional investment conduct paves the way for clearer regulative steers affecting institutions' corporate governance roles. Arguably, the imposition on large investment firms and funds to disclose 'principal adverse impact' on a double materiality basis is arguably the clearest form of public policy imposition on these investment entities to achieve broader social good by monitoring sustainability cost apart from impact on investment performance, and to implicitly influence their investee companies to count and make transparent such cost. However, investment intermediaries are likely to be responsive to market appetites and signals, and it remains to be seen how far such disclosures can produce a form of social signalling that affects their behaviour. There is still a significant amount of market-based regulation in the sustainable finance reforms in terms of subjecting smaller investment intermediaries to only single materiality considerations and disclosures. Regulatory provisions that facilitate the building of the market for sustainably-labelled investment products intended to be superior to industry labelled 'SRI' or 'ESG' products are also framed as market-based initiatives. The EU is not yet at a point where institutional shareholders are being comprehensively regulated, and it may be argued that market-based actors, and regulating them, are only one piece of the mosaic in securing behavioural change, which is more often directly impacted by business activity regulation.[137]

137. Rupert Allen, Hugues Letourneau, & Tessa Hebb, 'Shareholder Engagement in the Extractive Sector' (2012) 2 J. Sustainable Fin. & Inv. 3.

CHAPTER 13

The Market for Corporate Control in the EU

Blanaid Clarke

§13.01 INTRODUCTION

The theory of the market for corporate control (MCC) suggests that a company which is poorly managed will fail to maximise its performance potential leading to shareholders selling their shares with a consequent reduction in share price. This renders the company vulnerable to a takeover at a price below its real value by a bidder who will replace existing management, turn the company around, and reap the rewards. This has been referred to as 'the pruning of managerial deadwood'.[1] The most renowned proponent of the MCC was Henry Manne, an eminent American scholar and one of the founders of the Law and Economics movement. In his seminal article *Mergers and the Market for Corporate Control* in 1965, Manne suggested that corporate control constitutes a valuable asset which exists independently of any interest in either economies of scale or monopoly power.[2] Manne's positive perspective of hostile takeovers reached a receptive audience in the United States (US) during the 1980s when junk bonds fuelled a takeover boom following the easing of takeover regulations in the Williams Act 1968.[3] He argued that there is a high positive correlation between corporate managerial efficiency and the market price of shares. This creates opportunities for bidders able to revitalise targeted companies as 'the lower the stock price, relative to what it could be with more efficient management, the more attractive the takeover becomes to those who believe that they can manage the company more efficiently'.[4]

1. James Walsh and John Ellwood, *Mergers, Acquisitions, and the Pruning of Managerial Deadwood,* 12 Strategic Management Journal 201 (1991).
2. Henry Manne, *Mergers and the Market for Corporate Control* 73 J. Pol. Econ. 110 (1965).
3. Sue Konzelmann, Frank Wilkinson, Marc Fovargue-Davies, and Duncan Sankey, *Governance, Regulation and Financial Market Instability: The Implications for Policy,* 34 Camb. J. Econ 929 (2010).
4. Manne, *supra* n. 2, 113.

The strength of the MCC lies in its disciplinary effect. It is not necessary for a takeover to actually occur to reap the benefits of the MCC. The theory suggests that even the threat of losing their managerial positions in such circumstances will act as an incentive to managers to raise their game. Manne thus described the MCC as 'par excellence the market discipline for wayward managers'.[5] Examined through the prism of the 'pure agency relationship' between shareholders and managers, the MCC was thus hailed as a mechanism to constrain agency costs.[6] Jensen argued that the MCC plays an important role in 'protecting shareholders when the corporation's internal controls and board-level control mechanisms are slow, clumsy or defunct.'[7] The idea is that this 'reduction in agency costs, renders the target's assets worth more in the hands of the acquirer' and justifies the premium it can afford to pay to the targets' shareholders.[8] Easterbrook and Fischel opined that:

> 'All parties benefit from the process. The offeree's shareholders gain because they receive a premium over the market price. The offeror obtains the difference between the new value of the firm and the payment to the old shareholders.'[9] Although the premium received by the target shareholders was viewed by Manne as a discount on the true potential value of the shares causing them considerable opportunity losses, he suggested that the MCC avoided even greater capital losses.

It is worthwhile at the outset to identify the different theories which seek to explain hostile bids, and in particular, the ability of a bidder to pay above the market price to obtain control. *Efficiency theories* suggest that the bidder can do so because it can use the target's assets more efficiently. The MCC suggests that this is done by replacing inefficient managers. By contrast, the synergy hypothesis suggests that takeovers lead to operational efficiencies where the value of the target and the bidder combined is greater than the two individual companies.[10] Synergies may, for example, enhance revenues, reduce production or distribution costs, lower the cost of capital, generate economies of scale or finance, or minimise tax costs. *Exploitation theories* suggest that the premium can be met by extracting wealth from third parties at unacceptable costs. In this scenario, takeovers are the consequence not of wealth

5. Henry Manne, *Corporate Governance – Getting Back to Market Basics*, Paper to Seminario Consob, 11 (2008). https://www.consob.it/documents/46180/46181/sem_20081110_manne.pdf/f25f9186-e4c9-45b9-a5bf-8831ed93d1d6.
6. Michael Jensen and William Henry Meckling, *Theory of the Firm: Managerial Behavior, Agency Costs and Ownership Structure*, 3 Journal of Financial Economics 305 (1976).
7. Michael Jensen, *The Takeover Controversy: Analysis and Evidence*, 318 in *Knights, Raiders, and Targets: The Impact of the Hostile Takeover*, John Coffee, Louis Lowenstein and Susan Rose-Ackerman, eds. (Oxford University Press, 1988).
8. Frank Easterbrook and Daniel Fischel, *The Proper Role of a Offeree's Management in Responding to a Tender Offer* 94 Harv. L. Rev. 1161, 1173 (1981).
9. *Ibid.*, 1173–1174.
10. *See* Michael Bradley, Anand Desai, and E. Han Kim, *The Rational Behind Interfirm Tender Offers: Information or Synergy?* 11 J. Fin. Econ. 183 (1983), John McConnell and Timothy Nantell, *Corporate Combinations and Common Stock Returns: The Case of Joint Ventures*, 40 J. Fin. 519 (1985), Richard Roll, *Empirical Evidence on Takeover Activity and Shareholder Wealth* in *Knights, Raiders, and Targets: The Impact of the Hostile Takeover*, John Coffee, Louis Lowenstein and Susan Rose-Ackerman, eds. (Oxford University Press, 1988) and Michael Bradley, Anand Desai, and E. Han Kim, *Synergistic Gains From Corporate Acquisitions and Their Division Between the Stockholders of Offeree and Acquiring Firms*, 21 J. Fin. Econ. 3 (1988).

creation or preservation but rather of wealth transfer from the targets' shareholders at a cost to third parties. Such costs may include the exploitation of monopoly power or the breaching of implicit contracts between shareholders and creditors, employees or directors. Takeovers are often criticised in this context for their detrimental effect on employees who lose their jobs or are dislocated after the acquisition. While the empirical evidence indicates that shareholders of target companies reap benefits, as Parkinson noted: 'it is not clear to what extent these [gains] result from increased efficiency and hence represent net social gains, or are the product of what may be socially detrimental increases in market power or gains made at the expense of other groups such as employees'.[11] Donald has suggested that the MCC 'theory is sold very well, not just by academics, but mainly by investment banks' and that it might be viewed less as a good corporate governance instrument and more as 'a tool for rent extraction through financial fees'. [12] He suggests that this theory 'while effectively focusing executive management's attention on share price, turns corporations into raw material for the financial industry – material that can be acquired, divided, merged, spun off and consolidated to generate fees.'[13] By contrast, a number of studies have found that companies with more takeover exposure have higher firm value suggesting that the MCC's disciplinary effect exists and is valued.[14] An alternative theory explains the premium paid to the targets' shareholders as an *overpayment*. This frames a hostile takeover as a straightforward transfer of wealth from the bidders' shareholders to the targets' shareholders.[15] This overpayment may be caused, for example, by the management of the bidder overestimating their own abilities to manage the target more efficiently[16] or overestimating the value of the target as a result of poor information.[17] Marris' concept of 'managerial capitalism' explained this willingness to overpay on the basis of the personal ambition, self-identification, and class orientation of the bidders' directors.[18] A behavioural perspective is also evident in the writings of such economists as Baumol and Williamson who argued that directors seek to maximise growth even

11. John Parkinson, *Corporate Power and Responsibility: Issues in the Theory of Company Law* 125 (Clarendon Press, 1993).
12. David C. Donald, Keep Your 'Invisible Hands' to Yourself: Freeing Corporate Governance from the Cult of the 'Efficient Market' (November 13, 2020). The Chinese University of Hong Kong Faculty of Law Research Paper No. 2020-35, 17, https://ssrn.com/abstract=3729922.
13. *Ibid. See also* Karen Ho, *Liquidated: An Ethnography of Wall Street* (Duke University Press, 2009).
14. Matthew Cain, Stephen McKeon, and Steven Solomon, *Do Takeover Laws Matter? Evidence from Five Decades of Hostile Takeovers*, 124 J. Fin. Econ. 464 (2017) and Pattanaporn Chatjuthamard, Viput Ongsakul, and Pornsit Jiraporn *Do Hostile Takeover Threats Matter?Evidence from Credit Ratings*. 17 PloS ONE (2021).
15. John Coffee, *Regulating the Market for Corporate Control: A Critical Assessment of the Tender Offer's Role in Corporate Governance* 84 Col. L. Rev. 1145,1224 (1984).
16. Bernard Black, *Bidder Overpayment in Takeovers,* 41 Stan. L. Rev. 597, 624 (1989), Nikhil Varaiya, *The 'Winners Curse' Hypothesis and Corporate Takeovers*, 9 Managerial & Decision Econ. 311 (1988) and Robert Hayes and William Abernathy, *Managing Our Way to Economic Decline,* Harv. Bus. Rev. 67, 76 (1980).
17. Coffee, *supra* n. 15, 1230–1231.
18. Robin Marris, *The Economic Theory of Managerial Capitalism* (Palgrave Macmillan, 1964).

when it is contrary to the shareholders' best interests.[19] This may involve: adopting a strategy of 'empire building' to leave a legacy; seeking to increase performance related perquisites; increasing the likelihood of promotion; improving their standing in the business community; or increasing oligopolistic market power.[20] Takeovers may also be used by companies in the later stages of their lifecycle to avoid the slowdown in growth that product maturity brings.[21]

It is submitted that Baumol is correct in his statement that there is no 'correct model that captures the whole truth about managerial goals in all their subtle shading and complexity'.[22] It is not possible to adopt a monolithic approach to takeovers. Certain takeovers may be beneficial and certain detrimental depending on many factors, among them the relative skills of bidder and target control groups. Under a pluralistic interpretation, each theory may thus have a partial validity and may accurately describe motivations underlying some but not all takeovers. The implication of this conclusion is that a delicate balance needs to be struck by regulators between safeguarding the needs of the targets' shareholders and other relevant stakeholders and ensuring that unnecessary obstacles are not placed in the way of parties intending to make takeover offers.

This chapter commences with an examination of the MCC theory itself in §13.02 and the preconditions which exist to its effective operation. It also explores a number of inconsistencies in the theory as well as the rather mixed empirical evidence to support it. Section 13.03 of the chapter considers the importance of a competitive MCC and examines the role of defensive measures introduced by management. The value of the MCC has been acknowledged outside the US, and it has had a significant influence on the development of takeover regulation across the world. Section 13.03 also considers the extent to which the MCC is enshrined in Directive 2004/25/EC ('the Takeover Bids Directive') and the manner in which it has been implemented in Member States. Finally, §13.04 explores whether the MCC has stood the test of time, and in particular, how the 2008 Global Financial Crisis (GFC), the emergence of private equity, and the Pandemic has added to our understanding of the MCC and its

19. William Baumol, *Business Behaviour, Value and Growth* (Macmillan, 1959) and Oliver Williamson, *The Economics of Discretionary Behaviour: Managerial Objectives in a Theory of the Firm* (Prentice-Hall, 1964).
20. Michael Jensen, *Agency Costs of Free Cash Flow, Corporate Finance and Takeovers* 76 *Am. Econ. Rev.* 323, 323 (1986). *See also* Michael Jensen and Kevin Murphy, *Performance Pay and Top Management Incentives*, 98 *J. Pol. Econ.* 225 (1990); Richard Lambert and David Larcker, *Executive Compensation Effects of Large Corporate Acquisitions* 6 J. Account. Public Policy 231 (1987); Martin Conyon and Dennis Leech, *Top Pay, Company Performance and Corporate Governance* 56 Oxf. Bull. Econ. Stat. 229 (1994); Black, *supra* n. 16, 627 and Henry Agyei-Boapeah, Collins Ntim, and Samuel Fosu, *Governance Structures and the Compensation of Powerful Corporate Leaders in Financial Firms During M&As*, 37 J. Int. Account. Audit. Tax. 1 (2019).
21. Robin Marris and Dennis Mueller, *The Corporation, Competition, and the Invisible Hand* 18 J. Econ. Lit. 32, 44–45 (1980), Dennis Mueller, *A Theory of Conglomerate Mergers*, 83 Quart. J. Econ. 643 (1969), and Dennis Mueller *A Life Cycle Theory of the Firm*, 20 J. Ind. Econ. 199 (1972).
22. William Baumol, *The Stock Market and Economic Efficiency*, 51 (Fordham Univ. Press, 1965).

implications. It emphasises the choice between open markets and protectionism which these crises have intensified.

§13.02 POTENTIAL DEFICIENCIES IN THE MCC THEORY

The MCC depends on a number of assumptions, and any weakness in these assumptions might be considered to undermine the theory itself. These assumptions are examined in turn followed by an exploration of a number of unresolved issues in the theory. A review of the empirical research shedding light on these issues is then undertaken.

[A] Correlation Between Share Price and Managerial Efficiency

The first assumption upon which the MCC rests was one expressly addressed by Manne. He acknowledged that 'a fundamental premise underlying the market for corporate control is the existence of a high positive correlation between corporate managerial efficiency and the market price of shares of that company.'[23] Donald has described thus how Manne 'gave the takeover theoretical pedigree' by embedding it within what he described as 'the assumed cult of market efficiency'.[24] Fama's original description of the efficient market suggests that, in its semi-strong form, a company's share price reflects all publicly available information and is based on the market's evaluation of its past performance, its present state, and on the market's expectations of its future.[25] In 1978, Jensen argued that 'there is no other proposition in economics which has more solid empirical evidence supporting it than the Efficient Market Hypothesis'.[26] However, since the early studies of market efficiency, the securities markets have undergone significant changes including in terms of the disclosure of information and the nature of trading itself. For the poor performance of the managers of a target to lead to the under-valuation of its shares, share prices must reflect the relative expected profitability of the company under existing management. Hughes in his research found that whilst the market pricing mechanism may be efficient in the sense of responding rapidly to changes in information, there is little to suggest that share price movements are systematically related to the current, past, or subsequent underlying performance variables of companies.[27] In addition, other features of the market have since been revealed as significant. For example, the idea of 'noise', referring to pricing influences unrelated to rational expectations about asset values, has

23. Manne, *supra* n. 2, 112.
24. Donald, *supra* n. 12, 15.
25. Eugene Fama, *Efficient Capital Markets: A Review of Theory and Empirical Work*, 35 J. Fin. 383 (1970).
26. Michael Jensen, *Some Anomalous Evidence Regarding Market Efficiency*, 6 J. Fin. Econ. 95, 95 (1978).
27. Alan Hughes, *Mergers and Economic Performance in the UK: A Survey of the Empirical Evidence 1950–1990* in Matthew Bishop and John Kay (eds.), *European Mergers and Merger Policy* (OUP, 1993).

been put forward to explain stock market behaviour.[28] Shiller noted that while the depiction of the financial markets as rational and efficient is widely taught, it does not explain bubbles or Ponzi schemes.[29] His research has demonstrated that traders follow biases and often behave in irregular, erratic, value-destroying ways inconsistent with an efficient discovery of underlying value.[30] In the wake of the 2007–2008 GFC, Alan Greenspan, the then Chairman of the Federal Reserve and previously a leading proponent of the Efficient Market Hypothesis described his recognition that 'the whole intellectual edifice [of rational market theory] collapsed'.[31] Our understanding of the nature of the markets and the factors which influence share prices is arguably more sophisticated now than when the MCC was first mooted. However, that is not to say that this has rendered the theory obsolete. One might recall the advice of Voltaire that 'Le mieux est l'ennemi du bien'.[32] In criticising such an influential theory, one must be conscious of the nirvana fallacy in the context of efficiency which warns against comparing an 'ideal norm' and 'an existing 'imperfect' institutional arrangement'.[33] This view is shared by Kuhn who has cautioned against imprudent abandonment of a theory simply because an anomaly is present in its supporting data.[34]

[B] Shareholders Will Exit an Inefficiently Managed Company and Bidders Will Buy

A second premise underlying the MCC is that shareholders will sell their shares when they become dissatisfied with the manner in which the company is being operated. Using terms coined by Hirschman,[35] they will choose to 'exit' thus rather than to use their 'voice' to control the inefficiencies of their managers or to replace their directors. Is this plausible? One might consider that there are two possible reasons why shareholders might opt to sell in such circumstances. First, they may not appreciate the nature of the problem and may not attribute their companies' poor performance to their directors' inefficiencies. Scharfstein maintained that shareholders simply cannot distinguish between low corporate value caused by management shirking or that caused by an unfavourable environment.[36] It might seem anomalous to accept such a lack of awareness from target shareholders whilst simultaneously attributing great prescience

28. Donald C. Langevoort *Theories, Assumptions, and Securities Regulation: Market Efficiency Revisited* 140 U. Pa. L. Rev. 851 (1992).
29. Robert James Shiller, *Irrational Exuberance,* 78 (Princeton University Press, 2005).
30. *Ibid.,* 180.
31. *The Financial Crisis and the Role of Federal Regulators,* Committee on Oversight and Government Reform (hearing transcript), U.S. House of Representatives, October 23, 2008. *See* Justin Fox, *The Myth of the Rational Market: A History of Risk, Reward, and Delusion n Wall Street* (Harper Business, 2011).
32. Voltaire, *La Bégueule,* 50, Œuvres complètes de Voltaire, (Garnier, 1877) translated as 'Perfection is the enemy of the Good'.
33. Harold Demsetz, *Information and Efficiency: Another Viewpoint,* 12 J. Law. Econ. 1 (1969).
34. Thomas Kuhn, *The Structure of Scientific Revolution,* 81 (University of Chicago Press, 1970).
35. Albert Hirschman, *Exit, Voice and Loyalty* (Harvard University Press, 1970).
36. David Scharfstein, *The Disciplinary Role of Takeovers,* 55 Review of Economic Studies 185 (1988).

to the shareholders or management of the bidder. For the MCC to apply, we assume a bidder must be able to identify the cause of the low share price and to realise that the value of the company, if run properly, is higher than its current market value. Scharfstein argued that where corporate value is low simply because the environment is unfavourable, the probability of a takeover is low because although the shareholders still tender their shares at a low price, other companies who in other circumstances might bid for the company do not do so because they do not value the shares as highly. He argued that the takeover mechanism provides a means of penalising the director precisely when he or she should be penalised - when corporate value is low because the director shirked not because the environment was unfavourable. It is submitted that this attributes great foresight and expert knowledge to bidders and little insight to shareholders. It is not really a question of having good news before the market as in the private information theory, it is more a question of analysing the performance and being able to attribute it to the management of the company rather than anything else. Herman and Lowenstein have described this as 'implausible as a general rule, given the frequent lack of familiarity of the acquirer with the offeree's business, the lack of access to sometimes crucial inside knowledge, the great speed with which major decisions are sometimes made, and the considerable evidence of unpleasant ex post surprises'.[37] Coffee argued that internal monitoring should detect the inefficiencies before outsiders acting as 'an earlier trip-wire' and that a truly independent board would not tolerate sub-optimal performance by directors resulting in a share discount large enough to elicit a premium.[38] There is research to suggest that boards look at other companies in the same industry to evaluate the performance of their executive management and replace inefficient management. [39] That said, the number of cases in which internal governance has proven ineffective is of course significant.

A second and more plausible possibility is that shareholders become aware of managerial inefficiencies, but they are unwilling to take direct action to remedy the situation. Instead, they make the decision to sell their shares and exit the company. Writing in 1970, in *Exit, Voice and Loyalty*[40] Hirschman identified a fundamental schism between the exit option, where shareholders choose to escape from an objectionable state of affairs and the voice option where shareholders express their dissatisfaction directly to directors in an attempt to change the objectionable state of affairs. Describing exit as 'neat' and 'impersonal', he suggested that many shareholders choose it over voice which is a more 'messy' and expensive concept'.[41] It requires that dispersed shareholders be informed and organised rather than apathetic, time-poor, and subject to the free-riding problem.[42] Over fifty years later, the markets are very

37. Edward Herman and Louis Lowenstein, *The Efficiency Effects of Hostile Takeovers* 215 in *Knights, Raiders, and Targets: The Impact of the Hostile Takeover*, John Coffee, Louis Lowenstein, and Susan Rose-Ackerman, eds. (Oxford University Press, 1988).
38. Coffee, *supra* n. 15, 1202–1203.
39. Randall Morck, Andrei Shleifer, and Robert Vishny, *Alternative Mechanisms for Corporate Control*, 79 Am. Econ. Rev. 842 (1989).
40. Albert Hirschman, *Exit, Voice and Loyalty* (Harvard University Press, 1970).
41. *Ibid.*, 16.
42. Easterbrook and Fischel, *supra* n. 8, 1171.

different, and institutional investors play a greater role in corporate governance. Although there are challenges with shareholder engagement, empirical evidence suggests that shareholders are exercising the voice option to a greater extent now than at the time the MCC was first proposed, and a number of initiatives have been introduced since then to improve shareholder engagement, including stewardship codes and improved disclosure of voting policies. One might deduce thus both that share prices may not necessarily fall in the face of inefficient managers and also that the disciplinary effects of the MCC may not be the only or most effective means of controlling inefficient management. In addition, it is submitted that the MCC's reliance on the exit option overlooks the fact that many individual investors are simply not in a position to exit. Owners of large blocks of shares or index funds generally cannot make a quick exit without depressing the share price and precipitating a substantial loss. Because securities are unique commodities, institutional investors may not be able to duplicate their positions in the marketplace without considerable cost.

[C] Sufficient Reward for Bidders

A third premise of the MCC is that a bidder would be able to reap a sufficient reward from replacing inefficient management to be able to afford the acquisition. This obviously depends on the cost of the target reflecting its under-performance and not being inflated in other ways, and the bidder being able to turn it around and improve performance. This may be affected, for example, by assimilation problems post-takeover which are often more serious than anticipated or as a result of cultural issues.[43] Coffee suggested that this may be one reason why relatively few bidders make repeated hostile takeovers. Attempting to integrate new personnel from outside to a new corporate culture can also be difficult.[44]

The bidder's reward also depends on managerial inefficiency being significant enough to be reflected in a large reduction in the share price. Inefficiency stemming from mismanagement in the context of the MCC may result from ineptitude, negligence, or more deliberate self-dealing. Most instances of inefficiency will not result in a significant enough discounted share price to justify the substantial takeover premium that normally prevails, or it may lead only to a temporary reduction. Thus, the MCC may not apply to small amounts of mismanagement. Coffee suggested that 'no matter how venal or self-interested the management', it is unlikely that they could have misappropriated a sufficiently large proportion of the company's value to cause the market to discount the shares by more than half. Also, the misbehaviour must be viewed by a bidder as reversible. However, substantial losses caused by a self-dealing management may not be capable of being reversed. For this reason, Coffee argued that

43. Ali Bayat, Marc Goergen, and Peter Kawalek, *The Cultural Foundations of Corporate Control: An Empirical Enquiry* European Corporate Governance Institute – Finance Working Paper No. 816/2022 (2022) https://ssrn.com/abstract=4035025.
44. Paul Lawrence and Jay Lorsch, *Organization and Environment: Managing Differentiation and Integration*, 231–232 (Harvard Business Bks, 1967).

the discipline of the capital market is only effective within a limited range.[45] He also pointed out that the level of risk required to accept a financially-distressed company is high. Extremely badly managed companies may be perceived as carrying excessive risk and may thus become indigestible and survive. They are immune from attack precisely because of their pervasive inefficiency.[46] As a result, Coffee stated, companies where the level of inefficiency is either 'not extreme enough to justify the necessary premium or so extreme as to surpass the offeror's level of risk aversion' fall outside the range and will not be considered as targets.[47] It has been argued thus that the MCC is 'sufficiently limited that it can serve only as a remedy of last resort for massive managerial failures and not as the principal enforcer of corporate accountability'.[48]

[D] Empirical Evidence

If the empirical evidence supports the MCC, one would expect to find lower pre-acquisition performance of the target prior to a hostile takeover. One would also expect to see an improved performance following a successful offer and new management but a return to the target's pre-offer share price in the event of an unsuccessful offer. As indicated below, the evidence is mixed, making it difficult to conclusively prove more than a weak version of the MCC which may be valid at least in some acquisitions.

In terms of pre-acquisition performance, while some studies indicated that targets have significantly worse share price performance in the pre-merger period than the average company in the market,[49] contrary results were reported in other studies.[50] Schwert in his study of takeovers of US listed companies found no significant differences in pre-bid performance between targets of hostile takeovers and those of friendly takeovers.[51] A number of other studies concluded that the pre-takeover profitability of targets were not or only slightly inferior to that of their industry peers.[52]

45. Coffee, *supra* n. 15, 1200.
46. *Ibid.*, 1204.
47. *Ibid.*
48. *Ibid.*, 1153.
49. Gershon Mandelker, *Risk and Return: The Case of Merging Firms*, 1 *J. Fin. Econ.* 303 (1974), Donald Kummer and J. Ronald Hoffmeister, *Valuation Consequences of Cash Tender Offers*, 33 *J. Fin.* 505 (1978), Michael Firth, *The Profitability of Takeovers and Mergers* 89 *Econ. J.* 316 (1979), Krishna Palepu, *Predicting Takeover Offerees: A Methodological and Empirical Analysis* 8 *J. Acc & Econ.* 3 (1986), and Morck, Shleifer and Vishny, *supra* n. 39.
50. Julian Franks and Colin Mayer, *Hostile Takeovers and the Correction of Managerial Failure'* 40 *J. Fin. Econ.* 163 (1996), Gerald Newbould, *Management and Merger Activity* (Guthstead, 1970) and Peter Dodd and Richard Ruback, *Tender Offers and Stockholder Returns: An Empirical Analysis*, 5 *J. Fin. Econ.* 351 (1977).
51. William Schwert, *Hostility in Takeovers: In the Eyes of the Beholder?* 55 Journal of Finance 2599 (2000).
52. Ajit Singh, *Takeovers, Their Relevance to the Stock Market and Their Theory of the Firm* (Cambridge University Press, 1971), Douglas Kuehn, *Takeovers and the Theory of the Firm* (Palgrave Macmillan, 1975), Terence Langetieg, *An Application of a Three-Factor Performance Index to Measure Stockholder Gains from Merger* 6 *J. Fin. Econ.* 365 (1978), David Ravenscraft and Frederic Michael Scherer, *Life After Takeover*, 36 *J. Ind. Econ.* 147 (1987), Franks and Mayer, *supra*. n. 50; and Anup Agrawaal and Jeffrey Jaffe, *Do Takeover Targets Underperform Evidence from Operating and Stock Return*, 38 J. Fin. & Quant. Anal. 721 (2003).

Even if there is a decline in a company's performance, this may not of course be attributable to poor management. Denis and Sarin, for example, found that a sharp reduction in operating profitability preceding board changes is frequently caused by an industry-wide shock.[53] Such a shock could include, for example, deregulation, changes in input costs, or innovations in financing technologies. This would help to explain cyclical industry specific takeovers.[54]

In terms of management changes following a takeover, some studies have indicated that management turnover increased following completed takeovers, and that turnover occurred more often following acquisitions of companies that previously under-performed industry counterparts.[55] However, a study by Markham found that two-thirds of bidders granted 'virtual autonomy' to the acquired companies in respect of operating decisions and only in one-fifth of cases studied were there more than incidental reorganisation of the management structure.[56] Surveys that have asked bidders to explain the characteristics that they have sought in a potential acquisitions have reported that strong management is one of the main priorities.[57] Bidders also seem to claim a strong preference towards targets whose organisational structure fits with their own suggesting synergies rather than the MCC. Jenkinson and Mayer studied every hostile takeover in the United Kingdom (UK) between January 1989 and March 1990 and found no evidence of a disciplinary function of hostile takeovers. Bids, they found, were made according to the strategic objectives of the bidders rather than to control poorly performing directors. Unsurprisingly perhaps, Franks and Mayer found that hostile takeovers were associated with a high level of board turnover.[58] In such cases where the management have mounted robust defences, relationships are likely to be strained and clearly management are more likely to be dismissed.[59]

53. David Denis and Atulya Sarin, *Ownership and Board Structures in Publicly Traded Corporations* 52 J. Fin. Econ. 187 (1999). *See also* Mark Mitchell and J.Harold Mulherin, *The Impact of Industry Shocks on Takeover and Restructuring Activity*, 41 J. Fin. Econ. 193 (1996).
54. *Ibid.*, 1207. *See* Gregor Andrade, Mark Mitchell, and Erik Stafford, *New Evidence and Perspectives on Mergers* 15 Journal of Economic Perspectives 103 (2001) and Jarrad Harford, *What Drives Merger Waves?* 77 J. Fin. Econ. 529 (2005).
55. Kenneth Martin and John McConnell, *Corporate Performance, Corporate Takeovers and Management Turnover*, 46 *J. Fin.* 671 (1991), Ralph Walking and Michael Long, *Agency Theory, Managerial Welfare and Takeover Bid Resistance*, 15 Rand J. Econ. 54 (1984) and reported by Colin Mayer in Monitoring and Disciplining Mechanisms, a Paper to the First European Conference on Corporate Governance, Brussels, November 2000.
56. Jesse Markham, *Conglomerate Enterprise and Public Policy* (Harvard University, 1973). *See also* Harry Lynch, *Financial Performance of Conglomerates* (1971).
57. Touche Ross & Co, *The Effect of Mergers, Acquisitions and Tender Offers on American Business: A Touche Ross Survey of Corporate Directors' Opinions* (1981) and CFM Capital/Chapman Flood, *Acquisition Surveys 1989–1999* (1990–2000).
58. Franks and Mayer, *supra* n. 50.
59. David Hirshleifer and Anjan Thakor, *Managerial Performance, Boards of Directors and Takeover Bidding*, 1 J. Corp. Fin. 63 (1994), Franks and Mayer, *supra* n. 50, David Denis and Diane Denis, *Performance Changes Following Top Management Dismissals* 50 *J. Fin.* 1029 (1995), David Denis and Timothy Kruse, *Managerial Discipline and Corporate Restructuring Following Performance Declines*, 55 *J. Fin. Econ.* 391 (2000), Wayne Mikkelson and Megan Partch, *The Decline of Takeovers and Disciplinary Managerial Turnover*, 44 J. Fin. Econ. 205 (1997), Anil Shivdasani, *Board Composition, Ownership Structure, and Hostile Takeovers*, 16 J. Account. Econ 167 (1993)

In terms of improved efficiency, a number of studies have indicated that merged firms had increases in post-merger operating cash flow returns in comparison with their industries.[60] However, there is some evidence to suggest that merged firms have no operating improvements and that the bidder's shareholders make no gain or incur a loss.[61] This would suggest that any gains from acquiring inefficient companies are insufficient to offset the premiums which have to be paid. A review by Mueller and Sirower of distributions and gains in 168 mergers between large companies from 1978 through 1990 found considerable support for the managerial discretion and hubris hypotheses leading to a wasteful acquisition and some small support for the MCC. [62] This would appear to support the overpayment or exploitation theories but not the idea of synergies. However, there is also some evidence of increased firm performance post-leveraged buyouts.[63] In a study of takeovers in Australia where defensive measures are prohibited, bidders were found to have earned significant value for their shareholders, in terms of both announcement returns and long-run operating performance improvements. Takeover premiums which were substantially lower than those reported for takeovers in the US and UK were positively correlated with long-run operating performance, supporting the idea that takeovers are the result of real synergies rather than hubris or overpayment.[64]

§13.03 DEFENSIVE MEASURES AND THE BOARD NEUTRALITY RULE

[A] Theory

Acceptance of the MCC leads to an acknowledgement of the importance of open markets for takeovers and a corresponding reluctance to allow any measures which

---

and Jarrad Harford, *Takeover Bids and Target Directors' Incentives: The Impact of a Bid on Directors' Wealth and Board Seats*, 69 J. Fin. Econ. 51 (2003).

60. Julian Franks, Jack Broyles, and Michael Hecht, *An Industry Study of the Profitability of Mergers in the United Kingdom*, 32 *J. Fin.* 1513 (1977); Andrew Cosh, Alan Hughes, and Ajit Singh, *The Causes and Effects of Takeovers in the United Kingdom: An Empirical Investigation for the Late 1960s at the Microeconomic Level*, in Dennis Mueller, *The Determinants and Effects of Mergers* (1980); and Paul Healy, Krishna Palepu, and Richard Ruback, *Does Corporate Performance Improve After Mergers ?* (1992) 31 J. Fin. Econ. (1992).
61. George Alexandridis, Kathleen Fuller, Lars Terhaar, and Nickolaos Travlos, *Deal size, Acquisition Premia and Shareholder Gains* 20 J. Corp. Fi. 1 (2013), Mark Sirower, *The Synergy Trap* (Free Press, 2007), Elazar Berkovitch and M. Narayanan, *Motives for Takeovers: An Empirical Investigation* 28 J. Fin. & Quan. Anal. 347 (1993), Michael Bradley, Anand Desai, and E. Han Kim, *Synergistic Gains from Corporate Acquisitions and Their Division Between the Stockholders of Offeree and Acquiring Firms*, 21 J. Fin. Econ. 3 (1988), Nikhil Varaiya and Kenneth Ferris, *Overpaying in Corporate Takeovers: The Winner's Curse* J. Fin. Anal. 64 (1987), Herman and Lowenstein, *supra* n. 37, Michael Jensen and Richard Ruback, *The Market for Corporate Control: The Scientific Evidence*, 11 J Fin. Econ. 5 (1983).
62. Dennis Mueller and Mark Sirower, *The Causes of Mergers: Tests Based on the Gains to Acquiring Firms' Shareholders and the Size of Premia* 24 Manage. Decis. Econ. 373 (2003),
63. Shourun Guo, Edith Hotchkiss, and Weihong Song, *Do Buyouts (still) Create Value?* 66 J. Finance 479 (2011).
64. Mark Humphery-Jenner and Ronan Powell, *Firm Size, Takeover Profitability, and the Effectiveness of the Market for Corporate Control: Does the Absence of Anti-takeover Provisions Make a Difference?*, 17 J. Corp. Fin. 418 (2011).

might impede such markets. There may be a number of obstacles to a free market, including statutory restrictions, financial constraints, imperfect information, the free-rider problem, and short-termism. However, one of the most obvious impediments in this context is the introduction by target companies or potential target companies of defensive measures designed to frustrate a hostile bid. As the Organisation for Economic Co-operation and Development (OECD) Corporate Governance Principles state, 'The markets for corporate control should be allowed to function in an efficient and transparent manner'.[65]

The role of takeover defensive measures has been the subject of a major debate in academia since the emergence of hostile takeovers. One view, the 'shareholders' welfare hypothesis', is that such measures are selfless actions taken by a dedicated and expert group of directors acting in their shareholders' best interests. Such measures empower directors to negotiate larger premiums or to negotiate higher-value bids from third-party bidders.[66] This hypothesis is consistent with the 'management know best' premise and the idea that, left to their own devices, shareholders may make the wrong decision and accept a sub-optimal offer. An alternative view, the 'managerial entrenchment hypothesis', suggests that defensive measures are used as a form of management entrenchment to shield the conflicted management or board from the disciplinary effect of the MCC. This hypothesis is consistent with a jaundiced view of hostile boards as 'the villains of the story'[67] whose ability to shirk or consume excessive perquisites is seen as a central rationale for the hostile takeover. This entrenchment may lead to a lower firm value[68] and facilitate undisciplined management in engaging in empire building making value-destroying acquisitions.[69] For this reason the OECD Corporate Governance Principles also state that 'Anti-takeover devices should not be used to shield management and the board from accountability.'[70] The introduction of a board neutrality rule (BNR) in the UK and in the Takeover Bids Directive (as discussed below) prohibiting target boards from adopting any defensive measures which might frustrate a bid is consistent with such an hypothesis. Interestingly, Manne himself dismissed the need for an academic debate on the BNR on the basis that such an 'organizational decision ...is best left to private decision makers and the vagaries of infinite circumstances'.[71]

65. OECD Corporate Governance Principles, Principle II.H.2, 27.
66. Scott Linn and John McConnell, *An Empirical Investigation of the Impact of 'Antitakeover' Amendments on Common Stock Prices*, 11 *J. Fin. Econ.* 361 (1983) and Sanjeev Bhojraj, Partha Sengupta, and Suning Zhang,
Takeover defenses: Entrenchment and efficiency, 63 J. Account. Econ 142 (2017).
67. John Coffee, *Shareholders Versus Managers: The Strain in the Corporate Web*, 106 in John Coffee, Louis Lowenstein, and Susan Rose-Ackerman (eds.), *Knights, Raiders and Targets* (Oxford University Press, 1988).
68. Lucian Bebchuk, Alma Cohen, and Allen Ferrell, *What Matters in Corporate Governance?* 22 Rev. Fin. Stud. 783 (2009)
69. Ronald Masulis, Cong Wang, and Fei Xie, *Corporate Governance and Acquirer Returns*. 62 J. Finance 1851 (2007) and Jarrad Harford, Mark Humphery-Jenner, and Ronan Powell, *The Sources of Value Destruction in Acquisitions by Entrenched Managers*, 106 J. Fin. Econ. 247 (2012).
70. Principle II.H.2, 27.
71. Manne, *supra* n. 5, 8–9.

The empirical evidence on defensive measures too is mixed and often inconclusive. A number of studies point to their detrimental effects indicating that shareholders typically lose large tender premiums and experience large share value declines when a sole bidder withdraws in the face of resistance by incumbents.[72] A recent study by Carlinea, Linn, and Yadav of hostile bids in the UK over a fifteen-year period concluded that, based on market-adjusted returns, frustrating actions are motivated by bad-faith entrenchment motivations rather than good-faith efforts to maximize the potential for price improvement. [73] They found that 41% of bids, involved defensive measures 'intended to frustrate the takeover bid, potentially lethally, by making the target less attractive and/or more difficult to acquire for the initial bidder'. The remainder involved robust defence or what the authors termed 'passive resistance'. Taken together with other studies which indicated that defensive measures consistently lead to bid failure,[74] this would seem to lend support to the managerial entrenchment hypothesis. Other research, however, failed to demonstrate any link between defensive mechanisms and the likelihood that the targets in a contested bid are ultimately acquired.[75] There is also research in support of the shareholder welfare hypothesis indicating that defensive mechanisms improve the allocation of bid surpluses to target shareholders in completed deals[76] and are motivated by price improvement incentive and not managerial entrenchment.[77]

[B] The Takeovers Bids Directive 2004/25/EC

The Takeover Bids Directive is comprised of a framework of six general principles and a number of general requirements which Member States were required to respect through detailed implementing rules. In the lengthy negotiations which preceded its introduction, the question of whether, and/or how, to introduce a BNR was the focus of significant debate.[78] Aside from accepting either the shareholders welfare hypothesis or the managerial entrenchment hypothesis, a further concern was that a mandatory BNR would create an unlevel playing field for takeover bids within the European Union

72. Larry Dann and Harry DeAngelo, *Corporate Financial Policy and Corporate Control,* 20 J. Fin. Econ. 87 (1988), Frank Easterbrook and Gregg Jarrell, *Do Targets Gain from Defeating Tender Offers?* 59 N.Y.U.L. Rev. 277 (1984).
73. Nicholas Carline, Scott Linn, and Pradeep Yadav, *Severely Obstructive Resistance in Takeover Bids: Is a Board Passivity Rule Effective?,* American Finance Association Meetings Working Paper (2021) https://ssrn.com/abstract=1785364.
74. Lucian Bebchuk, John Coates IV, and Guhan Subramanian, *The Powerful Antitakeover Force of Boards: Theory, Evidence, and Policy,* 54 Stan. L. Rev. 887 (2002).
75. Randall Heron and Erik Lie, *On the Use of Poison Pills and Defensive Payouts by Takeover Targets,* 79 J. Bus.1783 (2006).
76. Thomas Bates, David Becher, and Michael Lemmon, *Board Classification and Managerial Entrenchment: Evidence from the Market for Corporate Control,* 87 J. Fin. Econ. 656 (2008).
77. Robert Comment and William Schwert, *Poison or Placebo? Evidence on the Deterrence and Wealth Effects of Modern Antitakeover Measures* 39 J. Fin. Econ. 3 (1995) and Thomas Bates and David Becher, *Bid Resistance by Takeover Targets: Managerial Bargaining or Bad Faith?* 52 J. Fin. Quant. Anal. 837 (2017).
78. Blanaid Clarke, *Takeover Regulation: Through the Regulatory Looking Glass,* CLPE Research Paper No. 18/2007 (2007) https://ssrn.com/abstract=1002675.

(EU). Different lawful company-specific barriers to takeovers applied in the various Member States which meant that in those Member States hostile takeover bids were less likely to succeed, and shareholders would not have equivalent opportunities to tender their shares.[79] A related fear was that a mandatory BNR would lead to an unlevel playing field between the EU and the US. This fear stemmed from the broad discretion afforded to the boards of American companies to utilise defensive measures pursuant to the business judgment rule and also the stakeholder statutes which apply in many individual states.[80] The European Commission ('Commission') appointed a high-level group of company law experts under the chairmanship of Jap Winter to consider this matter alongside a number of other issues raised by the European Parliament. The group concluded that 'in the light of available economic evidence', the availability of a mechanism to facilitate takeover bids would be beneficial.[81] It justified this on the basis of three factors: the exploitation of synergies, the opportunity to sell at a premium on market price, and the MCC.[82] On the latter, the group noted that 'actual and potential takeover bids are an important means to discipline the management of listed companies with dispersed ownership' and that such 'discipline of management' is in the long term best interests of 'all stakeholders and society at large.'[83] Acknowledging that defensive measures are controversial even in the US, reference was made to 'a large body of both economic and legal literature arguing that directors should be prohibited from engaging in defensive actions and that the ultimate decision should be made by shareholders.[84] The group strongly argued that the US approach would not be beneficial to the development of efficient integrated capital markets in the EU.[85] Thus, it concluded, 'any regime which confers discretion on a board to impede or facilitate a bid inevitably involves unacceptable cost and risk.'[86] This acknowledgement can be interpreted as a resounding approval of the MCC.

The BNR is set out in Article 9 of the Takeover Bids Directive. As with many of the provisions in the Takeover Bids Directive, the rule is based on a rule in the UK's Takeover Code, Rule 21 which prohibits frustrating actions by the board without shareholder approval. Article 9(2) commences:

> During the period referred to in the second subparagraph, the board of the offeree company shall obtain the prior authorization of the general meeting of shareholders given for this purpose before taking any action, other than seeking alternative bids, which may result in the frustration of the bid and in particular before issuing any shares which may result in a lasting impediment to the offeror's acquiring control of the offeree.

79. Report of the High Level Group of Company Law Experts on Issues Related to Takeover Bids (2002), Annex 4.
80. *Ibid.*, 39–42. *See* Blanaid Clarke, *The Takeovers Directive – Is a Little Regulation Better Than No Regulation*? 15 Eur. Law J. 174 (2009).
81. High Level Group of Company Law Experts, *supra* n. 79, 19.
82. *Ibid.*
83. *Ibid.*
84. *Ibid.*, 42.
85. *Ibid.*, 39–42.
86. *Ibid.*, 21.

The target board is thus prevented from taking any action which might frustrate a bid without seeking the approval of its shareholders. It builds upon one of the General Principles set out in Article 3 of the Takeover Bids Directive that 'the board of the offeree company…must not deny the holders of securities the opportunity to decide on the merits of the bid'.[87] This is a wide-ranging prohibition which applies to any potential action which might frustrate a bid with the exception of seeking alternative bids. In a hostile situation, it is not uncommon for the target's board to seek a competing bid from a preferred bidder or 'white knight' with a view to thwarting the hostile bidder. There is some evidence that the ability to do this may reduce the probability of an offer being made in the first place as bidders may wish to avoid a competitive situation and the auction which might ensue.[88] The promotion of an auction might also lead to the frustration of a hostile offer. However, their benefits were considered to outweigh these potential negatives. The crucial difference is that with auctions, shareholders are still afforded an opportunity to sell their shares. Bebchuk and Gilson maintained thus that auctions increase both shareholders' and society's wealth serving to allocate resources to their highest-valuing prospective users.[89] Although not expressly excluded in Article 9(2), it was acknowledged at the drafting stage that the prohibition would also not exclude the sort of passive resistance referred to earlier which would include communicating a robust response denigrating the offer terms or price, releasing strategic information such as a profit forecast statement, or seeking to persuade shareholders or relevant stakeholders of the need to reject the offer. In practice, although there are rules regarding such communications in many jurisdictions[90], this is considered to fall outside the scope of the BNR.

The period referred to in Article 9(2) during which the BNR applies is from the time the target's board receives the information from a bidder that a bid is to be made[91] and until the result of the bid is made public or the bid lapses. Member States may require that such authorisation be obtained at an earlier stage, and Article 9(2) cites as an example the time the target board becomes aware that the bid is imminent. This is the period the prohibition commences in the aforementioned Rule 21 of the UK's Takeover Code. Prior to this period thus, there is nothing in Article 9 to prevent companies introducing poison pills or other anti-takeover devices into their constitutions or shareholders agreeing such frustrating tools with a view to those measures being triggered by a hostile bid. However, Article 11 introduces the concept of a 'breakthrough rule' with the intention of eliminating certain corporate governance arrangements which might otherwise impede takeovers.[92] Article 11(2) and (3) also dis-apply certain mechanisms and structures which may frustrate a bid, as defined in

87. Art. 3(1)(c).
88. Easterbrook and Fischel, *supra* n. 8.
89. Lucian Bebchuk, *The Case for Facilitating Competing Tender Offers,* 95 Harv. L. Rev 1028 (1982) and Ronald Gilson, *Seeking competitive Bids Versus Pure Passivity in Tender Offer Defense* 35 Stan. L Rev.51 (1983).
90. *See,* for example, Rules 19 (Communications) and 20 (Equality of Information) of both the Irish Takeover Panel Act, 1997, Takeover Rules, 2022 and the UK Takeover Code.
91. Art. 6(1).
92. High Level Group of Company Law Experts, *supra* n. 79, 29.

the articles of association and related constitutional documents, when a bid has been made public.

Although Article 9(1) requires Member States to ensure compliance with the rules laid down in Article 9(2)–(5), Article 12(1) renders the introduction of the prohibition in Article 9(2) and (3) and/or Article 11 optional. The European Council viewed this optionality as necessary to accommodate the existing differences in Member States' company law mechanisms and structures. However, if Member States 'make use of this option', they must still grant companies the reversible option of applying the prohibition and/or breakthrough.[93] In what might be seen as a further weakening of the rules, Article 12(3) introduced reciprocity allowing Member States 'to exempt companies which apply' the aforementioned articles 'if they become the subject of an offer launched by a company which does not apply the same Articles as they do' or a company controlled by such a company. To do so, however, they need the authorisation of their shareholders at a meeting granted no more than eighteen months before the bid.[94] Although the introduction of the optionality in Article 12 may have been necessary to secure sufficient agreement to reach a consensus, the Irish Internal Markets Commissioner at the time, Commissioner McCreevy described how 'the protectionist attitude of a few seems to have had a knock-on effect on others' and that 'if this trend continues, then there is a real risk that companies launching a takeover bid will face more barriers, not fewer'.[95]

The Commission published in 2012 a report on the application of the Takeover Bids Directive[96] together with an external study[97] by Marccus Partners and the Centre for European Policy Studies. It noted that nineteen Member States had transposed the BNR describing this as a 'relative success'.[98] A total of 89% of stakeholders responding to a survey as part of the external study acknowledged that the restrictions on takeover defences had contributed to the openness of the EU MCC. Defensive measures were viewed as having a duel effect of sometimes preventing the occurrence of hostile bids but sometimes simultaneously leading to higher bid prices. The empirical analysis conducted as part of the external study found that while the BNR may increase incentives to launch an offer by removing post-bid defences, only a slight decrease in cumulative abnormal returns was noted. It suggested that this is because the BNR may also have reduced the potential premium paid by the bidder 'since it also reduces the

93. Art. 12(2).
94. Art. 12(5).
95. Press Release 27 February 2007 (IP/07/251).
96. European Commission, *Application of Directive 2004/25/EC on takeover bids* (2012) COM(2012) 347 final. https://eur-lex.europa.eu/LexUriServ/LexUriServ.do?uri=COM:2012:0347:FIN:EN:PDF Such a report was required by Art. 20.
97. Marccus Partners, in cooperation with the Centre for European Policy Studies, *Study on the Application of Directive 2004/25/EC on Takeover Bids* (2012). An abridged version with additional commentary to the
original study is available as Christophe Clerc, Fabrice Demarigny, Diego Valiante, and Mirzha de Manuel Aramendía, *A Legal and Economic Assessment of European Takeover Regulation* at http://aei.pitt.edu/47685/1/Takeover_Bids_Directive_book_-_Final.pdf.
98. European Commission, *supra* n. 96 at 8. In addition, only three Member States had transposed the breakthrough rule and thirteen Member States provided for reciprocity in accordance with Art. 12(3).

extent to which future controlling shareholders may extract benefits from the company' and it may also have induced incumbent shareholders to entrench pre-bid thus 'raising the cost of acquiring control'. [99] The overall impact of the rule thus was considered to be more balanced and 'moderate'.[100] The Commission concluded that there was no reason to make the optional articles mandatory on the basis that there was a lack of economic evidence available to justify changing the situation and stakeholders had indicated that breaking through takeover defences was possible.[101] The potential weakness of takeover defence mechanisms was also evident in the aforementioned study by Carlinea, Linn, and Yadav which revealed that despite the UK's Takeover Code's strict BNR, 41% of hostile bids in their fifteen-year sample involve frustrating actions. The authors are undoubtedly correct in suggesting that this raises serious doubts as to the effectiveness of such a rule.

§13.04 STANDING THE TEST OF TIME

[A] The Global Financial Crisis

The author has written in greater detail elsewhere[102] about the role of the MCC in the run-up to the GFC. Given the poor risk management and the misaligned remuneration policies in place in a significant number of credit institutions preceding the GFC, one might have expected the MCC to lead to share price reductions and subsequent takeovers in those firms. Indeed, the fear that this would happen, according to the MCC, should have constituted a sufficient deterrent to prevent this poor management in the first place. Quite to the contrary, share prices increased prior to the GFC, and the Turner Review in the UK commented that the UK banks 'delivered strong market price reinforcement to management's convictions that their aggressive growth strategies were value creative'.[103] Even those who might have had their doubts as to the sustainability of their actions appeared to believe they could not deviate from their high-risk strategies for fear of losing competitive edge and causing a reduction in share prices. The Turner Review concluded that 'a strong case can be made that the events of the last five years have illustrated the inadequacy of market discipline: indeed, they suggest that in some ways market prices and market pressures may have played positively harmful roles.'[104] Similarly, a governmental commission into the Irish Banking Crisis in 2008 found that banks pursued strategies with the objective of achieving higher growth, higher reported profits, and higher bank valuations. It concluded that a primary reason for this was 'to prevent a predatory takeover by

99. Clerc et al., *supra* n. 97, 126.
100. *Ibid.*
101. European Commission, *supra* n. 96, 10.
102. Blanaid Clarke, *Where was the 'Market for Corporate Control' When We Needed It?* UCD Working Papers in Law, Criminology & Socio-Legal Studies Research Paper No. 23/2009 (2009) https://ssrn.com/abstract=1524785.
103. The Turner Review, *A Regulatory Response to the Global Banking Crisis*, 46 (FSA, 2009). http://www.fsa.gov.uk/pubs/other/turner_review.pdf
104. *Ibid.*

another bank (either domestic or foreign) and thus maintain independence.'[105] This is consistent with the theory that rather than discipline managers, the threat of a takeover might cause them to behave myopically and is discussed further in §13.04[D] below. There are other views, however, which paint the MCC in a more benign light. In the context of the US markets, for example, Chew attributed the failure of General Motors which necessitated a USD 10 billion bail-out not to the MCC but to its absence. He noted:

> GM was simply so large, and politically entrenched ... that it was essentially immune to takeover or shareholder activism of any kind until faced with absolute disaster. And it was this absence of market discipline that 'enabled' the extreme mismanagement that Jensen foresaw would lead to the company's elephantine condition.[106]

[B] Private Equity

Private equity has become an increasingly active participant in the takeover market. The LexisNexis Market Tracker reported that in respect of public to private transactions, 64% (34) of the firm offers announced during 2021 in the UK (and 67% (28) in 2020) were made by bidders backed by private equity, financial investors, and/or individuals/family offices.[107] This followed a trend prior to the outbreak of the Pandemic and demonstrates such investors are 'comfortable with the technicalities and tactical considerations' of the takeover-bid process.[108] Private equity bidders also have access to deep pockets which may be particularly important if, as noted above, the operation of a BNR makes it more expensive for a bidder to obtain control. Private equity funds have been the focus of significant scrutiny for their role in determining the success of a bid and the allocation of resources. Private equity's appetite to engage on larger transactions continued to grow with P2P transactions in 2021 having an aggregate deal value of £41.1bn (2020: £20.5bn) and average deal value of £1.2bn (2020: £733m).[109] This represented 63% of total deal value in 2021 (2020: 58%). Since the BNR was first proposed in the negotiations preceding the Takeover Bids Directive, the manner in which it was meant to be implemented has changed as a result of the tendency of private equity to favour the bidder during a bid.[110] Davies et al. point out that hedge funds 'acting as arbitrageurs' are likely to favour the bidder and seek to secure the success of the bid by accepting the offer and voting against defensive

105. Nyberg Commission of Investigation into the Banking Sector in Ireland, 21 (Department of Finance, 2011), https://www.gov.ie/en/publication/31dab8-t/.
106. Don Chew, *Misreading Michael Jensen: The Case of Nicholas Lemann's Transaction Man: The Rise of the Deal and the Decline of the American Dream*. 33 J. Appl. Corp. Finance 130, 136 (2021).
107. LexisNexis, *Market Tracker Trend Report*, Trends in UK Public M&A in 2021, 4. https://www.lexisnexis.co.uk/blog/docs/default-source/corporate-law-documents/lexis-psl-public-m-a-2021-trend-report-final.pdf?sfvrsn=3819ce04_2.
108. *Ibid.*, quoting James Bole, Clifford Chance.
109. *Ibid.*, 20.
110. Clerc et al., *supra* n. 97, 79.

measures in any vote necessitated by the BNR.[111] This is particularly significant given that after the announcement of a bid, the proportion of more passive institutions/private investors decreases and that of activist shareholders, particularly event-driven hedge funds, increases. An example of this was seen following the hostile bid for Cadbury Plc by Kraft Foods Inc. in the UK in 2009. In the nineteen weeks of resistance before the offer was finally recommended, hedge funds and other short-term investors increased their share ownership from 5% to almost 30%.[112] Lord Mandelson, the Business Secretary at the time complained that the company's fate was decided by 'people who had not owned the company a few weeks earlier, and probably had no intention of owning it a few weeks later'.[113]

The role of private equity on the other side of the transaction is also noteworthy. Research suggests that private equity bidders pay lower premiums than public acquirers, and that they do this and ensure successful deal completion in part by avoiding targeting firms with strong defensive measures.[114] Whereas the MCC anticipates the replacement of inefficient managers and the making of operating improvements, there is also evidence that upon completion of a leveraged buyout, private equity firms typically retain the target management team albeit they replace non-executive directors with individuals employed by private equity sponsors.[115] This evidence does not provide support for the MCC as an explanation of takeovers. Indeed, the exploitation theory would appear to have found greater favour in this regard. Gogineni and Upadhyay note 'skeptics argue that major sources of gains to private equity firms are unrelated to real improvements and include activities such as securing funds at favorable terms[116] and expropriation of target shareholders through lower premiums.[117,118] There are also concerns about the shift from public to private equity ownership. This arises particular in the context of the acquisition of targets viewed as strategically important nationally by well-funded private equity with dissatisfaction expressed as to both the adequacy of the consideration being paid and the future of the enterprises acquired. A recent example was the GBP 7 billion acquisition of UK

111. Paul Davies, Edmund Schuster, and Emilie van de Walle de Ghelcke, *The Takeover Directive as a Protectionist Tool?*, European Corporate Governance Institute Law Working Paper, 28 (2010) https://ssrn.com/abstract = 1554616.
112. Blanaid Clarke, *Duties During an Offer Period – Lessons from the Cadbury PLC Takeover*, UCD Working Papers in Law, Criminology & Socio-Legal Studies Research Paper No. 44/2011 (2011) https://ssrn.com/abstract = 1759953.
113. Peter Mandelson, Speech at the Trade and Industry dinner, Guildhall, the Mansion House, London (1 March 2010).
114. Sridhar Gogineni and Arun Upadhyay, *Target Governance Provisions and Acquisition Types*, 110 J. Bus. Res. 160 (2020) and Leonce Bargeron, Frederick Schlingemann, Rene Stulz, and Chad Zutter, *Why Do Private Acquirers Pay So Little Compared to Public Acquirers?* 89 J. Fin. Econ. 375 (2008).
115. Francesca Cornelli and Oguzhan Karakaş, *Corporate Governance of LBOs: The Role of Boards* (2012), https://ssrn.com/abstract = 1875649.
116. Cem Demiroglu and Christopher James, *The Information Content of Bank Loan Covenants*. 23 Rev. Financ. Stud 3700 (2010).
117. Ludovic Phalippou, *Venture Capital Funds: Flow-Performance Relationship and Performance Persistence*, 34 J. Bank. Fin. 568 (2010) and Micah Officer, Oguzhan Ozbas, and Berk Sensoy, *Club Deals in Leveraged Buyouts*, 98 J. Fin. Econ. 214 (2010).
118. Gogineni and Upadhyay, *supra*, n. 113 and Bargeron et al., *supra* n. 113.

supermarket chain Morrisons by US private equity group Clayton Dubilier & Rice in 2021. The tabloid media focused on 'pandemic plundering' and argued that this was not 'a good deal for consumers, employees and businesses in the supply chain' given that private equity 'has a habit of only paying minimum wage and not offering any security to the supply chain'.[119] A campaign by the Daily Mail 'to curb predatory private equity' spread the blame around also castigating 'venal boards of directors' and 'short-sighted City shareholders who roll over and sell out' having failed 'to take boards to task for underperformance'.[120] Despite, opposition from almost 22% in number of shareholders, the bid had strong support from institutional investors and was approved by 99.2% of shares voted. It is clear in this case, that even if the Morrisons' board had attempted to seek shareholder approval for defensive measures pursuant to Rule 21 of the UK Takeover Code, it would not have succeeded. Though beyond the scope of this chapter, this case also provides an insight into the complexity of the current debate on the purpose of a company and its obligations to its stakeholders.

[C] A Post-pandemic Protected Marketplace

As noted earlier, for the MCC to operate, there must be an open marketplace unhindered by defensive measures by target boards. Of course, the market may be obstructed not only by private actors but also by public law authorities. Bids must adhere to competition law and are often subject to preconditions to the making of a bid or the implementation of a bid which depend upon clearance from competition regulators, including the Commission. A study by Dissanaike, Drobetz, and Momtazshows concluded that an unintended and detrimental by-product of EU merger control is that it impedes an efficient MCC.[121] They explain that the uncertainty about merger control decisions reduces the likelihood of a bid thus amplifying managerial entrenchment. These effects were found to be more pronounced in concentrated industries and in countries with government-dependent supervisory authorities and lax criminal sanctions.

Over the years, however, concern has been expressed about the wisdom of open markets in the face of foreign bids for strategic national icons, such as Mannesman in Germany and Cadbury in the UK. These fears are exacerbated in times of low market values or volatile markets when the discussion turns to foreign companies acquiring undervalued national strategic assets. Indeed, Evenett has described how concerns that economic crises generate 'firesale' foreign direct investment (FDI) are perennial. Not surprisingly thus, there were calls for increased protectionism in the wake of the GFC

119. Lucy White, *Shoppers ''could pay the price': Morrisons Customers and Suppliers Could Lose Out After Board Backs Fresh Takeover Bid from US Investors*, Daily Mail, 5 July 2021.
120. Ruth Sunderland, *Ten Reasons Why We Mustn't Let Morrisons Fall to the Pandemic Predators*, Daily Mail, 23 June 2021.
121. Gishan Dissanaike, Wolfgang Drobetz, and Paul Momtaz, *Competition Policy and the Profitability of Corporate Acquisitions*, 62 J. Corp. Fin. (2020).

and the Pandemic.[122] In many jurisdictions, screening has been carried out on the grounds of national security, and this classification now covers an increasingly wide range of sectors and interests. One of the most stringent is the US regime where the Foreign Investment Risk Review Modernization Act 2018 (FIRRMA) has expanded the scope of the Committee on Foreign Investment in the United States (CFIUS) screening activity 'to address growing national security concerns over foreign exploitation of certain investment structures which traditionally have fallen outside of CFIUS jurisdiction'.[123] These include operations structured through private equities and 'other investments' in certain US businesses affording a foreign person access to material non-public technical information in the possession of the US business, membership on the board of directors, or other decision-making rights, other than through voting of shares. At an EU level, Regulation 2019/452 on FDI Screening[124] establishes a framework for the screening by Member States of foreign direct investments into the EU on the grounds of security or public order. Article 4 of Regulation 2019/452 lists a wide range of factors that may be taken into account in determining whether a FDI is likely to affect security or public order. These include: critical infrastructure and technologies; access to sensitive information, including personal data or the ability to control such information; and extent to which the foreign investor is directly or indirectly controlled by the government of a third country. The definition of 'FDI' applies to 'an investment of any kind by a foreign investor aiming to establish or to maintain lasting and direct links ... including investments which enable effective participation in the management or control of a company carrying out an economic activity'.[125] It is clear that the difficulty of balancing the EU's commitment to 'an open investment environment' with desire to restrict FDI on 'security or public order' grounds will become increasingly difficult. In the UK, the National Security and Investment Act 2021 is even more far-reaching and resembles FIRRMA. It introduces a mandatory notification regime for acquisitions in seventeen key sectors, including Advanced materials; Advanced robotics; AI, Communications; Computing hardware; Data infrastructure; Defence; Energy; Synthetic biology; Military and dual-use; and Transport. It applies to acquisitions of 25% or more of the shareholding or voting rights; increases through 25%, 50%, and 75% shareholding/voting rights thresholds; or acquisitions of voting rights that enable/prevent any class of resolution passing. It also allows the UK Government to impose conditions on, unwind or block an acquisition. The extra-territorial scope of this regime is extraordinarily wide as it extends to acquisitions of entities outside of the UK which carry on activities in the UK or supply goods or services to people in the UK. Looking at this direction of travel, exacerbated no doubt by global tensions and increased focus on supply chain security,

122. UNCTAD, *World Investment Report 2021* reported FDI flows declining globally by 35% in 2020 as a result of lockdowns caused by the COVID-19 pandemic and the prospects of a recession.
123. US Treasury, *Summary of the Foreign Investment Risk Review Modernization Act of 2018*, https://www.treasury.gov/resource-center/international/Documents/Summary-of-FIRRMA.pdf
124. As amended by Commission Delegated Regulation (EU) 2020/1298 and Commission Delegated Regulation (EU) 2021/2126.
125. Art.2(1).

it is arguable that FDI restrictions are likely to remain or increase. In addition to restricting an active MCC in cases where there genuinely are security or public interest issues, it is clear that because of their broad drafting, FDI restrictions will give rise to great uncertainty, even more so than that referred to in relation to EU Merger Control.

[D] Managerial Myopia

While acknowledging that the MCC 'provided constant pressure on managers at all levels, including the board, to maximize the share price', Manne in 2008 still maintained his view that 'there is no aspect of corporate governance that is not better left to private contracting and the play of market forces.'[126] He described the MCC as a less blunt force than such 'piddling governance devices as the shareholders' proposal rule or mandated independent directors'[127] and one capable of resolving deficiencies such as inattention to work matters which litigation restricted by the business-judgment could not. It could also, he opined correct 'misguided efforts (certainly from the shareholders' point of view) to benefit stakeholders at the expense of shareholders.'[128] In light of the increasing emphasis on sustainable long-term value, and the challenges 'enlightened shareholder value' can bring in terms of managerial accountability, this was an interesting observation.

The question as to whether managers will be less inclined to attend to the interests of non-shareholder stakeholders and more focused on projects yielding more immediate benefits if they feel vulnerable to a hostile offer has been the subject of ongoing debate.[129] In the context of EU's sustainability goals, Sjåfjell et al. argued that the MCC 'undermines the role of boards and senior management' requiring them to be overly short-termist in their focus requiring 'a comprehensive assessment' of the regulatory framework for listed companies.[130] The idea of managerial short-termism affecting corporate social governance more broadly was the subject of a fascinating study by Wongsinhirun et al. involving 9,200 US firm-year observations from 1997 to 2012.[131] The study supports the managerial myopia hypothesis study finding that an increase in takeover vulnerability by one standard deviation results in a decline in corporate social responsibility (CSR) by 3.3%. Exposed to hostile takeover threats, managers make investments to increase short-term gains at the expense of long-term projects. The authors conclude:

126. Manne, *supra* n. 5, 4.
127. *Ibid.*, 11.
128. *Ibid.*
129. Jeremy Stein, *Takeover Threats and Managerial Myopia*, 96 J. Political Econ 61 (1988).
130. Beate Sjåfjell, Jukka Mähönen, Tonia Novitz, Clair Gammage, and Hanna Ahlström, *Securing the Future of European Business: SMART Reform Proposals* (May 7, 2020). University of Oslo Faculty of Law Research Paper No. 2020-11, Nordic & European Company Law Working Paper No. 20-08, 80 (2020), https://ssrn.com/abstract=3595048.
131. Nopparat Wongsinhirun, Pattanaporn Chatjuthamard, Pornsit Jiraporn, and Piyachart Phiromswad, *Do Takeover Threats Influence Corporate Social Responsibility? Evidence from Hostile Takeover Vulnerability* (March 2022) Corp. Soc. Responsib. Environ. Manag. 1. *See also* Aleksandra Kacperczyk, *With Greater Power Comes Greater Responsibility? Takeover Protection and Corporate Attention to Stakeholders, 30* Strateg. Manag. J. 261 (2009).

> Less secure in their job because of a more active takeover market, managers are reluctant to invest in these long-term projects, which are more difficult for shareholders and investors to evaluate, choosing instead to invest in projects that produce results earlier. Therefore, more takeover susceptibility results in significantly reduced corporate social responsibility.[132]

Given the enormous societal challenges we face in terms of climate change, the idea that an active MCC might detract management's attention from projects considered 'long-term' would be a concern. That of course assumes that the market would not value such a focus leading to an undervaluation of their shares by the market. Whether this is the case remains moot, and the empirical evidence on relationship between CSR and financial performance is inconclusive.[133]

§13.05 CONCLUSION

It is evident that the MCC has been accepted as an important external governance mechanism but while it may compliment internal governance, it should not be seen as a complete substitute for it. Currently, hostile takeovers form a relatively small proportion of takeover activity. For example, in the UK, only three of the fifty-three firm offers (5.6%) made in 2021 were hostile from the outset with a further three becoming hostile after competing offers emerged. The previous year only one hostile offer was announced.[134] However, industry sources predicted an increase in hostile activity during 2022 as 'a number of target boards and prospective purchasers may be unable to reconcile differences in valuation, with strategic bidders seeking to make their case directly to shareholders if management teams elect not to engage in a constructive manner on the grounds of an insufficient premium being offered to the company's prevailing share price'.[135] This was consistent with expected global trends, encouraged by the availability of capital, particularly private equity, and number of prospective bidders. This however predated concerns about inflation and interest rate, the War in Ukraine and the subsequent economic and energy crises which slowed down M&A activity in the first quarter of 2022.[136] While evidence still suggests the potential for an active MCC, as has been described in this chapter, there are impediments to its free operation. Manne claimed 'literally all that is needed for near ideal corporate governance' was a totally unfettered market for corporate control.[137] By unfettered he explained this meant that 'No arguments about differential pricing of the same shares, lost opportunities for better offers, inefficient pricing by the stock market, antitrust

132. *Ibid.*, 18.
133. Sonia Boukattaya, Zyed Achour, and Zeineb Hlioui, *Corporate Social Responsibility and Corporate Financial Performance: An Empirical Literature Review*, 1 Int. j. sci. res. publ. 1 (2021).
134. Adam Cain, Pinsent Masons quoted in LexisNexis, *Market Tracker, supra* n. 107, 5.
135. *Ibid.*
136. *Market Tracker Trend Report: Trends in UK Public M&A deals in H1* 2022. https://www.lexisnexis.co.uk/blog/docs/default-source/corporate-law-documents/public-m-a-h1-report-2022-final.pdf?sfvrsn=3ad46a2c_3
137. Manne, *supra* n. 5, 14.

barriers to mergers, failure to disclose the raider's plans for the company or information about the raider generally or any other of the purely self-serving arguments made by incumbent managers will be allowed to prevail.'[138] Anything less than this, he argued would be 'an economically unwarranted interference in an otherwise highly beneficial, though never costless, competitive market'.[139] It is submitted that this requires enormous faith in the MCC in the face of ambivalent empirical evidence and concerns as to the consequences of an unrestricted market. A degree of balance is required as part of a holistic approach to takeover regulation so that the benefits to be derived from hostile takeovers are retained whilst some of the unintended consequences are avoided. Finding such a balance, particularly in the face of increased protectionism, a weakening of globalisation as a result of the pandemic and the war in Ukraine, and increased global tensions will be a significant challenge.

138. *Ibid.*
139. *Ibid.*

CHAPTER 14

Corporate Governance by Certification

Florian Möslein

§14.01 INTRODUCTION

Certification schemes do not only enable companies to demonstrate compliance of their products or services with certain technical standards. They also extend to processes, including internal management systems. As opposed to the more traditional product certification, that latter type of certification has an obvious, though rarely discussed overlap with corporate governance.[1] For example, ISO 9001 compliance certificates relate to certain standards for quality management systems, including questions of leadership, planning, and organisation. Various other prominent certification schemes relate to questions of sustainable corporate behaviour. Directed at companies as a whole, these certification schemes are likely to interact with corporate governance. In addition, they serve as regulatory instruments in order to achieve a specific policy goal, namely the fostering of corporate sustainability. In this chapter, sustainability-oriented certification schemes will therefore serve as examples for illustrating the interplay of certification and corporate governance more generally.

In times of climate change and dwindling natural resources, policy-makers and regulators try to set incentives for sustainable corporate behaviour.[2] In doing so, they increasingly take advantage of certification schemes and sustainability labelling. Such

---

1. *See*, however, William A. Stimson, *The Role of Sarbanes-Oxley and ISO 9001 in Corporate Management* (McFarland & Company 2011).
2. Recently, for example, at the European level: Commission Proposal for a Directive of the European Parliament and of the Council on Corporate Sustainability Due Diligence and amending Directive (EU) 2019/1937, COM(2022) 71 final of 2 February 2022. For a broader comparative law overview, *see also*, Florian Möslein & Karsten Engsig Sorensen, *Nudging for Corporate Long-Termism and Sustainability? Regulatory Instruments from a Comparative and Functional Perspective*, 24 Colum. J. Eur. L. 393 (2018).

schemes capitalize on the individual preferences of consumers, investors, and employees, which serve as a sort of transmission belt in order to achieve regulatory goals. The mode of operation of these regulatory instruments can briefly be described as follows: consumers who want to be ethically responsible ('political consumerism') will prefer companies that produce sustainably.[3] Similarly, many investors are no longer exclusively focused on increasing financial returns; rather, they also take ecological and social criteria into account ('impact investing').[4] Effective demand-based incentives for corporate sustainability do not only require that the companies in question compete in markets where corresponding preferences prevail, but they also presuppose that the respective market counterpart, especially consumers and investors, can accurately and easily determine the sustainability of the respective corporate activities, as quality criteria that matter to them. However, it is usually difficult for outsiders to evaluate the degree of sustainability because it depends on various details, such as production processes, use of resources, and working conditions. The sustainability of corporate activities therefore ranks among hidden characteristics, the quality of which consumers and investors cannot reliably assess *ex ante* or, at least, can only do so with considerable difficulty.[5] These information deficits involve considerable risks of adverse selection.[6] The certification of sustainable corporations can be qualified as a regulatory instrument that aims to overcome such risks arising from information asymmetries.[7]

Such a mode of operation requires, however, that market counterparties perceive the certification in question as a credible indication of the actual existence of sustainable corporate activity, i.e., as a true quality seal.[8] As a special form of signalling, which is not carried out by the provider itself but by third parties,[9] certification promises effective prevention of market failures (subject, however, to proper regulatory design of the respective certification scheme). In addition to the credibility of the certification

3. *See*, for example, Lauren Copeland & Shelley Boulianne, *Political Consumerism: A meta-analysis*, 43 Int. Political Sci. Rev. 3 (2022).
4. *Global Handbook of Impact Investing: Solving Global Problems Via Smarter Capital Markets Towards A More Sustainable Society* (Elsa De Morais Sarmento & R. Paul Herman eds., Wiley 2021); Judith Rodin & Margot Brandenburg, *The Power of Impact Investing: Putting Markets to Work for Profit and Global Good* (Wharton School Press 2014).
5. In more detail, *see* Florian Möslein, *Europäische Zertifizierung mitgliedstaatlichen GmbH-Rechts*, 176 Zeitschrift für das gesamte Handelsrecht und Wirtschaftsrecht (ZHR) 470, 483 et seq. (2012).
6. On the resulting danger of a 'market for lemons', *see* George A. Akerlof, *The Market for 'Lemons': Quality Uncertainty and the Market Mechanism*, 84 Q. J. Econ. 488 (1970); *see also* Joseph E. Stiglitz, *Markets, Market Failures, and Development*, 97 Am. Econ. Rev. 197 (1989).
7. In more detail, on the economic arguments: Georg von Wangenheim, *Certification as a Solution to the Asymmetric Information Problem?* in *Certification – Trust, Accountability, Liability* 143, 147 (Peter Rott ed., Springer 2019).
8. Möslein, *supra* n. 5, at 485–487; Florian Möslein, *Zertifizierung nachhaltiger Kapitalgesellschaften: Regimevergleich und flankierende Maßnahmen, in Zertifizierung nachhaltiger Kapitalgesellschaften* 3, 4 (Martin Burgi & Florian Möslein, eds, Mohr Siebeck 2021).
9. On so-called third-party certifiers, cf., extensively, Jan De Bruyne, *Third-Party Certifiers* (Kluwer Law International 2019); *see also* B. James Deaton, *A Theoretical Framework for Examining the Role of Third Party Certifiers*, 15 Food Control 615 (2004).

body,[10] a widespread acceptance of certification presupposes in particular that the certification requirements objectively correspond (at least in part) to those criteria according to which market participants make their decisions. Moreover, market participants must also subjectively associate the certificate with those requirements.[11]

For effective promotion of corporate sustainability, the procedural as well as substantive regulatory design of the specific certification scheme is therefore of crucial importance. Existing certification schemes show much variation, though. This diversity can be illustrated by an outline of the particularly widespread US scheme of Certified B Corporations (§14.02), which will also be followed by an overview of the design variants of other, alternative certification schemes (§14.03). From the perspective of corporate governance, it is important to contrast these various certification schemes with other, functionally comparable regulatory instruments that aim to promote sustainable entrepreneurship, and to briefly discuss potential interactions between these instruments (§14.04). This stocktaking will then facilitate assessment of the potential implications of certification schemes for corporate governance (§14.05).

§14.02 THE PARAGON OF 'CERTIFIED B CORPORATIONS' OR 'B CORPS'

A particularly successful and popular certification scheme was initially established in the United States (US) but nowadays operates globally. Its development and implementation have been promoted by B Lab, a non-profit organization, under private law, which was founded in Pennsylvania in 2006 with the support of numerous sponsors, including the *Rockefeller Foundation*.[12] Certification under this scheme is based on a so-called B Impact Assessment, and after successful completion of this, the status of a 'Certified B Corporation' (or briefly: B Corp) is awarded. The assessment criteria have become more and more differentiated over time. Depending on company size, geographical location (developed vs. emerging markets), and industry sector (service, wholesale/retail, manufacturing, agriculture, etc.), the impact assessment now

10. On this condition, and also on potential incentive conflicts with regard to B Lab: Dana Brakman Reiser, *Blended Enterprise and the Dual Mission Dilemma*, 35 Vermont L. Rev. 105, at 115 et seq. (2010).
11. Cf. Möslein, *supra* n. 5, at 485–487. Overall, the preconditions on which the credibility of certifications depends are surprisingly seldom researched in economic terms; cf., however, Gabriele Jahn, Matthias Schramm, & Achim Spiller, *The Reliability of Certification: Quality Labels as a Consumer Policy Tool*, 28 J. Consum. Policy 53 (2005); *see also*, Eva van der Zee, *Sustainability Labels in the Shadow of the Law* 21 et seq. (2022).
12. *See* https://www.bcorporation.net/ and the following: Dana Brakman Reiser, *Benefit Corporations – A Sustainable Form of Organization?* 46 Wake Forest L. Rev. 591, 594 (2011); Robert T. Esposito, *The Social Enterprise Revolution* in *Corporate Law*, 4 Wm. & Mary Bus. L. Rev. 639, 695 (2013); Florian Möslein & Anne Mittwoch, *Social Enterprise in US Corporate Law – Benefit Corporations and Certified B Corporations*, 80 Rabels Zeitschrift für ausländisches und internationales Privatrecht (RabelsZ) 399, 406–411 (2016); J. Haskell Murray, *Choose Your Own Master: Social Enterprise, Certifications, and Benefit Corporation Statutes*, 2 Am. U. Bus. L. Rev. 1, 21 et seq. (2012); Karsten Engsig Sorensen & Mette Neville, *Social Enterprises: How Should Company Law Balance Flexibility and Credibility?* 15 EBOR 267, 280 et seq. (2014).

comprises more than seventy different variants.[13] In order to obtain certification, companies must answer an extensive questionnaire and achieve at least 80 out of 200 points. If necessary, they must also adapt their articles of association and undergo a review procedure.

The substantive criteria that are queried in the process of certification relate, on the one hand, to the company's impact on certain interest groups and, on the other hand, to the company's corporate governance structure. The relevant stakeholders include employees, consumers, civil society, and the environment. With regard to employees, financial remuneration (compensation and opportunities for participation), non-financial benefits (training and work flexibility), the social dimension (communication between management and employees, as well as social culture), and the working environment (health and safety practices) count among the criteria that are assessed in particular. From the consumer perspective, the impact of products and services on users is the main focus, but the promotion of disadvantaged population groups, for example, is also taken into account. In terms of civil society, the company's commitment to diversity, its regional roots, and its charitable activities are among the aspects that are put to the test. In the environmental category, improvements in the production process (reduction of emissions, resource and energy consumption) are particularly important, but what also counts is the question of whether the company solves specific ecological problems with the products or services it offers.[14]

However, in a more holistic view of the company, the institutional foundations of sustainable corporate governance are examined, including company law aspects. This assessment builds on the assumption that these factors also have an influence on the extent to which the company's orientation towards common good interests is permissible and permanently guaranteed.[15] Relevant factors include, for example, the establishment and implementation of social and ecological corporate mission statements, adherence to compliance rules, and the structures as well as responsibilities, and appointment rules of members of the corporate board (e.g., participation of independent directors and stakeholders).[16] Given that companies with a wide variety of legal forms can apply for certification, these rules are not necessarily prescribed by law. As a consequence, the articles of association need to be drafted accordingly.[17] Certification therefore requires – in addition to achievement of the necessary assessment points – certain mandatory contents of the articles of association. On the one hand, the orientation towards the common good must form part of the company's purpose and therefore needs to be enshrined in the articles of incorporation so that deviations are

13. Michael B. Dorff, *Assessing the Assessment: B Lab's Efforts to Measure Companies' Benevolence*, 40 Seattle U. L. Rev. 515, 523 (2017).
14. For more details, cf. the various certification guides that are available at https://www.bcorporation.net/en-us/resources; *see also* Möslein & Mittwoch, *supra* n. 12, at 409.
15. Dorff, *supra* n. 13, at 523.
16. More closely, *see* Möslein & Mittwoch, *supra* n. 12, at 409.
17. The certification scheme creates, however, a sort of constraint with regard to the legal form because it aims to ensure that certified companies transform themselves into the legal form of a so-called benefit corporation. For more details of this requirement, *see* sub. §14.03 below; more specifically on the implications of legal policy, *see* Möslein & Mittwoch, *supra* n. 12, at 410 et seq.

not easily possible, even in the case of a change of control or personnel turnover in the management bodies. On the other hand, guiding principles need to be defined so that increased shareholder value does not necessarily take priority in the exercise of management discretion, but stakeholder interests can also be taken into account.[18] In order to avoid overly restricting the exercise of discretion, however, specific interests do not need to be specifically ranked in the articles of association. As a consequence, directors can make decisions on the basis of their own assessment, without having to fear a later challenge through derivative suits.[19]

To verify the information that is provided by companies, B Lab employs a number of control mechanisms.[20] First, answers to certain questions are to be supported by corresponding documents. Publication of the company profile, its assessment, and its impact report (i.e., the expert opinion prepared by B Lab) serve to ensure public monitoring. Furthermore, a percentage of all certified companies are audited annually in onsite inspections. In addition, re-certification is required every three years. All these arrangements are intended to ensure the validity and reliability of the certification.

In addition, these procedural arrangements, and the suitability and persuasiveness of the substantive certification requirements, are to be ensured by the institutional design of the certification scheme, namely not only through the involvement of external experts but also through dynamic development of the applicable criteria. On the one hand, these criteria are not formulated by B Lab itself but by a standards advisory council, which largely consists of independent experts and representatives of various interest groups, in order to minimize potential influence by B Lab or the companies that are certified.[21] On the other hand, the criteria are continuously reviewed and refined, in particular, on the basis of regularly requested feedback from users and interest groups, but also in interaction with other standardization organizations.[22] This interaction is aimed in particular at compatibility with the Global Impact Investing Rating System (GIIRS), which is of great importance for raising capital for the certified companies as it serves investors worldwide as a basis for assessing the social and ecological impacts of their investments.[23] The need for dynamic development and

18. The specific requirements, including pre-formulated articles of association clauses (in accordance with the legal system and form), are provided by a 'Legal Requirement Tool'; available at: https://www.bcorporation.net/en-us/about-b-corps/legal-requirements.
19. On this risk, which is particularly significant in the USA, cf. Möslein & Mittwoch, *supra* n. 12, at 424–426.
20. *See* Ryan Honeyman, *The B Corp Handbook* 162 et seq. (Berrett-Koehler Publishers 2014); *see also* https://bcorporation.net/certification and Möslein & Mittwoch, *supra* n. 12, at 410.
21. For its composition, *see* https://www.bcorporation.net/en-us/standards/advisory-council; *see also*, Dorff, *supra* n. 13, at 522; Fred P. Gale, *The Political Economy of Sustainability* 151 et seq. (Edward Elgar 2018).
22. Larry Hamermesh, Bart Houlahan, Rick Alexander, & Dan Osusky, *A Conversation with B Lab*, 40 Seattle U. L. Rev. 321, 335 (2017).
23. Dana Brakman Reiser & Steven A. Dean, *Social Enterprise Law* 130 et seq. (Oxford University Press 2017); Rodin & Brandenburg, *supra* n. 4, at 60. Under the US government-sponsored Small Business Investment Company programme, for example, about half of the impact funds use this rating to fulfil their reporting obligations; cf. US Small Business Administration, SBA Announces New Initiative with GIIRS Rating System for Private Funds and Companies, 21 January 2017;

differentiation of the certification criteria is, for example, particularly obvious in the case of multinational companies. The original focus of impact assessment on small and medium-sized enterprises has meant that factors such as networking with local suppliers, consumers, and organizations, as well as contributions to local economic development, were originally heavily weighted in the certification process.[24] Since these indicators are obviously unsuitable for large global companies, a modified catalogue of requirements has been developed and tested specifically for this target group.[25] In fact, Danone will be the first multinational to get fully certified in 2025, having worked in partnership with B Lab since 2015 in order to assist in defining a meaningful and manageable path to certification for multinationals and publicly traded companies.[26]

§14.03 VARIATIONS OF CERTIFICATION SCHEMES

The outlined certification scheme of 'Certified B Corporations', with its origins in the USA and with its aim to verify the sustainability of companies in a quantifiable way, has spread rapidly across the entire globe. Today, more than 5,000 companies in around 80 countries worldwide are certified accordingly.[27] Notwithstanding this wide dissemination, however, various other certification schemes have also come into being: in Germany, for example, the sustainable corporate governance certification of TÜV Rheinland (Zertifizierung 'Nachhaltige Unternehmensführung'), the audit of the association for the promotion of the 'Gemeinwohlökonomie' (common good economy), and the so-called PHINEO Wirkt! label;[28] in Great Britain, the Social Enterprise Mark and the Certified Social Enterprise Badge; in France, the original two-level ESS/ESUS certification system (qualité d'entreprise de l'économie sociale et solidaire or agrément entreprise solidairc d'utilitć social), as well as the recently introduced société à mission; and in South Korea, the Social Enterprises Certification.[29]

---

available at: https://www.sba.gov/about-sba/sba-newsroom/press-releases-media-advisories/sba-announces-new-initiative-giirs-rating-system-private-funds-and-companies.

24. On these factors, *see* Dorff, *supra* n. 13, at 524.
25. *See* B Lab's recommendations on B Corp Certification for eligible multinationals and large enterprise businesses; available at: https://www.bcorporation.net/en-us/certification/large-enterprise-multinational; *see also* Christopher Marquis, *Better Business: How the B Corp Movement Is Remaking Capitalism* 204 et seq. (Cambridge University Press 2020).
26. For an extensive case study, cf. Benjamin C. Esty & Emilie Bilaud, *Danone S.A.: Becoming a Mission-Driven Company* (26 August 2021), HBS Case No. 722–354; available at SSRN: https://ssrn.com/abstract = 3954533.
27. https://www.bcorporation.net/en-us.
28. Further information is available at https://www.phineo.org/wirkt-siegel; at https://web.ecogood.org/de/unsere-arbeit/gemeinwohl-bilanz/unternehmen/4-gemeinwohl-bericht-audit/; and at https://www.tuv.com/content-media-files/germany/pdfs/0397-tuv-rheinland-bsci-auditing/tuv-rheinland-broschuere-nachhaltige-unternehmensfuehrung-de.pdf.
29. For an overview of these and other (European) schemes: *A Map of Social Enterprises and Their Eco-Systems, in Europe – Synthesis Report* 79–86 (European Commission 2015); also Anna Triponel & Natalia Agapitova, *Legal Frameworks for Social Enterprise* (World Bank 2016); on the more recent French scheme: Jérôme Lasserre Capdeville, *Financement alternatif relevant des principes de l'économie sociale et solidaire*, in *Droit de la Finance Alternative* 33, 47–50 (Jean-Marc Moulin ed., Bruylant 2017); on the South Korean scheme, *see* Eric Bidet & Hyung-Sik

These various certification schemes differ from one another and from B Lab in four different dimensions, namely with regard to their institutional framework, their procedural design, their substantive certification criteria, and their respective legal consequences.[30]

[A] Institutional Framework

The first and fundamental difference between the various certification schemes relates to their institutional framework, as some of them operate as public schemes (e.g., in France and South Korea), whereas others - like B Lab - are purely private in nature. Public schemes are administered by state institutions and operate on the basis of legal rules. Some of these schemes are more of a political nature, namely when appointment of members of the certification bodies is carried out by ministries, for example (in South Korea).[31] Other public schemes are more of an administrative nature, in particular when certification is carried out by administrative authorities, for instance, when it is closely linked to the commercial register (like in France).[32] A general argument in favour of such public-law arrangements is the fact that efficiency-enhancing corrections of market failures, to be achieved through the certification of sustainable corporations, are traditionally considered to be an important task of legislation.[33] Moreover, in contrast to purely profit-oriented companies, companies that also serve the common good internalize costs that would otherwise have to be borne by the state. The state therefore has a legitimate interest in functional and

Eum, *Social Enterprise in South Korea: History and Diversity*, 7 Social Enterprise Journal 77 (2011). On the more recent introduction of the French société à mission by the Loi PACTE in 2019, *see* Errol Cohen, *La société à mission: la loi pacte, enjeux pratiques de l'entreprise réinventée* (Hermann 2019); Alain Pietrancosta, *Codification in Company Law of General CSR Requirements: Pioneering Recent French Reforms and EU Perspectives*, Working Paper (2022); available at SSRN: https://ssrn.com/abstract=4083398; cf. also Holger Fleischer, *Gesetzliche Zertifizierung nachhaltiger Unternehmen: Die französische 'société à mission' als Vorbild für Deutschland?* Neue Zeitschrift für Gesellschaftsrecht (NZG) 1525 (2021).

30. In detail, also *see* the following: Florian Möslein, *Certifying Good Companies – Regulatory Schemes for Corporate Sustainability in a Comparative Perspective, in Cambridge Handbook of Corporate Law, Corporate Governance and Sustainability* 669 (Christopher Bruner & Beate Sjåfjell eds., Cambridge University Press 2020).
31. Cf. Art. 4 of the Social Enterprise Promotion Act, enacted by Act No. 8217 of 3 January 2007, amended by Act No. 8361 of 11 April 2007; English version available at: http://www.icnl.org/research/library/files/South%20Korea/socent.pdf.
32. In detail: Loi n. 2014-856 du 31 juillet 2014 relative à l'économie sociale et solidaire, JORF n. 176 du 1 août 2014, p. 12666; Arrêté du 5 août 2015 fixant la composition du dossier de demande d'agrément 'entreprise solidaire d'utilité sociale', JORF n. 185 du 12 août 2015, p. 14004; and Décret du 23 juin 2015 relatif à l'agrément 'entreprise solidaire d'utilité sociale' régi par l'article L. 3332-17-1 du code du travail, JORF n. 145 du 25 juin 2015, p. 10676; all three texts are available at https://www.legifrance.gouv.fr.
33. *See*, for example, Richard A. Posner, *Economics, Politics, and the Reading of Statutes and the Constitution*, 49 Univ. Chic. Law Rev. 263, 265 (1982).

reliable certification of such companies, and in avoiding so-called greenwashing.[34] Moreover, states often compensate for the costs internalized by these companies through public support, for example, through subsidies or tax benefits.[35]

Private certification schemes, however, operate without any specific legal basis and predominantly without the involvement of public institutions.[36] Rather, these schemes emerge on a purely private, autonomous basis. Certification is undertaken by bodies organized under private law, such as associations or foundations like B Lab, and it is based on contractual arrangements. The certifying bodies are mostly financed by licensing income, while some of them are (additionally) funded by private sponsors.[37] These bodies can, however, be more or less strongly interlinked with state institutions. Links can relate to the substantive criteria of certification, for example, when states are granted an influence on their content through their sponsorship or through specific appointment rights. In general, the governance structures of private certification institutions differ considerably from one another. In part, they are highly formalized and almost resemble a state division of powers, for example, through division of regulatory and administrative tasks, as in the US B Corp scheme (Standard Advisory Council versus B Lab) or in the German PHINEO label (with an independent recommendation commission).[38] Other certification schemes, however, are much more informally organized, for example, Social Enterprise UK.[39] In this scheme, there is simply no need for an independent standard-setting body because the certification criteria are exactly congruent to a state requirement, namely the conceptual definition of social enterprises by the British Department of Trade and Industry.[40] In spite of these differences, the private form of schemes, in general, is supported by three core considerations. First, other information intermediaries such as rating agencies are also privately organized. Second, competition between different certifiers can facilitate the search for better, more suitable solutions, for example, more precise certification criteria. Third and most important, it ranks among the fundamental principles of a market economy that private autonomy prevails over state regulation as long as there are no compelling reasons for such regulation.

34. *See* William S. Laufer, *Social Accountability and Corporate Greenwashing*, 43 J. Bus. Ethics 253 (2003); cf. also Béatrice Parguel, Florence Benoit-Moureau, & Fabrice Larceneux, *How Sustainability Ratings Might Deter 'Greenwashing'*, 102 J Bus. Ethics 15 (2011).
35. On such state support in South Korea: Bidet & Eum, *supra* n. 29, at 78.
36. In detail Möslein, *supra* n. 30, at 671 et seq.
37. The UK Social Enterprise Mark Scheme, for example, is operated by a company whose shares are held by the RISE Legacy Trust; *see* Rory Ridley-Duff & Cliff Southcombe, *The Social Enterprise Mark: A Critical Review of Its Conceptual Dimensions*, 8 Social Enterprise Journal 178 (2012).
38. Cf. PHINEO Annual Report 2016, at pp. 18–22 (governance structure) and 29 (recommendation commission); available at: https://www.phineo.org/uploads/Downloads/PHINEO-Jahresbericht_2016.pdf.
39. *See* www.socialenterprise.org.uk and the overview in Social Enterprise UK: *Impact Report 2016–2017* (2017) 29 et seq.
40. UK Department of Trade and Industry, *Social Enterprise: A Strategy for Success* 13 (2002); differentiated further, for example, in: Department for Business, *Innovation & Skills, Small Business Survey 2014: SME employers* 35 (BIS Research Paper No. 214, 2015).

[B] Procedural Requirements

The procedures that companies need to follow in order to obtain certification also differ substantially among the various schemes. In this respect, too, the degree of formalization varies considerably, although private certification schemes do not necessarily operate less formally than their public counterparts in every single respect. While these procedural differences have no effect on the substantive understanding of sustainability, they certainly influence the reliability and credibility of certification.

The fundamental procedural difference concerns the question of whether the certification body carries out a substantive review of the sustainability criteria or whether the companies assess their sustainability by themselves. Certification in public schemes typically requires approval by the competent authority, which is only granted after a substantive review, or involves controls by third parties, for instance, according to Article L. 210-10, 4° C. com. in the French scheme of the *société à mission*. But in most private schemes, the companies are typically also reviewed by the certification bodies, at least in random samples, like in the case of B Lab.[41] For the most part, the intensity of verification hardly differs from public schemes. However, there are also specific private certification schemes that are satisfied with mere self-assessment. For example, Social Enterprise UK only requires companies to sign a declaration of achievement of some basic sustainability criteria.[42] If the accuracy of the company's statements is not checked at all by any third party, however, it seems highly questionable whether the respective certificates can actually prove what they claim. Moreover, the more general and sweeping the criteria of the (self-)assessment, the more difficult it is to assess and verify them. It is doubtful whether information asymmetries can be substantially reduced when intermediaries do not even validly check the information in question.[43]

Another procedural difference concerns the validity period of the certificates. In this respect, too, there are very different approaches. Most certification schemes either provide for a time limit on the validity of the certificates (e.g., B Lab in the USA but also the certification schemes in Great Britain and France) or require at least periodic reports from the certified companies in order to be able to check whether the certification requirements are still being met (e.g., in South Korea).[44] In some schemes, such as the German PHINEO label, however, certification is valid indefinitely and is not even periodically reviewed.[45] Insofar as certification is not only limited to sustainability projects that are limited in time but also includes companies that are founded for an indefinite period, such an arrangement appears highly problematic. After all, the prerequisites for certification are subject to change over time. It is therefore not

41. In more detail, *see* Möslein, *supra* n. 30, at 673 et seq.
42. The membership application form available at https://www.socialenterprise.org.uk/ requires only the signing of a short confirmation containing the relevant criteria.
43. Cf. De Bruyne, *supra* n. 9, at 3–5 (highlighting these differences) and 121–124 (describing the conditions of independence).
44. On this, in detail, with numerous references, *see* Möslein, *supra* n. 30, at 674.
45. Explicitly, in this sense ('keine Gültigkeitsdauer'), *see* the self-description of the PHINEO label at https://www.phineo.org/wirkt-siegel.

guaranteed that a company that was originally appropriately certified still meets the respective certification criteria after the passage of time. In such a case, the certificate provides outdated information, and it thus sends incorrect signals to the market.

Finally, the various schemes differ considerably in terms of the fees that they charge for certification. While the public schemes in South Korea and France charge no or only low administrative fees for certification,[46] many private certification bodies charge quite substantial fees. This observation relates, of course, to the means of funding, which differ substantially between private and public schemes. The respective fees are mostly calculated in relation to the turnover of the company to be certified; in the case of B Lab, they can amount to EUR 50,000.[47] However, the German PHINEO label constitutes an exception as it can be obtained entirely free of charge. While PHINEO is financed exclusively through the contributions of the sponsors, the other private certification bodies need to cover at least part of their operating costs through the fees that they collect from companies applying for certification. Yet such pricing models bear an obvious risk that 'certificates of convenience' are issued: They create an incentive for certification bodies to certify as many companies as possible in order to maximize their own profits. From a legal perspective, however, the certification agreement qualifies as a service contract that only obliges the certification body to carry out the certification procedure. It does not create any legal obligation to issue the certificate.[48] Companies must therefore be aware that they might not receive a certificate in the event of a negative assessment. From an economic perspective, the conflict of interest which may call the impartiality of private certification bodies into question is also mitigated due to the fact that these bodies are highly dependent on their own reputation. The more impartial their judgment, the higher the reliability and information quality of the certificates that they issue. Accordingly, their certificate becomes more attractive, so that demand will increase accordingly.[49] Except for in special circumstances (such as acute financial needs), these effects are likely to deter certification bodies from issuing certificates of convenience.

[C] Substantive Conditions

The substantive content of the certification criteria determines the core prerequisites for companies in order to obtain the respective sustainability certification. In this respect, too, the various certification schemes differ considerably. The diversity of possible certification criteria has already become clear in the B Lab example.[50] Methodologically, the individual criteria are combined in two different ways. Some certification schemes are rigid and require cumulative fulfilment of all criteria (e.g.,

46. For South Korea, *see* the information at http://www.socialenterprise.or.kr. In France, there is a fee of EUR 89.80 for the ESS registration (while the ESUS permit can apparently be obtained free of charge); cf. Möslein, *supra* n. 8, at 12 (n. 44).
47. For more details (including on the other schemes), *see* Möslein, *supra* n. 30, at 674.
48. Cf. Juan Yang, *Contract Law Aspects of Sustainable Companies' Certification in the Global Value Chain*, 15 ERCL 31 (2017).
49. Dorff, *supra* n. 13, at 550 et seq.
50. *See supra* §14.03[A].

those in France and South Korea),[51] while others follow a more flexible approach, similar to the US model, and only require an overall minimum score. In the latter case, deficits related to specific criteria can be compensated for by overachievements with regard to other criteria.[52] Most substantive criteria relate more or less obviously to corporate governance issues. In addition to the governance constitution of the respective company itself, its corporate business model, its legal form, and its financial constitution are also taken into account.

The governance constitution is relevant because it forms the institutional basis for the stipulation and realization of the corporate purpose. For instance, the French *société à mission* scheme requires companies to install a *comité à mission* that is responsible for controlling whether the company follows its social and ecological goals, and which reports accordingly to the shareholder meeting.[53] Beyond such control mechanisms, most certification schemes require the participation of different interest groups in the process of corporate decision-making, but the respective requirements vary gradually: while public certification schemes make relatively-specific stipulations in this respect, private schemes remain for the most part very vague.[54] Basically, two models of participation can be considered. One model requires representatives of the respective interest groups in specific governing bodies, such as the managerial board or, if applicable, the supervisory board. As is well known from the German debate on the *Mitbestimmung*, such a requirement can, however, give rise to conflicts of interest and possibly also to concerns about cuts in professional qualifications.[55] In contrast, the second participation model only grants information and consultation rights to the representatives of interest groups and is therefore significantly less intrusive.[56] In any event, it is obvious that such control mechanisms and participation models go to the very core of corporate governance.

The corporate business model plays a fundamentally important role for certification and also touches on corporate governance issues, at least indirectly. Generally speaking, certification is reserved for companies that are not solely focused on making a profit but which are also concerned about public and social welfare, for example, integration of disadvantaged persons or protection of the environment. The tricky challenge, however, is to define the vague concepts of social entrepreneurship and sustainability more concretely and in a manner that allows them to be meaningfully verified in the context of certifications. From a methodological perspective, two different starting points are conceivable. The assessment can either focus abstractly on

51. The provisions in Art. L. 3332-17-1 of the Code du Travail, as amended by Art. 11 Loi n. 2014-856 of 31 July 2014 (*supra* n. 32), and in Art. 8, para. 1, of the Social Enterprise Promotion Act (*supra* n. 31) both contain enumerative lists of criteria that must be fulfilled cumulatively ('conditions cumulatives').
52. For details, cf. https://www.bcorporation.net/en-us/programs-and-tools/b-impact-assessment.
53. Cf. Art. L. 210-10, 3° S. 2 C. com. In smaller companies, however, a single appointee (*référent de mission*) can replace the committee according to Art. L. 210-12 C. com; more extensively, *see* Bernard Teyssié, *Les sociétés à mission*, JCP G, 828, at 833 (2021).
54. Möslein, *supra* n. 30, at 676 et seq., with further references.
55. *See* J. Haskell Murray, *Adopting Stakeholder Advisory Boards*, 54 Am. Bus. Law J. 61, 89 (2017).
56. Murray, *Ibid.*, suggests establishing an advisory commission of stakeholder representatives.

the business purposes embodied in the company's articles of association, or alternatively, it can measure the concrete outcomes of company activities. Overall, public schemes predominantly follow the first path.[57] For instance, the French scheme of the *société à mission* requires a corresponding formulation in the *raison d'être* of the company, but it turns out that most formulations remain rather blurred and evanescent.[58] In any event, only internal company documents (such as the articles of association, specific resolutions, or corporate policy guidelines) have to be examined in this alternative approach during the certification process. As a consequence, the assessment effort is comparatively low. However, verification of concrete impacts (such as environmental emissions) requires intensive inspections and measurements. It also presupposes specific and sometimes very technical expertise. Private schemes predominantly pursue a broader approach, but they are also often not very specific. PHINEO, for example, focuses on the 'social impact', whereas Social Enterprise UK checks whether companies are characterized by a 'clear social or environmental mission that is set out in its governing documents'.[59] In comparison to these schemes, the catalogue of criteria in the B Impact Assessment, as outlined earlier, appears to be both more differentiated and more profound. In addition to the corporate purpose, it examines the corporate policy with regard to very specific individual criteria.[60] Both certification approaches are at least indirectly linked to corporate governance, for it is now widely accepted that corporate governance is not 'simply about aligning managerial interests with those of their shareholders but with their corporate purposes'.[61]

With regard to legal form, no certification scheme is limited to a single, specific form of company. Rather, the relevant certifications are available for companies of different legal forms. However, almost all schemes target commercial companies, even if some of them are more focused on non-profit organizations (or at least originally had such a focus).[62] For example, the French ESS scheme was only accessible to associations, foundations, and cooperatives until 2014 but has since been expanded.[63] PHINEO, however, apparently remains focused on non-profit companies.[64] In contrast, the B Impact Assessment is quite different, as foundations and non-profit organizations are explicitly excluded. This scheme is therefore limited to cooperatives and for-profit

57. On this, in detail, *see* Möslein, *supra* n. 30, at 675.
58. Rémi Dalmau, *Les sociétés à mission: quelle nature et quelles sanctions?* JCP E, 1136 n. 7 (2020): 'Les exemples actuels de ces raison d'être démontrent bien souvent qu'il s'agit d'objectifs flous et évanescents'.
59. Cf. www.socialenterprise.org.uk (in the application form) or https://www.phineo.org/magazin/was-ist-soziale-wirkung ('Soziale Wirkung').
60. In addition, Honeyman, *supra* n. 20, at 118 et seq.; Möslein & Mittwoch, *supra* n. 12, at 409.
61. Colin Mayer, *The Governance of Corporate Purpose*, ECGI Working Paper 609/2021, p. 7, available at https://ecgi.global/sites/default/files/working_papers/documents/mayerfinal_1.pdf.
62. *See also* Möslein, *supra* n. 30, at 675 et seq.
63. For an overview of the historical development, *see* Yves Blein & Daniel Fasquelle, *Rapport d'information sur la mise en application de la loi n 2014-856 du 31 juillet 2014 relative à l'économie sociale et solidaire* 9 (Assemblée nationale, 2016).
64. The information materials only refer to projects ('Projekte'); *see*, for example, https://www.phineo.org/downloads/?filename=PHINEO_Hintergrund_Methode_05.pdf.

companies.[65] The two UK certification schemes provide for similar restrictions.[66] The French *société à mission* is also now open to all types of commercial companies.[67] Finally, it is noteworthy that the public schemes are (or must be) territorially limited to companies in their respective jurisdictions, whereas private schemes are not subject to any comparable limitation. As a consequence, the B Impact Assessment can market itself as being available 'to any business in the world, regardless of its existing legal structure or location of incorporation'.[68] In this respect, the relation to corporate governance is relatively loose. If certification schemes focus on business corporations, however, their scope of application overlaps with that of corporate governance.

Finally, the financial constitution also ranks among the criteria that are frequently queried in the certification process. Many certification schemes contain limitations on dividends to shareholders and investors, or restrictions on the distribution of residual assets in the event of a company's dissolution.[69] The idea is that it should be possible for social enterprises to use a substantial part of their profits or assets for the promotion of respective social purposes. Only the PHINEO scheme does without a corresponding requirement, but it focuses on non-profit enterprises anyway.[70] In other schemes, the requirements vary between 50% and 66%; the US Benefit Impact Assessment scheme is much more flexible and only requires a reserve of 20% of annual profits or 2% of turnover.[71] Such requirements reflect a fundamentally different model of corporate governance in which profit incentives of shareholders are gradually less relevant, much like in non-profit companies.[72] However, strict restrictions seem justified if respective companies enjoy special advantages such as subsidies or tax benefits. However, they make certification potentially unattractive for traditional business enterprises, and they also make it more difficult for certified enterprises to raise equity capital on financial markets.[73]

---

65. *See* Honeyman, *supra* n. 20, at 175.
66. They require, in each case, that more than half of the income must come from trading activities; cf. Möslein, *supra* n. 30, at 675, with further references.
67. Stanislas Guerini, *in* Rapport Roland Lescure et al., n. 1237, *Assemblée Nationale, Enregistré* à la Présidence de l'Assemblée nationale le 15 septembre 2018, Tome II, p. 127 ('[C]e statut se cumulera avec les statuts existants: société anonyme à mission; société par actions simplifiée (SAS) à mission; société à responsabilité limitée (SARL) à mission; entreprise unipersonnelle à responsabilité limitée (URL) à mission.').
68. Honeyman, *supra* n. 20, at 5. On the territorial limitation of public schemes, cf. also Möslein, *supra* n. 30, at 675, with further references.
69. In detail Möslein, *supra* n. 30, 677.
70. For the comparatively generous requirements (sources and use of funds traceable, and long-term stability of the organization), *see* https://www.phineo.org/downloads/?filename=PHINEO_Hintergrund_Methode_05.pdf, p. 2 et seq.
71. Honeyman, *supra* n. 20, at 139.
72. This conceptual difference is also evident, for example, in the design of specific legal forms for sustainable enterprises; *see* Jacques Defourny & Marthe Nyssens, *Conceptions of Social Enterprise and Social Entrepreneurship in Europe and the United States: Convergences and Divergences*, 1 J. Soc. Entrepreneurship 32 (2010); *see also*, Möslein & Mittwoch, *supra* n. 12, at 426–431.
73. *See also*, Elodie Thirion, *Statute for Social and Solidarity-Based Enterprises – European Added Value Assessment* 26 (2017); available at: http://www.europarl.europa.eu/RegData/etudes/STUD/2017/611030/EPRS_STU%282017%29611030_EN.pdf.

[D] Legal Consequences

Companies that have successfully completed the respective certification procedure are exclusively allowed to use certain symbols and designations in business transactions in order to express their sustainability or social orientation as clearly as possible. However, this exclusivity of use of the respective labels can be protected in various ways that fundamentally differ from a legal perspective. As opposed to the procedural design and the substantive certification requirements, a categorial difference can be observed between public and private certification schemes in this respect. While public certification schemes can provide the respective protection by legal provisions,[74] private schemes need to base it on private autonomy. In the case of private schemes, two different variants can be found. In some cases, protection is established by means of copyright law, so that the symbols and designations used to represent certification in the outside world are registered accordingly. This approach is followed, in particular, by certification schemes, such as B Corp and the UK Social Enterprise Mark.[75] Other schemes are not protected by trademark law (as in the case of PHINEO and Social Enterprise UK) but rely instead on unfair competition law, in particular on the prohibition of misleading advertising.[76]

In addition to these rights to use the respective label, further legal consequences can be attached to certification. In some public schemes, for example, certified enterprises receive state support, for example, in the form of subsidies, tax benefits, or advantages in public procurement procedures.[77] A prime example is the South Korean scheme, but in view of the high-insolvency rates, doubts have arisen over whether long-term competitiveness is actually increased by such financial support.[78] In private certification schemes, however, comparable privileges are not entirely excluded. English public procurement law, for example, is thought to attribute certain advantages to (private) certification. However, this link is not explicit but formulated in general terms, so that certification merely has an indicative effect.[79] The European Social

74. Cf. Art. 19 (restriction of use) and Art. 21, para. 1, n. 2 (sanctioning), of Social Enterprise Promotion Act, *supra* n. 31; and Art. 1, para. 3, of Loi n. 2014-856 du 31 juillet 2014 (*supra* n. 32).
75. Cf. the respective agreements, which are available at https://www.bcorporation.net and https://www.socialenterprisemark.org.uk/wp-content/uploads/2021/06/Licence-Terms-and-Conditions_June-2021.pdf. In the case of B Lab, additional brand guidelines apply; cf. the so-called *Global Brand Book*; available at: https://www.bcorporation.net/en-us/resources.
76. For a more general account of the protection of corporate social responsibility statements under competition law, *see* the contributions in *Corporate Social Responsibility – Binding Standards of Competition Law?* (Reto Hilty & Frauke Henning-Bodewig eds., 2014).
77. On those benefits in South Korea, cf. Bidet and Eum, *supra* n. 29, at 78. For France, *see* the *Communication* from the Conseil National des Chambres Régionales de l'Économie Sociale et Solidaire; available at: http://www.cncres.org/upload/iedit/12/529_2008_CNCRESS_Note_Societes_commerciales_de_lESS_2016.pdf, at p. 3.
78. According to a 2014 study, 58.6% of the certified enterprises either went bankrupt, were transformed into normal enterprises or cut jobs after the public subsidies ended; cf. Insun Kim, *Institutional Development of Social Economy: A Case of Korea's Social Enterprise Promotion Act*, Science of Science and Management of Science and Technology 38, at 43 (2016).
79. Art. 1(3) of the Public Services (Social Value) Act 2011 provides that procurement decisions should 'consider (a) how what is proposed to be procured might improve the economic, social and environmental well-being of the relevant area, and (b) how, in conducting the process of

Entrepreneurship Fund and the European Commission's Social Entrepreneurship Initiative operate in a similar way.[80] In these cases, certification serves as an indicative approximation criterion for funding measures, not as a necessary prerequisite. Overall, the linkage with state-support measures therefore appears to be significantly less robust than in the case of public certification schemes. Nonetheless, despite all differences between private and public schemes, both are able to set incentives for companies to opt into certification. However, certification can also have negative effects, in particular, where companies do not comply with their respective promises or where certification is based on false statements. Similar to product certification, such circumstances can give rise to liability issues.[81] If creditors and shareholders base their investment decisions on their trust in the certificate, for example, the question will arise whether directors or the company can be held liable for wrongful certification.[82] While courts did not yet have opportunities to clarify the difficult legal problems that relate to liability for wrongful certification of companies, at least in Germany, it is obvious that liability sanctions can serve as (negative) incentives for companies and their directors to comply with the substantive certification criteria. As a consequence, such legal consequences are likely to ensure compliance also with the corporate governance criteria that form part of certification schemes.

[E] Towards Hybrid Schemes?

The differences between private and public certification schemes are smaller than might be assumed given their fundamental institutional differences. Public schemes have some advantages, though. In particular, they are usually considered to safeguard an impartial assessment. At least, their implementation is carried out by public authorities (which usually charge low administrative fees), and such schemes do not depend on respective funding. In addition, rule-makers that are democratically legitimized are in a good position to define certification criteria and thus to credibly determine the respective steering effects. Last but not least, the public character of certification schemes makes it easier to justify linkages to related state-support measures.

---

procurement, it might act with a view to securing that improvement'. *See*, for example, Jo Barraket, Robyn Leigh Keast, & Craig W. Furneaux, *Social Procurement and New Public Governance* 115 (Routledge 2016): 'The Social Enterprise Mark makes it easy for commissioners and procurement managers to identify when social value is being delivered.'

80. *See* Regulation (EU) No. 346/2013 of the European Parliament and of the Council of 17 April 2013 on European Social Entrepreneurship Funds, OJ EU 2013 L 115/18, and Communication from the European Commission to the European Parliament the Council, European Economic and Social Committee ant the Committee of the Regions Social Business Initiative: Creating an 'ecosystem' to promote social enterprises as key actors in the social economy and social innovation, COM(2011) 682 final of 25 October 2011.
81. For an extensive discussion on the basis of German law, *see* Florian Möslein, *Privatrechtsfragen eines hybriden Zertifizierungsregimes*, in *Zertifizierung nachhaltiger Kapitalgesellschaften* 411–428 (Martin Burgi & Florian Möslein eds., Mohr Siebeck 2021).
82. Möslein, *supra* n. 81, at 425.

Private certification schemes, however, are prone to dangers of 'greenwashing' due to their financing through certification fees. But given their embeddedness in the private sector, they are usually in a better position than state authorities when it comes to mapping and dynamically developing sector-, company- and market-specific certification criteria. In addition, they can provide impulses to overcome the traditional distinction between for-profit and non-profit legal forms, which is reflected in the typologies of state company law. In the US, 'Certified B Corporations' used to serve as a decisive driving force for the widespread introduction of new, hybrid corporate forms.[83]

Against the backdrop of these respective advantages, the challenge lies in combining private and public elements in order to design certification schemes in such a way that the benefits of both worlds can be achieved. In some certification schemes, there are already certain hybrid approaches that mix public and private elements. One example is Social Enterprise UK, the certification criteria of which are based on public government guidelines. Similarly, a legal framework for private certification was recently created in the USA. The state of Delaware introduced sustainability certification frameworks that, while not mandating certification or specific certification schemes, nonetheless require Delaware-registered companies seeking certification to formally adopt mandatory certification and to assess and monitor it at the highest corporate level.[84]

§14.04 INTERACTIONS WITH OTHER SUSTAINABILITY-RELATED REGULATORY INSTRUMENTS

In addition, certification schemes interact with the institutional framework of existing measures which do not themselves operate with the certification of companies but which equally serve to promote sustainable and social businesses and which also have corporate governance implications. Among the extremely diverse and multi-faceted measures that serve such regulatory goals, three instruments stand out from a company-law perspective because their relationships and references to the certification of sustainable companies appear particularly intense: (1) the introduction of new, sustainability-oriented corporate forms; (2) disclosure of non-financial corporate information; and (3) certification of sustainable (financial) products.

[A] Hybrid Legal Forms

In addition to certification, the development and indeed the innovation of new legal forms is another current trend in corporate law.[85] Some of these new forms

83. For more details, *see* §14.03[A] *supra*.
84. Cf. Certification of Adoption of Sustainability and Transparency Standards Act, House Bill No. 310; available at: http://legis.delaware.gov/json/BillDetail/GenerateHtmlDocument?legislationId=26304&legislationTypeId=1&docTypeId=2&legislationName=HB310.
85. On the general advantages of these regulatory innovations, cf. Joseph A. McCahery, Erik P.M. Vermeulen, Masato Hisatake, & Jun Saito, *The New Company Law – What Matters in an*

complement private certification schemes, but remarkably, they are also promoted by them. In the US, for example, Certified B Corporations have significantly contributed to the triumph of a new legal form of company. There are now so-called Benefit Corporations in almost all US-American states.[86] The certification and the legal form are closely linked because companies that are certified as Certified B Corporations need to enter into a contractual obligation to either transform into the legal form of benefit corporations or promote legislative introduction into their own company law jurisdiction if such a legal form is not yet available in that jurisdiction.[87] Moreover, most regulations that provide for such a legal form are each based on the blueprint of a model law,[88] drafted by numerous practitioners under the B Lab initiative.[89] In addition to the benefit corporation, various other similar hybrid legal forms have emerged in the US. Among these are the so-called L3C (low-profit limited liability company), as a smaller, closed corporate form,[90] as well as the so-called FPC (flexible purpose corporation) or SPC (social purpose corporation), which, like benefit corporations, are based on the legal form of a joint-stock company, but which are more flexible due to the lack of a public benefit purpose and which are also subject to less-stringent disclosure obligations.[91] Over the last fifteen years, numerous European countries have also introduced new legal forms that are intended to promote social entrepreneurship and sustainable corporate activity. Benefit corporations can now be found in Italy; the UK

Innovative Economy? in *Private Company Law Reform* 71 (Joseph A. McCahery, Levinus Timmermann, & Erik P.M. Vermeulen eds., Asser Press 2010).

86. For an overview of the applicable legislation and its entry into force, *see* Christopher Geczy, Jessica S. Jeffers, David K. Musto, & Anne M. Tucker, *Institutional Investing When Shareholders Are Not Supreme*, 5 Harv. Bus. L. Rev. 73, 138 et seq.: Appendix D (2015); *see also*, the 'Social Enterprise Law Tracker' that is hosted and maintained by the Grunin Center for Law and Social Entrepreneurship at NYU School of Law; available at: https://socentlawtracker.org/#/map. Benefit corporations are conceived as a legal form in their own right, not as a special form of the corporation; nevertheless, the general rules of corporate law apply on a subsidiary basis; *see* Brakman Reiser, *supra* n. 12, at 595 et seq.; Kyle Westaway & Dirk Sampselle, *The Benefit Corporation: An Economic Analysis with Recommendations to Courts, Boards, and Legislatures*, 62 Emory Law J. 999, 1033 et seq. (2013) (also on the disadvantages of this regulatory technique).
87. In detail Möslein & Mittwoch, *supra* n. 12, at 410 f. (qualifying the mechanism as a collusive legal form constraint).
88. B Lab used to recommend (on its website) use of the Model Law as the 'basis of any new legislation'; cf. Möslein, *supra* n. 8, at 20, n. 79.
89. Model Benefit Corporation Legislation, 17 April 2017 version, reprinted as Appendix A in: Frederick Alexander, *Benefit Corporation Law and Governance* (Berrett-Koehler Publishers 2017).
90. This legal form has so far been introduced in about ten US states; for more details on the debate, *see* especially J. William Callison & Allan Vestal, *The L3C Illusion: Why Low-Profit Limited Liability Companies Will Not Stimulate Socially Optimal Private Foundation Investment in Entrepreneurial Ventures*, 35 Vermont L. Rev. 273 (2010); Carter G. Bishop, *The Low-Profit LLC (L3C): Program-Related Investment by Proxy or Perversion*, 63 Arkansas L. Rev. 243 (2010); Daniel S. Kleinberger, *A Myth Deconstructed: The 'Emperor's New Clothes' on the Low-Profit Limited Liability Company*, 35 Del. J. Corp. Law 879 (2010).
91. *See* Dana Brakman Reiser, *The Next Big Thing: Flexible Purpose Corporations*, 2 Am. U. Bus. L. Rev. 55 (2012); Christen Clarke, *California's Flexible Purpose Corporation: A Step Forward, a Step Back, or No Step at All?* 5 J. Bus. Entrepreneurship & L., Iss. 301 (2012). California, which was originally the only state to adopt the FPC, later changed its designation to SPC; this has been the designation (from the outset) in the states of Florida, Texas, and Washington.

has introduced the community interest company, which is comparable in many respects; and the social cooperatives that have been introduced in France and Italy, among others, serve very similar purposes.[92]

A common characteristic of all these new forms of companies is that, in contrast to the traditional dichotomy of (purely) profit-oriented and (purely) non-profit forms of organization, they enable new, overarching categories of hybrid companies. Similar to certification, common good orientation and profit-making are no longer considered to be mutually incompatible but rather alternatives to be reconciled by lawmakers.[93] The new corporate forms are aptly referred to as 'profit and purpose' companies.[94] In the US, the hybrid character finds its legal expression above all in the fact that benefit corporations are supposed to act in the public interest even when making profits, i.e., in their actual business activities, but conversely are not limited in their distribution of profits. This approach is diametrically different from the understanding of the common good that used to prevail in Europe and also from most recent European approaches to company law reform.[95]

Under most European company laws, company directors of public limited companies are not primarily obliged to pursue shareholder value but are allowed (though to different extents) to serve the broader interests of their company. They therefore enjoy greater discretion to also take stakeholder interests into account in their business decisions.[96] Moreover, profit-oriented and public interest-oriented forms of companies are often combined in corporate groups that can themselves be qualified as hybrid forms of organization.[97] Conversely, however, specific legal forms can help to anchor the hybrid character not only at board level but also in the corporate constitution itself, so that this character develops into a much stronger guiding principle for the respective company. Legal forms also have important signalling effects, similar to certification. While these are reasons to argue that the legal innovation of benefit

92. *See* Social Impact Investment Taskforce, Impact Investment: The Invisible Heart of Markets: Final Report 39 (Italy) and 41 et seq. (France) (2014); available at: http://www.socialimpactinvestment.org/reports/Impact%20Investment%20Report%20FINAL%5B3%5D.pdf; Sorensen & Neville, *supra* n. 12, at 277 (UK) and 279 f. (Denmark); Jacques Defourny & Marthe Nyssens, *Social Enterprise in Europe; Recent Trends and Developments*, 4 Journal of Social Entrepreneurship 202, at 206 (2008) (Belgium); for a broader comparative law overview, *see* Antonio Fici, *A European Statute for Social and Solidarity-Based Enterprises – Study for the JURY Committee* 17–20 (2017); available at: http://www.europarl.europa.eu/RegData/etudes/STUD/2017/583123/IPOL_STU(2017)583123_EN.pdf.

93. Cf. Möslein & Mittwoch, *supra* n. 12, at 404–406.

94. *See* especially Kyle Westaway, *Profit & Purpose: How Social Innovation Is Transforming Business for Good* (Wiley 2014).

95. Similarly, and also in comparison with more recent hybrid legal forms in English and Danish company law: Sorensen & Neville, *supra* n. 12, at 298 (a 'radically different approach').

96. For an overview and discussion of the historical development, *see* Sabrina Bruno, *Directors' Versus Shareholders' Primacy in U.S. Corporations Through the Eyes of History: Is Directors' Power 'Inherent'?* ECFR 421 (2012), with further references.

97. *See*, for example, with respect to German law: Lars Leuschner, *Das Konzernrecht des Vereins* (Mohr Siebeck 2011). On the spin-off of economic activities to independent subsidiaries, cf. also the so-called ADAC ruling of the German Federal Court: BGHZ 85, 84 Neue Juristische Wochenschrift (NJW) 569 (1983). However, the need for such constructs has decreased considerably since its so-called Kita decision; *see* BGHZ 215, 69 Neue Juristische Wochenschrift (NJW) 1943 (2017).

corporations can be a useful addition to the existing corporate forms in Europe, they do not imply that its introduction forms a necessary prerequisite for the effective operation of certification schemes. As long as existing company laws give company directors sufficient discretion and contractual freedom to enable companies to comply with the substantive requirements of certification schemes, the latter will not depend on the existence of hybrid legal forms. In fact, in some countries where attempts to introduce benefit corporation legislation have turned out to be unsuccessful, the number of B Corps has nonetheless managed to increase.[98] If successfully implemented, however, hybrid legal forms have obvious corporate governance implications. In fact, their requirements are typically more rigid and also more robust than the corporate governance requirements of certification schemes, not least because respective impact assessments typically do not demand all substantive criteria to be fulfilled. In the case of B Corp, for example, they are satisfied with an overall score of 80 out of 200 points. In comparison with legal forms, the corporate governance requirements of certification schemes are therefore of a relatively flexible nature.

[B] Non-financial Reporting

Moreover, there exist functional links between certification of sustainable corporations and disclosure of non-financial corporate information. Both regulatory instruments serve to reduce information asymmetries and, moreover, contain similar sustainability-related information. At the same time, disclosure provides and guarantees some of the information that serves as the basis for certification, so that both instruments are closely intertwined in operational terms. In contrast to certification, however, disclosure does not condense the information in question into a concise certificate. Its signal effect may therefore be lower; conversely, its message is not merely binary and therefore more nuanced. In addition, non-financial disclosure is generally less focussed on corporate governance conditions but aims at specific ESG (environmental, social, and governance) factors.

At European level, the CSR (corporate social responsibility) directive obliges large companies of public interest to report on environmental, social, and organizational aspects of their activities.[99] Its German transposition, for example, stipulates an obligation to go beyond a brief description of the business model of the respective company, and to at least address the concerns of the environment and employees,

---

98. With regard to Australia, for example, *see* Ian Ramsay & Mihika Upadhyaya, *The Failed Attempt to Enact Benefit Company Legislation in Australia and the Rise of B Corps* in *The International Handbook of Social Enterprises Law* (Henry Peter, Carlos Vargas Vasserot & Jaime Alcalde Silva eds., forthcoming Springer 2022); working paper available at: https://papers.ssrn.com/sol3/papers.cfm?abstract_id=3795039. Cf. also Guido Ferrarini & Shanshan Zhu, *Is There a Role for Benefit Corporations in the New Sustainable Governance Framework?* in *Festschrift in honour of Rolf Skog* (Ronald J. Gilson, Mats Isaksson, Erik Lidman, Johan Munck & Erik Sjöman eds., Norstedts Juridik 2021); working paper available at: https://papers.ssrn.com/sol3/papers.cfm?abstract_id=3869696.
99. Directive 2014/95/EU of the European Parliament and of the Council of 22 October 2014 amending Directive 2013/34/EU as regards disclosure of non-financial and diversity information by certain large companies and groups, OJ L 330/1, 15.11.2014.

social aspects, respect for human rights, and the fight against corruption by the company.[100] The comparability of this information, however, depends on European provisions for procedural implementation of the substantive requirements of the directive. Without a EU-wide standard for preparation and presentation of information, the lack of comparability risks being detrimental to the desired signal effects.[101] The Commission has therefore published two different guidelines for non-financial reporting in accordance with Article 2 of the CSR directive for the guidance of companies,[102] but these recommendations are non-binding and therefore do not seem suitable for bringing about the necessary harmonization effects. In its recent proposal for a corporate sustainability reporting directive (CSRD), [103] however, the Commission proposes to amend the existing reporting requirements, in particular, by requiring an audit of reported information and by introducing more detailed reporting requirements. More specifically, the proposal stipulates a requirement to report according to mandatory EU sustainability reporting standards to be developed by the European Financial Reporting Advisory Group (EFRAG). According to the Commission, these standards will be tailored to EU policies, while building on and contributing to international standardization initiatives. An initial set of standards has been announced, to be adopted by October 2022.[104] While the focus of these current reform proposals is clearly on improving the method and procedure of reporting, the Commission should also consider what role the certification of sustainable corporations can possibly play in interaction with sustainability reporting. After all, it is precisely this certification that is best suited to concisely 'get to the nub' of sustainability information. At the same time, it is fair to say that the corporate governance effects of disclosure are likely to be less intensive than those of certification. This is due both to the substantive focus of disclosure and to its more detailed and complex format.

[C] Certification of (Financial) Products

While certification of sustainable companies is largely new territory in Europe, various other forms of certification have been tested in other regulatory areas for quite some

100. As opposed to the Action Plan for Financing Sustainable Growth, the CSR directive thus emphasizes not only the ecological dimension of sustainability but also its social objective; in more detail, *see* Florian Möslein & Anne Mittwoch, *Der Europäische Aktionsplan zur Finanzierung nachhaltigen Wachstums*, Wertpapier-Mitteilungen (WM) 481 (2019).
101. In this sense, for example, *see* Birgit Spießhofer, *Die neue europäische Richtlinie über Offenlegung nichtfinanzieller Informationen – Paradigmenwechsel oder Papiertiger?* Neue Zeitschrift für Gesellschaftsrecht (NZG) 1281, at 1285 (2014).
102. European Commission, Guidelines on reporting non-financial information, OJ C 215/1, 5.7.2017; and European Commission, Guidelines on non-financial reporting: Supplement on reporting climate-related information, OJ C 209/1, 20.6.2019.
103. Commission *Proposal for a directive of the European Parliament and of the Council amending Directive 2013/34/EU, Directive 2004/109/EC, Directive 2006/43/EC and Regulation (EU) No 537/2014, as regards corporate sustainability reporting*, COM(2021) 189 final of 21 April 2021.
104. More information about the preparatory work is available at https://www.efrag.org/Lab2.

time, for example, in product safety law and also in environmental law.[105] As with the certification of sustainable companies, these certification schemes are also focused on quality control, more precisely at the verification and disclosure of otherwise hidden (product) characteristics. However, there is a fundamental difference with regard to the object of certification, which, in these other schemes, concerns products and services, not intangible legal products such as companies. In this respect, there is greater similarity with the certification of sustainable financial products, which the Commission has recently proposed in its 'Action Plan for Financing Sustainable Growth'.[106] With the much-debated taxonomy, the action plan aims to provide a uniform classification scheme, intended to give the concept of sustainability more-precise contours. But the action plan also aims to introduce labelling schemes for environmentally friendly financial products.[107] The point of reference, however, is financial products and (specific) corporate activities, not the corporate entity as a whole. As a consequence, corporate governance aspects play a relatively limited role in that type of certification.

Overall, a decisive advantage of the regulatory approach of certification and labelling is that it deliberately refrains from banning products that do not meet certain pre-defined criteria. Certification, it is therefore said, is a particularly market-based control mechanism: instead of direct state intervention, it only creates an incentive to rely on certain quality criteria.[108] Which actor carries out the quality control is also extremely variable in these other, product-oriented certification schemes. Certification is often understood as a non-governmental instrument because, especially at the global level, powerful certification schemes are of a private nature, for example, in the environmental and forestry sectors.[109] At the European level, however, accreditation of products is sovereignly defined by a framework regulation,[110] and the accreditation

105. On these areas in detail: Hans Christian Röhl, *Akkreditierung und Zertifizierung im Produktsicherheitsrecht* (Springer 2000); Christoph Leifer, *Das europäische Umweltmanagementsystem EMAS als Element gesellschaftlicher Selbstregulierung* 143–184 (Mohr Siebeck 2007).

106. Communication from the European Commission to the European Parliament, the European Council, the European Central Bank, European Economic and Social Committee and the Committee of the Regions Action Plan: Financing Sustainable Growth, COM(2018) 97 final of 8 March 2018; *see also*, Commission *Proposal for a Regulation of the European Parliament and of the Council on the establishment of a framework to facilitate sustainable investment*, COM(2018) 353 final of 24 May 2018.

107. In detail, *see* Möslein & Mittwoch, *supra* n. 12.

108. Sonja Mühlenbruch & Benedikt Buchner, *Kosten und Nutzen der (Nicht-)Prävention durch Recht - Prävention durch Recht (legal opinion commissioned by the Bertelsmann Foundation)* 41 (2007); available at: http://www.igmr.uni-bremen.de/deutsch/projekte/praevention.pdf.

109. Stéphane Guéneau, *Certification as a New Private Global Forest Governance System: The Regulatory Potential of the Forest Stewardship Council*, in *Non-State Actors as Standard-Setters* 379 (Anne Peters, Lucy Koechlin, Till Förster, & Gretta Fenner Zinkernagel eds., Cambridge University Press 2009); Joyeeta Gupta, *The Role of Non-State Actors in International Environmental Affairs* 63 Zeitschrift für ausländisches öffentliches Recht und Völkerrecht (ZaöRV) 459, at 470 et seq. (2003); cf. also the monograph by Lars H. Gulbrandsen, *Transnational Environmental Governance – The Emergence and Effects of the Certification of Forests and Fisheries* (Edward Elgar 2010).

110. Regulation (EC) No. 765/2008 of the European Parliament and of the Council of 9 July 2008 setting out the requirements for accreditation and market surveillance relating to the marketing

bodies themselves do not necessarily have to be state authorities.[111] Moreover, there are decidedly public schemes at European level, such as the organic seal in the food sector, the conditions and control of which are defined in the EC Regulation on Organic Agriculture. The actual control, however, can again be carried out by private, state-approved control bodies.[112] In general, state and private actors work together in many certification schemes, often in very different roles.[113] Certification is therefore increasingly seen as 'supranationally regulated self-regulation'.[114] Even if certification is not characterized by its governmental or private nature, the trustworthiness of quality labels depends on the institutional design. Consumers must be able to rely on the fact that the certification criteria are set and controlled by a reputable and independent body.[115]

§14.05 RELATIONSHIP WITH CORPORATE GOVERNANCE (CODES)

In addition to its interplay with these other, specifically sustainability-related regulatory instruments, the certification of companies is also likely to interact with the broader framework of corporate governance. While both certification and corporate governance codes can be seen as alternative regulatory instruments, but their respective impact on the corporate governance of companies can also overlap or even contradict. It has already become clear that most certification schemes provide for certain governance arrangements, such as the *comité à mission* that the French scheme requires in order to control whether the company follows its social and ecological goals.[116] In general, the term corporate governance refers to the way in which companies are directed and controlled. According to the definition in the G20/Organisation for Economic Co-operation Development (OECD) Principles of Corporate Governance, it 'involves a set of relationships between a company's management, its board, its shareholders and other stakeholders'.[117] By identifying the attribution of decision-making power and accountability, corporate governance also

---

of products and repealing Council Regulation (EEC) No. 339793, OJ No. L 218, 13.08.2008, p. 30; in more detail, *see* Hanna Schebesta, *Control in the Label: Self-Declared, Certified, Accredited?* in *Certification – Trust, Accountability, Liability* 143, 147 (Peter Rott ed., 2019).

111. Cf. recital 11 and Art. 8 of the Regulation.
112. Council Regulation (EC) No. 834/2007 of 28 June 2007 on organic production and labelling of organic products and repealing Regulation (EEC) No. 2092/91, OJ No. L 189, p. 1. 1; in detail, *see* Alberto Alemanno, *Regulating Organic Farming in the European Union – Balancing Consumer Preferences and Free Movement Imperatives,* 1 European Consumer Law Journal 87, 103–106 (2009).
113. In this sense, *see* Hermann Pünder, *Zertifizierung und Akkreditierung – private Qualitätskontrolle unter staatlicher Gewährleistungsverantwortung,* 170 Zeitschrift für das gesamte Handels- und Wirtschaftsrecht (ZHR) 567, 593–596 (2006).
114. Georgios Dimitropoulos, *Zertifizierung und Akkreditierung im Internationalen Verwaltungsverbund* 128 (Mohr Siebeck 2012).
115. Möslein, *supra* n. 5, at 485 et seq.
116. Cf. references *supra* n. 67.
117. G20/OECD, Principles of Corporate Governance 9 (2015); available at: https://www.oecd.org/corporate/principles-corporate-governance/.

serves as a 'toolkit that enables management and the board to deal more effectively with the challenges of running a company'.[118]

More specifically, the framework of corporate governance is described and, to some extent, also defined in corporate governance codes. This regulatory instrument is of relatively recent origins. Its history started with various scandals in the UK, which led to appointment of the Cadbury Committee.[119] This committee elaborated the Cadbury Report, which urged that contemporary best practices be promulgated among listed companies. Its recommendations led not only to the UK Combined Code but also to adoption of the OECD Principles of Corporate Governance and to the widespread emergence of corporate governance codes in company law jurisdictions all around the globe.[120] As with certification schemes, however, these codes vary substantially from a regulatory perspective, with different procedures of elaboration, different substantive approaches, and also different modes of enforcement. Several studies have identified different regulatory modes of corporate governance codes, ranging from genuine self-regulation to pure regulation, including various degrees of statutory and non-statutory support in between.[121] These regulatory variations in corporate governance codes and certification schemes turn any abstract analysis of interactions between both into a calculation with many unknowns, although some general observations can be made.

[A] Similarities in Substantive Contents

To begin with, the substantive content of corporate governance codes and certification schemes has significant overlaps. As has already been described earlier, certain corporate governance requirements form crucial elements of certification schemes' substantive criteria.[122] These requirements not only serve as control mechanisms for tracking social and ecological goals but also enable the participation of certain stakeholders, in particular employees. Also, other, non-sustainability oriented schemes such as ISO 9001 compliance certificates build on governance-related criteria, namely with regard to management systems. However, the establishment of corporate bodies with control rights and the appointment of certain members of the board are also integral elements of the corporate governance framework. Such requirements have an

---

118. Chartered Governance Institute (ICSA), What is Corporate Governance?; available at: https://www.cgi.org.uk/about-us/policy/what-is-corporate-governance.

119. *See* Brian Cheffins, *The History of Corporate Governance*, in *The Oxford Handbook of Corporate Governance* 46, 57 (Douglas M. Wright, Donald S. Siegel, Kevin Keasey, & Igor Filatotchev eds., Oxford University Press 2013).

120. For a more extensive account, *see* Florian Möslein, *Genuine Self-Regulation in Germany: Drawing the Line*, in *Self-Regulation in Private Law in Japan and Germany* 83, at 100 et seq. (Harald Baum, Moritz Bälz, & Marc Dernauer eds., 2018).

121. Annika Galle, *'Comply or Explain' in Belgium, Germany, Italy, the Netherlands and the UK: Insufficient Explanations and an Empirical Analysis*, 12 Corporate Ownership & Control 862 (2014); Alain Pietrancosta, *Enforcement of Corporate Governance Codes – A Legal Perspective*, in *Festschrift für Klaus J. Hopt 1109* (Stefan Grundmann et al. eds., de Gruyter 2010); Eddy Wymeersch, *The Enforcement of Corporate Governance Codes*, 6 J. Corp. L. Stud. 113 (2006).

122. Cf. *supra* at n. 15 et seq.

obvious impact on the way in which companies are directed and controlled, and they also affect the relationships between a company's management, its board, its shareholders, and other stakeholders. This substantive overlap is not surprising, though. On the contrary, it is commonly assumed that governance structures, with their incentive effects, have an important impact on the behaviour of companies. In fact, the abbreviation ESG already indicates the close relationship between sustainability issues and the corporate governance framework.[123]

Vice versa, corporate governance codes also increasingly take sustainability considerations into account. For instance, such considerations form a crucial element of the current reform of the German Corporate Governance Code. Once it has been promulgated by the Federal Ministry of Justice, the 2022 version will (in its preamble) stress that in addition to long-term economic goals, the corporate strategy should also take appropriate account of ecological and social goals.[124] The rationale is that in the long term, economic, environmental, and social goals are often mutually dependent. According to the reasoning of the Code Committee, ecological and social sustainability is just as much a prerequisite for long-term value enhancement as economic strength and stability are prerequisites for investments and other measures serving ecological and social goals.[125] Even before the current reform, sustainability considerations received considerable (though less emphatic) attention in the German Corporate Governance Code.[126] In a similar vein, section 87, paragraph 1, of the German Stock Corporation Act provides that remuneration structures have to be oriented towards the promotion of long-term and sustainable development of companies.[127] While this double-sided similarity between governance codes and certification schemes can be explained in both directions, it is by no means frictionless. Even if there are similarities in substance, specific divergences and contradictions are conceivable and even likely. They will arise whenever governance codes and certification schemes formulate different criteria, for instance, with respect to employee participation at board level. As both sets of requirements are formulated by different institutions with different objectives and different members, deviations are almost inevitable; all the more so in view of the institutional varieties of both governance codes and certification schemes.

123. For a comparison of ESG scores and the B Impact Assessment, cf. Katarzyna Bachnik & Justyna Szumniak-Samolej, *Impact: Meaning, Scope, and Measurement Methods*, in *Corporate Social Responsibility and Sustainability* 26, 33–35 (Katarzyna Bachnik et al. eds., Routledge 2022); for a broad overview, *see also*, Peter Yeoh, *Environmental, Social and Governance (ESG) Laws, Regulations and Practices in the Digital Era* (Kluwer Law International 2022).
124. In detail, *see* Birgit Spießhofer, *Sustainable Corporate Governance*, Neue Zeitschrift für Gesellschaftsrecht (NZG) 435 (2022); Jakob Timmel, *Der Entwurf zum DCGK 2022 – Nachhaltigkeit im Fokus*, Zeitschrift für Rechtspolitik (ZRP) 70 (2022).
125. Cf. the foreword of the current reform proposal; available at: https://www.dcgk.de/en/consultations/current-consultations.html ('Social and environmental factors influence the performance of the company, and its activities have an impact on people and the environment. The Management Board and the Supervisory Board take this into account when managing and supervising the enterprise.').
126. Gregor Bachmann, *Commentary on G23, para. 50*, in *Deutscher Corporate Governance Kodex* (Thomas Kremer, Gregor Bachmann, Marcus Lutter, & Axel von Werder eds., 8th edition, C.H. Beck 2021).
127. *Ibid.*, para. 51.

[B] Parallelisms of Regulatory Mechanisms

At the same time, governance codes and certification schemes operate on the basis of similar regulatory mechanisms. First, both instruments are elaborated by rule-makers that cannot be clearly assigned to either the public or private sphere. The German Corporate Governance Committee, for example, consists exclusively of private actors, but the rule-making procedure is initiated by the state.[128] Moreover, the provisions of the Code become valid with their publication in the official section of the Federal Gazette: published as if they were laws.[129] Second, the substance of both governance codes and certification schemes consists of a mixture of replicated (and sometimes modified) legal requirements and extra-legal standards that reflect certain market expectations. Even for those seemingly genuinely self-regulated sets of rules, however, the 'shadow of the legislator'[130] and interactions with (future) legal rules play an important role, albeit in an indirect and informal manner. Third and most important, both governance codes and certification schemes refrain from formulating mandatory rules but allow for deviations. Instead, their mode of regulation is of a more subtle nature, which builds on reputational effects. For example, the most prominent regulatory mechanism of corporate governance originates in the comply-or-explain principle, which is, in German law, for example, laid down in section 161 of the German Stock Corporations Act.[131] This principle, which is also well known in many other jurisdictions, requires companies to disclose deviations from the governance code's recommendations.[132] Such deviations have to be explained in an annual declaration of conformity.[133] Much akin to the operation of certification schemes, the comply-or-explain principle thereby establishes a kind of social enforcement mechanism, which operates on the basis of reputational effects. It builds on the idea that companies that comply with the respective rules enjoy a better reputation with investors, and that this reputation will ultimately translate into higher stock market rates and better economic success.[134] A core regulatory characteristic of both certification schemes and governance codes is their function as an instrument of conformity

128. In more detail, *see* Möslein, *supra* n. 120, at 102 et seq.
129. Cf. its rules of procedure: Geschäftsordnung der Regierungskommission Deutscher Corporate Governance Kodex, p. 4 (sub. 3.4.); available at: https://www.dcgk.de/de/kommission.html.
130. Similarly, this can be seen in the wording of its title: Marc Moore, *Corporate Governance in the Shadow of the State* (Bloomsbury Publishing 2013).
131. For detailed accounts, *see*, for example, Marcus Lutter, *Die Erklärung zum Corporate Governance Kodex gemäß § 161 AktG*, 166 Zeitschrift für das gesamte Handels- und Wirtschaftsrecht (ZHR) 523, 525 et seq. (2002); Matthias Schüppen, *To Comply or Not to Comply – That's the Question!* Zeitschrift für Wirtschaftsrecht (ZIP) 1269 (2002).
132. With regard to that principle in UK Corporate Governance, cf. Marc Moore & Martin Petrin, *Corporate Governance: Law, Regulation and Theory* 58 et seq. (Bloomsbury Publishing 2017).
133. Cf. Lutter, *supra* n. 131, 530 et seq.
134. In the corporate governance debate, it is broadly assumed, however, that the effectiveness of this mechanism depends on a broad range of circumstances; *see*, for instance, Olaf Ehrhard & Eric Nowak, *Die Durchsetzung von Corporate-Governance-Regeln*, Die Aktiengesellschaft (AG) 336 (2002). In general, on the interplay of rules and companies' reputation: Lars Klöhn & Klaus Ulrich Schmolke, *Unternehmensreputation (Corporate Reputation)*, Neue Zeitschrift für Gesellschaftsrecht (NZG) 689 (2015); cf. also the contributions in: *The Oxford Handbook of Corporate Reputation* (Michael L. Barnett & Timothy G. Pollock eds., Oxford University Press 2012).

assessment and quality control.[135] Both certification and code compliance signal conformity with a multitude of substantive criteria, which also promises a certain quality on the part of the company in question.[136] By making the fulfilment of such criteria transparent for investors and consumers, both regulatory instruments also create incentives for companies to fulfil these requirements in spite of their non-mandatory character. Both instruments are by no means only mechanisms of quality assurance, but they also constitute a mode of social regulation.[137]

[C] The Challenge of Consistency

From a regulatory perspective, the likely substantive divergences or even contradictions between the requirements of governance codes and certification schemes appear highly problematic. Legal theory stresses the general and fundamental requirement that law 'has to be consistent, that is to say, it must lack contradictions'.[138] In the German debate, for instance, this idea of consistency and coherence has been strongly emphasized ever since *Karl Engisch* stressed the unity of the legal order ('Einheit der Rechtsordnung')[139] and *Claus-Wilhelm Canaris* laid the ground for system thinking by postulating that value contradictions and systemic incoherences ('Wertungswidersprüche' and 'Systembrüche') need to be avoided at all costs.[140] The same requirements not only apply for the law itself but are also relevant for systems of norms in general. If governance codes and certification schemes point in different, contradictory directions, they are both likely to diminish their regulatory impact because the reputational mechanisms which enable these instruments to operate risk being impaired. After all, these mechanisms thrive on the conviction that the respective standards enjoy broad social recognition and mirror the preferences of the respective target group. Imagine, for example, a company that explains its non-compliance with an applicable corporate governance code by referring to the need to fulfil certain (divergent) certification requirements in order to obtain the respective certificate. Whenever such cases arise, the gain in reputation on the certification side cannot simply be offset against the loss of reputation on the governance compliance side. In

135. With regard to certification systems, *see* Karin Bieback, *Zertifizierung und Akkreditierung – Das Zusammenwirken staatlicher und nichtstaatlicher Akteure in gestuften Prüfsystemen* 199–201 (Nomos 2008), describing certification as an instrument of quality control ('Instrument der Qualitätssicherung'); similarly, *see* Pünder, *supra* n. 113, at 589–593 ('Qualitätssicherungsverfahren'); *see also*, recital No. 8 of Regulation (EC) No. 765/2008 (*supra* n. 110): accreditation as 'part of an overall system, including conformity assessment and market surveillance, designed to assess and ensure conformity with the applicable requirements'.
136. Mühlenbruch & Buchner, *supra* n. 108, at 41.
137. In this sense: Tim Bartley, *Certification as a Mode of Social Regulation*, in *Handbook on the Politics of Regulation* 441 (David Levi-Faur ed., Edward Elgar 2011).
138. Ricardo Alberto Caracciolo, *Contradictions in the Legal System*, 65 Archiv für Rechts- und Sozialphilosophie (ARSP) 457 (1979).
139. Karl Engisch, *Die Einheit der Rechtsordnung* (C. Winter 1935); for a thorough discussion of the significance of that argument, *see* Dagmar Felix, *Die Einheit der Rechtsordnung* (Mohr Siebeck 1998).
140. Claus-Wilhelm Canaris, *Systemdenken und Systembegriff in der Jurisprudenz* 112 et seq., 116 (2nd edition, Duncker & Humblot 1983).

view of such norm contradictions, the addressees of the information in question will rather be likely to question the value of the corresponding signals as such, and both regulatory instruments risk losing their ability to provide reliable quality signals and steer corporate behaviour. The requirements of consistency and coherence are, however, much more difficult to fulfil in the absence of a single, uniform lawmaker. Any plurality of standard-setters involves the risk of inconsistencies because different institutions are likely to pursue different regulatory objectives.[141] The risk of inconsistencies is likely to increase when the respective standard-setters are not embedded in a uniform regulatory framework, even more so if they are themselves very different, be it with regard to the information addressees that they focus on or with regard to the jurisdictions they are embedded in, for example. The future challenge will therefore be to find ways to reconcile the substance of certification schemes and governance codes – in spite of the plurality of respective rule-makers and of their significant variation in terms of institutional arrangements, procedural requirements, substantive conditions, and legal consequences.

§14.06 CONCLUSION

The certification of companies is closely linked to corporate governance. Most certification schemes are based on a variety of requirements that relate to corporate governance, even though to various degrees. The most obvious example not only concerns the governance constitution of the respective company itself but also requirements relating to the corporate business model of a company, to its legal form, and to its financial constitution take aspects of corporate governance into account. Given that the certification of companies often serves the regulatory goal of fostering corporate sustainability, certification schemes can also be compared with other regulatory instruments that serve similar functions. Such comparison reveals variations in the regulatory, governance-related impact of the different regulatory instruments: While the governance requirements of certification schemes are less rigid than those of hybrid legal forms, for example, they are likely to have greater impact than disclosure requirements or even the certification of financial products. Last but not least, certification schemes and corporate governance codes share similarities both with respect to their substance as well as functions. However, it is precisely due to these similarities that their regulatory relationship is delicate: They can overlap and even contradict with each other, thereby causing risks of regulatory inconsistencies. If both instruments are to achieve their regulatory (sustainability) goals, they need to be reconciled with each other. Given the variety of private and public rule-setters and regulatory approaches, such regulatory consistency is, however, difficult if not impossible to reach.

141. Cf., for instance, Möslein, *supra* n. 120, at 86–89.

PART III Enforcement and Its Effect on Governance

CHAPTER 15

Directors' Liability

Carsten Gerner-Beuerle

§15.01 INTRODUCTION

Conventional wisdom posits that shareholder litigation is a powerful corporate governance tool that allows shareholders to hold directors and managers to account if they do not act in the best interest of the shareholders. Strong shareholder enforcement rights mitigate the managerial agency problem by both deterring managerial misconduct *ex ante* and providing an avenue to recover any loss suffered by the corporation (or, depending on the cause of action, the shareholders individually) *ex post*.[1] The normative lesson is thus clear: the rights of shareholders to enforce breaches of directors' duties should be strengthened. A trend towards facilitating shareholder litigation could indeed be observed in the European Union (EU) and elsewhere over the last decades. For example, in Germany, the standing threshold to bring a derivative action was gradually reduced from 20% to 1% in 2005[2] and in Italy for listed companies to 2.5% in 2003.[3]

However, recently, the orthodox view on shareholder litigation has come under sustained attack from empirical scholarship. Most empirical studies focus on the United States (US) and here, in particular, on the staggered adoption of so-called

1. Rafael La Porta, Florencio Lopez-de-Silanes, Andrei Shleifer, and Robert Ward Vishny, *Legal Determinants of External Finance*, 52 J. Finance 1131, 1136 (1997).
2. The most recent reforms were introduced by Gesetz *zur Unternehmensintegrität und Modernisierung des Anfechtungsrechts* (UMAG), Law of 22 September 2005, Federal Law Gazette I, p. 2802, which also established a claims admission procedure and changed the cost rules (§ 148 German Stock Corporation Act).
3. Guido Ferrarini, Mario Stella Richter, and Paolo Giudici, *Company Law Reform in Italy: Real Progress?*, 69 Rabels Zeitschrift für ausländisches und internationales Privatrecht 658, 681–82 (2005).

universal demand laws by US states.[4] Several of these studies find that an increased risk of litigation is associated with efficiency *losses* and reduced information provision. For example, empirical evidence indicates that *weaker* shareholder litigation rights are associated with higher financial leverage and firm value,[5] a lower level of corporate cash reserves and increased investment in value-enhancing projects,[6] increased engagement in explorative innovation activities,[7] improved corporate takeover efficiency,[8] improvements in outside director experience and reputation,[9] and more frequent and comprehensive corporate disclosures.[10]

On the other hand, at least one study finds that weaker shareholder litigation rights are related to lower corporate social responsibility (CSR) scores (however, these are, in turn, associated with higher firm value),[11] and several studies provide evidence of further harmful consequences of creating obstacles to derivative lawsuits. These include a deterioration in information quality, increased risk-taking, and a greater risk of insider expropriation, which translate into a higher cost of capital for corporations,[12] lower stock market liquidity,[13] an increase in corporate governance arrangements that

4. An overview of the empirical literature is given by Dain C. Donelson, Laura Kettell, John McInnis, and Sara Toynbee, *The Need to Validate Exogenous Shocks: Shareholder Derivative Litigation, Universal Demand Laws and Firm Behavior*, 73 J. Account. Econ. 101427 (2022) (listing 25 papers published since 2018). Research with a broader comparative scope is rare. One of the few studies compiling a broad cross-country sample is Matteo P. Arena and Stephen P. Ferris, *A Global Analysis of Corporate Litigation Risk and Costs*, 56 Int. Rev. Law Econ. 28 (2018) (finding no evidence of a significant relation between probability of litigation and economic indicators of firm performance for a sample of companies incorporated in 16 developed economies). For a comparison of shareholder lawsuits in the US and UK, *see also* John Armour, Bernard Black, Brian Cheffins, and Richard Nolan, *Private Enforcement of Corporate Law: An Empirical Comparison of the U.K. and the U. S.*, 6 J. Empir. Leg. Stud. 687 (2009) (concluding that formal private enforcement of corporate law plays a minor role in protecting shareholders in both countries).
5. Nam H. Nguyen, Hieu V. Phan, and Eunju Lee, *Shareholder Litigation Rights and Capital Structure Decisions*, 62 J. Corp. Finance 101601 (2020).
6. Hien T. Nguyen, Hieu V. Phan, and Lingna Sun, *Shareholder Litigation Rights and Corporate Cash Holdings: Evidence from Universal Demand Laws*, 52 J. Corp. Finance 192 (2018).
7. Chen Lin, Sibo Liu, and Gustavo Manso, *Shareholder Litigation and Corporate Innovation*, 67 Management Science 3321 (2021).
8. Yongqiang Chu and Yijia Zhao, *The Dark Side of Shareholder Litigation: Evidence from Corporate Takeovers*, 50 Financial Management 845 (2021) (measuring takeover efficiency based on announcement returns for acquirers and post-merger operating performance).
9. Ronald W. Masulis, Sichen Shen, and Hong Zou, *Director Liability Protection and the Quality of Outside Directors*, ECGI Working Paper N° 672/2020, available at SSRN: http://ssrn.com/abstract_id = 3329220 (2020).
10. Audra Boone, Eliezer M. Fich, and Thomas Griffin, *Shareholder Litigation Risk and the Information Environment: Revisiting Evidence from Two Natural Experiments*, available at SSRN: https://ssrn.com/abstract = 3106086 (2022); Thomas Bourveau, Yun Lou, and Rencheng Wang, *Shareholder Litigation and Corporate Disclosure: Evidence from Derivative Lawsuits*, 56 J. Account. Res. 797 (2018).
11. Steven Freund, Nam H. Nguyen, and Hieu V Phan, *Shareholder Litigation and Corporate Social Responsibility*, J. Financ. Quant. Anal 1 (2022).
12. Joel F. Houston, Chen Lin, and Wensi Xie, *Shareholder Protection and the Cost of Capital*, 61 J. Law Econ. 677 (2018).
13. Benedikt Downar and Mario Keiling, *Shareholder Rights and Capital Structure: Evidence from Derivative Lawsuits*, available at SSRN: https://ssrn.com/abstract = 3511349 (2019).

are traditionally opposed by shareholders, for example, staggered boards,[14] a tendency to engage in empire building,[15] and more frequent instances of real earnings management.[16]

The picture is further complicated by the possibility that these empirical studies overstate the legal changes brought about by universal demand laws and their impact on litigation risk, as asserted by some commentators.[17] On this view, the adoption of universal demand laws is an inappropriate instrument leading to spurious findings of an association between litigation risk and firm outcomes.[18] The empirical literature is therefore at an impasse. If the methodological criticism of studies relying on the adoption of universal demand laws to isolate the effects of shareholder litigation rights is correct, a more promising avenue is the exploitation of clear legal differences that exist between countries.[19] However, the challenge with this approach is that it is difficult to account for all potentially confounding variables.[20] In particular, in contrast to a sample that is limited to the US, where certain elements of investor protection laws are federal law, such as disclosure obligations under the Securities Act of 1933 and the Securities Exchange Act of 1934, and others are broadly similar even though they are state law, such as directors' duties, shareholder rights across countries are different in very different ways and thus difficult to translate into proxies for shareholder protection.

This contribution seeks to develop a framework that can be used to compare shareholder enforcement rights meaningfully across countries and thus assist in testing the effect of differences in the legal design of enforcement rights empirically. A good understanding of the link between the enforcement of directors' duties and firm outcomes is also important in light of recent initiatives establishing, or proposing to establish, 'due diligence duties', which require companies to take appropriate measures to identify and prevent or mitigate adverse human rights and environmental

---

14. Ian Appel, *Governance by Litigation*, available at SSRN: https://ssrn.com/abstract=2532278 (2019).
15. Chune Young Chung, Incheol Kim, Monika K. Rabarison, Thomas Y. To, and Eliza Wu, *Shareholder Litigation Rights and Corporate Acquisitions*, 62 J. Corp. Finance 101599 (2020); Leye Li, Gary S. Monroe, and Jeffrey J. Coulton, *Litigation Risk and Cost Behavior: Evidence from Derivative Lawsuits*, AAA 2018 Management Accounting Section Midyear Meeting, available at SSRN: https://ssrn.com/abstract=3020842 (2018).
16. Sterling Huang, Sugata Roychowdhury, and Ewa Sletten, *Does Litigation Deter or Encourage Real Earnings Management?*, 95 Account. Rev. 251 (2020).
17. Donelson et al., *supra* n. 4.
18. Specifically, Donelson et al., *supra* n. 4, observe that derivative litigation against public companies was very rare in states that adopted universal demand laws ('UD states') both before and after the adoption. Differences-in-differences in litigation rates that other studies have found between UD states and control states can be explained with different trends in litigation that predated the adoption of universal demand laws. Donelson et al. conclude that universal demand laws, accordingly, have little to do with changes in derivative litigation.
19. Compare, for example, differences in the EU highlighted in Carsten Gerner-Beuerle and Edmund-Philipp Schuster, *The Evolving Structure of Directors Duties in Europe*, 15 EBOR 191, 214–222 (2014).
20. Houston et al., *supra* n. 12, 682.

effects of business operations.[21] While due diligence obligations are imposed on corporations,[22] they are closely linked to directors' duties, since directors have overall responsibility for implementing due diligence procedures and ensuring that they are effective.[23] Moreover, under proposed EU legislation and the laws of some countries, they must consider the impact of their decisions on sustainability factors when discharging their duty to act in the best interest of the company.[24] This form of regulatory intervention is only justified if the regulatory burden imposed by due diligence duties is outweighed by a reduction in the adverse impact of business operations on societal interests. Whether this is the case requires that duties shape firm behaviour in positive ways. However, robust empirical evidence establishing a link between diligence duties, their enforcement, and sustainability outcomes is largely lacking.[25]

The remainder of this chapter is organised as follows. Section 15.02 identifies three challenges to capturing and quantifying legal rules, termed the problems of 'substitutability', 'complementarity', and 'complexity', and explains how they call into question the reliability of existing attempts to test the association between legal rules and economic outcomes. Section 15.03 gives a comparative overview of the building blocks of a system regulating directors' duties and their enforcement, covering the laws of Delaware, the United Kingdom (UK), Germany, and France. Section 15.04 takes the duty of care as an example to suggest a mapping of the interdependencies of the building blocks discussed in §15.03 that can be translated into legal variables. Section 15.05 concludes.

§15.02 IDENTIFYING CORRELATION AND CAUSATION

Traditionally, correlation and causation between certain aspects of the legal environment and economic outcomes, on the level of either the economy or the firm, have been tested by compiling 'legal indices'. Influential indices include the 'Anti-Director

21. European Commission, Proposal for a Directive on Corporate Sustainability Due Diligence, COM(2022) 71 final, Arts 6–8. Comparable national initiatives include the French duty of vigilance (Loi no 2017-399 relative au devoir de vigilance des sociétés mères et des entreprises donneuses d'ordre, 27 March 2017) and the German law on corporate due diligence obligations in supply chains (Gesetz über die unternehmerischen Sorgfaltspflichten in Lieferketten, 16 July 2021). On due diligence duties, *see also*, Beate Sjåfjell, Chapter 3 in this volume.
22. *See, e.g.*, Proposal for a Directive on Corporate Sustainability Due Diligence, Art. 4. The proposal envisages that companies are liable for damages if they fail to comply with their due diligence obligations and an adverse impact that should have been identified, prevented, or mitigated occurred and led to damage as a result of this failure, *ibid.* Art. 22.
23. *Ibid.*, recital 64 and Art. 26.
24. *Ibid.*, Art. 25. The proposed Directive conceptualises the above obligation as part of the directors' duty of care and stipulates that this duty shall be 'understood and applied in a manner which is coherent and consistent with the due diligence obligations introduced by this Directive', *ibid.*, recital 63. On the duty to act in the best interest of the company from a comparative perspective, *see*, Jessica Östberg, Chapter 2 in this volume.
25. Some existing studies suffer from the methodological challenges outlined earlier, e.g., Freund et al., *supra* n. 11.

Rights index' ('ADR index') introduced by La Porta et al.,[26] the 'anti-self-dealing index' by Djankov et al.,[27] the 'Governance index' ('G-index') by Gompers, Ishii, and Metrick,[28] the 'entrenchment index' ('E-index') by Bebchuk, Cohen, and Ferrell,[29] which builds on the G-index, and the 'Management Insulation index' ('MI-index') by Ferreira et al.[30]

Most of these indices are based on a list of legal and regulatory variables that quantify certain shareholder rights and other aspects of the regulatory environment relevant to outside investor protection. These are either simply aggregated, usually without weighting and without any attempt to explore possible interconnections between index components or added as separate explanatory variables. For example, the ADR index contains several proxies for the strength of shareholder rights generally, such as the existence of pre-emption rights or the right of shareholders to call a general meeting, and one proxy that concerns enforcement, namely the availability of a judicial venue to challenge management decisions (termed 'oppressed minorities mechanism').[31] The relevant rules are coded in a binary manner and aggregated to form the ADR index. Similarly, the anti-self-dealing index equals the average of scores for approval and disclosure requirements for related-party transactions and provisions concerning the enforcement of liability provisions, which each range from 0 to 1 (partly with incremental steps).[32] The E-index condenses the G-index into six provisions that capture different aspects of an investor protection regime. Sample firms are then given a score ranging from 0 to 6 that represents the number of provisions that apply to them.[33]

This approach to capturing the essence of legal rules faces several challenges, which may be termed the problems of 'substitutability,' 'complementarity', and 'complexity'. They are addressed below. The only exception to this methodology among the above indices is the MI-index, which captures the time it takes for a majority

26. Rafael La Porta, Florencio López-de-Silanes, Andrei Shleifer, and Robert W. Vishny, *Legal Determinants of External Finance*, 52 J.Finance 1131 (1997); Rafael La Porta, Florencio López-de-Silanes, Andrei Shleifer, and Robert W. Vishny, *Law and Finance*, 106 J. Political Econ. 1113 (1998); Rafael La Porta, Florencio López-de-Silanes, and Andrei Shleifer, *What Works in Securities Laws?*, 61 J. Finance 1 (2006). The literature relying on and criticising the anti-director rights index is voluminous. *See*, among others, John Armour, Simon Deakin, Priya Lele, and Mathias M. Siems, *How Do Legal Rules Evolve? Evidence from a Cross-Country Comparison of Shareholder, Creditor, and Worker Protection*, 57 Am. J. Comp. Law 579 (2009); Mathias M. Siems, *What Does Not Work in Comparing Securities Laws: A Critique on La Porta et al.'s Methodology*, 16 ICCLR 300 (2005); Holger Spamann, *The 'Antidirector Rights Index' Revisited*, 23 Rev. Financ Stud. 467 (2009).
27. Simeon Djankov, Rafael La Porta, Florencio López-de-Silanes, and Andrei Shleifer, *The Law and Economics of Self-dealing*, 88 J. Financ. Econ. 430 (2008).
28. Paul Gompers, Joy Ishii, and Andrew Metrick, *Corporate Governance and Equity Prices*, 118 Q. J.Econ. 107 (2003).
29. Lucian Bebchuk, Alma Cohen, and Allen Ferrell, *What Matters in Corporate Governance*, 22 Rev. Financ. Stud. 783 (2009).
30. Daniel Ferreira, David Kershaw, Tom Kirchmaier, and Edmund Schuster, *Corporate Governance and Bank Failures, ECGI Working Paper* No 345/2013 (2020).
31. La Porta et al., *Law and Finance*, *supra* n. 26, 1122–23.
32. Djankov et al., *supra* n. 27, 434–435.
33. Bebchuk, Cohen, and Ferrell, *supra* n. 29, 785.

group of shareholders to gain control of the board.[34] In contrast to the other indices, it does not award scores by assessing the presence or absence of a set of governance provisions but the *interaction* of different legal rules. For this reason, the authors call the MI a 'contingent index'. It takes account of the fact that 'certain governance arrangements can be rendered functionally irrelevant by the presence or absence of other rules' and seeks to measure how *combinations* of governance provisions affect the insulation of board members.[35]

[A] Substitutability

The problem of substitutability arises where legal institutions are compared across jurisdictions, as in the case of the ADR or anti-self-dealing indices. Such a comparison faces the problem that legal systems are structured in different ways, use different terminology, and sometimes employ different mechanisms to address the same social conflicts. Thus, the compilation of legal data cannot proceed based on legal concepts that exist in one jurisdiction, then search for the same legal instrument in other jurisdictions and conclude, if it cannot be found, that the respective issue is less comprehensively regulated.

Enforcing directors' duties is a case in point. All legal systems rely on a combination of public or semi-public and private enforcement mechanisms. In some jurisdictions, the two forms of enforcement function effectively as substitutes, and policy goals are achieved by relying predominantly on either public or private enforcement. For example, in the UK, the possibility to disqualify directors under the Company Directors Disqualification Act (CDDA) 1986[36] is more important than private enforcement through a derivative action.[37] The latter had long been ineffective because of the rule in *Foss v. Harbottle*,[38] which generally allowed minority shareholders to bring a lawsuit only if the act complained of 'amount[ed] to ... a fraud on the minority and the wrongdoers [were] themselves in control of the company'.[39] The Companies Act 2006 now contains a codified derivative action mechanism that is more conducive to minority shareholder litigation but directors' disqualification remains of greater practical relevance.[40] Under the Company Directors Disqualification Act 1986, the relevant government minister or the liquidator if a company is being wound up can make an application for a disqualification order. The court will disqualify a director, among other reasons, if it is satisfied that the director is 'unfit to be concerned in the

34. Ferreira et al., *supra* n. 30, 3.
35. *Ibid.*
36. 1986, c. 46.
37. On directors' disqualification, *see also* Jesper Lau Hansen, Public Enforcement of Directors' Duties, Chapter 17 in this volume, § 17.08.
38. (1843) 2 Hare 461.
39. *Ibid.*, 1067.
40. Annually, between 1,000 and 1,400 directors are disqualified and, as a consequence, prohibited from serving as a director of a company or participating directly or indirectly in the formation or management of a company, Carsten Gerner-Beuerle and Michael Schillig, *Comparative Company Law* 717 (Oxford University Press 2019).

management of a company.'[41] Unfitness 'may be shown by conduct which is dishonest (including conduct showing a want of probity or integrity) or by conduct which is merely incompetent'.[42] The concept thus encompasses breaches of directors' duties, including breaches of the duty of care in situations where a director acts in good faith and without a conflict of interest.[43] Director disqualification mechanisms can therefore be seen as a functional substitute for purely private enforcement. They have the advantage of relieving shareholders of any litigation risk and the requirement to pay court fees, which may otherwise disincentivise them from bringing a minority shareholder lawsuit.[44]

Shareholders benefit from similar advantages if corporate misconduct is qualified as a criminal offence and consequently enforced in criminal proceedings.[45] This is particularly relevant in France, where the criminal offence of *abus de biens sociaux* complements traditional directors' duties in cases where a director uses corporate assets in bad faith for private purposes.[46] These conditions are interpreted broadly by the courts and cover not only cases of outright embezzlement or the exploitation of a corporate opportunity but also management decisions that result in a waste of assets, for example, the decision to enter into a transaction that does not provide for any, or not for adequate, consideration for the company.[47] Abuse of corporate assets entails not only criminal liability but, generally, also civil liability.[48] This gives minority shareholders the opportunity to file a criminal complaint and combine this with a claim for damages on behalf of the company (*plainte avec constitution de partie civile*).[49] The judge will open criminal proceedings if the shareholders can show that 'the existence of a loss and the direct link between the loss and a criminal offence' (that is, the

41. CDDA 1986, ss. 6(1)(b), 8(2). Other grounds for disqualification include the commission of an indictable offence in relation with the promotion, formation, management, or liquidation of a company, persistent breaches of reporting requirements under the Companies Acts and the Insolvency Act 1986, or the finding that a director is liable to contribute to the company's assets because of wrongful or fraudulent trading, CDDA 1986, ss. 2–4, 10.
42. *Re Barings plc and Others* (No 5) [1999] 1 BCLC 433, 483.
43. Barings, *supra* n. 42. However, it is important to note that a disqualification order will not be issued in all instances of a breach of duty. Rather, the courts require a showing of recklessness or 'negligence in a very marked degree', for example, where a director repeatedly fails to keep proper accounting records, fails to file annual returns, and causes loan transactions to be made between companies of a corporate group that were in severe financial difficulties, *Re Sevenoaks Stationers (Retail) Ltd* [1991] Ch 164, 184. For further details, *see* Gerner-Beuerle and Schillig, *supra* n. 40, 717–18.
44. On this problem, *see also* §15.03.
45. This paragraph is adapted from Gerner-Beuerle and Schillig, *supra* n. 40, 720.
46. French Commercial Code, Article L242-6.
47. This has been held to be the case where a director receives excessive remuneration (Cass. Crim., 22 September 2004, no 03-82266, *Bull. Joly Sociétés* 2005, 45) or remuneration that has not been authorised (Cass. Crim., 22 March 2017, no 15-84229, *Revue des sociétés* 2017, 591), assets are transferred, or services rendered, at rates below market value within a corporate group (Cass. Crim., 25 October 2006, no 05-85998, *Bull. Joly Sociétés* 2007, 243), or a director enters a self-dealing transaction that is of no economic value to the company (Cass. Crim., 12 September 2001, no 01- 80895, *Droit des sociétés* 2002, no 6).
48. French Commercial Code, Article L225-251.
49. French Code of Criminal Procedure, Articles 2, 3, 85.

conditions for being able to act as *partie civile* in the criminal proceedings[50]) are 'possible'.[51] Thus, the evidentiary burden is relatively easy to satisfy, and if the necessary link has been shown, the judge is under a duty to investigate.[52] This enforcement mechanism is important in practice, with several hundred convictions for abuse of corporate assets per year. Its function within the French enforcement architecture is somewhat comparable to the UK directors' disqualification regime, insofar as the latter allows creditors to obtain compensation for a loss suffered by the company because of the misconduct of a director.[53] In both cases, private parties can take advantage of a public enforcement mechanism to obtain damages. However, crucially, parties to the French *action civile* have control over the proceedings, whereas the creditors of companies falling within the scope of the UK Company Directors Disqualification Act 1986 must rely on the Secretary of State to seek first a disqualification order and then compensation.

The problem of substitutability arises not only in relation to public and private enforcement mechanisms but also within the realm of private enforcement. As a basic principle, directors' duties are in most legal systems and under most circumstances owed to the company and not to shareholders individually.[54] The question, therefore, is how the company's damages claim can be enforced. Legal systems give different answers, which are partly a function of differences in prevalent corporate governance structures and partly of policy preferences regarding the perceived desirability of private enforcement and court supervision. In legal systems where companies predominantly operate under a one-tier board structure, the board of directors is typically empowered to take enforcement decisions,[55] with the general meeting having a subsidiary or complementary power to commence proceedings.[56] In two-tier board

50. *Ibid.*, Art. 2.
51. Cass crim, 5 November 1991, no 90-82605 (*Société Industrielle et Financière Bertin*), *Revue des sociétés* 1992, 91. For a brief discussion of the decision in English, *see* Pierre-Henri Conac, Luca Enriques, and Martin Gelter, *Constraining Dominant Shareholders' Self- Dealing: The Legal Framework in France, Germany, and Italy*, 4 ECFR 491, 518 (2007).
52. Conac, Enriques, and Gelter, *supra* n. 51, 518, with references.
53. Pursuant to the CDDA 1986, Arts 15A and 15B, the Secretary of State may seek compensation from the director for the benefit of the creditors if the company is insolvent and the conduct that has given rise to the disqualification order or disqualification undertaking has caused a loss to the company's creditors.
54. *See*, for example, the UK Companies Act 2006, s. 170(1) and the German Stock Corporation Act, § 93(2) sentence 1 (liability of the members of the management board); §116 (liability of the members of the supervisory board).
55. For example, in the UK, US, and France, enforcement decisions are regarded as falling within the general management powers of the board, *see*, e.g., *John Shaw & Sons v Shaw and Shaw* [1935] 2 KB 113 (UK); *Zapata Corp v Maldonado*, 430 A.2d 779 (Del. 1981).
56. On this point, there is considerable variation across legal systems. In the UK, enforcement powers of the general meeting are subsidiary: The general meeting, 'in the absence of an effective board, has a residual authority to use the company's powers. ... Moreover, although the general meeting cannot restrain the directors from conducting actions in the name of the company, it still seems to be the law that the general meeting can commence proceedings on behalf of the company if the directors fail to do so.' *Alexander Ward & Co Ltd v Samyang Navigation* [1975] 1 WLR 673, 679 (per Lord Halisham). In Italy, it is complementary. Shareholders can always direct the board to commence litigation by way of ordinary resolution, Article 2364(1) no 4 Italian Civil Code. Under Delaware law, the shareholders enjoy neither a

systems, this power is generally vested in the supervisory board, which also represents the company in legal proceedings.[57] Again, the general meeting may enjoy a subsidiary or complementary power to bring litigation or request the company to do so.[58]

Because of the conflict of interest that exists if the board of directors in a unitary board system and, to a lesser extent, the supervisory board in a dual board system are entrusted with making enforcement decisions concerning one or more board members, the basic rules sketched in the previous paragraph are complemented in most legal systems by ancillary mechanisms designed to safeguard the interests of shareholders if the board does not act and the general meeting is unable to step in for practical or legal reasons. Here, substitutability becomes relevant. Many legal systems provide for a derivative action mechanism that enables individual shareholders or groups of shareholders to bring a lawsuit and enforce claims of a company against its directors. The design of the minority shareholder lawsuit differs considerably across jurisdictions. How to quantify this variation is a non-trivial question, to which we return in §15.03 and §15.04. For present purposes, it is important to note that the derivative action is not the only mechanism employed by legal systems to alleviate the conflict of interest that affects board enforcement decisions.

As an alternative,[59] some legal systems permit minority shareholders to petition a court to appoint a special auditor who is empowered to investigate potential misconduct, which may then form the basis of a liability claim.[60] An example of such a mechanism that has received considerable attention are the Dutch inquiry proceedings.[61] These proceedings are conducted by the Enterprise Chamber of the Amsterdam Court of Appeal. They are different from other shareholder rights to appoint a special auditor in that the proceedings, once initiated on the application of shareholders holding at least 10% of the issued share capital or shares with a nominal value of EUR 225,000,[62] are largely reliant on public resources. If shareholders can substantiate the claim that the company has not been managed properly, the court will appoint an independent investigator, who is empowered to inspect the corporate books and

complementary nor a subsidiary power to bring a lawsuit, but must always make a demand on the board, *Zapata Corp v Maldonado*, 430 A.2d 779, 782 (however, a derivative action is possible when demand was refused in breach of directors' duties or demand is excused, *see* §15.03).

57. For example, German Stock Corporation Act, § 112.
58. German Stock Corporation Act, § 147(1). For further examples, *see*, Carsten Gerner-Beuerle, Philipp Paech, and Edmund Schuster, *Study on Directors' Duties and Liability*, prepared for the European Commission DG Markt 194 (2013).
59. The paragraph that follows is adapted from Gerner-Beuerle and Schillig, *supra* n. 40, 719–20.
60. For example, under German law, shareholders representing at least 1% of the legal capital or EUR 100,000 have the right to apply to the court to appoint a special auditor, German Stock Corporation Act, §142(2). A similar right exists in France for shareholders holding at least 5% of the share capital, French Commercial Code, Article L225-231. A precondition for the exercise of the right under German, but not French, law is a prima facie showing that the conduct complained of involved dishonesty or a gross violation of the law. Importantly, pursuant to both German and French law, the court can decide that court fees and the remuneration of the special auditor must be borne by the company. For a discussion of both provisions, *see* Conac, Enriques, and Gelter, *supra* n. 51, 512–13.
61. Dutch Civil Code, Articles 2:344 to 2:359.
62. Dutch Civil Code, Article 2:346(b). The request can also be made by the advocate general at the court, if this is in the public interest, Article 2:345(2), or by a workers' union, Article 2:347.

records and request any other relevant information from the company's directors.[63] The Enterprise Chamber can adopt a range of measures to remedy problems identified in the investigator's report, including the annulment of resolutions, dismissal of directors, appointment of external auditors or independent directors, disapplication of specific provisions of the articles, and, as a last resort, winding up of the company.[64] It has been argued that this flexibility, combined with the power of the court to grant injunctive relief in a fast-track procedure, explains the success of the inquiry proceeding.[65] The procedure is also cost-efficient for investors, provided they meet the filing threshold, since costs are imposed on the company, and the court oversees the investigation.[66]

Finally, on a more fundamental level, a degree of substitutability (as well as complementarity[67]) also exists between the formulation of directors' duties and their enforcement. If it is believed that the correct benchmark to measure the effectiveness of a regulatory regime in constraining managerial misconduct is the threat that directors who engage in misconduct are found liable to pay damages, both the strictness of duties and the ease of their enforcement play a role. This point is explored further in §15.03 below.

[B] Complementarity

Some legal instruments are ineffective if not complemented by others. Complementarity of legal rules has a substantive and a procedural dimension. An example of both facets is the right of minority shareholders to challenge decisions of the board of directors or the general meeting, which is mentioned by La Porta et al., as part of their 'oppressed minorities' variable (a component of the ADR index).[68] This right has little relevance if the law does not provide for substantive requirements to which decisions of the general meeting or the board must conform and that reflect the interests of the shareholders.[69] In addition, the law must ensure that minority shareholders can enforce their right without unreasonable difficulties. This is, for example, the crucial problem of appraisal rights in the US, where several structural and procedural deficiencies render the remedy largely ineffective.[70] Legal coding that does not take

63. Dutch Civil Code, Articles 2:350(1), (4), 2:351.
64. *Ibid.*, Arts 2:355, 2:356.
65. Erik P.M. Vermeulen and Dirk A. Zetzsche, *The Use and Abuse of Investor Suits: An Inquiry into the Dark Side of Shareholder Activism* (2010) 7 ECFR 1, 18–19. Injunctive relief is set out in Art. 2:349a(2) Dutch Civil Code.
66. Dutch Civil Code, Art. 2:350(3).
67. On this latter point, *see* §15.02[B].
68. *See* the text Rafael La Porta et al., *Law and Finance*, *supra* n. 31.
69. The German Stock Corporation Act provides for an example of such a substantive requirement in § 243(2), which allows a resolution adopted by the shareholders in general meeting to be challenged on the ground 'that a stockholder, by exercising the voting right, sought to obtain special benefits for himself or for a third party to the detriment of the company or of the other stockholders and that the resolution is suited to serve this purpose'.
70. For an overview of these deficiencies, *see*, Arthur R. Pinto and Douglas M. Branson, *Understanding Corporate Law* § 6.06 (5th ed., LexisNexis 2018).

these substantive and procedural complementarities into consideration, such as, arguably, La Porta et al.'s 'oppressed minorities' variable, fails to assess the effectiveness of an instrument correctly.[71]

These considerations are of direct relevance to the present analysis. Starting point of an inquiry into the effectiveness of a regulatory regime establishing directors' duties and regulating their enforcement is the observation that the risk of monetary liability sets incentives and thus influences the behaviour of directors and managers.[72] If calibrated correctly, it will minimise the sum of agency costs, enforcement costs (particularly through litigation), and principal costs (costs incurred by the shareholders because of risk averse behaviour of the directors or a higher level of compensation demanded by directors because of heightened liability standards).[73] It is not the purpose of this contribution to examine under which conditions legal rules are optimal in this sense – for example, whether it is more efficient to limit liability to situations where directors are conflicted, act in bad faith, or without appropriate information (business judgment rule) than holding them liable for any loss caused by a negligent act[74] – or which legal system provide for the most efficient solution to the problem of managerial misconduct.

Rather, the important point is that an optimal regulatory solution can be reached through different routes. If it is correct that there is a trade-off between agency costs, enforcement costs, and principal costs (that is, a minimisation of, say, agency costs considered in isolation through high liability standards is not optimal), as argued in the literature, a regime is optimal if it facilitates shareholder enforcement but at the same time limits the liability exposure of directors in some form.[75] This can be achieved either through an appropriate formulation of directors' duties, notably the business judgment rule, or limitations on enforcement. However, reforms that seek to strengthen enforcement against the backdrop of stringently formulated duties, or vice versa, may create an inefficiently high risk of liability.[76] It is important to be aware of this interdependence between the content of duties and their enforcement.

71. The original definition of the variable can be found in La Porta et al., *Law and Finance, supra* n. 26, 1122, and a revised version in Djankov et al., *supra* n. 27, 455.
72. It is debatable whether the mere pronouncement of a behavioural standard without the threat of liability in case of non-compliance is sufficient to incentivise directors to act according to that behavioural standard. Under US law, for example, the standard of conduct of directors is different from the standard applied by courts to review the behaviour of directors. The former is informed by the 'amount of care which ordinarily careful and prudent men would use in similar circumstances', *Re Walt Disney Co. Derivative Litigation*, 907 A.2d 693, 749 (Del. Ch. 2005). The latter is known as the business judgment rule. However, it is plausible to assume that the formulation of a behavioural standard that is unenforceable will have a limited effect on behaviour. This is indeed a standard assumption in the literature, *see*, e.g., Holger Spamann, *Monetary Liability for Breach of the Duty of Care?*, 8 J. Leg. Anal. 337, 343 (2016).
73. On the concept of principal costs, *see* Zohar Goshen and Richard Squire, *Principal Costs: A New Theory for Corporate Law and Governance*, 117 Columbia Law Rev. 767 (2017).
74. For formal models exploring this question, *see* Spamann, *supra* n. 72; Andreas Engert and Susanne Goldlücke, *Why Agents Need Discretion: The Business Judgment Rule as Optimal Standard of Care*, 13 Rev. Law Econ. 1 (2017).
75. *See* Spamann, *supra* n. 72; Engert and Goldlücke, *supra* n. 74.
76. Engert and Goldlücke, *supra* n. 74, 5.

[C] Complexity

Necessarily, any model of the real world needs to operate at a sufficiently abstract level to have explanatory value. The question is how to balance the need for simplification and the risk of over-simplification. As mentioned, legal indices initially often quantified legal rules in a binary and linear fashion. More recently, revised indices developed by La Porta et al. and other researchers seek to capture nuances of legal rules by introducing incremental steps between 0 and 1. For example, the anti-self-dealing index uses smaller increments of, for example, one-half, one-third, or one-fifth points.[77] This method addresses partly the fact that a quantification of legal rules needs to account for gradual differences in how rules are formulated across countries, but it continues to be subject to concerns. First, it is based on the implicit assumption that each transition from one incremental step to the next is equally important in assessing the effectiveness of a legal rule, since all steps are weighted equally. The same assumption underlies the use of indices that aggregate or average the scores allocated to index components, as is the case with most of the indices discussed earlier.[78]

Second, and arguably even more importantly, legal rules (and elements of rules, where an index disaggregates them) are often meaningless if assessed in isolation. The effectiveness of a legal systems in regulating a particular economic conflict generally only becomes clear if the full set of relevant rules is analysed holistically. The reason is partly that some rules have substitutes and complements, as discussed in §15.02[A] and §15.02[B], but also that rules operate differently depending on decisions of economic actors – issuers, shareholders, directors – at earlier stages, which, in turn, are constrained or enabled by other legal rules. An illustrative example is a variable from Djankov et al.'s self-dealing index that measures the ease with which an interested director can be held liable. The variable ranges from 0 to 1 and receives the following values:[79]

Equals 0 when the interested director is either not liable or liable only in cases of bad faith, intent, or gross negligence. Equals 1/2 when the interested director is liable if he either influenced the approval or was negligent. Equals 1 if the interested director is liable if the transaction is unfair, oppressive, or prejudicial.

This definition is difficult to apply to the duty of loyalty as formulated under Delaware law (and in many other jurisdictions). Pursuant to Delaware law, an interested director is liable if a related-party transaction is not entirely fair to the corporation (thus, the variable should arguably receive the value 1), *unless* the transaction was approved by the disinterested directors or shareholders.[80] The latter point, approval by disinterested shareholders, is a separate component of the self-dealing index, which '[e]quals 1 if the transaction must be approved by disinterested shareholders, and zero otherwise'.[81] Under Delaware law, transactions do not have to

77. Djankov et al., *supra* n. 27, 434–435.
78. *See* the text to notes 26–33 *supra*.
79. Djankov et al., *supra* n. 27, 434.
80. Delaware General Corporation Law, § 144(a).
81. Djankov et al., *supra* n. 27, 434.

be approved by disinterested shareholders, but they can, in which case interested directors are generally not liable even if the transaction is unfair.[82] The self-dealing index does not capture this interaction effect.

The next two sections analyse in more detail how legal rules interact in the context of liability for managerial misconduct. The next section gives an overview of legal rules relevant to this question, regarding both the substantive formulation of duties and their enforcement. Section 15.04 takes one duty, the duty of care, as an example to illustrate a possible mapping of interactions and offer a framework for quantifying different legal and contractual arrangements concerning directors' duties.

§15.03 DIRECTORS' DUTIES AND THEIR ENFORCEMENT

The risk of monetary liability is a function of the content of directors' duties (for example, the formulation of the standard of care), their enforcement, and ancillary legal rules that allow or disallow private ordering that affects the liability exposure of directors. In particular, shareholders and directors may seek to curtail the reach of duties, authorise or ratify certain acts, indemnify directors against liability, or arrange for the company to take out insurance for the benefit of the directors.

Table 15.1 summarises these aspects of directors' duties in four influential jurisdictions: Delaware, the UK, Germany, and France. It includes information on the content of the two main fiduciary duties that impose behavioural expectations on directors - care and loyalty - and the availability of contractual mechanisms that could limit the liability of directors. The duties of care and loyalty can be found, in one form or another, in virtually all legal systems, including Delaware, the UK, Germany, and France.[83] They differ to some extent in their conceptual design and the standards of conduct they impose on directors, but in all four jurisdictions directors are expected to exercise the care of a reasonably diligent person and avoid conflicts of interest. In all four jurisdictions, liability can furthermore be modified or limited through private ordering. Again, legal systems differ in the extent to which this is possible, but no jurisdiction prohibits all arrangements that would limit the liability exposure of directors. Table 15.1 distinguishes between *ex ante* limitations, for example, a broad authorisation of certain types of conduct by the shareholders or in the articles of association, such as the exploitation of specified categories of corporate opportunities, indemnification against liability or expenses incurred by a director in an action of the company against the director, *ex post* limitations, in particular, the ratification of acts that amount to a breach of duty, and directors and officers (D&O) insurance.

82. If disinterested shareholder or director approval has been obtained, courts will not enter into a full fairness review. *See*, e.g., *Marciano v. Nakash*, 535 A.2d 400, 405 (Del. 1987): '[A]pproval by fully-informed disinterested directors under section 144(a)(1) [Delaware General Corporation Law], or disinterested stockholders under section 144(a)(2), permits invocation of the business judgment rule and limits judicial review to issues of gift or waste with the burden of proof upon the party attacking the transaction'.
83. Gerner-Beuerle and Schuster, *supra* n. 19, 199.

Table 15.1 Directors' Duties in Comparative Perspective

	Delaware	*UK*	*Germany*	*France*
Duty of care	Business judgment rule: no liability unless plaintiffs can show a conflict of interest, bad faith, or that the defendants did not act on an informed basis;[84] if the business judgment rule does not apply, directors must show entire fairness[85]	Directors must exercise reasonable care, skill, and diligence;[86] no business judgment rule	Directors must exercise the care of a diligent and conscientious manager; business judgment rule applies: no liability if directors show that they acted in good faith in the best interest of the company and based on appropriate information[87]	Directors must act as prudent and diligent managers; no business judgment rule[88]

84. *See*, for example, *Aronson v Lewis*, 473 A.2d 805, 812 (Del. 1984)): 'The business judgment rule … is a presumption that in making a business decision the directors of a corporation acted on an informed basis, in good faith and in the honest belief that the action taken was in the best interests of the company. … Absent an abuse of discretion, that judgment will be respected by the courts. The burden is on the party challenging the decision to establish facts rebutting the presumption.'
85. For example, in *In re Walt Disney Co. Derivative Litigation*, 906 A.2d 27, 52 (Del. 2006), the Supreme Court of Delaware explained: The presumptions of the business judgment rule 'can be rebutted if the plaintiff shows that the directors breached their fiduciary duty of care or of loyalty or acted in bad faith. If that is shown, the burden then shifts to the director defendants to demonstrate that the challenged act or transaction was entirely fair to the corporation and its shareholders.'
86. UK Companies Act 2006, s. 174.
87. German Stock Corporation Act, § 93(1), (2).
88. For example, Cass. Com., 30 March 2010, FP-P + B + R + I, n° 08–17.841, *Fonds de garantie des dépôts (FGD) c/ Sté Caribéenne de conseil et d'audit (Crédit Martiniquais)*, *Revue des sociétés* 2010, 304.

	Delaware	*UK*	*Germany*	*France*
Duty of loyalty	Related-party transactions must be entirely fair unless approved by disinterested directors or shareholders[89]	Related- party transactions must be disclosed; default rule is that interested directors abstain from decisions;[90] shareholder approval under some conditions[91]	Supervisory board decides on related- party transactions between the company and members of the management board, but no explicit disclosure requirement[92]	Certain types of transaction (regulated agreements) require board and shareholder approval, but complex and non-transparent procedure[93]

89. Delaware General Corporation Law, § 144.
90. UK Companies Act 2006, s. 177.
91. For example, companies with a premium listing on the London Stock Exchange are required to obtain disinterested shareholder approval of related-party transactions that exceed certain size thresholds, FCA Handbook, Listing Rule 11.1.7.
92. German Stock Corporation Act, § 112.
93. French Commercial Code, Articles L225–38 to L225–42.

	Delaware	*UK*	*Germany*	*France*
***Ex ante* limitation of liability**	Exclusion of liability for monetary damages for breach of the duty of care possible in the certificate of incorporation, except for acts in bad faith;[94] corporation may waive any interest in specified business opportunities or classes or categories of opportunities in the certificate of incorporation[95]	Liability for breach of the duty of care cannot be contractually excluded *ex ante*; authorisation of transactions that would violate the duty of loyalty can be given *ex ante* by the disinterested directors if permitted in the articles[96]	Impermissible to contractually alter liability *ex ante*;[97] if the management board lays a resolution before the general meeting authorising an act of a director, and shareholders vote accordingly, the company cannot claim damages based on that act, but creditors continue to be able to enforce the company's claim under certain conditions[98]	Impermissible to contractually alter liability *ex ante*[99]

94. Delaware General Corporation Law, § 102(b)(7).
95. Delaware General Corporation Law, § 122(17).
96. UK Companies Act 2006, s. 175(4)(b), (5).
97. This follows from the principle of limited contractual freedom in the law on stock corporations, German Stock Corporation Act, § 23(5).
98. German Stock Corporation Act, § 93(4), sentence 1, (5). Creditors are entitled to enforce the company's damages claim if the company is unable to satisfy the creditors' claim(s) and the directors acted grossly negligently or violated certain capital maintenance provisions listed in § 93(3).
99. French Commercial Code, Article L225-53.

	Delaware	*UK*	*Germany*	*France*
Indemnification in an action *of the company* against a director	Indemnification against expenses and attorney's fees permissible, provided the director is held not to be liable, acted in good faith, and reasonably believed that the challenged conduct was in the best interest of the company[100]	Indemnification against expenses and attorney's fees permissible, provided the director is held not to be liable[101]	Not explicitly addressed in the Stock Corporation Act, but predominantly regarded as impermissible[102]	Indemnification regarded as impermissible[103]

100. Delaware General Corporation Law, § 145(b).
101. UK Companies Act 2006, s. 234(b)(ii).
102. It has been argued that indemnification by the company would be tantamount to a violation of § 93(4) Stock Corporation Act. *See* text to n. 107 and Gerner-Beuerle and Schillig, *supra* n. 40, 673 for references.
103. Bernard Black et al., *Legal Liability of Directors and Company Officials Part 2: Court Procedures, Indemnification and Insurance, and Administrative and Criminal Liability*, Colum. Bus. L. Rev. 1, 58 (2008).

	Delaware	*UK*	*Germany*	*France*
***Ex post* waiver of liability**	Ratification by fully informed disinterested shareholder vote permissible, unless the act is non-ratifiable (i.e., *ultra vires*, fraudulent, or a waste of corporate assets);[104] however, note that ratification does not extinguish liability, but reinstates business judgment rule review[105]	Ratification of conduct by a director amounting to negligence, default, or breach of duty by shareholder resolution permissible; votes of interested directors and connected members are disregarded[106]	The company can only waive claims three years after they arose and only if approved by shareholders and no objection is registered by minority shareholders holding at least 10% of the share capital;[107] the waiver has no effect in relation to creditors, who may be able to enforce the company's claim under certain conditions[108]	No *ex post* waiver of liability claims permissible[109]

104. *Michelson v Duncan*, 407 A.2d 211, 219 (Del. 1979). Ultra vires acts have been defined as 'acts specifically prohibited by the corporation's charter, for which no implicit authority may be rationally surmised, or those acts contrary to basic principles of fiduciary law', *Solomon v. Armstrong*, 747 A.2d 1098, 1114, fn. 45 (Del. Ch. 1999).
105. *Gantler v. Stephens*, 965 A.2d 695 (Del. 2009). If the business judgment rule implies, shareholder plaintiffs can only succeed if they are able to show that the challenged conduct amounts to a waste of corporate assets, *see*, e.g., *Fliegler v. Lawrence*, 361 A.2d 218, 221 (Del. 1976): '[S]hareholder ratification of an 'interested transaction', although less than unanimous, shifts the burden of proof to an objecting shareholder to demonstrate that the terms are so unequal as to amount to a gift or waste of corporate assets.'
106. UK Companies Act 2006, s. 239.
107. German Stock Corporation Act, § 93(4).
108. German Stock Corporation Act, § 93(5). *See, also, supra* n. 98 on the position of creditors.
109. French Commercial Code, Article L225-253.

	Delaware	*UK*	*Germany*	*France*
Insurance	Company can take out insurance for the benefit of its directors, including for damages claims of the company against a director and where indemnification would not be permissible[110]	Company can take out insurance for the benefit of its directors, including for damages claims of the company against a director and where indemnification would not be permissible[111]	Company can take out insurance for the benefit of its directors, including for damages claims of the company against a director, but the insurance policy must provide for an excess of at least 10% of the damage, capped at not less than 1.5 times the director's fixed annual remuneration[112]	Company can take out insurance for the benefit of its directors, including for damages claims of the company against a director,[113] except against criminal liability and liability arising from intentional or fraudulent conduct[114]

Source: Author's own.

110. Delaware General Corporation Law, § 145(g). However, it is worth noting that insurance policies typically provide for deductibles and exclude coverage for intentional or reckless behaviour and violations of securities regulation, Pinto and Branson, *supra* n. 70, § 14.11[H].
111. UK Companies Act 2006, s 233.
112. German Stock Corporation Act, § 93(2) sentence 3.
113. Cass. Civ., 1 June 2011, decision no 10–18143, *Bull. Joly Sociétés* 2011, 860.
114. French Insurance Code, Art. L113-1(2).

If the risk of monetary liability is key to calibrating behaviour, as suggested in §15.02[B], the effectiveness of directors' duties is a function of (1) the range of conduct amounting to a breach of duty (first two rows of Table 15.1); (2) conduct excluded *ex ante* from the set of behaviour that potentially amounts to a breach of duty (third row of Table 15.1); (3) the right of directors to be indemnified by the company (fourth row of Table 15.1); (4) conduct that can be excluded *ex post* from the set of behaviour that potentially amounts to a breach of duty (fifth row of Table 15.1); (5) the coverage of D&O insurance (sixth row of Table 15.1); and (6) the ease with which potential breaches of duties can be enforced. Points (1) and (6) are governed by a country's legal system, whereas points (2) to (5) are governed by the private arrangements between a company, its shareholders, and directors within the limits on private ordering drawn by a legal system. Data compiled according to this methodology is therefore firm-level data that will exhibit variation at both the country and firm level.

Since directors' duties are generally owed to the company, and not to shareholders directly, the company is the proper plaintiff in an action enforcing duties.[115] In most jurisdictions, the body authorised to take enforcement decisions on behalf of the company is the board of directors.[116] Entrusting the board of directors (or even the supervisory board in companies with a two-tier board structure[117]) with the decision to enforce a potential claim of the company against a director gives rise to an evident conflict of interest. For this reason, legal systems have developed mechanisms that allow minority shareholders to instigate enforcement actions. In many cases, these are designed as a derivative action, that is, a lawsuit in which shareholders have standing to bring a cause of action in the company's name, although substitute mechanisms exist.[118] The conditions under which minority shareholders can bring a derivative action can be divided into three groups: standing requirements, further conditions (or screening mechanisms) that serve to distinguish between meritorious and frivolous claims or between efficient and inefficient enforcement actions, and cost rules.[119] Standing rules specify whether anyone holding at least one share can file a derivative action, or claimants must satisfy a holding threshold expressed in percentage terms or as a minimum nominal value amount. Further conditions may relate to minimum holding periods, the requirement that an enforcement of the company's claim must be in the best interest of the company, or, most restrictively, the defendant director is in control of the general meeting.[120] Procedural rules that determine whether the company or the claimant bears the costs of the proceedings and, if the latter is the case, whether the claimant has a right to be indemnified by the company, are important

115. *See supra* n. 54.
116. For a more detailed discussion of this point, *see* Paul L. Davies, Sarah Worthington, and Christopher Hare, *Gower: Principles of Modern Company Law* 15-002 (11th ed., Sweet & Maxwell 2021); Gerner-Beuerle and Schillig, *supra* n. 40, 678–81.
117. *See*, for example, § 112 German Stock Corporation Act.
118. *See* §15.02[A].
119. Gerner-Beuerle and Schuster, *supra* n. 19, 215–216.
120. This is the famous rule in *Foss v. Harbottle* (1843) 67 ER 189 that applied in the UK until the derivative action was codified in the Companies Act 2006: The defendant directors must have committed a wrong that benefitted them personally and have de jure or de facto control of the general meeting.

because enforcement through minority shareholders faces a collective action and free-rider problem. If the company's claim is successfully enforced, it is the company who recovers damages, and the payoff accrues only indirectly to the shareholders in proportion to their shareholdings. The shareholders' incentives to bring a derivative action are, therefore, inefficiently low if they bear the litigation risk. Table 15.2 summarises Delaware, UK, German, and French law along these three dimensions.

Table 15.2 Comparative Effectiveness of the Derivative Action

	Delaware	*UK pre-2006*	*UK post-2006*	*Germany pre-2005*	*Germany post-2005*	*France*
Size of share-holding	1 share	1 share	1 share	1884: 20% 1965: 10% 1998: 5%	1% or EUR 100,000	1 share
Additional conditions	Demand refused or excused	Fraud on the minority	Claim admission procedure	1998: Bad faith or gross negligence	Claim admission procedure	Company refuses to take action
Cost rules	Court decides (corporation if lawsuit beneficial); contingency fee possible	Indemnification order if good faith and reasonable grounds	Indemnification order if good faith and reasonable grounds	Shareholder bears litigation risk	Plaintiff can generally claim reimbursement	Shareholder bears litigation risk

Source: Adapted from Gerner-Beuerle and Schillig (n 40) 714.

The relationship between the three types of legal requirement is not self-evident. Martin Gelter has argued that several preconditions must be satisfied simultaneously for a derivative action to be an efficient shareholder protection tool, and the absence of any of them renders the derivative action largely ineffective.[121] This observation is important because it underlines that a construction of legal indices based on a simple aggregation of scores or averages may introduce bias and misrepresent the true operation of legal rules.

In Table 15.2, the dark grey shaded entries represent aspects of a legal system's derivative action mechanism that are either difficult to satisfy by minority shareholders or likely to deter them from bringing a derivative action. In the UK, until a codification

121. *See* Martin Gelter, *Why do Shareholder Derivative Suits Remain Rare in Continental Europe?*, 37 Brook, J. Int'l L. 843, 856–880 (2012) (arguing that standing requirements must be favourable and not include a minimum ownership threshold, the claimant must not bear the litigation risk, access of shareholders to information must be secured, and it must be possible to include controlling shareholders as potential defendants).

of derivative actions in the Companies Act 2006,[122] the common law position was known as the rule in *Foss v. Harbottle*, which required that the challenged act constituted a fraud on the minority and the defendants were in control of the company.[123] This rule effectively made minority shareholder lawsuits in public companies, which were unlikely to have a controlling shareholder, impossible. The 'fraud on the minority' and 'wrongdoers in control' requirements have not been retained by the Companies Act 2006,[124] and minority shareholder lawsuits have become more common now.[125]

Similarly, in Germany, a high threshold of initially 20% of the share capital, which was gradually reduced to 5% in 1998, as a prerequisite to bring a derivative action made it difficult for minority shareholders to enforce a claim of the company. This threshold was further reduced to 1% or EUR 100,000 in 2005,[126] but it is questionable whether this change goes far enough. In addition, cost rules were unfavourable until 2005 and continue to impose a certain litigation risk on claimants. Until the reforms of 2005, claimant-shareholders bore the full litigation risk under Germany's 'loser pays' system. The 2005 reforms introduced a claims admission procedure similar to the one established by the Companies Act 2006 in the UK.[127] Claimants now bear the costs of the proceedings if the court dismisses the petition to grant leave.[128] If leave is granted, but the lawsuit is dismissed, the claimants have a right to be reimbursed for their costs by the company.[129] The litigation risk is therefore partly shifted to the company. However, since the decision of the court whether to grant leave depends on an assessment of what is in the best interest of the company,[130] the outcome of the procedure will often not be easy to predict. This may explain why derivative actions have remained rare in Germany even after the reforms of 2005.[131]

122. UK Companies Act 2006, ss. 260–269.
123. *See supra* n. 38 and accompanying text. The courts had developed several exceptions to this rule, *see*, *Edwards v. Halliwell* [1950] 2 All ER 1064, but these were of limited scope.
124. Some ambivalence remains, *see* David Kershaw, *The Rule in Foss v Harbottle is Dead; Long Live the Rule in Foss v. Harbottle*, (2015) J. Bus. L. 274 (arguing that wrongdoer control continues to be a threshold condition to derivative litigation). A different position is taken by John Armour, *Derivative Actions: A Framework for Decisions*, 135 Law Q. Rev. 412, 423–26 (2019). A version of the rule in *Foss v. Harbottle* also remains in force in some other common law jurisdictions, for example, Ireland, *see Fanning v. Murtagh* [2008] IEHC 277.
125. Armour et al., *supra* n. 4, 690 (observing that before 2006, 'the chances of a director of a publicly traded U.K. company being sued under corporate law [were] virtually nil'). While the rate of derivative litigation has increased since the adoption of the Companies Act 2006, the absolute number of minority shareholder lawsuits in the UK remains small in comparison with Delaware and some other common law and East Asian jurisdictions, Armour *supra* n. 124, 426–28.
126. Stock Corporation Act, § 148(1). *See also* the reference in n. 2 *supra*.
127. Stock Corporation Act, § 148. For similarities and differences between the German and UK derivative action mechanisms, *see* Gerner-Beuerle and Schuster, *supra n.* 19, 217–18.
128. Stock Corporation Act, § 148(6).
129. *Ibid.*
130. Stock Corporation Act, § 148(1), sentence 2, no. 4.
131. Sebastian Mock in Gerald Spindler and Eberhard Stilz (eds.), *Grosskommentar Aktienrecht* § 148 AktG para. 28 (5th ed., C.H. Beck 2022) (observing that only two decisions on a petition to grant leave have been reported since 2005).

UK law has developed a similar cost rule. In *Wallersteiner v. Moir*,[132] a decision that predates the Companies Act 2006, the Court of Appeal held that 'where a shareholder has in good faith and on reasonable grounds sued as plaintiff in a minority shareholder's action, the benefit of which, if successful, will accrue to the company and only indirectly to the plaintiff as a member of the company, and which it would have been reasonable for an independent board of directors to bring in the company's name',[133] it is appropriate for the courts to make use of their judicial discretion to grant minority shareholders a cost indemnification. When leave is granted under the statutory derivative action mechanism that now applies, the *Wallersteiner v. Moir* test will typically be satisfied.[134] However, the outcome of an application for permission to continue a claim cannot be predicted with certainty. In addition, even where an application is successful, an indemnification order is within the discretion of the court, and there is thus a residual financial risk for the claimants.[135] Given the misaligned incentives in derivative actions, *any* litigation risk that is borne by the claimant-shareholders likely operates as a deterrent to enforcing a claim.

In Table 15.2, the fact that the post-2005 German rules and the *Wallersteiner v. Moir* test in the UK do not fully shift the litigation risk to the company is represented by light grey shaded entries. Admittedly, the financial disincentive is greater if general civil procedure rules apply, as in Germany before the reforms of 2005 and in France still today. The French rules are a particularly illustrative example, since the French minority shareholder lawsuit is in principle permissively regulated. Any shareholder can bring an *action ut singuli*; claimants do not have to apply for permission to continue the claim, and the law does not establish any other restrictive conditions. The fact that minority shareholder litigation is almost non-existent in France is thus presumably attributable to the French cost rules.[136]

This leaves Delaware law as the only jurisdiction of the sample analysed here that regulates minority shareholder lawsuits appropriately across all three dimensions depicted in Table 15.2. It is worth emphasising that the Delaware courts have developed a relatively stringent screening mechanism to distinguish between meritorious and frivolous claims. The authority to bring a lawsuit lies with the board of directors. Shareholders must therefore make a demand on the board to enforce a claim.[137] A claim brought by shareholders will be dismissed if directors decide, in compliance with their fiduciary duties, to refuse demand or the shareholders failed to

132. [1975] QB 373.
133. *Ibid.*, 403–404.
134. *Iesini v Westrip Holdings Ltd* [2010] B.C.C. 420, 450.
135. For references to the relevant case law, *see* Davies, Worthington, and Hare, *supra* n. 116, 15–19.
136. Conac, Enriques, and Gelter, *supra* n. 51, 508–509.
137. *See Aronson v. Lewis*, 473 A.2d 805, 811–12 (Del. 1984): 'By its very nature the derivative action impinges on the managerial freedom of directors. Hence, the demand requirement of Chancery Rule 23.1 exists at the threshold, first to insure that a stockholder exhausts his intracorporate remedies, and then to provide a safeguard against strike suits. Thus, by promoting this form of alternate dispute resolution, rather than immediate recourse to litigation, the demand requirement is a recognition of the fundamental precept that directors manage the business and affairs of corporations.'

make a demand, unless 'the directors are under an influence which sterilizes their discretion [such that] they cannot be considered proper persons to conduct litigation on behalf of the corporation.'[138] While the demand requirement pursues the same goal as the claims admission procedure under UK and German law, it therefore uses a different technique that presents, arguably, a bigger hurdle to plaintiffs than the UK and German rules: The evaluation of whether the enforcement of a claim is in the best interest of the company is left to the board of directors rather than a court, unless plaintiffs create a reasonable doubt that the directors could have formed an independent and disinterested business judgment.

On the other hand, cost rules are more favourable to plaintiffs than in any of the other jurisdictions. The possibility to enter into a contingency fee agreement combined with the 'American rule', according to which each party pays its own fees and expenses, allows plaintiffs to eliminate the litigation risk almost completely. As an additional incentive, Delaware law allows fees to be calculated based not only on the monetary fund produced by an action but also the value of a non-monetary benefit conferred on the company or its shareholders if an action does not result in a monetary recovery, for example, the annulment of an election or the production of amendments to corporate bylaws (so-called corporate benefits doctrine).[139]

§15.04 TOWARDS A CONCEPTUALISATION OF THE DUTY-LIABILITY NEXUS: THE DUTY OF CARE

This section takes the duty of care as an example to develop a framework for capturing the interdependence between the elements of directors' duties and their enforcement that were discussed in §15.03. Figure 15.1 visualises this interdependence. It charts paths that depend on the formulation of directors' duties, the permissiveness of a legal system regarding arrangements to limit the liability exposure of directors, and enforcement mechanisms. These paths determine a Duty of Care Index (DCI) ranging from 0 to 6 and an Enforcement Index (EI) ranging from 0 to 4, with higher scores indicating a greater liability exposure of directors. If directors do not face liability for any type of behaviour, that is, the DCI is equal to zero, the EI must also be zero. In other cases, there is no evident a priory relationship between the degree of liability exposure stemming from legal rules and contractual arrangements associated with directors' duties (points (1) to (5) as set out in §15.03) and the enforcement of duties. For

138. *Ibid.*, 814. To establish whether this is the case and demand is excused, courts ask three questions on a director-by-director basis: '(i) whether the director received a material personal benefit from the alleged misconduct that is the subject of the litigation demand; (ii) whether the director faces a substantial likelihood of liability on any of the claims that would be the subject of the litigation demand; and (iii) whether the director lacks independence from someone who received a material personal benefit from the alleged misconduct that would be the subject of the litigation demand or who would face a substantial likelihood of liability on any of the claims that are the subject of the litigation demand. If the answer to any of the questions is 'yes' for at least half of the members of the demand board, then demand is excused as futile.' *United Food & Commer. Workers Union v. Zuckerberg*, 262 A.3d 1034, 1059 (Del. 2021).

139. Pinto and Branson, *supra n.* 70, § 14.08[B], [C].

example, it is not clear how a low DCI/high EI combination compares with a high DCI/low EI combination. It is therefore sensible to treat both as separate variables.

Figure 15.1 Duty of Care-Enforcement Interdependence

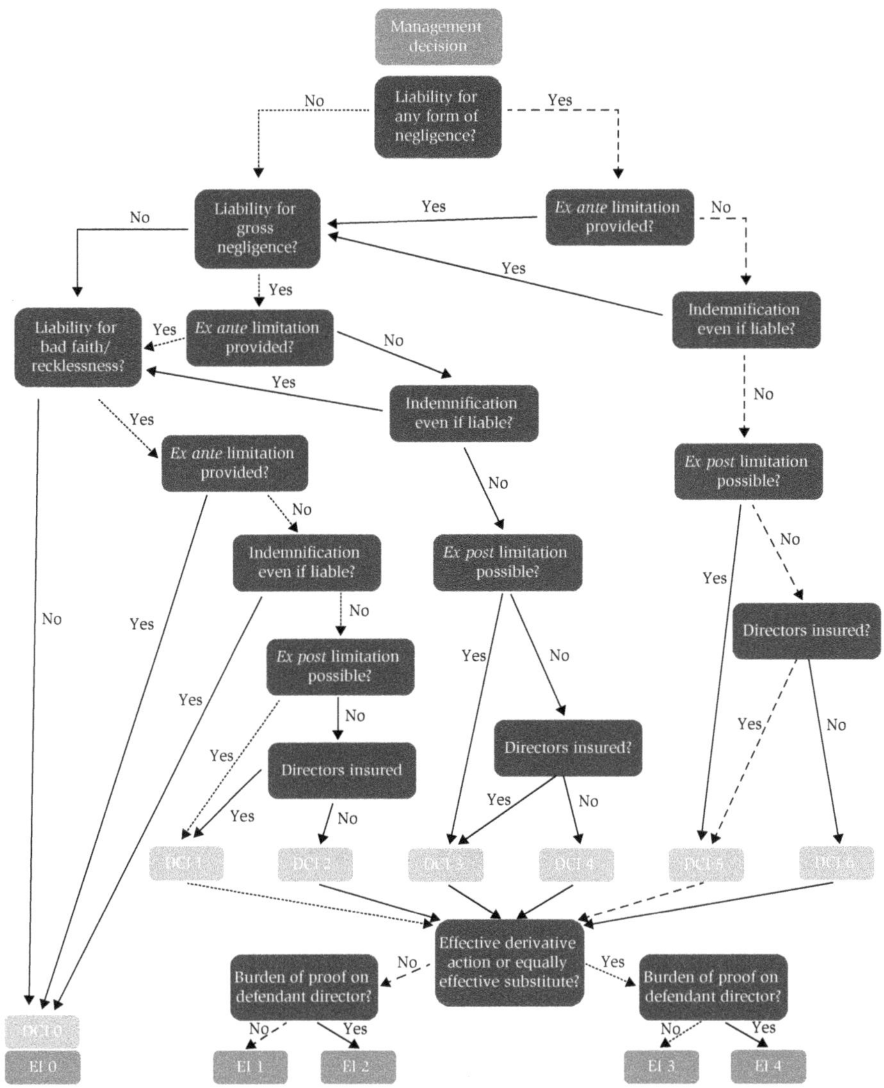

Figure 15.1 first outlines three broad standards of care that cover the spectrum of conceivable standards: a negligence standard, a gross negligence standard, and a bad faith/recklessness standard. Then, it makes allowance for the possibility that legal systems permit an *ex ante* modification of the applicable standard of care by limiting

liability to conduct that amounts to the most demanding standard (such as Delaware) or excluding liability for conduct not exceeding the least demanding standard. If liability can be excluded even for bad faith or reckless behaviour (which is not the case in any of the legal systems analysed here), directors face no liability, and the DCI thus equals zero. Likewise, if directors have a right to be indemnified fully for certain types of conduct (e.g., negligence), even if they are found liable, they face no threat of liability for that type of conduct, and Figure 15.1 shifts the analysis to the next standard of care.[140]

Figure 15.1 then asks whether the liability exposure of directors can be limited *ex post*, through ratification of an act amounting to either a breach of the duty of care or a waiver of the company's claim. Some legal systems, for example, Delaware and the UK, allow ratification by a vote of disinterested shareholders. Others do so only with significant hurdles (Germany[141]), and yet others prohibit any *ex post* waiver of liability (France).[142] The liability exposure of directors is higher than in the case of an *ex ante* limitation of liability, even if ratification results in directors being regarded as not having committed a breach of duty,[143] because the *ex ante* threat of liability conditions the behaviour of directors, and there is no guarantee that disinterested shareholders will ratify a breach in a particular case. In addition, a legal system may provide that some acts are non-ratifiable, or ratification does not extinguish liability, but may instead result in the activation of a review standard that is more favourable to directors. Notably, this is the case under Delaware law, where acts amounting, for example, to a waste of corporate assets cannot be ratified, and shareholder ratification of other acts reinstates the business judgment rule standard, rather than fully exculpating directors.[144]

D&O insurance, likewise, does not offer full protection against personal liability. Some legal systems provide for a legally mandated excess (for example, pursuant to German law, at least 10% of the damage with a cap of not less than 1.5 times the director's fixed annual remuneration[145]) or exclude coverage for certain types of conduct (for example, under French law, a company cannot insure its directors against liability arising from intentional or fraudulent conduct[146]). Even where no deductible is legally required, insurance policies will only offer limited coverage.[147] Furthermore, insurance undertakings are responsive to changes in the probability of a director being

140. Again, full indemnification is not permitted in any of the legal systems analysed here. *See*, for example, the UK Companies Act 2006, ss. 232(2) and 234(b)(ii), which provide that the articles of association or other contractual arrangements must not provide any indemnity against liability incurred by a director in proceedings brought by the director's company in which judgment is given against the director.
141. Claims can only be waived three years after they arose and only if no objection is registered by minority shareholders holding at least 10% of the share capital, German Stock Corporation Act, § 93(4).
142. *See* Table 15.2.
143. On the meaning and consequences of ratification and waiver, *see* Davies, Worthington, and Hare, *supra* n. 116, 10–112.
144. *See* the references in Table 15.2.
145. German Stock Corporation Act, § 93(2) sentence 3.
146. French Insurance Code, Art L113-1(2).
147. *See* the *references supra* n. 110.

held liable, which may be a result of either legal changes or an updated assessment of the probability of future non-compliant behaviour by a director.[148] Directors may therefore face monetary consequences for a breach of duty even if they are insured. For purposes of the DCI, this means that if insurance is in place, the index should be lower than without insurance, but higher than in cases where liability is excluded *ex ante*. However, it is difficult to see how the incentive difference (if any) between the possibility of an *ex post* ratification of a breach of duty or waiver of the company's claim and the partial protection against monetary liability from insurance can be quantified in a rationally defensible manner. The DCI therefore treats both identically (DCI 1, 3, and 5).

To illustrate the operation of the DCI, assume that a company is incorporated under Delaware law and has made use of all possibilities granted under the law of Delaware to limit the liability exposure of directors. Pursuant to the Delaware duty of care, directors face no liability unless plaintiffs can show that the defendants acted in bad faith, disregarded material information reasonably available to them, or sought to derive a personal benefit from a transaction, for example, by engaging in self-dealing.[149] Whether directors availed themselves of all material information and then acted with the requisite care is assessed against a gross negligence standard.[150] However, Delaware law allows companies to exclude liability for monetary damages for a breach of the duty of care in the certificate of incorporation, except for acts in bad faith.[151] Such acts are also non-indemnifiable,[152] but shareholders have the possibility to ratify them (provided directors have not acted fraudulently[153]). Insurance policies, on the other hand, are unlikely to cover bad faith conduct. This sequence of considerations is depicted by dotted arrows in Figure 15.1. The resulting DCI equals 1.

In contrast, under French law, directors are liable for any form of negligence. Liability cannot be excluded or limited *ex ante*, directors cannot be indemnified and claims of the company cannot be waived *ex post*.[154] Companies are able to take out D&O insurance, which typically covers negligence. If insurance has indeed been

148. *See*, e.g., Roberta Romano, *Corporate Governance in the Aftermath of the Insurance Crisis* 39 Emory Law J. 1155, 1157–9 (1990) (explaining that D&O insurance became difficult to obtain in the United States after an explosion of liability actions in the first half of the 1980s that seemed to usher in a substantial increase in the risk of liability for good-faith breaches of the duty of care).
149. *Aronson v Lewis*, 473 A.2d 805, 812 (Del. 1984).
150. *Ibid.* From more recent case law, *see also Brehm v. Eisner*, 746 A.2d 244, 259 (Del. 2000); *Re Walt Disney Co. Derivative Litigation*, 907 A.2d 693, 749 (Del. Ch. 2005).
151. Delaware General Corporation Law, § 102(b)(7).
152. Delaware General Corporation Law, § 145(b).
153. Fraudulent acts constitute acts in bad faith, but whether acts in bad faith amount to fraud is a matter of definition. Under Delaware law, fraud and bad faith are not synonymous. Bad faith is defined as an 'intentional dereliction of duty, a conscious disregard for one's responsibilities', *In re Walt Disney Co. Derivative Litigation*, 906 A.2d 27, 66 (Del. 2006). Fraud, also referred to as subjective bad faith, is a narrower category that also requires 'an actual intent to do harm', *ibid.*, 64.
154. *See* Table 15.2.

purchased, the DCI therefore equals 5.[155] The relevant analytical steps are depicted by dashed arrows in Figure 15.1.

Enforcement questions are generally independent of the DCI, except where the DCI equals zero. In other cases, it is not clear why a DCI of a particular value (say, a particularly stringently formulated duty of care) should influence the ease of enforcing a breach of the duty (that is, there are no obvious interaction effects between the DCI and EI). It is therefore sensible to compute both variables separately. However, as discussed in §15.03, individual legal elements that determine how a potential breach of duty can be enforced are not independent of one another.

For purposes of the EI, it is assumed that an effective enforcement regime must provide for the possibility of an action being brought by persons or bodies other than the board of directors, which will often be conflicted, or the general meeting, which may suffer from a similar conflict of interest or, if shareholders are dispersed, from coordination problems. Primarily, effective enforcement will therefore require that minority shareholders are able to bring a derivative claim without undue difficulties. If it is correct, as argued in §15.03, that this is only the case if a derivative action mechanism is conducive to minority shareholder litigation along *all* dimensions identified as relevant in that section, the EI should not represent an aggregation of scores assigned to these dimensions (for example, the EI takes the value 3 if all three dimensions are favourable to minority shareholder lawsuits, and the value 2 if one of the three dimensions creates an obstacle to litigation). Rather, it is suggested that the EI operates in a binary fashion at this level: either an effective enforcement mechanism exists that allows an independent body or person to sidestep the potentially conflicted board of directors and general meeting, or it does not exist.

In the absence of an effective derivative action, other legal mechanisms may, in principle, function as substitutes. Whether these are effective depends on the legal mechanism in question. Of those examined in §15.02[A], arguably only the Dutch inquiry proceedings may qualify as an effective substitute. Criminal law is limited to particularly grievous misconduct and has a high evidentiary threshold, and directors' disqualification typically only becomes relevant once a company has been placed into insolvency proceedings.

In a second stage, the EI captures how the burden of proof is distributed. This question is again formulated in a binary fashion. A legal rule that shifts the burden on the directors (as, for example, German law[156]) facilitates recovery. It is suggested that the focus of the inquiry at this level should be on the initial allocation of the burden of proof. Legal system may provide that the burden shifts under certain conditions, but if claimant-shareholders need to meet an initial threshold of showing misconduct,

155. It is worth repeating that the DCI reflects a firm-level assessment. Thus, if insurance was unavailable or had not been purchased by a French company, the DCI for that company would equal 6.

156. German Stock Corporation Act, § 93(2), sentence 2.

recovery is appreciably more difficult than if directors had to show that they complied with their duties.[157]

For the two legal systems used to illustrate the operation of the DCI and EI, Delaware and France, these considerations mean the following. Only Delaware law provides for a derivative action that does not stymie minority shareholder litigation.[158] The French minority shareholder action plays a negligible role in practice because of the financial disincentives that it creates, and French law has not developed an effective substitute mechanism. In both legal systems, claimant-shareholders must show that directors breached their fiduciary duties, although the burden shifts to the directors if the shareholders meet this threshold.[159] In Figure 15.1, these analytical steps are again depicted by dotted arrows for Delaware and dashed arrows for France. The resultant EI equals 3 for Delaware and 1 for France.

It is interesting to note that the scores for the DCI and EI in the two countries are roughly reversed. France scores in the top third in the DCI and the bottom quartile in the EI, and Delaware in the bottom quartile in the DCI and the top half in the EI. Whether this means that the overall environment for a protection of minority shareholders in the two countries is roughly comparable can de doubted. The impact of the EI on minority shareholder protection is likely non-linear. An EI below 3 means that enforcement actions will be rare. An EI of 3 or 4, on the other hand, means that potential breaches of fiduciary duties will be litigated regularly, and shareholders will recover damages in at least some cases even if the DCI is low.[160]

§15.05 CONCLUSION

This chapter has suggested a theoretical framework to capture and quantify the effects of fiduciary duties and legal mechanisms governing their enforcement. It is for future research to extend the framework in two respects. First, from a theoretical angle, the interdependence of legal rules that address further typical scenarios of managerial conduct should be conceptualised similarly to what this contribution did for the duty of care. In particular, the regulation of related-party transactions between a director and the company and the exploitation of corporate opportunities by directors for their

157. For example, the Delaware business judgment rule operates as a presumption that the defendant directors acted in good faith, without a conflict of interest, and based on appropriate information. If plaintiff-shareholders rebut the presumption, the burden shifts to the directors to demonstrate that the challenged act or transaction was entirely fair to the corporation, *In re Walt Disney Co. Derivative Litigation*, 906 A.2d 27, 52 (Del. 2006). Similarly, under French law, shareholders bear the burden of proving that a decision of the directors constituted a management mistake. If they meet this burden, it falls on the defendant directors to establish that they exercised the care of a cautious and prudent director, notably by opposing the challenged decision, Cass. Com., 30 March 2010, FP-P + B + R + I, n° 08-17.841, *Fonds de garantie des dépôts (FGD) c/ Sté Caribéenne de conseil et d'audit (Crédit Martiniquais)*, *Revue des sociétés* 2010, 304. For an English translation and analysis of this case, *see* Gerner-Beuerle and Schillig, *supra* n. 40, 523–26.
158. *See* the discussion in §15.03.
159. *See supra* n. 157.
160. A high DCI-EI combination may, in any case, not be optimal, *see* the discussion in §15.02[B].

personal gain are likely to follow patterns partially different from those depicted in Figure 15.1, although many of the considerations that have informed the development of Figure 15.1 (such as the possibility to limit liability exposure *ex ante* or *ex post* through private ordering) will be equally applicable to this context.

In a second step, the legal variables constructed according to the methodology suggested here can be used to investigate several empirical questions that this contribution has touched upon. In particular, it is not well understood how the fiduciary duties-enforcement nexus should be calibrated to improve economic outcomes. A variable capturing enforcement regimes is unlikely to have a linear effect, but this needs to be investigated further. Likewise, it is unclear how substantive rules interact with enforcement mechanisms and whether, for example, strong enforcement rights combined with limited liability exposure are more efficient than strong enforcement rights combined with stringent fiduciary duties.

CHAPTER 16

Auditors' Role in Corporate Governance

Jukka Mähönen[*]

§16.01 INTRODUCTION

There are numerous reasons for firms[1] undergoing an audit.[2] As described by accounting historians Ross Watts and Jerold Zimmerman, auditing is a mechanism to enable management teams to add credibility to their position as stewards and to confirm the reliability of information issued to investors.[3] Others argue that audits are not market-driven: undertakings will undergo an audit when it suits them, for instance, as

* I would like to thank the organizers of the January 2022 conference and the editors of the volume, Hanne Birkmose, Mette Neville, and Karsten Engsig Sørensen. I would also like to acknowledge all the inspiring comments and suggestions made by the participants. For their helpful comments on a draft of this chapter, my thanks go to Karsten Engsig Sørensen and Hanne Birkmose. This chapter is based on research of the University of Oslo UiO: Nordic initiative funded research project Futuring Sustainable Nordic Business Models.

1. In this chapter, 'firm' and 'undertaking' are used interchangeably. Undertaking is a concept used in the EU legislation on audit and accounting, e.g., the following three EU legal instruments central to this chapter: Directive 2006/43/EC of the European Parliament and of the Council of 17 May 2006 on statutory audits of annual accounts and consolidated accounts, amending Council Directives 78/660/EEC and 83/349/EEC and repealing Council Directive 84/253/EEC, OJ L 157, 9.6.2006, pp. 87–107 (Audit Directive); Regulation (EU) No. 537/2014 of the European Parliament and of the Council of 16 April 2014 on specific requirements regarding statutory audits of public-interest entities and repealing Commission Decision 2005/909/EC, OJ L 158, 27.5.2014, pp. 77–112 (Audit Regulation); and Directive 2013/34/EU of the European Parliament and of the Council of 26 June 2013 on annual financial statements, consolidated financial statements, and related reports of certain types of undertakings, amending Directive 2006/43/EC of the European Parliament and of the Council and repealing Council Directives 78/660/EEC and 83/349/EEC, OJ L 182, 29.6.2013, pp. 19–76 (Accounting Directive).
2. I have previously discussed the EU accounting and audit regulatory framework, for instance, in Jukka Mähönen, *Comprehensive Approach to Relevant and Reliable Reporting in Europe: A Dream Impossible?* 12 Sustainability 5277 (2020).
3. Ross L. Watts & Jerold L. Zimmerman, *Agency Problems, Auditing, and the Theory of the Firm: Some Evidence*, 26 J. Law Econ. 613, 614 (1983).

a means of avoiding stringent regulation of their financial reports or to obtain professional advice. However, audits do not exist in a vacuum: they are subject to regulation and undertakings' duty to provide information based on a political process involving various interests and interest groups seeking some kind of advantage or trying to avoid the auditing process. So, auditing depends on the prevailing legal and economic environment.[4] At the same time, audits of private and public entities are an important part of society, creating accountability for those in power and trust in the legitimacy of use of such power.[5]

Notwithstanding the complexity of their duties,[6] auditors must focus on auditing financial accounts.[7] Auditing and accounting are inseparable, and development of the auditing process follows the development of accounting and reporting. Financial accounting and reporting constitute the cornerstone of traditional corporate infrastructure and, accordingly, of capitalism itself. Today's capitalism would not even exist without financial reporting.[8] Financial accounting and reporting and corporate governance are also interlinked: modern accounting and, through this, corporate reporting began developing at the end of the fifteenth century, for instance, in Venice, England, and the Netherlands, paving the way for creation of the modern company of the nineteenth century.[9] Technological changes in manufacturing created by innovations

4. Josephine Maltby & Roy Chandler, *Auditing*, in *The Routledge Companion to Accounting History* 252 (John Richard Edwards & Stephen Walker eds., Routledge 2020).
5. On the history of auditing, *see* John R. Edwards, *A History of Financial Accounting* (RLE Accounting) (2013); Maltby & Chandler, *supra* n. 4. *See also*, Felix I. Lessambo, *Overview, History, and Overall Objectives of Auditing*, in *Auditing, Assurance Services, and Forensics: A Comprehensive Approach* 3–16 (Springer International Publishing 2018); *see also*, Thomas Alexander Lee (ed.), *The Evolution of Audit Thought and Practice* (Routledge Library Editions 1989); and Thomas Alexander Lee, *Corporate Audit Theory* (Chapman & Hall 1993).
6. In this chapter, 'auditor' refers to a statutory auditor or an audit firm auditing financial statements. In the EU, statutory audits are defined in the Audit Directive. In the Directive, a statutory audit means an audit of annual financial statements or consolidated financial statements as (a) required by Union law; (b) required by national law for small undertakings; (c) voluntarily carried out at the request of small undertakings, meeting national legal requirements that are equivalent to those for an audit under point (b), where national legislation defines such audits as statutory audits; *see* Art. 2(1) of the Audit Directive, as amended by Directive 2014/56/EU of the European Parliament and of the Council of 16 April 2014 amending Directive 2006/43/EC on statutory audits of annual accounts and consolidated accounts, OJ L 158, 27.5.2014, pp. 196–226 (Amended Audit Directive). A statutory auditor is defined as a person who is approved in accordance with the Audit Directive by competent authorities in a Member State to carry out statutory audits, and an audit firm is a legal person or any other entity (regardless of its legal form) approved in accordance with the Directive by competent authorities in a Member State to carry out statutory audits; *see* Art. 2(2) and (3) of the Audit Directive. The definitions in the Audit Directive are also applied in the Audit Regulation.
7. Auditing can be defined, for instance, as it is done in Art. 2(1) of the Audit Directive as a 'statutory audit', meaning 'an audit of annual financial statements or consolidated financial statements as (a) required by Union law, (b) required by national law as regards small undertakings, (c) voluntarily carried out at the request of small undertakings which meets national legal requirements that are equivalent to those for an audit under point (b), where national legislation defines such audits as statutory audits'.
8. Robert G. Eccles & Birgit Spiesshofer, *Integrated Reporting for a Re-Imagined Capitalism*, in *Re-Imagining Capitalism* 207–225 (Dominic Barton, Dezsö Horváth, & Matthias Kipping, eds., Oxford University Press 2016).
9. Mähönen, *supra* n. 2, at 3.

from the Industrial Revolution facilitated introduction and expansion of capital markets, and the evolution of capital-intensive business enterprises contributed to accounting-related functions, such as financial reporting and auditing, which, in turn, became part of corporate regulation and business legislation designed to make corporate managers accountable to shareholders. Unsurprisingly, public accountants from the mid-nineteenth century onwards organized themselves collectively to create associations to defend their economic and social interests in such matters.[10]

Until the separation of companies and their members, the role of accounting was to serve owner-manager partners. With separation of ownership and control, the focus of financial reporting changed from within-company owner-managers to outside shareholders. However, without the modern company and its legal persona, there would have been no entity on which to report (with the separation of capital from income distinguishing a company from a partnership). From the early 1900s, the entity concept was expanded to encompass groups with consolidated accounts.[11]

Due to these origins, corporate reporting has, since the nineteenth century, been centred on providers of financial capital and creation of classifications between different groups of capital providers (including controlling shareholders, minority shareholders, and creditors), based on taxonomies of the financial assets they provide to the enterprise (classified as equity, debt, or derivatives) serving to protect them.[12] The objectives of traditional continental accounting regulation can be summarized as[13] (1) maintenance of capital – regulation of dividends; (2) monitoring of management – stewardship; (3) information for investors; (4) information for the state; (5) information for employees; (6) information for the general public; and (7) computation of tax. These seven classes do not apply equally to every country, and their relative importance in each country will have varied significantly over time as well. However, there has been (and still is) a strong link between accounting rules and company law, and due to this link, corporate reporting is invariably an opportunity for financial capital providers to count the 'value' of their investments and the surplus distributable (e.g., the difference between commodities sold and production costs).[14] Internationalization of financial reporting has emphasized the focus on investor usefulness. Since the 1970s, the US Financial Accounting Standards Board (FASB) and International Accounting Standards Committee (IASC; later the International Accounting Standards Board, IASB) have developed financial reporting standards based on decisions in the interests of investors.[15]

---

10. Thomas A. Lee, *Financial Accounting Theory*, in *The Routledge Companion to Accounting History* 159, 161–162 (John Richard Edwards & Stephen P. Walker, eds., 2nd edition, Routledge 2020).
11. Starting with the United States Steel Corporation in 1902; *see ibid.*, 163.
12. Mähönen, *supra* n. 2, at 3.
13. John Flower, *European Financial Reporting: Adapting to a Changing World* (Palgrave Macmillan 2004), 29–30. *See also* Stephen A. Zeff, *The Objectives of Financial Reporting: A Historical Survey and Analysis*, 43 Accounting and Business Research 262, 309 (2013).
14. Mähönen, *supra* n. 2, at 3.
15. Zeff, *supra* n. 13, at 264.

Accounting has a central role in corporate governance, as a tool to control the flow of information between different constituencies of an undertaking: the management, members of the undertaking (primarily) (including partners, members of a cooperative, and shareholders in a company), contractual and semi-contractual parties (secondarily) as creditors, and the state as the collector of tax revenues. Any tension between management needs and investor needs will be reflected in an audit: an auditor's primary responsibility is to ensure that the interests of shareholders (and maybe those of other constituencies) are protected or to act as an adviser to the management, but are these two roles complementary or competing? The answer to this question has implications for audit objectives: should the audit primarily be directed at statement verification, or fraud detection *ex post*, or at preventing error and misstatement *ex ante*? The desired audit objective also has an impact on audit technique, e.g., the relative importance of testing the substance of transactions or the testing of accounting controls, the use of sampling and the emphasis on risk in planning audit work.[16]

Auditing plays an important and varying role in corporate governance, and the history of different kinds of audits is as long as the history of modern enterprises.[17] In Europe, auditing is now understood to be an activity performed by auditors or audit firms.[18] However, this is not necessarily the case. Originally, accounts were audited by the management itself, shareholders or their representatives as supervisory boards, before the duty was transferred to external experts (auditors) at the end of the nineteenth century and early twentieth century.[19] At the same time, auditors became subject to regulation for the first time, first by regulation of auditor accreditation and then also by regulation of the audit process.[20]

A never-ending flow of financial scandals has impacted on the course of auditing regulation. The world economic crisis of 1929 and the Great Depression that followed affected both accounting regulation (for example, the US Securities Act and Securities Exchange Act of 1933 and 1934, and the German Stock Companies Act (*Aktiengesetz*) of 1937) and the professionalization of auditing practices.[21] Similarly, a consolidation process began, starting voluntarily in the early twentieth century, with the help of

---

16. Maltby & Chandler, *supra* n. 4, at 252.
17. Watts & Zimmerman, *supra* n. 3, at 613; Josephine Maltby & Roy Chandler, *Auditing* (Routledge, 2009); Lessambo, *supra* n. 5.
18. According to Art. 3(1) of the Audit Directive, a statutory audit may only be carried out by statutory auditors or audit firms approved by the Member State requiring the statutory audit.
19. In this chapter, auditor and auditing firm are used interchangeably unless otherwise indicated in the text; *see supra* n. 6.
20. For instance, auditor authorization was introduced in Denmark in 1909, in Norway in 1910, in Sweden in 1910, and in Finland in 1912; *see* Arne Fagerström & Simon Lundh, *Accounting development in the Nordic Countries: A Comparative Study*, 2 Journal for Global Business Advancement 4–27 (2009); Peter Öhman & Eva Wallerstedt, *Audit Regulation and the Development of the Auditing Profession: The Case of Sweden*, 17 Accounting History 241–257 (2012); Claus Holm, *Civil and Common Law Influences on the Danish Auditor's Responsibilities in Relation to Fraud*, 24 Account. Hist. Rev. 7–26 (2014).
21. Walther Busse von Colbe & Rolf U. Fülbier, *Accounting and the Business Economics Tradition in Germany*, in *Accounting and Business Economics: Insights from National Traditions* 45–46 (Yuri Biondi & Stefano Zambon, eds., Routledge 2013).

auditors,[22] which then gradually became compulsory in various jurisdictions (for instance, in the United Kingdom in 1947,[23] in Germany in 1965,[24] and finally in the European Union (EU) in 1983).[25] The internationalization of consolidated accounts also began on a voluntary basis, for instance, in Germany, triggered by the first listing of a German company on the New York Stock Exchange and introduction of the FASB standards (US generally accepted accounting principles (GAAP)),[26] triggering the (then) IASC (later the IASB International Financial Reporting Standards (IFRS)) initiative. This replaced the option to prepare consolidated accounts according to the US GAAP with compulsory IFRS consolidated accounts for European publicly traded companies from the beginning of 2005, and it raised the IAS/IFRS and IASC/IASB to their current position and likewise the role of auditors in listed multinational companies.[27] Although the emphasis of international accounting standards and international audits applies to listed companies only, they have crystallized the focus on regulation of accounting and auditing of domestic companies and other undertakings.

During the last 150 years or so, regulation of auditors, auditing firms, and auditing has grown within the context of a jungle of national, transnational, and international; public, private, and semi-public; legal and social norms and market structures. Although auditors have been challenged by competing assurance providers,[28] auditing has survived as a part of corporate governance, and its enduring presence suggests that it is a vital part of efficient organizations.[29]

In the EU, for instance, legislation requires that the corporate financial statements (comprising annual financial statements or consolidated financial statements) of public-interest entities, including listed undertakings,[30] credit institutions, insurance

22. Starting with the United States Steel Corporation in 1902, with the help of Price, Waterhouse & Co.; *see* Lee, *supra* n. 10, at 163.
23. Zeff, *supra* n. 13, at 290.
24. Busse von Colbe & Fülbier, *supra* n. 21, at 53.
25. Seventh Council Directive 83/349/EEC of 13 June 1983, based on Art. 54(3) (g) of the Treaty on consolidated accounts, OJ L 193, 18.7.1983, pp. 1–17.
26. Daimler Benz AG in 1993, followed by, e.g., Deutsche Telekom in 1995, SAP in 1998, and finally Deutsche Bank and Siemens in 2001; *see* Busse von Colbe & Fülbier, *supra* n. 21, at 54–55.
27. Regulation (EC) No. 1606/2002 of the European Parliament and of the Council of 19 July 2002 on the application of international accounting standards, OJ L 243, 11.9.2002, pp. 1–4; *see* Leo G. van der Tas, *American Hegemony or Mutual Recognition with Benchmarks? A Comment*, 4 European Accounting Review 255–260 (1995); Karel van Hulle, *From Accounting Directives to International Accounting Standards*, in *The Economics and Politics of Accounting* (Oxford University Press 2004); Stephen A. Zeff, *The Evolution of the IASC into the IASB, and the Challenges It Faces*, 87 T Account. Rev. 807–837 (2012); Zeff, *supra* n. 13, at 310.
28. *See*, for instance, Art. 34(3) of the Commission's proposal for the Corporate Sustainability Reporting Directive, granting Member States the right to also allow independent assurance services providers to express an opinion regarding sustainability reporting compliance with the requirements of the proposed Directive; *see* European Commission, Proposal for a Directive of the European Parliament and of the Council amending Directive 2013/34/EU, Directive 2004/109/EC, Directive 2006/43/EC, and Regulation (EU) No. 537/2014, regarding corporate sustainability reporting, COM(2021) 189 final (Corporate Sustainability Reporting Directive proposal).
29. Watts & Zimmerman, *supra* n. 3, at 614.
30. In this chapter, the terms 'listed undertaking', 'firm', and 'company' are used, meaning (for instance, in the EU) companies whose securities are listed or dealt with in a regulated market in an EU Member State, defined as 'a multilateral system operated and/or managed by a market

undertakings, issuers of securities trading in a regulated market, payment institutions, undertakings for collective investment in transferable securities (UCITS), electronic money institutions, and alternative investment funds, as well medium-sized and large undertakings, be audited by one or more persons entitled to carry out such audits in accordance with Union law.[31] Measures for certification of auditors are an important part of the regulations,[32] and the introduction of this EU legislation ended a centuries-old tradition of amateur (peer) auditing in the EU, starting from 2008.[33]

However, tensions can still exist in accounting, so for verification purposes, an audit is a useful tool for management of efficient business decisions and for 'stewardship', to help members of the undertaking (and other interested parties) evaluate how well management teams have fulfilled their duties as custodians of their investments.[34]

---

operator, which brings together or facilitates the bringing together of multiple third-party buying and selling interests in financial instruments – in the system and in accordance with its non-discretionary rules – in a way that results in a contract, in respect of the financial instruments admitted to trading under its rules and/or systems, and which is authorized and functions regularly and in accordance with Title III of this Directive'; Art. 4(1)(21) of Directive 2014/65/EU of the European Parliament and of the Council of 15 May 2014 on markets in financial instruments and amending Directive 2002/92/EC and Directive 2011/61/EU, OJ L 173, 12.6.2014, pp. 349–496.

31. Art. 34(1) of the Accounting Directive; Art. 1(1) of Council Directive 86/635/EEC of 8 December 1986 on the annual accounts and consolidated accounts of banks and other financial institutions, OJ L 372, 31.12.1986, pp. 1–17; Art. 1(1) of Council Directive 91/674/EEC of 19 December 1991 on the annual accounts and consolidated accounts of insurance undertakings, OJ L 374, 31.12.1991, pp. 7–31; Art. 4(4) of Directive 2004/109/EC of the European Parliament and of the Council of 15 December 2004 on the harmonization of transparency requirements in relation to information about issuers whose securities are admitted to trading on a regulated market and amending Directive 2001/34/EC, OJ L 390, 31.12.2004, pp. 38–57; Art. 17(2) of Directive (EU) 2015/2366 of the European Parliament and of the Council of 25 November 2015 on payment services in the internal market, amending Directives 2002/65/EC, 2009/110/EC, and 2013/36/EU and Regulation (EU) No. 1093/2010, and repealing Directive 2007/64/EC, OJ L 337, 23.12.2015, pp. 35–127; Art. 73 of Directive 2009/65/EC of the European Parliament and of the Council of 13 July 2009 on the coordination of laws, regulations, and administrative provisions relating to undertakings for collective investment in transferable securities (UCITS), OJ L 302, 17.11.2009, pp. 32–96; Art. 3(1) of Directive 2009/110/EC of the European Parliament and of the Council of 16 September 2009 on the taking up, pursuit and prudential supervision of the business of electronic money institutions, amending Directives 2005/60/EC and 2006/48/EC and repealing Directive 2000/46/EC, OJ L 267, 10.10.2009, pp. 7–17; and Art. 22(3) of Directive 2011/61/EU of the European Parliament and of the Council of 8 June 2011 on Alternative Investment Fund Managers and amending Directives 2003/41/EC and 2009/65/EC and Regulation (EC) No. 1060/2009 and (EU) No. 1095/2010, OJ L 174, 1.7.2011, pp. 1–73. Moreover, Art. 4(1)(1)(2)I of Directive 2014/65/EU of the European Parliament and of the Council of 15 May 2014 on markets in financial instruments and amending Directive 2002/92/EC and Directive 2011/61/EU, OJ L 173, 12.6.2014, pp. 349–496 requires that the investment firm's annual accounts be audited by one or more persons empowered, under national law, to audit accounts.
32. In the EU, the conditions for approval of persons responsible for carrying out statutory audits, as well as the minimum requirements for carrying out such statutory audits, are laid down in the Audit Directive; *see* especially Chapters II and V.
33. Watts & Zimmerman, *supra* n. 3. As an example of implementation of the Directive, *see* the Finnish government's proposal for an Audit Act and accompanying legislation (HE 194/2006 vp, Hallituksen esitys Eduskunnalle tilintarkastuslaiksi ja siihen liittyväksi lainsäädännöksi).
34. *See*, e.g., Zeff, *supra* n. 13, at 264, 277, 290, 305–306; Vincent O'Connell, *Reflections on Stewardship Reporting*, 21 Accounting Horizons 215, 216–217 (2007). Stewardship can be understood in different ways, from management's honesty in husbanding the enterprise's resources to its efficiency in utilizing them, providing shareholders with a suitable return on

The second question is whether the focus is on members' or investors' needs or on the needs of society as a whole, and how well it fulfils their expectations.[35] The path to modern international accounting as reflected in the FASB US GAAP and IFRS, based on usefulness to investors, has had a long path, however,[36] and more and more demands are being made for stricter stewardship and accountability for the usefulness of verified economic information – not only to management and investors but also to other groups whose position is affected by the activities of the undertaking, as well as society and the ecosystem as a whole.[37]

As the role of accounting and auditing in corporate governance has become even more important due to development of modern undertakings and markets for securities during the last 150 years or so, corporate governance has also become more important, along with a corresponding need for credible assurance of accounting information. This has led auditing to focus on corporate governance as an enforcement mechanism in the verification of accounting data.[38] A key role of auditing is to constrain opportunistic managerial behaviour involving manipulation of accounting numbers and to render accounting reliable for contracting and for credible communication with investors and other constituencies.[39] However, the relationship between accounting's role both as a tool for management and as a tool for stewardship is reflected in the *ex ante* and *ex post* objectives of auditing, both to help management verify its statements and also to support stewardship in detecting flaws in management.

Auditors have an important role in corporate governance, but they are not part of an undertaking's management, including the board and the chief executive officer (CEO) or the general manager.[40] They are not, legally speaking,

---

management's employment of resources, enabling the shareholders to take actions to remunerate, promote or dismiss management or to make rational decisions about buying and selling their shares; *see* Zeff, *supra* n. 13, at 264.

35. *Ibid.*
36. George J. Staubus, *The Residual Equity Point of View in Accounting*, 34 Account. Rev. 3, 4 (1959); George J. Staubus, *A Theory of Accounting to Investors*, 3 (University of California Press 1961); George J. Staubus, *The Decision Usefulness Theory of Accounting: A Limited History* (1st edition, Routledge 1999).
37. O'Connell, *supra* n. 34, at 223–224.
38. Ross L. Watts & Jerold L. Zimmerman, *Positive Accounting Theory*, 196 (Prentice Hall 1986); Jere R. Francis, Inder K. Khurana, & Raynolde Pereira, *The Role of Accounting and Auditing in Corporate Governance and the Development of Financial Markets Around the World*, 10 Asia-Pacific Journal of Accounting & Economics 1, 8 (2003).
39. Francis, Khurana, & Pereira, *Ibid.*
40. There is no uniform definition, not even in the EU, of management of corporations as it is based on national legislation, which varies from country to country and from business form to business form. However, according to a recent definition in the EU Shareholders' Rights Directive, applied to listed companies (i.e., companies whose securities are listed or dealt with in a regulated market in an EU Member State, Art. 4(1)(21) of Directive 2014/65/EU of the European Parliament and of the Council of 15 May 2014 on markets in financial instruments and amending Directive 2002/92/EC and Directive 2011/61/EU, OJ L 173, 12.6.2014, pp. 349–496, *see supra* n. 30), a 'director' means (i) any member of the administrative, management, or supervisory bodies of a company; (ii) where they are not members of the administrative, management, or supervisory bodies of a company, the CEO and, if such function exists in a company, the deputy CEO; (iii) where so determined by a Member State, other persons who perform functions similar to those performed under point (i) or (ii); *see* Art. 2(i) of Directive 2007/36/EC of the European Parliament and of the Council of 11 July 2007 on the exercise of certain rights of shareholders in

'agents'[41] for the members of the undertaking either, although they are often elected by members. However, auditors are not agents for the management either, despite their fees being based on a contract between themselves and the management – acting on behalf of the undertaking – whose work they scrutinize. In the case of firms with societal importance, in particular, they are seen as guardians of public interests, albeit not directly, by communities of people and institutions relying on auditors' work (including the state in its many roles) but also in a more abstract way, given that auditing contributes to the reliability and orderly functioning of markets and society generally by enhancing the integrity and efficiency of corporate information. In this way, auditors fulfil a particularly important societal role.[42] This role can also be seen as one that ensures accountability to a firm's stakeholders.[43]

Traditionally, research into auditing in corporate governance has focused on how corporate governance affects auditing, rather than how auditing affects corporate governance.[44] However, the abovementioned changes in regulatory frameworks all over the world show that the role of external auditors reflects the increasing focus on corporate governance and internal control not only on the part of companies and regulators but also its heterogeneousness.[45] In listed companies, we have seen a change in auditors' roles for various reasons, such as limitations on audit firms as full-scale service providers, increased pressure on the perceived credibility of auditors, increased importance of audit committees, their independence, and their role in communicating with auditors.[46] In closed companies, the auditor is still the primary

listed companies, OJ L 184, 14.7.2007, pp. 17–24, as amended by Directive (EU) 2017/828 of the European Parliament and of the Council of 17 May 2017 amending Directive 2007/36/EC regarding the encouragement of long-term shareholder engagement, OJ L 132, 20.5.2017, pp. 1–25. The definition is also used in Art. 3(o) of the European Commission Proposal for a Directive of the European Parliament and of the Council on Corporate Sustainability Due Diligence and amending Directive (EU) 2019/1937, COM(2022) 71 final. In Art. 3(p) of the Proposal, a 'board of directors' is defined as 'the administrative or supervisory body responsible for supervising the executive management of the company, or, if no such body exists, the person or persons performing equivalent functions'.

41. Viewing the problematics of agency theory as a normative theory, *see*, e.g., Beate Sjåfjell & Jukka Mähönen, Corporate Purpose and the Misleading Shareholder vs Stakeholder Dichotomy (21 February 2022), available at https://papers.ssrn.com/abstract=4039565 (accessed 8 July 2022). In this chapter, agency is used as a description of the relationships between different parties in a business undertaking, including auditors. On agency theory, *see* John W. Pratt & Richard Zeckhauser (eds) *Principals and Agents: The Structure of business* (Harvard Business School Press 1985).
42. Preamble 1 of the Audit Regulation.
43. As with agency (*see* Lee, *supra* n. 10), I have reservations about the concept of stakeholders as it is often misleading, creating false dichotomies between corporate constituencies; *see* Sjåfjell & Mähönen, *supra* n. 41. The concept is used in the EU corporate regulatory framework. For instance, according to Preamble 13 of the Audit Regulation, the results of the statutory audit of a public-interest entity should be presented to stakeholders in the audit report. Stakeholder is not, however, defined in the regulation.
44. C. Richard Baker & Dwight M. Owsen, *Increasing the Role of Auditing in Corporate Governance*, 13 Critical Perspectives on Accounting 783–795 (2002).
45. Claus Holm & Peter Birkholm Laursen, *Risk and Control Developments in Corporate Governance: Changing the Role of the External Auditor?* 15 Corporate Governance: An International Review 322, 324 (2007).
46. *Ibid.*

adviser to the management and the controlling members in matters relating to good governance. This tension can be seen in resistance to extend full-scale auditing to small, closed undertakings.[47] Tension can also arise from the way in which audits are conducted. Listed companies can find it difficult to follow the IFRS (at least in their consolidated accounts), with audit markets restricted to those auditors and audit firms working to the standards, and requiring strict regulation of the process. The leading set of standards regulating auditing is the International Standards on Auditing (ISA), issued by the International Auditing and Assurance Standards Board (IAASB), a body supported by the International Federation of Accountants (IFAC).[48]

In the remaining parts of this chapter, I discuss in more detail the *ex ante* and *ex post* roles of auditors in governance of different kinds of undertakings, both large and small, multinational and local. What is common to all undertakings is the auditors' task of maintaining both the cooperation of the management and their oversight, or in other words, the informal and formal role of auditors in corporate governance structures. I limit the discussion here to external auditors or proper auditors only, though not because internal audits and compliance play a lesser role. Indeed, successful management entails both.

I pay special attention to auditors as overseers of firm management, how they fulfil this role in different kinds of firms, the kind of regulatory framework within which this role is fulfilled, and what effect their involvement is likely to have on corporate governance. I focus on undertakings with member-limited liability and legal standing, with separation of control between the meeting of the members, the board and the possible CEO or general manager, i.e., mainly companies and cooperatives. Of key concern is the question of the relationship of auditors to boards and also to the internal constituencies of an undertaking, especially not only members but also other financiers as creditors.

The main question to be answered is whether the auditors are enhancing good corporate governance and could do this job even better. The latter part of the question is approached through discussion of the scope of the audit, e.g., will it be focused on financial reports only or will the auditors also audit reports on management, governance, environmental, and social impact of undertakings? As an example, I use the

47. *See* Art. 34(1) of the Accounting Directive, narrowing auditing of financial statements to public-interest entities (listed companies, banks and other credit institutions, and insurance undertakings; Art. 2(1) of the Accounting Directive) and medium-sized (as defined in Art. 3(3) of the Accounting Directive) and large (as defined in Art. 3(4) of the Accounting Directive) undertakings.
48. According to original Art. 26 of the Audit Directive, EU Member States must require statutory auditors and audit firms to carry out statutory audits in compliance with the international auditing standards adopted by the Commission. The Commission, however, has not adopted any ISAs so far, so, according to the Directive, Member States may apply a national auditing standard if the Commission has not adopted an international auditing standard covering the same subject matter. The present Art. 26 uses different wording but has the same meaning; *see* Art. 26 of the Audit Directive, as amended by Directive 2014/56/EU of the European Parliament and of the Council of 16 April 2014 amending Directive 2006/43/EC on statutory audits of annual accounts and consolidated accounts, OJ L 158, 27.5.2014, pp. 196–226.

European Commission proposal for sustainability reporting, which expands the duties of auditors to include audits of sustainability reports.[49]

§16.02 AUDITORS IN MODERN CORPORATE GOVERNANCE

As with the history of accounting, the history of audit regulation is one of crises and regulatory responses to these. For instance, in the United States (US), the emergence of an accounting profession, with the attendant privileges afforded professions, occurred in the last third of the nineteenth century.[50] Professionalization was seen as a solution to the succession of financial scandals and crises that followed the US Civil War, associated with the growing significance of corporations and all the attendant problems of the corporate form.[51] At that time, presumably all that financial markets lacked was sufficient 'information' to enable those markets to hold in check abuses of corporate power to the detriment of the public. Publicity of accounts or transparency was the solution, with audited financial statements prepared in accordance with appropriate accounting procedures based on GAAP, allowing investors to make sound investment decisions. The proposed solution to the financial crises of the 1870s and '80s was 'publicity of accounts', and this was a major impetus for establishing an accounting profession in the US.[52] As already mentioned in §16.01, prior to the regulatory response to the Great Depression, there were no written accounting standards in the US. Accounting was a practice whose excellence was formed both by accountants' social norms (including moral norms or virtues) and by law.[53] Formal accounting standards and auditing in line with these was triggered by the US securities regulation of 1933 and 1934.[54]

Similarly, the German stock market crash of 1929 triggered the Emergency Corporate Law Measures of 1931,[55] ensuring greater transparency in accounting practices and in the information provided in the annual return, balance sheet, and profit and loss account, and by requiring an examination of the accounts by independent auditors.[56] In Sweden, for instance, the Kreuger Crash and an audit scandal caused the Swedish Institute of Authorized Public Accountants (*Föreningen Auktoriserade Revisorer*) to realize the need for a more explicit code of ethics and rules, which

49. *See* Corporate Sustainability Reporting Directive proposal, *supra* n. 28.
50. Paul F. Williams, *Unreliable Accounts: Governing Behind a Veil*, 12 Accounting, Economics, and Law: A Convivium 211–231 (2022).
51. Adolf A. Berle et al., The Modern Corporation and Private Property (1933), available at http://books.google.com/books?id = zaZZAAAAYAAJ (last visited 4 June 2022).
52. Williams, *supra* n. 50.
53. *Ibid.*
54. *See* Securities Act, Pub. L. 73–22, 48 Stat. 74, 15 U.S.C. § 77a et seq. and Securities Exchange Act, Pub. L. 73–291, 48 Stat. 881, 15 U.S.C. § 78a et seq.; *See* Williams, *supra* n. 50, 215–216.
55. Verordnung des Reichspräsidenten über Aktienrecht, Bankenaufsicht und über eine Steueramnestie vom 19 September 1931, Reichsgesetzblatt [RGBl], 19 September 1931.
56. Peter Muchlinski, *The Development of German Corporate Law Until 1990: An Historical Reappraisal*, 14 Ger. Law J. 339, 365 (2013); Sebastian Hoffmann & Dominic Detzen, *The Regulation of Asset Valuation in Germany*, 18 Accounting History 367, 389 (2013).

began being issued from 1933. More importantly, the Swedish authorities took tighter control of the licensing of audit practitioners.[57]

The financial scandals of the first decade of the twenty-first century (e.g., *Enron* and *Parmalat*) and the financial crisis again triggered major changes in the role of auditor and audit regulation, especially in listed firms, starting in the US with the Sarbanes-Oxley Act of 2002 and the Dodd-Frank Wall Street Reform Act of 2010,[58] followed by the EU's Audit Directive of 2006, Amended Audit Directive of 2014, and Audit Regulation of 2014.[59] Important elements of the reforms were prohibiting the provision for non-audit services,[60] audit committees,[61] rotation of auditors,[62] and surveillance of auditors,[63] elements that have dominated discussion of the role of auditors in corporate governance during the last two decades.

Tension between the informal and formal role of auditors is evident in this regulation. The option for auditors to act in their traditional non-auditing role as advisors to management, while simultaneously acting as a verifier of their stewardship towards members is, on the one hand, limited by fewer possibilities for offering non-audit services; on the other hand, the scope for this is broadened by emphasizing constant cooperation and communication between the auditor, the board and its audit committee. There is both market and regulatory pressure to use auditors more broadly, not only for formal audits of financial accounts in listed firms, as shown in the European Commission Sustainability Reporting Directive proposal.[64]

The EU regulation shows the multifaceted and evolving roles of auditors in corporate governance. For as long as audit institutions have existed, auditors have been used to filling gaps in the legal system, especially in jurisdictions with weak legal

---

57. Öhman & Wallerstedt, *supra* n. 20.
58. Sarbanes-Oxley Act, Pub. L. No. 107-204, 116 Stat. 745 (2002); Dodd-Frank Wall Street Reform and Consumer Protection Act, Pub. L. No. 111-203, 124 Stat. 1376 (2010); *see* Jeffrey Cohen, Ganesh Krishnamoorthy, & Arnie Wright, *Corporate Governance in the Post-Sarbanes-Oxley Era: Auditors' Experiences*, 27 Contemporary Accounting Research 751–786 (2010).
59. Directive 2006/43/EC of the European Parliament and of the Council of 17 May 2006 on statutory audits of annual accounts and consolidated accounts, amending Council Directives 78/660/EEC and 83/349/EEC and repealing Council Directive 84/253/EEC, OJ L 157, 9.6.2006, pp. 87–107 (Audit Directive); Directive 2014/56/EU of the European Parliament and of the Council of 16 April 2014 amending Directive 2006/43/EC on statutory audits of annual accounts and consolidated accounts, OJ L 158, 27.5.2014, pp. 196–226 (Amended Audit Directive); Regulation (EU) No. 537/2014 of the European Parliament and of the Council of 16 April 2014 on specific requirements regarding statutory audits of public-interest entities and repealing Commission Decision 2005/909/EC, OJ L 158, 27.5.2014, pp. 77–112 (Audit Regulation), *see supra* n. 1 and n. 6.
60. Art. 5 of the Audit Regulation.
61. Arts 11 and 16 of the Audit Regulation and Art. 39 of the Audit Directive, as amended by Directive 2014/56/EU of the European Parliament and of the Council of 16 April 2014 amending Directive 2006/43/EC on statutory audits of annual accounts and consolidated accounts, OJ L 158, 27.5.2014, pp. 196–226.
62. Art. 17 of the Audit Regulation.
63. Title IV of the Audit Regulation.
64. European Commission, Proposal for a Directive of the European Parliament and of the Council amending Directive 2013/34/EU, Directive 2004/109/EC, Directive 2006/43/EC, and Regulation (EU) No. 537/2014, regarding corporate sustainability reporting, COM(2021) 189 final (Corporate Sustainability Reporting Directive proposal), *see supra* n. 28.

systems: in contrast with countries with strong legal systems, auditors serve an even more significant governance function in weak legal environments.[65] Moreover, auditors' roles in non-listed firms are different from the highly regulated status of auditors in public-interest entities. Although auditors remains auditors, their independence is not as strictly regulated as it is for public-interest entities in the post-*Enron* world, and the auditors' role in corporate governance is more direct as an advisor to the management and members of the undertaking. The role of auditors has, however, been diminished by rules that exempt small undertakings from audits and so from their services in governance.[66]

Generally, auditors are an important part of the corporate governance 'mosaic' of the management, board, and CEO/general manager, ensuring the quality of corporate reporting, both in public-interest entities and in private undertakings.[67] The role of auditors in corporate governance varies, however, from jurisdiction to jurisdiction. For instance, in Sweden, auditors have, since the 1940s, been seen as a separate company law organ, along with general meetings, the board, and CEO/general manager.[68] However, the legislative trend starting with the Sarbanes-Oxley Act has increased corporate governance obligations for auditors in public-interest entities, ensuring their independence.[69] Although auditors are not seen as agents in legal terms,[70] the role of an auditor in an undertaking, and especially, auditor independence rely on the same agency-theory justifications as board member independence in listed firms.

§16.03 AUDITORS AS AGENTS

One of the most powerful economic theories in corporate governance is agency theory. At the same time, it is one of the most controversial as an economic explanation of the role of different players in corporate governance game does not fit the legal framework.[71] Neoclassical economics explains a firm as a set of contracts among providers of different factors of production. These sets of contractual arrangements (for example, alternative property structures) incentivize contractual parties to engage in opportunistic behaviour to the detriment of the firm. The most important providers of factors of production are the investors providing financial capital and the management

65. Jong-Hag Choi & T.J. Wong, *Auditors' Governance Functions and Legal Environments: An International Investigation*, 24 Contemporary Accounting Research 13–46 (2007).
66. Art. 34(1)(1) of the Audit Directive exempts other undertakings from auditing of financial statements, namely public-interest entities and medium-sized and large undertakings.
67. Cohen, Krishnamoorthy, & Wright, *supra* n. 58.
68. *See* Swedish Government proposal for Companies Act etc., No. 1944:5 [Kungl. Maj:ts proposition nr 5 till riksdagen med förslag till lag om aktiebolag, m. m., given Stockholms slott den 22 december 1943], 286.
69. Holm & Laursen, *supra* n. 45.
70. Sjåfjell & Mähönen, *supra* n. 41.
71. *See*, e.g., Beate Sjåfjell, *Sustainability and Law and Economics: An Interdisciplinary Redefinition of Agency Theory*, in *Interdisciplinary Research for Sustainable Business: Perspectives of Women Business Scholars* (Beate Sjåfjell, Roseanne Russell, & Maja van der Velden, eds., Springer 2022) (forthcoming).

running the firm for them. To explain the relationship between investors, the management, and the firm in this contractual arrangement, economics sees the management of a firm as agents of the members.[72] The management's opportunistic behaviour reduces the total of the firm and hence its value, so an efficient contractual arrangement reduces opportunism. The financial scandals discussed in §16.01 were foremostly caused by opportunistic management behaviour.

In economics, corporate governance rules are primarily understood as tools with which to reduce management opportunism. The most important opportunism-reducing contractual and regulatory tools are the management's duties. Another is financial accounts provided by the management to the members to reduce their management monitoring costs. The role of the auditor and the audit is connected to this monitoring; with audits, auditors enforce the contract between those responsible for management and stewardship and the members.[73]

From an agency theory point of view, an audit fulfils its objectives if it is successful in changing negative expectations of management opportunism and hence in reducing opportunistic behaviour costs (agency costs) borne by the management. However, an audit is only a success if it is expected that the auditor will report to the members at least some discovered breaches of contract. The probability that the auditors will report a discovered breach is effectively the auditing profession's definition of independence. So, although the management contracts the auditor on the firm's behalf, it is in its interest to secure auditor independence in a way that fulfils member and general market expectations.[74]

Independence is not enough, however. Auditors also need skills to perform their duties. Auditor professionalism and independence are therefore interlinked. The requirement for professionalism and independence increases with increases in the size and number of firms in the markets, the complexity of their financial accounts, and the liability of the management for wrongdoings.[75] Agency theory not only explains the specific requirements for audits of listed firms described in §16.01 above but also problematizes the role of auditors in closed firms where managers are also members, and so auditors' roles deviate from the ideal of a listed firm with dispersed control.

The efficiency of auditing as a tool for agency not only depends on professionalism and independence but also on auditors' monitoring behaviour and enforcement of private and public penalties for wrongdoings, creating incentives for auditors to report breaches of the contracts that they monitor.[76] Sanctions might be based on public law (administrative in nature, e.g., withdrawal of approval) or could be criminal sanctions.

72. Michael C. Jensen & William H. Meckling, *Theory of the Firm: Managerial Behavior, Agency Costs and Ownership Structure*, 3 J. Financ. Econ. 305, 356 (1976).
73. *Ibid.*; Watts & Zimmerman, *supra* n. 3, at 614–615; Richard Baker & Owsen, *supra* n. 15, at 784; Josephine Maltby & Roy Chandler, *Auditing*, in *The Routledge Companion to Accounting History* 252, 255 (Routledge 2020).
74. Watts & Zimmerman, *supra* n. 3, at 615.
75. *Ibid.*, at 630.
76. *Ibid.*, at 633.

They could also be based on private law, including auditors' duties to identify damage compensation, as well as social costs, such as loss of reputation and clientele.[77]

Another variable affecting auditors' behaviour is the quality of the tools they use in their work, be they law-based, social norm-based, or a hybrid. This is, of course, connected to professionalism as regulation of audit quality reflects the characteristics of the business environment and legal system; consequently, regulation varies across countries.[78] One such example is control of the audit risk: auditors of companies with independent boards and audit committees are perceived by auditors as lower risk.[79]

However, what is seen as important is how the audit is conducted. In recent decades, an increasing number of countries have adopted a uniform set of *standards*: the ISAs, issued by the IAASB, a body supported by the IFAC. According to original Article 26 of Audit Directive, EU Member States must require statutory auditors and audit firms to carry out statutory audits in compliance with international auditing standards adopted by the Commission. However, the Commission has not adopted any ISAs so far, so, according to the Directive, Member States may apply a national auditing standard if the Commission has not adopted an international auditing standard covering the same subject matter. The present Article 26 uses a different wording but has the same meaning.[80]

However, formal adoption of the ISAs may amount to little more than 'window dressing' for countries in which economic, political, legal, and institutional features do not represent a good fit for the standards.[81] Audit standards, therefore, function only if the corporate governance framework is functioning. However, standardized auditing is a prerequisite for audits achieving their objectives.

§16.04 WHAT DO AUDITORS AUDIT?

Standards alone – irrespective of how good they might be – are not enough if there is no clear view of what auditors are to audit. The recent German *Wirecard* scandal concretizes the problem. The *Wirecard* scandal was a ten-year-long series of corrupt business practices and fraudulent financial reporting, which led to insolvency of the

77. *See*, for instance, Art. 30 and Preamble 19 of the Audit Directive, stating that statutory auditors and audit firms 'are responsible for carrying out their work with due care and thus should be liable for the financial damage caused by a lack of the care owed. However, the auditors' and audit firms' ability to obtain professional indemnity insurance cover may be affected by whether they are subject to unlimited financial liability. For its part, the Commission intends examining these issues, considering the fact that liability regimes of the Member States may vary considerably.' For these reasons, the financial liability of auditors is not harmonized in the EU.
78. Dan A. Simunic, Minlei Ye, & Ping Zhang, *The Joint Effects of Multiple Legal System Characteristics on Auditing Standards and Auditor Behavior*, 34 Contemporary Accounting Research 7, 8 (2017).
79. Jeffrey R. Cohen & Dennis M. Hanno, *Auditors' Consideration of Corporate Governance and Management Control Philosophy in Preplanning and Planning Judgments*, 19 Auditing: A Journal of Practice & Theory 133–146 (2000).
80. *See* Art. 26 of the Audit Directive, as amended by Directive 2014/56/EU of the European Parliament and of the Council of 16 April 2014 amending Directive 2006/43/EC on statutory audits of annual accounts and consolidated accounts, OJ L 158, 27.5.2014, pp. 196–226.
81. Simunic, Ye, & Zhang, *supra* n. 78.

payment processor and financial services provider *Wirecard* AG. Allegations of accounting malpractices have haunted the company since the early days of its incorporation, reaching a peak in 2019, after the *Financial Times* published a series of investigations, along with whistle-blower complaints and internal documents. On 25 June 2020, *Wirecard* filed for insolvency after revelations that EUR 1.9 billion was 'missing' and the termination and arrest of its CEO Markus Braun. Questions have been raised about regulatory failure on the part of the Federal Financial Supervisory Authority (BaFin) and possible malpractice on the part of *Wirecard*'s long time auditor Ernst & Young.[82]

The main question relating to auditors' duties was to what extent auditors must review financial reports at all. According to German law,[83] auditors must review the annual and consolidated accounts to determine whether they are in accordance with the applicable legal provisions and corporate charter. Moreover, the review must be performed to detect any errors and irregularities in these accounts.[84] *Wirecard*'s problem was that the financial statements were not only false or misleading but also based on a large-scale fraud beyond the scope of the auditors' duties.[85]

The *Wirecard* case highlights one of the most crucial questions relating to audit usefulness: to what extent auditors can or cannot rely on the documents and information presented by the undertaking.[86] *Wirecard* also shows the problematics of auditing a multinational, as the key problems lay with bank accounts in East Asia, out of reach of the company's German auditors.[87]

Auditors' ability to fulfil their role in corporate governance is not only weakened by fraud and internationalization. Financial reports do not depict stewardship fully or how well the management fulfils its duties and meets its purpose. Auditing historical financial accounts is also still the primary role of auditors in the EU regulatory framework. According to Article 34(1)(1) of the EU Accounting Directive, Member States must ensure that the financial statements of public-interest entities and medium-sized and large undertakings are audited by one or more statutory auditors or audit firms approved by Member States to carry out statutory audits based on the Audit Directive. According to Article 34(2), Article 34(1)(1) applies *mutatis mutandis* with respect to consolidated financial statements.

Auditors' traditional role to audit *financial accounts* only is a historical paradox: financial accounts represent the past by definition as they are drafted several weeks after the end of the fiscal year. The members' or shareholders' meeting takes place several months after the end of financial year, so audit reports are relevant for investment decisions.[88] In this sense, the financial reports that auditors audit are

82. *See*, e.g., Sebastian Mock, *Wirecard and European Company and Financial Law*, 18 Eur. Co. Financial Law Rev. 519–554 (2021); Thomas M.J. Möllers, *The Wirecard Accounting Scandal in Germany, and How the Financial Industry Failed to Spot It*, 54 Int. Lawyer 325–360 (2021).
83. S. 317(1)(2) of the German Commercial Code (Handelsgesetzbuch).
84. S. 317(1)(3) of the German Commercial Code.
85. Mock, *supra* n. 82, at 536, with extensive references to German legal literature.
86. Mock, *supra* n. 82, at 537.
87. Mock, *supra* n. 82, at 519–554.
88. Baker & Owsen, *supra* n. 44.

almost useless for constituencies as far as the future is concerned. Instead, investors get information relevant to their investments from management through unaudited interim earnings reports, financial analysts' forecasts, and privately obtained information, all beyond the scope of auditor influence.

While the financial report has lost its position as the only source when assessing corporate governance, there are increasing demands for reports on the quality of corporate governance, including the efficiency of internal controls.[89] In the EU, the *management report* referred to in Article 19 of the Accounting Directive should include a fair review of the development and performance of the undertaking's business and of its position, together with a description of the principal risks and uncertainties that it faces.[90] Large public-interest entities which (on their balance sheet) have an average number of employees exceeding 500 during the financial year must include in the management report a *non-financial statement* containing sufficient information to clearly convey the undertaking's development, performance, position, and the impact of its activity relating to, as a minimum, environmental, social, and employee matters, respect for human rights, anti-corruption, and bribery matters.[91] However, instead of including statement in the management report, an undertaking can prepare a separate report covering the information required for the non-financial statement.[92] In addition, listed companies must include a *corporate governance statement* in their management report or a separate report, in accordance with Article 20 of the Accounting Directive.

The *Wirecard* scandal also has a corporate governance statement side.[93] As a listed German company, it was obliged to issue an annual statement concerning its corporate governance, as described in the German Corporate Governance Code (*Deutscher Corporate Governance Kodex*), based on the comply-or-explain principle.[94] In its corporate governance statement of 2018, *Wirecard* stated that the company complied with the recommendations of the German Corporate Governance Code, except that the Chair of the Supervisory Board was also the Chair of the audit committee. (There was no actual audit committee in reality as this is not mandatory under German law,[95] although it is recommended by the Code,[96] and the financial statement might not necessarily be published within the timeframes set out in the Code.[97]) *Wirecard* did neither report the non-existence of committees, as recommended by the Code, nor the reasons for a very small supervisory board of only five (later six) members, despite the Code requiring members to collectively have the

89. Holm & Laursen, *supra* n. 45.
90. Art. 19(1) of the Accounting Directive.
91. Art. 19a(1) of the Accounting Directive.
92. Art. 19a(4) of the Accounting Directive.
93. Mock, *supra* n. 82, at 528–529.
94. S. 161 of the German Stock Corporation Act (Aktiengesetz).
95. S. 107(4) of the German Stock Corporation Act, using the option in Art. 39(1) of the Audit Directive.
96. No. 5.3.2 of the German Corporate Governance Code of 2017 and Principle 14 of the German Corporate Governance Code of 2022.
97. Deviation of No. 7.1.2 of the German Corporate Governance Code of 2017 and Recommendation F.2 of the German Corporate Governance Code of 2022.

knowledge, skills, and professional expertise to properly perform all of their duties.[98] The deviations and peculiarities of *Wirecard* corporate governance did not fall under the scrutiny of Ernst & Young as the corporate governance statement is not subject to review by auditors under German law.[99]

German law is in accordance with the Accounting Directive regarding not requiring an audit of the management report, non-financial report, or corporate governance statement. The Accounting Directive is of particular importance for corporate governance as it shows that reporting forms other than financial reports serving as management reports (as per Article 19), non-financial statements (as per Article 19a), and corporate governance statements (as per Article 20) have not been subject to 'full auditing' as financial statements.

According to Article 34(1)(2) of the Accounting Directive, statutory auditors or audit firms must also (a) express an opinion on (i) whether the management report meant in Article 19 of the Directive is consistent with the financial statements for the same financial year, and (ii) whether the management report has been prepared in accordance with the applicable legal requirements; and (b) state whether, in light of the knowledge and understanding of the undertaking and its environment, obtained in the course of the audit, he, she, or it has identified material misstatements in the management report and must give an indication of the nature of any such misstatements. According to Article 34(2), Article 34(1)(2) will apply *mutatis mutandis* with respect to consolidated management reports.

Even less strict rules apply to corporate governance statements. Although Article 20(3) of the Accounting Directive[100] stipulates that the statutory auditor or audit firm must express an opinion in accordance with Article 34(1)(2), regarding information presented in specific parts of the corporate governance statement, the auditor is only required to check that the necessary information has been provided.

An even more dramatic difference can be seen with other corporate reports regarding the non-financial report meant in Article 19a(1) and (4), and consolidated non-financial report meant in Article 29a(1) and (4) of the Accounting Directive. According to Article 34(3), the provisions of Article 34(1) and (2) do not apply to the non-financial statement referred to in Article 19a(1), the consolidated non-financial statement referred to in Article 29a(1), or to the separate reports referred to in Articles 19a(4) and 29a(4). According to Article 19a(5) and 29a(5) of the Directive, Member States only need to ensure that the statutory auditor or audit firm checks

98. No. 5.4.1 of the German Corporate Governance Code of 2017 and Principle 11 of the German Corporate Governance Code of 2022.
99. S. 317(2)(6) of the German Commercial Code.
100. As amended by Directive 2014/95/EU of the European Parliament and of the Council of 22 October 2014 amending Directive 2013/34/EU regarding disclosure of non-financial and diversity information by certain large undertakings and groups, OJ L 330, 15.11.2014, pp. 1–9 (Non-Financial Reporting Directive).

whether the non-financial statement or consolidated non-financial statement referred to in Article 19a(1) and (4) and in Article 29a(1) and (4) has been provided.[101]

The differences are important for efficient scrutiny of corporate governance as auditors' roles are still different in terms of verifying the financial report and other reports whose importance has increased during the last decade. Relaxation of the EU regulations has even backfired on auditors' roles in governance. Although Member States could have taken the opportunity to strengthen the sustainability reporting requirements and assurance possibilities that the rules on non-financial statements afforded them in the Accounting Directive in 2014,[102] it led to an unfortunate reversal of requirements, with, for example, Norway (as a European Economic Area country) removing its pre-2003 Directive on sustainability reporting requirements, which it had already put in place for all companies except for the largest ones, and Finland removing its auditing requirement for management reports.[103] In Finland, where the management report has traditionally been subject to a full audit, due to implementation of Article 19a of the Accounting Directive, only the minimum requirements of the Directive are applied to the management report and other reports.[104]

This change in the legal framework is crucial as auditors are especially important in economies where share ownership is highly concentrated, as in emerging and Nordic markets like Finland and Norway.[105] In concentrated control environments, control holders tend to employ reputable information intermediaries as auditors in order to assure minority investors and other contractual parties of the credibility of information and governance and to mitigate agency problems between the majority and the minority and between the management and the minority when acquiring shares from secondary markets.[106]

---

101. As amended by the Non-Financial Reporting Directive, *see supra* n. 100. According to Arts 19a(6) and 29a(6) of the Accounting Directive, as amended by the Non-Financial Reporting Directive, Member States *may* require that information in the non-financial statement and consolidated non-financial statement referred to in Arts 19a(1) and (4), and 29a(1) and (4), be verified by an independent assurance services provider.
102. Ar. 19a and 29a of the Accounting Directive, as amended by the Non-Financial Reporting Directive; *see supra* n. 100.
103. Beate Sjåfjell, Jukka Mähönen, Tonia A. Novitz, Clair Gammage, Hanna Ahlström, Securing the Future of European Business: SMART Reform Proposals (7 May 2020). University of Oslo Faculty of Law Research Paper No. 2020-11, Nordic & European Company Law Working Paper No. 20-08, available at SSRN: https://ssrn.com/abstract=3595048, at 45.
104. Government proposal 70/2016 for Act amending the Auditing Act and other related Acts [Hallituksen esitys 70/2016 vp eduskunnalle laiksi tilintarkastuslain muuttamisesta ja eräiksi siihen liittyviksi laeiksi], p. 19; *see* Jukka Mähönen, *Kestävyysraportointi* [Sustainability Reporting], in Yritysvastuu & oikeus [Corporate responsibility & law] 125, 142–143 (Anne Vanhala & Michael Ristaniemi, eds., 2022).
105. Joseph P.H. Fan & T.J. Wong, *Do External Auditors Perform a Corporate Governance Role in Emerging Markets? Evidence from East Asia*, 43 J. Account. Res. 35–72 (2005); Jukka Mähönen & Guðrún Johnsen, *Law, Culture and Sustainability: Corporate Governance in the Nordic Countries*, in *The Cambridge Handbook of Corporate Law*, Corporate Governance and Sustainability 218–231 (Beate Sjåfjell & Christopher M. Bruner, eds., 1st edition, Cambridge University Press 2019).
106. Fan & Wong, *ibid.*

§16.05 THE ROLE OF AUDITORS' LIABILITY FOR CORPORATE GOVERNANCE

As mentioned in §16.03, auditors' liability, be it joint liability (with management and auditors held jointly responsible for the full amount of damages sought in a lawsuit), several liability (with each party responsible for its proportionate share of damages), or joint and several liability (with each party independently liable for the full extent of the injuries stemming from the tortious act, but where the compensating party may seek contributions from other tortfeasors), is an important part of the enforcement mechanism of auditors' duty. Auditors' liability creates an incentive to issue modified (qualified) auditor reports, and vice versa: when auditor liability is relaxed, the probability of issuing a 'clean' (unqualified) report increases.[107]

However, auditors see their liability differently, viewing auditor liability as too harsh an incentive. For decades, auditors have claimed to be unfair victims of lawsuits and have campaigned to secure liability concessions: for instance, depending on the jurisdiction, by replacing 'joint and several liability' with proportional liability, 'capping' auditor liability, and creating a statutory right to negotiate liability limits with boards.[108] An example of contractual limitations and capping is the German law allowing auditors contractual limits on their liability and limiting auditors' liability per audit.[109] However, scandals always trigger stricter regulation. Following the *Wirecard* scandal, the caps were raised considerably and abolished in the case of gross negligence.[110]

In light of this debate, it is clear that from a legal and political point of view, the question of auditors' liability is not a question of giving auditors more incentives to fulfil their duty of care but rather vice versa: auditors attempting to free themselves from liability.[111] However, in jurisdictions where there are no specific limitations on

107. Divya Anantharaman, Jeffrey A. Pittman, & Nader Wans, *State Liability Regimes within the United States and Auditor Reporting*, 91 Account. Rev. 1545–1575 (2016). According to Art. 28(2)I of the Audit Directive, the audit report should include an audit opinion, which should be unqualified, qualified, or an adverse opinion and should clearly state the opinion of the statutory auditor(s) or the audit firm(s) as to (i) whether the annual financial statements give a true and fair view in accordance with the relevant financial reporting framework; and (ii) where appropriate, whether the annual financial statements comply with statutory requirements.
108. Jim Cousins, Austin Mitchell, & Prem Sikka, *Auditor Liability: The Other Side of the Debate*, 10 Critical Perspectives on Accounting 283–312 (1999).
109. S. 54a of the German Public Accountant Act (Wirtschaftsprüferordnung) and section 323(2) of the German Commercial Code (Handelsgesetzbuch). Auditors' liability is not harmonized in the European Union; *see* Mock, *supra* n. 82. Harmonization attempts have also failed, as indicated in a proposal by the European Commission in 2007; *see* Walter Doralt et al., *Auditors' Liability and Its Impact on the European Financial Markets*, 67 C.L.J. 62–68 (2008).
110. *See* Act to Strengthen Financial Market Integrity (Gesetz zur Stärkung der Finanzmarktintegrität Finanzmarktintegritätsstärkungsgesetz), 3. Juni 2021 BGBl. I S. 1534 (Nr. 30). On the *Wirecard* scandal and its legal consequences, *see* Mock, *supra* n. 82, 541.
111. *See*, e.g., Cousins, Mitchell, & Sikka, *supra* n. 108; Marshall A. Geiger, K. Raghunandan, & Dasaratha V. Rama, *Auditor Decision-Making in Different Litigation Environments: The Private Securities Litigation Reform Act, Audit Reports and Audit Firm Size*, 25 J. Account. Public Policy 332–353 (2006); Steven E. Kaplan & David D. Williams, *Do Going Concern Audit Reports Protect Auditors from Litigation? A Simultaneous Equations Approach*, 88 Account. Rev. 199–232

auditors' liability, the general rules of tort law or those relating to their obligations regarding negligence and causality limit auditors' liability. Audit standards like the ISAs also limit auditors' liability by setting a cap on auditors' duty of care.[112]

There is some truth in the criticism of limitless auditors' liability. Although high liability will incentivize auditors to take their duty of care more seriously, it may be morally hazardous to both management and investors.[113] Auditors' liability in relation to firms and third parties is likely to be less severe when they provide clear audit opinions on financial statements that are subsequently alleged to have been misstated, but more severe if an audit is found to be negligent or fraudulent.[114] Due to auditor liability, auditors share the governance risk with the management of the firm. Some individuals may take a greater risk if they think that someone other than themselves will suffer the consequences. Shareholders and contractual parties (including non-contractual creditors) may think auditors have 'deep pockets' and can insure their losses in corporate insolvency, especially when the likelihood of managers being able to meet liability sums from their personal resources is seen as low.[115] Similarly, management teams may take a moral risk if they can rely on the auditors' ability to pay compensation.

This moral hazard has several negative consequences. As only big audit firms can bear the risk, companies will switch to larger auditing firms, and the number of audit firms will decrease.[116] A moral hazard can also increase insurance costs. By using auditors in this way, contractual parties can attempt to obtain insurance against business risk which is unavailable in the conventional insurance market.[117] However, at the end of the day, the risk is transferred to insurers as the moral hazard increases insurance premiums, and auditors transfer their increased risk to their insurers.[118] Increased auditors' liability increases audit costs and also demands to exempt even more undertakings from audit.[119]

The question of whether auditors are jointly liable along with management and third parties is distinctive for corporate governance: in systems where there is joint liability, a moral hazard is created for insolvent management 'insured' by supposedly

(2012); Reiner Quick, *Can Prohibitions of Non-Audit Services and An Expanded Auditor Liability Improve Audit Quality?* 26 Int. J. Audit. 18–22 (2022). A poem by Gin Chong aptly describes the relationship between auditors and their liability: Gin Chong, *Auditors' liabilities*, 15 Critical Perspectives on Accounting 330–32 (2004).

112. *See*, e.g., Rachel Schwartz, *Auditors' Liability, Vague Due Care, and Auditing Standards*, 11 Rev. Quant. Finance Account. 183–207 (1998).
113. Quick, *supra* n. 111, at 18–22.
114. Simunic, Ye, & Zhang, *supra* n. 78, at 12.
115. Noel O'Sullivan, *Auditors' Liability: Its Role in the Corporate Governance Debate*, 23 Accounting and Business Research 412–420 (1993).
116. Sasson Bar-Yosef & Joshua Livnat, *Auditor Selection: An Incentive-Signalling Approach*, 14 Accounting and Business Research 301–309 (1984); Quick, *supra* n. 111, at 18–22.
117. O'Sullivan, *supra* n. 115.
118. Quick, *supra* n. 111, at 18–22.
119. *Ibid.*

'deep pocket' auditors.[120] However, lack of joint liability will increase the management's vigilance when it comes to preparation of disclosures.[121] If a lack of joint liability encourages error prevention, then joint liability encourages error detection.[122] In this sense, audit liability increases audit quality, and restrictions on audit liability decrease it.[123] From an economic point of view, proportionate liability is superior to joint and several liability, and strict liability, in contrast to negligence liability, results in socially optimal auditor effort level.[124] However, strong[125] joint and several liability creates an incentive to align auditor interests with corporate interests.

There is also a direct link between audit quality, auditing standards, and the characteristics of legal systems, including rules on audit liability, and how optimal standards are affected by legal systems. When the expected damage award based on audit liability is low, even optimal audit standards may not be able to induce the first-best effort, particularly if the vagueness of the court system increases. Furthermore, simply adopting a set of auditing standards such as the ISAs, without a proper legal enforcement system, will not achieve the desired audit quality.[126] For these reasons, auditors' liability as an enforcement mechanism for good corporate governance is a complex issue, and it is not surprising that there is no harmonization in the EU.

§16.06 THE ROLE OF CONTROL HOLDERS AND AUDITORS IN CORPORATE GOVERNANCE

The previous sections have shown that as reporting has become more important in corporate governance, there has been a greater need for credible auditing in corporate governance as an enforcement mechanism in the verification of accounting data.[127] Additional regulation of reporting might also backfire in relaxed auditing and assurance, as we have seen in the EU non-financial reporting regulation that carved out auditing of management reports and non-financial statements. The amount of reporting is, however, not the only relevant variable for audits; corporate control also plays a role. The importance of accounting and reporting is such that auditing is dependent on the concentration of corporate control. The more dispersed control in an undertaking, the bigger role formal assured information must have to narrow the information asymmetry between insiders and outsiders and vice versa; fewer outside shareholdings

120. *Ibid.*
121. *Ibid.*
122. *Ibid.*
123. Stephen A. Hillegeist, *Financial Reporting and Auditing under Alternative Damage Apportionment Rules*, 74 Account. Rev. 347–69 (1999).
124. Quick, *supra* n. 111.
125. *See* examples from the Supreme Court of Sweden: NJA 1996:35 (*Scandinavian Clinics – Första Sparbanken case*), NJA 1998:110 (*Årstadal Metallhandel – Gotabanken case*) and NJA 2014 s. 272 (*BDO case*); and also, from the Supreme Court of Finland: KKO:1999:118, KKO:2001:36, and KKO:2008:115.
126. Simunic, Ye, & Zhang, *supra* n. 78, at 9.
127. Watts & Zimmerman, *supra* n. 38, at 196.

will mean a relatively lesser need for strong corporate governance that includes credible, transparent, and timely accounting.[128]

Share ownership concentration is a feature of publicly listed companies, not only in emerging markets but also in Nordic countries and even in the US. A controlling shareholder (blockholder) can more efficiently monitor the board and management than minority shareholders. In emerging markets, control facilitates transactions in weak property rights and judicial systems: through concentrated ownership, controlling shareholders obtain power and incentives to negotiate and enforce corporate contracts with various contractual parties.[129] However, concentrated control creates an entrenchment problem, which allows controlling shareholders' self-dealings to go unchallenged internally by boards or externally by takeover markets. This entrenchment problem can come at a price to the controlling owners and their firms: outside investors anticipate the problem; hence, they discount the share prices and make it more difficult for firms to issue equities in the future.[130]

However, a controlling shareholder may introduce monitoring or bonding mechanisms not available to the minority that limit his or her ability to hold up minority shareholders and hence mitigate the agency conflict.[131] In general, monitoring or bonding behaviours are observed when (1) effective mechanisms are available and (2) the benefits of imposing the mechanisms (reduced agency costs or lowered capital-raising costs) outweigh the costs of using the mechanisms (the premium paid to employ these mechanisms and any forfeited benefits due to the governance constraint).[132]

To mitigate potential conflicts of interest between the controlling shareholder(s) and the minority, especially concerns about containing the controlling owners' self-interested activities and weakness of conventional internal and external governance mechanisms such as takeover markets, the controlling shareholders try to find other ways to employ credible monitoring and bonding mechanisms to assure the minority shareholders that their interests will be protected. External independent auditors are seen as important when it comes to playing this role.[133]

According to comparative law and finance research, there is more demand for credible accounting and auditing enforcement in corporate governance systems of countries with strong investor protection laws. Credible accounting facilitates contracting and resolves information asymmetries between firms (managers and inside shareowners) and outside investors. Countries with stronger investor protection, such as the Nordic countries,[134] have traditionally had national accounting standards that are

128. Francis, Khurana, & Pereira, *supra* n. 38.
129. Fan & Wong, *supra* n. 105; Rafael La Porta, Florencio Lopez-De-Silanes, & Andrei Shleifer, *Corporate Ownership Around the World*, 54 J. Financ. 471–517 (1999); Andrei Shleifer & Robert W. Vishny, *A Survey of Corporate Governance*, 52 J. Financ. 737–783 (1997).
130. Stijn Claessens et al., *Disentangling the Incentive and Entrenchment Effects of Large Shareholdings*, 57 J. Financ. 2741–2771 (2002); Rafael La Porta et al., *Investor Protection and Corporate Valuation*, 57 J. Financ. 1147–1170 (2002).
131. Jensen & Meckling, *supra* n. 72.
132. Fan & Wong, *supra* n. 105.
133. *Ibid.*
134. Mähönen & Johnsen, *supra* n. 105.

of a higher quality than in countries with weaker protection, are more accrual-based, have greater transparency through public financial disclosure and where higher quality auditing serves as an enforcement mechanism. Countries with higher quality accounting and auditing in corporate governance also have more developed financial markets.[135] An example of this is the Finnish accounting regime before direct[136] and indirect[137] adoption of International Financial Reporting Standards.[138]

However, 'strong' accounting cannot compensate for 'weak' investor protection laws,[139] although 'better than expected' auditing can be seen as being associated with more developed financial markets. The adoption of developed accounting standards (along with rigorous auditing to enforce proper application of accounting standards) is, politically speaking,[140] a more promising path to pursue than trying to change investor protection laws and the legal infrastructure underlying corporate governance.[141]

§16.07 THE WAY FORWARD REGARDING AUDITORS' ROLES IN CORPORATE GOVERNANCE

In §16.06 above, I discussed the regulatory weaknesses of efficient auditing in governance. The most important weakness is exclusion of small, unlisted undertakings from the audit process. For instance, in the EU, Member States only have to ensure that the financial statements of public-interest entities, medium-sized and large undertakings are audited by one or more statutory auditors or audit firms approved by Member States to carry out statutory audits on the basis of the Audit Directive (Article 34(1) of the Accounting Directive). Small, non-listed undertakings (undertakings which, on their balance sheets, do not exceed the limits of at least two of the following three criteria: (a) balance sheet total: EUR 4 million; (b) net turnover: EUR 8 million; (c) average number of employees during the financial year: 50) are excluded unless they are listed undertakings, credit institutions, insurance undertakings, or undertakings

135. Francis, Khurana, & Pereira, *supra* n. 38.
136. Regulation (EC) No. 1606/2002 of the European Parliament and of the Council of 19 July 2002 on the application of international accounting standards, OJ L 243, 11.9.2002, pp. 1-4.
137. Directive 2003/51/EC of the European Parliament and of the Council of 18 June 2003 amending Directives 78/660/EEC, 83/349/EEC, 86/635/EEC and 91/674/EEC on the annual and consolidated accounts of certain types of companies, banks and other financial institutions and insurance undertakings, OJ L 178, 17.7.2003, pp. 16-22; Government Proposal 126/2004 for Act Amending the Accounting Act and other related Acts [Hallituksen esitys 126/2004 vp eduskunnalle laiksi kirjanpitolain muuttamiseksi sekä eräiksi siihen liittyviksi laeiksi]; Act Amending the Accounting Act 1304/2004.
138. *See* Pekka Pirinen, *Economic and Normative Pressures as Drivers for the Adoption of International Accounting Standards in Finland Since 1976* (2005), 14 Eur. Account. Rev. 213; Kati Pajunen, *Changing Reporting Models: A Summary of the Experience in Finland* (2013), 25 Research in Accounting Regulation 260; Jukka Mähönen, Tulo ja pääoma: kirjanpidon merkitys osakeyhtiön säätelyssä [Income and Capital: The role of accounting in corporate regulation] (Edita, 2001).
139. Rafael La Porta et al., *Law and Finance*, 106 J. Political Econ. 1113-1155 (1998).
140. Rafael La Porta et al., *Agency Problems and Dividend Policies Around the World*, 55 J. Financ. 1-33 (2000).
141. Francis, Khurana, & Pereira, *supra* n. 38.

designated by Member States as public-interest entities (Article 2(1) and 3(2)(1) of the Accounting Directive).

The second problem is limited assurance of reports other than financial statements. Management reports and corporate governance statements crucial for corporate governance fall under limited assurance. In addition, Member States may exempt totally small undertakings from the obligation to prepare management reports and so from assurance of the information included in them (Article 19(3) of the Accounting Directive). The duty to prepare a corporate governance statement is applied to listed undertakings only (Article 20(1) of the Accounting Directive). Non-financial statements do not fall under any kind of assurance. In addition, rules on non-financial statements apply only to large undertakings (undertakings which, on their balance sheet, exceed at least two of the following three criteria: (a) balance sheet total: EUR 20 million; (b) net turnover: EUR 40 million; (c) average number of employees during the financial year: 250; Article 3(4) of the Accounting Directive) and are public-interest entities exceeding on their balance sheet dates the criterion of the average number of 500 employees during the financial year, have an average number of employees exceeding 500 during the financial year (Article 19a(1) of the Accounting Directive). Across the whole EU, this means only 11,000 undertakings.[142] Other undertakings are denied the benefits of non-financial statements in their governance and all undertakings from its assurance.

In April 2021, the Commission submitted its proposal for a Corporate Sustainability Reporting Directive.[143] Compared with the Non-Financial Reporting Directive of 2014,[144] adding rules on non-financial statement to the Accounting Directive, the proposal includes important changes in the regulatory framework and especially to the duties of auditors, directly relevant for their role in governance. For this reason, although still a proposal under discussion in the European Parliament and in the Council, this proposed reform is of interest to the topic here.

The proposal extends the scope to all large companies[145] and all listed companies in regulated markets (except for listed micro-enterprises[146]), requires auditing (assurance) of reported information, introduces more-detailed reporting requirements, and a requirement to report according to mandatory EU sustainability reporting standards, and requires companies to digitally 'tag' the reported information so that it is

142. European Commission, Questions and Answers: Corporate Sustainability Reporting Directive proposal, available at https://ec.europa.eu/commission/presscorner/detail/en/qanda_21_1806.
143. *See* Corporate Sustainability Reporting Directive proposal, *supra* n. 28.
144. Non-Financial Reporting Directive; *see supra* n. 100.
145. Defined in Art. 3(4) of the Accounting Directive as undertakings which, according to their balance sheet dates, exceed at least two of the following three criteria: (a) balance sheet total: EUR 20 million; (b) net turnover: EUR 40 million; and (c) average number of employees during the financial year: 250.
146. Defined in Art. 3(1) of the Accounting Directive as undertakings which, according to their balance sheet dates, do not exceed the limits of at least two of the following three criteria: (a) balance sheet total: EUR 350 000; (b) net turnover: EUR 700 000; and (c) average number of employees during the financial year: 10.

machine-readable and feeds into the European single access point envisaged in the Capital Markets Union Action Plan.[147]

For our topic, the most interesting proposals include amendments to Article 34 of the Accounting Directive about assurance of sustainability reporting. It requires statutory auditors to perform a 'limited assurance engagement' on companies' sustainability reporting, including compliance of the sustainability reporting with the proposed sustainability reporting standards, a check of the process carried out by companies to identify the information reported pursuant to the standards, a check of the mark-up for sustainability reporting, and a check of the indicators reported pursuant to Article 8 of the Taxonomy Regulation.[148] In addition, it allows Member States to allow any independent assurance services provider accredited in accordance with Regulation (EC) No 765/2008 of the European Parliament and of the Council[149] to provide an opinion on sustainability reporting on the basis of a limited assurance engagement. It also requires Member States to ensure that consistent requirements are set out for all persons and firms, including statutory auditors and audit firms who are allowed to provide an opinion on the assurance of sustainability reporting.

It is proposed that Article 1 of the Audit Directive will be amended to include assurance of annual and consolidated sustainability reporting, where carried out by the statutory auditor or audit firm carrying out the statutory audit of financial statements. A new article is being proposed (Article 26a), to be added to the Audit Directive, providing that Member States will require auditors to carry out assurance engagements for sustainability reporting in accordance with assurance standards adopted by the Commission and to apply national assurance standards, procedures, or requirements (unless the Commission has adopted an assurance standard covering the same subject matter). It will empower the Commission to adopt assurance standards by means of delegated acts, setting out the procedures that auditors perform in order to draw their conclusions on the assurance of sustainability reporting, including engagement planning, risk consideration, and response to risks, and the type of conclusions to be included in the audit report. It will also require auditors to base their opinions on sustainability reporting on a reasonable assurance engagement, should the Commission use the option to adopt standards for reasonable assurance. It is proposed that Article 48a be amended to set out conditions for delegation of powers to the Commission to adopt assurance standards for sustainability reporting pursuant to Article 26a(2).

147. European Commission, Communication from the Commission to the European Parliament, the Council, the European Economic and Social Committee and the Committee of the Regions: A Capital Markets Union for people and businesses – new action plan, COM(2020) 590 final.

148. Regulation (EU) 2020/852 of the European Parliament and of the Council of 18 June 2020 on the establishment of a framework to facilitate sustainable investment, and amending Regulation (EU) 2019/2088, PE/20/2020/INIT, OJ L 198, 22.6.2020, pp. 13–43 (Taxonomy Regulation).

149. Regulation (EC) No. 765/2008 of the European Parliament and of the Council of 9 July 2008, setting out the requirements for accreditation and market surveillance relating to the marketing of products and repealing Regulation (EEC) No. 339/93, OJ L 218, 13.8.2008, pp. 30–47.

Article 27a will extend the rules on statutory assurance of consolidated sustainability reporting for groups of companies, where carried out by the statutory auditor.

It is proposed that Article 28 will be amended to require the statutory auditors or audit firms carrying out the assurance of sustainability reporting to present their results in the audit report, and to prepare the report in accordance with the requirements for assurance standards adopted by the EU or Member State concerned. In particular, audit reports should specify the annual or consolidated sustainability reporting and date and period they cover. The sustainability reporting framework applied during the audit will also need to be identified. The audit report should include a description of the scope of the assurance of sustainability reporting and identify the assurance standards in accordance with which the assurance of sustainability reporting was conducted. Finally, it should include the statutory auditor's opinion on sustainability reporting.

Article 39 of the Audit Directive will be amended to clarify the tasks of the audit committee in assurance of sustainability reporting. In particular, the audit committee should inform the audited entity's administrative or supervisory body of the outcome of the assurance of sustainability reporting and explain how the audit committee contributed to the integrity of sustainability reporting and what the role of the audit committee was in this process. It should monitor the sustainability reporting process (including the digital reporting process) and the process carried out by the company to identify information reported according to the relevant sustainability reporting standards and submit recommendations or proposals to ensure its integrity. It should monitor the effectiveness of the company's internal quality control and risk management systems and, where applicable, its internal audit of the sustainability reporting of the audited entity, including its digital reporting (as will be required under the amended Accounting Directive), without breaching its independence. Finally, the audit report should monitor assurance of annual and consolidated sustainability reporting, and review and monitor the independence of statutory auditors or audit firms.

As this chapter has shown, these proposals signal important moves to strengthen auditors' role in governance. First, the proposal introduces, for the first time, a standardized 'nearly full audit' for reports other than financial statements. Second, the scope of undertakings preparing and finally being subject to auditing is much broader than for existing non-financial reports. Third, auditing of sustainability reports is to be standardized. Fourth, fear of a concentration of audit service providers and decreased competition will, at least partly, be eliminated by creating the possibility for non-audit assurance provider markets. Finally, auditing of sustainability reports will require advanced professionalism on the part of auditors, assured by regulated training and certification.

However, the proposals still constitute a modest advance in expansion of auditors' assurance duties to approximately 49,000 undertakings in the EU.[150] However, it is a good start, compared to 11,000 undertakings without any kind of auditor assurance under the present Non-Financial Reporting Directive regime.

150. Corporate Sustainability Reporting Directive proposal, p. 10; *see supra* n. 28.

§16.08 CONCLUSIONS

The role of auditors in corporate governance is connected to what information they audit and assure, and the importance of such information in corporate governance. While still providing the basis for assessing the performance and accountability of board and management, it is apparent that financial reports have lost their position as the only source for members and outsiders when assessing company governance. Outsiders or stakeholders – if we want to call them like that[151] – demand reports on the quality of corporate governance that include the efficiency of internal controls. Tension between auditors' traditional role in assuring financial accounts and demands for audits to also include other reports (in the EU regime), such as the management report, sustainability report, and corporate governance statement, show the ever-developing role of auditors in corporate governance.

The moves to expand auditors' assurance duties to include other reports such as sustainability reports, as proposed by the European Commission in its Corporate Sustainability Reporting Directive proposal discussed earlier, are a step in the right direction.[152] In order to increase the credibility of reports on internal control, they must be audited or at least assured by an external auditor. This, in turn, is likely to lead to not only an increase in the cost of control for the companies but also strengthening of the role of external auditors as agents in the corporate governance context.[153] The cost can be controlled by auditing and assurance standards taking into consideration the scalability of standards to the scale and complexity of the activities of an undertaking.[154]

Auditors are likely to play a pivotal role in corporate governance in the future. Their sceptical observation, questioning, reasoning, and demands for documentation all serve to ensure the reliability of financial and 'non-financial' sustainability information. In fulfilling their duties, auditors make a fundamental contribution to corporate governance, and this contribution will become even greater in the future, depicting the precise relationship between sustainability and performance. The question is how proactive auditors are in the long run. The *Wirecard* scandal showed that the regulatory changes were ten years late. Auditors are the ones who provide the knowledge and have the liability that management lacks. However, although they are subject to strict rules and regulations, for example, governing their duties and independency requests, the preparation of reports is generally not subject to any specific regulatory frameworks.[155] If auditors are only called in after the financial and sustainability information has been prepared, it is too late to fully use their expertise. Auditors should therefore resume their multi-role position as both advisors and supervisors of management teams.

---

151. *See* Sjåfjell & Mähönen, *supra* n. 41.
152. *See also*, Mähönen, *supra* n. 2, and Sjåfjell et al., *supra* n. 103, with similar proposals.
153. Holm & Laursen, *supra* n. 45, 330.
154. *See* Sjåfjell et al., *supra* n. 103, especially pp. 70–71.
155. Gabriela Figueiredo Dias, *Sustainability and Sustainable Finance: A Regulator's Perspective and Beyond*, in *The Palgrave Handbook of ESG and Corporate Governance* 217, 221 (Paulo Câmara & Filipe Morais, eds., Palgrave Macmillan 2022).

Assurance of sustainability information is not only important for corporate governance but also expands auditors' societal role or, to be more precise, re-enlarges it. Rather than verifying reports relevant for investments, the role of auditing in corporate governance is to improve management controls and processes and assist management in maximizing the economic performance of their undertakings, for the benefit of the undertaking itself, its management, members, and other key constituencies.[156]

All in all, auditors are crucial in corporate governance for all kinds of undertakings. The tendency to free small and even medium-sized undertakings from auditing is a double-edged sword: although this may be justified in terms of business costs, a lack of auditing deprives them of an important agent in corporate governance. The Nordic examples described in this chapter have illustrated how the flexible Non-Financial Reporting Directive backfired, highlighting the need for harmonization of stringent and clear requirements at EU level in the interests of the undertakings themselves.[157] The problems with more rigid regulation could be solved by giving auditors tools that fit the scale and complexity of undertakings' activities. However, as can be seen from the EU's proposal for the Corporate Sustainability Reporting Directive, its scope is being enlarged very gradually, with inclusion of provisions for small- and medium-sized enterprises (SMEs). Although this is a step in the right direction, there is still a long way to go.

A recent example of how to respond to the challenge of auditing SMEs is the ongoing work focused on formulating a standard for auditing of 'less complex entities' (LCEs) by the IAASB.[158] The new standard is specifically designed for audits of LCEs but, at the same time, is based on the underlying concepts of the ISAs. Public consultation on the draft standard was open until the end of January 2022 and is now in the final stages.

156. Cadbury Report, Oxford Reference, available at https://www.oxfordreference.com/view/10.1093/oi/authority.20110803095540752 (last visited 30 April 2022); Publications Office of the European Union, *GREEN PAPER: The Role, the Position and the Liability of the Statutory Auditor Within the European Union, CELEX1* (1996), http://op.europa.eu/en/publication-detail/-/publication/51543ef5-17f8-4850-99d9-3a78cca64fca/language-en (last visited 30 April 2022).
157. Sjåfjell et al., *supra* n. 103, at 45.
158. IAASB, International Standard on Auditing: Proposed International Standard on Auditing of Financial Statements of Less Complex Entities (ISA for LCE), July 2021, available at https://www.ifac.org/system/files/publications/files/IAASB-Exposure-Draft-Audits-Less-Complex-Entities.pdf.

CHAPTER 17

Public Enforcement of Directors' Duties

Jesper Lau Hansen

§17.01 INTRODUCTION

Economists are said to assume away most practical problems when they build their models. A similar and probably more just critique could be levelled at company law scholars: that we focus on the content of regulation, for example, what exactly should constitute directors' duties, but ignore the drearier question of how that regulation is supposed to be enforced. There can be no doubt that enforcement matters. In fact, we habitually refer to a piece of legislation without prospect of enforcement as *lex imperfecta*. The purpose of this contribution is to ensure that the question of enforcement does not entirely escape our attention.

Enforcement within the sphere of corporate governance is mostly done by private parties, but this contribution was invited to focus on *public* enforcement as distinct from private enforcement and examine its comparable merits and deficiencies. As explored later, the notion of public enforcement covers two separate issues: what kind of enforcement and by whom? In each case, one can make a distinction between public and private.

§17.02 CORPORATE GOVERNANCE

Enforcement of directors' duties is seen as pivotal to the proper functioning of any corporate governance model. Hence, it is useful to briefly examine what is meant by corporate governance.

There are many definitions of corporate governance. Some are *normative* statements on how to behave and are usually based on the presumption that the prescribed behaviour leads to optimal outcomes when measured by certain values. In the field of corporate governance, such statements are often labelled *best practise* or *good corporate governance*; the hopeful adjectives signalling the normative character of this endeavour. Normative statements like these are usually slightly patronising but always well-intentioned. As long as they are in no way mandatory, there is no need to insist on any democratic legitimacy of them.[1]

Other definitions tend to be more *descriptive*, simply describing the applicable normative regulation in place, usually in the form of legislative instruments, such as instruments of corporate governance, which is the theme of this book. Here, the main task is not to ask what would be the best way to design company law regulation, which is debated in other chapters of this book, but to take the regulation already in place as it is, which for this author is the Danish corporate governance system shared with the other four Nordic countries.[2] However, the analyses of enforcement by public means or authorities may also apply to other corporate governance models.

§17.03 DIRECTORS' FUNCTIONS AND CORRESPONDING DUTIES

Although this contribution does not explore the normative questions of how best to design corporate governance, it is useful for a chapter on the enforcement of such duties to dwell for a moment on how to design directors' duties because the choice of design may have a bearing on *who* will or should do the enforcing, when said duties are violated.

A duty is usually a reflection of a function, that is, a power to act in a certain way, and directors' duties mostly reflect their functions within the company and the general distribution of powers within the company. The inherent connection between a function, a duty, and liability is well-known in everyday parlance: this job is my responsibility. Consequently, company law legislation, typically in the form of a Companies Act, will contain provisions that describe the distribution of powers within the company, including the functions that different company organs can perform.[3]

1. Normative standards of corporate governance of this kind can be presented by anyone, who think they have the sufficient experience and knowledge, and the market for CG literature is substantial. Another source for such standards is national codes on corporate governance. Although these codes are subject to oversight by various private actors, usually stock exchanges (regulated markets under EU law), they remain private instruments and are as such voluntary and not subject to direct enforcement, although the comply-or-explain principle often applied to these code does have a certain coercive character, since non-compliance must be explained, that is, excused in public. These voluntary normative standards are not examined further in this chapter.
2. For a survey in English of the Danish model, *see* Jesper Lau Hansen & Carsten Lønfeldt, *Corporate Governance in Denmark*, Annex A in Per Lekvall (ed.), *The Nordic Corporate Governance Model* (SNS Förlag 2014, available at SSRN.com). As the 2014 Lekvall Report shows, Danish corporate governance is part of the unique Nordic model, so foreign readers are advised to skip the country reports in the annexes of the Report and read Per Lekvall's Chapter III, which presents a consolidated Nordic version.
3. In the Danish Companies Act, such fundamental provisions on competence are notably § 111, which describes the company organs involved in running the company and §§ 115–118 describing each company organ's functional responsibilities. Similar provisions in the Act provide the general meeting of shareholders with competence as a non-permanent company organ, e.g., § 106 on amendments to the statutes or § 120 on election of directors in public limited companies.

It is questionable, whether it is necessary to have statutory provisions on directors' duties beyond these provisions on functions to be performed. As C. Northcote Parkinson observed, if you advertise for an acrobat capable of crossing a slack wire 200 feet above a raging furnace, it is not necessary to add that the applicant should have an excellent sense of balance.[4]

At least since the 1930s, when Ronald Coase wrote about the theory of the firm,[5] it has been understood that it is not possible to fully describe what the employees of a company should do in every detail. If that was possible, there would be no need to employ them in the first place; their services could be acquired and performed under contract. Employment, on the other hand, is necessary where it is not possible to explicitly describe the performance wanted, which necessitates instructions to be given on a continuous basis. Employment, or rather the prospect of losing it, makes it possible to instruct the employees ad hoc and respond if their performance of these instructions is not good enough. This goes for the lowliest part-time employee working in the basement up to the magnificent CEO in the top corner office and the directors on the board. Consequently, whenever somebody is employed by a company, it is because it is not possible to describe their functions sufficiently exact, and it is necessary to subject them to the instructions of somebody within the company up to and including the general meeting of shareholders.

The lack of any explicit description of the performance required usually provides the employees with a certain level of discretion, except for the most menial tasks. Nonetheless, depending on the particular jurisdiction, it is not uncommon to see statutory provisions that attempt to govern the discretion to be exercised by directors when performing their function either generally or in respect of certain functions. This can be done in a *positive* way, thus instructing the directors to exercise their discretion in a way that take specific consideration of interests that are in fashion among legislators, e.g., that the directors should take consideration of creditors, shareholders, stakeholders and society, the environment, etc. In other jurisdictions, where legislators are less inclined to think that they know better than the average director and have more trust in the faculties of their fellow man, directors' duties may be described more in the *negative*, thus preventing directors from taking specific action or pursue naked self-interest that may result in harm.

Directors' duties that are described negatively and preventive tend to be short and couched in general terms, whereas duties that are described positively and instructive tend to be long and detailed. This observable difference is probably brought about by the fact that there are many good causes to champion for the legislator once they first start to think about it, and probably also due to the unfortunate habit of jurists to think that if something is described by a list of considerations, then any absence from the list is intentional, and the absentee consideration is not to be considered, which may then necessitate its formal inclusion and thus an ever-expanding legislative text.[6]

4. Cyril Northcote Parkinson, *Parkinson's Law* (Houghton Mifflin; Sentry Edition, 1957).
5. Ronald Coase, *The Nature of the Firm*, 4 Economica 386 (1937).
6. For example, the UK Companies Act s. 172 lists in subss. 1(a)–(f) six considerations a director must take into account when promoting the success of the company. One may ask whether British

Regardless of how directors' duties are described in national company law legislation, the question remains *who* should enforce said duties. In this context, it should be noted that where a directors' duty concerns a specific interest, it is likely that the interested private party will have sufficient incentive to enforce it, though it is not certain as we shall see. Conversely, if the duty concerns more general societal interests, there may not be any private parties that have the necessary incentive to enforce it because each party may not be sufficiently interested or at least not enough to accept the costs of enforcement. This is the problem of collective action and is revisited later in this contribution. Or it may simply be unclear who exactly is supposed to enforce a duty of the directors to safeguard, say, the environment. Thus, if the legislator opts for inserting such broad duties, the legislator also has to make clear whether the duty is a mere aide to the persons already empowered by the Companies Act to discipline directors, ultimately the shareholders in general meeting, or whether it is intended to allow other parties, private or public, *outside* the company to interfere with the *internal* decision-making process inside the company.[7]

§17.04 IS THERE A PROBLEM?

Before embarking on a quest to ensure public enforcement as opposed to private, it is probably wise first to consider whether there is any problem at all. Are directors' duties effectively safeguarded by private enforcement? Some voices in the public discourse appear to believe that business is rife with nefarious practices, and that companies are run only to defraud the public, oppress workers, exploit consumers, and ruin the environment. However, they appear to be in a minority, at least in the Nordics, and can safely be ignored. The public discourse as recorded by daily media, however, does neither appear to support the contention that company directors are able to violate their legal duties without consequences, nor, and more importantly, are there any specific scandals that could lend support to such a contention.

It is possible that banks constitute an exemption to this otherwise rather benign view of business in Denmark. The Financial Crisis of 2008 fanned a belief that bank directors were particularly to blame for the crisis, and the public view of banks in Denmark is so poor that our government has been able to levy a tax specifically on banks as a 'societal contribution', which, apparently, comes on top of the many billions the Danish State took in from acting as a lender of last resort to the banking sector when liquidity froze as a consequence of the crisis.[8] As observed elsewhere, it is not obvious that the crisis should be blamed entirely on the banks that did the lending and not on

directors would likely fail to observe one or more of the enumerated considerations if they had not been included by statute, or whether the list in subs. 1 should be considered exhaustive so that directors may disregard considerations not listed, but relevant in the case at hand? Probably not.

7. The potential of having non-transparent parties external to the company serving as enforcers of the company's internal decision-making process is among the criticism vested with the Commission's proposal for a directive on Corporate Sustainability Due Diligence, *see* COM (2022) 71 final, discussed in n. 15 *infra*.
8. The special tax on banks was recently criticised by the Danish Economic Council, an independent body that monitors public economic policy, in its recent report published on 29 March 2022. They

the customers that formed the other side of the same transactions, or, indeed, on the legislators and regulators who were responsible for the legal framework in place at the time.[9] Furthermore, some of the criticism that bank directors were not sufficiently liable for their actions appeared to be based on a banal misreading of the Danish Supreme Court's decision in the *Capinordic* case.[10]

If these flimsier views of banks are ignored in favour of the case law that actually emerged in the aftermath of the crisis, there is no indication that bank directors were immune to the legal consequences of their behaviour, often resulting in multimillion damages in personal liability for the involved directors. These cases involved civil litigation most of them brought by Finansiel Stabilitet A/S, a public limited company owned by the Danish State and set up to take over failed banks and litigate instances of suspected illegal behaviour, which they have done with considerable vigour and with substantial litigation costs.

There appeared to be substantially fewer *criminal* cases prosecuted by the State, and in the Danish Green Paper No. 1575/2021, new legislation is proposed to enable more criminal prosecutions.[11] These deliberations are subject to political negotiations at the moment, and it is not possible to predict their outcome. However, the Green Paper mostly proposes examples to illustrate existing offences based on bank directors' duties with perhaps only one notable expansion: that it should be a criminal offence to neglect duties prescribed by other parts of the financial legislation, if it increases the risk that the bank is used for money-laundering. However, as bank directors are already obliged to observe anti-money-laundering (AML)legislation, it is questionable whether this is an extension at all, even if it is made into law, which is in itself doubtful at the moment. These minor proposals suggest that criminal law is probably not the best instrument to enforce directors' duties because bank directors seldom act with the clear and provable intent to defraud or to cause economic harm that is necessary to establish criminal liability. More likely, they act recklessly or make mistakes, which may be sufficient to establish private liability in tort, but not criminal liability. This is not just the case in respect of financial regulation. Several of the directors' duties proscribed by the Danish Companies Act and as such applicable also to non-financial companies are made a criminal offence by § 367 of the Act, but it is hardly ever used.

---

criticise that special taxes are levied on certain branches of business, here banks, as it distorts competition. A less-economic argument would be to call the special tax unfair.

9. *See* Jesper Lau Hansen, *Director Liability in Banks: Business As Usual?*, 375–399 in *Festskrift till Jan Kleineman* (Stefan Lindskog, André Andersson, Axel Calissendorff & Jessika van der Sluijs (Eds), Jure Förlag AB 2021). The view that the public opprobrium of banks is mostly unwarranted is further argued in Michael Møller & Niels Christian Nielsen, *Fakta og fordomme om finanssektoren* (Samfunds Litteratur 2021).
10. In *Capinordic* (U 2019.1907 H), the Supreme Court mentioned in passing that the standard of liability was the same fault-based standard applicable to all limited liability companies, which some took to mean that there was no difference between running a pizza shop and a bank. Naturally, although the *standard* of liability may be the same, the *result* of applying said standard will be quite different because there are considerably more onerous legislations applicable to running a bank than a pizza shop, as indeed there ought to be.
11. Cf. *Betænkning om skærpet ansvarsvurdering forledelsesmedlemmer m.v. i finansielle virksomheder* [Green Paper on increased liability for directors etc. in financial institutions], Betænkning nr. 1575, January 2021.

The experience gained from the banking sector after the Financial Crisis should not be disregarded, but it is fair to distinguish this sector from the overall business and commercial sector that comprises the vast majority of companies. As noted earlier, there appears to be few scandals or other examples that directors in non-financial companies can violate their duties without consequences.

The absence of court cases involving director liability should not be interpreted as an indication that no enforcement takes place. That would be mistaken because the main instrument of private enforcement of directors' duties is occupational in nature as explained in §17.03 and relies on the private measures of company law. Thus, the primary instrument of enforcement of management's duties is removal from their position and the reputational damage that this brings. Considering how difficult it is to reach these senior and extremely well-paid positions, the risk of losing it all is probably a very efficient instrument of enforcement quite on par with any criminal sanctions.

There is every reason to think that this system of private enforcement by simply removing the directors and the concomitant damage to their occupational reputation and future career prospects is working fairly well, as it would appear to be more swift, nuanced, and discrete, than any system involving civil courts and open litigation of violations of statutory provisions would be.

Furthermore, the apparent absence of court cases involving enforcement of directors' duties may also be explained by the prevalence of arbitration as the preferred instrument of conflict solution. Arbitration offers a number of characteristics, e.g., speed of procedure, the ability to select experts with business experience as arbitrators, and confidentiality of proceedings, that parties in a commercial setting often prefer. Thus, it is difficult to accurately estimate the actual extent of enforcement of directors' duties by adversarial proceedings as the number of arbitrations is unknown.

However, all is not necessarily well in the state of Denmark. A recent survey by the think-tank Justitia showed that private enterprises do not rely on the courts to pursue pecuniary claims.[12] Among the main reasons, the respondents pointed to excessively long time to obtain judgments, and a failure by courts to compensate for the full costs incurred by the proceedings, even when a judgment was awarded. These costs can be considerable, especially because professional standards among practicing lawyers still mitigate against using no-cure, no-pay services.[13]

12. Henrik Rothe, Stine Brøsted Jensen, and Yas Farah Bakhsh Akbatani, *Erhvervslivets adgang til domstolene* Justitia, 2020, available at http://justitia-int.org/erhvervslivets-adgang-til-domstolene/.

13. There is no longer any prohibition of no-cure, no-pay practices by the standards applied by Danish lawyers, however, they are still obliged to only charge a fee based on the case at hand. Thus, they are not allowed to take a higher fee that would off-set the risk entailed by a no-cure, no-pay service. In other words, Danish lawyers may do it, but they would demonstrate their failure to understand basic economics if they did. The root course of this de facto denial of no-cure, no pay-system springs from the fact that the fee may eventually be charged to the losing party to the conflict, although this rarely happens in full as evidenced by the 2020 Justitia Report (Rothe, Jensen, and Bakhsh Akbatani, *supra* n. 12). What lacks is a right for a party to agree to pay out of his own pocket a higher fee to compensate the lawyer's promise not to charge in case of failure, which is how the system works in the US. An increased use of litigation financing by external parties may bring reform, *see* Carsten Fode, *Ledelsesansvar og ansvarsbegrænsning* (Jurist – og Økonomforbundets Forlag 2020).

Although the 2020 Justitia Report and analysis concerned something else, i.e., the courts as an instrument to enforce pecuniary claims and settle disputes in commercial matters, it is likely that these two problems, duration and costs, are also present in the enforcement of directors' duties. This is particularly likely to form a problem, where a transgression of a directors' duties is pursued by parties that cannot avail themselves of the more efficient enforcement connected with removal of directors offered by company law, that is, where creditors or minority shareholders are concerned. If there is a problem with courts as an instrument of conflict solution due to high costs, it is not likely to be mitigated by the use of arbitration as that is usually even costlier.

To conclude, there may be a problem with the enforcement of directors' duties worth considering. The problem does not appear to concern majority shareholders. They can exercise their powers to discipline management and if they feel that litigation is necessary, they can use their powers to persuade the board of directors to let the company sue former directors and officers for any failure to fulfil their duties. But other parties may be less fortunately positioned to address a perceived wrong committed by the management of a company.

If private enforcement is difficult, or perhaps even impossible due to practical or economical constrains, then it is natural to look to public enforcement to ensure the observance of directors' duties. This requires a contemplation of what, exactly, is the difference between private and public enforcement, or more basically between public and private.

§17.05 PRIVATE OR PUBLIC?

Although once popular, it is now generally accepted in legal studies that the dichotomy of public versus private is ill-suited as an analytical tool to distinguish between different disciplines of law. Public bodies may engage in private activities, such as contracts and commercial transactions, and the activities of private parties often take place on the basis of or within the framework of public regulation. The freedom of contract is still an important freedom, but it is increasingly fenced in by public considerations mandated by legislation.

However, the irrelevance of the distinction as an analytical tool to separate legal disciplines is due to the inseparability of the public and the private sphere, which does not in itself exclude that it is important to distinguish between the two; it is just not possible to do that on a more general scale as is necessary with legal disciplines. Thus, to observe that, for example, the legal discipline of Company Law comprises elements of both private law and public law does not mean that these elements are indistinguishable; they are.

One of the greatest achievements of our society has been the steady progress, at least since the age of Enlightenment and probably even before that, to curtail the reach and powers of the State in favour of an ever-increasing liberty of the individual. In modern democracies like ours, the perception of the State has changed significantly within the last three centuries. The State is no longer considered our master but our servant. Representatives of governments are even called ministers, which no longer means servants of the King, but of the People who elected them or the government they serve and who may remove them again in the next election.

This process has not been uncontested, notably by the totalitarian ideologies of communism, fascism, and national-socialism in the twentieth century. The mass popular support they once enjoyed shows that some people find individual freedom a burden they would happily trade for the security and order of a totalitarian state. [14] However, their defeat in their countries of origin, Russia, Italy, and Germany, have removed them as serious challengers, although some still favour authoritarian regimes that emphasise the importance of the State as a collective, 'embodying' its citizens in a commitment to a common purpose as an alternative to liberal democracy based on human rights for the individual.

In a modern democracy like ours, the State is provided with substantial powers, even, as Max Weber observed, with a monopoly on violence. It is exactly this concentration of power that necessitates a distinction between public and private. It is important to limit the power and reach of the State to avoid it from trampling its citizens. It is thus important to remember the gross asymmetry between the powers of the State as compared to individuals.

This observation leads to the first recognisable difference between the State as a public entity as opposed to the individual as a private person: private persons cannot legally coerce other individuals to follow their will but have to rely on voluntary contracts necessitating a consent, which is usually only provided where the other party sees a benefit in the contractual arrangement. The State, however, may use its powers to order people about, and it may extract the money it needs in the form of taxes without explicit consent from each taxpayer.

This arrangement is necessary for the State to operate and to uphold a civilised society that avoids a Hobbesian anarchy, but it plainly also presents a continuous risk of abuse and exploitation by whoever happens to be in control of the State at any given time. The State should continuously be reminded of its immense powers, so that they are exercised with appropriate respect to its citizens' wellbeing; nothing is more dangerous and prone to wreak havoc than an elephant that thinks it is a mouse.

Among the limitations on state power is the right of individuals to pursue the activities they like, including commercial activities, without the approval of the State. Gone is the mediaeval system of guilds and royal patronage, where the individual's right to pursue a commercial enterprise depended on the whimsical consent by authorities. How important this right to pursue your own interest, and how revolutionary a break with the past that it once was, is perhaps best understood by the fact that such a right was mentioned in the first democratic constitution of Denmark of 1849, and it still forms part of it today as § 74.

14. For a recent presentation of this emphasis of the collective before the individual (Gemeinnutz vor Eigennutz) in German company law that ended with the AktG of 1937 adopted by the National-Socialist regime but embodying widely held beliefs at the time, *see* Rolf Skog, *Talk Is cheap*, NTS 2021/4 83. For a contemporary review of the then new company law reform in Germany, *see* William Conrad Kessler, *The German Corporation Law of 1937*, 28 Am. Econ. Rev. 653 (1938).

Another important limitation of state power is that the State cannot use its citizens to achieve certain outcomes, no matter how benign they are believed to be. In a democracy, politicians may openly strive to move society in certain directions, but they cannot mandate that all citizens accept their policy and dedicate themselves to achieving it. It is legal to dissent and ignore, and even to oppose. Philosophers as different and distant as Immanuel Kant and John Rawls all agree: no human being should serve as a mere instrument for others. It is acceptable and common place for the State to regulate the activities of its citizens, but this regulation must take the form of distinct obligations or prohibitions, it cannot more openly require subservience to a specific political goal.

These observations of the inherent freedoms of the individual citizen in a modern democracy must also apply where individuals decide to exercise these rights together with others. There is no reason why the freedom of the individual in a democracy should not extend where citizens act collectively, as when acting within a company. Consequently, the company must be seen as a private entity as opposed to the State.[15]

The fact that a company must be registered by a public authority does not make it a public body to be governed by the State. To suggest that would be an atavistic throwback to the age of Absolutism, where formation of a company required royal consent and depended on the whim of the monarch. The registration of companies reflects other concerns, notably those of transparency, and do not involve an act of grace or permission. The too frequent use of the phrase 'a license to operate' should not obscure this. It is just a lame metaphor for the fact that, in a competitive economy, a company is dependent on the goodwill of its customers; it does not suggest that the company need permission from the public or anybody megalomanic enough to think they represent the public.

Even upon registration of its formation, the company remains a private entity to be governed by the private parties that set it up. How these parties have distributed their powers among them remains a private arrangement based on contract and payment within the confines of the applicable company law legislation, which in most

15. On 23 February 2022, the Commission finally published its proposal for a directive on Corporate Sustainability Due Diligence, *see* COM (2022) 71 final. Despite the fact that the subject is only 'due diligence', the proposal's Art. 15 commands that companies 'shall adopt a plan to ensure that the business model and strategy of the company are compatible with the transition to a sustainable economy and with the limiting of global warming to 1.5 °C in line with the Paris Agreement'. If the intent is to command the company to adhere to a zero-carbon strategy, that should have been clearly stated as an obligation on the company in Art. 15. But as it is written, Art. 15, more generally, obliges the company to strive for the political goal of the international treaty. This will open up the internal decision-making process of the company to scrutiny by outside non-transparent parties and make the company vulnerable to the inevitable complaint of 'more could be done'. Considering that the Commission's previous attempt at harmonising directors' duties was rejected by the Commission's own Regulatory Scrutiny Board, *inter alia,* because 'the impact assessment is not sufficiently clear about the need to regulate directors' duties on top of due diligence requirements', the continuation of this attempt under the label of 'sustainability due diligence' is in violation of Art. 5 of the EU Treaty. The vast criticism of the proposal makes it possible, however, that the provision is changed during the negotiations between the European Parliament and the Council.

jurisdictions afford the parties considerable discretion to arrange the company's internal affairs.

That this is a fair description of a company as a private entity is evidenced by the fact that company law legislation, notably in the Nordics, is dominated by default provisions allowing a wide discretion for alternative arrangements to be negotiated on what is effectively a contractual basis, whereas mandatory provisions are few and occur only where third parties are concerned, who do not have access to the internal decision-making process and therefore cannot fend for themselves, such as creditors in the case of a limited liability company or minority shareholders in respect of far-reaching decisions of the general meeting.

It should be noted that a company remains a private entity in this sense, even where it is referred to as a 'public' company as a consequence of it 'going public'. Of course, this parlance only means that the company has chosen to have its shares admitted to trading on a trading venue (stock exchange) that attracts the investing 'public' at large. As the trading of shares, and debentures for that matter, is exogenous to the company, it remains a private company in every sense here discussed regardless of how its financial instruments are traded. That also goes for the relatively new concept in EU company and accounting law known as 'public interest entities' or PIEs, where the alleged 'public interest' does not change the fact that companies covered by this concept are private entities in the sense that any attempt to take away or limit the ownership and governance rights would be an act of expropriation, something that cannot be done by EU law due to Article 345 of the Treaty on the Functioning of the European Union and Article 17 of the European Charter.

Equally, this is true of the distinction known in EU company law between public and private limited companies, as evidenced by Annex I on PLCs and Annex IIa of the Companies Directive 2017/1132, respectively. This distinction was originally intended to provide a protective capital regime to companies that might 'go public', that is, have their shares admitted to trading on a trading venue. This is, and has been for many years, quite unnecessary as an instrument of investor protection because that protection is today provided by EU legislation directly aimed at companies making using of trading venues and perhaps the Crowdfunding Regulation (2020/1503) that allows private companies to offer their shares to the public will prove to be the final nail in the coffin of this peculiar and outdated phenomenon. Either way, it does not change the fact that even a public limited company is a private entity that should enjoy the same rights of autonomy of the State that are afforded to the private individuals who set it up and run it on a daily basis.

To sum up, the State is vastly more powerful than individuals in every respect, be that personnel at its disposal, its powers, and its command of and access to funds and other resources. Even in respect of time, the State is eternal and can afford to spend it in a way no human being can endure. For this reason, public enforcement must be subjected to limitations that minimise the always present risk that these vast powers are abused. The vast array of treaties and legislation that serve this purpose include such different instruments as the 1950 European Convention on Human Rights (ECHR) and its supplementary protocols, the Charter of the EU, which would apply directly to any secondary EU legislation, including that which pertain to directors' duties, and, in national law, procedural safeguards pertaining to public administration and to criminal prosecutions.

We should never be blinded by our coincidental acceptance of a policy pursued by the State to lose sight of why these limitations on State power are important and must be observed at all times.

§17.06 THE AUSTRALIAN EXPERIENCE

Within the EU, company law has been harmonised to a great extent, which makes it necessary to look outside the Union to find examples that are truly different. One such example is Australia, which has experimented with a combination of public enforcement of directors' duties in a way that has not yet been experienced in Europe.

In 1998, as part of a reform of the Australian Corporations Act, the public supervisory authority was renamed the Australian Securities and Investments Commission (ASIC) and assigned new powers, notably for this Chapter these powers entailed public enforcement of directors' duties under what is now the 2001 Corporations Act.

The ASIC itself could be described as a public one-stop body under its own 2001 ASIC Act with federal responsibility for the public enforcement of the directors' duties enumerated in the 2001 Corporations Act, and with power to seek civil and criminal pecuniary penalties, compensation, disqualification of directors, and jail terms.[16] Directors' duties under the Corporations Act can broadly be described using the dichotomy derived from US jurisprudence of duties of care and duties of loyalty. The statutory provisions on directors' duties found in Sections 180–184 of the Act corresponds to those derived from common law, and the public enforcement powers of the ASIC do not preclude private enforcement by derivative suits.

Thus, the public enforcement system is a *supplement* to the private enforcement more traditionally relied upon in most other jurisdictions, not just in that it provides criminal sanctions, which is also known in the more traditional jurisdictions, but also by allowing 'civil penalties'. As the name would suggest, a civil penalty is first and foremost a penalty, that is, it has a punitive character. As one scholar describes it, it is 'concerned with public wrongs and moral culpability, and not merely conduct causing damage'.[17] It is thus different in nature from a claim based on tort, which merely pursues restitution of a loss.

The experience with the ASIC as a public enforcement of directors' duties appears to have satisfied the original expectations behind the reform that the existence of a

16. The literature on ASIC is considerable, for a presentation with an emphasis on the issues dealt with in this Chapter, *see* Vicky Comino, *Effective Regulation by the Australian Securities and Investments Commission: The Civil Penalty Problem*, 33 Melb. U. L. Rev. 803 (2009).
17. Cf. Thomas Middleton, *The Privilege against Self-Incrimination, the Penalty Privilege and Legal Professional Privilege under the Laws Governing ASIC, APRA, the ACCC and the ATO – Suggested Reforms*, 30 Austl. Bar Rev. 282, 310 (2008).

public authority to prosecute wrong doings would increase the number of enforcement cases before the courts and thus serve as a deterrent against future wrongs.

However, and probably only as a surprise to the very naïve, it has not entirely prevented director misconduct. A review conducted in 2017 by the Commonwealth's Senate Economics References Committee had as its first recommendation out of six to have the government 'consider reforms to provide greater clarity regarding the evidentiary standards and rules of procedure that apply in civil penalty proceedings involving white-collar offences.'[18] As pointed out in an academic survey some years before, 'an examination of the case law reveals the tendency of the courts to treat such proceedings more like criminal proceedings.'[19]

Evidently, the benefit of using the greater powers of a public authority to litigate private individuals like directors with so-called civil penalties is mitigated by judges' inclination to then apply the procedural safeguards normally associated with criminal proceedings. Or, to put it more bluntly, Australian judges appear not to have been fooled by the legislator's use of the euphemism, 'civil penalty' but have placed emphasis on the second half of the concept and used the corresponding safeguards applicable to criminal penalties.

§17.07 IS THERE ROOM FOR PUBLIC ENFORCEMENT OF DIRECTORS' DUTIES?

At least when the Australian experience is viewed from Europe, it is difficult not to side with the judges. It is the clear case law of the ECHR that Article 6 ECHR on the right of a fair trial in criminal proceedings must be subjected to a convention autonomous construction of what constitutes a 'criminal charge'.[20] Or to put it bluntly again: a contracting State cannot escape its convention bound duties to behave in a civilised manner simply by calling a criminal offence something else, like an 'administrative measure' or a 'civil penalty'. Forgive the punt, but that is not civil at all and should be avoided. The obligations that follow from said Article 6 is the price to pay for applying the immense powers of the State in proceedings against an individual, when the State is doing what a State is supposed to do with criminal law: fighting 'public wrongs and moral culpability, and not merely conduct causing damage'.[21]

Article 6 ECHR is neither easily circumvented, nor should it be. This treaty obligation necessitates a choice: to use either private law or criminal law when enforcing directors' duties, which is effectively a choice between litigation of a restorative nature to recoup a loss and litigation to punish behaviour that is deemed

18. Senate Economics References Committee, 'Lifting the fear and suppressing the greed': Penalties for white-collar crime and corporate and financial misconduct in Australia, 23 March 2017.
19. Comino, *supra* n. 16, 810.
20. For guidance, *see* the Court's own publication, *Guide on Article 6 of the European Convention on Human Rights: Right to a fair trial (criminal limb)*, 31 December 2021, which also contains a list of cases.
21. Middleton, *supra* n. 17.

anti-social irrespectively of whether the behaviour caused any economic consequences. The former can be done as civil enforcement, the latter only by criminal proceedings.

If criminal law is chosen, then prosecution is done by public authorities and the defendant is protected by the safeguards guaranteed by Article 6 ECHR and any additional provisions in national law on criminal proceedings. These safeguards comprise notably the prior existence of a clear statutory prohibition, a presumption of innocence, no self-incrimination, right of defence, proceedings before an impartial and organisationally independent court or tribunal, and placing the burden of proof to overcome the presumption of innocence squarely on the public prosecutor.

The current deliberations on the proposals discussed in the Danish Green Paper 1575/2021 on strengthening the criminal offence of a bank director causing considerable loss or risk thereof will show to which extent this is a possible route.[22] One major problem will probably turn out to be whether the unacceptable conduct by bank directors can be described sufficiently clear to serve as the basis of criminal proceedings. Even when linking the conduct to the causation of a loss or a serious risk of loss, it may be difficult to describe exactly what the director did wrong and should have done differently, which is necessary for a criminal prohibition to work. If it is the causation of the loss that constitutes the criminal conduct, then should all decisions that lead to a loss be punishable? Surely not, as a loss may simply be the unwanted outcome of careful risk-taking, and careful risk-taking is what businesses should be doing. And if the prohibition concerns the neglect to observe a certain conduct, shouldn't that be punishable in itself, even where it did not result in a loss or even the risk of a loss? This might end up with draconic sanctions for failure to observe more formal rules on behaviour, which again may serve to prevent necessary risk-taking and reduce bold entrepreneurs to box-ticking control freaks. The fact emphasised in the Green Paper that such criminal prohibitions already exist but are seldom used, which is the very reason reform is contemplated, would suggest that this is a very difficult exercise.

Perhaps a better route is to rely on private enforcement in respect of procedure and use the powers of the State to do the private enforcement. Thus, even where the procedure is purely private, it could be considered using public authorities as the enforcers in lieu of private parties; in other words, to rely on private means but used by public authorities. As just mentioned, this should not attempt to circumvent the obligation to observe certain safeguards in respect of criminal charges; on the contrary, it is to let the public authority use the traditional civil enforcement procedures in the same way as a private party would, that is, to pursue a claim that cannot be qualified as a 'criminal charge' under the 1950 ECHR, typically to recover a loss inflicted by company directors' violation of their duties.

As discussed in §17.04, a problem of private enforcement is that the parties harmed by directors' violations of their duties may not possess the time or resources to enforce their claims for damages in civil proceedings. They are understandably

22. Betænkning nr. 1575, *supra* n. 11.

reluctant to 'throw good money after bad' and involve themselves in lengthy court proceedings with negligent prospect of recouping their loss or the money spent on litigation.

One way of overcoming the problem of collective action is to authorise a public authority to commence litigation in the name and on behalf of individuals. It is similar to a class action in the way that many individuals are bundled together and raises similar concerns of how to establish the group of plaintiffs, e.g., to use an opt-in or opt-out model, and whether the defendant may challenge each individual of the group or only the common reason for their complaint. This can be a solution to the problem of collective action, where no one individual has sufficient incentive to respond to a problem. It is already in use in Danish law in respect of the Consumer Ombudsman, who may initiate private proceedings on behalf of consumers, cf. § 28 of the Act on Marketing, although it is a rarely used power, which may suggest that this kind of collective litigation is difficult.

However, to use a public authority in this way raise the problem of which public authority to use. Considering that these civil enforcement procedures would probably be infrequent, it is not likely that a new public body should be established for that sole purpose. Although the Danish State did set up Finansiel Stabilitet A/S to take over failed banks and then litigate claims of director misconduct by civil enforcement before the courts, that, however, was due to the number of failed banks in the aftermath of the Financial Crisis and the substantial sums involved and may not be replicated outside such extraordinary circumstances. It may even be counterproductive to establish a new public authority to pursue violations of directors' duties, since that public body would depend on a steady stream of complaints to secure its raison d'être and bolster its budgets, making it less likely to exercise the critical restraint that befits a public authority vested with such powers vis-à-vis private sector companies and the individuals that run them.[23] It is probably better to rely on a pre-existing public authority that is established and funded for other reasons.

It is thus more advisable that the relevant public authority should form part of the remit of one of the existing public bodies, e.g., in Denmark the Business Authority, which is the public authority in charge of company law, possibly with a divided responsibility with the Danish FSA, which supervises financial enterprises and is probably better equipped to enforce directors' duties of a financial nature.

Another way of overcoming the problem of collective action is to allow the public authority to pursue a private litigation on its own behalf, which is possible where the

23. Art. 17 of the proposal for a directive on corporate sustainability due diligence (*supra* n. 15) calls for Member States to designate one or more national public authorities to be competent to handle complaints about the exercise of directors' duties defined in Arts 25–26 and the compliance of Art. 15 on the design of the company's business model and strategy. This would allow the public authorities to challenge managerial decisions, which is far-reaching especially when considering that complaints can be filed by non-transparent foreign actors masquerading as aggrieved 'stakeholders' according to Art. 19. This would serve as an excellent tool to harass European companies and keep them out of foreign markets where standards of human rights and environmental protection are low. Again, it is to be hoped for that the negotiations of the proposal will lead to a more sensible outcome.

State has suffered a loss. Again, the establishment of Finansiel Stabilitet A/S is a case in point. The company acquired failed banks and was therefore able to enforce private claims arising out of these acquisitions, which were due to the rather unusual circumstances that are now mainly over.

More relevant is the litigation brought by the Tax Authorities because here the State is directly an aggrieved party with a private claim of payment of missing taxes and value-added tax (VAT). Such private enforcement of private claims on behalf of the State would not directly benefit other private parties, who may have suffered a loss due to the same circumstances, for example, the reckless conduct by a company's directors, but it would nonetheless have two major benefits: first, the enforcement action would in itself serve to discipline directors and prevent abuses, and, second, once the culpability of a director has been proven by the public authority in court this could also serve as a sufficient basis for other plaintiffs, who could either join their claims to the pending case or initiate new proceedings based on the established facts.

If one looks at Danish case law on liability in respect of directors' duties, it is noticeable how often the plaintiff has been the Tax Authorities pursuing a loss suffered due to unpaid taxes and VAT. It is probably no coincidence that the alarming growth in abuse of limited liability companies that has occurred in Denmark in recent years coincided with the break-down of the Danish Tax Authorities and their incapacity to claim and pursue unpaid taxes and VAT before the courts.[24]

Where public authorities are used to pursue private claims, the litigation would be conducted before civil courts and according to civil procedure. This would ensure some equality between the public authority as plaintiff and the director as defendant. However, the public authority would still have superiority in respect of resources and, notably, time. Consequently, it is necessary to protect the private party against frivolous litigation, and especially appeals of acquittals should be subject to close scrutiny by a superior and independent authority irrespectively of whether it is before the courts or in administrative proceedings. Lengthy proceedings do not constitute the same problem for a public authority as they do for private individuals, since civil servants leave their office and worries behind at the end of business hours, whereas the private party has to live with it every day and night until it is over. So, the public authority should be forced to show the necessary restraint also in its private enforcement actions.

24. Correlation is not causation, and it remains a subject worthy of dedicated research to explore whether the growth of the abuse of limited liability companies is caused by the break-down of the Danish Tax Authorities. The growth of abuse is only indirectly documented in Denmark by way of the report issued by the Danish Business Authority in September 2018 examining the abuse of the IVS, which was the Danish equivalent of the German UG, that is, a private type of company without a legal minimum capital upon formation. However, the report was drawn-up to provide the basis for the politically-desired outcome to abolish the IVS, and so the report did not explore in detail the extent of abuse of the two other types of limited liability companies, the ApS and the A/S, but only mentioned this in passing. *See* more generally on the report and the unfortunate abolition of the IVS, Jesper Lau Hansen, *Editors' Note: Companies Without Legal Capital and the Strange Case of Denmark*, ECFR 677 (2019).

§17.08 OTHER FORMS OF PRIVATE ENFORCEMENT BY PUBLIC AUTHORITIES

So far, private enforcement has been described as litigation pursuing claims for damages to recover losses suffered by the neglect of directors' duties. It is possible, however, to contemplate other enforcement actions that do not necessarily have the character of a 'criminal charge' as used in Article 6 ECHR.

One incremental step away from the clear case of a claim for damages is proceedings to establish responsibility but not to assign liability, that is, fact-finding. This is known in company law as *investigations*, and they form an independent step that may later be followed by other steps, such as litigation to establish liability.

Investigations are a well-known corporate governance instrument available to shareholders according to national company law legislation. As an instrument of corporate governance, it is available to the shareholders in general meeting, who may decide to apply it by a resolution passed with a simple majority. However, since the majority has appointed the management of the company, whose conduct would be the subject of the investigation, the instrument is also available to a minority of shareholders. It should be noted, though, that national company law usually only allows this instrument where the minority is substantial, in Danish law it is only available for a minority representing 25% of the subscribed capital.[25] This high threshold for an instrument of minority protection is due to the intrusive and disruptive effect of an ongoing investigation, which suggest that the instrument should not be made available, unless the petitioner represents considerable interests in the company. This would often rule out individual stakeholders external to the company but not necessarily major creditors.

In Danish company law, the decision to allow investigation by request of the minority of shareholders in the company is made by a court, and only once it is convinced that the request is merited. For this reason, the minority is not required to pay the expert(s) who carry out the investigation, but the costs are carried by the company. This makes sense, where the company is existing and can pay the costs, and it is not obvious that the instrument of investigations would be enhanced by letting a public authority examine the company or carry the cost. The involvement of a court is a sufficient safeguard to avoid abuse of the instrument of investigation. If reform should be considered in this regard, it would be to include major creditors as empowered to request investigation on par with a minority of shareholders. This may serve to prevent bankruptcies by exposing risky or unlawful behaviour at an early stage. It could also be contemplated to allow other stakeholders than creditors to request an investigation if the company is made subject to certain non-financial obligations, for example, of climate-related measures. However, to avoid harassment and interference with the decisions made by the company's legitimate decision-makers, such investigations should only concern clearly defined obligations to act in a certain way. In each case and irrespectively of what is the object of the investigation,

25. Investigation is governed in Danish company law by §§ 150–152 of the Companies Act.

the investigation should only be allowed if the court is presented with sufficient evidence to suggest that wrong-doing has taken place and by taking into account the disturbance and inconvenience to the company, its owners and its employees that it may entail.

Investigation is presently only used in existing companies that can pay the costs. However, the instrument should also be considered where a company has been deserted and left for mandatory winding-up by liquidation. Back in the 1990s, Denmark was plagued by a string of abusive takeovers, whereby a buyer would acquire the shares of a limited company that had ceased to do business and was left with some assets including unpaid taxes, take the money owed by the company to the Tax Authorities, and make a run for it, the so-called Emptying Companies Scams. This was possible because once a company fails to file its annual accounts, it will receive a warning from the Business Authority, and if no filing has been made, it will be subjected to mandatory liquidation courtesy of the State. To lower costs, the liquidation would be done without any investigation of the company as a simple administrative decision to delete the company from the register. However, after some years the Tax Authorities and the Business Authority began to inform each other, and the scams were discovered, eventually leading to the imprisonment of a few of the perpetrators.

Almost thirty years later it is still the case that abandoned companies are left for automatic liquidation and with a substantial cost to the State, that is, for the taxpayers. An important first step to stop this continuing loss to the State would be to make it an offence for owners and directors to abandon a company instead of seeing to its voluntary and orderly liquidation and making them personally liable for the costs of a mandatory liquidation. Due to AML legislation, the (ultimate) owners of even the smallest limited company in Denmark are today known to and registered by the Danish Business Authority, so it would most often simply be a question of sending a bill to cover the liquidation costs.

A next and possible step would then be for the Business Authority to select, either on a random or on a risk-based basis, abandoned companies and examine them for any violations, which could then be prosecuted. This would entail costs, which would have to be carried by the Authority, but the benefit would be the preventive effect among owners and directors of companies that there is a not insubstantial risk of being examined and any possible wrongdoings found out. It would then depend on the outcome of such an investigation by the Business Authority whether criminal proceedings would be justified, or whether the Tax Authorities or private parties have suffered a loss that might give rise to private proceedings. Such investigations by the Business Authority would entail further costs and thus a bigger budget, but it would be in line with the recent development that has seen the Business Authority change from mostly a register of companies to a supervisor and enforcer of company law.

The mere fact that an instrument does not entail a prison sentence or fine does not necessary preclude that it has the character of a criminal charge and as such is subject to the safeguards applicable by Article 6 ECHR, but it is clear from the case law of the ECHR that certain 'disciplinary' measures may not be considered a criminal charge. It is for this reason not clear that whether the instrument of *director disqualification* would be seen as a criminal charge, and as this particular instrument is not (yet) subject to harmonisation by EU company law, there is considerable difference in its application among Member States.

In Danish law, the instrument is treated as an instrument that involves the courts and is subject to public prosecution, which would satisfy the requirements of Article 6 ECHR. Considering the harsh consequences of the measure on the disqualified director, this is well-founded and may be considered an example of public enforcement of directors' duties by a public authority using a public procedure. The fact that it is not openly a measure of criminal law should not obscure that the courts should only apply it with the same caveats that would apply to traditional criminal measures like imprisonment, that is, a clear presumption of innocence and the strict observance of proportionality between crime and punishment. It is thus important that director disqualification is only used in cases of clear misconduct and not used to punish those who actively try but fail to salvage companies in distress, which is a high-risk activity but necessary to avoid financial loss to shareholders, creditors, employees, and society at large.

A less-drastic measure related to director disqualification is the measure of fit & proper, which is used in banking law.[26] Here, the measure seeks to ensure the directors' qualification and is thus an *ex ante* measure and not an *ex post*, as is disqualification. The restraint recommended above on the exercise of this power by public authorities is also advisable here, so authorities should only deny the status of fit & proper where there is clear reason to. In other words, the 'burden of proof' should be on the authority to overcome a presumption that those who want to appoint the director knows the directors' capabilities better than the public authority. However, such a measure is an intrusion into the right of private sector companies to govern themselves that can hardly be extended beyond the area of banks, if indeed it is necessary there. It would be much too costly and disproportionate to expand this regime to directors of all companies, even to a smaller subset, such as PLCs or listed companies.

§17.09 CONCLUSION

Directors' duties need to be enforced partly to address instances of abuse, partly to avoid future abuse. Most enforcement of directors' duties probably take place informally by removing the director, and the reputational consequences and the preventive effects of this should not be underestimated. On that background, the infrequency of court case concerning director's duties cannot be taken to signal that there is a lack of enforcement. It is thus not clear that there is any serious lack of enforcement, and hence it is not obvious that there is any need of reform.

---

26. A director of a credit institution is required to be fit and proper, *see* Capital Requirements Directive (CRD), notably CRD4 (2013/36) Art. 13 and CRD5 (2019/878) Art. 91.

However, it is reasonable to consider whether the costs connected with enforcement serve as a deterrence to private enforcement by private parties and whether the aforementioned need for enforcement thus necessitates public enforcement of some kind. The question of public enforcement covers two separate questions: what kind of enforcement and by whom?

Public enforcement is usually associated with criminal law, and the inherent asymmetry between the State and its powers vis-à-vis a private defendant requires certain limitations on the State's exercise of its powers in criminal proceedings, as evidenced by instruments such as the 1950 ECHR and the EU Charter. Some lessons can be learned from the Australian experiment of having a public body enforce directors' duties. However, a central tenet of this experiment is the application of so-called civil penalties, which is not transferable as they would constitute criminal charges under the said European instruments and require criminal proceedings.

Thus, the first question of what kind of enforcement is reasonably clear: either the enforcement concerns a criminal charge in which case criminal proceedings must be used, or the enforcement concerns something that is clearly not a criminal charge, usually a claim for damages, and then civil proceedings can be used even by a public authority, albeit with some discretion and oversight to avoid abuse of the public authorities' superior powers. Which public authority that should engage in this kind of private enforcement depends on whether the public authority acts on its own interest, i.e., that of the State, or on behalf of private parties. Most likely, it would be cost efficient to make use of existing public authorities already working with company law.

Another kind of public engagement that falls between criminal and private enforcement is investigation. At present, this measure is only available to shareholders, but it could be expanded to include creditors and even other stakeholders. However, considering the intrusive nature of the measure, its use should be curtailed and only applied when sufficient evidence can convince a court to allow the measure. The investigation can be done by a public authority to establish whether there is any violation that could justify criminal or civil proceedings. This could be useful especially in respect of abandoned companies that face mandatory liquidation and would have a preventive effect on abuse of companies.

CHAPTER 18

The Digitalisation of Corporate Governance

Alexandra Andhov

§18.01 INTRODUCTION

Companies have an essential position in our society. They contribute to innovation, societal development, and wealth. However, since Second World War, due to various monetary policy and regulatory decisions, we have observed an increasing concentration of economic activity and power in companies.[1] This has resulted in growth and significant impact of companies on society as well as a continuous concentration of market dominance of a handful of companies, generating market imbalance and unequal division of wealth and power.[2] One key factor that has allowed for corporate domination has been the paradigm theory of neoclassical economists and legal scholars asserting that the company's sole objective is maximising shareholder wealth – the shareholder primacy theory.[3]

Fast forward to 2022, the global society has transpired into a world that faces complex challenges, such as climate change, a continuous COVID-19 pandemic, a war in Ukraine, and omnipresent racial and economic inequality. These and other world events push organisations in every industry to re-think and re-design their businesses by embracing digital solutions. For example, the COVID-19 pandemic showed us that a lot could be digitised, from everyday work and board meetings to shareholder voting. New platforms have been introduced to facilitate collaborative work, decentralise management, and increase employee engagement.[4] At the same time, digitalisation gives the management novel and often powerful tools for collecting and analysing data

1. *See* David C. Korten, *When Corporations Rule the World,* European Business Review (1998).
2. *See,* e.g., Joshua Gans et al., *Inequality and Market Concentration, When Shareholding Is More Skewed Than Consumption,* 35 (3) Oxford Rev. of Econ. Pol. 550 (2019).
3. *See,* e.g., Sabeel K. Rahman, *Domination, Democracy, and Constitutional Political Economy in the New Gilded Age: Towards a Fourth Wave of Legal Realism?*, 94 Texas L. Rev. 1329 (2016).
4. As an example, *see* Achievers, Gtmhub, or Ascentis.

about their customers, employees, business partners, and competitors. Yet, machine learning and artificial intelligence (AI) can produce outcomes that are difficult to understand and thus to communicate. Many early AI solutions turned out as 'black boxes',[5] increasing distrust in AI systems. Therefore, the more recent trend in connection with AI has been to take advantage of human expertise that complements AI outcomes and thus increases transparency and trust in such systems.[6] Since the COVID-19 pandemic, the digitalisation of corporate governance has become an often-discussed topic. Yet, despite numerous initiatives, little has transpired.

Corporate law and corporate governance have evolved remarkably over the past decades. Yet, the changes were slow and planned. Over the decades, corporate law and governance introduced new tools and mechanisms to govern the relationships within the company and the relationships with outside stakeholders. Decisions that used to be within the hands of the interested parties became increasingly regulated, and novel governance mechanisms, obligations, and responsibilities have been introduced to balance the powers of various stakeholders.[7] These rules have been designed to govern physical, or one could say analogue activities, and as such, the digital solutions might often be outside of the scope. For example, in Germany, the German Bundestag needed to adopt COVID-19 emergency legislation to allow public limited companies to hold their general meetings virtually, given that their existing rules did not permit virtual general meetings.[8] Yet, this exemption was only for the duration of the COVID-19 pandemic, as general meetings can be held online only until 31 August 2022.[9] Thus, it seems that the German government prefers the analogue general meetings instead of offering new forms of collaboration or digital solutions.

As this chapter intends to show, technology offers additional flexibility and opens new possibilities, but it also has the ability to distort the adopted rules and their purpose. Even if some may believe that technology is neutral, it is not. That being said, technology has a lot of potential; presumably, we may not entirely escape it. Neither could we escape COVID-19. Therefore, when addressing the digitalisation of corporate governance and designing a framework to adopt new technological solutions, it is necessary to address the capabilities and risks of technology through the aims that corporate governance envisions achieving. Simultaneously, we need to consider our regulation's state of the art. Is the law offering companies to grow international? Does it provide space for online shareholder meetings or for shareholders to vote across multiple jurisdictions and time zones?

---

5. The term black box means an AI system whose inputs and operations are not transparent or understandable by the user or another party. Often, black boxes after being utilised for a longer period of time may render outputs that are not even explainable by the original engineer.
6. *See* Thomas H. Davenport, *Can We Solve AI's 'Trust Problem'?*, 60(2) MIT Sloan Management Review, 1–5 (2019).
7. *See* generally on the development of corporate governance and current governance mechanisms, Jeffrey N. Gordon & Wolf-Georg Ringe, *The Oxford Handbook of Corporate Law and Governance* (Oxford University Press 2018).
8. *See* German COVID-19 Mitigation Act, *Gesetz zur Abmilderung der Folgen der Covid-19 Pandemie im Zivil-, Insolvenz- und Strafverfahrensrecht*, 27 March 2020, §1.
9. *Ibid.*, §6.

Digitalisation, similarly to regulation, needs to be assessed in a specific context, and that context is the purpose of corporate governance. Through this lens, we can review and analyse various novel technological solutions, their promises, possible deliverables, and risks. Contemporary technical solutions offer new approaches to inherent problems of corporate governance, including agency costs, related parties' transactions or shareholder activism/passivity. In this publication, the authors have addressed various corporate governance instruments, from regulating managerial procedures to certification. This chapter addresses some of the existing corporate governance instruments and their possible digitalisation. Yet, before we adopt various digital solutions to digitise corporate governance, we must be aware of inherent technological risks and limitations. With technology and its design, we can knowingly or unknowingly affect the rights and obligations of the involved parties.

This chapter examines the impact of corporate governance digitalisation from both positive and normative perspectives by critically reviewing novel technological corporate governance solutions through the lens of corporate governance purpose. Reflecting on both the United States (US) and European corporate governance practices, this chapter aims to offer insights into the practices on both sides of the Atlantic; where necessary, the distinction is outlined. This chapter ultimately asks whether technology can provide a solution for particular corporate governance 'pain points'. The term 'pain point' is commonly used in the start-up world, and they represent specific problems faced by current or prospective users of the technological solution. Often, when new digital solutions are developed, the first question that the start-up team needs to answer is what are 'the pain points' that this solution attempts to solve. What are the problems that we try to fix? For example, during the COVID-19 pandemic, we needed to figure out how shareholders could meet and how they could digitally sign various documents with admissible signatures while maintaining the lockdowns.

Before designing a technological tool, we need to understand what problems the technology attempts to solve. Subsequently, we need to analyse that if the technology is applied, what are the possible foreseen and unforeseen risks that this solution brings. Does the solution meet the needs of the target users? Is it retaining the users, which means do the users continue to use the solution? And more importantly, for any contemporary start-up, the critical question is whether the solution is scalable. Scalability means how quickly the group of users can grow and across how many jurisdictions. Digital tools that are to serve the legal community, in general, are extremely hard to scale, given the distinctions in laws and regulations. Thus, as you can see, any company that wishes to design a solution to address corporate governance pain points needs to consider multiple elements.

The digitalisation of corporate governance is a complex topic, which I hope to address from various perspectives throughout this chapter. Yet, before diving into the content, a couple of disclosures. This chapter focuses on publicly-traded companies, also referred to as companies and is structured in the following manner. First, a brief discourse is offered on the purpose of corporate governance through the analysis of company's purpose and the need for corporate governance. This section aims to reflect for whose benefit the corporate governance instruments have been designed and whether these can be advanced by and with technology. Once we understand the aim of corporate governance, we can review the inherent corporate governance pain points independently and address the plausibility of technological solutions. However, as mentioned, technology is not omnipresent, and thus, before adopting digital corporate governance tools, we need to be aware of potential and unintentional risks. Finally, this chapter concludes with perspectives on the limitations of technology and calls for adequate technology reviews and audits before implementing digital tools for corporate governance purposes. Consider this chapter as an introduction to corporate governance digitalisation. Further in-depth analyses into the individual corporate governance challenges are necessary, and undoubtedly more critical work must be carried out in this area.[10]

§18.02 FRAMING THE CORPORATE GOVERNANCE PURPOSE

Corporate governance represents an inherent part of corporate law. It correspondingly extends to the formation of the East India Company, the Levant Company, and other major chartered companies in the sixteenth and seventeenth centuries.[11] However, according to legal historians, the first discussions around corporate governance, without necessarily calling it as such, only go back to the 1920s and '30s,[12] as the new large-scale enterprises were created. The term 'corporate governance' was used in the *New York Times* in 1972.[13] The US Securities and Exchange Commission (SEC) used the term corporate governance later in the 1970s – when it brought corporate governance to the official reform agenda.[14] The SEC referred to managerial accountability, board structure, and shareholder's rights as corporate governance. The SEC started to treat corporate governance as part of its regulatory remit from this moment on. It is worth mentioning that in the 1970s, a major corporate governance scandal at Penn Central took place, further incentivising the SEC to drive a new regulatory wave in corporate governance.[15] This became the trait of corporate governance. One could argue that every major regulatory development has gone hand in hand with a significant,

10. *See generally* Iris H-Y Chiu & Ernest WK Lim, *Technology vs. Ideology: How Far Will Artificial Intelligence and Distributed Ledger Technology Transform Corporate Governance and Business?*, 18 Berkeley Bus. Law J. 1 (2021); Martin Petrin, *Corporate Management in the Age of AI*, 3 Columbia Bus. Law Rev. 965 (2019); Carla Reyes, Nizan G. Packin, & Benjamin Edwards, *Distributed Governance*, 59(1) Wm. & Mary L. Rev. (2017); David Yermack, *Corporate Governance and Blockchains*, 21(1) Rev. Financ. (2017); and Alexandra Andhov, *Corporations on Blockchain: Opportunities and Challenges*, 53(1) Cornell Int. Law J. (2020).
11. *See* Brian R. Cheffins, *The History of Corporate Governance* in *Oxford Handbook of Corporate Governance* (Mike Wright et al. ed., Oxford University Press 2013).
12. *See*, e.g., Harwell Wells, *The Birth of Corporate Governance*, 33 Seattle Uni. Law Rev. 1247–1249 (2010).
13. *See* Mariana Pargendler, *The Corporate Governance Obsession*, 42 J. Corp. Law 373 (2016).
14. *See* Cheffins, *supra* n. 11.
15. *See* Joel Seligman, *The Transformation of Wall Street: A History of the Securities and Exchange Commission and Modern Corporate Finance*, 535–542 (Boston: Houghton, Mifflin 1982).

sometimes even a global corporate scandal that uncovered that the existing rules and principles were unsatisfactory.[16]

By the second half of twentieth century, the term corporate governance spread from the US worldwide. Corporate governance became an essential part of corporate law within a reasonably short period, yet governed through different tools. These include corporate governance guidelines issued by stock exchanges[17] or the international corporate governance codes.[18] Corporate governance remains one field that is substantially affected by scandals and crises. We have never discussed corporate governance reforms as much as after events such as the East Asian financial crisis in 1997, the Enron Scandal in 2001, or the financial crisis of 2007–2008. Nonetheless, corporate governance remains dispersed through numerous fields of laws and governed by soft law instruments to a great extent. So, what is corporate governance?

[A] What Is Corporate Governance?

To understand corporate governance and its purpose, we need a brief historical review. In the traditional corporate law view, going back to the nineteenth century, corporate law aimed to solve a narrow set of problems related to formation and management. Historically, corporate law's key notions have been legal personality, limited liability, minimum capital requirements, rights and obligations connected to the ownership of shares, board structure, its rights, and accountability. We could further include agency problems and questions associated with fiduciary duties. Traditional corporate law has perceived all the other questions about the rights of employees, creditors, debtors, environmental concerns, or financial accountability to be outside the realms of corporate law. Translated into a straightforward language, the 'traditional' corporate law was only concerned with how a group of shareholders could establish a company, while their personal wealth would not be affected if things went wrong.[19] Developing the concept of a separate legal entity was fundamental to supporting and fostering business activities and risk-taking, often leading to innovation. Legal fiction is the underlying theory upon which corporate law and governance have been built.[20]

Yet, the formal structures laid down by laws and implemented through articles of association or statutes were inefficient for operating businesses. As Professor Gilson once stated, a company is a structure that allows a legal fiction to operate a business

16. The scandals include, for example, Enron, Volkswagen, Lehman Brothers, or Siemens.
17. In 1976, After the Penn Central scandal, the SEC persuaded the New York Stock Exchange to amend its listing requirements and oblige listed companies to maintain an audit committee composed of independent directors.
18. *E.g.*, OECD Principles of Corporate Governance, which were first issued in 1999.
19. *See* Katharina Pistor, *The Code of Capital: How the Law Creates Wealth and Inequality* 54–67 (Princeton University Press, 2019).
20. *See* Michael C. Jensen & William H. Meckling, *Theory of the Firm: Managerial Behaviour, Agency Costs and the Theory of the Firm*, 3 J. Fin. Econ. 310 (1976).

and make it possible for third parties to do business with it confidently.[21] This structure consists of different elements, including legal rules and obligations, which are greatly complemented by business operations. These business operations consist of various processes that allow information flow and decision-making. This part is seen as corporate governance – the tools and procedures through which the management governs the company.

Different regional and international institutions adopt various definitions of corporate governance. For example, the Business Roundtable, an organisation composed of the chief executive officers (CEOs) of many multinational companies, described corporate governance in the following way:

A good corporate governance structure is a working system for principled goal setting, effective decision making, and appropriate monitoring of compliance and performance. Through this vibrant and responsive structure, the CEO, the senior management team and the board of directors can interact effectively and respond quickly and appropriately to changing circumstances, within a framework of solid corporate values, to provide enduring value to the shareholders who invest in the enterprise.[22]

Other descriptions or definitions are similar and ultimately accept corporate governance as a set of principles and rules that help companies and their decision-makers design the internal processes to govern the company. For example, the Group of Twenty (G20)/Organisation for Economic Co-operation and Development (OECD) Principles of Corporate Governance (OECD Principles) define corporate governance as a set of relationships between a company's management, its board, its shareholders and other stakeholders, whereas the corporate governance provides *the structure* through which *the objectives* of the company are set, and *the means* of attaining those objectives and monitoring performance are determined.[23]

Corporate governance is an organic and flexible concept constantly evolving in response to a changing corporate environment. Therefore, any narrow definition would soon become obsolete.[24] Professor Gilson offered an interesting explanation of corporate governance, who stated that corporate governance is the corporation's operating system.[25] This metaphor is well-suited for discussing the digitalisation of corporate governance. However, such depiction limits the scope of corporate governance. If we see corporate governance as just an operating system, we should undoubtedly proceed and introduce digital tools for faster and more efficient governance. However, if, similarly to the Business Roundtable, we see corporate governance also as a tool to interact effectively with other stakeholders and respond quickly and appropriately to changing circumstances, such as the COVID-19 pandemic, climate

21. *See* Ronald J. Gilson, *From Corporate Law to Corporate Governance* in *The Oxford Handbook of Corporate Law and Governance* 7 (Jeffrey N. Gordon & Wolf-Georg Ringe eds, Oxford University Press 2018).
22. *See Business Roundtable, Principles of Corporate Governance 2005* 6 (November 2005).
23. *See G20/OECD Principles of Corporate Governance*, 9 (2015).
24. *See generally* Janet Dine and Marios Koutsias, *The Nature of Corporate Governance: The Significance of National Cultural Identity* 67–70 (Edward Elgar 2013).
25. *See* Gilson, *supra* n. 21, at 8.

change, and others, while reflecting on corporate values, such as diversity, sustainability, and accountability,[26] then to translate these processes into a digital solution is a much more complex task.[27]

[B] Corporate Purpose in Corporate Governance

Given the path dependence between companies and corporate governance, the purpose of corporate governance is directly connected to the company purpose. Over the past years, a lot has been written about the corporate purpose and whether its purpose is to benefit the shareholders or the stakeholders.[28]

In early 2001, two recognised corporate scholars, Hansmann and Kraakman, eagerly proclaimed the 'end of history for corporate law.'[29] The company's purpose is to benefit the shareholders predominantly – shareholder corporate governance has dominated the Western corporate law theory. Hansmann, Kraakman, and other scholars believed that the model would become the dominant corporate law paradigm.[30] However, just a few months after their imprudent proclamation, Enron collapsed, initiating a new wave of research into corporate governance and accounting. It was acknowledged that corporate governance failed to address not only the interest of shareholders, creditors, and other stakeholders but also completely disregarded any corporate or personal accountability.[31] Recommendations were replaced with

---

26. The OECD also stipulates that the purpose of corporate governance is to help build an environment of trust, transparency, and accountability necessary for fostering long-term investment, financial stability, and business integrity, thereby supporting stronger growth and more inclusive societies.
27. *See* Alexandra Andhov, *Corporate Governance in Developing: Lessons from Covid-19 and EU Green Deal*, 3 Erhvervsjuridisk Tidsskrift, 15–17 (2021).
28. *See*, e.g., Lynn Stout, *The Shareholder Value Myth: How Putting Shareholders First Harms Investors, Corporations, and the Public* (Berrett-Koehler Publishers 2012); Mark J. Roe, *Missing the Target: Why Stock-Market Short-Termism Is Not the Problem* (Oxford University Press 2022); Stephen M. Bainbridge, *The New Corporate Governance Theory and Practice* (Oxford University Press 2008); Hillary A. Sale, *The Corporate Purpose of Social License*, Georgetown Law Faculty Publications and Other Works (2019); Alexandra Andhov & Lela Melon, *Policy Coherence for Corporate Sustainability in the EU: Can We Achieve Sustainable Corporate Governance Without Sustainable Finance?* in *Money Law, Capital, and the Changing Identity of the European Union* (Gabriella Gimigliano and Valentino Cattelan eds, Hart Publishing 2022).
29. *See* Henry Hansmann & Reiner Kraakman, *The End of History for Corporate Law*, 89 Georgetown Law J. 439, 454 (2001).
30. *See*, e.g., Stephen M. Bainbridge, *The Globalization of Corporate and Securities Law in the Twenty-First Century: Director v. Shareholder Primacy in the Convergence Debate*, Transnational Law 16 (45) (2002); John C. Coffee, Jt., *The Future as History: The Prospects for Global Convergence in Corporate Governance and Its Implications*, 93 Northwestern Univ. L. Rev. 641 (1999) or Jeswald W. Salacuse, *Corporate Governance, Culture and Convergence: Corporations American Style or With a European Touch?*, 9 L. & Bus. Rev. of the Americas 33 (2003).
31. In the early 2000s, a group of progressive corporate law scholars has published on this issue, *see* Lawrence E. Mitchell, *Corporate Irresponsibility: America's Newest Export* (2002); Kellye Y. Testy, *Linking Progressive Corporate Law with Progressive Social Movement*, 76 Tulane L. Rev. 1227 (2002); Kent Greenfield, *September 11 and the End of History of Corporate Law*, 76 Tulane L. Rev. 1409 (2002).

regulations.[32] Several years later, the financial crisis of 2007–2008 showed another corporate governance deficiency – *the financial intermediaries*. Scholars have realised that market watchdogs and governmental institutions have failed to oversee financial intermediaries' activities properly. Moreover, governments failed to introduce incentives and accountability to protect the interest of those who have entrusted their economic well-being to banks, investment, and insurance companies. Thus, another wave of scholarship and regulation took place that nudged the companies towards stakeholder theory.[33]

Currently, in the European Union (EU), we discuss the corporate purpose from another perspective – climate change. In December 2019, the European Commission initiated its growth strategy and introduced – the EU Green Deal.[34] The EU Green Deal aims to 'transform the EU into a fair and prosperous society, with a modern resource-efficient and competitive economy where there are no net emissions of greenhouse gases in 2050 and where economic growth is decoupled from resource use.'[35] With the adoption of the EU Green Deal, the EU aims to re-design its policies and legislative tools across all industries to transform the economy and secure the EU's climate neutrality. The EU Green Deal represents a preparatory material for significant changes that will, similarly to the COVID-19 pandemic, affect us all, including corporate governance. Regulations regarding environmental, societal, and governance (ESG) disclosure have been introduced, including the Proposal on Corporate Due Diligence and Corporate Accountability[36] and other initiatives also mentioned in the Circular Economy Action Plan.[37]

Whether these proposals will be adopted and in which form and shape, is to be seen. Nonetheless, these and other regulatory changes affect the notion of corporate governance and its everyday application by companies.[38] Even if there is no agreement on the corporate purpose among scholars and policymakers or even if we agree that

32. E.g., The Sarbanes-Oxley Act of 2002, Pub. L. 107–204, 116 Stat 745;
33. For a comprehensive analysis of the history of corporate purpose, *see* Dorothy S. Lund & Elizabeth Pollman, *The Corporate Governance Machine,* Colum. L. Rev. 121 (2021). For understanding the specifics of stakeholder theory, *see* Virginia Harper Ho, *'Enlightened Shareholder Value': Corporate Governance Beyond the Shareholder-Stakeholder Divide*, J. of Corp. Law 36 (2010); Ann M. Lipton, *What We Talk About When We Talk About Shareholder Primacy*, Case Western Reserve L. Rev. 69 (2019); and Edward Rock, *For Whom Is the Corporation Managed in 2020?: The Debate Over Corporate Purpose*, Law and Economic Research Paper Series Working Paper No. 20-16 (2020).
34. European Commission, Communication from the Commission to the European Parliament, the European Council, the European Economic and Social Committee and the Committee of the Regions, Brussels 11.12.2019, COM (2019) 640 final.
35. *Ibid.*, at 2.
36. European Parliament, Draft Report with Recommendations to the Commission on Corporate Due Diligence and Corporate Accountability (2020/2129(INL)).
37. Communication from the Commission to the European Parliament, the Council, the European Economic and Social Committee and the Committee of the Regions, A New Circular Economy Action Plan: For a Cleaner and More Competitive Europe (COM/2020/98 final).
38. Regulation of corporate governance is not solely EU's phenomenon. Corporate Governance is being regulated all over the world. *See*, e.g., Marc I. Steinberg, *The Federalization of Corporate Governance* (Oxford University Press 2018) or Andreas M. Fleckner and Klaus J. Hopt, *Comparative Corporate Governance: A Functional and International Analysis* (Cambridge University Press 2013).

possibly companies, in general, should not even have a purpose,[39] the recent regulatory proposals affect corporate governance. As a consequence, they affect which parts and elements of corporate governance can or cannot be carried out with or by technology. The rest of this chapter is built on acknowledging that corporate governance is more than just a set of tools and procedures and that corporate governance aims to protect the company's values and other stakeholders.

[C] Pain Points of Corporate Governance

In the world of technology, there is generally a belief that any new solution, technical or not, should be conceptualised through specific pain points. This means that before proposing particular solutions, we should understand the existing problems and challenges of corporate governance. Similarly, before we try to assess whether and how digitalisation can improve corporate governance, we need to understand the issues, or the pain points that (a) corporate governance aims to solve and (b) corporate governance remains unsuccessful in solving.

If we review and epitomise the leading literature[40] on corporate governance and internationally recognise corporate governance principles, i.e., OECD Principles or Business Roundtable Principles, the critical pain points of corporate governance are the following:

- Division of control and ownership between management, boards, shareholders (and other stakeholders);
- Role of the boards, their composition, and accountability;
- Disclosure, transparency, and market manipulation; and
- Compliance, sustainability, and protection of (diverse) stakeholders;

These pain points are addressed through a mix of various regulatory and non-regulatory tools that aim to solve the omnipresent information asymmetry and discrepancy of incentives. The following subchapter analyses the above pain points and their plausible digital solutions.

§18.03 CAN TECHNOLOGY SOLVE THE CORPORATE GOVERNANCE PAIN POINTS?

Some believe that a revolutionary paradigm shift is well underway in how we think about corporate governance because of the new and emanating technologies. A new

39. *See* Jill E. Fisch & Steven Davidoff Solomon, *Should Corporations Have a Purpose?*, 99 Texas L. Rev. 1309 (2021) for a critical discourse on the value of corporate purpose for theoretical and practical application of corporate law.
40. *See* Jonathan R. Macey, *Corporate Governance: Promises Kept, Promises Broken* (Princeton University Press 2008); Reinier Kraakman et al., *The Anatomy of Corporate Law: A Comparative and Functional Approach* (Oxford University Press 2017); Gordon & Ringe, supra n. 7; Beate Sjåfjell et al., *The Cambridge Handbook of Corporate Law, Corporate Governance and Sustainability* (Cambridge University Press 2019); and Fleckner & Hopt, *supra* n. 38.

term, 'CorpTech,' which refers to practices that include distributed ledger technology, data analytics, or AI in corporate governance, has already been introduced.[41] Scholars and practitioners have become excited by the latest technological possibilities that can utilise anything from a simple management platform for easier administration of board's activities, to abstract ideas where the decision-making is carried out on a distributed ledger that utilises the power of AI with data-driven analytics. Those scholars sometimes referred to as 'tech proponents,' share the view that technology will fundamentally change the existing corporate governance and may even eradicate long-standing corporate governance problems. They believe that technology is the panacea to a diverse set of issues that have been present in corporate governance since the times of modern corporations. Yet, the more we learn about the technologies and their limitations, the more we realise that the technological solution needs to be genuinely well thought through, from the moment the engineers start to design it, through the use of the data up until a human begins to use it.

The scholarship has addressed the great potential of technology, including blockchain, big data, or AI, but not always with a careful review and understanding of the underlying reasons for the corporate governance pain points, and thus possibly not reflecting on the entire puzzle. After discussing the key challenges of modern corporate governance, this chapter assesses how can technology be utilised to solve some of these. The following section starts with analysing the 'pain points' and then it moves to reflect on the existing tech solutions, their possibilities and limitations.

[A] Division of Control and Ownership Between Boards, Shareholders (and Other Stakeholders)

The division of control and power between the management and shareholders has been discussed for centuries. Already in 1776, Adam Smith observed the tension as 'the directors of such companies, however, being the managers rather of other people's money than of their own, it cannot well be expected, that they should watch over it with the same anxious vigilance with which the partners in a private copartnery frequently watch over their own.' [42] One hundred and fifty years later, amidst the economic growth and the rise of large companies with dispersed stock in the US, Berle and Means analysed the phenomena of separation of ownership and weakening of shareholder control.[43] In Europe, we might not have seen such obvious tension between the shareholders and managers, as many large companies have been for decades in the hands of their owners – families.[44] Yet, we observe a tension between

41. *See* Luca Enriques and Dirk Zetzsche, *Corporate Technologies and the Tech Nirvana Fallacy*, 72 Hastings Law J. (2020).
42. *See* Adam Smith, *An Inquiry into the Nature and Causes of the Wealth of Nations* 193 (Liberty Classics 1776).
43. *See* Adolf A. Berle & Gardiner C. Means, *The Modern Corporation and Private Property* 7–9 (Transaction Publishers 1932).
44. Sometimes referred to as 'family capitalism' in Italy, France, or Germany. *See* Ugo Pagano and Sandro Trento, *Continuity and Change in Italian Corporate Governance: The Institutional Stability of One Variety of Capitalism*, University of Siena Department of Economics Working

diverse groups of shareholders (often referred to as 'blockcholdings') and simultaneously between managers and other influential stakeholders (i.e., banks, governments, or employees or corporate elites).[45]

Irrespective of the groups in control and those having ownership, the underlying challenge is the misalignment of interests and incentives, which is very well known under the agency theory.[46] As Jensen and Meckling asserted, 'the relationship between the stockholders and manager of a corporation fits the definition of a pure agency relationship.'[47] Jensen believed that minimising agency costs between shareholders and management are a crucial goal of corporate governance.[48] However, agency costs appear among all groups with power or control over the company, with different interests and incentives. Historically, we have attempted to introduce new legal and non-legal solutions for incentives alignment from independent directors,[49] institutional investors, [50] and remuneration policies.[51] However, none of them has proved to be bulletproof. Thus, could technology offer help to manage and possibly align these interests and motivations?

[1] Digital Asset Management Systems

A technological solution that could help with information asymmetry and design a space where stakeholders could align their interests could be a digital asset management system. A digital asset management system is software that allows companies to securely organise, communicate, collaborate, store, and share digital files.[52] The majority of these systems are used in project management or within specific departments, whether it is HR, marketing, or product development.[53] However, such tool could be re-thought for the purposes of clear communication within a company with

---

Paper (2002) or Prem Sikka, *Corporate Governance and Family-owned Companies*, in *Corporate Governance in Contention* 90–97 (Ciaran Driver and Grahame Thompson, eds, Oxford University Press 2018).

45. *See* Roger M. Barker, *Corporate Governance, Competition, and Political Parties: Explaining Corporate Governance Change in Europe* 7–10 (Oxford University Press 2010).
46. *See generally* Ronald J. Gilson & Jeffrey N. Gordon, *The Agency Costs of Agency Capitalism: Activist Investors and the Revaluation of Governance Rights*, 113 Columbia L. Rev. (2013).
47. *See* Jensen & Meckling, supra n. 20, at 309.
48. *See* Brian R. Cheffins, 'What Jensen and Meckling Really Said About the Public Company', *Legal Studies Research Paper* no. 29/2020, University of Cambridge 3 (2020).
49. *See*, e.g., Stephen M. Bainbridge, *Independent Directors and the ALI Corporate Governance Project*, 61 George Washington L. Rev. (1993); Jeffrey N. Gordon, *The Rise of Independent Directors in the United States, 1950–2005: Of Shareholder Value and Stock Market Prices*, 59 Stanford L. Rev. (2007).
50. *See*, e.g., Bernard S. Black, *Agents Watching Agents: The Promise of Institutional Investor Voice*, 39 UCLA Law Rev. (1992).
51. *See*, e.g., Guido Ferrarini & Maria Cristina Ungureanu, *Executive Remuneration'* in *The Oxford Handbook of Corporate Law and Governance* (Jeffrey N. Gordon & Wolf-Georg Ringe eds, Oxford University Press 2018).
52. *See* IBM, *Digital Asset Management*, available online at: < https://www.ibm.com/topics/digital-asset-management > last accessed 18 August 2022.
53. *See*, for example, Sales Layer, *Digital Asset Management*, available online at: https://saleslayer.com/digital-asset-management-dam last accessed 18, August 2022.

their shareholders, employees, and other relevant stakeholders that have the right to be informed.

If such tool or technology is to be introduced, the computer scientists and designers must be aware of all involved parties, their rights, their obligations, and the purpose of such a tool. The tool would need to reflect the existing disclosure rules and market abuse regulations. The software would have to have a clear purpose, so that *the parties* that should utilise this technology are aware of its aim, possibilities, and limitations. Transparency must be part of the journey to use the technology.

If we aim to improve communication and distribution of information, technology can quickly solve the problem. Whether it is a simple email with pdf attachments or a particular online platform for shareholders, where they can access different information about the company, we can and should use technology to communicate.[54] Not only is such communication efficient, but it also often keeps a record should any future dispute arise. However, this is also why many companies might not wish to maintain a digital trace of their communications, decisions, and actions. Furthermore, shareholder management software can be designed to mirror the company's bylaws and national regulations. It can allow for voting and decision-making to take place and include almost everyone without limitations to their physical presence. The rights and obligations of the parties can be relatively easily translated into a code. Computer scientists can create different accounts, depending on types of shares, common, preferred, or other, to which they can assign rights and obligations. They can develop mechanisms for the board to communicate with a particular class of shareholders, notify shareholders when their vote is requested, or even facilitate dividends payments.[55]

In addition, in many European countries that have employee representation, the software can provide access to employee representatives and other selected groups of stakeholders who have the right to participate in the governance according to the bylaws, national laws, and corporate governance codes. The options are almost limitless as to which level the parties could embrace much more active governance. Many start-ups and smaller companies have embraced such tools to facilitate and empower their investors and employees. Start-ups regularly inform their investors and key employees of their business and product development. Some crowdfunding platforms also offer those who have invested through their platforms continuous access to information.[56] These solutions should be offered by classical centralised software or decentralised tools, such as a distributed ledger technology (also known as 'blockchain').[57] The choice of one or the other solution would depend on the size of the company, the features that should be implemented, and the desire to automate the activities through, for example, smart contracts.

54. Examples of such technology include SharesInside or Equvista.
55. For example, Fidelity Investments has developed an in-house solution called SOCOACT, a blockchain-based voting designed to authenticate shareholders and ensure the origin and truthfulness of the submitted vote.
56. *See*, e.g., Seedinvest.
57. For a comprehensive analysis of blockchain, *see* Primavera De Filippo & Aaron Wright, *Blockchain and the Law: The Rule of Code* (Harvard University Press 2018).

A smart contract is a computer program similar to a contract. A smart contract shares theoretical similarities with a legal contract as they are both aimed at regulating the interaction between different parties.[58] However, a smart contract is much simpler than a classical contract. A smart contract encodes logic that runs when predetermined conditions are met. They are used to automate the execution of an agreement so that all parties can be immediately certain of the outcome. They enable transactions of any size with minimal transaction costs and high transaction security levels. Smart contracts could be incorporated into corporate governance to help with decision processes, voting, or distribution of dividends, if the conditions were clearly stipulated. For example, during an Annual General Meeting, shareholders need to vote on agendas and often make key decisions for the company and vote on board members. Different smart contracts could be developed for each one.

Regarding the election of board members, smart contracts could easily collect the names of the candidates for a particular position, including ascertaining that these candidates comply with the existing requirements. Using smart contracts could limit third-party interference and, at the same time, provide all parties with the same access to such a position. The possibility of people nominating themselves and others for various functions would suddenly become much more democratised. As long as they fulfilled the requirements, they could be on the list. The process would possibly gain a layer of transparency.

The risk of implementing smart contracts lies in the inability to change the specifications indicated in the smart contract after one is created and the possible security breach.[59] However, as with any technological solution, there are specific smart contract audits and insurance protocols, if needed.

From a transparency perspective (more in §18.03[C]), such software keeps track and records of communication and decisions that the management or shareholders took. This overview of past actions could also improve the quality of governance. Thus, such tools could, on the one hand, facilitate communication and decision-making, and on the other, they can provide the basis for a review and improvements in governance and possible accountability, if needed. Therefore, going back to the incentives, we should ask whether it is in the board's interest to introduce such a tool. If the interest is there, shareholders should be able to compel their boards to adopt such tools. From the perspective of shareholders' participation, such devices' quality and UIX (user interface) would greatly determine whether the individual shareholders would use this tool.

---

58. *See* Wulf A. Kaal, *Blockchain-Based Corporate Governance*, Stan. J. Blockchain L. & Pol'y (2021).
59. In 2016, the first Decentralised Autonomous Organisation (DAO) was created through numerous smart contracts, without any central leadership. The idea was to create an organisation that would be governed by a community organised around a specific set of rules. DAO was meant to operate like a venture capital fund for the crypto and decentralised space. DAO was built on the Ethereum blockchain and during its formation, anyone was allowed to buy DAO tokens - aka DAO shares - which encoded in themselves the rights and obligations of the DAO's shareholders. The formation was extremely successful as DAO raised around USD150 million. The smart contract infrastructure allowed for the entire organisation to be run automatically. The smart contracts were codes that would be executed when a set of criteria would be met.

Institutional shareholders should welcome such software, as it would shorten the time they spend on information collection, management overview, and subsequent analytics. Institutional investors have been using various technological tools to map and analyse corporate activities for some time. Such tools help them streamline access to fundamental and technical data about the ecosystems, network activity, trading, social media activity, news, and other research on their assets while providing additional data analytics. Bloomberg has been dominating business and market analytics for many years. However, the more prominent institutional investors, including investment firms and pension funds, have been investing in their own digital asset management systems to help them manage their portfolios.[60] They provide them with the necessary information to understand what is happening with the companies they invested. They compare these data with market data and carry out business analytics, based on which they are able to make informed (better) decisions. Thus, one could say that technology is already there for some shareholders with a slightly different purpose. The question remains whether we are interested in re-thinking this technology, and creating easier access to such information for general shareholders and other stakeholders or not. Depending on whether companies undertake a centralised or decentralised approach, they can choose among a variety of technology, including also decentralised ledger technology (DLT).[61]

[2] DLT and New Market Architecture

DLT as technology could potentially have a revolutionary character. First, it is essential to indicate a disclaimer that DLT today is still in the phase of development, and even though we already see DLT used across some sectors, it is still a technology that needs to be substantially improved and/or altered before we can apply it as some foresee.[62] Second, before we get into specifics, we should briefly familiarise ourselves with what DLT actually is.

The most known DLT is blockchain. But blockchain is a type of DLT with a specific set of features. Thus, DLT is a broader term. First, it is distributed, which encompasses the technological infrastructure and protocols on DLT that allow simultaneous access, validation, and updating of records. For example, if we imagined that a company's shares would be on a DLT, there would not be a centralised register of shares, but the moment someone would purchase a share, and this ownership would be recorded, the same moment this person would be able to actively take on the rights and obligations that stem from such ownership. Second, ledger can be translated as a

60. *See*, for example, the Sherlock SM, a digital asset data and analytics solution developed by Fidelity Investment or independent analytics solution, such as Bynder.
61. For example, DLT Company Corda has been building a variety of digital assets solutions for issuance, trading as well as settlement, allowing digital assets to be moved more easily between diverse parties. Companies such as HSBC or Nasdaq have been using such technology.
62. For an overview of the possible applications of DLT technology, *see* Horst Treiblmaier & Roman Beck (eds), *Business Transformation Through Blockchain* (Springer 2019); or Andhov, *supra* n. 27. For a critical assessment of blockchain, *see* Marco Iansiti & Karim R. Lakhani, *The Truth About Blockchain*, Harv. Bus. Rev. (January–February 2017).

form of a digital database. Thus, whenever thinking about DLT, think about a digital database that stores information in a distributed, decentralised manner while using high-level cryptography and securing that the information, once stored cannot be deleted, and any updates are permanently recorded for posterity.[63]

DLT offers, in theory, a possibility to re-think and re-design the entire capital market architecture. Currently, we have a centralised architecture with numerous powerful financial intermediaries governing and navigating the rights and obligations of companies, their shareholders, and other stakeholders. DLT architecture could represent a significant change in how data are collected and communicated from a centralised location (management or company) to a decentralised system, in which all relevant entities (shareholders or possibly other major stakeholders) can access and view and engage with the data. The existing capital market transactions remain to a great extent, centrally governed, where only a few intermediaries have an overview and understanding of which activities are taking place and thus, in reality, limiting access to the market for the majority.

In theory, this technology could offer a new market infrastructure. It could offer increased transparency and eliminate the chance of fraudulent activities directly affecting disclosure or market manipulation. Furthermore, DLT removes the need for using different intermediaries, which can decrease various agency costs and also eliminates entities that have an active role in managing the interests of the stakeholders. DLT could directly provide the individual shareholders with a multitude of rights and automatically enforce some of them through smart contracts while facilitating a more transparent and accessible market.[64] For example, while the transfer of a share of stock can take up to a week, in some jurisdictions much longer, with DLT, it could happen in a few seconds. DLT could substantially slash the cost of transactions. Yet, this scenario would first require broad coordination and complete re-design of the existing systems. Moreover, it would require, or incentivise, active shareholders who have an interest in active participation and who have an interest in governance. Neither DLT nor any other technology is bulletproof, and the design of the technology can introduce additional worries down the line, including different forms of governance disputes, new forms of agency costs, or market manipulation. The speed of the transactions would substantially increase. Suddenly, the market, which today is similar to the railway infrastructure from the nineteenth century, would transform into *shinkansen*. Thus, the entire systemic design needs to be considered in detail before introducing partial solutions.

[B] Role of the Boards, Their Composition and Accountability

Technology in boards' activities is nothing new. Since the introduction of computers, boardrooms have adopted different tools and software to help them carry out their

63. For an in-depth analysis into DLT and blockchain technologies, *see* De Filippo & Wright, *supra* n. 57; or Arvind Narayanan et al., *Bitcoin and Cryptocurrency Technologies: A Comprehensive Introduction* (Princeton University Press 2016).
64. For more in-depth analysis of how this could work, *see* Andhov, *supra* n. 10.

tasks more efficiently. With a greater amount and access to data, boards will use various AI-driven market advisory software to help them carry out their advisory and supervisory roles. Regarding the concern of board composition, the technology currently offers no creative solution. One could consider transforming platforms like LinkedIn or Glassdoors into an open market for possible board members. The question is whether there will be a product-market fit for such solution. Interestingly, Petrin claimed that deploying AI on boards may indirectly increase diversity.[65] Regarding boards' accountability, technology is already being used, whether in various compliance tools (*see* §18.03[D]) or simply when enforcement agencies collect data and employ analytical technology.[66]

One of the most exciting technologies for the daily activities of boards is undoubtedly AI which might support boards in their decision-making but potentially could one day replace some of the board members. AI represent numerous sets of diverse applications. However, the core of an AI system is the ability to process a substantial amount of data in a short period, which a human brain would not be able to carry out and analyse or apply these data in a pre-defined manner.[67] AI promises to decrease agency costs, improve monitoring efficiency, and enhance decision-making processes.[68] The AI systems can support the board in one or more of the following ways:

> Data-driven decision-making – The bigger the company, the more data it collects. Boards might be able to collect and use relevant data across different levels of the company and collect data about their clients to make more informed decisions. Boards have been using data analyses over the past two decades. However, with the introduction of big data, data analytics through the hands of AI has become highly impactful.
>
> Market predictions – AI is extremely good at seeing and recognising patterns. Various companies have been collecting data about financial markets for decades and utilising these data to predict market developments and possibly identify the next financial crisis or downturn. Naturally, some events are unforeseeable or highly improbable, such as world pandemic or war in Europe and yet can happen;
>
> Risk-management – Lies between data science and risk modelling, where AI systems can act as risk-management assistance to the board and flag potential

---

65. *See* Petrin, *supra* n. 10.
66. The challenge of big data in the EU. In the EU, enforcement agencies or any public authorities must comply with the existing General Data Protection Regulation (GDPR) rules and provide the necessary privacy protection. However, there is currently a tension between the European Data Protection Supervisor and Europol as to the strictness of the interpretation and subsequent limitations on effective enforcement. *See*, e.g., Vincent Manancourt, *Europe's Surveillance Crisis*, Politico (11 January 2022).
67. For better understanding of AI and automation processes, *see* Alexandra Andhov, *Computational Law* (Karnov 2022) Chapter six.
68. *See*, in general, Florian Möslein, *Robots in the Boardroom: Artificial Intelligence and Corporate Law*, in *Research Handbook on the Law of Artificial Intelligence* (Woodrow Barfield & Ugo Pagallo eds, Edward Elgar 2018).

conflicts or problems for the company. The added value of AI in this regard is the speediness and the real-time deployment.

The above AI's promises are highly plausible, but before deploying AI in a boardroom, boards and shareholders need to consider additional factors, which are both legal and technical.[69] First, regarding the legal concerns, multiple layers are connected to the AI system's accountability and potential liability. The first layer is the liability for its advice (if we agree that before exchanging board members for AI, we test them as an assistance tool). The second layer is the liability of the existing board for using AI. As a bare minimum, the board would need to be aware of how the AI works, how it has been trained, and where the data come from. It would be the board member who is responsible for the decision. So, if they are to use any AI system, they need to consider not only the final outcome – the advice or the risk assessment – but also the possibility of the AI system being incorrect. However, such mental activity would need to be based on the board member's capability of AI's critical assessment. For example, the Monetary Authority of Singapore has suggested that companies need to review and approve the highly material AI decision at the board level and should periodically update the board on the use of AI within the company so that the board maintains a central view of all material AI-driven decisions.[70] The board would need to adopt specific procedures to address unforeseen or possibly unwelcome AI recommendations or observations that may uncover unflattering data and expose the board or the company to further scrutiny.[71] Moreover, with greater use of AI, we are also getting closer to AI's regulation, which aims to introduce a new set of obligations and compliance requirements, including the adoption codes of conduct.[72] It is not an understatement to foresee the EU AI Act as a similar standard-setter as the General Data Protection Regulation (GDPR).

On the technical side, for many people, AI is a black box that they do not fully understand. This is, however, solvable by employing data and AI specialists, who can assist when an AI system is introduced to support the board's activities. The key technological questions that the companies need to address are connected with the system's design and control. The first question to consider is whether a company is going to design its own solution or is it going to purchase a ready-made tool. The first option is more expensive, possibly takes several months or years. The second option is riskier. How exactly was the AI system built and trained might not be disclosed. It is

---

69. The promise of AI is evident from the recent corporate spending. In 2021, the total of USD93.5 billion was invested in AI projects. *See* Stanford University, *Artificial Intelligence Index Report 2022* (2022).
70. *See* Avi Gesser, Bill Regner, & Anna Gressel, *AI Oversight is Becoming a Board Issue*, Harvard Law School Forum on Corporate Governance (April 26, 2022).
71. Google has experienced one of the more recent controversies of use of AI after the Stanford Professor Timnit Gebru exposed in her research Google's vulnerability and approach to AI regarding its diversity efforts. *See* Bob Copeland & Parmy Olson, *Artificial Intelligence Will Define Google's Future. For Now, It's a Management Challenge*, The Wall Street Journal (January 26, 2021).
72. *See* Article 69 of the Proposal for a Regulation of the European Parliament and of the Council Laying down Harmonised Rules on Artificial Intelligence (AI Act) and Amending Certain Union Legislative Acts, COM/2021/206/final.

highly doubtful that the company selling the AI system would not attach a long list of disclosure and liability limitations. Moreover, such a generic AI might provide only rudimentary added value. If many companies use the same AI, will they not all get the same advice?

On the other hand, the challenge of the AI systems' design, data and purpose remain relevant even if a company designs such a system from scratch. The board would need to appoint a committee of diverse experts and company representatives to design such a solution and actively manage the underlying structure, sources of data, and analysis of such data. And this is just the beginning of the considerations that a board needs to review and agree upon. One could even argue that the decision to use AI for the board's decision-making should be agreed upon during a general meeting. In the same way, the general meeting appoints the board member, the general meeting should be able to nominate and appoint the AI member.

[C] Disclosure, Transparency, and Market Manipulation

Disclosure and transparency are related directly to the power of information and its proper timing. The misuse of confidential or classified information is linked with market manipulation. But it became almost impossible to control the external information flows given the speed at which we communicate and share information. Many companies interact with investors, suppliers, customers, and government regulators worldwide and do so in an era in which instant communication is the norm and where technology has to a great extent, taken over. For example, information in the age of Twitter has substantially changed the form and materiality of disclosure. The SEC is currently investigating Musk for his late Twitter purchase disclosure.[73] Yet previously, the technology mogul has settled several SEC fraud charges for his numerous public disclosures of material information on Twitter.[74] The ability to disclose material information in various forms and change the market's behaviour has never been so easy. Thus, boards need to recognise this new sharing phenomenon and consider it more appropriate *forum* for disclosure.

The nature of the information that interests shareholders and markets differs from the practice just ten years ago. For example, companies must disclose information on conflict minerals, payments to foreign governments, or reports on modern slavery. Information that may be relevant in a social context but might have little relevance to material information that a shareholder would need to make an investment decision. Nonetheless, these new regulatory obligations increase compliance and disclosure duties. For some of these disclosures, companies need to embrace additional technological solutions that help them collect, review, and analyse the data – similarly described in §18.03[B] In addition, companies will need to also disclose more and more

73. *See* Gerrit De Vynck, *SEC Confirms Probe of Elon Musk's Twitter Share Purchase Disclosure*, The Washington Post (May 27, 2022).
74. *See*, e.g., *SEC, Elon Musk Settles SEC Fraud Charges; Tesla Charged with and Resolves Securities Law Charge* (Press Release, 29 September 2018).

about the technology (i.e., AI) that they use. Thus, a possible vicious circle is to be expected.[75]

[D] Compliance, Corporate Sustainability, and Protection of (Diverse) Stakeholders

Over the last several years, the environment in which companies operate has become increasingly complex. The rise of multinational companies and globalisation has been accompanied and shaped by legal documents and factors outside the classical corporate law framework. International treaties, bilateral treaties, and numerous voluntary codes of conduct issued by international organisations introduced new duties for companies. These included human rights and environmental and social obligations.[76] Even though the academic opinions on the enforcement of such codes remain divided,[77] prescriptively and normatively, these codes became widely proliferated through contracts, codes of conduct, and other measures.[78] Moreover, governments in numerous countries adopted laws on modern slavery, conflict minerals, or corruption directly enforceable against companies.[79] The increased regulatory burdens imposed on public companies have added to the costs and complexity of overseeing and managing business activities and bring new challenges from operational, regulatory, and compliance perspectives. Considerations for sustainability, climate change, and other interests have become part of this picture.

As a consequence, a specialised area of technology has formed. Some refer to it as RegTech (regulatory technology) or Legal Tech, a more general term that often includes compliance technology. In general, compliance technology is ultimately anything that helps with diverse regulatory obligations, such as anti-money laundering (AML) compliance, environmental compliance, GDPR protection cybersecurity. For example, the majority of companies in the financial industry are obliged to comply with AML regulations.[80] Yet, they do not build their compliance systems in-house, and they rather outsource to third parties their AML compliance. There are solutions that have access to various beneficial owners lists, multijurisdictional company registries, or sanctions lists where they can collect a variety of data to determine whether the person

75. *See*, e.g., Article 52 of the AI Act that stipulated transparency and disclosure requirements for AI systems with human interaction. An increased duty of disclosure will also apply to AI systems that generate deep fakes manipulated pictures, sound, and video.
76. *See* Rosemary Teele Langford, *Purpose-Based Governance: A New Paradigm*, 43 (3) U. N.S.W. L.J. (2020).
77. *See*, e.g., Anna Beckers, *Enforcing Corporate Social Responsibility Codes: On Global and Self-Regulation and National Private Law* (Hart Publishing 2015).
78. *See* Vibe Ulfbeck, Ole Hansen, and Alexandra Andhov, *Contractual Enforcement of CSR Clauses and the Protection of Weak Parties in the Supply Chain* in *Law and Responsible Supply Chain Management: Contract and Tort Interplay and Overlap* (Vibe Ulfbeck, Alexandra Andhov, and Katerina Mitkidis eds, Routledge 2019).
79. *See*, e.g., the California Transparency in Supply Chains Act 2010 on human trafficking, the United Kingdom's Modern Slavery Act 2015, the United Kingdom's Bribery Act 2010, or the EU Conflict Minerals Regulation.
80. This obligation is not just regarding the larger players, such as banks or pension institutions, but also smaller investment firms or fintech companies.

might represent a higher risk for terrorist financing. Numerous systems have developed KYC (know your customer) analytics to monitor transactions and possibly determine money laundering.

As such, these technologies are not always used at the board level, but they are part of the board's decision-making when choosing, implementing, and maintaining such tools. Some of these tools are purely data collection tools with incorporated SaaS,[81] and some incorporate more-sophisticated AI analytics.

Many legal tech companies started with compliance tools addressing the complexities of AML and KYC compliance. However, they are moving towards designing solutions that will help with risk analysis, bankruptcy alerts, or (the forthcoming) sustainability compliance. The algorithm behind this business decision is simple. The moment that the EU, the US federal government, or any other major market adopts a new regulation that obliges millions of companies to comply with new regulations, there is a hole in the market that good data analytics can help manage. I have no doubt that many of current AML tools will integrate additional risk and sustainability metrics to provide an additional layer of analytics. Compliance data from all relevant business units will be combined into an easy-to-read management interface to offer systematic board-level monitoring. Yet, similarly to the above discussion, any Board must understand where the data come from, how they are analysed, and what the limitations are before they onboard them.

§18.04 CONCLUSION

The beauty of corporate governance is that it is one of the fields that continues to evolve and change over time. There are constantly new challenges; even if we find reasonable solutions, new ones will arise. Corporate governance consists of instruments that help the company interact effectively with other stakeholders and respond quickly and appropriately to changing circumstances, such as the COVID-19 pandemic, climate change, and others, actively while reflecting on corporate values, such as diversity, sustainability, and accountability. These instruments include mechanisms from independent directors, through rules on executive remuneration to procedural rights given to minority shareholders. These and many others represent a specific tool or process. We should similarly reflect on technology. It is a tool that aims to achieve the goal of good corporate governance.

Digital corporate governance is already the reality in practice to some extent, and the law, as usual, needs to catch up and reflect on the new rules of the game and how to advise and navigate companies through this new challenge while maintaining the primary aim of corporate governance. Provisions in laws across the globe need to be changed to allow for this digital transformation to be much more effective. The annual personal shareholder meetings requirement simply does not make much more sense.

81. SaaS refers to Software as a Service.

Contemporary technical solutions offer new approaches to inherent corporate governance problems, including agency costs, related-parties transactions, or shareholder activism/passivity. Tools that help companies with compliance, data analytics, or effective business communication are already in place. Many of them could be slightly re-designed and offer possibly great added value to millions of shareholders and investors. The infrastructure of our markets could be re-thought to open the markets and provide greater access to a variety of financial solutions for both companies and individuals. However, we should never blindly trust any technology. We have seen that AI can be even more discriminatory and racist than humans. The patterns, the data, and the used algorithms must be understood, reviewed, and regularly audited. The same way we carry out tests and safety procedures for cars, we must do so with any broadly applied and used technology.

The underlying technology and its design can knowingly or unknowingly affect the rights and obligations of the involved parties. Thus, before we adopt novel digital solutions to digitise corporate governance further, we must be aware of inherent technological risks and limitations. Boards need to understand the technology they use and possibly limit the variety of the risks it brings. Naturally, we cannot stop evolution. Still, we can be prepared for it, carry out a proper risk assessment, and conduct adequate technology reviews and audits before implementing digital tools for corporate governance. Ultimately, boards need to take an active role when adopting and implementing technology that carries out any part of the corporate governance. They cannot just simply say that it is the fault of AI. Even if some may hope for technical nirvana, there is no panacea for flawed human behaviour.

Bibliography

Articles, Essays, Working Papers, Etc.

Aboi, Joshua & Charles K.D. Adjasi, *Corporate Governance and Small and Medium Enterprises Sector: Theory and Implications*, 7(2) Corporate Governance 111 (2007)

Agrawaal, Anup & Jeffrey Jaffe, *Do Takeover Targets Underperform Evidence from Operating and Stock Return*, 38 Journal of Financial & Quantitative Analysis 721 (2003)

Aguilera, Ruth & Alvaro Cuervo Cazurra, *Codes of Good Governance Worldwide: What Is the Trigger?*, 25 Organization Studies 415 (2004)

Aguilera, Ruth & Alvaro Cuervo-Cazurra, *Codes of Good Governance*, 17 Corporate Governance. An International Review 376 (2009)

Agyei-Boapeah, Henry, Collins Ntim & Samuel Fosu, *Governance Structures and the Compensation of Powerful Corporate Leaders in Financial Firms During M&As*, 37 Journal of International Accounting, Auditing & Taxation 1 (2019)

Ahern, Deirdre, *The Mythical Value of Voice and Stewardship in the EU Directive on Long-Term Shareholder Engagement: Rights Do Not an Engaged Shareholder Make* 20 Cambridge Yearbook of European Legal Studies 88 (2018)

Akerlof, George A., *The Market for 'Lemons': Quality Uncertainty and the Market Mechanism*, 84 Quarterly Journal of Economics 488 (1970)

Alchian, Armen A. & Harold Demsetz, *Production, Information Costs and Economic Organisation*, 62 American Economics Review 777 (1972)

Alemanno, Alberto, *Regulating Organic Farming in the European Union – Balancing Consumer Preferences and Free Movement Imperatives*, 1 European Consumer Law Journal 87, 103 (2009)

Allen, Rupert, Hugues Letourneau & Tessa Hebb, *Shareholder Engagement in the Extractive Sector*, 2 Journal of Sustainable Finance & Investment 3 (2012)

Almlöf, Hanna, *Regulation of Shareholder Exits in Closely Held Companies – Reflections from Sweden*, 19(2) European Company and Financial Law Review 175-202 (2022)

Anantharaman, Divya, Jeffrey A. Pittman, & Nader Wans, *State Liability Regimes Within the United States and Auditor Reporting*, 91 Accounting Review 1545 (2016)

Alexandridis, George, Kathleen Fuller, Lars Terhaar & Nickolaos Travlos, *Deal Size, Acquisition Premia and Shareholder Gains*, 20 Journal of Corporate Finance 1 (2013)

Ammann, Manuel, Christopher Bauer, Sebastian Fischer & Philipp Müller, *The Impact of the Morningstar Sustainability Rating on Mutual Fund Flows*, 25(3) European Financial Management 520-553, https://ssrn.com/abstract=3068724 (2018)

Andersen, Paul Krüger, *Nye Anbefalinger for god selskabsledelse i Danmark, 2020*, 2021:1 Nordisk Tidsskrift for Selskabsret, 95 (2021)

Andhov, Alexandra, *Corporations on Blockchain: Opportunities and Challenges*, 53(1) Cornell International Law Journal (2020)

Andhov, Alexandra, *Corporate Governance in Developing: Lessons from Covid-19 and EU Green Deal*, 3 Erhvervsjuridisk Tidsskrift, 15 (2021)

Andrade, Gregor, Mark Mitchell & Erik Stafford *New Evidence and Perspectives on Mergers*, 15 Journal of Economic Perspectives 103 (2001)

Apostolakis, George, Gert Van Dijk, Robert J Blomme, Frido Kraanen & Athanasios P. Papadopoulos, *Predicting Pension Beneficiaries' Behaviour When Offered a Socially Responsible and Impact Investment Portfolio*, 8 Journal of Sustainable Finance & Investment 213 (2018)

Apostolakis, George, Frido Kraanen & Gert van Dijk, *Pension Beneficiaries' and Fund Managers' Perceptions of Responsible Investment: A Focus Group Study*, 16 Corporate Governance 1 (2016)

Appel, Ian, *Governance by Litigation*, https://ssrn.com/abstract=2532278 (2019)

Arena, Matteo P. & Stephen P. Ferris, *A Global Analysis of Corporate Litigation Risk and Costs*, 56 International Review of Law & Economics 28 (2018)

Armour, John, Ginataus Bartkus, Blanaid J. Clarke, Pierre-Henri Conac, Harm Jan De Kluver, Holger Fleischer, Mónica Fuentes, Jesper Lau Hansen, Vanessa Knapp, Marco Lamandini, Arkadiusz Radwan Christoph Teichmann, R.H. van Het Kaar & Martin Winner, *Report on the Recognition of the Interest of the Group*, https://papers.ssrn.com/abstract=2888863 (2016)

Armour, John, *Derivative Actions: A Framework for Decisions*, 135 Law Quarterly Review 412 (2019)

Armour, John, Bernard Black, Brian Cheffins & Richard Nolan, *Private Enforcement of Corporate Law: An Empirical Comparison of the U.K. and the U.S.*, 6 Journal of Empirical Legal Studies 687 (2009)

Armour, John, Simon Deakin, Priya Lele & Mathias M. Siems, *How Do Legal Rules Evolve? Evidence from a Cross-Country Comparison of Shareholder, Creditor, and Worker Protection*, 57 American Journal of Comparative Law 579 (2009)

Arosa, Blanca, Txomin Iturralde & Amaia Maseda, *Outsiders on the Board of Directors and Firm Performance: Evidence from Spanish Non-listed Family Firms*, 1(4) Journal of Family Business Strategy 236

Asplund, Aino, *Who Should Say on Pay and for the Sake of Whom in a Listed Company?*, 12 European Company Law 286 (2015)

Avgouleas, Emilios & Jay Cullen, *Market Discipline and EU Corporate Governance Reform in the Banking Sector: Merits, Fallacies, and Cognitive Boundaries*, 41 Journal of Law & Society 28 (2014)

Ayres, Ian, *Regulating Opt-Out: An Economic Theory of Altering Rules*, 121 Yale Law Journal 2032 (2012)

Ayres, Ian & Robert Gertner, *Filling Gaps in Incomplete Contracts: An Economic Theory of Default Rules*, 99 Yale Law Journal 91 (1989)

Bahagat, Sanjai & Brian Bolton, *Director Ownership, Governance, and Performance*, 48 Journal of Financial and Quantitative Analysis 105 (2013)

Bainbridge, Stephen M., *Director Primacy and Shareholder Disempowerment*, 119 Harvard Law Review 1745 (2006)

Bainbridge, Stephen M., *In Defense of the Shareholder Wealth Maximization Norm: A Reply to Professor Green*, 50(4) Washington & Lee Law Review 1423 (1993)

Bainbridge, Stephen M., *The Globalization of Corporate and Securities Law in the Twenty-First Century: Director v. Shareholder Primacy in the Convergence Debate*, 16(45) Transnational Law (2002)

Bainbridge, Stephen M., *Independent Directors and the ALI Corporate Governance Project*, 61 George Washington Law Review (1993)

Bammens, Yannick, Wim Voordecker & Anita Van Gils, *Board of Directors in Family Businesses: A Literature Review and Research Agenda*, 13 International Journal of Management Reviews 134 (2011)

Bar-Yosef, Sasson, & Joshua Livnat, *Auditor Selection: An Incentive-Signalling Approach*, 14 Accounting and Business Research 301 (1984)

Bargeron, Leonce, Frederick Schlingemann, Rene Stulz & Chad Zutter, *Why do Private Acquirers Pay So Little Compared to Public Acquirers?*, 89 Journal of Financial Economics 375 (2008)

Barker, Sarah, Mark Baker-Jones, Emilie Barton & Emma Fagan, *Climate Change and the Fiduciary Duties of Pension Fund Trustees – Lessons from the Australian Law*, 6 Journal of Sustainable Finance & Investment 211 (2016)

Barney, Jay, *Firm Resources and Sustained Competitive Advantage*, 17 Journal of Management 99 (1991)

Bates, Thomas, David Becher & Michael Lemmon, *Board Classification and Managerial Entrenchment: Evidence from the Market for Corporate Control*, 87 Journal of Financial Economics 656 (2008)

Bates, Thomas & David Becher, *Bid Resistance by Takeover Targets: Managerial Bargaining or Bad Faith?*, 52 Journal of Financial and Quantitative Analysis 837 (2017)

Baumüller, Josef & Michaela-Maria Schaffhauser-Linzatti, *In Search of Materiality for Nonfinancial Information – Reporting Requirements of the Directive 2014/95/EU*, 26(4) NachhaltigkeitsManagementForum, Sustainability Management Forum 101-111 (2018)

Bayat, Ali, Marc Goergen & Peter Kawalek, *The Cultural Foundations of Corporate Control: An Empirical Enquiry*, European Corporate Governance Institute – Finance Working Paper No. 816/2022 (2022) https://ssrn.com/abstract=4035025

Bayer, Walter & Jessica Schmidt, *BB-Gesetzgebungs- und Rechtsprechungsreport zum Europäischen Unternehmensrecht 2018/19 – Teil I: Company Law Package*, Betriebs-Berater, 1922 (2019)

Bebchuk, Lucian Arye, *The Case for Facilitating Competing Tender Offers*, 95 Harvard Law Review 1028 (1982)

Bebchuk, Lucian Arye, Alma Cohen, & Allen Ferrell, *What Matters in Corporate Governance*, 22 Review of Financial Studies 783 (2009)

Bebchuk, Lucian Arye, Kobi Kastiel & Roberto Tallarita, *For Whom Corporate Leaders Bargain*, 94 (6) Southern California Law Review 1467 (2021)

Bebchuk, Lucian Arye, Alma Cohen & Allen Ferrell, *What Matters in Corporate Governance?*, 22 Review of Financial Studies 783 (2009)

Bebchuk, Lucian Arye & Roberto Tallarita, *Will Corporations Deliver Value to All Stakeholders?*, 75 Vanderbilt Law Review 1031 (2021)

Bebchuk, Lucian Arye & Roberto Tallarita, *The Illusory Promise of Stakeholder Governance*, Harvard Law School Program on Corporate Governance Working Paper 2020-1 (December 2020)

Bebchuk, Lucian Arye & Roberto Tallarita, *The Illusory Promise of Stakeholder Governance*, 106 Cornell Law Review 19 (2020)

Bebchuk, Lucian Arye & Mark J. Roe, *A Theory of Path Dependence in Corporate Ownership and Governance*, 52 Stanford Law Review 127 (1999)

Bebchuk, Lucian Arye & Roberto Tallarita, *The Perils and Questionable Promise of ESG-Based Compensation*, 48 The Journal of Corporation Law (forthcoming 2022)

Bebchuk, Lucian Arye & Jesse Fried, *Executive Compensation as an Agency Problem*, 17 Journal of Economic Perspectives 3 (2003)

Bebchuk, Lucian Arye, John Coates IV & Guhan Subramanian, *The Powerful Antitakeover Force of Boards: Theory, Evidence, and Policy*, 54 Stanford Law Review 887 (2002)

Belinfanti, Tamara & Lynn Stout, *Contested Visions: The Value of Systems Theory for Corporate Law*, 166 University of Pennsylvania Law Review 591 (2018)

Beltratti, Andrea & René M. Stultz, *Why Did Some Banks Perform Better During the Credit Crisis? A Cross-Country Study of the Impact of Governance and Regulation*, NBER Working Paper, http://papers.ssrn.com/sol3/papers.cfm?abstract_id=1433502 (2009)

Benston, George, *The Self-Serving Management Hypothesis – Some Evidence*, 7 Journal of Accounting and Economics, 67 (1985)

Berkovitch, Elezar & M. P. Narayanan, *Motives for Takeovers: An Empirical Investigation*, 28 Journal of Financial and Quantitative Analysis 347 (1993)

Berle, Adolf A., *Corporate Powers as Powers in Trust*, Harvard Law Review 1049 (1931)

Bertoni, Michele & Bruno De Rosa, *The Evolution of Financial Reporting for Private Entities in the European Union*, https://papers.ssrn.com/sol3/papers.cfm?abstract_id=1536065 (2010)

Bhagat, Sanjai & Bernard Black, *The Uncertain Relationship Between Board Composition and Firm Performance*, 54 The Business Lawyer 921 (1999)

Bhojraj, Sanjeev, Partha Sengupta & Suning Zhang, *Takeover Defenses: Entrenchment and Efficiency*, 63 Journal of Accounting and Economics 142 (2017)

Bianchi, Marcello, Angela Ciavarella, Valerio Novembre & Rossella Signoretti, *Comply or Explain? Investor Protection Through Corporate Governance Codes*, ECGI Finance Working Paper N. 278/2010, https://www.ecgi.org (2010)

Bidet, Eric & Hyung-Sik Eum, *Social Enterprise in South Korea: History and Diversity*, 7 Social Enterprise Journal 77 (2011)

Binder, Jens-Henrich, *'Proceduralisierung' und Corporate Governance*, Zeitschrift für Unternehmens- und Gesellschaftsrecht 745 (2007)

Birch, Kean & Vlad Mykhnenko, *Lisbonizing Versus Financializing Europe? The Lisbon Agenda and the (un)Making of the European Knowledge-Based Economy*, 32(1) Environment and Planning C: Government and Policy 108 (2014)

Birkmose, Hanne Søndergaard, *European Challenges for Institutional Shareholder Engagement: Is Mandatory Disclosure the Way Forward?*, European Company & Financial Law Review 214 (2014)

Bishop, Carter G., *The Low-Profit LLC (L3C): Program-Related Investment by Proxy or Perversion*, 63 Arkansas Law Review 243 (2010)

Black, Bernard, *Bidder Overpayment in Takeovers'*, 41 *Stanford Law Rev*iew 597 (1989)

Black, Bernard, *Agents Watching Agents: The Promise of Institutional Investor Voice*, 39 UCLA Law Review (1992)

Black, Bernard, *Corporate Law and Residual Claimants*, Stanford Law and Economics Olin Working Paper No. 217 (2001)

Black, Bernard, Brian R. Cheffins, Martin Gelter, Hwa-Jin Kim, Richard Nolan, Mathias Siems & Linia Prava, *Legal Liability of Directors and Company Officials Part 2: Court Procedures, Indemnification and Insurance, and Administrative and Criminal Liability*, 1 Columbia Business Law Review 58 (2008)

Black, Julia, *Paradoxes and Failures: 'New Governance' Techniques and the Financial Crisis* 75 Modern Law Review 1037 (2012)

Blommestein, Hans J., Lex Hoogduin & J.J.W. Peeters, *Uncertainty and Risk Management after the Great Moderation: The Role of Risk (Mis)Management by Financial Institutions*, http://papers.ssrn.com/sol3/papers.cfm?abstract_id=1489826 (2009)

Boone, Audra, Eliezer M. Fich & Thomas Griffin, *Shareholder Litigation Risk and the Information Environment: Revisiting Evidence from Two Natural Experiments*, https://ssrn.com/abstract=3106086 (2022)

Borch, Odd J. & Morten Huse, *Informal Strategic Networks and Boards of Directors*, 18(1) Entrepreneurship: Theory and Practice 23 (1993)

Boukattaya, Sonia, Zyed Achour & Zeineb Hlioui, *Corporate Social Responsibility and Corporate Financial Performance: An Empirical Literature Review*, 1 International Journal of Scientific & Research Publications 1 (2021)

Bourveau, Thomas, Yun Lou & Rencheng Wang, *Shareholder Litigation and Corporate Disclosure: Evidence from Derivative Lawsuits*, 56 Journal of Accounting Research 797 (2018)

Gibson Brandon, Rajna & Philipp Krüger, *The Sustainability Footprint of Institutional Investors* (ECGI Working Paper 2018) at https://ssrn.com/abstract = 2918926

Bradley, Michael, Anand Desai & E. Han Kim, *The Rational Behind Interfirm Tender Offers: Information or Synergy?*, 11 Journal of Financial Economics 183 (1983)

Bradley, Michael, Anand Desai & E. Han Kim, *Synergistic Gains from Corporate Acquisitions and Their Division Between the Stockholders of Offeree and Acquiring Firms*, 21 Journal of Financial Economics 3 (1988)

Broccardo, Eleonora, Olivia Hart & Luigi Zingales, *Exit vs. Voice*, Harvard Law School John M. Olin Center Discussion Paper # 1061 (22 April 2022), available at https://ssrn.com/abstract = 3671918

Brummer, Chris & Leo E. Strine Jr., *Duty and Diversity*, 75(1) Vanderbilt Law Review (2022)

Brundin, Ethel, Emilia Florin Samuelsson & Leif Melin, *Family Ownership Logic: Framing the Core Characteristics of Family Business*, 20(1) Journal of Management and Organization 6 (2014)

Bruner, Christopher M., *Center-Left Politics and Corporate Governance: What Is the 'Progressive' Agenda?* 2018(2) Brigham Young University Law Review (2018)

Brunninge, Olof, Mattias Nordquist & Johan Wirklund, *Corporate Governance and Strategic Change in SMEs: The Effects of Ownership in SMEs: The Effect of Ownership, Board Composition and Top Management Teams*, 29 Small Business Economics 295 (2007)

Bruno, Sabrina, *Directors' Versus Shareholders' Primacy in U.S. Corporations Through the Eyes of History: Is Directors' Power 'Inherent'?*, European Company and Financial Law Review 421 (2012)

Buhr, Bob, *Assessing the Sources of Stranded Asset Risk: A Proposed Framework* 7 Journal of Sustainable Finance & Investment 37 (2017)

Byrd, John & Elizabeth S. Cooperman, *Investors and Stranded Asset Risk: Evidence from Shareholder Responses to Carbon Capture and Sequestration (CCS) Events*, 8 Journal of Sustainable Finance & Investment 185 (2018)

Cai, Jie & Ralph Walkling, *Shareholders' Say on Pay: Does It Create Value*, 46 Journal of Financial and Quantitative Analysis 2, 299 (2011)

Cain, Matthew, Stephen McKeon & Steven Solomon, *Do Takeover Laws Matter? Evidence from Five Decades of Hostile Takeovers*, 124 Journal of Financial Economics 464 (2017)

Cairns, David, *Financial Reporting in Europe: Future Challenges*, 12(2) Accounting in Europe 187 (2015)

Callison, J. William & Allan Vestal, *The L3C Illusion: Why Low-Profit Limited Liability Companies Will Not Stimulate Socially Optimal Private Foundation Investment in Entrepreneurial Ventures*, 35 Vermont Law Review 273 (2010)
Caracciolo, Ricardo Alberto, *Contradictions in the Legal System*, 65 Archiv für Rechts- und Sozialphilosophie 457 (1979)
Carline, Nicholas, Scott Linn & Pradeep Yadav, *Severely Obstructive Resistance in Takeover Bids: Is a Board Passivity Rule Effective?*, American Finance Association Meetings Working Paper (2021) https://ssrn.com/abstract=1785364
Carroll, Archie B., *A Three-Dimensional Conceptual Model of Corporate Social Performance*, 4 Academy of Management Review 497 (1979)
Carroll, Archie B., *Corporate Social Responsibility: Evolution of a Definitional Construct*, 38(3) Business & society 268 (1999)
Castaldi, Richard & Max S. Wortman Jr., *Boards of Directors in Small Corporations: An Untapped Resource*, 9(2) American Journal of Small Business 1 (1984)
Chalaczkiewicz-Ladna, Katarzyna, *Failed Reform of Say on Pay in the UK? The Future of Shareholder Engagement with Executive Pay*, 40 Company Law 47 (2019)
Chambers, Rachel & Anil Yilmaz-Vastardis, *The New EU Rules on Non-financial Reporting: Potential Impacts on Access to Remedy*, 10 Human Rights & International Legal Discourse 18 (2016)
Charny, David, *Hypothetical Bargains: The Normative Structure of Contract Interpretation*, 89(7) Michigan Law Review 1821 (1991)
Chatjuthamard, Pattanaporn, Viput Ongsakul & Pornsit Jiraporn, *Do Hostile Takeover Threats Matter? Evidence from Credit Ratings*, 17 PloS ONE (2021)
Cheffins, Brian R., *Did Corporate Governance 'Fail' During the 2008 Stock Market Meltdown? The Case of the S&P 500*, 65 Business Law 1 (2009)
Cheffins, Brian R., *What Jensen and Meckling Really Said about the Public Company*, Legal Studies Research Paper no. 29/2020, University of Cambridge 3 (2020)
Cheffins, Brian, *Stop Blaming Milton Friedman*, ECGI Law Working Paper No 523/2020 (4 June 2020) available at https://ssrn.com/abstract=3552950
Cheffins, Brian R., *Does Law Matter? The Separation of Ownership and Control in The United Kingdom*, ESRC Centre for Business Research, University of Cambridge Working Paper No. 172, (2000)
Cheffins, Brian & Bobby Reddy, *Thirty Years and Done – Time to Abolish the UK Corporate Governance Code*, ECGI Law Working Paper N. 654/2022, https://www.ecgi.org
Cheng, Ing-Haw, Harrison G. Hong & Jose A. Scheinkman, *Yesterday's Heroes: Compensation and Creative Risk-Taking*, NBER Working Paper July 2010, http://papers.ssrn.com/sol3/papers.cfm?abstract_id=1502762
Chew, Don, *Misreading Michael Jensen: The Case of Nicholas Lemann's Transaction Man: The Rise of the Deal and the Decline of the American Dream*, 33 Journal of Applied Corporate Finance 130 (2021)
Chiu, Iris H.-Y., *Unpacking the Reforms in Europe and UK Relating to Mandatory Disclosure in Corporate Social Responsibility: Instituting a Hybrid Governance Model to Change Corporate Behaviour?*, European Competition Law, 193 (2017)

Chiu, Iris H-Y, *Turning Institutional Investors into 'Stewards' – Exploring the Meaning and Objectives in 'Stewardship'*, 66 Current Legal Problems 443 (2013)
Chiu, Iris H-Y, *The EU Sustainable Finance Agenda – Developing Governance for Double Materiality in Sustainability Metrics*, 23 European Business Organization Law Review 87-123 (2022)
Chiu, Iris H-Y, *Building a Single Market for Sustainable Finance in the EU- Mixed Implications and the Missing Link of Digitalisation*, 18(5) European Company & Financial Law Review (2022)
Chiu, Iris H-Y & Anna Donovan, *A New Milestone in Corporate Regulation: Procedural Legislation, Standards of Transnational Corporate Behavior and Lessons from Financial Regulation and Anti-bribery Regulation*, Journal of Corporate Law Studies 427 (2017)
Chiu, Iris H-Y & Ernest W.K. Lim, *Technology vs. Ideology: How Far Will Artificial Intelligence and Distributed Ledger Technology Transform Corporate Governance and Business?*, 18 Berkeley Business Law Journal 1 (2021)
Chiu, Iris H-Y & Dionysia Katelouzou, *Making a Case for Regulating Institutional Shareholders' Corporate Governance Roles*, Journal of Business Law 67 (2018)
Choi, Jong-Hag & T.J. Wong, *Auditors' Governance Functions and Legal Environments: An International Investigation*, 24 Contemporary Accounting Research 13 (2007)
Chong, Gin, *Auditors' liabilities*, 15 Critical Perspectives on Accounting 330 (2004)
Chu, Yongqiang & Yijia Zhao, *The Dark Side of Shareholder Litigation: Evidence from Corporate Takeovers*, 50 Financial Management 845 (2021)
Chung, Chune Young, Incheol Kim, Monika K. Rabarison, Thomas Y. To & Eliza Wu, *Shareholder Litigation Rights and Corporate Acquisitions*, 62 Journal of Corporate Finance 101599 (2020)
Chrisman, James J., Jess Huan Chua & Reginald A. Litz, *Comparing the Agency Costs of Family Firms and Non-Family Firms – Conceptual Issues and Exploratory Evidence*, 28(4) Entrepreneurship Theory and Practice 339 (2004)
Christiansen, Charlotte, Thomas Jansson, Malene Kallestrup-Lamb & Vicke Noren, *Who Are the Socially Responsible Mutual Fund Investors?* (2019), http://ssrn.com/abstract=3128432
Claessens, Stijn, Simeon Djankov, Joseph P.H. Fan & Larry H.P. Lang, *Disentangling the Incentive and Entrenchment Effects of Large Shareholdings*, 57 The Journal of Finance 2741 (2002)
Clark, Gordon L., Andreas Feiner & Michael Viehs, *From the Stockholder to the Stakeholder, How Sustainability Can Drive Financial Outperformance* (5 March 2015), available at https://papers.ssrn.com/abstract_id=2508281
Clarke, Blanaid, *Takeover Regulation: Through the Regulatory Looking Glass*, CLPE Research Paper No. 18/2007 (2007) https://ssrn.com/abstract=1002675
Clarke, Blanaid, *The Takeovers Directive – Is a Little Regulation Better Than No Regulation?*, 15 European Law Journal 174 (2009)
Clarke, Blanaid, *Where Was the 'Market for Corporate Control' when We Needed It?* UCD Working Papers in Law, Criminology & Socio-Legal Studies Research Paper No. 23/2009 (2009) https://ssrn.com/abstract=1524785

Clarke, Blanaid, *Duties During an Offer Period – Lessons from the Cadbury PLC Takeover*, UCD Working Papers in Law, Criminology & Socio-Legal Studies Research Paper No. 44/2011 (2011) https://ssrn.com/abstract=1759953

Clarke, Christen, *California's Flexible Purpose Corporation: A Step Forward, a Step Back, or No Step at All?*, 5 The Journal of Business, Entrepreneurship & the Law 301 (2012)

Coase, Ronald, *The Nature of the Firm*, 4 Economica 386 (1937)

Coffee, John, *Shareholders Versus Managers: The Strain in the Corporate Web*, 85 Michigan Law Review 1 (1986)

Coffee, John, *The Future as History: The Prospects for Global Convergence in Corporate Governance and Its Implications*, 93 Northwestern University Law Review 641 (1999)

Coffee, John, *Regulating the Market for Corporate Control: A Critical Assessment of the Tender Offer's Role in Corporate Governance*, 84 Columbia Law Review 1145 (1984)

Coglianese, Cary & David Lazer, *Management-Based Regulation: Prescribing Private Management to Achieve Public Goals*, Law & Society Review 691 (2003)

Cohen, Jeffrey, Ganesh Krishnamoorthy & Arnie Wright, *Corporate Governance in the Post-Sarbanes-Oxley Era: Auditors' Experiences*, 27 Contemporary Accounting Research 751 (2010)

Cohen, Jeffrey R. & Dennis M. Hanno, *Auditors' Consideration of Corporate Governance and Management Control Philosophy in Preplanning and Planning Judgments*, 19 Auditing: A Journal of Practice & Theory 133 (2000)

Cole Jensen, Michael & William H. Meckling, *Theory of the Firm: Managerial Behavior, Agency Costs and Ownership Structure*, 3 Journal of Financial Economics 305 (1976)

Collins, Denton L., William R. Pasewark & Mark E. Riley, *Financial Reporting Outcomes under Rules-Based and Principles-Based Accounting Standards*, 26(4) Accounting Horizons 681 (2012)

Comino, Vicky, *Effective Regulation by the Australian Securities and Investments Commission: The Civil Penalty Problem*, 33 Melbourne University Law Review 803 (2009)

Comment, Robert, William Schwert, *Poison or Placebo? Evidence on the Deterrence and Wealth Effects of Modern Antitakeover Measures*, 39 Journal of Financial Economics 3 (1995)

Conac, Pierre-Henri, Luca Enriques & Martin Gelter, *Constraining Dominant Shareholders' Self- Dealing: The Legal Framework in France, Germany, and Italy*, 4 European Company & Financial Review 491 (2007)

Conlon, Thomas, *Industrial Democracy and EEC Company Law: A Review of the Draft Fifth Directive*, 24(2) The International and Comparative Law Quarterly 348 (1975)

Conrad Kessler, William, *The German Corporation Law of 1937*, 28 American Economic Review 653 (1938)

Conyon, Martin & Dennis Leech, *Top Pay, Company Performance and Corporate Governance*, 56 Oxford Bulletin of Economics & Statistics 229 (1994)

Cools, Sofie, *The Dividing Line Between Shareholder Democracy and Board Autonomy: Inherent Conflict of Interest as Normative Criterion*, 11(2) European Company and Financial Law Review 271 (2014)

Copeland, Lauren & Shelley Boulianne, *Political Consumerism: A Meta-analysis*, 43 International Political Science Review 3 (2022)

Corbetta, Guido & Carlo Salvato, *Self-Serving or Self-Actualizing? Models of Man and Agency Costs* in *Different Types of Family Firms – A Commentary on 'Comparing the Agency Costs of Family and Non-Family Firms: Conceptual Issues and Exploratory Evidence'*, 28(4) Entrepreneurship Theory and Practice, 360 (2004)

Cornelli, Francesca & Oğuzhan Karakaş, *Corporate Governance of LBOs: The Role of Boards*, https://ssrn.com/abstract=1875649 (2012)

Cousins, Jim, Austin Mitchell & Prem Sikka, *Auditor Liability: The Other Side of the Debate*, 10 Critical Perspectives on Accounting 283 (1999)

Cunăt, Vicente, Mireia Gine & Maria Guadalupe, *Say Pays! Shareholder Voice and Firm Performance*, Review of Finance 1799 (2016)

Dahlsrud, Alexander, *How Corporate Social Responsibility Is Defined: An Analysis of 37 Definitions*, 15 Corporate Social Responsibility and Environmental Management 4 (2008)

Daily, Catarine M., Dan R. Dalton & Albert Canalla, *Corporate Governance: Decades of Dialogue and Data*, 28 Academy of Management Review 379 (2003)

Daily, Catherine M. & Dan R. Dalton, *Board of Directors Leadership and Structure: Control and Performance Implications*, 1 Journal of Financial Economics 55 (1993)

Dalmau, Rémi, *Les sociétés à mission: quelle nature et quelles sanctions?*, JCP E, 1136 (2020)

Dalton, Dan R., Catherine M. Daily, Travis S. Certo & Rungpen Roengpitya, *Meta-analyses of Financial Performance and Equity: Fusion or Confusion?*, 46 Academy of Management Review 13 (2003)

Dalton, Dan R., Catherine M. Daily, Allan E. Ellstrand & Jonathan L. Johnson, *Meta-analytic Reviews of Board Composition, Leadership Structure and Financial Performance*, 19(3) Strategic Management Journal 269 (1998)

Dann, Larry & Harry DeAngelo, *Corporate Financial Policy and Corporate Control*, 20 Journal of Financial Economics 87 (1988)

Davenport, Thomas H., *Can We Solve AI's 'Trust Problem'?*, 60(2) MIT Sloan Management Review, 1 (2019)

Davies, Paul, *Shareholders in the United Kingdom*, ECGI Working Paper in Law, Working Paper No 280/2015 (2015)

Davies, Paul L., *Struktur der Unternehmensführung in Großbritannien und Deutschland: Konvergenz oder fortbestehende Divergenz?*, Zeitschrift für Unternehmens- und Gesellschaftsrecht 30 282 (2001)

Davies, Paul, Edmund Schuster & Emilie van de Walle de Ghelcke, *The Takeover Directive as a Protectionist Tool?*, European Corporate Governance Institute Law Working Paper, 28 (2010) https://ssrn.com/abstract=1554616

Davies, Paul L. & Klaus J. Hopt, *Corporate Boards in Europe: Accountability and Convergence*, American Journal of Comparative Law 301 (2013)

Davies, Paul L., Susan Emmenegger, Guido Ferrarini, Klaus Hopt, Adam Opalski, Alain Pietrancosta, Andrés Recalde Castells, Markus Roth, Michael Schouten, Rolf Skog, Martin Winner & Eddy Wymeersch, *The European Parliament's Draft Directive on Corporate Due Diligence and Corporate Accountability*, 2021(2) Nordisk Tidsskrift for Selskabsret 30 (2021)

Davis, Keith, *The Case for and Against Business Assumption of Social Responsibilities*, 16(2) Academy of Management Journal 312 (1973)

Deaton, B. James, *A Theoretical Framework for Examining the Role of Third Party Certifiers*, 15 Food Control 615 (2004)

de Jongh, Matthijs, *Tussen societas en universitas. De beursvennootschap en haar aandeelhouders in historisch perspectief* (IVOR nr. 94; diss. Rotterdam) (2014)

de Kluiver, Harm-Jan, *Private Ordering and Buy-Out Remedies Within Private Company Law: Towards a New Balance Between Fairness and Welfare?*, 8(1) European Business Organization Review 103 (2007)

de Vries, Manfred F.R. Kets, *The Dynamics of Family Controlled Firms: The Good and the Bad News*, 21 (3) Organizational Dynamics 59 (1993)

Deakin, Simon F., *Reflexive Governance and European Company Law*, 15(2) European Law Journal 224 (2009)

Defourny, Jacques & Marthe Nyssens, *Conceptions of Social Enterprise and Social Entrepreneurship in Europe and the United States: Convergences and Divergences*, 1 Journal of Social Entrepreneurship 32 (2010)

Defourny, Jacques & Marthe Nyssens, *Social Enterprise in Europe; Recent Trends and Developments*, 4 Journal of Social Entrepreneurship 202 (2008)

Delsen, Lei & Alex Lehr, *Value Matters or Values Matter? An Analysis of Heterogeneity in Preferences for Sustainable Investments*, 9 Journal of Sustainable Finance & Investments 240 (2019)

Demiroglu, Cem & Christopher James, *The Information Content of Bank Loan Covenants*, 23 Review of Financial Studies 3700 (2010)

Demsetz, Harold, *Information and Efficiency: Another Viewpoint*, 12 Journal of Law & Economics 1 (1969)

Denis, David & Atulya Sarin, *Ownership and Board Structures in Publicly Traded Corporations'* 52 Journal of Financial Economics 187 (1999)

Denis, David & Diane Denis, *Performance Changes Following Top Management Dismissals*, 50 Journal of Finance 1029 (1995)

Denis, David & Timothy Kruse, *Managerial Discipline and Corporate Restructuring Following Performance Declines*, 55 Journal of Financial Economics 391 (2000)

Dent Jr, Georg W., *Stakeholder Governance: A Bad Idea Getting Worse*, 58 Case Western Reserve Law Review, 1109 (2008)

Dissanaike, Gishan, Wolfgang Drobetz & Paul Momtaz, *Competition Policy and the Profitability of Corporate Acquisitions*, 62 Journal of Corporate Finance (2020)

Dittmann, Ingolf, Ernst Maug & Dan Zhang, *Restricting CEO Pay*, 17 Journal of Corporate Finance 1200 (2011)

Djankov, Simeon, Rafael La Porta, Florencio López-de-Silanes & Andrei Shleifer, *The Law and Economics of Self-Dealing*, 88 Journal of Financial Economics 430 (2008)

Dodd, Peter & Richard Ruback, *Tender Offers and Stockholder Returns: An Empirical Analysis*, 5 Journal of Financial Economics 351 (1977)

Donald, David C., *Keep Your 'Invisible Hands' to Yourself: Freeing Corporate Governance from the Cult of the 'Efficient Market'* (November 13, 2020). The Chinese University of Hong Kong Faculty of Law Research Paper No. 2020-35, 17, https://ssrn.com/abstract=3729922 (2020)

Donelson, Dain C., Laura Kettell, John McInnis & Sara Toynbee, *The Need to Validate Exogenous Shocks: Shareholder Derivative Litigation, Universal Demand Laws and Firm Behavior*, 73 Journal of Accounting Economics 101427 (2022)

Doralt, Walter, et al., *Auditors' Liability and Its Impact on the European Financial Markets*, 67 Current Law Journal 62 (2008)

Dorff, Michael B., *Assessing the Assessment: B Lab's Efforts to Measure Companies' Benevolence*, 40 Seattle University Law Review 515 (2017)

Downar, Benedikt & Mario Keiling, *Shareholder Rights and Capital Structure: Evidence from Derivative Lawsuits,* available at SSRN: https://ssrn.com/abstract=351 1349 (2019)

Drygala, Tim, *Harte Quote, weiche Quote und die Organpflichten von Vorstand und Aufsichtsrat*, NZG: Neue Zeitschrift für Gesellschaftsrecht 1129 (2015)

Dusepulchre, Gaëlle, Sacha Feierabend & Maddelena Neglia, *Europe Can Do Better – How EU Policy Makers Can Strengthen the Corporate Sustainability Due Diligence Directive*, FIDH N°794a, https://www.fidh.org/IMG/pdf/duediligence.pdf (2022)

E. Kaplan, Steven & David D. Williams, *Do Going Concern Audit Reports Protect Auditors from Litigation? A Simultaneous Equations Approach*, 88 Accounting Review 199–232 (2012)

Easterbrook, Frank Hoover & Daniel R. Fischel, *Close Corporations and Agency Costs*, 38(2) Stanford Law Review 271 (1986)

Easterbrook, Frank Hoover & Daniel R. Fischel, *The Corporate Contract*, 89(7) Columbia Law Review 1430 (1989)

Easterbrook, Frank Hoover & Daniel Fischel, *The Proper Role of a Offeree's Management in Responding to a Tender Offer*, 94 Harvard Law Review 1161 (1981)

Easterbrook, Frank Hoover & Gregg Jarrell, *Do Targets Gain from Defeating Tender Offers?*, 59 New York University Law Review 277 (1984)

Ehrhard, Olaf & Eric Nowak, *Die Durchsetzung von Corporate-Governance-Regeln*, Die Aktiengesellschaft 336 (2002)

Ehrlich, Isaac & Richard Allen Posner, *An Economic Analysis of Legal Rulemaking*, 3(1) The Journal of Legal Studies 267 (1974)

Eijsbouts, A. Jan A.J. & Bastiaan Kemp, *Over maatschappelijk verantwoord ondernemen, waardecreatie, ondernemingsrecht en vennootschappelijk belang*, TvOB 5 (2012)

Eldar, Ofer, *Designing Business Forms to Pursue Social Goals*, 106 Virginia Law Review 937 (2020)

Engert, Andreas & Tim Florstedt, *Which Related Party Transactions Should Be Subject to Ex Ante Review? Evidence from Germany*, 20 Journal of Corporate Law Studies 263 (2020)

Engert, Andreas & Susanne Goldlücke, *Why Agents Need Discretion: The Business Judgment Rule as Optimal Standard of Care*, 13 Review of Law & Economics 1 (2017)

Enriques, Luca, *EU Corporate Law: Time for Cutting Red Tape*, 9 European Company Law 172 (2012)

Enriques, Luca, *The Business Roundtable CEOs' Statement: Same Old, Same Old, Promarket*, https://www.promarket.org/2019/09/09/the-business-roundtable-ceos-statement-same-old-same-old/ (2019)

Enriques, Luca, *Related Party Transactions: Policy Options and Real-World Challenges (with a Critique of the European Commission Proposal)*, 16(1) European Business Organization Law Review 1 (2015)

Enriques, Luca & Paolo F. Volpin, *Corporate Governance Reforms in Continental Europe*, 21(1) Journal of Economic Perspective 117 (Winter 2007)

Enriques, Luca & Dirk Zetzsche, *The Risky Business of Regulating Risk Management in Listed Companies*, 10(3) European Company and Financial Law Review 271-303 (2013)

Enriques, Luca & Dirk Zetzsche, *Corporate Technologies and the Tech Nirvana Fallacy*, 72 Hastings Law Journal (2020)

Eding, Erwin & Bert Scholtens, *Corporate Social Responsibility and Shareholder Proposals*, 24 Corporate Social Responsibility & Environmental Management 648 (2017)

Esposito, Robert T., *The Social Enterprise Revolution*, in *Corporate Law*, 4 William & Mary Business Law Review 639 (2013)

Esty, Benjamin C. & Emilie Bilaud, *Danone S.A.: Becoming a Mission-Driven Company*, Harvard Business School Case No. 722–354, https://ssrn.com/abstract=395 4533 (2021)

European Company Law Experts Group, *The European Parliament's Draft Directive on Corporate Due Diligence and Corporate Accountability*, NTS 2021:4 30

Fagerström, Arne & Simon Lundh, *Accounting Development in the Nordic Countries: A Comparative Study*, 2 Journal for Global Business Advancement 4 (2009)

Fama, Eugene, *Efficient Capital Markets: A Review of Theory and Empirical Work*, 35 Journal of Finance 383 (1970)

Fama Eugene F. & Michael Cole Jensen, *Separation of Ownership and Control*, 26(2) Journal of Law & Economics 301 (1983)

Fan, P.H. Joseph & T.J. Wong, *Do External Auditors Perform a Corporate Governance Role in Emerging Markets? Evidence from East Asia*, 43 Journal of Accounting Research 35 (2005)

Fabry, James Hansen, Brian Walker, Diana Liverman, Katherine Richardson, Paul Crutzen & Jonathan Foley, *Planetary Boundaries: Exploring the Safe Operating Space for Humanity* 14(2) Ecology and Society (2009)

Fannon, Irene L., *The Corporate Social Responsibility Movement and Law's Empire: Is There a Conflict?* 58(1) Northern Ireland Legal Quarterly 12 (2007)

Feltham, Tammi S., Glen D. Feltham & James L. Barnett, *The Dependence of Family Businesses on a Single Decision-Maker*, 43 Journal of Small Businesses 1 (2005)

Ferrarini, Guido, Mario Stella Richter & Paolo Giudici, *Company Law Reform in Italy: Real Progress?*, 69 Rabels Zeitschrift für ausländisches und internationales Privatrecht 658 (2005)

Ferrarini, Guido, *Corporate Purpose and Sustainability*, ECGI Working Paper, Working Paper No 559/2020 (7 December 2020) available at https://ssrn.com/abstract=3753594

Ferrarini, Guido, Michele Siri & Shanshan Zhu, *The EU Sustainable Governance Consultation and the Missing Link to Soft Law*, ECGI Law Working Paper No 576/2021, https://www.ecgi.org

Ferreira, Daniel, David Kershaw, Tom Kirchmaier & Edmund Schuster, *Corporate Governance and Bank Failures*, ECGI Working Paper No 345/2013 (2020)

Ferri, Fabrizio & David Maber, *Say on Pay Votes and CEO Compensation: Evidence from the UK*, 17 Review of Finance 527 (2013)

Finkelstein, Sydney & Ann C. Mooney, *Not the Usual Suspects: How to Use Board Process to Make Boards Better*, 17(3) The Academy of Management Executive 101 (2003)

Finnemore, Martha & Kathryn Sikkink, *International Norm Dynamics and Political Change*, 52(4) International Organization 887 (1998)

Firth, Michael, *The Profitability of Takeovers and Mergers*, 89 The Economic Journal 316 (1979)

Fisch, Jill E., *Purpose Proposals*, ECGI Law Working Paper No. 638/2022 (4 April 2022) https://papers.ssrn.com/abstract_id=4079135

Fisch, Jill E. & Steven Davidoff Solomon, *Should Corporations Have a Purpose?*, 99 Texas Law Review 1309 (2021)

Fisch, Jill E. & Steven Davidoff Solomon, *Should Corporations Have a Purpose?*, ECGI Working Paper No 510/2020 (September 2021) https://ssrn.com/abstract=3561164

Fleischer, Holger, *Corporate Purpose: A Management Concept and Its Implications for Company Law*, ECGI Law Working Paper No 561/2021, 7–8 (January 2021)

Fleischer, Holger, *Family Firms and Family Constitutions: A Legal Primer*, 15(1) European Company Law 16 (2018)

Fleischer, Holger, *Zum Inhalt des « Unternehmensintresses » im GmbH-Recht*, GmbH-Recht, 1307 (2010)

Fleischer, Holger, *Gesetzliche Zertifizierung nachhaltiger Unternehmen: Die französische 'société à mission' als Vorbild für Deutschland?* NZG: Neue Zeitschrift für Gesellschaftsrecht 1525 (2021)

Francis, R., Jere, Inder K. Khurana & Raynolde Pereira, *The Role of Accounting and Auditing in Corporate Governance and the Development of Financial Markets Around the World*, 10 Asia-Pacific Journal of Accounting & Economics 1 (2003)

Franks, Julian & Colin Mayer, *Hostile Takeovers and the Correction of Managerial Failure*, 40 Journal of Financial Economics 163 (1996)

Franks, Julian, Jack Broyles & Michael Hecht, *An Industry Study of the Profitability of Mergers in the United Kingdom*, 32 Journal of Finance 1513 (1977)

Freeman, Robert Edward, *Managing for Stakeholders*, 9 (January 2007), available at http://ssrn.com/abstract=1186402

Freund, Steven, Nam H. Nguyen & Hieu V Phan, *Shareholder Litigation and Corporate Social Responsibility*, Journal of Financial Quantitative Analysis 1-31 (2022)

Friede, Gunnar, Timo Busch & Alexander Bassen, *ESG and Financial Performance: Aggregated Evidence from More Than 2000 Empirical Studies*, 5 Journal of Sustainable Finance & Investment 210 (2015)

Fried, Jesse, *The Roundtable's Stakeholderism Rhetoric Is Empty, Thankfully*, Harvard Law School Forum on Corporate Governance (22 November 2019)

Fried, Jesse M. & Charles C.Y. Wang, *Short-Termism, Shareholder Payouts, and Investment in the EU* (ECGI Law Working Paper No 544/2020) (October 2020)

Friedman, Milton, *The Social Responsibility of Business Is to Increase Its Profits*, The New York Times Magazine 32 124 (13 September 1970)

Frishammar, Johan & Vinit Parida, *Circular Business Model Transformation: A Roadmap for Incumbent Firms*, 61 California Management Review 5 (2019)

Frost, Ina Anne & Leena Linnainmaa, *Corporate Governance: Frauen im Aufsichtsrat – Könnenwir von unseren skandinavischen Nachbarn lernen?*, Die Aktiengesellschaft 601 (2007)

Frydman, Carola & Raven Saks, *Executive Compensation: A New View from a Long-Term Perspective, 1936*, 23 The Review of Financial Studies 5, 2100 (2010)

Fuller, Joseph & Michael Cole Jensen, *Just Say No to Wall Street*, 14(4) Journal of Applied Corporate Finance 41 (2002)

Gabrielsson, Jonas & Morten Huse, *Outside Directors in SME Boards: A Call for Theoretical Reflections*, 1(1) Corporate Board: Role, Duties & Composition, 28–37 (2005)

Galle, Annika, *'Comply or Explain' in Belgium, Germany, Italy, the Netherlands and the UK: Insufficient explanations and an Empirical Analysis*, 12 Corporate Ownership & Control 862 (2014)

Gammage, C., *The EU's Evolving Commitment to Promoting Sustainability in Its External Actions: Policy (In)Coherence for Development?* SMART working paper on file with current authors, University of Oslo (2020)

Gans, Joshua, Martin Schmalz & Adam Triggs, *Inequality and Market Concentration, When Shareholding Is More Skewed Than Consumption*, 35(3) Oxford Review of Economic Politics 550 (2019)

Gaspar, Jose-Miguel, Massimo Massa & Pedro Matos, *Shareholder Investment Horizons and the Market for Corporate Control*, 76 Journal of Financial Economics 135 (2005)

Geczy, Christopher, Jessica S. Jeffers, David K. Musto & Anne M. Tucker, *Institutional Investing when Shareholders Are Not Supreme*, 5 Harvard Business Law Review 73 (2015)

Geiger, Marshall A., K. Raghunandan & Dasaratha V. Rama, *Auditor Decision-Making in Different Litigation Environments: The Private Securities Litigation Reform Act, Audit Reports and Audit Firm Size*, 25 Journal of Accounting Public Policy 332 (2006)

Gelter, Martin & Alexandra M. Reif, *What Is Dead May Never Die: The UK's Influence on EU Company Law*, 40 Fordham International Law Journal 1413 (2017)

Gerner-Beuerle, Carsten & Tom Kirchmaier, *Say on Pay: Do Shareholders Care?*, Finance Working Paper No 579/2018, ECGI

Gerner-Beuerle, Carsten, *Diffusion of Regulatory Innovations: The Case of Corporate Governance Codes*, Journal of Institutional Economics 271–303 (2017)

Gerner-Beuerle, Carsten, & Edmund-Philipp Schuster, *The Evolving Structure of Directors Duties in Europe*, 15 European Business Organization Law Review 191 (2014)

Gesser, Avi, Bill Regner & Anna Gressel, *AI Oversight Is Becoming a Board Issue*, Harvard Law School Forum on Corporate Governance (26 April 2022)

Ghezzi, Federico & Corrado Malberti, *The Two-Tier Model and the One-Tier Model of Corporate Governance in the Italian Reform of Corporate Law*, European Company and Financial Law Review 1 (2008)

Goergen, Marc & Luc Renneboog, *Managerial Compensation*, 17 Journal of Corporate Finance 1068–1077 (2011)

Gompers, Paul, Joy Ishii & Andrew Metrick, *Corporate Governance and Equity Prices*, 118 Quarterly Journal Economics 107 (2003)

Gorriz, Carlos, *EU Company Law: Past, Present and … Future?*, Global Jurist (2018)

Goshen, Zohar & Richard Squire, *Principal Costs: A New Theory for Corporate Law and Governance*, 117 Columbia Law Review 767 (2017)

Gilson, Ronald, *Seeking Competitive Bids Versus Pure Passivity in Tender Offer Defense*, 35 Stanford Law Review 51 (1983)

Gilson, Ronald J., *Controlling Shareholders and Corporate Governance: Complicating the Comparative Taxonomy*, 119(6) Harvard Law Review 1663–1664 (2006)

Gilson, Ronald J. & Jeffrey N. Gordon, *The Agency Costs of Agency Capitalism: Activist Investors and the Revaluation of Governance Rights*, 113 Columbia Law Review (2013)

Gilson, Ronald & Jeffrey Gordon, *Board 3.0: An Introduction*, 74 The Business Lawyer 351 (2019)

Goergen, Marc &Luc Renneboog, *Strong Managers and Passive Institutional Investors in the UK*, http://ssrn.com/abstract = 137068 (1998)

Goergen, Marc, Luc Renneboog & Chendi Zhang, *Do UK Institutional Shareholders Monitor Their Investee Firms?*, http://ssrn.com/abstract_id = 1124406 (2007)

Gogineni, Sridhar & Arun Upadhyay, *Target Governance Provisions and Acquisition Types*, 110 Journal of Business Research 160 (2020)

Gomstian, Suren, *Voting Engagement by Large Institutional Shareholders*, 45 Journal of Corporate Law 659 (2020)

Gordon, Jeffrey N., *The Mandatory Structure of Corporate Law*, 89(7) Columbia Law Review 1557–1562 (1989)

Gordon, Jeffrey N., *The Rise of Independent Directors in the United States, 1950–2005: Of Shareholder Value and Stock Market Prices*, 59 Stanford Law Review (2007)

Goshen, Zohar & Richard Squire, *Principal Costs: A New Theory for Corporate Law and Governance*, 117 Columbia Law Review 767 (2017)

Green, Jemma & Peter Newman, *Disruptive Innovation, Stranded Assets and Forecasting: The Rise and Rise of Renewable Energy*, 7 Journal of Sustainable Finance & Investment 169 (2017)

Greenfield, Kent, *The Puzzle of Short-Termism*, Boston College Law School Legal Studies Research Paper Series (3 October 2011)

Greenfield, Kent, *September 11 and the End of History of Corporate Law*, 76 Tulane Law Review 1409 (2002)

Grewal, Jody, George Serafeim, & Aaron Yoon, *Shareholder Activism on Sustainability Issues* Harvard Business School Working Paper, 2016

Groenland, Irene C.P., *Related Party Transactions in the Revised Shareholders' Rights Directive: The EU Perspective and Implementation in National Law*, 16 European Company Law 44 (2019)

Gropp, Reint & Matthias Köhler, *Bank Owners or Bank Managers: Who Is Keen on Risk? Evidence from the Financial Crisis*, European Business School Research Paper No 10-02, http://ssrn.com/abstract=1555663 (January 2010)

Gulin, Danimir, Spajić Ferdo, Vesna Vašiček & Žager Lajoš, *History of Accounting Regulation in the Europe and Its Effects on the Accounting Regulation in Croatia* (2004) https://citeseerx.ist.psu.edu/viewdoc/download?doi=10.1.1.544.8685&rep=rep1&type=pdf

Guo, Shourun, Edith Hotchkiss & Weihong Song, *Do Buyouts (Still) Create Value?*, 66 Journal of Finance 479 (2011)

Gupta, Joyeeta, *The Role of Non-State Actors in International Environmental Affairs*, 63 Zeitschrift für ausländisches öffentliches Recht und Völkerrecht (ZaöRV) 459 (2003)

Gözlügöl, Alperen Afsin, *The Political Economy of the Related Party Transactions Regulation in the Shareholders' Rights Directive II*, 39 Yearbook of European Law 497 (2020)

Habersack, Mathias, *Das Aktiengesetz und das Europäische Recht*, ZIP: Zeitschrift für Wirtschaftsrecht 445 (2006)

Habersack, Mathias & Jens Kersten, *Chancengleiche Teilhabe an Führungspositionen in der Privatwirtschaft – Gesellschaftsrechtliche Dimensionen und verfassungsrechtliche Anforderungen*, 47 Betriebs-Berater 2819 (2014)

Hachigian, Heather & Sarah M. McGill, *Reframing the Governance Challenge for Sustainable Investment*, 2 Journal of Sustainable Finance & Investment 166 (2012)

Hainsworth, Anthony, *The Shareholder Rights Directive and the Challenge of Re-enfranchising Beneficial Shareholders*, 1 Law & Financial Market Review 11 (2007)

Hale, Kathleen, *Corporate Law and Stakeholders: Moving Beyond Stakeholder Statutes*, 45 Arizona Law Review 823 (2003)

Hall, Matthew, *Accounting Information and Managerial Work*, 35(3) Accounting, Organizations and Society 301–315 (2010)

Hallemeesch, Nick, *Self-Dealing by Controlling Shareholders: Improving Minority Protection in the Light of Article 9c SRD*, European Company & Financial Law Review 197 (2018)

Hambrick, Donald C. & Phyllis A. Mason, *Upper Echelons: The Organization as a Reflection of Its Top Managers*, 9(2) Academy of Management Review 193–206 (1984)

Hamermesh, Larry, Bart Houlahan, Rick Alexander & Dan Osusky, *A Conversation with B Lab*, 40 Seattle University Law Review 321 (2017)

Hansen, Jesper Lau, *A Scandinavian Approach to Corporate Governance,* 50 Scadinavian Studies in Law 125 (2007), https://scandinavianlaw.se/pdf/50-8.pdf

Hansen, Jesper Lau, *Editors' Note: Companies Without Legal Capital and the Strange Case of Denmark*, European Company and Financial Law Review 677 (2019)

Hansmann, Henry, *Corporation and Contract*, 8(1) American Law and Economics Review 12 (2006)

Hansmann, Henry & Reinier H. Kraakman, *The End of History of Corporate Law*, 89 Georgetown Law Journal (2001)

Harford, Jarrad, *What Drives Merger Waves?*, 77 Journal of Financial Economics 529 (2005)

Harford, Jarrad, *Takeover Bids and Target Directors' Incentives: The Impact of a Bid on Directors' Wealth and Board Seats*, 69 Journal of Financial Economics 51 (2003)

Harford, Jarrad, Mark Humphery-Jenner & Ronan Powell, *The Sources of Value Destruction in Acquisitions by Entrenched Managers,* 106 Journal of Financial Economics 247 (2012)

Hart, Oliver & Luigi Zingales, *Companies Should Maximize Shareholder Welfare Not Market Value*, 2(2) Journal of Law, Finance, and Accounting 247 (2017)

Hayes, Robert & William Abernathy, *Managing Our Way to Economic Decline,* Harvard Business Review 67 (1980)

Healy, Paul, Krishna Palepu & Richard Ruback, *Does Corporate Performance Improve after Mergers?*, 1992(31) Journal of Financial Economics (1992)

Heron, Randall & Erik Lie, *On the Use of Poison Pills and Defensive Payouts by Takeover Targets*, 79 Journal of Business 1783 (2006).

Herremans, Irene M., Jamal A. Nazari & Fareshteh Mahmoudian, *Stakeholder Relationships, Engagement, and Sustainability Reporting*, 138(3) Journal of Business Ethics 417–435 (2016)

Hillegeist, Stephen A., *Financial Reporting and Auditing under Alternative Damage Apportionment Rules*, 74 Accounting Review 347–369 (1999)

Hillman, Amy J. & Thomas Dalziel, *Boards of Directors and Firm Performance: Integrating Agency and Resource Dependence Perspectives*, 28 Academy Management Review 383–396 (2003)

Hirshleifer, David & Anjan Thakor, *Managerial Performance, Boards of Directors and Takeover Bidding*, 1 Journal of Corporate Finance 63 (1994)

Ho, Virginia Harper, *'Enlightened Shareholder Value': Corporate Governance Beyond the Shareholder-Stakeholder Divide*, Journal of Corporate Law 36 (2010)

Ho, Virginia, Harper, *From Public Policy to Materiality: Non-financial Reporting, Shareholder Engagement, and Rule 14a-8's Ordinary Business Exception*, 76 Washington & Lee Law Review 1231 (2019)

Hoffmann, Sebastian & Dominic Detzen, *The Regulation of Asset Valuation in Germany*, 18 Accounting History 367 (2013)

Hoffmann-Becking, Michael, *Unabhängigkeit im Aufsichtsrat*, NZG: Neue Zeitschrift für Gesellschaftsrecht 801 (2014)

Holm, Claus, *Civil and Common Law Influences on the Danish Auditor's Responsibilities in Relation to Fraud*, 24 Accounting History Review 7–26 (2014)

Holm, Claus & Peter Birkholm Laursen, *Risk and Control Developments in Corporate Governance: Changing the Role of the External Auditor?*, 15 Corporate Governance: An International Review 322 (2007)

Hommelhoff, Peter, *Einige Bemerkungen zur Organisationsverfassung der Europäischen Aktiengesellschaft*, Die Aktiengesellschaft 279 (2001)

Hong, Fidy Xiangxin, *Protection of Shareholders' Rights at EU Level: How Far Does It Go?*, 3 European Company Law 124 (2009)

Hopt, Klaus J., *Vergleichende Corporate Governance*, 175 ZHR: Zeitschrift für das gesamte Handels- und Wirtschaftsrecht 444–526 (2011)

Hopt, Klaus J., *Board oder Vorstand und Aufsichtsrat?*, 27 Europäische Zeitschrift für Wirtschaftsretcht 201 (2016)

Hopt, Klaus J. & Patrick Leyens, *Board Models in Europe – Recent Developments of Internal Corporate Governance Structures in Germany, the United Kingdom, France, and Ita*ly, European Company and Financial Law Review 135 (2004)

Hopt, Klaus J. & Patrick Leyens, *The Structure of the Board of Directors: Boards and Governance Strategies in the US, the UK and Germany*, ECGI Law Working Paper 567/2021, https://papers.ssrn.com/sol3/papers.cfm?abstract_id=3804717

Horn, Laura, *Corporate Governance in Crisis? The Politics of EU Corporate Governance Regulation*, 18(1) European Law Journal 93 (2012)

Houston, Joel F., Chen Lin & Wensi Xie, *Shareholder Protection and the Cost of Capital*, 61 Journal of Law and Economics 677 (2018)

Hsieh, Nien-hê, Marco Meyer, David Rodin & Jens Van't Klooster, *The Social Purpose of Corporations*, 6(1) Journal of the British Academy 58 (2018)

Hu, Henry T.C. & Bernard Black, *The New Vote Buying: Empty Voting and Hidden (Porphable) Ownership*, 79 Southern California Law Review 811 (2006)

Huang, Sterling, Sugata Roychowdhury & Ewa Sletten, *Does Litigation Deter or Encourage Real Earnings Management?*, 95 Accounting Review 251 (2020)

Humphery-Jenner, Mark & Ronan Powell, *Firm Size, Takeover Profitability, and the Effectiveness of the Market for Corporate Control: Does the Absence of Antitakeover Provisions Make a Difference?*, 17 Journal of Corporate Finance 418 (2011)

Huse, Morten, *Corporate Governance: Understanding Important Contingencies*, 4(2) Corporate Governance & Control 41–50 (2005)

Huse, Morten, et al., *Power Shift, Strategic Change and Board Roles in SMEs: A Portfolio Approach,* ECMLG 2016 – Proceedings of the 12th European Conference on Management (2016)

Huse, Morten, *Board Composition in Small Enterprises*, 2(4) Entrepreneurship & Regional Development 363–374 (1990)

Huse, Morten, *Researching the Dynamics of Board-Stakeholder Relations*, 31 Long Range Planning 218 (1998)

Häyhä, Tina, Sarah Elisabeth Cornell, Holger Hoff, Paul L. Lucas & Detlef P. van Vuuren, *Operationalizing the Concept of a Safe Operating Space at the EU Level – First Steps and Explorations*, Stockholm Resilience Centre, Stockholm University, Sweden, https://www.sei.org/publications/operationalizing-concept-safe-operating-space-eu/ (2018)

Iansiti, Marco & Karim R. Lakhani, *The Truth About Blockchain*, Harvard Business Review (January–February 2017)

Ielasi, Federica & Monica Rossolini, *Responsible or Thematic? The True Nature of Sustainability-Themed Mutual Funds*, 11 Sustainability Journal 3304 (2019)

Ioannou, Ioannis & George Serafeim, *Corporate Sustainability: A Strategy?*, Harvard Business School Accounting and Management Unit, Working Paper 19-065 (1 January 2019)

Ingley, C.B. & N.T. van der Walt, *Corporate Governance, Institutional Investors and Conflicts of Interest*, 12 Corporate Governance: An International Review 534 (2004)

Ingley, Coral, Wafa Khlif & Lotfi Karouri, *SME Growth Trajectories, Transitions and Board Role Portfolios: A Critical Review and Integrative Model,* 35(6) International Small Business Journal 729–750 (2017)

Ingley, Coral, Lotfi Karoui & Wafa Khlif, *Power Shift, Strategic Change and Board Roles in SMEs: A Portfolio Approach*, ECMLG 2016 – Proceedings of the 12th European Conference on Management (2016)

Ismail, Raisal & Arun Kumar Tarofder, *Corporate Governance Structure and Firm Performance in Small and Medium-Sized Enterprises (SMEs) in Sri Lanka: A Path to Access the Credit*, 12(1) Journal of Management 28 (2015)

Jackson, Gregory, Julia Bartosch, Emma Aventlsyan, Daniel Kiderman & Jette Steen Knudsen, *Mandatory Non-financial Disclosure and Its Influence on CSR: An InternationalComparison*, 162 Journal of Business Ethics 323-342 (2020)

Jahn, Gabriele, Matthias Schramm & Achim Spiller, *The Reliability of Certification: Quality Labels as a Consumer Policy Tool*, 28 Journal of Consumer Policy 53 (2005)

Jakobsen, Lisa Charlotte, *Vinningsformålet i norsk aksjeselskabsrett*, 2018(2) Nordisk tidsskrift for Selskabsret (2018)

Jansson, Magnus Jans & Anders Biel, *Investment Institutions' Beliefs about and Attitudes Toward Socially Responsible Investment (SRI): A Comparison Between SRI and Non-SRI Management*, 22 Sustainable Development 33 (2014)

Jensen, H. O., *Træk af den danske Aktierets Udvikling i det syttende og attende Aarhundrede*, Ugeskrift for Retsvæsen Online (U.1944B.221)

Jensen, Michael C., *Value Maximization, Stakeholder Theory, and the Corporate Objective Function*, Tuck Business School Working Paper No. 01-09

Jensen, Michael C., *Value Maximization, Stakeholder Theory, and the Corporate Objective Function*, 12 Business Ethics Quarterly 235 (2002)

Jensen, Michael C., *Some Anomalous Evidence Regarding Market Efficiency*, 6 Journal of Financial Economics 95 (1978)

Jensen, Michael C., *Agency Costs of Free Cash Flow, Corporate Finance and Takeovers*, 76 The American Economic Review 323 (1986)

Jensen, Michael C. & Kevin Murphy, *Performance Pay and Top-Management Incentives*, 98(2) Journal of Political Economy 225–264 (1990)

Michael C. Jensen & William H. Meckling, *Theory of the Firm: Managerial Behaviour, Agency Costs and the Theory of the Firm*, 3 Journal of Financial Economics 305–360 (1976)

Jensen, Michael C. & Richard Ruback, *The Market for Corporate Control: The Scientific Evidence*, 11 Journal of Financial Economics 5 (1983)

Jin, Ick, *Is ESG a Systematic Risk Factor for US Equity Mutual Funds?*, 8 Journal of Sustainable Finance & Investment 72 (2018)

Johnson, Matthew, Friederike Redlbacher & Stefan Schaltegger, *Stakeholder Engagement for Corporate Sustainability: A Comparative Analysis of B2C and B2B Companies*, 25(4) Corporate Social Responsibility and Environmental Management, 659-673 (2018)

Johnston, Andrew, Jeroen Veldman, Robert G. Eccles, Simon Deakin, Jerry Davis, Marie-Laure Djelic, Katharina Pistor, Blanche Segrestin, Cynthia A. Williams, David Millon, Paddy Ireland, Beate Sjåfjell, Christopher M. Bruner, Lorraine E. Talbot, Hugh Christopher Willmott, Charlotte Villiers, Carol Liao, Bertrand Valiorgue, Jason Glynos, Todd L. Sayre, Bronwen Morgan, Rick Wartzman, Prem Sikka, Filip Gregor, David Carrol Jacobs, Roger Gill, Roger Brown, Vincenzo Bavoso, Neil Lancastle, Julie Matthaei, Scott Taylor, Ulf Larsson-Olaison, Jay Cullen, Alan J. Dignam, Thomas Wuil Joo, Ciarán O'Kelly, Con Keating, Roman Tomasic, Simon Lilley, Kevin Tennent, Keith Robson, Willy Maley, Iris H.-Y. Chiu, Ewan McGaughey, Chris Rees, Nina Boeger, Adam Leaver, Marc T. Moore, Leen Paape, Alan D. Meyer, Marcello Palazzi, Nitasha Kaul, Juan Felipe Espinosa-Cristia, Timothy Kuhn, David J. Cooper, Susanne Soederberg, Andreas Jansson, Susan Watson, Ofer Sitbon, Joan Loughrey, David Collison, Maureen McCulloch, Maureen McCulloch, Navajyoti Samanta, Daniel J. H. Greenwood, Grahame F. Thompson, Andrew R. Keay, Alessia Contu, Andreas Rühmkorf, Richard Hull, Irene-Marie Esser & Nihel Chabrak, *Corporate Governance for Sustainability*, https://papers.ssrn.com/sol3/papers.cfm?abstract_id=3502101 (2019)

Joos, Peter & Mark Lang, *The Effects of Accounting Diversity: Evidence from the European Union*, 32 Journal of Accounting Research 141–168 (1994)

Josefy, Amanda Bree, *An Examination of Director Stock Ownership Requirements* (Texas A&M University), https://oaktrust.library.tamu.edu/bitstream/handle/1969.1/156916/JOSEFY-DISSERTATION-2016.pdf;sequence=1 (2016)

Kaal, Wulf A., *Blockchain-Based Corporate Governance*, 4(1) Stanford Journal of Blockchain Law & Policy (2021)

Kacperczyk, Aleksandra, *With Greater Power Comes Greater Responsibility? Takeover Protection and Corporate Attention to Stakeholders, 30* Strategement Management Journal 261 (2009)

Kalss, Susanne, *The Transfer of Shares of Private Companies,* 1(3) European Company and Financal Law Review 347–349 (2004)

Kampel, Carl, *Why Privately Held and Family-Owned Businesses Should Have Independent Boards of Directors*, 28 Financial Executive 18 (2012)

Kaplow, Louis, *Rules Versus Standards: An Economic Analysis*, 42 Duke Law Journal 588–596 (1992)

Karim, Khondkar, Eunju Lee & Sanghuyn Suh, *Corporate Social Responsibility and CEO Compensation Structure*, 40 Advances in Accounting, 27–41 (2018)

Kay, Ira, *The Perils and Questionable Promise of ESG-Based Compensation: A Response to Bebchuk and Tallarita*, https://corpgov.law.harvard.edu/2022/04/27/the-perils-and-promise-of-esg-based-compensation-a-response-to-bebchuk-and-tallarita/ (2022)

Keay, Andrew, *Ascertaining the Corporate Purpose: An Entity Maximisation and Sustainability Model*, 71 Modern Law Review 663 (2008)

Keay, Andrew R., *Stakeholder Theory in Corporate Law: Has It Got What It Takes?*, 9 Richmond Journal of Global Law & Business 249 (2010)

Kemp, Bastiaan, *Developments in Stakeholder Governance: Lessons from the Netherlands* (editorial), 3 European Company Law (2022)

Kemp, Bastiaan & Sebastian Renshof, *The Limited Power to Appoint and Dismiss Management Board Members in Dutch Listed Companies*, 17(2) European Company Law (2020)

Kershaw, David, *The Rule in Foss v Harbottle Is Dead; Long Live the Rule in Foss v Harbottle*, Journal of Business Law 274 (2015)

Kershaw, David & Edmund Schuster, *The Purposive Transformation of Company Law*, LSE Law, Society and Economy Working Papers 4/2019

Keys, Patrick W., Victor Galaz, Michelle Dyer, Nathaniel Matthews, Carl Folke, Magnus Nyström & Sarah E. Cornell, *Anthropocene Risk*, 2 Nature Sustainability 667 (2019)

Kim, Insun, *Institutional Development of Social Economy: A Case of Korea's Social Enterprise Promotion Act*, Science of Science and Management of Science and Technology 38 (2016)

Kindermann, Daniel, *Corporate Social Responsibility in the EU, 1993–2013: Institutional Ambiguity, Economic Crises, Business Legitimacy and Bureaucratic Politics*, 51 Journal of Common Market Studies 702 (2013)

Kleinberger, Daniel S., *A Myth Deconstructed: The 'Emperor's New Clothes' on the Low-Profit Limited Liability Company*, 35 Delaware Journal of Corporate Law 879 (2010)

Klöhn, Lars & Klaus Ulrich Schmolke, *Unternehmensreputation*, NZG: Neue Zeitschrift für Gesellschaftsrecht 689 (2015)

Knapp, Vanessa, *The Requirements of the Shareholders' Rights Directive*, 9 ERA Forum 377 (2008)

Kolk, Ans *Sustainability, Accountability and Corporate Governance: Exploring Multinationals Reporting Practices*, 17(1) Business Strategy and the Environment 1–15 (2008)

Konzelmann, Sue, Frank Wilkinson, Marc Fovargue-Davies & Duncan Sankey, *Governance, Regulation and Financial Market Instability: The Implications for Policy*, 34 Cambridge Journal of Economics 929 (2010)

Korkea-aho, Emilia, *Legal Interpretation of EU Framework Directives: A Soft Law Approach* 40(1) European Law Review 70–88 (2015)

Korten, David C., *When Corporations Rule the World*, European Business Review (1998)

Kotzé, Louis J., *The Anthropocene, Earth System Vulnerability and Socio-ecological Injustice in an Age of Human Rights*, 10 Journal of Human Rights and the Environment (2019)

Krajewski, Markus, Kristel Tonstad & Franziska Wohltmann, *Mandatory Human Rights Due Diligence in Germany and Norway: Stepping, or Striding, in the Same Direction?*, 6 Business and Human Rights Journal (2021)

Kumar, N.C. Ashwin, Camille Smith, Leïla Badis, Nan Wang, Paz Ambrosy & Rodrigo Tavares, *ESG Factors and Risk-Adjusted Performance: A New Quantitative Model*, 6 Journal of Sustainable Finance & Investment 292 (2016)

Kummer, Donald & J. Ronald Hoffmeister, *Valuation Consequences of Cash Tender Offers*, 33 Journal of Finance 505 (1978)

La Porta, Rafael, Florencio Lopez-de-Silanes & Andrei Shleifer, *The Economic Consequences of Legal Origins* (November 2007), available at https://ssrn.com/abstract=1028081

La Porta, Rafael, Florencio López-de-Silanes & Andrei Shleifer, *What Works in Securities Laws?*, 61 Journal of Finance 1 (2006)

La Porta, Rafael, Florencio Lopez-De-Silanes & Andrei Shleifer, *Corporate Ownership Around the World*, 54 Journal of Finance 471–517 (1999)

La Porta, Rafael, Florencio López-de-Silanes, Andrei Shleifer & Robert W. Vishny, *Investor Protection and Corporate Valuation*, 57 Journal of Finance 1147–1170 (2002)

La Porta, Rafael, Florencio Lopez-de-Silanes, Andrei Shleifer & Robert Ward Vishny, *Agency Problems and Dividend Policies Around the World*, 55 Journal of Finance 1–33 (2000)

La Porta, Rafael, Florencio Lopez-de-Silanes, Andrei Shleifer & Robert Ward Vishny, *Legal Determinants of External Finance*, 52 Journal of Finance 1131 (1997)

La Porta, Rafael, Florencio López-de-Silanes, Andrei Shleifer & Robert W. Vishny, *Law and Finance*, 106 Journal of Political Economy 1113 (1998)

Lafarre, Anne, *Consequences of Significant Minority Shareholder Revolt over Executive Pay*, 16 European Company Law 114 (2019)

Lambert, Richard & David Larcker, *Executive Compensation Effects of Large Corporate Acquisitions*, 6 Journal of Accounting and Public Policy 231 (1987)

Lando, Henrik, *Shareholder eller stakeholder value? En retsøkonomisk analyse af loyalitetspligten i aktieselskaber*, 2001(1) Nordisk Tidsskrift for Selskabsret (2001)

Langetieg, Terence, *An Application of a Three-Factor Performance Index to Measure Stockholder Gains from Merger*, 6 Journal of Finance and Economics 365 (1978)

Langevoort, Donald C., *Theories, Assumptions, and Securities Regulation: Market Efficiency Revisited*, 140 University of Pennsylvania Law Review 851 (1992)

Langford, Teele, Rosemary, *Purpose-Based Governance: A New Paradigm*, 43(3) The University of New South Wales Law Journal (2020)

Laufer, William S., *Social Accountability and Corporate Greenwashing*, 43 Journal of Business Ethics 253 (2003)

LeCournu, Mark R., Richard G.P. McMahon, David M. Forsaith, & Anthony M.J. Stanger, *The Small Enterprise Financial Objective Function: An Exploratory Study*, 34(3) Journal of Small Business Management 1–16 (1996)

Lekvall, Per, Ronald J. Gilson, Jesper Lau Hansen, Carsten Lønfeldt, Manne Airaksinen, Tom Berglund, Tom von Weymarn, Gudmund Knudsen, Harald Norvik, Rolf R. Skog, and Erik Sjöman, *The Nordic Corporate Governance Model*, Nordic & European Company Law Working Paper No. 14-12 (2014) https://papers.ssrn.com/abstract_id=2534331

Li, Leye, Gary S. Monroe & Jeffrey J. Coulton, *Litigation Risk and Cost Behavior: Evidence from Derivative Lawsuits*, AAA 2018 Management Accounting Section Midyear Meeting, https://ssrn.com/abstract=3020842 (2018)

Lin, Chen, Sibo Liu & Gustavo Manso, *Shareholder Litigation and Corporate Innovation*, 67 Management Science 3321 (2021)

Lindholm, Tomas & Jakob Storå, *Begreppet corporate benefit i finsk aktiebolags- och insolvensrätt*, 4 JFT (2010)

Liang, Hao & Luc Renneboog, *On the Foundations of Corporate Social Responsibility*, ECGI Finance Working Paper No 394/2013, available at https://ssrn.com/abstract=2360633

Linn, Scott & John McConnell, *An Empirical Investigation of the Impact of 'Antitakeover' Amendments on Common Stock Prices*, 11 Journal of Financial Economics. 361 (1983)

Lipton, Ann M., *What We Talk About When We Talk about Shareholder Primacy*, Case Western Reserve Law Review 69 (2019)

Lund, Dorothy S. & Elizabeth Pollman, *The Corporate Governance Machine*, Columbia Law Review 121 (2021)

Lutter, Marcus, *Die Erklärung zum Corporate Governance Kodex gemäß § 161 AktG*, 166 ZHR: Zeitschrift für das gesamte Handels- und Wirtschaftsrecht 523 (2002)

Macey, Jonathan, *The Central Role of Myth in Corporate Law*, ECGI Law Working Paper No 519/2020, 22–32 (May 2020)

Macey, Jonathan R., *Corporate Law and Corporate Governance – A Contractual Perspective*, Journal of Corporate Law 187 (1992/93)

MacNeil, Iain & Xiao Li, *'Complay or Explain': Market Discipline and Non-compliance with the Combined Code*, 14 Corporate Governance: An International Review 486 (2006)

MacNeil, Iain & Irene-Marié Esser, *The Emergence of 'Comply or Explain' as a Global Model for Corporate Governance Codes*, 33 European Business Law Review 1 (2022)

Madsen, Marina B., *Behavioural Economics in European Corporate Governance – Much Ado about Nudging*, 32(2) European Business Law Review 295–316 (2021)

Madsen, Marina B., *Nudging Institutional Shareholders*, 32 European Business Law Review 295 (2021)

Madsen, Marina B., Mette Neville, Hanna Almlöf & Kajsa Haag, *Ejerskabsdynamik i SMV'er – Et svensk/dansk projekt om problemer og løsninger ved ændringer i ejerkredsen*, Nordisk Tidsskrift for selskabsret, 74–96 (2019:4)

Maitre-Ekern, Elénore, Mark B. Taylor & Maja van der Velden, *Towards a Sustainable Circular Economy. SMART Reform Proposals* (2020), University of Oslo Faculty of Law Research Paper No 2020-12, Nordic & European Company Law Working Paper No 20-10, https://ssrn.com/abstract=3596076

Mandelker, Gershon, *Risk and Return: The Case of Merging Firms*, 1 Journal of Financial Economy 303 (1974)

Mangano, Renato, *Improving the Quality of the Comply or Explain Approach and Introducing Self-Monitoring Through Online Feedbacks*, 14 European Company and Financial Law Review 435 (2017)

Manne, Henry, *Mergers and the Market for Corporate Control*, 73 Journal of Political Economy 110 (1965)

Manne, Henry, *Corporate Governance – Getting Back to Market Basics* (2008) https://www.consob.it/documents/46180/46181/sem_20081110_manne.pdf/f25f9186-e4c9-45b9-a5bf-8831ed93d1d6

Marris, Robin & Dennis Mueller, *The Corporation, Competition, and the Invisible Hand*, 18 Journal of Economic Literature 32 (1980)

Martin, Kenneth & John McConnell, *Corporate Performance, Corporate Takeovers and Management Turnover*, 46 Journal of Finance 671 (1991)

Masulis, Ronald, Cong Wang & Fei Xie, *Corporate Governance and Acquirer Returns*, 62 Journal of Finance 1851 (2007)

Masulis, Ronald W., Sichen Shen & Hong Zou, *Director Liability Protection and the Quality of Outside Directors*, ECGI Working Paper No. 672/2020 http://ssrn.com/abstract_id=3329220 (2020)

Matejun, Marek & Zdenek Mikolás, *Small Business Life Circle: Statics and Dynamics*, 9(6) Engineering Management in Production and Services (2017)

Magill, Michael, Martine Quinzil & Jean-Charles Rochet, *A Theory of the Stakeholder Corporation*, 83 Econometrica 1685 (2015)

Mayer, Collin, *Shareholderism Versus Stakeholderism – A Misconceived Contradiction: A Comment on 'The Illusory Promise of Stakeholder Governance' by Lucian Bebchuk & Roberto Tallarita*, European Corporate Governance Institute - Law Working Paper No 522/2020 (2020)

Mayer, Colin, Anette Mikes & Sudhir Rama Murthy, *Responsible Business Theory and Accounting*, Said Business School, University of Oxford (19 September 2021)

Mayer, Colin, *Ownership, Agency and Trusteeship*, ECGI Law Working Paper No 488/2020 (11 December 2019)

Mayer, Colin, *The Governance of Corporate Purpose*, ECGI Working Paper 609/2021, https://ecgi.global/sites/default/files/working_papers/documents/mayerfinal_1.pdf (2021)

McCahery, Joseph A. & Erik P.M. Vermeulen, *The Changing Landscape of EU Company Law* (TILEC Discussion Paper Series No 023, 2004)

McConnell, John & Timothy Nantell, *Corporate Combinations and Common Stock Returns: The Case of Joint Ventures*, 40 Journal of Finance 519 (1985)

Mensi-Klarbach, Heike, Stephan Leixnering & Michael Schiffinger, *The Carrot or the Stick: Self-Regulation for Gender-Diverse Boards via Codes of Good Governance*, 170 Journal of Business Ethics 577 (2021)

Middleton, Thomas *The Privilege against Self-Incrimination, the Penalty Privilege and Legal Professional Privilege under the Laws Governing ASIC, APRA, the ACCC and the ATO – Suggested Reforms*, 30 Australian Bar Review 282 (2008)

Mikkelson, Wayne & Megan Partch, *The Decline of Takeovers and Disciplinary Managerial Turnover*, 44 Journal of Financial Economics 205 (1997)

Millon, David K., *Why Is Corporate Management Obsessed with Quarterly Earnings and What Should Be Done about It?*, 70 George Washington Law Review 890 (2002)

Mitchell, Mark & J. Harold Mulherin, *The Impact of Industry Shocks on Takeover and Restructuring Activity*, 41 Journal of Financial Economics 193 (1996)

David Millon, *Theories of the Corporation*, Duke Law Journal 201 (1990)

Mock, Sebastian, *Wirecard and European Company and Financial Law*, 18 European Company and Financial Law Review 519–554 (2021)

Moore, Marc T., *'Whispering Sweet Nothings': The Limitations of Informal Conformance in UK Corporate Governance*, 9 Journal of Corporate Law Studies 35 (2009)

Monciardini, David, John Dumay & Lucia Biondi, *'IR' and EU Law. Competing, Converging or Complementary Regulatory Frameworks?*, Paper presented at the conference, Life-cycle based management and reporting for sustainable business, Oslo, Norway (29–30 November 2016)

Morck, Randall, Andrei Shleifer & Robert Vishny, *Alternative Mechanisms for Corporate Control*, 79 American Economic Review 842 (1989)

Mosca, Luigi, Martine Gianecchini & Diego Campagnolo, *Organizational Life Cycle Models: A Design Perspective*, 10(3) Journal of Organisation Design 18 (2021)

Muchlinski, Peter, *The Development of German Corporate Law Until 1990: An Historical Reappraisal*, 14 German Law Journal 339 (2013)

Mueller, Dennis, *A Theory of Conglomerate Mergers*, 83 The Quarterly Journal of Economics 643 (1969)

Mueller, Dennis, *A Life Cycle Theory of the Firm*, 20 The Journal of Industrial Economics 199 (1972)

Mueller, Dennis & Mark Sirower, *The Causes of Mergers: Tests Based on the Gains to Acquiring Firms' Shareholders and the Size of Premia*, 24 Managerial and Decision Economics 373 (2003)

Murphy, Kevin, *Corporate Performance and Managerial Remuneration – An Empirical Analysis*, 7 Journal of Accounting and Economics, 11–42 (1985)

Murray, J. Haskell, *Choose Your Own Master: Social Enterprise, Certifications, and Benefit Corporation Statutes*, 2 American University Business Law Review 1 (2012)

Murray, J. Haskell, *Adopting Stakeholder Advisory Boards*, 54 American Business Law Journal 61 (2017)

Mustakallio, Mikko, *Contractual and Relational Governance in Family Firms – Effects on Strategy Decision-Making Quality and Firm Performance* 166 (Helsinki University of Technology, Institute of Strategy and International Business, 2002)

Mustakallio, Mikko, Errko Autio & Shaker A. Zahra, *Relational and Contractual Governance in Family Firms: Effects on Strategic Decision Making*, 15 Family Business Review 205–222 (2002)

Möllers, Thomas M.J., *The Wirecard Accounting Scandal in Germany, and How the Financial Industry Failed to Spot It*, 54 International Lawyer 325 (2021)

Möslein, Florian, *Europäische Zertifizierung mitgliedstaatlichen GmbH-Rechts*, 176 ZHR: Zeitschrift für das gesamte Handelsrecht und Wirtschaftsrecht 470 (2012)

Möslein, Florian & Karsten Engsig Sørensen, *Sustainable Corporate Governance: A Way Forward*, European Company Law 7–14, Law Working Paper No 583/2021, ECGI (2021)

Möslein, Florian & Karsten Engsig Sørensen, *Nudging for Corporate Long-Termism and Sustainability? Regulatory Instruments from a Comparative and Functional Perspective*, Columbia Journal of European Law 391–454 (2018)

Möslein, Florian & Anne Mittwoch, *Social Enterprise in US Corporate Law – Benefit Corporations and Certified B Corporations*, 80 Rabels Zeitschrift für ausländisches und internationales Privatrecht (RabelsZ) 399 (2016)

Möslein, Florian & Anne Mittwoch, *Der Europäische Aktionsplan zur Finanzierung nachhaltigen Wachstums*, Wertpapier-Mitteilungen 481 (2019)

Mühlenbruch, Sonja & Benedikt Buchner, *Kosten und Nutzen der (Nicht-)Prävention durch Recht – Prävention durch Recht (legal opinion commissioned by the Bertelsmann Foundation)*, http://www.igmr.uni-bremen.de/deutsch/projekte/praevention.pdf (2007)

Mähönen, Jukka, *Comprehensive Approach to Relevant and Reliable Reporting in Europe: A Dream Impossible?*, 12 Sustainability 5277 (2020)

Nachemson-Ekwall, Sophie *Gör om gör rätt: Synpunkter på Kollegiets vinstfokus i den nya koden för bolagsstyrning 2020*, Tidningen Balans (24 January 2020)

Nadler, David A., *Building Better Boards*, 82(5) Harvard Business Review 102 (2004)

Nelen, Samuel B. Garcia, *De participantenvennootschap: gedachten over een mogelijke nieuwe rechtsvorm*, 3–4 Maandblad voor Ondernemingsrecht 120 (2021)

Neville, Mette & Karsten Engsig Sørensen, *Promoting Entrepreneurship – The New Company Law Agenda*, 15(4) European Business Organization Law Review 545–584 (2014)

Nguyen, Hien T., Hieu V. Phan & Lingna Sun, *Shareholder Litigation Rights and Corporate Cash Holdings: Evidence from Universal Demand Laws*, 52 Journal of Corporate Finance 192 (2018)

Nguyen, Nam H., Hieu V. Phan & Eunju Lee, *Shareholder Litigation Rights and Capital Structure Decisions*, 62 Journal of Corporate Finance 101601 (2020)

Nicholson, Gavin J. & Geoffrey Kiel, *Can Directors Impact Performance? A Case-Based Test of Three Theories of Corporate Governance*, 15(4) Corporate Governance: An International Review 585 (2007)

Nobes, Christopher, *The True and Fair View: Impact on and of the Fourth Directive*, Working Paper, University of Reading (1993)

Nordqvist, Mattias, *Understanding Strategy Processes in Family Firms: Exploring the Roles of Actors and Arenas*, 30(1) International Small Business Journal 36 (2012)

Novitz, Tonia, *Engagement with Sustainability at the International Labour Organization and Implications for Worker Voice*, 159(4) International Labour Review 463 (2020)

Nykvist, Björn, Åsa Persson, Fredrik Moberg, Linn Persson, Sarah Cornell & Johan Rockström, *National Environmental Performance on Planetary Boundaries*, Swedish Environmental Protection Agency (2013)

Obermann, Jörn & Patrick Velte, *Determinants and Consequences of Executive Compensation-Related Shareholder Activism and Say-on-Pay Votes: A Literature Review and Research Agenda*, 40 Journal of Accounting Literature 116 (2018)

O'Byrne, Stephen F., *Say on Pay: Is It Needed? Does It Work?* (Harvard Corporate Governance Forum, 25 January 2018), https://corpgov.law.harvard.edu/2018/01/25/say-on-pay-is-it-needed-does-it-work/

O'Connell, Vincent, *Reflections on Stewardship Reporting*, 21 Accounting Horizons 215 (2007)

Officer, Micah, Oguzhan Ozbas & Berk Sensoy, *Club Deals in Leveraged Buyouts*, 98 Journal of Financial Economics 214 (2010)

Öhman, Peter & Eva Wallerstedt, *Audit Regulation and the Development of the Auditing Profession: The Case of Sweden*, 17 Accounting History 241 (2012)

Östberg, Jessica, *Styrelseledamöters lojalitetsplikt: särskilt om förbudet att utnyttja affärsmöjligheter* 143 (Jure Förlag 2016)

O'Sullivan, Noel, *Auditors' Liability: Its Role in the Corporate Governance Debate*, 23 Accounting and Business Research 412–420 (1993)

Pagano, Ugo & Sandro Trento, *Continuity and Change in Italian Corporate Governance: The Institutional Stability of One Variety of Capitalism*, University of Siena Department of Economics Working Paper (2002)

Pajunen, Kati, *Changing Reporting Models: A Summary of the Experience in Finland* 25 Research in Accounting Regulation 260 (2013)

Parguel, Béatrice, Florence Benoit-Moureau & Fabrice Larceneux, *How Sustainability Ratings Might Deter 'Greenwashing'*, 102 Journal of Business Ethics 15 (2011)

Phalippou, Ludovic, *Venture Capital Funds: Flow-Performance Relationship and Performance Persistence*, 34 Journal of Banking and Finance 568 (2010)

Palepu, Krishna, *Predicting Takeover Offerees: A Methodological and Empirical Analysis*, 8 Journal of Accounting & Economics 3 (1986)

Pargendler, Mariana, *The Corporate Governance Obsession*, 42 Journal of Corporate Law 373 (2016)

Park, James, *From Managers to Markets: Valuation and Shareholder Wealth Maximization*, 47(2) Journal of Corporate Law 435 (2022)

Persson, Linn, Bethanie M. Carney Alroth, Christopher D. Collins, Sarah Cornel, Cynthia A. de Wit, Miriam L. Diamond, Peter Fantke, Martin Hassellöv, Matthew MacLeod, Morten W. Ryberg, Peter Søgaard Jørgensen, Patricia Villarrubia-Gómez, Zhanyun Wang & Michael Z. Hauschild, *Outside the Safe Operating Space of the Planetary Boundary for Novel Entities*, Environmental Science & Technology (2022)

Petrin, Martin, *Corporate Management in the Age of AI*, 3 Columbia Business Law Review 965 (2019)

Pieterse, Jan Nederveen, *Periodizing Globalization: Histories of Globalization*, 6(2) New Global Studies (2012)

Pietrancosta, Alain, *Codification in Company Law of General CSR Requirements: Pioneering Recent French Reforms and EU Perspectives*, ECGI Law Working Paper No 639/2022, https://papers.ssrn.com/abstract_id=4083398 (6 June 2022)

Pirinen, Pekka, *Economic and Normative Pressures as Drivers for the Adoption of International Accounting Standards in Finland Since 1976*, 14 European Accounting Review 213 (2005)

Porter, Michael Eugene & Mark R. Kramer, *Strategy and Society: The Link Between Competitive Advantage and Corporate Social Responsibility*, 84(12) Harvard Business Review 78 (2006)

Posner, Eric A., *Agency Models in Law and Economics*, John M. Olin Program in Law and Economics Working Paper No 92 (2000)

Posner, Richard A., *Economics, Politics, and the Reading of Statutes and the Constitution*, 49 University of Chicago Law Review 263 (1982)

Poutziouris, Panikkos, *The Strategic Orientation of Owner-Managers of Small Ventures: Evidence from the UK Small Business Economy*, 9(5) International Journal of Entrepreneurial Behaviour & Research 185–214 (2003)

Prahalad, C.K. & Gary Hamel, *The Core Competence of the Corporation*, Harvard Business Review 79–91 (1990)

Pünder, Hermann, *Zertifizierung und Akkreditierung – private Qualitätskontrolle unter staatlicher Gewährleistungsverantwortung*, 170 ZHR: Zeitschrift für das gesamte Handels-und Wirtschaftsrecht 567 (2006)

Quick, Reiner, *Can Prohibitions of Non-audit Services and an Expanded Auditor Liability Improve Audit Quality?*, 26 International Journal of Auditing 18–22 (2022)

Rahman, Sabeel K., *Domination, Democracy, and Constitutional Political Economy in the New Gilded Age: Towards a Fourth Wave of Legal Realism?*, 94 Texas Law Review 1329 (2016)

Ravenscraft, David & Frederic Michael Scherer, *Life after Takeover,* 36 Journal of Industrial Economics 147 (1987)

Raworth, Kate, *A Safe and Just Space for Humanity: Can We Live Within the Doughnut, Oxfam Discussion Papers* (2012)

Reddy Bobby V., *The Emperor's New Code? Time to Re-evaluate the Nature of Stewardship Engagement under the UK's Stewardship Code*, https://ssrn.com/abstract=3773156 (2021)

Brakman Reiser, Dana, *The Next Big Thing: Flexible Purpose Corporations*, 2 American University Business Law Review 55 (2012)

Brakman Reiser, Dana, *Blended Enterprise and the Dual Mission Dilemma*, 35 Vermont Law Review 105 (2010)

Brakman Reiser, Dana, *Benefit Corporations – A Sustainable Form of Organization?* 46 Wake Forest Law Review 591 (2011)

Brakman Reiser, Dana & Steven A. Dean, *Social Enterprise Law* 130 (2017)

Brakman Reiser, Dana & Anne Tucker, *Buyer Beware: Variation and Opacity in ESG and ESG Index Funds*, 41 Cardozo Law Review 1921 (2020)

Remenarić, Branka, Ivana Kenfelja & Ivo Mijoč, *Creative Accounting-Motives, Techniques and Possibilities of Prevention*, 31(1) Ekonomski vjesnik 193–199 (2018)

Reyes, Carla, Nizan G. Packin & Benjamin Edwards, *Distributed Governance*, 59(1) William & Mary Law Review (2017)

Reynisson, Kristin, *Related Party Transactions: Analysis of Proposed Article 9c of Shareholders' Rights Directive*, 5 European Company Law 175 (2016)

Richard Baker, Charles & Dwight M. Owsen, *Increasing the Role of Auditing in Corporate Governance*, 13 Critical Perspectives on Accounting 783 (2002)

Richardson, Benjamin, *From Fiduciary Duties to Fiduciary Relationships for Socially Responsible Investing: Responding to the Will of Beneficiaries*, 1 Journal of Sustainable Finance & Investment 5 (2011)

Ridley-Duff, Rory & Cliff Southcombe, *The Social Enterprise Mark: A Critical Review of Its Conceptual Dimensions*, 8 Social Enterprise Journal 178 (2012)

Ringe, Georg, *German Versus Nordic Board Models: Form, Function, and Convergence*, 65(1) Nordic Journal of Business 27, http://njb.fi/wp-content/uploads/2016/03/Ringe.pdf (2016)

Roberta Romano, *Corporate Governance in the Aftermath of the Insurance Crisis*, 39 Emory Law Journal 1155 (1990)

Rock, Edward, *For Whom Is the Corporation Managed in 2020?: The Debate over Corporate Purpose*, NYU Law and Economic Research Paper Series Working Paper No 20-16; European Corporate Governance Institute – Law Working Paper No. 515/2020 (2020)

Rockström, Johan, Will Steffen, Kevin Noone, Åsa Persson, F. Stuart, I. Chapin, Eric Lambin, Timothy Lenton, Marten Scheffer, Carl Folke, Hans Joachim Schellnhuber, Björn Nykvist, Cynthia A. de Wit, Terry Hughes, Sander van der Leeuw,

Henning Rodhe, Sverker Sörlin, Peter K. Snyder, Robert Costanza, Uno Svedin, Malin Falkenmark, Louise Karlberg, Robert W. Corell, Victoria J. Fabry, James Hansen, Brian Walker, Diana Liverman, Katherine Richardson, Paul Crutzen & Jonathan A. Foley, *A Safe Operating Space for Humanity*, Nature 461 (2009)

Roe, Mark J., *Corporate Purpose and Corporate Competition*, ECGI Law Working Paper No 601/2021 (13 July 2021), http://ssrn.com/abstract_id = 3817788

Roe, Mark J., Holger Spamann, Jesse M. Fried & Charles C.Y. Wang, *The EY Sustainable Corporate Governance Report's Major Flaws: Discussion and Analysis*, https://ec.europa.eu/info/law/better-regulation/have-your-say/initiatives/12548-Sustainable-corporate-governance/F594640 (2020)

Roland, Clift, Sarah Sim, Henry King, Jonathan L. Chenoweth, Ian Christie, Julie Clavreul, Carina Mueller, Leo Posthuma, Anne-Marie Boulay, Rebecca Chaplin-Kramer, Julia Chatterton, Fabrice DeClerck, Angela Druckman, Chris France, Antonio Franco, Dieter Gerten, Mark Goedkoop, Michael Zwicky Hauschild, Mark A. J. Huijbregts, Thomas Koellner, Eric F. Lambin, Jacquetta Lee, Simon Mair, Stuart Marshall, Michael S. McLachlan, Llorenc Mila i. Canals, Cynthia Mitchell, Edward Price, Johan Rockstrom, James Suckling & Richard Murphy, *The Challenges of Applying Planetary Boundaries as a Basis for Strategic Decision-Making in Companies with Global Supply Chain*, 9 Sustainability 279 (2017)

Rose, Caspar, *The New European Shareholder Rights Directive: Removing Barriers and Creating Opportunities for More Shareholder Activism and Democracy*, 16 Journal of Management & Governance 269 (2012)

Rose, Jacob, Cheri Mazza, Carolyn Norman & Anna Rose, *The Influence of Director Stock Ownership and Board Discussion Transparency on Financial Reporting Quality*, 38(5) Accounting, Organizations and Society 397–405 (2013)

Rosenstein, Stuart & Jeffrey G. Wyatt, *Outside Directors, Board Independence, and Shareholder Wealth*, 26(2) Journal of Financial Economics (1990)

Rothe, Henrik, Stine Brøsted Jensen & Yas Farah Bakhsh Akbatani, *Erhvervslivets adgang til domstolene*, Justitia, http://justitia-int.org/erhvervslivets-adgang-til-domstolene/ (2020)

Ryabota, Vladislava, Alexey Volynets, Axel Kravatzky & Helen Carrington, *IFC Corporate Governance Knowledge Publication*, 43 Private Sector Opinion, https://openknowledge.worldbank.org/handle/10986/32363 (2019)

Salacuse, Jeswald W., *Corporate Governance, Culture and Convergence: Corporations American Style or with a European Touch?*, 9 Law & Business Review of the Americas 33 (2003)

Sale, Hillary A., *The Corporate Purpose of Social License*, Georgetown Law Faculty Publications and Other Works, https://papers.ssrn.com/sol3/papers.cfm?abstract_id = 3403706 (2019)

Sanchez-Marin, Gregorio, Gabriel Lozano-Reina, Samuel Baixauli-Soler & Maria Ernacion Lucas-Perez, *Say on Pay Effectiveness, Corporate Governance Mechanisms, and CEO Compensation Alignment*, 20 Business Research Quarterly, 226–239 (2017)

Sauerwald, Steve, J. (Hans) Van Oosterhout & Marc Van Essen, *Expressive Shareholder Democracy: A Multilevel Study of Shareholder Dissent in 15 Western European Countries*, 53 Journal of Management Studies 520 (2016)

Scharfstein, David, *The Disciplinary Role of Takeovers*, 55 Review of Economic Studies 185 (1988)

Schmid, Alexander Koeberle, Karsten Schween & Peter May, *Governance Kodex für Familienunternehmen in der Praxis – Ergebnisse einer Studie über Familienverfassungen*, 41 Betriebs-Berater 2499 (2011)

Schmidt, Jessica, *SE and SCE: Two New European Company Forms – And More to Come*, 27 Company Lawyer 99 (2006)

Schmidt, Jessica, *DiRUG-RefE: Ein Digitalisierungs-Ruck für das deutsche Gesellschafts- und Registerrecht*, ZIP: Zeitschrift für Wirtschaftsrecht 112 (2021)

Schmidt, Jessica, *BB-Gesetzgebungs- und Rechtsprechungsreport zum Europäischen Unternehmensrecht 2021/22*, Betriebs Berater, 1859 (2022)

Schmolke, Klaus Ulrich, *Expulsion and Valuation Clauses – Freedom of Contract vs. Legal Paternalism in German Partnership and Close Corporation Law*, 9(3) European Company and Financial Law Review 388 (2012)

Schüppen, Matthias, *To Comply or Not to Comply – That's the Question!* ZIP: Zeitschrift für Wirtschaftsrecht 1269 (2002)

Schwartz, Rachel, *Auditors' Liability, Vague Due Care, and Auditing Standards*, 11 Review of Quantitative Finance and Accounting 183 (1998)

Schwert, William, *Hostility in Takeovers: In the Eyes of the Beholder?*, 55 Journal of Finance 2599 (2000)

Scoones, Ian, *The Politics of Sustainability and Development*, 41 Annual Review of Environment and Resources 293 (2016)

Sealy, Leonard *The Disclosure Philosophy and Company Law Reform*, 2 The Company Lawyer 51–56 (1981)

Segismundo Álvarez Royo-Villanova, *Proposal Regarding the Use of Digital Tools and Processes in Company Law: The Practitioner's Perspective*, European Company and Financial Law Review 149 (2019)

Sergakis, Konstantinos, *Deconstruction and Reconstruction of the 'Comply or Explain' Principle in EU Capital Markets*, 5 Journal of Accounting, Economics, and Law: A Convivium 233 (2015)

Sharfman, Bernard S., *How the Strong Negotiating Position of Wall Street Employees Impacts the Corporate Governance of Financial Firms*, 5 Virginia Business & Law Review 350 (2011)

Shivdasani, Anil, *Board Composition, Ownership Structure, and Hostile Takeovers*, 16 Journal of Accounting and Economics 167 (1993)

Shleifer, Andrei, & Robert W. Vishny, *A Survey of Corporate Governance*, 52 The Journal of Finance 737 (1997)

Siems, Mathias M., *What Does Not Work in Comparing Securities Laws: A Critique on La Porta et al.'s Methodology*, 16 International Company and Commercial Law Review 300 (2005)

Sikka, Prem & John Stittle, *Debunking the Myth of Shareholder Ownership of Companies: Some Implications for Corporate Governance and Financial Reporting*, 63 Critical Perspective on Accounting 101992 (2019)

Silver, Nicholas, *Blindness to Risk: Why Institutional Investors Ignore the Risk of Stranded Assets*, 7 Journal of Sustainable Finance and Investment 99 (2017)

Simunic, Dan A., Minlei Ye & Ping Zhang, *The Joint Effects of Multiple Legal System Characteristics on Auditing Standards and Auditor Behavior*, 34 Contemporary Accounting Research 7 (2017)

Singh, Kuldeep & Deepa Pillai, *Corporate Governance in Small and Medium Enterprises: A Review*, 22(1) Corporate Governance: International Journal of Business in Society 23–41 (2022)

Sjåfjell, Beate & Jukka Mähönen, *Corporate Purpose and the Misleading Shareholder vs Stakeholder Dichotomy*, https://papers.ssrn.com/abstract=4039565 (21 February 2022)

Sjåfjell, Beate *If Not Now, When? European Company Law in a Sustainable Development Perspective*, 7(5) European Law Journal 187 (2010)

Sjåfjell, Beate, *Sustainable Companies: Possibilities and Barriers in Norwegian Company Law*, 11(1) International and Comparative Corporate Law Journal 1 (2014)

Sjåfjell, Beate, *Sustainable Value Creation Within Planetary Boundaries – Reforming Corporate Purpose and Duties of the Corporate Board*, University of Oslo, Faculty of Law Legal Studies Research Paper Series No. 2020-20 (4 August 2020)

Sjåfjell, Beate, *The Financial Risks of Unsustainability: A Research Agenda*, University of Oslo Faculty of Law Research Paper No 2020-18 (2020)

Sjåfjell, Beate, *How Company Law Has Failed Human Rights – And What to Do about It*, 5(2) Business and Human Rights Journal (2020)

Sjåfjell, Beate & Jukka Mähönen, *Corporate Purpose and the Misleading Shareholder vs Stakeholder Dichotomy*, University of Oslo Faculty of Law Legal Studies Research Paper Series No 2022-43 (21 February 2022)

Sjåfjell, Beate, Tiina Häyhä & Sarah Cornell, *A Research-Based Approach to the UN Sustainable Development Goals. A Prerequisite to Sustainable Business*, University of Oslo Faculty of Law Research Paper No 2020-02, Nordic & European Company Law Working Paper No 21-12, SSRN: https://ssrn.com/abstract=3526744 (28 January 2020)

Beate Sjåfjell, Jukka Mähönen, Tonia Novitz, Clair Gammage & Hanna Ahlström, *Securing the Future of European Business: SMART Reform Proposals* (7 May 2020). University of Oslo Faculty of Law Research Paper No 2020-11, Nordic & European Company Law Working Paper No 20-08, https://ssrn.com/abstract=3595048 (2020)

Sjåfjell, Beate & Jukka Mähönen, *Corporate Purpose and the Misleading Shareholder vs Stakeholder Dichotomy*, University of Oslo Faculty of Law Research Paper No 2022-43, https://ssrn.com/abstract=4039565 (2022)

Skadden, Arps, Meagher Slate & Flom LLP and Affiliates, *2021 Compensation Committee Handbook*, https://www.skadden.com/insights/publications/2021/02/2021-compensation-committee-handbook (15 April 2022)

Skog, Rolf, *The Importance of Profit in Company Law – A Comment from a Swedish Perspective*, 12(4) European Company and Financial Law Review (2015)

Skog, Rolf, *Talk Is Cheap*, 2021(4) Nordisk Tidsskrift for Selskabsret 83 (2021)

Smit, Lisa, Claire Bright, Robert McCorquodale, Matthias Baur, Hanna Deringer, Daniella Baeza-Breinbauer, Francisca Torres Cortes, Frank Alleweldt, Sendra Kara, Héctor Tejero Tobed & Camille Salinier, *Study on Due Diligence Requirements Through the Supply Chain*, Final Report https://op.europa.eu/sv/publication-detail/-/publication/8ba0a8fd-4c83-11ea-b8b7-01aa75ed71a1/language-en (20 February 2020)

Smit, Lise & Claire Bright, *The Concept of a 'Safe Harbor' and Mandatory Human Rights Due Diligence*, CEDIS Working Papers, www.cedis.fd.unl.pt/wp-content/uploads/2020/12/CEDIS_working-paper_the-concept-of-safe-harbour.pdf (December 2020)

Smythe, Donald J., *Shareholder Democracy and the Economic Purpose of the Corporation*, 63 Washington and Lee Law Review 1407 (2006)

Sonnenberger, Hans Jürgen, *Die Organisation der Aktiengesellschaften im Gemeinsamen Markt*, 19 AG: Die Aktiengesellschaft 1 (1974)

Spamann, Holger, *Monetary Liability for Breach of the Duty of Care?*, 8 Journal of Legal Analysis 337 (2016)

Spamann, Holger, *The 'Antidirector Rights Index' Revisited*, 23 Review of Financial Studies 467 (2009)

Spießhofer, Birgit, *Die neue europäische Richtlinie über Offenlegung nichtfinanzieller Informationen – Paradigmenwechsel oder Papiertiger?*, NZG: Neue Zeitschrift für Gesellschaftsrecht 1281 (2014)

Spießhofer, Birgit, *Sustainable Corporate Governance*, NZG: Neue Zeitschrift für Gesellschaftsrecht 435 (2022)

Sroufe, Robert, *Integration and Organizational Change Towards Sustainability*, 162 Journal of Cleaner Production 315 (2017)

Staubus, George J., *The Residual Equity Point of View in Accounting*, 34 The Accounting Review 3 (1959)

Stevenson, Howard H. & David E. Gumpert, *The Heart of Entrepreneurship*, 64(2) Harvard Business Review 85–94 (1985)

Stein, Jeremy, *Takeover Threats and Managerial Myopia*, 96 Journal of Political Economy 61 (1988)

Stiglitz, Joseph E. *Markets, Market Failures, and Development*, 97 American Economic Review 197 (1989)

Storey, David J. *Optimism and Chance: The Elephants in the Entrepreneurship Room*, 29(4) International Small Business Journal 303–323 (2011)

Stout, Lynn A, Jean-Philippe Robé, Paddy Ireland, Simon Deakin, Kent Greenfield, Andrew Johnston, Harm Schepel, Magaret M. Blair, Lorraine E. Talbot, Alan J. Dignam, Janet Dine, David Millon, Beate Sjåfjell, Charlotte Villiers, Cynthia A. Williams, Marios Koutsias, Andrew Pendleton, Gerald F. Davis, Michael Galanis, David Chandler, Andrew R. Keay, Marc T. Moore, Jean Du Plessis, Andrea J. Bather, Beau Linton Lefler, Carrie Bradshaw, Christopher M. Bruner, Thomas

Wuil Joo, Daniel J. H. Greenwood, Thomas Clarke, Lyman Johnson, Floriana Mulazzi, Martin Lipton, Carol Liao, Rebecca Johnson, Anat Alon-Beck, Greg Markel, Wendy Currie, Frank Partnoy, Leonardo F. Peklar, Alexandre Di Miceli da Silveira, Ofer Sitbon, Cesar González-Cantón, Jean-Pierre Chanteau, Angela Rita Franco Donaggio, Irene-Marie Esser, Gill North, Sergio Alberto Gramitto Ricci, Roman Tomasic, Renginee G. Pillay, Ciarán O'Kelly, Con Keating, Hugh Christopher Willmott, Jeroen Veldman & Paige Morrow, *The Modern Corporation Statement on Company Law*, https://papers.ssrn.com/sol3/papers.cfm?abstract_id=2848833 (2016)

Strand, Therese, *EU and Sustainable Corporate Governance*, 2021(3) Nordisk Tidsskrift for Selskabsret 1–18 (2021)

Strine Jr, Leo, *Toward Fair and Sustainable Capitalism*, University of Pennsylvania, Institute for Law & Economy, Research Paper No 19-39, Harvard John M. Olin Discussion Paper No 1018 (August 2020)

Strine Jr, Leo E., *The Dangers of Denial: The Need for a Clear-Eyed Understanding of the Power and Accountability Structure Established by the Delaware General Corporation Law*, University of Pennsylvania Law School, Institute for Law and Economics, Research Paper No 15-08 (2016)

Strätling, Rebecca, *General Meetings: A Dispensable Tool for Corporate Governance of Listed Companies?*, 11 Corporate Governance: An International Review 74–82 (2003)

Sullivan, Kristen & Maureen Bujno, *Incorporating ESG Measures into Executive Compensation Plans*, Harvard Law School Forum on Corporate Governance, https://corpgov.law.harvard.edu/2021/05/24/incorporating-esg-measures-into-execu
tive-compensation-plans/ (24 May 2021)

Szabó, Daniel Gargely & Karsten Engsis Sørensen, *Integrating Corporate Social Responsibility in Corporate Governance Codes in the EU*, 24 European Business Law Review 781 (2013)

Sørensen, Karsten Engsig & Mette Neville, *Social Enterprises: How Should Company Law Balance Flexibility and Credibility?*, 15 European Business Organization Law Review 267 (2014)

Talbot, Lorraine E., *Polanyi's Embeddedness and Shareholder Stewardship: A Contextual Analysis of Current Anglo-American Perspectives on Corporate Governance*, 62 Northern Ireland Legal Quarterly 451 (2011)

Taub, Jennifer S., *Able but Not Willing: The Failure of Mutual Fund Advisers to Advocate for Shareholders' Rights*, 34 Journal of Corporate Law 102 (2009)

Taylor, Mark B., *Litigating Sustainability – Towards a Taxonomy of Counter-Corporate Litigation*, University of Oslo Faculty of Law Research Paper No 2020-08 (2020) www.ssrn.com/abstract=3530768

Taylor, Mark B. & Maja van der Velden, *Resistance to Regulation: Failing Sustainability in Product Lifecycles*, 11(22) Sustainability 6526 (2019)

Teece, David J., Gary Pisano & Amy Shuen, *Dynamic Capabilities and Strategic Management*, 18(7) Strategic Management Journal 509 (1997)

Testy, Kellye Y., *Linking Progressive Corporate Law with Progressive Social Movement*, 76 Tulane Law Review 1227 (2002)

Teubner, Günther, *Unternehmensinteresse – das gesellschaftliche Interesse des Unternehmens 'an sich'?*, ZHR: Zeitschrift für das gesamte Handels- und Wirtschaftsrecht 148, 470–488 (1984)

Thirion, Elodie, *Statute for Social and Solidarity-Based Enterprises – European Added Value Assessment* 26, http://www.europarl.europa.eu/RegData/etudes/STUD/2017/611030/EPRS_STU%282017%29611030_EN.pdf (2017)

Thomas, Randall & Christoph Van der Elst, *Say on Pay Around the World*, 92 Washington University Law Review 671–673 (2015)

Thomä, Jakob & Hugues Chenet, *Transition Risks and Market Failure: A Theoretical Discourse on Why Financial Models and Economic Agents May Misprice Risk Related to the Transition to a Low-Carbon Economy*, 7 Journal of Sustainable Finance & Investment 82 (2017)

Timmel, Jakob, *Der Entwurf zum DCGK 2022 – Nachhaltigkeit im Fokus*, ZPR: Zeitschrift für Rechtspolitik 70 (2022)

Triponel, Anna & Natalia Agapitova, *Legal Frameworks for Social Enterprise*, https://openknowledge.worldbank.org/bitstream/handle/10986/26397/114405-18-4-2017-15-11-50-DesignLegalFrameworksforSEsApr.pdf?sequence=1&isAllowed=y (2016)

Tröger, Tobias H. & Uwe Walz, *Does Say on Pay Matter? Evidence from Germany*, European Company and Financial Law Review 381–414 (2019)

Tsagas, Georgina & Charlotte Villiers, *Why 'Less Is More' in Non-financial Reporting Initiatives – Concrete Steps Towards Sustainability*, 10(2) Accounting, Economics & Law: A Convivium (2020)

Tsang, Albert, Kun Tracy Wang, Simeng Liu & Li Yu, *Integration Corporate Social Responsibility Criteria into Executive Compensation and Firm Innovation: International Evidence*, 70 Journal of Corporate Finance 102070 (2021)

Umakanth, Varottil, *Proliferation of Corporate Governance Codes in the Backdrop of Divergent Ownership Structure*, 24 Competition & Change 471 (2020)

van Bekkum, Jaron, Steven Hijink, Michael C. Schouten & Jaap W. Winter, *Corporate Governance in the Netherlands*, International Congress on Comparative Law, Washington (2010), https://papers.ssrn.com/abstract=1507633

Van den Heuvel, Jeroen, Anita Van Gils & Wim Voordeckers, *Board Roles in Small and Medium Sized Family Businesses: Performance and Importance*, 14(5) Corporate Governance: An International Review 467 (2006)

Van der Elst, Christoph & Anne Lafarre, *Shareholder Voice on Executive Pay: A Decade of Dutch Say on Pay*, 18 European Business Organization Law Review 56–58 (2017)

Van der Elst, Christoph, *Shareholders Holding the Reins on Remuneration: The European Say on Pay*, 14 European Company Law 114 (2017)

van der Elst, Christoph & Anne Lafarre, *Shareholder Stewardship in the Netherlands: The Role of Institutional Investors in a Stakeholder Oriented Jurisdiction* (ECGI

Working Paper 2020), https://ecgi.global/sites/default/files/working_papers/documents/final_2.pdf
Van Gils, Anita, *Management and Governance in Dutch SMEs*, 23(5) European Management Jounal 583–589 (2005)
Varaiya, Nikhil, *The 'Winners Curse' Hypothesis and Corporate Takeovers*, 9 Managerial and Decision Economics 311 (1988)
Varaiya, Nikhil & Kenneth Ferris, *Overpaying in Corporate Takeovers: The Winner's Curse*, 64 Financial Analysts Journal (1987)
Velte, Patrick, *Wechsel vom Vorstand in den Aufsichtsrat mit oder ohne Cooling Off als 'gute' Corporate Governance?*, Wertpapier-Mitteilungen 537 (2012)
Ventoruzzo, Marco, *On 'Prosperity' by Colin Mayer: Brief Critical Remarks on the (Legal) Relevance of Announcing a Multi-Stakeholders 'Corporate Purpose*, https://iris.unibocconi.it/handle/11565/4037291 (2020)
Vermeulen, Erik P.M. & Dirk A. Zetzsche, *The Use and Abuse of Investor Suits: An Inquiry into the Dark Side of Shareholder Activism*, 7 European Company and Financial Law Review 1 (2010)
Villiers, Charlotte, *Executive Pay: A Socially Oriented Distributive Justice Framework*, 37(5) The Company Lawyer 139 (2016)
Villiers, Charlotte, *Boardroom Culture – An Argument for Compassion*, 2 European Business Law Review 253 (2019)
Villiers, Charlotte, *New Directions in Sustainability Reporting and Due Diligence in the EU – The Problem of Complexity*, European Journal of Risk Regulation 1-19 (2022)
Villiers, Charlotte L., *Sustainable Companies: Barriers and Possibilities in UK Company Law*, 11(1) International and Comparative Corporate Law Journal (21 November 2010), University of Oslo Faculty of Law Research Paper No. 2010-03, available at SSRN: https://ssrn.com/abstract=1712791
Walker, David, *A Review of Corporate Governance in UK Banks and Other Financial Industry Entities. Final Recommendations* (2009), https://www.ecgi.org
Walking, Ralph & Michael Long, *Agency Theory, Managerial Welfare and Takeover Bid Resistance*, 15 The Rand Journal of Economics 54 (1984)
Walsh, James & John Ellwood, *Mergers, Acquisitions, and the Pruning of Managerial Deadwood*, 12 Strategic Management Journal 201 (1991)
Wang, Calvin, Elizabeth A. Walker & Janice Redmond, *Explaining the Lack of Strategy Planning in SMEs: The Importance of Owner Motivation*, 12(1) International Journal of Organisational Behavior (2007)
Wang-Erlandsson, Lang, Arna Tobian, Ruud J. van der Ent, Ingo Fetzer, Sofie te Wierik, Miina Porkka, Arie Staal, Fernando Jaramillo, Heindriken Dahlman, Chandrakant Singh, Peter Greve, Dieter Gerten, Patrick W. Keys, Tom Gleeson, Sarah E. Cornell, Will Steffen, Xuemei Bai & Johan Rockström, *A Planetary Boundary for Green Water*, 3 Nature Reviews Earth and Environment 380 (2022)
Ward, John L. & L. James, *A Survey of Board Practices*, 1(3) Family Business Review 289–308 (1988)

Warren, Ben, *Why Investors Are Putting Sustainability at the Top of the Agenda* (EY 19 May 2020), https://www.ey.com/en_gl/power-utilities/why-investors-are-putting-sustainability-at-the-top-of-the-agenda

Watts, Ross L. & Jerold L. Zimmerman, *Agency Problems, Auditing, and the Theory of the Firm: Some Evidence*, 26 Journal of Law and Economics 613 (1983)

Weber-Rey, Daniela, *Effects of the Better Regulation Approach on European Company Law and Corporate Governance*, 4(3) European Company and Financial Law Review 370–416 (2007)

Weller, Marc-Phillippe, *Corporate Governance in geschlossesenen Gesellschaften: Status Quo und Anforderungen*, 41(2–3) ZGR: Zeitschrift für Unternehmens- und Gesellschaftsrecht 386–417 (2012)

Wells, Harwell, *The Birth of Corporate Governance*, 33 Seattle University Law Review 1247 (2010)

Westergård-Nielsen, Niels, *Danske bestyrelser og deres medlemmer – hvem bestemmer i danske selskaber?* (Center for Corporate Governance. Copenhagen Business School 2020)

Will, Steffen, Katherine Richardson, Johan Rockström, Sarah E. Cornell, Ingo Fetzer, Elena M. Bennett, Reinette Biggs, Stephen R. Carpenter, Wim de Vries, Cynthia A. de Wit, Carl Folke, Dieter Gerten, Jens Heinke, Georgina M. Mace, Linn M. Persson, Veerabhadran Ramanathan, Belinda Reyers & Sverker Sörlin, *Planetary Boundaries: Guiding Human Development on a Changing Planet Science* 1259855 (2015)

Williams, Paul F., *Unreliable Accounts: Governing Behind a Veil*, 12 Accounting, Economics, and Law: A Convivium 211–231 (2022)

Wins, Anett & Bernhard Zwergel, *Comparing Those Who Do, Might and Will Not Invest in Sustainable Funds: A Survey among German Retail Fund Investors*, 9 Business Research 51 (2016)

Winter, Jaap, *Addressing the Crisis of the Modern Corporation: The Duty of Societal Responsibility of the Board* (13 April 2020), available at https://papers.ssrn.com/abstract_id=3574681

Winter, Jaap, *Towards a Duty of Societal Responsibility of the Board*, European Company Law 192–200 (2020)

Wongsinhirun, Nopparat, Pattanaporn Chatjuthamard, Pornsit Jiraporn & Piyachart Phiromswad, *Do Takeover Threats Influence Corporate Social Responsibility? Evidence from Hostile Takeover Vulnerability*, Corporate Social Responsibility and Environmental Management 1 (2022)

Wouters, Jan, *European Company Law: Quo Vadis?*, 37(2) Common Market Law Review 257–307 (2000)

Westaway, Kyle & Dirk Sampselle, *The Benefit Corporation: An Economic Analysis with Recommendations to Courts, Boards, and Legislatures*, 62 Emory Law Journal 999 (2013)

Wu, Betty H.T., Iain MacNeil & Katarzyna Chalaczkiewicz-Ladna, *Say on Pay' Regulations and Director Remuneration: Evidence from the UK in the Past Two Decades*, 20(2) Journal of Corporate Law Studies 541 (2020)

Wymeersch, Eddy, *The Enforcement of Corporate Governance Codes*, 6 Journal of Corporate Law Studies 113 (2006)

Yang, Juan, *Contract Law Aspects of Sustainable Companies' Certification in the Global Value Chain*, 15 European Review of Contract Law 31 (2017)

Yermack, David, *Corporate Governance and Blockchains*, 21(1) The Review of Financial Studies (2017)

Yikun, Zhu, *The Legal Regulation of Irrational Elements in the Operation of Board of Directors*, 38(2) Social Sciences in China 95 (2017)

Yoon, Kyoung-Soo & Yangsoo Jin, *Related Party Transactions, Agency Problem, and Exclusive Effects*, 51 The European Journal of Law & Economics 1 (2021)

Zahra, Shaker A. & John A. Pearce, *Boards of Directors and Corporate Financial Performance: A Review and Integrative Model*, 15 Journal of Management 291 (1989)

Zeff, Stephen A., *The Objectives of Financial Reporting: A Historical Survey and Analysis*, 43 Accounting and Business Research 262, 309 (2013)

Zetzsche, Dirk A., *Shareholder Passivity, Cross-Border Voting and the Shareholder Rights Directive*, 8 Journal of Corporate Law Studies 289 (2008)

Zhao, Jingchen & Zhihui Li, *The Regulatory Framework of Executive Remuneration: Contribution from Shareholder Activism and Board Accountability*, 15(2) Hastings Business Law Journal 203 (2019)

Books

Altmeppen, Holger & Günter H. Roth, *Gesetz betreffend die Gesellschaften mit beschränkter Haftung – GmbHG* § 60 (C.H. Beck 10. Auflage 2021)

Andersen, Paul Krüger, Aktie- og anpartsselskabsret (15th ed., Jurist og Økonomiforbundets Forlag 2021)

Andersson, Sten, Svante Johansson & Rolf Skog, *Aktiebolagslagen: en kommentar* (JUNO version 16, Norstedts Juridik 2021)

Andhov, Alexandra, *Computational Law* (Karnov 2022)

Armour, John, Dan Awry, Paul Davies, Luca Enriques, Jeffry N. Gordon, Colin Mayer & Jennifer Payne, *Principles of Financial Regulation* (Oxford University Press 2016)

Bainbridge, Stephen M., *Corporate Governance after the Financial Crisis* (Oxford University Press 2012)

Bainbridge, Stephen M., *The New Corporate Governance Theory and Practice* (Oxford University Press 2008)

Bainbridge, Stephen M. & Matthew Todd Henderson, *Limited Liability: A Legal and Economic Analysis* (Edward Elgar Publishing 2016)

Baldwin, Robert, Martin Cave & Martin Lodge, *Understanding Regulation: Theory, Strategy, and Practice* (Oxford University Press 2011)

Barker, Roger M., *Corporate Governance, Competition, and Political Parties: Explaining Corporate Governance Change in Europe* (Oxford University Press 2010)

Barker, Roger & Iris H-Y Chiu, *Corporate Governance and Investment Management* (Edward Elgar Publishing 2017)

Barnett, Michael L. & Timothy G. Pollock eds, *The Oxford Handbook of Corporate Reputation* (Oxford University Press 2012)

Barraket, Josephine, Robyn Keast & Craig Furneaux, *Social Procurement and New Public Governance* (Routledge 2016)

Baumol, William, *The Stock Market and Economic Efficiency* (Fordham University Press 1965)

Baumol, William, *Business Behaviour, Value and Growth* (Macmillan 1959)

Bebchuk, Lucian Arye & Jess Fried, *Pay Without Performance: The Unfulfilled Promise of Executive Compensation* (Harvard University Press 2004)

Beckers, Anna, *Enforcing Corporate Social Responsibility Codes: On Global and Self-Regulation and National Private Law* (Hart Publishing/Bloomsbury Publishing 2015)

Bénéplanc, Gilles & Jean-Charles Rochet, *Risk Management in Turbulent Times* (Oxford University Press 2011)

Berle, Adolf A. & Gardiner C. Means, *The Modern Corporation and Private Property* (The Macmillan 1932)

Berle, Adolf A. & Gardiner C. Means, *The Modern Corporation and Private Property* (1933)

Bieback, Karin, *Zertifizierung und Akkreditierung – Das Zusammenwirken staatlicher und nichtstaatlicher Akteure in gestuften Prüfsystemen* (Nomos 2008)

Birkmose, Hanne Søndergaard & Konstantinos Sergakis (eds), *SRD II – Political Ambitions and Regulatory Rationale* (Edward Elgar Publishing 2021)

Birkmose, Hanne Søndergaard & Konstantinos Sergakis eds, *The Shareholder Rights Directive II: A Commentary* (Edward Elgar Publishing 2021)

Blair, Margaret M., *Ownership and Control, Rethinking Corporate Governance for the Twenty-First Century* (Brookings Institution Press 1995)

Bråthen, Tore, *Selskapsrett* (6th ed. Gyldendal, Focus Forlag, 2019)

Bøhren, Øyvind, *Eierne, styret og ledelsen: corporate governance i Norge* (Fagbokforlaget, 2011)

Cameron, Kim S. & Robert E. Quinn, *Diagnosing and Changing Organizational Culture – Based on the Competing Values Framework* (Wiley 2011)

Canaris, Claus-Wilhelm, *Systemdenken und Systembegriff in der Jurisprudenz* (2nd ed., Duncker & Humblot 1983)

Carroll, Archie B. ed., *Managing Corporate Social Responsibility* (Scott Foresman & Co. 1977)

Cheffins, Brian R., *Company Law: Theory, Structure and Operation* (Oxford University Press 1997)

Chiu, Iris H-Y, *Regulating (from) the Inside: The Legal Framework for Internal Control in Banks and Financial Institutions* (Hart Publishing 2015)

Clark, Robert Charles, *Corporate Law* (Aspen Publishers 1986)

Coffee, John, Louis Lowenstein & Susan Rose-Ackerman (eds), *Knights, Raiders, & Targets: The Impact of the Hostile Takeover* (Oxford University Press 1988)

Cohen, Errol, *La société à mission: la loi pacte, enjeux pratiques de l'entreprise réinventée* (Hermann 2019)

Davies, Howard, *The Financial Crisis – Who Is to Blame* (Polity Press 2010)
Davies, Paul L., Sarah Worthington & Christopher Hare, *Gower: Principles of Modern Company Law* (11th ed., Sweet & Maxwell 2021)
Davies, Paul, Klaus J. Hopt, Richard Nowak & Gerard van Solinge eds, *Corporate Boards in Law and Practice* (Oxford University Press 2013)
De Bruyne, Jan, *Third-Party Certifiers* (Wolters Kluwer 2019)
De Filippo, Primavera & Aaron Wright, *Blockchain and the Law: The Rule of Code* (Harvard University Press 2018)
De Lacy, John, *The Reform of United Kingdom Company Law* (Routledge-Cavendish 2002)
de Vries, Paul, *Exit Rights of Minority Shareholders in a Private Limited Company* (Kluwer 2010)
Dimitropoulos, Georgios, *Zertifizierung und Akkreditierung im Internationalen Verwaltungsverbund* (Morh Siebeck 2012)
Dine, Janet & Marios Koutsias, *The Nature of Corporate Governance: The Significance of National Cultural Identity* (Edward Elgar Publishing 2013)
Donaldson, Thomas, *Corporations and morality* (Prentice-Hall 1982)
Donaldson, Thomas & Thomas W. Dunfee, *Ties That Bind. A Social Contracts Approach to Business Ethics* (Harvard Business Review Press 1999)
Dorresteijn, Adriaan F.M., Christoph Teichmann, Erik Werlauff, Tiago Monteiro & Nadia Pocher eds, *European Corporate Law* (Wolters Kluwer 2016)
Dotevall, Rolf, *Aktiebolagsrätt: fördjupning och komparativ belysning* (Norstedts Juridik 2015)
Easterbrook, Frank H. & Daniel R. Fischel, *The Economic Structure of Corporate Law* (Harvard University Press 1996)
Edmans, Alex, *Grow the Pie: How Great Companies Deliver Both Purpose and Profit* (Cambridge University Press 2020)
Edwards, John R., *A History of Financial Accounting* (Routledge 2013)
Engisch, Karl, *Die Einheit der Rechtsordnung* (C. Winter 1935)
Felix, Dagmar, *Die Einheit der Rechtsordnung* (Morh Siebeck 1998)
Fleckner, Andreas Martin, *Antike Kapitalvereinigungen: ein Beitrag zu den konzeptionellen und historischen Grundlagen der Aktiengesellschaft* (Böhlau Verlag Köln Weimar 2010)
Fleckner, Andreas Martin & Klaus J. Hopt, *Comparative Corporate Governance: A Functional and International Analysis* (Cambridge University Press 2013)
Flower, John, *European Financial Reporting: Adapting to a Changing World* (Palgrave Macmillan 2004)
Fode, Carsten, *Ledelsesansvar og ansvarsbegrænsning* (Jurist- og Økonomforbundets Forlag 2020)
Fode, Carsten & Mette Neville, *SMV-bestyrelsen. Hele vejen rundt* (Karnov 2018)
Fox, Justin, *The Myth of the Rational Market: A History of Risk, Reward, and Delusion on Wall Street* (Harper Business 2011)
Freeman, Robert Edward, *Strategic Management: A Stakeholder Approach* (Cambridge University Press 1984)

Gale, Fred P., *The Political Economy of Sustainability* (Edward Elgar 2018)
Gepken-Jager, Ella, Gerard van Solinge & Levinus Timmerman eds, *VOC 1602-2002, 400 Years of Company Law* (Kluwer Law International 2005)
Gerner-Beuerle, Carsten & Michael Schillig, *Comparative Company Law* (Oxford University Press 2019)
Gordon, Jeffrey N. & Wolf-Georg Ringe, *The Oxford Handbook of Corporate Law and Governance* (Oxford University Press 2018)
Greenfield, Kent, *The Failure of Corporate Law: Fundamental Flaws and Progressive Possibilities* (University of Chicago Press 2006)
Greenfield, Kent, *The Failure of Corporate Law: Fundamental Flaws and Progressive Possibilities* (University of Chicago Press 2008)
Gulbrandsen, Lars H., *Transnational Environmental Governance – The Emergence and Effects of the Certification of Forests and Fisheries* (Edward Elgar Publishing 2010)
Habersack, Mathias, Marc Löbbe & Peter Ulmer, *GmbHG Großkommentar* (3rd ed., Mohr Siebeck 2020)
Hart, Herbert Lionel Adolphus, *The Concept of Law* (Clarendon 1961)
Hilty, Reto & Frauke Henning-Bodewig eds, *Corporate Social Responsibility – Binding Standards of Competition Law?* (Springer 2014)
Hickel, Jason, *The Divide: A Brief Guide to Global Inequality and its Solutions* (William Heinemann 2017)
Hirschman, Albert, *Exit, Voice and Loyalty* (Harvard University Press 1970)
Ho, Karen, *Liquidated: An Ethnography of Wall Street* (Duke University Press 2009)
Hoffmann-Becking, Michael ed., *Münchener Handbuch des Gesellschaftsrechts, Band 4* (5th ed., C.H. Beck 2020)
Honeyman, Ryan, *The B Corp Handbook* (Berrett-Koehler Publishers 2014)
Hutchinson, Brian, *Keane on Company Law* (5th ed., Bloomsbury Professional 2017)
Jacobi, Jolande, *The Psychology of C.G. Jung* (Yale University Press 1973)
Janis, Irving Lester, *Groupthink: Psychological Studies of Policy Decisions and Fiascoes* (2nd ed., Houghton Mifflin 1983)
Keay, Andrew, *The Enlightened Shareholder Value Principle and Corporate Governance* (Routledge 2013)
Kershaw, David, *The Foundations of Anglo-American Corporate Fiduciary Law* (Cambridge University Press 2018)
Kersting, Christian, et al., eds, *Gesetz betreffend die Gesellschaften mit beschränkter Haftung: GmbHG* (C.H. Beck 2022)
Koch, Jens, *Aktiengesetz* (16th ed., C.H. Beck 2022)
Kraakman, Reinier, John Amour, Paul Davies, Luca Enriques, Henry Hansmann, Gerad Hertig, Klaus Hopt, Hideki Kanda, Mariana Pargendler, Wolf-Georg Ringe & Edward Rock, *The Anatomy of Corporate Law: A Comparative and Functional Approach* (Oxford University Press 2017)
Krarup, Mathias Dahlerup, *Interessekonflikter i små og mellemstore selskaber* (Djøf Forlag 2019)
Kremer, Thomas, Gregor Bachmann, Marcus Lutter & Axel von Werder eds, *Deutscher Corporate Governance Kodex* (8th ed., C.H. Beck 2021)

Kuehn, Douglas, *Takeovers and the Theory of the Firm* (Palgrave Macmillan 1975)
Kuhn, Thomas, *The Structure of Scientific Revolution* (University of Chicago Press 1970)
Lafarre, Anne, *The AGM in Europe: Theory and Practice of Shareholder Behaviour* (Emerald Publishing 2017)
Lambert, Thomas, *How to Regulate. A Guide for Policymakers* (Cambridge University Press 2017)
Lawrence, Paul & Jay Lorsch, *Organization and Environment: Managing Differentiation and Integration* (Harvard Business Books 1967)
Lee, Thomas Alexander ed., *The Evolution of Audit Thought and Practice* (Routledge Library Editions 1989)
Lee, Thomas Alexander, *Corporate Audit Theory* (Chapman & Hall 1993)
Leifer, Christoph, *Das europäische Umweltmanagementsystem EMAS als Element gesellschaftlicher Selbstregulierung* (Mohr Siebeck 2007)
Lekvall, Per ed., *The Nordic Corporate Governance Model* (SNS Förlag 2014)
Lessambo, Felix I., *Auditing, Assurance Services, and Forensics: A Comprehensive Approach* (Springer International Publishing 2018)
Leuschner, Lars, *Das Konzernrecht des Vereins* (Mohr Siebeck 2011)
Lowenstein, Louis & Susan Rose-Ackerman eds, *Knights, Raiders and Targets* (Oxford University Press 1988)
Lutter, Marcus, Walter Bayer & Jessica Schmidt, *Europäisches Unternehmens- und Kapitalmarktrecht* (6th ed., De Gruyter 2018)
Lynch, Harry, *Financial Performance of Conglomerates* (Division of Research, Graduate School of Business Administration, Harvard University 1971)
Macey, Jonathan R., *Corporate Governance: Promises Kept, Promises Broken* (Princeton University Press 2008)
Marquis, Christopher, *Better Business: How the B Corp Movement Is Remaking Capitalism* (Yale University Press 2020)
Markham, Jesse, *Conglomerate Enterprise and Public Policy* (Harvard University 1973)
Marris, Robin, *The Economic Theory of Managerial Capitalism* (Palgrave Macmillan 1964)
Mayer, Colin, *Prosperity: Better Business Makes the Greater Good* (Oxford University Press 2018)
McCahery, Joseph A. & Erik P.M. Vermeulen, *Corporate Governance of Non-Listed Companies* (Oxford University Press 2008)
Mitchell, Lawrence E., *Corporate Irresponsibility: America's Newest Export* (Yale University Press 2001)
Mitchell, Lawrence E, *Progressive Corporate Law* (Routledge 2019)
Moore, Marc, *Corporate Governance in the Shadow of the State* (Cambridge University Press 2013)
Moore, Marc & Martin Petrin, *Corporate Governance: Law, Regulation and Theory* (Bloomsbury Publishing 2017)
Moore, Wilbert, *The Conduct of the Corporation* (Random House 1962)
Mähönen, Jukka & Seppo Villa, *Aktiebolag I: Allmänna läror* (Alma Talent 2016)

Mähönen, Jukka, *Tulo ja pääoma: kirjanpidon merkitys osakeyhtiön säätelyssä [Income and Capital: The Role of Accounting in Corporate Regulation]* (Edita 2001)
Møller, Michael & Niels Christian Nielsen, *Fakta og fordomme om finanssektoren* (Samfunds Litteratur 2021)
Narayanan, Arvand, Joseph Bonneau, Edward Felten, Andrew Miller & Steven Goldfeder, *Bitcoin and Cryptocurrency Technologies: A Comprehensive Introduction* (Princeton University Press 2016)
Nelen, Samuel B. Garcia, *De beursvennootschap, corporate governance en strategie* (Wolters Kluwer 2020)
Newbould, Gerald, *Management and Merger Activity* (Guthstead 1970)
Nordberg, Donald, *Corporate Governance: Principle and Issues* (SAGE 2011)
Osterwalder, Alexander & Yves Pigneur, *Business Model Generation* (Wiley 2010)
Parker, Christine, *The Open Corporation* (Cambridge University Press 2000)
Parkinson, Cyril Northcote, *Parkinson's Law* (Houghton Mifflin; Sentry Edition, 1957)
Parkinson, John Edward, *Corporate Power and Responsibility: Issues in the Theory of Company Law* (Clarendon Press 1993)
Pfeffer, Jeffry & Gerald Salancik, *The External Control of Organisations: A Resource Dependence Perspective* (Stanford University Press 1978)
Pinto, Arthur R. & Douglas M. Branson, *Understanding Corporate Law* (5th ed., LexisNexis 2018)
Pistor, Katharina, *The Code of Capital: How the Law Creates Wealth and Inequality* (Princeton University Press 2019)
Posner, Richard, *Economic Analysis of Law* (9th ed., Aspen Law & Business 2014)
Pratt, John W. & Richard Zeckhauser eds, *Principals and Agents: The Structure of Business* (Harvard Business School Press 1985)
Ritzer, George & Paul Dean, *Globalization: A Basic Text* (John Wiley & Sons 2015)
Rodin, Judith & Margot Brandenburg, *The Power of Impact Investing: Putting Markets to Work for Profit and Global Good* (Wharton School Press 2014)
Roe, Mark J., *Missing the Target: Why Stock-Market Short-Termism Is Not the Problem* (Oxford University Press 2022)
Röhl, Hans Christian, *Akkreditierung und Zertifizierung im Produktsicherheitsrecht* (Springer 2000)
Sandström, Torsten, *Svensk aktiebolagsrätt* (7th ed., Wolters Kluwer 2020)
Sarmento, Elsa De Morais & R. Paul Herman eds, *Global Handbook of Impact Investing: Solving Global Problems Via Smarter Capital Markets Towards a More Sustainable Society* (Wiley 2021)
Schaumburg-Müller, Peer & Erik Werlauff, *Selskabsloven med kommentarer* 792 (DJØF Forlag 2020)
Schouten, Michael C., *The Decoupling of Voting and Economic Ownership* (Wolters Kluwer 2012)
Seligman, Joel, *The Transformation of Wall Street: A History of the Securities and Exchange Commission and Modern Corporate Finance* (Mifflin 1982)
Shiller, Robert James, *Irrational Exuberance* (Princeton University Press 2005)

Singh, Ajit, *Takeovers, Their Relevance to the Stock Market and Their Theory of the Firm* (Cambridge University Press 1971)
Sirower, Mark, *The Synergy Trap* (Free Press 2007)
Sjåfjell, Beate & Christopher M. Bruner, *The Cambridge Handbook of Corporate Law, Corporate Governance and Sustainability* (Cambridge University Press 2019)
Smith, Adam, *An Inquiry into the Nature and Causes of the Wealth of Nations* (Liberty Classics 1776)
Sofsrud, Thorbjørn, *Bestyrelsens beslutning og ansvar* (DJØF Forlag 1999).
Spindler, Gerard, *Münchener Kommentar zum Aktiengesetz*, AktG § 76 Rn 67–70 (5th ed. C.H. Beck 2019)
Staubus, George J., *A Theory of Accounting to Investors*, 3 (University of California Press 1961)
Staubus, George J., *The Decision Usefulness Theory of Accounting: A Limited History* (1st ed., Routledge 1999)
Steinberg, Marc I., *The Federalization of Corporate Governance* (Oxford University Press 2018)
Stimson, William A., *The Role of Sarbanes-Oxley and ISO 9001 in Corporate Management* (McFarland 2011)
Strand, Therese, *The Owners and the Power: Insights from Annual General Meetings*, PhD series No. 25.2012 (2012)
Stout, Lynn, *The Shareholder Value Myth: How Putting Shareholders First Harms Investors, Corporations, and the Public* (Berrett-Koehler 2012)
Szekely, Francisco & Zahir Dossa, *Beyond the Triple Bottom Line: Eight Steps Toward a Sustainable Business Model* (MIT Press 2017)
Taxell, Lars-Erik, *Aktiebolagets organisation* (Åbo Akademi 1983)
Treiblmaier, Horst & Roman Beck (eds), *Business Transformation Through Blockchain* (vol. 2, Springer 2019)
van der Zee, Eva, *Sustainability Labels in the Shadow of the Law* (Springer 2022)
Ventoruzzo, Marco, Pierre-Henri Conac, Gen Gotō, Sebastian Mock, Mario Notari & Arad Resiberg, *Comparative Corporate Law* (West Academic 2015)
Verde, Antimo, *Is Globalisation Doomed?* (Palgrave Macmillan 2017)
Villiers, Charlotte, *European Company Law: Towards Democracy?* (Ashgate/Dartmouth 1998)
Vogel, David, *The Market for Virtue: The Potential and Limits of Corporate Social Responsibility* (Brookings 2006)
Watts, Ross L. & Jerold L. Zimmerman, *Positive Accounting Theory* (Prentice Hall 1986)
Wells, Harwell ed., *Research Handbook on the History of Corporate and Company Law* (Edward Elgar 2018)
Werlauff, Erik, *Selskabsret* (11th ed., Karnov Group Denmark 2019)
Wicke, Hartmut, *Gesetz betreffend die Gesellschaften mit beschränkter Haftung (GmbHG)*, Anh. § 34: Austritt und Ausschließung eines Gesellschafters (C.H. Beck, 4. Auflage 2020)
Williamson, Oliver, *The Economics of Discretionary Behaviour: Managerial Objectives in a Theory of the Firm* (Prentice-Hall 1964)

Westaway, Kyle, *Profit & Purpose: How Social Innovation Is Transforming Business for Good* (John Wiley & Sons 2014)

Yeoh, Peter, *Environmental, Social and Governance (ESG) Laws, Regulations and Practices in the Digital Era* (Kluwer Law International 2022)

Contributions to Edited Volumes

Airaksinen, Manne, *Conflicts Between Shareholders and How to Solve Them in the Legislation*, in *Shareholder Conflicts* 249 (Paul Krüger Andersen, Nis Jul Clausen & Rolf Skog eds, Thomson Reuters, 2006)

Almlöf, Hanna, *Insynsrätt i ägarledda aktiebolag*, in *Festskrift Rolf Dotevall* (Marie Karlsson-Tuula, Annina H. Persson & Patrick Lindskoug eds, Juristförlaget i Lund 2020)

Andersson, Jan, *Minority Shareholder Protection in SMEs: A Question of Information Ex Post and Bargaining Power Ex Ante?*, in *Company Law and SMEs* (Mette Neville & Karsten Engsig Sørensen eds, Thomson Reuters 2010)

Andhov, Alexandra & Lela Melon, *Policy Coherence for Corporate Sustainability in the EU: Can We Achieve Sustainable Corporate Governance Without Sustainable Finance?*, in *Money Law, Capital, and the Changing Identity of the European Union* (Gabriella Gimigliano & Valentino Cattelan eds, Hart Publishing 2022)

Armour, John, Henry Hansmann & Reinier H. Kraakman, *Agency Problems and Legal Strategies*, in *The Anatomy of Corporate Law: A Comparative and Functional Approach* (Kraakman, Reinier, John Armour, Paul Davies, Luca Enriques, Henry B. Hansmann, Gérard Hertig & Klaus J. Hopt eds, Oxford University Press 2017)

Armour, John, Henry Hansmann & Reinier Kraakman, *What Is Corporate Law?*, in *The Anatomy of Corporate Law: A Comparative and Functional Approach* (Kraakman, Reinier, John Armour, Paul Davies, Luca Enriques, Henry B. Hansmann, Gérard Hertig & Klaus J. Hopt eds, Oxford University Press 2017)

Arnold, Mark, *General Duties of Directors*, in *Company Directors: Duties, Liabilities and Remedies* (Simon Mortimore QC, ed., 2nd ed., Oxford University Press 2013)

Arnold, Mark & Marcus Haywood, *Duty to Promote the Success of the Company*, in *Company Directors: Duties, Liabilities and Remedies* (Simon Mortimore QC, ed., 2nd ed., Oxford University Press 2013)

Arvidsson, Niklas & Per Samuelsson, *Ett och annat om vinstsyftet, generalklausulen, företagsvärdering och likhetsprincipen*, in *Festschrift in Honour of Rolf Skog* (Ronald J. Gilson, Mats Isaksson, Erik Lidman Johan Munck & Erik Sjöman eds, Norstedts Juridik 2021)

Bachmann, Gregor, *Disclosure of Corporate Governance by Codes*, in *Transparency of Stock Corporations in Europe* (Vassilios Tountopoulos & Rüdiger Veil eds, Hart Publishing 2019)

Bachnik, Katarzyna & Justyna Szumniak-Samolej, *Impact: Meaning, Scope, and Measurement Methods*, in *Corporate Social Responsibility and Sustainability* (Katarzyna Bachnik, Magdalena Kaźmierczak, Magdalena Rojek-Nowosielska, Magdalena Stefańska & Justyna Szumniak-Samolej eds, Routledge 2022)

Barotini, Roberto, Stefano Bozzi, Guido Ferranini & Maria-Cristina Ungureanu, *Directors' Remuneration Before and After the Crisis: Measuring the Impact of Reforms in Europe* in *Boards and Shareholders in European Listen Companies* (Massimo Belcredi & Guido Ferranini eds, Cambridge University Press 2013)

Bartley, Tim, *Certification as a Mode of Social Regulation,* in *Handbook on the Politics of Regulation* (David Levi-Faur ed., Edward Elgar Publishing 2011)

Belcredi, Massimo & Guido Ferranini, *Corporate Boards, Incentive Pay and Shareholder Activism in Europe: Main Issues and Policy Perspectives* in *Boards and Shareholders in European Listed Companies* (Massimo Belcredi & Guido Ferranini eds, Cambridge University Press 2013)

Bianchi, Marcello & Mateja Miliê, *Article 9C: Transparency and Approval of Related Party Transactions* in *The Shareholder Rights Directive II: A Commentary* (Hanne Søndergaard Birkmose & Konstantinos Sergakis eds, Edward Elgar Publishing 2021)

Bolton, Patrick, Marco Becht & Alisa Roell, *Corporate Governance and Control,* in *Handbook of the Economics of Finance* (George M. Constantinides, Milton Harris & René Stulz eds, Elsevier 2003)

Bril, Herman, Georg Kell & Andreas Rasche, *Sustainable Investing: A Path to a New Horizon* in *Sustainable Investing: A Path to a New Horizon* (Herman Bril, Georg Kell & Andreas Rasche eds, Routledge 2021)

Bråthen, Tore, *The Myth of Shareholder Ownership – The Norwegian Legal Perspective* in *Festschrift in Honour of Rolf Skog* (Ronald J. Gilson, Mats Isaksson, Erik Lidman Johan Munck & Erik Sjöman eds, Norstedts Juridik 2021)

Busse von Colbe, Walther & Rolf U. Fülbier, *Accounting and the Business Economics Tradition in Germany,* in *Accounting and Business Economics: Insights From National Traditions* (Yuri Biondi & Stefano Zambon, eds, Routledge 2013)

Båvestam, Urban, *Några frågor kring den särskilda insynsrätten enligt 7 kap. 36 § aktiebolagslagen,* in *Vänbok till Anders Lagerstedt – Studier i associationsrätt och förmögenhetsrätt* (Jan Andersson, Karin Blad, Clara Ehn & Jessica Östberg eds, Jure 2020)

Capdeville, Jérôme Lasserre, *Financement alternatif relevant des principes de l'économie sociale et solidaire,* in *Droit de la Finance Alternative* 33 (Jean-Marc Moulin ed., Primento Digital Publishing 2017)

Cheffins, Brian R., *The History of Corporate Governance,* in *The Oxford Handbook of Corporate Governance* (Douglas M. Wright, Donald S. Siegel, Kevin Keasey & Igor Filatotchev eds, Oxford University Press 2013)

Chiu, Iris H-Y & Dionysia Katelouzou, *From Shareholder Stewardship to Shareholder Duties: Is the Time Ripe?* in *Shareholder's Duties* (Hanne Søndergard Birkmose ed., Kluwer Law International, 2016)

Clark, Robert Charles, *Agency Costs Versus Fiduciary Duties,* in *Principals and Agents: The Structure of Business* (John W. Pratt & Richard Zeckhauser eds, Harvard Business School Press 1991)

Conac, Pierre-Henri, *Public Versus Private Enforcement in Corporate Governance*, in *Comparative Corporate Governance* (Afra Afsharipour & Martin Gelter eds, Edward Elgar 2021)

Conac, Pierre-Henri, *France*, in *Comparative Corporate Governance*, 463 (Andreas M. Fleckner & Klaus Hopt eds, Cambridge University Press 2013)

Cosh, Andrew, Alan Hughes & Ajit Singh, *The Causes and Effects of Takeovers in the United Kingdom: An Empirical Investigation for the Late 1960s at the Microeconomic Level*, in *The Determinants and Effects of Mergers* (Dennis C. Mueller ed., Oelgeschlager, Gunn & Hain 1980)

Crouhy, Michel, *Risk Management Failures During the Financial Crisis*, in *Lessons from the Financial Crisis: Causes, Consequences, and Our Economic Future* (Robert W. Kolb ed., John Wiley 2010)

Edmans, Alex, Xavier Gabaix & David Jenter, *Executive Compensation: A Survey of Theory and Evidence*, in *The Handbook of the Economics of Corporate Governance*, 390 (Benjamin E. Hermalin & Michael S. Weisbach eds, Elsevier 2017)

Enriques, Luca, Henry Hansmann, Reinier Kraakman & Mariana Parglender, *The Basic Governance Structure: Minority Shareholders and Non-shareholder Constituencies*, in *The Anatomy of Corporate Law. A Comparative and Functional Approach* (Reinier Kraakmann, John Amour, Paul Davies, Luca Enriques, Henry Hansmann, Gerad Hertig, Klaus Hopt, Hideki Kanda, Mariana Pargendler, Wolf-Georg Ringe & Edward Rock eds, Oxford University Press 2017)

Esty, Dan & Todd Cort, *The Data Challenges That Remain*, in *Sustainable Investing* (Cary Kronsinsky & Sophie Purdom eds, Routledge 2017)

Fairfax, Lisa, *The Elusive Quest for Director Independence*, in *Research Handbook on the Economics of Corporate Law* (Claire Hill & Brett McDonnell eds, Edward Elgar 2012)

Ferrarini, Guido & Maria Cristina Ungureanu, *Executive Remuneration*, in *The Oxford Handbook of Corporate Law and Governance* (Jeffrey N. Gordon & Wolf-Georg Ringe eds, Oxford University Press 2018)

Ferrarini, Guido & Shanshan Zhu, *Is There a Role for Benefit Corporations in the New Sustainable Governance Framework?*, in *Festschrift in Honour of Rolf Skog* (Ronald J. Gilson, Mats Isaksson, Erik Lidman, Johan Munck & Erik Sjöman eds, Norstedts Juridik 2021)

Figueiredo Dias, Gabriela, *Sustainability and Sustainable Finance: A Regulator's Perspective and Beyond*, in *The Palgrave Handbook of ESG and Corporate Governance* 217 (Paulo Câmara & Filipe Morais eds, Palgrave Macmillan 2022)

Fisch, Jill & Steven Davidoff Solomon, *The 'Value' of a Public Benefit Corporation*, in *Research Handbook on Corporate Purpose and Personhood* (Elizabeth Pollman & Robert B. Thompson eds, 2021)

G. Eccles, Robert & Birgit Spiesshofer, *Integrated Reporting for a Re-imagined Capitalism*, in *Re-imagining Capitalism* 207 (Dominic Barton, Dezsö Horváth & Matthias Kipping eds, Oxford University Press 2016)

Gabrielsson, Jonas, Morten Huse & Carl Åberg, *Corporate Governance in Small and Medium Sized Enterprises*, in *Advances in Corporate Governance: Comparative*

Perspectives, (Helmut K. Anheier & Theodor Baums eds, Oxford University Press 2020)

Gallo, Miguel Angel & Denise Kenyon-Rouvinez, *The Importance of Family and Business Governance*, in *Family Business: Key Issues* (Denise Kenyon-Rouvinez & John L. Ward eds, Palgrave Macmillan 2005)

García-Ramos, Rebeca & Belén Díaz Díaz, *Chief Executive Officer (CEO Duality)*, in *Encyclopedia of Sustainable Management* (Samuel Idowu, René Schmidpeter, Nicholas Capaldi, Liangrong Zu, Mara Del Baldo & Rute Abreu eds, Springer 2020)

Gerner-Beuerle, Carsten & Edmund-Philipp Schuster, *Mapping Directors' Duties: Strategies and Trends in the EU*, in *Boards of Directors in European Companies – Reshaping and Harmonising Their Organisation and Duties* (Hanne Birkmose, Mette Neville & Karsten Engsig Sørensen eds, Kluwer Law International 2013)

Gilson, Ronald J., *From Corporate Law to Corporate Governance*, in *The Oxford Handbook of Corporate Law and Governance* (Jeffrey N. Gordon & Wolf-Georg Ringe eds, Oxford University Press 2018)

Goel, Sanjay, Iiro Jussila & Tuuli Ikäheimonen, *Governance in Family Firms: A Review and Research Agenda*, in *The Sage Handbook of Family Business* (Leif Melin, Mattias Nordqvist & Pramodita Sharma eds, SAGE Publications 2014)

Gomstian, Suren, *Transparency of Asset Managers*, in *The Shareholder Rights Directive II: A Commentary* (Hanne S. Birkmose & Konstantinos Sergakis eds, Edward Elgar 2021)

Gordon, Jeffrey N. *Convergence and Persistence in Corporate Law and Governance*, in *The Oxford Handbook of Corporate Law and Governance* (Jeffrey N. Gordon & Wolf-Georg Ringe eds, Oxford University Press 2018)

Goshen, Zohar & Assaf Hamdani, *Corporate Control and the Regulation of Controlling Shareholders*, in *The Law and Finance of Related Party Transactions* 28 (Luca Enriques & Tobias Tröger eds, Cambridge University Press 2019)

Gray, Colin, *Growth Orientation and the Small Firm*, in *Small Enterprise Development Policy and Practice in Action* (Kevin Caley, Elizabeth Chell, Francis Chittenden & Colin Mason eds, Sage Publications 1992)

Grossi, Poracchia & Raynouard, *France*, in *Company Laws of the EU* (Andrea Vicari & Alexander Schall eds C.H. Beck 2020)

Guéneau, Stéphane, *Certification as a New Private Global Forest Governance System: The Regulatory Potential of the Forest Stewardship Council*, in *Non-State Actors as Standard-Setters* (Anne Peters, Lucy Koechlin, Till Förster & Gretta Fenner Zinkernagel eds, Cambridge University Press 2009)

Hall, Peter A. & David Soskice, *An Introduction to Varieties of Capitalism*, in *Varieties to Capitalism: The Institutional Foundations of Comparative Advantage* (Peter A. Hall & David Soskice eds, Oxford University Press 2001)

Hansen, Jesper Lau, *Director Liability in Banks: Business as Usual?*, in *Festskrift till Jan Kleineman* (Stefan Lindskog, André Andersson, Axel Calissendorff & Jessika van der Sluijs eds, Jure Förlag AB 2021)

Hansen, Jesper Lau, *The Nordic Corporate Governance Model – A European Model?*, in *Perspectives in Company Law and Financial Regulation: Essays in Honour of Eddy Wymeersch* (Michel Tison, Hans de Wulf, Christoph van der Elst & Reinhard Steennot eds, Cambridge University Press 2009)

Hansen, Jesper Lau & Carsten Lønfeldt, *Corporate Governance in Denmark*, Annex A, in *The Nordic Corporate Governance Model* (Per Lekvall ed., SNS Förlag 2014).

Herman, Edward & Louis Lowenstein, *The Efficiency Effects of Hostile Takeovers*, in *Knights, Raiders, and Targets: The Impact of the Hostile Takeover* (John Coffee, Louis Lowenstein & Susan Rose-Ackerman eds, Oxford University Press 1988)

Hommelhoff, Peter, *Corporate Governance: Directors' Duties, Financial Reporting and Liability – Remarks from a German Perspective*, in *Perspectives in Company Law and Financial Regulation* (Michel Tison, Hans de Wulf, Christoph Van der Elst & Reinhard Steennot eds, Cambridge University Press 2009)

Hopt, Klaus J., *Groups of Companies: A Comparative Study of the Economics, Law, and Regulation of Corporate Groups*, in *The Oxford Handbook of Corporate Law and Governance* (Jeffrey N. Gordon & Wolf-Georg Ringe eds, Oxford University Press 2018)

Hopt, Klaus J., *Comparative Corporate Governance: The State of the Art and International Regulation*, in *Comparative Corporate Governance. A Functional and International Analysis* (Andreas M. Fleckner & Klaus J. Hopt eds, Cambridge University Press 2013)

Hughes, Alan, *Mergers and Economic Performance in the UK: A Survey of the Empirical Evidence 1950–1990*, in *European Mergers and Merger Policy* (Matthew Bishop & John Kay eds, Oxford University Press 1993)

Humphrey, Jacquelyn, *Socially Responsible Screening in Mutual Funds*, in *The Routledge Handbook of Responsible Investment* (Tessa Hebb, James Hawley, Andreas Hoepner, Agnes Neher & David Wood eds, Routledge 2015)

Jensen, Michael C., *The Takeover Controversy: Analysis and Evidence*, in *Knights, Raiders, and Targets: The Impact of the Hostile Takeover* (John Coffee, Louis Lowenstein & Susan Rose-Ackerman eds, Oxford University Press 1988)

Johnston, Andrew, *Market-Led Sustainability Through Information Disclosure: The UK Approach*, in *Cambridge Handbook of Corporate Law, Corporate Governance and Sustainability* (Sjåfjell Beate & Christopher M. Bruner eds, Cambridge University Press 2019)

Johnston, Andrew & Beate Sjåfjell, *The EU's Approach to Environmentally Sustainable Business: Can Disclosure Overcome the Failings of Shareholder Primacy?*, in *Research Handbook on EU Environmental Law* (Marjan Peeters & Mariolina Eliantonio eds, Edward Elgar 2020)

Katelouzou, Dionysia, *Shareholder Stewardship: A Case of (Re)Embedding the Institutional Investors and the Corporation?*, in *Cambridge Handbook of Corporate Law, Corporate Governance and Sustainability* (Beate Sjåfjell & Christopher M. Bruner eds, Cambridge University Press 2019)

Keay, Andrew, *An Analytical Study of Board Accountability in Transnational Codes of Corporate Governance*, in *Corporate Governance Codes for the 21st Century.*

International Perspectives and Critical Analyses (Jean du Plessis & Chee Keong Low eds, Springer 2017)

Lee, Thomas Alexander, *Financial Accounting Theory*, in *The Routledge Companion to Accounting History* (John Richard Edwards & Stephen P. Walker eds, 2nd ed., Routledge 2020)

Lekvall, Per, *On Company Purpose, Directors' Duties and Corporate Sustainability*, in *Festschrift in Honour of Rolf Skog* (Ronald J. Gilson, Mats Isaksson, Erik Lidman, Johan Munck & Erik Sjöman eds, Norstedts Juridik 2021)

Lidman, Erik, *The Purpose of the Corporations a Contractarian Perspective*, in *Festschrift in Honour of Rolf Skog* (Ronald J. Gilson, Mats Isaksson, Erik Lidman, Johan Munck & Erik Sjöman eds, Norstedts Juridik 2021)

Liao, Carol, *Regulation by Litigation on the Path to Sustainable Corporations*, in *Innovating Business for Sustainability: Regulatory Approaches in the Anthropocene* (Beate Sjåfjell, Carol Liao & Aikaterini Argyrou eds, Edward Elgar Publishing 2022)

Liu Junhai, *Globalisation of Corporate Governance Depends on Both Soft Law and Hard Law*, in *Corporate Governance Codes for the 21st Century. International Perspectives and Critical Analyses* (Jean du Plessis & Chee Keong Low eds, Springer 2017)

Mähönen, Jukka, *Kestävyysraportointi*, in *Yritysvastuu & oikeus* (Anne Vanhala & Michael Ristaniemi eds, Kauppakamari 2022)

Mähönen, Jukka & Gurún Johnsen, *Law, Culture and Sustainability: Corporate Governance in the Nordic Countries*, in *The Cambridge Handbook of Corporate Law, Corporate Governance and Sustainability* (Beate Sjåfjell & Christopher M. Bruner eds, Cambridge University Press 2019)

Malberti, Corrado, *The Proposed Directive on the Encouragement of Long-Term Shareholder Engagement*, in *European Listed Companies: A Critical Appraisal* (P.M. Vasudev & Susan Watson eds, Edward Elgar 2017)

Maltby, Josephine & Roy Chandler, *Auditing*, in *The Routledge Companion to Accounting History* (John Richard Edwards & Stephen P. Walker eds, Routledge 2020)

Mares, Radu, *Business and Human Rights after Ruggie: Foundations, the Art of Simplification and the Imperative of Cumulative Progress*, in *The UN Guiding Principles on Business and Human Rights – Foundations and Implementation* (Radu Mares ed., Martinus Nijhoff Publishers 2012)

McCahery, Joseph A., Erik P.M. Vermeulen, Masato Hisatake & Jun Saito, *The New Company Law – What Matters in an Innovative Economy?*, in *Private Company Law Reform* (Joseph A. McCahery, Levinus Timmermann & Erik P.M. Vermeulen eds, T.M.C. Asser Press 2010)

McNulty, Terry, *Process Matters: Understanding Board Behavior and Effectiveness*, in *The Oxford Handbook of Corporate Governance* (Douglas Michael Wright, Donald S. Siegel, Kevin Keasey & Igor Filatotchev eds, Oxford University Press 2013)

Micheler, Eva, *Intermediated Securities from the Perspective of Investors: Problems, Quick Fixes and Long-Term Solutions*, in *Intermediation and Beyond* (Louise Gullifer & Jennifer Payne eds, Hart Publishing 2019)

Mock, Sebastian, *Kommentierung der §§ 142-149*, in *Grosskommentar Aktienrecht* (5th ed., Gerald Spindler & Eberhard Stilz eds, C.H. Beck 2022)

Möslein, Florian, *Robots in the Boardroom: Artificial Intelligence and Corporate Law*, in *Research Handbook on the Law of Artificial Intelligence* (Woodrow Barfield & Ugo Pagallo eds, Edward Elgar 2018)

Möslein, Florian, *Zertifizierung nachhaltiger Kapitalgesellschaften: Regimevergleich und flankierende Maßnahmen*, in *Zertifizierung nachhaltiger Kapitalgesellschaften* (Martin Burgi & Florian Möslein eds, Mohr Siebeck 2021)

Möslein, Florian, *Genuine Self-Regulation in Germany: Drawing the Line*, in *Self-Regulation in Private Law in Japan and Germany* (Harald Baum, Moritz Bälz & Marc Dernauer eds, Carl Heymanns Verlag 2018)

Möslein, Florian, *Certifying Good Companies – Regulatory Schemes for Corporate Sustainability in a Comparative Perspective*, in *The Cambridge Handbook of Corporate Law, Corporate Governance and Sustainability* (Christopher Bruner & Beate Sjåfjell eds, Cambridge University Press 2020)

Möslein, Florian, *Privatrechtsfragen eines hybriden Zertifizierungsregimes*, in *Zertifizierung nachhaltiger Kapitalgesellschaften* (Martin Burgi & Florian Möslein eds, Mohr Siebeck 2021)

Murphy, Kevin, *Executive Compensation: Where We Are, and How We Got There*, in *Handbook of Economics of Finance* (George M. Constantinides, Milton Harris & Rene M. Stulz eds, Elsevier 2013)

Napier, Christopher J., *The History of Financial Reporting in the UK*, in *A Global History of Accounting, Financial Reporting and Public Policy* (Gary Previts, Peter Walton & Peter Wolnizer eds, Emerald 2010)

Neville, Mette, *Conflicts in Small and Medium-Sized Enterprises*, in *Shareholder Conflicts* (Paul Krüger Andersen, Nis Jul Clausen & Rolf Skog eds, Thomson Reuters 2006)

Neville, Mette, *Corporate Governance and Strategic Change in SMEs in a Digital Age – The Board as a Digital Catalyst?*, in *Festschrift in Honour of Rolf Skog* (Ronald J. Gilson, Mats Isaksson, Erik Lidman Johan Munck & Erik Sjöman eds, Norsteds Juridik 2021)

Mette Neville, *Corporate Governance i mindre og mellemstore virksomheder*, in *Corporate Governance i Danmark: Om god selskabsledelse i et dansk og internationalt perspektiv* (Jens Valdemar Krenchel & Steen Thomsen eds, Dansk Industri 2004)

Neville, Mette, *A Statutory Buy-Out Right in SMEs – An Important Corporate Governance Mechanism and Minority Protection?*, in *Company Law and SMEs* (Karsten Engsig Sørensen & Mette Neville eds, Thomson Reuters 2010)

Neville, Mette, *Konfliktløsning*, in *Den nye selskabslov* (Mette Neville & Karsten Engsig Sørensen eds, Jurist- og Økonomforbundet 2009)

Neville, Mette, *The Many Roles of Boards in SMEs*, in *Board of Directors in European Companies: Reshaping and Harmonising Their Organisations and Duties* (Hanne S. Birkmose, Karsten Engsig Sørensen & Mette Neville eds, Kluwer Law International 2013)

Neville, Mette, *Fremtidens SMV-bestyrelse - værdiskabelse i en turbulent verden* in *Festskrift for Rolf Doteval* (Maria Karlsson-Tuula, Annika H. Persson, & Patrik Lindskoug eds, Juristförlaget i Lund 2020)

Nitsche, Christin & Michael Schröder, *Are SRI Funds Conventional Funds in Disguise or Do They Live Up to Their Name?*, in *Research Handbook of Finance and Sustainability* (Sabri Boubaker, Douglas Cumming & Duc Khuong Nguyen eds, Edward Elgar 2018)

Östberg, Jessica, *Några tankar kring aktiebolagslagens vinstsyfte*, in *Vänbok till Anders Lagerstedt* (Jan Andersson et al. eds, Jure Förlag 2020)

Östberg, Jessica, *Något om skyldigheten att iaktta bolagets intresse vid insolvens*, in *Festskrift till Lars Pehrson* (Jan Kleineman, Jori Munukka & Jessika van der Sluijs eds, Jure Förlag 2016)

Osthoff, Peer, *What Matters to SRI Investors?*, in *The Routledge Handbook of Responsible Investment* (Tessa Hebb, James P. Hawley, Andreas G. F. Hoepner, Agnes L. Neher & David Wood eds, Routledge 2015)

Oxelheim, Lars, Clas Wihlborg & Jianhua Zhang, *How to Avoid Compensating the CEO for Luck: The Case of Macroeconomic Fluctuations*, in *Research Handbook on Executive Pay* (Randall Thomas & Jennifer Hill eds, Edward Elgar 2015)

Pacces, Alessio M., *Procedural and Substantive Review of Related Party Transactions*, in *The Law and Finance of Related Party Transactions* (Luca Enriques & Tobias H. Tröger eds, Cambridge University Press 2019)

Pietrancosta, Alain, *Enforcement of Corporate Governance Codes – A Legal Perspective*, in *Festschrift für Klaus J. Hopt zum 70. Geburtstag am 24. August 2010* (Stefan Grundmann, Brigitte Haar, Hanno Merkt, et al. eds, De Gryuyter 2010)

Poelzig & Bärnreuther, *Germany*, in *Company Laws of the EU* (Andrea Vicari & Alexander Schall eds, Beck/Hart 2020)

Pratt, John Winsor & Richard Jay Zeckhauser, *Principals and Agents: An Overview*, in *Principals and Agents: The Structure of Business* (John W. Pratt & Richard Jay Zeckhauser eds, Harvard Business School Press 1991)

Raiser, Thomas, *Führungsstruktur und Mitbestimmung in der Europäischen Aktiengesellschaft nach dem Verordnungsvorschlag der Kommission vom 25. August 1989*, in *Festschrift für Ernst Steindorff zum 70. Geburtstag am 13. März 1990* (Jürgen F. Baur, Klaus J. Hopt & K. Peter Mailänders eds, Walter de Gruyter 1989)

Ramsay, Ian & Mihika Upadhyaya, *The Failed Attempt to Enact Benefit Company Legislation in Australia and the Rise of B Corps*, in *The International Handbook of Social Enterprises Law* (Henry Peter, Carlos Vargas Vasserot & Jaime Alcalde Silva eds, Springer International Publishing AG 2022)

Redenius-Hövermann, Julia, *Behavioural Economics, Neoroeconomics, and Corporate Law*, in *Advances in Corporate Governance: Comparative Perspectives* (Helmut K. Anheier & Theodor Baums eds, Oxford University Press 2020)

Renneboog, Luc & Peter Szilagyi, *Shareholder Engagement at European General Meetings*, in *Board and Shareholders in European Listed Companies* (Massimo Belcredi & Guido Ferranini eds, Cambridge University Press 2013)

Renssen, Samantha, *Extra Ordinary Corporate Transactions: Liquidation and Winding Up*, in *Company Laws of the EU: A Handbook* (Andrea Vicari & Alexander Schall eds, C.H. Beck 2020)

Roe, Mark J. & Massimiliano Vatiero, *Corporate Governance and Its Political Economy*, in *The Oxford Handbook of Corporate Law and Governance* (Jeffrey N. Gordon & Wolf-Georg Ringe eds, Oxford University Press 2018)

Roll, Richard, *Empirical Evidence on Takeover Activity and Shareholder Wealth*, in *Knights, Raiders, and Targets: The Impact of the Hostile Takeover* (John Coffee, Louis Lowenstein & Susan Rose-Ackerman eds, Oxford University Press 1988)

Schall, Alexander, *Stock Corporations: Corporate Governance and Internal and External Control*, in *Company laws of the EU* (Andrea Vicari & Alexander Schall eds, C.H. Beck, Hart 2020)

Schebesta, Hanna, *Control in the Label: Self-Declared, Certified, Accredited?*, in *Certification – Trust, Accountability, Liability* 143 (Peter Rott ed., Springer 2019)

Sikka, Prem, *Corporate Governance and Family-Owned Companies*, in *Corporate Governance in Contention* (Ciaran Driver & Grahame Thompson eds, Oxford University Press 2018)

Siri, Michele & Shanshan Zhu, *Integrating Sustainability in EU Corporate Governance Codes*, in *Sustainable Finance in Europe* (Danny Busch, Guido Ferrarini & S. Grünewald eds, Palgrave Macmillan 2021)

Sjåfjell, Beate, *Sustainability and Law and Economics: An Interdisciplinary Redefinition of Agency Theory*, in *Interdisciplinary Research for Sustainable Business: Perspectives of Women Business Scholars* (Beate Sjåfjell, Roseanne Russell & Maja van der Velden eds, Springer forthcoming)

Sjåfjell, Beate, *When the Solution Becomes the Problem: The Triple Failure of Corporate Governance Codes*, in *Corporate Governance Codes for the 21st Century. International Perspectives and Critical Analyses* (Jean du Plessis & Chee Keong Low eds, Springer 2017)

Sjåfell, Beate, *Capitalism, the Sustainability Crisis, and the Limitations of Current Business Governance*, in *Company Law and Sustainability: Legal Barriers and Opportunities* (Beate Sjåfjell & Benjamin J. Richardson eds, Cambridge University Press 2015)

Sjåfell, Beate, *Redefining Agency Theory to Internalize Environmental Product Externalities: A Tentative Proposal Based on Life Cycle Thinking*, in *Preventing Environmental Damage from Products* (Eleonore Maitre-Ekern, Carl Dalhammar & Hans Christian Bugge eds, Cambridge University Press 2018)

Sjåfjell, Beate, Andrew Johnston, Linn Anker-Sørensen & David Millon, *Shareholder Primacy: The Main Barrier to Sustainable Companies*, in *Company Law and Sustainability: Legal Barriers and Opportunities* (Beate Sjåfjell & Benjamin J. Richardson eds, Cambridge University Press 2015)

Sjåfjell, Beate & Benjamin J. Richardson, *The Future of Company Law and Sustainability*, in *Company Law and Sustainability: Legal Barriers and Opportunities* (Beate Sjåfjell & Benjamin J. Richardson eds, Cambridge University Press 2015)

Sjåfjell, Beate & Georgina Tsagas, *Integrating Sustainable Value Creation in Corporate Governance: Company Law, Corporate Governance Codes and the Constitution of the Company*, in *Sustainable Value Creation in the European Union: Towards Pathways to a Sustainable Future Through Crises* (Beate Sjåfjell, Georgina Tsagas & Charlotte Villiers eds, Cambridge University Press 2022)

Skog, Rolf, *Talet om 'bolagets intresse' som något mer än aktieägarnas intresse – i vems intresse?*, in *Festskrift till Jan Kleineman* (Stefan Lindskog, André Andersson Axel Calissendorff & Jessika van der Sluijs eds, Jure Förlag 2021)

Sørensen, Karsten Engsig & Mette Neville, *Interessentskabslignende anpartsselskaber*, in *Selskabers organisation* (Paul Krüger Andersen ed., DJØF Forlag 1997)

Stattin, Daniel, *Aktieägares rätt till information*, in *Aktieägares rättigheter* (Carl Svernlöv ed., Stockholm Centre for Commercial Law, Iustus, 2009)

Stout, Lynn, *The Economic Nature of the Corporation*, in *The Oxford Handbook of Law and Economics. Volume II: Private and Commercial Law* (Francesco Parisi ed., Oxford University Press 2017)

Ungureanu, Cristina, *Engagement of Institutional Shareholders*, in *Governance of Financial Institutions* (Danny Busch, Guido Ferrarini & Gerard van Solinge eds, Oxford University Press 2019)

van Bekkum, Jaron, Steve Hijink, Michael C. Schouten & Jaap W. Winter, *Corporate Governance in the Netherlands*, in *Comparative Corporate Governance: A Functional and International Analysis* (Andreas M. Fleckner & Klaus Jürgen Hopt eds, Cambridge University Press 2013)

Van der Elst, Christoph, *Shareholder Engagement and Corporate Voting in Action: The Comparative Perspective*, in *Shareholder Engagement and Voting* (Harpreet Kaur, Chao Xi, Christoph Van der Elst & Anne Lafarre eds, Cambridge University Press 2022)

Van der Elst, Christoph & Anne Lafarre, *Article 9a and 9b: Say on Pay*, in *The Shareholder Rights Directive II: A Commentary* (Hanne S. Birkmose & Konstantinos Sergakis eds, Edward Elgar 2021)

Veldman, Jeroen, *Self-Regulation in International Corporate Governance Codes*, in *Corporate Governance Codes for the 21st Century. International Perspectives and Critical Analyses* (Jean du Plessis & Chee Keong Low eds, Springer 2017)

Vibe, Ulfbeck, Ole Hansen & Alexandra Andhov, *Contractual Enforcement of CSR Clauses and the Protection of Weak Parties in the Supply Chain*, in *Law and Responsible Supply Chain Management: Contract and Tort Interplay and Overlap* (Vibe Ulfbeck, Alexandra Andhov & Katerina Mitkidis eds, Routledge 2019)

Villiers, Charlotte, Beate Sjåfjell & Georgina Tsagas, *Pathways Towards Sustainable Value Creation in the EU*, in *Sustainable Value Creation in the EU: Towards Pathways to a Sustainable Future Through Crises* (Beate Sjåfjell, Georgina Tsagas & Charlotte Villiers eds, Cambridge University Press, 2022)

von Wangenheim, Georg, *Certification as a Solution to the Asymmetric Information Problem?*, in *Certification – Trust, Accountability, Liability* 143 (Peter Rott ed., Springer 2019)

Whiteman, Gail & Amanda Williams, *Systemic Planetary Risks: Implications for Organization Studies*, in *The Routledge Companion to Risk, Crisis and Emergency Management* (Robert P. Gephart Jr, C. Chet Miller & Karin Svedberg Helgesson eds, Routledge 2019)

Williams, Cynthia A., *Corporate Social Responsibility and Corporate Governance*, in *The Oxford Handbook of Corporate Law and Governance* (Jeffrey N. Gordon & Wolf-Georg Ringe eds, Oxford University Press 2018)

Willson, William, *Directors' Decision-Making and Delegation*, in *Company Directors* (Simon Mortimore ed., Oxford University Press 2017)

Winter, Jaap, *A Behavioral Perspective on Corporate Law and Corporate Governance*, in *The Oxford Handbook of Corporate Law and Governance* (Jeffry N. Gordon & Wolf-Georg Ringe eds, Oxford University Press 2018)

Wundenberg, Malte, *§ 34* in *Europäisches und Deutsches Kapitalmarktrecht* (Rüdiger Veil ed., 3rd ed. Mohr Siebeck 2010)

Wymeersch, Eddy, *European Corporate Governance Codes and Their Effectiveness*, in *Boards and Shareholders in European Listed Companies* (Massimo Belcredi & Giudo Ferrarini eds, Cambridge University Press 2013)

Reports, Etc.

Bennedsen, Morten & Kasper Meisner Nielsen, *Ejerledelse i Danmark – Rapport 1: Ejerledelse – baggrund og udbredelse* (Center for Ejerledede Virksomheder, Copenhagen Business School 2015) https://www.cbs.dk/files/cbs.dk/ejerledelse_i_danmark_rapport.pdf.

Blein, Yves & Daniel Fasquelle, *Rapport d'information sur la mise en application de la loi n 2014-856 du 31 juillet 2014 relative à l'économie sociale et solidaire* 9 (Assemblée nationale, 2016)

Clerc, Christophe, Fabrice Demarigny, Diego Valiante & Mirzha de Manuel Aramendía, *A Legal and Economic Assessment of European Takeover Regulation*, http://aei.pitt.edu/47685/1/Takeover_Bids_Directive_book_-_Final.pdf

Dao, Quoc-Hy, Pascal Peduzzi, Bruno Chatenoux, Andrea De Bono, Stefan Schwarzer & Damien Friot, *Environmental Limits and Swiss Footprints Based on Planetary Boundaries*, Swiss Federal Office for the Environment (FOEN) (2015)

Dinh Tami, Anna Husmann & Gaia Melloni, *The Role of Non-financial Performance Indicators and Integrated Reporting in Achieving Sustainable Value Creation* (European Parliament, 24 September 2021) https://www.europarl.europa.eu/RegData/etudes/ATAG/2021/662943/IPOL_ATA(2021)662943_EN.pdf

European Coalition for Corporate Justice (ECCJ), *Suing Goliath: An Analysis of Civil Cases Against EU Companies for Overseas Human Rights and Environmental Abuses* (28 September 2021), https://corporatejustice.org/wp-content/uploads/2021/09/Suing-Goliath-FINAL.pdf

Ferry, Korn, *Non-Executive Directors in Europe 2019*

Fici, Antonio, *A European Statute for Social and Solidarity-Based Enterprises – Study for the JURY Committee*, 17 (2017) available at http://www.europarl.europa.eu/RegData/etudes/STUD/2017/583123/IPOL_STU(2017)583123_EN.pdf

Freshfields Bruckhaus Deringer, *A Legal Framework for the Integration of Environmental, Social and Governance Issues into Institutional Investment* (Report for the UNEP Finance Initiative, 2005), https://www.unepfi.org/fileadmin/documents/freshfields_legal_resp_20051123.pdf

Gerner-Beuerle, Carsten, Philipp Paech & Edmund Schuster, *Study on Directors' Duties and Liability*, prepared for the European Commission DG Markt 194, https://papers.ssrn.com/sol3/papers.cfm?abstract_id = 3886382 (2013)

Heidrick & Struggles and the INSEAD Corporate Governance Centre, *Changing the Climate in the Boardroom* (December 2021)

Leach, Melissa, Kate Raworth & Johan Rockström, *Between Social and Planetary Boundaries: Navigating Pathways in the Safe and Just Space for Humanity*, World Social Science Report 2013 (OECD Publishing 2013)

Lucas, Paul L. & Harry C. Wilting, *Using Planetary Boundaries to Support National Implementation of Environment-Related Sustainable Development Goals*, PBL Netherlands Environmental Assessment Agency (2018)

Neville, Mette & André Falsig, *SMV-bestyrelsen i en digital tidsalder*, https://mgmt.au.dk/fileadmin/SMVbestyrelsenIenDigitalTidsalder_Rapport.pdf

Neville, Mette & André Falsig, *Krise som digital driver i SMV-bestyrelser* https://mgmt.au.dk/fileadmin/MGMT/Subsites/Centre/SMV/Reports/Digital-Katalysator-2021-Rapport-170x240mm_Indholdssider_08.pdf

Nykredit, *Ejerlederanalyse 2010 – Potentiale for vækst i ejerledede virksomheder* 26 (2010)

PricewaterhouseCoopers LLP, *Corporate Governance. Towards Best-Practice Corporate Reporting*, in *Corporate Governance for Main Market and AIM Companies* (London Stock Exchange ed., 2012), https://www.londonstockexchange.com (last accessed 15 April 2022)

Shearman & Sterling, *Corporate Governance & Executive Compensation Survey 2021*, 59–62 (Shearman & Sterling LLP 2021)

Touche Ross & Co, *The Effect of Mergers, Acquisitions and Tender Offers on American Business: A Touche Ross Survey of Corporate Directors' Opinions* (1981)

Turner Review, *A Regulatory Response to the Global Banking Crisis*, 46 (FSA, 2009). http://www.fsa.gov.uk/pubs/other/turner_review.pdf

UN General Assembly, *General Assembly Resolution 70/1. Transforming Our World: the 2030 Agenda for Sustainable Development*, A/RES/70/1 (25 September 2015), www.undocs.org/A/RES/70/1

UNEPFI, *Fiduciary Duty in the 21st Century* (2019), https://www.unepfi.org/wordpress/wp-content/uploads/2019/10/Fiduciary-duty-21st-century-final-report.pdf

Corporate Governance Codes and collections of best practices

CACG Principles: Commonwealth Association for Corporate Governance, Principles for Corporate Governance in the Commonwealth. Towards global competitiveness and economic accountability (1999), https://ecgi.org

Code Banken: NVB (Nederlandse Vereniging van Banken), Code Banken (2010), https://www.nvb.nl
Dutch CGC: monitoring Committee Corporate Governance Code, The Dutch Corporate Governance Code (2016), https://www.mccg.nl
French CGC: Afep and Medef, Corporate Governance Code of Listed Coporation – Consultation, https://consultation.codeafepmedef.fr
German CGC: Regierungskommission Deutscher Corporate Governance Kodex, German Corporate Governance Code (2019), https://www.dcgk.de
Italian CGC: Comitato Corporate Governance, Corporate Governance Code (2020), https://www.borsaitaliana.it/comitato-corporate-governance
ICGN Principles: International Corporate Governance Network, Global Governance Principles (2021), https://www.icgn.org
Middlenext CGC: Middlenext, Code de gouvernement d'entreprise, Cahier n° 14 (2021), https://www.middlenext.com
OECD Principles: OECD, G20/OECD Principles of Corporate Governance (Paris: OECD Publishing, 2015)
OECD Guidelines: OECD, Guidelines for Multinational Enterprises (2011), available at http://mneguidelines.oecd.org
UK CGC: FRC (Financial Reporting Council), UK Corporate Governance Code (2018), available at https://www.frc.org.uk
UN Guiding Principles: United Nations, Guiding Principles on Business and Human Rights (2011), available at https://www.ohchr.org

EUROPEAN COMPANY LAW SERIES

1. Steef M. Bartman (ed.), *European Company Law in Accelerated Progress*, 2006 (ISBN 978-90-411-2529-3)
2. Karen Vandekerckhove, *Piercing The Corporate Veil: A Transnational Approach*, 2007 (ISBN 978-90-411-2591-0)
3. Beate Sjåfjell, *Towards a Sustainable European Company Law: A Normative Analysis of the Objectives of EU Law, with the Takeover Directive as a Test Case*, 2009 (ISBN 978-90-411-2768-6)
4. Cornelis de Groot, *Corporate Governance as a Limited Legal Concept*, 2009 (ISBN 978-90-411-2873-7)
5. Adriaan Dorresteijn, Mieke Olaerts, Bastiaan Kemp, Thomas Biermeyer, Marcus Meyer-Erdmann & Tomas Arons, *European Corporate Law*, Fourth Edition, 2022 (ISBN 978-94-035-3223-3)
6. Gert-Jan Vossestein, *Modernization of European Company Law and Corporate Governance: Some Considerations on its Legal Limits*, 2010 (ISBN 978-90-411-2592-7)
7. Catalin Stefan Rusu, *European Merger Control: The Challenges Raised by Twenty Years of Enforcement Experience*, 2010 (ISBN 978-90-411-3259-8)
8. Sabrina Bruno & Eugenio Ruggiero, *Public Companies and the Role of Shareholders: National Models Towards Global Integration*, 2011 (ISBN 978-90-411-3423-3)
9. Hanne S. Birkmose, Mette Neville & Karsten Engsig Sørensen (eds), *The European Financial Market in Transition*, 2012 (ISBN 978-90-411-3360-1)
10. Hanne S. Birkmose, Mette Neville & Karsten Engsig Sørensen (eds), *Boards of Directors in European Companies: Reshaping and Harmonising Their Organisation and Duties*, 2013 (ISBN 978-90-411-4141-5)
11. Christoph Van der Elst, *Executive Directors' Remuneration in Comparative Corporate Perspective*, 2015 (ISBN 978-90-411-5607-5)
12. Hanne S. Birkmose, *Shareholders' Duties*, 2017 (ISBN 978-90-411-6670-8)
13. Alan S. Gutterman, *Sustainability and Corporate Governance: A Practice Guide to Implementing a Sustainability Governance System*, 2018 (ISBN 978-90-411-9975-1)
14. Jan De Bruyne, *Third-Party Certifiers*, 2019 (ISBN 978-94-035-1091-0)
15. Hanne S. Birkmose, Mette Neville & Karsten Engsig Sørensen (eds), *Abuse of Companies*, 2019 (ISBN 978-94-035-0892-4)
16. Ivan Romashchenko, *Related Party Transactions and Corporate Groups: When Eastern Europe Meets the West*, 2020 (ISBN 978-94-035-1701-8)

17. Patryk Filipiak & Anna Hrycaj, *European Insolvency Proceedings: Commentary on Regulation (EU) 2015/848 of the European Parliament and of the Council of 20 May 2015 on Insolvency Proceedings (Recast)*, 2021 (ISBN 978-94-035-3410-7)
18. Alexandros Seretakis, *Regulating Hedge Funds in the EU*, 2022 (ISBN 978-94-035-3512-8)
19. Hanne S. Birkmose, Mette Neville & Karsten Engsig Sørensen (eds), *Instruments of EU Corporate Governance: Effecting Changes in the Management of Companies in a Changing World*, 2023 (ISBN 978-94-035-4162-4)

www.ingramcontent.com/pod-product-compliance
Ingram Content Group UK Ltd.
Pitfield, Milton Keynes, MK11 3LW, UK
UKHW020257051026
15470UKWH00020B/385

9 789403 541624